Cisco ISE for BYOD and Secure Unified Access

Aaron T. Woland, CCIE No. 20113

Jamey Heary, CCIE No. 7680

Cisco Press

800 East 96th Street

Indianapolis, IN 46240

Cisco ISE for BYOD and Secure Unified Access

Aaron Woland
Jamey Heary

Copyright© 2013 Cisco Systems, Inc.

Published by:

Cisco Press
800 East 96th Street
Indianapolis, IN 46240 USA

Printed in the United States of America 1 2 3 4 5 6 7 8 9 0
First Printing June 2013

Library of Congress Cataloging-in-Publication Number: 2013938450

ISBN-13: 978-1-58714-325-0
ISBN-10: 1-58714-325-9

Warning and Disclaimer

This book is designed to provide information about Cisco Identity Services Engine. Every effort has been made to make this book as complete and as accurate as possible, but no warranty or fitness is implied.

The information is provided on an "as is" basis. The authors, Cisco Press, and Cisco Systems, Inc., shall have neither liability nor responsibility to any person or entity with respect to any loss or damages arising from the information contained in this book or from the use of the discs or programs that may accompany it.

The opinions expressed in this book belong to the author and are not necessarily those of Cisco Systems, Inc.

Trademark Acknowledgments

All terms mentioned in this book that are known to be trademarks or service marks have been appropriately capitalized. Cisco Press or Cisco Systems, Inc. cannot attest to the accuracy of this information. Use of a term in this book should not be regarded as affecting the validity of any trademark or service mark.

Corporate and Government Sales

The publisher offers excellent discounts on this book when ordered in quantity for bulk purchases or special sales, which may include electronic versions and/or custom covers and content particular to your business, training goals, marketing focus, and branding interests. For more information, please contact **U.S. Corporate and Government Sales** 1-800-382-3419, corpsales@pearsontechgroup.com.

For sales outside of the U.S., please contact **International Sales** international@pearsoned.com.

Feedback Information

At Cisco Press, our goal is to create in-depth technical books of the highest quality and value. Each book is crafted with care and precision, undergoing rigorous development that involves the unique expertise of members from the professional technical community.

Readers' feedback is a natural continuation of this process. If you have any comments regarding how we could improve the quality of this book, or otherwise alter it to better suit your needs, you can contact us through email at feedback@ciscopress.com. Please make sure to include the book title and ISBN in your message.

We greatly appreciate your assistance.

Publisher: Paul Boger	**Business Operation Manager, Manager Global Certification: Cisco Press:** Jan Cornelssen
Associate Publisher: Dave Dusthimer	**Senior Development Editor:** Christopher Cleveland
Executive Editor: Brett Bartow	**Development Editor:** Marianne Bartow
Managing Editor: Sandra Schroeder	**Technical Editors:** Brad Spencer, Chad Sullivan
Project Editor: Mandie Frank	**Editorial Assistant:** Vanessa Evans
Copy Editor: Sheri Replin	**Indexer:** Lisa Stumpf
Proofreader: Sarah Kearns	**Composition:** Jake McFarland
Cover Designer: Mark Shirar	

CISCO.

Americas Headquarters
Cisco Systems, Inc.
San Jose, CA

Asia Pacific Headquarters
Cisco Systems (USA) Pte. Ltd.
Singapore

Europe Headquarters
Cisco Systems International BV
Amsterdam, The Netherlands

Cisco has more than 200 offices worldwide. Addresses, phone numbers, and fax numbers are listed on the Cisco Website at **www.cisco.com/go/offices**.

CCDE, CCENT, Cisco Eos, Cisco HealthPresence, the Cisco logo, Cisco Lumin, Cisco Nexus, Cisco StadiumVision, Cisco TelePresence, Cisco WebEx, DCE, and Welcome to the Human Network are trademarks; Changing the Way We Work, Live, Play, and Learn and Cisco Store are service marks; and Access Registrar, Aironet, AsyncOS, Bringing the Meeting To You, Catalyst, CCDA, CCDP, CCIE, CCIP, CCNA, CCNP, CCSP, CCVP, Cisco, the Cisco Certified Internetwork Expert logo, Cisco IOS, Cisco Press, Cisco Systems, Cisco Systems Capital, the Cisco Systems logo, Cisco Unity, Collaboration Without Limitation, EtherFast, EtherSwitch, Event Center, Fast Step, Follow Me Browsing, FormShare, GigaDrive, HomeLink, Internet Quotient, IOS, iPhone, iQuick Study, IronPort, the IronPort logo, LightStream, Linksys, MediaTone, MeetingPlace, MeetingPlace Chime Sound, MGX, Networkers, Networking Academy, Network Registrar, PCNow, PIX, PowerPanels, ProConnect, ScriptShare, SenderBase, SMARTnet, Spectrum Expert, StackWise, The Fastest Way to Increase Your Internet Quotient, TransPath, WebEx, and the WebEx logo are registered trademarks of Cisco Systems, Inc. and/or its affiliates in the United States and certain other countries.

All other trademarks mentioned in this document or website are the property of their respective owners. The use of the word partner does not imply a partnership relationship between Cisco and any other company. (0812R)

About the Authors

Aaron Woland, CCIE No. 20113, is a Senior Secure Access Engineer at Cisco Systems and works with Cisco's largest customers all over the world. His primary job responsibilities include secure access and ISE deployments, solution enhancements, futures, and escalations. Aaron joined Cisco in 2005 and is currently a member of numerous security advisory boards. Prior to joining Cisco, he spent 12 years as a consultant and technical trainer. His areas of expertise include network and host security architecture and implementation, regulatory compliance, and routing and switching. Aaron is the author of many white papers and design guides, including the *TrustSec 2.0 Design and Implementation Guide* and the *NAC Layer 3 OOB Using VRFs for Traffic Isolation* design guide. He is also a distinguished speaker at Cisco Live for topics related to identity and is a security columnist for *Network World*, where he blogs on all things related to identity. Additional certifications include CCSP, CCNP, CCDP, Certified Ethical Hacker, MCSE, and many other industry certifications.

Jamey Heary, CCIE No. 7680, is a Distinguished Systems Engineer at Cisco Systems, where he works as a trusted security advisor to Cisco customers and business groups. He is also a featured security columnist for *Network World*, where he blogs on all things security. Jamey sits on the PCI Security Standards Council-Board of Advisors, where he provides strategic and technical guidance for future PCI standards. Jamey is the author of *Cisco NAC Appliance: Enforcing Host Security with Clean Access*. He also has a patent pending on a new DDoS mitigation technique. Jamey sits on numerous security advisory boards for Cisco Systems and is a founding member of the Colorado Healthcare InfoSec Users Group. His other certifications include CISSP, and he is a Certified HIPAA Security Professional. He has been working in the IT field for 19 years and in IT security for 15 years.

About the Technical Reviewers

Brad Spencer, CCIE No. 25971 (Security), has worked as a senior security engineer and architect in a consulting capacity for multiple fortune 100 companies since 1997. In the last 16 years, Brad has concentrated on Cisco Security products through consulting as being a Cisco Certified Systems Instructor (CCSI). Brad is currently the Program Manager of Identity Solutions at Priveon, with the primary focus on Cisco Security and Identity products.

Chad Sullivan is CEO and co-owner of Priveon, Inc., a networking and security consulting organization that works with customers globally to deploy and integrate various solutions into customer environments. Prior to starting Priveon, Chad was a Security Consulting Systems Engineer (CSE) at Cisco Systems in Atlanta, GA. Chad holds many certifications, including a triple CCIE (Route-Switch, SNA/IP, and Security). Chad is known across the networking and security industries for his experience, which also includes endpoint security where he has written two books (Cisco Security Agent). Chad has also assisted by contributing to other books as well, by providing content for a NAC Appliance book available from Cisco Press. Today, Chad spends most of his professional time consulting with customers, researching current security trends, and speaking at various public events and seminars.

Dedications

This book is dedicated first to my Mom and Dad, who have always believed in me and supported me in everything I've ever done, encouraged me to never stop learning, taught me the value of hard work, and to pursue a career in something I love. Secondly to my wife, Suzanne, without her continued love, support, guidance, wisdom, encouragement, and patience, this book would surely not exist. To my two awesome children—Eden and Nyah—who are my inspiration, my pride and joy, and who continue to make me want to be a better man. Lastly, to my grandparents, who have taught me what it means to be alive and the true definition of courage and perseverance.

—Aaron

This book is dedicated to my loving wife and two incredible sons, Liam and Conor. Without your support and sacrifice, this book would not have been possible. Thanks for putting up with the late nights and weekends I had to spend behind the keyboard instead of playing games, Legos, soccer, or some other fun family activity. You are all the greatest!

—Jamey

Acknowledgments

From Aaron:

To Thomas Howard and Allan Bolding from Cisco for their continued support, encouragement, and guidance. I could not have done it without you.

To Craig Hyps, a Senior Technical Marketing Engineer at Cisco, for his deep technical knowledge on absolutely everything and his guidance on content found throughout this book. Craig, you are a true inspiration and you drive me to be better every day.

To Jamey Heary, Distinguished Systems Engineer: Thank you for being crazy enough to agree to take the plunge with me. You've been a terrific writing partner and friend.

To Christopher Heffner, a Technical Marketing Engineer at Cisco, for convincing me to step up and take a swing at this book. Without his words of encouragement and guidance, this book would not exist.

To Paul Forbes, a Product Owner at Cisco, who sets an example to aspire to. Without Paul's continued passion, focus, dedication, and drive to make ISE the best product ever, none of us would have this amazing solution to work with.

To Darrin Miller and Nancy Cam-Winget, Distinguished Engineers who set the bar so incredibly high. You are both truly inspirational people to look up to, and I appreciate all the guidance you give me.

To the original cast members of the one and only SSU, especially Jason Halpern, Danelle Au, Mitsunori Sagae, Fay-Ann Lee, Pat Calhoun, Jay Bhansali, AJ Shipley, Joseph Salowey, Thomas Howard, Darrin Miller, Ron Tisinger, Brian Gonsalves, and Tien Do.

To Jonny Rabinowitz, Mehdi Bouzouina, Eddie Mendonca, Pramod Badjate, and all the other members of the world's greatest engineering team. You guys continue to show the world what it means to be "world class."

To my colleagues Naasief Edross, Jeremy Hyman, Kevin Sullivan, Mason Harris, David Anderson, Luc Billot, Jesse Dubois, Jay Young Taylor, Hsing-Tsu Lai, Dave White Jr., Nevin Absher, Ned Zaldivar, Mark Kassem, Greg Tillett, Chuck Parker, Jason Frazier, Shelly Cadora, Ralph Schmieder, Corey Elinburg, Scott Kenewell, Larry Boggis, Chad Sullivan, Dave Klein, and so many more! The contributions you make to this industry inspire me.

To the technical reviewers, Chad Sullivan and Brad Spencer, who provided excellent technical coverage and kept this book accurate and easy to navigate. Your suggestions and guidance are evidenced on nearly every page!

Finally, to the Cisco Press team: Brett Bartow, the executive editor, for seeing the value and vision provided in the original proposal and believing enough to provide me the opportunity to build this book. In addition, Marianne Bartow (Neil), Christopher Cleveland, Mandie Frank, and Sheri Replin, who have put up with my inability to utilize the English language in the manner deemed appropriate by Cisco Press, and who have been there every step of the way. Your guidance, perseverance, and ability to constantly remind Jamey and I of our deadlines are much appreciated! Lastly, everyone else in the Cisco Press team who spent countless hours normalizing the manuscript, its technical drawings and content; their effort can be seen throughout this book pertaining to my ideas, words, and pictures, presented in ways that I could never have imagined.

From Jamey:

I echo Aaron's sentiments, which are previously shown. So many people have made it possible for this book to exist, and for that matter, for this most excellent solution to exist to write about in the first place. Great job to SAMPG, your tireless efforts are bearing fruit. Thank you.

Thank you to Aaron Woland, for pushing the idea of us writing this book and making it real. Your technical kung fu is impressive, as is your ability to put pen to paper so others can understand and follow along. Lastly, a huge thanks for picking up my slack when things got crazy, thus allowing us to publish this on time. It was a fun ride.

Thank you, Tony Kelly and John Graham. Without your coaching, backing, and support as my manager, this book wouldn't have happened. Thanks for making it possible.

Thank you to Greg Edwards, for your mentorship and advice as I transitioned into the DSE role and contemplated whether writing another book was a good fit. You got it right again; it was a good idea and good fit.

Thank you to the tech editors and Cisco Press team. As Aaron stated, your contributions and tireless efforts are supremely appreciated.

I know I must have forgotten some people; so many have helped me along this journey. Thank you.

Contents at a Glance

Contents

Command Syntax Conventions

The conventions used to present command syntax in this book are the same conventions used in the IOS Command Reference. The Command Reference describes these conventions as follows:

- **Boldface** indicates commands and keywords that are entered literally as shown. In actual configuration examples and output (not general command syntax), boldface indicates commands that are manually input by the user (such as a **show** command).

- *Italic* indicates arguments for which you supply actual values.

- Vertical bars (|) separate alternative, mutually exclusive elements.

- Square brackets ([ ]) indicate an optional element.

- Braces ({ }) indicate a required choice.

- Braces within brackets ([{ }]) indicate a required choice within an optional element.

Introduction

Today's networks have evolved into a system without well-defined borders/perimeters that contain data access from both trusted and untrusted devices. Cisco broadly calls this trend borderless networking. The Cisco Secure Unified Access Architecture and Cisco Identity Services Engine (ISE) were developed to provide organizations with a solution to secure and regain control of borderless networks in a Bring Your Own Device (BYOD) world.

A few basic truths become apparent when trying to secure a borderless network. First, you can no longer trust internal data traffic. There are just too many ingress points into the network and too many untrusted devices/users inside the network to be able to trust it implicitly. Second, given the lack of internal trust, it becomes necessary to authenticate and authorize all users into the network regardless of their connection type—wired, wireless, or VPN. Third, because of the proliferation of untrusted and unmanaged devices connecting to your internal network, device control and posture assessment become critical. Each device must be checked for security compliance before it is allowed access to your network resources. These checks vary according to your security policy, but usually involve the device type, location, management status, operating-system patch level, and ensuring anti-malware software is running and up to date.

This book addresses the complete lifecycle of protecting a modern borderless network using Cisco Secure Unified Access and ISE solutions. Secure Access and ISE design, implementation, and troubleshooting are covered in depth. This book explains the many details of the solution and how it can be used to secure borderless networks. At its heart, this solution allows organizations to identify and apply network security policies based on user identity, device type, device behavior, and other attributes, such as security posture. Technologies such as 802.1X, profiling, guest access, network admission control, RADIUS, and Security Group Access are covered in depth.

The goal is to boil down and simplify the architectural details and present them in one reference without trying to replace the existing design, installation, and configuration guides already available from Cisco.

Objectives of This Book

This book helps the reader understand, design, and deploy the next-generation of Network Access Control: Cisco's Secure Unified Access system. This system combines 802.1X, profiling, posture assessments, device onboarding, and Guest Lifecycle management. Cisco ISE for Secure Unified Access teaches readers about the business cases that an identity solution can help solve. It examines identifying users, devices, security policy compliance (posture), and the technologies that make all this possible. This book details the Secure Unified Access solution and how to plan and design a network for this next generation of access control, and all it can offer a customer environment, from device isolation to protocol-independent network segmentation. This book gives readers a single reference to find the complete configuration for an integrated identity solution. All sections of this book use both best practices and real-world examples.

Who Should Read This Book?

The book is targeted primarily to a technical audience involved in architecting, deploying, and delivering secure networks and enabling mobile services. It can help them make informed choices, and enable them to have an engaging discussion with their organization, on how they can achieve their security and availability goals, while reaping the benefits of a secure access solution.

This book is helpful to those looking to deploy Cisco's ISE and 802.1X, as well as Bring Your Own Device (BYOD) or Choose Your Own Device (CYOD) information-technology models.

How This Book Is Organized

This book is organized into 30 chapters distributed across 7 sections. Although it can be read cover to cover, readers can move between chapters and sections, covering only the content that interests them. The seven sections on the book are

Section I, "The Evolution of Identity-Enabled Networks": Examines the evolution of identity-enabled networks. It provides an overview of security issues facing today's networks and what has been the history of trying to combat this problem. This section covers 802.1X, NAC framework, NAC appliance, the evolution into Secure Unified Access, and the creation of the ISE. It discusses the issues faced with the consumerization of information technology, the mass influx of personal devices, ensuring only the correct users, correct devices, with the correct software are allowed to access the corporate network unfettered.

Section II, "The Blueprint, Designing an ISE-Enabled Network": Covers the high-level design phase of a Secure Unified Access project. Solution diagrams are included. This section covers the different functions available on the ISE, how to distribute these functions, and the rollout phases of the solution: Monitor Mode, Low-Impact Mode, and Closed Mode. Additionally, the solution taxonomy is explained. It discusses the enforcement devices that are part of this solution and ones that are not. Change of Authorization (CoA) is introduced. All these concepts are clarified and reinforced throughout the other sections.

Section III, "The Foundation, Building a Context-Aware Security Policy": Describes how to create a context-aware security policy for the network and devices. This is often the hardest part of a secure access project. This section covers the departments that need to be involved, the policies to be considered, and best practices. Coverage includes some lessons learned and landmines to watch out for. Screenshots and flow diagrams are included in this section to aid in the readers' understanding of the process, how communication occurs and in what order, as well as how to configure the miscellaneous device supplicants.

Section IV, "Configuration": Details the step-by-step configuration of the ISE, the network access devices, and supplicants. The goal of this section is to have the entire infrastructure and policy management configured and ready to begin the actual deployment in Section V.

Section V, "Deployment Best Practices": Walks readers through a phased deployment. It starts by explaining the different phases of deployment and how to ensure zero downtime. This section begins with a description followed by the actual step-by-step deployment guides, how to use the monitoring tools to build out the correct policies and profiling tuning, and how to move from phase to phase. This section provides the reader with insight into the best practices, caveats, common mistakes, deployment lessons learned, tricks of the trade, and rules to live by.

Section VI, "Advanced Secure Unified Access Features": Details some of the more advanced solution features that truly differentiate Secure Unified Access as a system.

Section VII, "Monitoring, Maintenance, and Troubleshooting": Examines the maintenance of ISE, backups, and upgrades. It covers how to troubleshoot not only ISE, but the entire Secure Unified Access system, and how to use the tools provided in the ISE solution. Common monitoring and maintenance tasks, as well as troubleshooting tools, are explained from a help-desk support technician's point of view.

Here is an overview of each of the 30 chapters:

- **Chapter 1, "Regain Control of Your IT Security":** Introduces the concepts that brought us to the current evolutionary stage of network access security. It discusses the explosion of mobility, virtualization, social networking, and ubiquitous network access coupled with the consumerization of information technology.

- **Chapter 2, "Introducing Cisco Identity Services Engine":** Cisco ISE makes up the backbone of Cisco's next-generation context-aware identity-based security policy solution. This chapter introduces this revolutionary new product and provides an overview of its functions and capabilities.

- **Chapter 3: "The Building Blocks in an Identity Services Engine Design":** This chapter covers the components of the Secure Unified Access solution, including ISE personas, licensing model, and the policy structure.

- **Chapter 4: "Making Sense of All the ISE Deployment Design Options":** This chapter examines all the available personas in ISE and design options with the combination of those personas.

- **Chapter 5: "Following a Phased Deployment":** Implementing secure access with a phased approach to deployment is critical to the success of the project. Cisco provided three modes to assist with this phased approach: Monitor Mode,

Low-Impact Mode, and Closed Mode. This chapter briefly summarizes the importance of following this phased approach to deployment.

■ **Chapter 6: "Building a Cisco ISE Network Access Security Policy":** In order for any network-centric security solution to be successful, a solid network access security policy (NASP) must first be in place. Once a policy is in place, ISE enforces that policy network-wide. This chapter focuses on the creation of that NASP.

■ **Chapter 7: "Building a Device Security Policy":** This chapter explores Host Security Posture Assessment and Device Profiling features in some detail in order to disclose the different ways in which ISE identifies device types and determines their security posture.

■ **Chapter 8: "Building an ISE Accounting and Auditing Policy":** This chapter delves into the creation of accounting and audit policies, including administrator configuration changes, ISE system health, processing of ISE rules, and full logging of authentication and authorization activities.

■ **Chapter 9: "The Basics: Principal Configuration Tasks for Cisco ISE":** This chapter provides a high-level overview of the ISE personas, walks the reader through the initial configuration (called bootstrapping) of ISE itself, and role-based access control (RBAC).

■ **Chapter 10: "Profiling Basics":** This chapter introduces the concepts of profiling and configuration choices needed to create a foundation to build upon. It examines the different profiling mechanisms and the pros and cons related to each, discussing best practices and configuration details.

■ **Chapter 11: "Bootstrapping Network Access Devices":** This key chapter examines the configuration of the network access devices (NAD) themselves and focuses on best practices to ensure a successful ongoing deployment.

■ **Chapter 12: "Authorization Policy Elements":** This chapter examines the logical roles within an organization and how to create authorization results to assign the correct level of access based on that role.

■ **Chapter 13: "Authentication and Authorization Policies":** This chapter explains the distinct and important difference between Authentication and Authorization Policies, the pieces that make up the policy, and provides examples of how to create a policy in ISE that enforces the logical policies created out of Chapter 12.

■ **Chapter 14: "Guest Lifecycle Management":** Guest access has become an expected resource at companies in today's world. This chapter explains the full secure guest lifecycle management, from Web Authentication (WebAuth) to sponsored guest access and self-registration options.

■ **Chapter 15: "Device Posture Assessments":** This chapter examines endpoint posture assessment and remediation actions, the configuration of the extensive checks and requirements, and how to tie them into an Authorization Policy.

- **Chapter 16: "Supplicant Configuration":** This chapter looks at configuration examples of the most popular supplicants.

- **Chapter 17: "BYOD: Self-Service Onboarding and Registration":** This critical chapter goes through a detailed examination of Bring Your Own Device (BYOD) concepts, policies, and flows. Both the user and administrative experiences are detailed, as well as introducing the new integration between ISE and third-party MDM vendors.

- **Chapter 18: "Setting Up a Distributed Deployment":** Cisco ISE can be deployed in a scalable distributed model as well as a standalone device. This chapter examines the way ISE may be deployed in this distributed model, and the caveats associated, as well as detailing high availability (HA) with technologies such as load balancing.

- **Chapter 19: "Inline Posture Node":** This chapter overviews the Inline Posture Node and its deployment into a network.

- **Chapter 20: "Deployment Phases":** This key chapter builds on Chapter 5, going into more detail and beginning the foundational configuration for a phased deployment approach.

- **Chapter 21: "Monitor Mode":** This chapter details the configuration and the flow during the Monitor Mode phase of deployment to ensure zero downtime for the end users.

- **Chapter 22: "Low-Impact Mode":** This chapter examines the configuration and the flow for the Low-Impact Mode end-state of deployment.

- **Chapter 23: "Closed Mode":** This chapter details the configuration and the flow for the Low-Impact Mode end-state of deployment.

- **Chapter 24: "Advanced Profiling Configuration":** This chapter builds on what was learned and configured in Chapter 10, examining how to profile unknown endpoints and looking deeper into the profiling policies themselves.

- **Chapter 25: "Security Group Access":** This chapter introduces the next-generation tagging enforcement solution, examining classification, transport, and enforcement.

- **Chapter 26: "MACSec and NDAC":** This chapter covers the layering of Layer 2 encryption on top of the deployment to secure the traffic flows and the Security Group Tags from Chapter 25. It also examines the network device admission control features that provide access control for network devices and forms domains of trusted network devices.

- **Chapter 27: "Network Edge Access Topology":** This chapter discusses the concept and configuration of this unique capability for extending secure access networks beyond the wiring closet.

- **Chapter 28: "Understanding Monitoring and Alerting":** This chapter explains the extensive and redesigned monitoring, reporting, and alerting mechanisms built into the ISE solution.

- **Chapter 29: "Troubleshooting":** This chapter aids the reader when having to troubleshoot the Secure Unified Access system and its many moving parts.

- **Chapter 30: "Backup, Patching, and Upgrading":** Provides a detailed discussion and procedural walk-through on the available backup, restore, patching, and upgrading of ISE.

- **Appendix A: Sample User Community Deployment Messaging Material**

- **Appendix B: Sample ISE Deployment Questionnaire**

- **Appendix C: Configuring the Microsoft CA for BYOD**

- **Appendix D: Using a Cisco IOS Certificate Authority for BYOD Onboarding**

- **Appendix E: Sample Switch Configurations**

Chapter 1

Regain Control of Your IT Security

The explosion of mobility, virtualization, social networking, and ubiquitous network access coupled with the consumerization of Information Technology brings new security challenges to organizations, including:

- Insufficient security controls for non-corporate-owned devices, especially consumer-class devices such as the iPhone and iPad. This is known as the Bring Your Own Device (BYOD) phenomenon.

- An increased potential for the loss of sensitive data, which can cause an array of problems for your business, customers, and partners.

- Dissolution of network security boundaries (borderless networks), resulting in an increased number of entry points to your network and, therefore, an increased risk to your business.

- Increased complexity in maintaining compliance with security and privacy regulations, laws, and other enforced standards such as Payment Card Industry (PCI).

IT network and security policies, budgets, and resources are not keeping pace with the rapid innovations happening in our business models, workplace, and technology. With today's security challenges and threats growing more sophisticated and broad, traditional network security approaches are no longer sufficient without augmentation. Organizations require security systems that can provide more actionable intelligence, that are pervasively deployed, and that are more tightly integrated with other installed networking and security tools than they have been in the past. The purpose of this chapter is to define the major focus areas that will need to be considered in order to take back and continue to maintain control of your IT security. This must be accomplished in the face of the recent technology trends while still enabling businesses to function efficiently. The secret lies in centralized, pervasive security policy control.

Security: A Weakest-Link Problem with Ever More Links

The bad guys are always looking for the path of least resistance to their targets. Why waste effort attacking a hardened target system directly when you can get there by quickly compromising something weaker and using its privileges to exploit your target? This is the basic principle of the weakest-link problem. The information you are trying to protect is only as secure as the weakest entry point (link) to that information. This has always been true in IT security. The big change is in the increase of the sum total of "links" that must be dealt with.

Never before have networks and their data been more accessible by external untrusted individuals. Also, the number of devices in today's typical network has grown dramatically over time with the addition of network capable nodes such as IP phones, IP videoconferencing systems, and mobile devices such as cell phones and tablets. Today's networks allow access from literally anywhere on the globe via a combination of wireless, wired, virtual private networks (VPN), guest portals, consumer devices, mobile devices, B2B connections...and the list goes on.

Prior to the expansion of cost-effective mobile computing and networkable handheld devices, networks were composed of stationary corporate-owned desktop PCs, each of which often had only one employee assigned to it for dedicated usage. Now employees have several network-attached devices each, most or all of which are highly mobile. For example, one of this book's authors has an iPhone, an iPad, a Windows 7 PC, a MacBook Pro, a Verizon MiFi device, a Wi-Fi corporate IP Phone, and a desk IP Phone, some of which are personal devices (for example, the iPad and iPhone), while others are corporate-owned assets. Those are just the mobile devices the author uses that can store and share information; add to this the online "cloud" services, and the security scope explodes!

Very few organizations today are closed entities with well-defined network security perimeters. This leads us to the concepts of ubiquitous access and borderless networks. Gone are the days of a nicely defined network security perimeter made up of a firewall that guards against unauthorized access from the "outside." Security architecture is changing from a point defense perimeter approach to a defense-in-depth network design that is security policy driven.

So what happens to security now that networks are borderless and full of mobile devices? Here are some fundamental shifts:

- You can no longer simply trust the packets on your internal networks.

- The network must become identity and context aware at all ingress points (internal and external).

- Security policies must become identity and context aware.

- Security policies need to be application, Layer 7, aware. Traditional 5-tuple ACL match alone is no longer sufficient.

- Security controls need to be policy based, context aware, identity aware, and controlled centrally by a single source of truth.

Today, networks are most secure at their traditional network perimeter, namely the Internet-facing access points. However, the security of the internal networks, especially wired networks, behind those impressive perimeter fortress walls is sorely lacking. By and large, once a user gains access to the internal networks, they are given free and unrestricted network access. In addition, the pervasiveness of mobility has thrown the concept of internal vs. external out the window. Mobile devices roam between both internal and external networks while sometimes connecting to both simultaneously. Never before has the average employee been so connected in so many ways in so many places. Effectively dealing with the security risks that spring forth from this new networking reality by using the Cisco Identity Services Engine (ISE) and Cisco Secure Unified Access are the focus of this book.

Cisco Identity Services Engine

Cisco describes its Identity Services Engine solution in this way:

> The Cisco Identity Services Engine is a next-generation identity and access control policy platform that enables enterprises to facilitate new business services, enhance infrastructure security, enforce compliance, and streamline service operations. Its unique architecture allows enterprises to gather real-time contextual information from networks, users, and devices to make proactive governance decisions by enforcing policy across the network infrastructure—wired, wireless, and remote.

As noted in the "Cisco Identity Services Engine (ISE) Data Sheet" (http://tinyurl.com/amugy4x), to policy enable your network and devices, the Cisco ISE and Secure Unified Access solution provides the following services:

- Network identity awareness.

- Network and device context awareness.

- A common security policy across wired, wireless, and VPN access for simpler corporate governance.

- Centralized guest access management that is common across wired and wireless access methods.

- System-wide visibility into who, where, and what is on a network.

- Authentication, authorization, and accounting (AAA), device profiling, device posture, mobile device onboarding, and guest services into a single solution to simplify deployments and cut operational costs via ISE.

- Automated device profiling/identification using ISE-based traffic probes, Cisco IOS device sensors included in Cisco switches, and active endpoint scanning.

- Simplified BYOD onboarding through self-service device registration and provisioning.

- Identity- and context-aware Secure Unified Access tagging of data frames as they enter the Secure Unified Access–capable network. These packet tags can then be used by any tag-aware device to enforce differentiated policy on the network.

To summarize, the Cisco ISE solution allows you to connect any user on any device to any segment of your network more easily, reliably, and securely. The rich policy-based nature of the ISE solution provides you with identity- and context-based access differentiation.

Sources for Providing Identity and Context Awareness

Having *identity awareness* in the network simply means that you are able to determine and authenticate the individuality of the user or group of users trying to gain access to your network. To establish individuality, combine both a username (or equivalent) and any other available user attributes. For example, Jamey Heary successfully authenticated onto the network using his Active Directory account JHeary. JHeary is a member of both the *Users* and *Contractors* groups. There is now an identity for the user JHeary that can be utilized to determine which network policy ISE should assign to the network.

ISE can obtain identity information and validate its authenticity using several sources, including its own local database. Here are the most common ways ISE will gather identity information:

- **802.1X:** 802.1X is an IEEE standard for Layer 2 access control to wired and wireless networks. As an example, WPA2 Enterprise uses 802.1X plus Extensible Authentication Protocol (EAP) for authentication. 802.1X can use either user identity or machine identity, or it can use both. 802.1X offers the capability to permit or deny Layer 2 network connectivity, assign a VLAN, and apply various other traffic- and network-related policies.

- **MAC address authentication:** ISE uses the machine's hardware MAC address of its network interface card to gain access to the network. Because of the ease of MAC forgery, it is recommended to use additional device-profiling context information to ensure authenticity.

- **Web redirect to portal:** A user's web browser is automatically redirected to a user authentication web page (in other words, a web portal) where they can input their identity via a customized web form.

- **Guest access:** Users are identified as guest users in various ways. Most typically this happens when the user does not have valid credentials to log in to any restricted network. Guest access can also be defined based on connection information. For example, anyone who connects to the *public-net* wireless service set identifier (SSID) is considered a guest user.

- **VPN authentication:** Users enter their credentials before a VPN tunnel or a Secure Sockets Layer (SSL) VPN is allowed to pass traffic.

Now that identity awareness has been established, you need to gather real-time contextual information from networks, users, and devices. The Cisco Identity Services Engine has several ways of collecting and using contextual information. Here are some of the more common context sources:

■ User authorization attributes from identity sources such as Lightweight Directory Access Protocol (LDAP), Active Directory, RADIUS, or the internal ISE user database.

■ An integrated device profiling engine that will actively and/or passively scan a device or monitor its network behavior to determine what kind of device it is. For example, if a device has a MAC address owned by Apple and its browser user-agent string includes the words "Apple iPad," then the profiling engine will classify it as an Apple iPad.

■ Location information such as physical location, network access type (wired, wireless, VPN), GPS location, and switch port location.

■ Device Posture which gathers posture information from the host. Posture information can include OS type and version, service pack, security software, application inventory, running processes, registry keys, digital certificates, and many others.

Unleash the Power of Centralized Policy

The final step is putting identity and context information to work via ISE's policy framework. Cisco ISE provides a centralized view from which you can administrate the policy of up to 250,000 endpoints enterprise wide regardless of their network access type—wired, wireless, or VPN. The policies you create will monitor and enforce users' compliance with any written security policy and other corporate governance regulations your organization has in place. The Cisco Identity Services Engine is capable of performing simple or complex, yet elegant, policy rules that are both identity and context aware. Once a policy rule is matched, its permissions are applied to the network and/or device. It is in this way that ISE's centralized policy structure is able to greatly simplify and restore your control and governance of the network.

The kinds of permissions that ISE can grant once a policy match is obtained are extensive. Here are a few of the popular ones:

■ Deny any network access

■ Permit all network access

■ Restrict network access by downloading an access control list (ACL) to the access device (switch, wireless controller, VPN headend)

■ Assign a VLAN to a switch or wireless controller

■ Redirect client for web authentication

- Provision the device's 802.1X supplicant or client

- Assign a Security Group Tag (SGT) to all data frames

- Execute an Auto Smartports macro on a Cisco switch

Figure 1-1 depicts some of the permissions that are available using Cisco ISE. In the pro-ceeding chapters of this book, we will explore permissions and the other topics of this chapter in more detail.

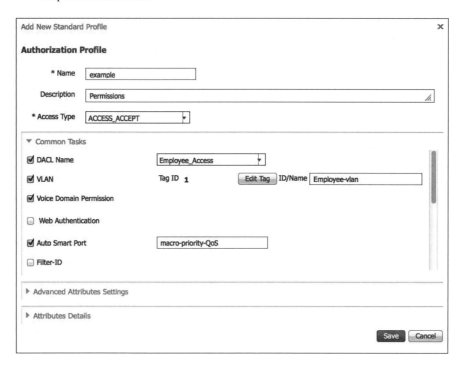

Figure 1-1   *Cisco ISE Permission Authorization Profile Example*

Summary

This chapter examined the increasing security risks and corporate governance challenges being faced in our borderless networks that are filled with highly mobile corporate-owned and personally owned devices, such as iPhones and iPads. This chapter focused on net-work security as a weakest-link problem in an environment where the number of "links" is exponentially expanding due to mobility, virtualization, and the consumerization of IT. Cisco Identity Services Engine and Cisco Secure Unified Access were introduced to help alleviate these risks and challenges. The secret to efficiently tackling these tasks is perva-sive and centralized policy control of all devices and network access methods. This chap-ter discussed the policy structure and options provided by Cisco ISE and gave examples of ways to provide identity- and context-aware differentiated network access. In the ensu-ing chapters of this book, we will explore the topics of this chapter in more detail.

Chapter 2

Introducing Cisco Identity Services Engine

The Cisco Identity Services Engine (ISE) makes up the backbone of Cisco's next-generation, context-aware, identity-based security policy solution. To give you some historical context, ISE will be providing the next-generation functionality that was formally accomplished by both the Cisco Network Admission Control (NAC) Appliance Suite and Cisco Access Control Server (ACS) RADIUS-only product functions.

Systems Approach to Centralized Network Security Policy

A bit of history is required to understand how the NAC and AAA server markets have evolved to date. This will set the stage for a discussion of the systems approach that the Cisco Identity Services Engine now implements. Prior to 2004, Cisco developed a NAC solution called Cisco NAC Framework. It was heavily based on 802.1X and integration with network services. Unfortunately, it was ahead of its time and never widely deployed. It can be argued that it was the right approach to security, but back then, the clients, devices, switches, operating systems, and just about everything else in the network weren't capable or ready for an 802.1X-based integrated solution.

In response to the slow adoption of the NAC Framework, Cisco acquired Perfigo, and released the Cisco NAC Appliance solution that was based on the Perfigo technology in 2004. Cisco NAC Appliance provided an overlay NAC solution that did not require, nor use, 802.1X or a systems approach. It was a pure overlay technology using SNMP and inline NAC appliances to get the job done. Over the years, this solution gained traction and quickly became the most deployed and highest rated NAC solution on the market. As the maturation and proliferation of support for 802.1X has grown over the years, it became clear to Cisco that it was time to reintroduce a next-generation NAC solution that was based on 802.1X and embraced a systems approach instead of an overlay design.

In 2011, Cisco released the Cisco Identity Services Engine to provide its customers with an 802.1X-based NAC solution. ISE is a new, built from the ground up, security policy control system. But Cisco didn't stop there. As shown in Figure 2-1, ISE drastically reduces the number of appliances needed.

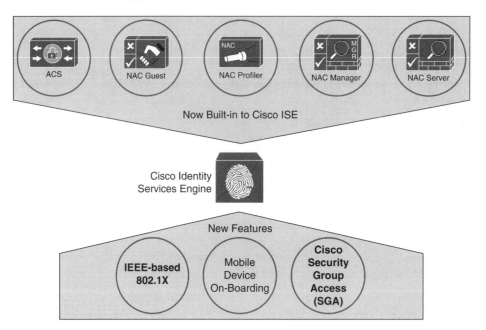

Figure 2-1   *Cisco ISE Centralized Policy Control Functionality*

Figure 2-1 depicts the previously separate functionality along with the new functionality that is now integrated into the ISE solution. What used to require up to five separate appliances and up to four separate administrative interfaces to configure is now available within a single appliance and administrative interface. Let's examine what this integrated functionality actually means in more detail:

- **Cisco ACS:** ISE is able to perform all of the RADIUS functionality currently found on the Cisco AAA server. As of this writing, Cisco ISE does not yet support the ACS TACACS+ functionality.

- **Cisco NAC Guest Server:** Cisco ISE provides full guest user lifecycle management. Both authenticated guest and unauthenticated guest access is supported.

- **Cisco NAC Profiler:** Cisco ISE provides greatly enhanced profiling functionality over the previous offering. ISE ships with predefined device profiles for hundreds of endpoints, such as IP phones, printers, IP cameras, smartphones, network devices, and tablets. The predefined profile templates are automatically updated and revised via an Internet update feed from Cisco. Custom profiles can also be created. These profiles can be used to deterministically detect, classify, and associate policy to endpoints in real time as they connect to the network. Cisco ISE collects endpoint attribute data via passive network telemetry, by querying the actual endpoints, and from the device sensors embedded in Cisco Catalyst switches.

- **Cisco NAC Manager:** ISE extends the previous NAC functionality found in Cisco NAC Manager. The biggest change is the new systems-based approach that utilizes a centralized policy-based architecture. ISE verifies endpoint posture assessment for both PCs and mobile devices connecting to the network. It works via either a persistent client-based agent or a temporal web agent. ISE provides the ability to create powerful policies that include, but are not limited to, checks for the latest OS patches, antivirus and antispyware software packages, registry entries, running processes, and applications. ISE also supports auto-remediation of PC clients and periodic reassessment to make sure the endpoint is not in violation of company policies.

- **Cisco NAC Server:** In most cases, to perform any of the ISE functions, a separate inline appliance is not needed or recommended. This is because ISE integrates itself into the network instead of overlaying inline appliances on top of the network. In rare cases where the overlay is still required, ISE does provide the ability for it to assume an Inline Posture Node (IPN) capability.

- **IEEE 802.1X:** The 802.1X standard describes a communication framework to use Extensible Authentication Protocol (EAP) over LAN. This is the defacto industry mechanism for providing network authentication. Cisco has enhanced the authentication mechanisms above and beyond the industry standard to include advanced authorization mechanisms and authentication methods.

- **Mobile Device On-Boarding:** ISE provides native capabilities for self-service personal device registration and onboarding, including Native Supplicant Provisioning, Certificate Issuance, and Mobile Device Management (MDM) integration.

- **Cisco Security Group Access (SGA):** SGA provides for advanced authorization enforcement techniques that provide much greater scale than what is available with the standard 802.1X enforcement mechanisms of today.

What Is the Cisco Identity Services Engine?

The Cisco ISE product line was first introduced in 2011. Cisco created it to provide businesses with an integrated systems approach to their network access and policy requirements. The ISE solution provides consolidated and comprehensive network visibility using identity and contextual awareness. This includes the who, what, where, when, and how of network access. Figure 2-2 illustrates the policy-based nature of ISE.

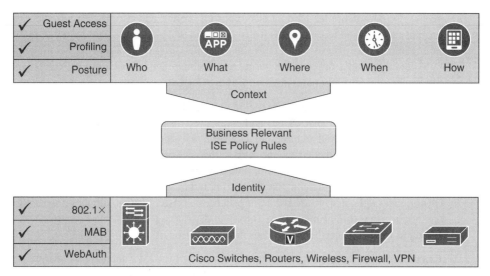

Figure 2-2   *Cisco ISE Visibility*

Let's break down the information found in Figure 2-2 into its constituent parts. The two main parts are Context and Identity. Identity provides knowledge of the user or device; this gives us the who. Context extends the amount of information we have about an identity to provide additional information such as what, where, when, and how. The consolidation of identity and context allows the creation of business-relevant policies. Here is a good example of what this would look like: Jamey Heary (who) logged in to the network in building 4 (where) using Cisco AnyConnect (what) today at 9 p.m. (when) using his iPhone (how).

Now that you know what information you want to include in your ISE policies, you need to figure out how to gather that data. A major strength of Cisco ISE is its ability to support all access methods, wired, wireless, and VPN, into a single policy table. To do this, ISE relies on network systems for both the collection of identity and context and the enforcement of policy. The left side of Figure 2-2 provides some examples of how identity and context information can be collected by the ISE architecture. Let's take a look at each of these in some detail, starting with identity. Identity can be gathered in multiple ways using the ISE solution. The following methods are available, in order of preference:

■ **802.1X:** IEEE 802.1X is the standard for port-based network access control. The protocol uses Extensible Authentication Protocol (EAP), a flexible authentication framework defined in RFC-3748. The protocol defines three components in the authentication process:

   ■ **Supplicant:** The agent on the device/PC that is used to access the network. The supplicant is either built in or added onto the operating system. It requests authentication by the authenticator.

- **Authenticator:** The device that controls the status of a link; typically a wired switch or Wireless LAN Controller.

- **Authentication server:** A backend server that authenticates the credentials provided by supplicants. For example, the Wireless LAN Controller passes credentials from the supplicant via RADIUS to ISE for authentication.

- **VPN/RADIUS authentication:** By using ISE to authenticate your VPN clients, ISE then knows the identity of your VPN users. For example, Cisco ASA sends credentials from the VPN client via RADIUS to ISE for authentication.

- **ASA identity firewall:** Cisco ASA supports identity firewalling (IDFW). ASA can use ISE as an authentication server for this purpose. In this way, ISE will learn the identity of all users passing through the IDFW-enabled Cisco ASA.

- **Web authentication:** Provides authentication via web page, usually via a URL redirect of the user's browser. The built-in Guest Server functionality of ISE provides this web portal service. For example, a user attaches to a wireless network without authentication, that is, open mode. The user's browser is then redirected to the login page hosted by ISE. ISE collects the credentials and performs the authentication.

- **MAC Authentication Bypass (MAB):** MAB relies on a MAC address for authentication. A MAC address is a globally unique identifier that is assigned to all network-attached devices, and therefore it is often referred to as a *hardware* or *physical address*. Because it is a globally unique identifier, it can be used in authentication. However, the ability to assign your own MAC address to your device means that, by itself, a MAC address is not a strong form of authentication. Later on, you will read about how ISE Profiler functionality with MAB will provide you with a much more secure alternative to just MAB.

  Let's look at a MAB example. A printer that does not support 802.1X attaches to the wired network. 802.1X authentication times out and MAB takes over. The printer sends its MAC address to ISE. ISE then verifies the MAC address is allowed using its MAC address database or some external database containing a list of approved MAC addresses.

Caution   MAB by itself is not a secure authentication mechanism. MAB with ISE Profiler should be implemented instead.

- **Unauthenticated/authenticated guest access:** ISE includes a Guest Server functionality that will provide a guest user splash page and, optionally, a user agreement page and/or a page that asks for information from the user such as their email address, name, company, and so forth. Guests are allowed access without providing identity information, which is usually termed "unauthenticated guest access." This is what you would find at your local café that provides free Internet access. Guests are not authenticated by ISE, but, instead, any actions or information they provide will be cataloged. In contrast, authenticated guest access will allow Internet access to guests using temporary credentials that expire after a set time period. Guests are provided with these credentials through SMS, a printed handout, or other means. In almost all cases, the network access that a guest receives is severely restricted in comparison to what an authenticated employee receives, and usually allows only Internet access.

The most secure methods, which we recommend that you implement in your network, are 802.1X, VPN authentication, and ASA Identity Firewall logins. All of these techniques provide a robust and seamless user experience. If these are not available for use in specific scenarios within your own network, then employ MAB with ISE Profiler, use web authentication through a browser-based web portal page, or offer an unauthenticated or authenticated guest access option.

ISE Authorization Rules

After authentication is complete, ISE performs its policy enforcement, also known as *authorization*. ISE can utilize dozens of policy attributes to each policy rule in a consolidated policy rule table for authorization. Here is a sampling of some of the more popular policy attributes available for use in ISE:

- Posture assessment results

- Active Directory group membership

- Active Directory user-based attributes (company name, department, address, job title, and so on)

- Location

- Access method (MAB, 802.1X, wired, wireless, and so on)

- Time and date

- Profiler match for device type

- If device has been registered with ISE

- Digital certificate information (commonly used to determine corporate vs. noncorporate assets)

- Hundreds of RADIUS attributes and values

The ISE policy rule table can be evaluated on a first-match basis (most common) or multiple-match basis. If there are no matches, then a default "catch all" rule is enforced. Figure 2-3 shows an example ISE authorization policy.

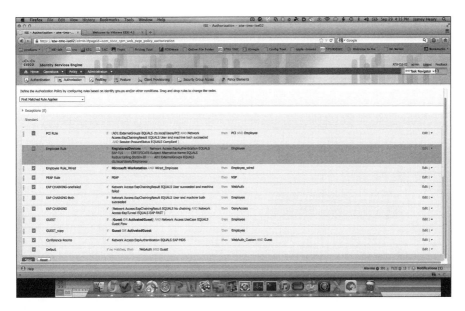

Figure 2-3 *Cisco ISE Authorization Policy Example*

Summary

Cisco ISE has integrated and consolidated the functionality of what used to be five separate products with four separate GUI front ends. ISE has also moved to 802.1X and an integrated solution instead of the previous overlay solution. Cisco ISE provides a fully functional Network Access Control solution, managed by a central Administrator GUI.

Chapter 3

The Building Blocks in an Identity Services Engine Design

This chapter covers the following topics:

- ISE solution components
- ISE personas
- ISE licensing, requirements, and performance
- ISE policy-based structure

Knowing how to properly design security solutions is what separates the professional from the amateur. Without a proper design, the eventual implementation will most likely be a disaster. One of the keys to success when designing a security solution is to first understand all of the pieces, or building blocks, you have to work with. After you understand the building blocks, you need to become skilled at manipulating them in ways that best fit your environment. This chapter focuses on the building blocks that are available with the ISE for Secure Unified Access solution. The purpose and function of each building block are covered in this chapter. Chapter 4, "Making Sense of All the ISE Design Options," discusses your options for manipulating these building blocks.

ISE Solution Components Explained

At a high level, the following are the three product component groups that make up the ISE solution:

- Infrastructure components
- Policy components
- Endpoint components

Each group has a distinct role to play in the ISE solution. Let's examine the roles and functions of these groups in more detail.

Infrastructure Components

Infrastructure components supported by Cisco ISE are numerous, with more added regularly. These network infrastructure devices include both Cisco-branded devices and non-Cisco devices. However, the Cisco-branded devices, predictably, provide more functionality with better integration into the ISE solution.

Note   Certain advanced use cases, such as those that involve posture assessment, profiling, and web authentication, are not consistently available with non-Cisco devices or may provide limited functionality, and are therefore not supported with non-Cisco devices. In addition, certain other advanced functions, such as Centralized Web Authentication (CWA), Change of Authorization (CoA), Security Group Access, and downloadable Access Control Lists (dACL), are supported only on Cisco devices.

Note   For the latest support list of infrastructure components, refer to the most recent release of *Cisco Identity Services Engine Network Component Compatibility* at http://www.cisco.com/en/US/products/ps11640/products_device_support_tables_list.html.

Table 3-1 provides a partial list of the core infrastructure components that are most likely to be used in an ISE deployment. The table shows each device's capabilities for the following features:

- **MAC Authentication Bypass (MAB):** Using the MAC Address of an endpoint that cannot authenticate itself to the network.

- **802.1X:** The IEEE standard for communicating identity credentials using Extensible Authentication Protocol (EAP) over LAN.

- **Web Authentication:** Authenticating users attempting network access via a web page. Web Authentication has two deployment modes:

  - **Central Web Authentication (CWA):** The most popular option, controlled by ISE.

  - **Local Web Authentication (LWA):** Performed by the switch or Wireless LAN Controller (WLC) and cannot perform CoA (described next), modify the port VLAN, or support session ID.

- **Change of Authorization (CoA):** RADIUS attribute that ISE issues to an access device in order to force the session to be reauthenticated. CoA forms the backbone of the 802.1X ISE solution.

- **VLAN:** Virtual LAN. The layer-2 broadcast domain that might be assigned to incoming devices.

- **Downloadable ACL (dACL):** An access control list that is sent from ISE to the access device to restrict the session.

- **Security Group Access (SGA):** SGA architecture builds secure networks by establishing a domain of trusted network devices. SGA also uses the device and user identity information acquired during authentication to classify the packets as they enter the network. This packet classification is maintained by tagging packets on ingress to the SGA-based network. The tag, called the Security Group Tag (SGT), allows the network to enforce the access control policy by enabling the network device to act upon the SGT to control/restrict traffic.

- **Cisco IOS Device Sensor:** Enables profiling functionality built into the Cisco IOS Catalyst switch or Cisco WLC hardware. This allows profiling to occur locally at the access device instead of centrally at an ISE node.

Table 3-1 *ISE Supported Infrastructure Components*

Device	Minimum OS Version	MAB	802.1X	Web Auth (CWA)	Web Auth (LWA)	CoA	VLAN	DACL	SGA	IOS Sensor
Access Switches										
Catalyst 2940	IOS v12.1(22) EA1	Yes	Yes	No	No	No	Yes	No	No	No
Catalyst 2950	IOS v12.1(22) EA1	No	Yes	No	No	No	Yes	No	No	No
Catalyst 2955	IOS v12.1(22) EA1	No	Yes	No	No	No	Yes	No	No	No
Catalyst 2960[1], Catalyst 2960-S[1], ISR EtherSwitch ES2	IOS v12.2(52)SE LAN Base	Yes	Yes	Yes	Yes	Yes	Yes	Yes	No	No
Catalyst 2960[1], Catalyst 2960-S[1], Catalyst 2960-C	IOS v12.2(52)SE LAN Lite[2]	Yes	Yes	No	No	No	Yes	No	No	No
Catalyst 2970	IOS v12.2(25)SE	Yes	Yes	No	No	No	Yes	No	No	No
Catalyst 2975	IOS v12.2(52)SE	Yes	Yes	Yes	Yes	Yes	Yes	Yes	No	No

Device	Minimum OS Version	MAB	802.1X	Web Auth (CWA)	Web Auth (LWA)	CoA	VLAN	DACL	SGA	IOS Sensor
Catalyst 3550	IOS v12.2(44)SE	Yes	Yes	No	No	No	Yes	Yes	No	No
Catalyst 3560[1], Catalyst 3560-C[1]	IOS v12.2(52)SE	Yes	Yes	Yes	Yes	Yes	Yes	Yes	Yes	Yes 15.0 (1) SE
Catalyst 3560-E[1], ISR EtherSwitch ES3	IOS v12.2(52)SE	Yes	Yes	Yes	Yes	Yes	Yes	Yes	Yes	Yes 15.0 (1) SE
Catalyst 3560-X[1]	IOS v12.2(52)SE	Yes	Yes	Yes	Yes	Yes	Yes	Yes	Yes	Yes 15.0 (1) SE
Catalyst 3750[1]	IOS v12.2(52)SE	Yes	Yes	Yes	Yes	Yes	Yes	Yes	Yes	Yes 15.0 (1) SE
Catalyst 3750-E[1]	IOS v12.2(52)SE	Yes	Yes	Yes	Yes	Yes	Yes	Yes	Yes	Yes 15.0 (1) SE
Catalyst 3750 Metro[1]	IOS v12.2(52)SE	Yes	Yes	Yes	Yes	Yes	Yes	Yes	Yes	Yes 15.0 (1) SE
Catalyst 3750-X[1]	IOS v12.2(52)SE	Yes	Yes	Yes	Yes	Yes	Yes	Yes	Yes	Yes 15.0 (1) SE
Catalyst 4500/4500X	IOS v12.2(54) SG1 IOS-XE 3.3SG	Yes	Yes	Yes	Yes	Yes	Yes	Yes	Yes	Yes 15.1.1SG/3.3SG
Catalyst 6500	IOS v12.2(33) SXI6	Yes	Yes	Yes	Yes	Yes	Yes	Yes	Yes	No
Data Center Switches										
Catalyst 4900	IOS v12.2(54) SG1	Yes	Yes	Yes	Yes	Yes	Yes	Yes	Yes	—
Nexus 7000[3]	—	—	—	—	—	Yes	—	Yes	—	
Wireless[4, 5]										
WLC 2100, 4400	7.0.116.0	No[6]	Yes	No	Yes	Yes	Yes	Yes	No	No

Device	Minimum OS Version	MAB	802.1X	Web Auth (CWA)	Web Auth (LWA)	CoA	VLAN	DACL	SGA	IOS Sensor
WLC 2500, 5500	7.2.103.0	No[6]	Yes	Yes	Yes	Yes	Yes	Yes	Yes	No
WLC 7500 Series	7.2.103.0	Yes[6]	Yes	No	Yes (local only)	No	Yes	No	No	No
WiSM1 Blade for 6500	7.0.116.0	No[6]	Yes	No	Yes	Yes	Yes	Yes	No	No
WiSM2 Blade for 6500	7.2.103.0	No[6]	Yes	Yes	Yes	Yes	Yes	Yes	Yes	No
WLC for ISR (ISR2 ISM, SRE700, and SRE900)	7.0.116.0	No[6]	Yes	No	Yes	Yes	Yes	Yes	No	No
WLC for 3750	7.0.116.0	No[6]	Yes	No	Yes	Yes	Yes	Yes	No	No
Routers										
ISR 88x, 89x Series	15.2(2)T	Yes	Yes	No	LWA (L3)	Yes	Yes	No	Yes (IPsec)	No
ISR 19x, 29x, 39x Series	15.2(2)T	Yes	Yes	No	LWA (L3)	Yes	Yes	Yes	Yes (IPsec)	No

1. For 802.1X authentications, you need IOS version 12.2(55)SE3.

2. Does not support posture and profiling services.

3. SGA only.

4. WLCs do not support dACLs, but do support named ACLs. WLCs prior to release 7.0.116.0 do not support CoA and require deployment of an ISE Inline Posture Node to support posture services. Use of an Inline Posture Node requires WLC version 7.0.98 or later. Autonomous AP deployments (no WLC) also require deployment of an Inline Posture Node for posture support. Profiling services are currently supported for 802.1X-authenticated WLANs only on the WLC with CoA support. Hybrid Remote Edge Access Point (HREAP), which is also referred to as FlexConnect, is supported starting with WLC version 7.2. WLCs added support for "Wireless MAB" in version 7.2.

5. An issue has been observed during wireless login scenarios where the WLC is running firmware version 7.0.116.0. Unless you require features available only in version 7.0.116.0, Cisco recommends returning your WLC firmware version to 7.0.98.218 or upgrading your WLC firmware version to 7.0.220.0. For more information, see the Release Notes for Cisco Identity Services Engine, Release 1.1.1.

6. WLCs support MAC filtering with RADIUS lookup. For WLCs that support version 7.2.103.0, there is support for session-ID and CoA with MAC filtering, so it is more MAB-like. Cisco ISE refers to this as "Wireless MAB".

Table 3-2 lists the most capable and recommended infrastructure components for each category (at the time of writing).

Table 3-2 *Recommended Infrastructure Components*

Access Switches	Campus Core Switches	Data Center Switches	Wireless Controllers	Routers	Firewall
Catalyst 3650X/3750X	Catalyst 6500 Supervisor 2T	Nexus 7000 Series	WLC 5500/2500	ISR G2 Models	ASA 5585 9.X
Catalyst 3850	Catalyst 4500 Supervisor 7-E	Nexus 5500 Series	WLC 5760	ISR G3 Models	ASA 5500-X 9.x
Catalyst 4500/4500x			WiSM 2 for Catalyst 6500	ASR 1000 Models	

Policy Components

The Cisco Identity Services Engine comprises the one and only policy component in the ISE solution. Having a single centralized policy engine signifies the power inherent in the ISE solution. Cisco ISE provides a highly powerful and flexible attribute-based access control solution that combines on a single platform authentication, authorization, and accounting (AAA); posture; profiling; and guest management services. Administrators can centrally create and manage access control policies for users and endpoints in a consistent fashion, and gain end-to-end visibility into everything that is connected to the network. Cisco ISE automatically discovers and classifies endpoints, provides the right level of access based on identity, and provides the ability to enforce endpoint compliance by checking a device's posture. Cisco ISE also provides advanced enforcement capabilities, including SGA through the use of Security Group Tags (SGT), Security Group Firewalls such as the Cisco ASA, and Security Group ACLs (SGACL).

Endpoint Components

The network endpoints play an integral role in the total ISE solution. It is the endpoint that provides authentication using 802.1X, MAB, or web authentication. It is also the endpoint that provides posture information to ISE to ensure it is in compliance with security policies. Here are the recommended endpoint components (these are recommended, not required):

- **802.1X Supplicant/Agent:** A supplicant is basically just software that understands how to communicate via Extensible Authentication Protocol over LAN (EAPoL). There are many supplicants available for use. A supplicant is built into Windows and Mac OS-X. Also available via Cisco AnyConnect and other, third-party supplicant software agents. Cisco IP Phones, video equipment, printers, and many other devices now come with built-in supplicants. Nearly any device that is able to use WiFi will have a native supplicant.

■ **Cisco NAC Agent:** For Windows, Mac OS X, and Linux. Provides host posture information to ISE.

In many cases, you will not have the option of adding the recommended endpoint components. This is typically the case with printers, IP-Phones, badge readers, HVAC, and other industrial or biomedical endpoints. It is for this reason that ISE has a profiler service that can automate the process of properly identifying and categorizing devices that can't do it by themselves.

ISE Personas

The ISE architecture has many personas to help it scale to large networks and large numbers of users and devices. Cisco ISE has a highly available and scalable architecture that supports standalone and distributed deployments. ISE has three main personas. The persona or personas of an ISE node determine the services it will provide. An ISE node can assume any or all of the following personas:

■ **Administration:** Allows you to perform all administrative operations in a standalone or distributed Cisco ISE deployment. The Administration node provides a single pane of glass for management. It handles all system-related and policy-based configuration. In a distributed ISE deployment, you can have only one, or a high-availability (HA) pair, of nodes running the Administration persona. An ISE node dedicated to the administration persona is known as a Policy Administration Node (PAN).

■ **Policy Service:** Provides network access, posture, guest access, client provisioning, web portals, and profiling services. This persona evaluates the policies and makes all the decisions. You can have more than one node assume this persona. When a node is dedicated to the Policy Service persona, it is referred to as a Policy Service Node (PSN). Typically, a distributed deployment would have more than one PSN.

■ **Monitoring:** Enables Cisco ISE to function as the log collector and store log messages from all the Administration and Policy Service Nodes in your network. This persona provides advanced monitoring and troubleshooting tools that you can use to manage your network and resources effectively. A node with this persona aggregates and correlates the data that it collects to provide you with meaningful information in the form of reports. Cisco ISE allows you to have a maximum of two nodes with this persona, both of which can take on primary or secondary roles for high availability. Both the primary and secondary Monitoring nodes collect log messages. If the primary Monitoring node goes down, the secondary Monitoring node automatically becomes the primary Monitoring node. When an ISE node is dedicated to the Monitoring persona, it is referred to as a Monitoring & Troubleshooting Node (MnT).

Note   Due to the high performance requirements of the Monitoring persona, in midsize to large deployments, it is recommended that you dedicate a node to specifically run this persona.

ISE also has two node types that determine the node's functions:

- ISE node
- Inline Posture Node (IPN)

Only the ISE node type can be configured with one or more of the previously discussed personas. The inline posture node must be a dedicated node and cannot assume any of the personas. As an inline posture node, it is logically or physically inline in the network. Typically, this means it is behind a VPN headend device or behind a non-Cisco WLC that cannot support CoA or another required feature. While inline, this node type can block traffic and apply other network policies as per the ISE policy rule table.

Figure 3-1 provides an idea of how these personas and node types look logically. Only the primary connections are shown, for simplicity.

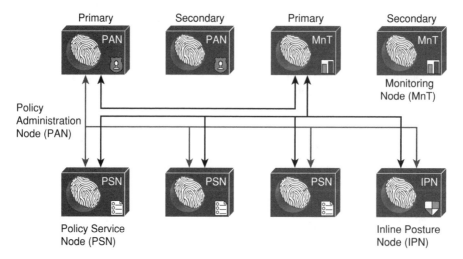

Figure 3-1   *ISE Persona and Node Types*

ISE Licensing, Requirements, and Performance

This section discusses the centralized ISE licensing model, hardware and virtual machine requirements, and the published performance of an ISE node.

ISE Licensing

Identity Services Engine licensing is fairly straightforward. There are only three licenses, and each license is sized for concurrent authenticated users and devices. Figure 3-2 depicts the three ISE license types: Base, Advanced, and Wireless Only.

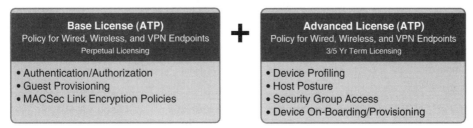

Figure 3-2 *ISE Licensing*

The licenses shown in Figure 3-2 would additionally include a user count. For example, L-ISE-ADV3Y-100= means a 100-user advanced license that is valid for 3 years.

Note   The Advanced license requires the purchase of the Base license as well. The Wireless license includes both Base and Advanced licenses.

ISE Requirements

Cisco ISE comes in two form factors: physical appliance and virtual appliance. The physical appliance comes with the server hardware. The virtual appliance comes as a VMware virtual appliance package that you can load onto a VMware ESX server. The physical appliance comes in three form factors: small, medium, and large (as of this writing). Table 3-3 provides the hardware details.

Table 3-3 *ISE Physical Appliance Specifications*

Platform	Cisco Identity Services Engine Appliance 3415 (Small) UCS-C220-M3	Cisco Identity Services Engine Appliance 3495 (Large)
Processor	Xeon E5-2609 4 core processor @ 2.4 GHz	2 x QuadCore Intel Xenon E5-2609 @ 2.4 GHz

Platform	Cisco Identity Services Engine Appliance 3415 (Small) UCS-C220-M3		Cisco Identity Services Engine Appliance 3495 (Large)
Memory	16 GB		32 GB
Hard disk	1 x 600-GB SAS		2 x 600-GB SAS
RAID	No		Yes (RAID 0+1)
Ethernet NICs	4x 1 Gigabit NICs		4 x Integrated Gigabit NICs
			Dual Pwr, SSL Acceleration card

Platform	Cisco Identity Services Engine Appliance 3315 (Small)	Cisco Identity Services Engine Appliance 3355 (Medium)	Cisco Identity Services Engine Appliance 3395 (Large)
Processor	1 x QuadCore Intel Core 2 CPU Q9400 @ 2.66 GHz (4 total cores)	1 x QuadCore Intel Xeon CPU E5504 @ 2.00 GHz (4 total cores)	2 x QuadCore Intel Xeon CPU E5504 @ 2.00 GHz (8 total cores)
Memory	4 GB	4 GB	4 GB
Hard disk	2 x 250-GB SATA HDD (250 GB total disk space)	2 x 300-GB SAS drives (600 GB total disk space)	4 x 300-GB SFF SAS drives (600 GB total disk space)
RAID	No	Yes (RAID 0)	Yes (RAID 0+1)
Ethernet NICs	4x Integrated Gigabit NICs	4 x Integrated Gigabit NICs	4 x Integrated Gigabit NICs

Given that the physical appliances will be upgraded once or twice a year by Cisco, be sure to check Cisco.com for the latest specifications.

For the virtual appliance, the specifications for the virtual machine (VM) host should be sized at or above the specifications for the physical appliance you are trying to match. For example, if you want to have performance similar to that of a Medium physical appliance, then you would build a VM with the specifications of a Medium appliance shown in Table 3-3. Hard drives with 10-KB or higher RPM are highly recommended for ISE VM. VMware VMotion and cloning are only supported in ISE version 1.2 or later. It is possible to decrease the HD requirements in certain situations. Here are the ISE persona minimum disk space requirements for production VM deployments:

- Standalone ISE: 600 GB

- Administration: 200 GB

- Monitoring: 600 GB

- Administration and Monitoring: 600 GB

- Administration, Monitoring, and Policy Service: 600 GB

- Policy Service: 100 GB (200 GB strongly recommended)

Note   Do not use Intel Hyper-Threading Technology for the ISE VM. Ensure that the correct number of Cores are allocated per VM; it is the Cores that matter in the configuration.

Note   ISE version 1.2 (and later) moved to a 64-bit OS, thus enabling it to address more than 4 GB of RAM memory. ISE 3495 includes 32 GB of RAM.

ISE Performance

ISE performance is dependent on several factors and, unfortunately, is not a straightforward or precise calculation. It is dependent on the node type, persona(s), policy complexity, bandwidth requirements, and several other variables. Table 3-4 through Table 3-6 dissect the different performance specs for ISE. Use typical design guidance when using performance metrics: never exceed 80 percent of stated capacity, and design for 50 percent or less out of the gate. This allows you to build growth into the architecture and ensures that you have a healthy buffer in case your environment doesn't mirror the performance metrics tested and documented by Cisco.

Table 3-4   *ISE Performance*

Platform	Maximum Endpoints	Profiler Events	Posture Authentications
Cisco Identity Services Engine 3315 Appliance	3000	500 per second	70 per second
Cisco Identity Services Engine 3355 Appliance	6000	500 per second	70 per second

Platform	Maximum Endpoints	Profiler Events	Posture Authentications
Cisco Identity Services Engine 3395 Appliance	10,000	1200 per second	110 per second
Cisco Identity Services Engine 3415	5000		
Cisco Identity Services Engine 3495	20,000		

Table 3-5 shows the maximum possible performance per ISE *deployment*, not per ISE node. It assumes Large appliances unless otherwise stated.

Table 3-5   *ISE 1.2 Performance (Maximum per Deployment)*

Description	Number
Maximum number of endpoints with separate Administration, Monitoring, and Policy Service nodes	200,000
Maximum number of endpoints with Administration and Monitoring on a single node	10,000
Maximum number of endpoints with Administration, Monitoring, and Policy Service all on a single node	2000 for all 33x5 platforms, 5000 for 3415, and 10,000 for 3495
Maximum number of Policy Service nodes with separate Administration, Monitoring, and Policy Service nodes	40
Maximum number of Policy Service nodes with Administration and Monitoring on a single node	5
Maximum number of Network Access Devices (NAD)	10,000

When building a distributed ISE deployment, you need to consider the bandwidth requirements that are needed for the ISE personas to exchange information, as outlined in Table 3-6.

Table 3-6   *ISE Bandwidth Requirements*

Description	Requirement
Minimum bandwidth between Monitoring and Policy service	1 Mbps
Minimum bandwidth between Monitoring and Admin	256 Kbps
Minimum bandwidth between client and Policy Service with posture	125 bps per endpoint

Description	Requirement
Minimum bandwidth between Monitoring and Monitoring (redundant)	256 Kbps
Minimum bandwidth between Admin and Policy Service (redundant Admin)	256 Kbps

ISE Policy-Based Structure Explained

The Identity Services Engine solution relies on a policy-driven rule set to make its decisions. ISE has several different policy types that are all consolidated into a policy set. A *policy set* is a grouping of several different policy rules from both authentication and authorization policies. You can then have multiple policy sets that are processed in order, top down. Finally, you can have global exception rules across the entire ISE deployment. The following policy rule types can be called within an ISE policy set:

- Authentication Policy

- Authorization Policy

- Profiling Policy

- Device Posture Policy

- Client Provisioning Policy

- Security Group Access Policy

- Guest Policy

Each policy type will be explained in the configuration section of this book. To enable the policy set view, choose **Administration > System > Settings > Policy** and select Policy set. Given the power of policy sets, it is a best practice to enable this feature.

For now, just realize that, as part of preparing for your ISE deployment, you have these policy types at your disposal. Figure 3-3 shows a simple example of a Policy Set.

In the left pane of Figure 3-3, you can see the Policy Sets. These policy sets are processed from the top down, beginning with the Global Exceptions policy set, followed by the ThirdParty Policy Set, and finally the Default policy set. The Policy Set selected in Figure 3-3, ThirdParty, shows you the Authentication Policies and Authorization Policies that make up this set. These policy rules are also processed from the top down, thus making the ordering of rules very important.

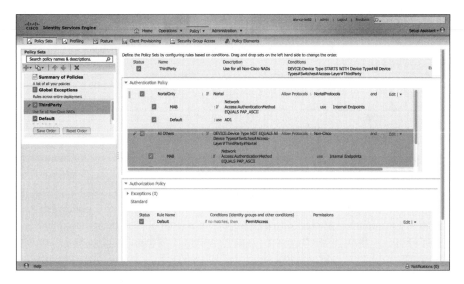

Figure 3-3   *ISE Policy Set Example*

Summary

This chapter provided a baseline to understand all of the building blocks you have to work with inside of ISE. With this knowledge, you can begin to understand your ISE options for the following:

- ISE solution components

- ISE personas

- ISE licensing, requirements, and performance

- ISE policy structure

Chapter 4 explores all of the details of the various deployment options for ISE.

Making Sense of All the ISE Deployment Design Options

Cisco Identity Services Engine supports many different design and deployment options. This chapter explains the options with the goal of helping you to select the best one for your environment. The deployment options are broken down into two main topics to consider: centralized and distributed. This chapter will examine these and other ISE design options.

As discussed in Chapter 3, all ISE node types, such as Administration, Monitoring, and Policy Service, can be made highly available. The node types are broken out from standalone mode to distributed mode when scaling beyond 2000 simultaneous endpoints is required. When ISE is deployed in standalone mode, with all node types running on one ISE appliance, you can deploy a secondary standalone ISE node to act as a backup to the original primary server and all of its running services/nodes. When deploying Cisco ISE in a high-availability scenario, it is important to know how to configure each node type's high availability. Both the Admin and Monitoring nodes work in a primary/standby configuration whereby one active node does all of the work until it fails, at which time the other, backup node takes over. The Policy Service Node (PSN) is different in that it is made resilient either by load balancing between several PSNs or by configuring your Network Access Devices (NAD) with a list of available PSNs to choose from. In the latter case, if the NAD detects a failure of a PSN, it will choose the next one in its list.

Centralized Versus Distributed Deployment

A *centralized deployment* is one in which all of your ISE nodes are physically located in one location, usually adjacent to each other at Layer 2. All local and any remote sites will connect to the centrally deployed ISE nodes.

A *distributed deployment* is one in which your ISE policy services nodes are physically and strategically dispersed in multiple locations. Your Administration and Monitoring nodes remain at your most robust central network location, and only your PSNs are distributed.

In either deployment mode, your configuration, monitoring, and all ISE admin functions will have a consolidated, single pane of glass look and feel for the administrators. Also, both deployment types support the maximum endpoints that can be supported by ISE, which in version 1.2 is 250,000.

Note   The final deployment configuration doesn't need to be determined at the outset of your ISE deployment. In almost all cases, you will do your initial ISE deployment, also known as a proof of concept, in centralized mode.

Whenever you have more than one Policy Services Node that are Layer 2 adjacent, you should use the Node Group function in ISE, which not only enables you to load-balance between multiple PSNs within the same group but also enables you to detect a failure of a PSN within the group. It is recommended that you do not exceed a maximum of four PSNs per node group. All PSNs in a group will exchange multicast update packets in order to detect a failure of a server within the group. If a PSN fails, then the group will send a Change of Authorization (CoA) to the NAD for any sessions in the pending state. A session is in the pending state if it has been authorized but posture assessment is not yet complete. The CoA will force the client to reauthenticate to a new available ISE PSN.

Node Groups and High Availability are both covered in greater detail in Chapter 18, "Setting Up a Distributed Deployment."

Centralized Deployment

Centralized deployment is the most popular method. In a centralized deployment, all ISE nodes are located in the same physical location, with LAN-like bandwidth and latency expected between all ISE nodes. It should be used for small, medium-sized, or large deployments that have a single physical location. Centralized deployment mode also works best if you have remote sites that already connect to a common central site for the vast majority of their services. Figure 4-1 shows an example diagram of a centralized ISE deployment.

Deploying ISE in a campus or other area where all clients and ISE nodes are connected via LAN transport is the ideal situation for a centralized ISE deployment. However, this doesn't exclude you from using this method when you have remote sites that are not using a LAN-like transport. The following are things to consider for centralized deployment with remote attached clients:

- Bandwidth available between the client NADs and the ISE PSN

- Reliability of WAN links/circuits between client NADs and ISE nodes

- Resiliency requirements if the WAN goes down between the client NADs and ISE

- Whether quality of service (QoS) is deployed on the networks between the client NADs and ISE

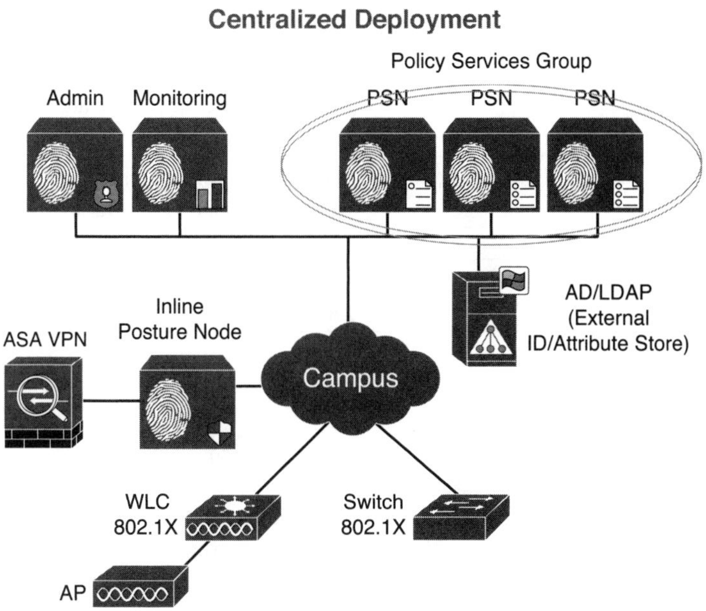

Centralized Deployment

Figure 4-1 *ISE Centralized Deployment*

Calculating exact ISE bandwidth requirements is not a simple or straightforward exercise. There are just too many variables in the mix for that to be the case. However, there are some general guidelines available for estimating your bandwidth needs. The minimum bandwidth required between a client and its PSN with posture assessment enabled is 128 bps per endpoint. You can, and should, use QoS to ensure the ISE traffic is prioritized appropriately over the WAN. Table 4-1 provides some general guidance on bandwidth requirements.

Table 4-1 *Centralized ISE Deployment Bandwidth Guidance*

Process	Flow	Bandwidth Guidance
Min. BW client to PSN with posture	Client to PSN	128 bps per endpoint
AAA RADIUS functions	NAD to PSN	Very low
Posture no remediation	Client to PSN	Low
Web Authentication/Guest Services	Client to PSN	Low (be sure to keep any custom web page graphics to small sizes)
Posture remediation	Client to Remediation Sources	Depends on size and location of remediation files
Profiling with DHCP, SNMP, DNS, HTTP	NAD to PSN	Low

Process	Flow	Bandwidth Guidance
Profiling with NetFlow, SPAN[1]	NAD to PSN	Medium to very high depending on the capture filters and amount of netflow
Syslog monitoring traffic	NAD to Monitoring Node	Low to medium when set to informational and no logging of ACLs
NAC client install or upgrade	Client to PSN	Medium (client software is approx. 30 Mb in size)

1. SPAN = Switched Port Analyzer.

For centralized deployment to work over a WAN, you must have highly reliable WAN links. To ensure your critical ISE communication is successful end to end every time, you will want to use QoS. You should use QoS to prioritize all radius and SNMP communications between NADs and ISE PSNs such that other traffic will not saturate the links to the point that ISE traffic is delayed or dropped, causing authentication and posturing issues for those active clients.

Centralized mode depends on the availability of communications between clients, NADs, and ISE nodes at all times. If this communication is broken temporarily, the Cisco ISE solution does have some resiliency features that can ensure a working solution during the failure. Having robust WAN redundancy in your network greatly reduces the risk of this problem. During an outage, your currently connected clients typically are not impacted, but new clients coming on are impacted. It is up to the local NAD (switch or WLC) to determine how to treat new devices connecting during a WAN outage. Catalyst switches support several failure scenario solutions: fail open, fail closed, or fail to a specific VLAN.

Distributed Deployment

Even though the centralized deployment method is generally recommended, there are some use cases where a distributed deployment works better. Here are some examples:

- You want to increase ISE resiliency by distributing ISE nodes across redundant data centers.

- You want to ensure Remote site resiliency against a WAN outage.

- You need the ISE PSN profiler to be local to the clients it is serving. This is typically for cases when you are forced to use Switched Port Analyzer (SPAN) or netflow probes to access client traffic.

Note   You must use ISE version 1.2 or greater for a distributed deployment.

In a distributed ISE deployment, the Admin and Monitoring nodes are both centralized, while the policy services nodes are geographically dispersed.

> **Note**   The nodes in an Admin HA pair or Monitoring HA pair do not need to be Layer 2 adjacent to each other; they can be multiple Layer 3 hops away from each other. However, low-latency, high-bandwidth links must be available between the primary and secondary nodes.

In this model, you are placing your PSNs closer to both your NADs and your clients. This results in better performance and a more scalable ISE deployment, especially when working with high-latency, long-distance, or bandwidth-constrained WAN connections. Figure 4-2 depicts an example ISE distributed deployment model.

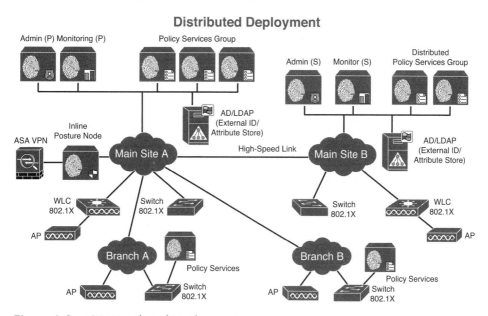

Figure 4-2   *ISE Distributed Deployment*

In a distributed deployment such as the one shown in Figure 4-2, the databases between all of the ISE nodes are automatically synchronized. The Primary Admin node is the source of all database replication traffic. Its job is to replicate the database to all other ISE nodes, including monitoring, policy services, and a secondary admin node. Upon registering a secondary node (that is, as any node that is not the Admin primary) with the primary admin node, a database sync connection is automatically set up between the two nodes. A full copy of the database is kept up to date in near real time on all nodes by the primary admin node. This includes configuration changes. You can view the status of replication from the Deployment pages of the ISE Administrative user interface.

Of course, this synchronization also happens in a centralized deployment, but because these nodes have LAN connectivity, you don't need to worry about its performance. Over a WAN, however, you do need to consider the ramifications of database replications, especially as they pertain to latency and bandwidth requirements. To this end, Cisco has developed a bandwidth and latency calculator to help you determine the correct specifications required. Unfortunately, this calculator is only available to Cisco resellers and employees. In lieu of the calculator, Table 4-2 provides some general guidance.

Table 4-2 *Minimum Bandwidth Requirements*

Description	Requirement
Minimum bandwidth between Monitoring and Policy Service	1 Mbps
Minimum bandwidth between Monitoring and Admin	256 Kbps
Minimum bandwidth between Client and Policy Service with posture	125 bps per endpoint
Minimum bandwidth between Monitoring and Monitoring (redundant)	256 Kbps
Minimum bandwidth between Admin and Policy Service (redundant admin)	256 Kbps

Table 4-2 lists the absolute minimum, so be sure to scale up as required. Additionally, all database sync and replication traffic should be given QoS priority just below radius, voice, and video but above normal traffic types.

A partial database replication is triggered whenever a PSN sends a database update to the primary Admin node. The primary admin node then initiates an update replication to all other ISE nodes. When deploying ISE distributed PSNs, note that AAA/RADIUS and posture-assessment features cause very minimal database replication traffic. ISE profiling and Guest Services, however, can cause lots of database replication traffic due to their frequent database writes and updates. As a result, lower latency and higher bandwidth WAN links are necessary when using these services within your ISE deployment.

Note   NetFlow and SPAN-based collection methods are *not* supported for distributed deployments due to the potentially high volume of data replication required by these methods.

In the event of a loss of connectivity to the Administration node, distributed policy services nodes will continue to provide full authentication and authorization services to their local NADs and endpoints. This assumes that the cut-off PSN still has access to its AAA resources. Note that the following disruptions occur on the PSN until the Admin node is brought back online:

■ Cannot authenticate new sponsored or self-service Guest user accounts.

■ Cannot profile new endpoints.

- Logging is interrupted if connectivity between the PSN and Monitoring node is also lost.

- Automatic client provisioning services will not function.

Summary

This chapter examined the centralized deployment mode and the distributed deployment mode. It suggested that in most cases, the centralized mode should be used. However, it also presented use cases in which the distributed mode is preferable. See Chapter 18, "Setting Up a Distributed ISE Deployment," for details on the configuration when distributing the ISE personas.

Chapter 5

Following a Phased Deployment

One of the most common mistakes that you can make in any 802.1X deployment is to perform a quick and incomplete proof of concept and then deploy too much technology, too fast. There is so much power that can be enabled in a Secure Access deployment. More often than not an organization will attempt the deployment all at once, instead of deploying the technology in more manageable portions.

This chapter examines deployment concepts, and discusses a framework that will allow you to deploy Secure Access in a manageable way, with little to no impact on the end users. This chapter provides an overview of the phases of deploying the Secure Access solution. The details and configuration involved in each phase are covered in Chapters 21 through 23.

Why Use a Phased Deployment Approach?

Let's introduce this topic with a fun little history lesson. Back in the late 1990s and early 2000s, a new technology was introduced to the world, called IEEE 802.1X. This technology allows a device to authenticate to the network at Layer 2, using the Extensible Authentication Protocol (EAP) over the LAN. At the time, it was a revolutionary concept that was going to change current networking as we all knew it. The predictions were that, within a few years, there would not be a single switch port in the world where a user/device could plug in without the network knowing the identity of that device or user.

Well, there are some very interesting and complex dependencies required to deploy 802.1X in a successful manner. For example, it not only requires a switch that is able to communicate with EAP over LAN (EAPoL), which is what 802.1X actually defines, but also requires that the endpoint system have software that can communicate with EAPoL. This software is called a *supplicant*.

As you can imagine, there are a number of devices that could be deployed that may not have a supplicant, or that may not have a supplicant that can be easily configured. Examples include printers, fax machines, cameras, thin clients, conference room scheduling tools, digital signage devices, and many more.

A phased approach to deployment allows the network administration team to enable authentication in a controlled manner on a definable portion of the network over a period of time. Moreover, it allows the network administration team to initially place a section of the network into Monitor Mode. Monitor Mode allows an administrator to audit which endpoints or users would have failed authentication without denying access to that user or device.

Cisco has developed three modes that are used throughout a phased deployment: Monitor Mode, Low-Impact Mode, and Closed Mode. The concept is to begin the deployment in Phase 1 using Monitor Mode and then transition to Phase 2 using either of the two end-state modes, Low-Impact Mode or Closed Mode, as shown in Figure 5-1. These modes are discussed in turn in the following sections.

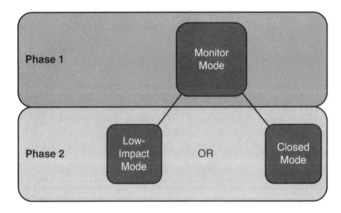

Figure 5-1   *Phase from Monitor Mode to Low-Impact or Closed Mode*

Monitor Mode

It's very important to understand that Monitor Mode is much more than a command; it's a process. Think back to the history lesson from the previous section, when companies would enable 802.1X on the switch ports. Only a certain percentage of the devices would successfully authenticate.

The success of any identity-related project typically requires the cooperation and coordination of several different teams within the company. The desktop team should be responsible for the supplicant deployment and configuration of company workstations. The network team must be involved to configure 802.1X on the switches and wireless controllers. If there is a separate team that manages Active Directory, that team must also be included.

There have been many cases of 802.1X deployments in which even managed systems failed authentication. In such cases, the issue may have been something very simple. For example, perhaps the Windows XP workstations were not successfully rebooted after the Group Policy pushed the new configuration to the built-in supplicant, and therefore those systems failed authentication, or perhaps those managed systems did not receive the software package that installed the third-party supplicant.

In addition to the managed workstations, there will typically be a number of noninteractive and nonauthenticating devices. These are the devices that either do not have an end user who will be logged in to them in an interactive fashion or do not have a supplicant to authenticate to the network.

There are usually a number of devices that the IT department did not know existed in their network. These are the "one-off" deployments where a group within the company have deployed a nonstandard technology. For example, Linux workstations may have been deployed for a specific group, or a thin client solution may have been deployed only for a "special project."

The purpose of Monitor Mode is to allow an organization to enable authentication on the network ports in an audit phase without any danger of denying access to the endpoint. In other words, devices that can authenticate will authenticate, and devices that fail authentication (or simply cannot authenticate at all) will not be denied access but instead will be logged as failing authentication.

The administrator can then use the logged failures to identify devices that have been denied access, and remediate any existing issues prior to enabling authentication as a requirement for network access. Remediation may involve correcting misconfigured supplicants, or configuring Cisco Identity Services Engine (ISE) to permit specific nonauthenticating devices via MAC Authentication Bypass (MAB). When deploying Monitor Mode, most organizations are surprised to find devices connected to the network that they were unaware of previously.

The key to Monitor Mode is that no enforcement should be applied. As previously stated, Monitor Mode is not a command on a device; rather, it ensures that the policy server (ISE) will not send any authorization other than RADIUS Access-Accept or RADIUS Access-Reject (and device-traffic-class=voice for phones). Any other authorization result, such as VLAN assignment or ACL assignment, will in fact take effect.

The flow of Monitor Mode is displayed in Figure 5-2.

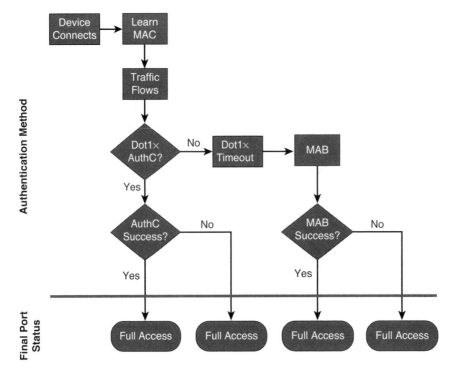

Figure 5-2   *Monitor Mode Always Results in Full Access*

Choosing Your End-State Mode

As previously discussed, Monitor Mode is implemented during the first phase of any deployment and is considered the "audit mode." However, the goal of any identity-related project is to eventually provide security. This process begins with Phase 2 when you transition to an end state of either Low-Impact Mode or Closed Mode.

Originally, 802.1X was designed to be binary, with either Full Access or No Access as the only possible outcome, as illustrated in Figure 5-3.

This concept is most likely very familiar to you if you have experience connecting to a wireless network. When you configure your device's wireless supplicant to connect to a Wi-Fi network, the authentication first must succeed. If that authentication fails, your device simply does not associate to the wireless network and you are denied access.

That behavior has been quite successful in wireless networks for many reasons, some of which are

■ The wireless network must be chosen (that is, which SSID you are configuring your laptop to connect to).

■ A guest selects the specific GUEST network (whatever that SSID may be called).

■ It is expected to provide authentication to the corporate (non-GUEST) network.

■ A device does not "plug into" a wireless network; it must be configured. The wireless network may require authentication. Once completed, the end user enters credentials into the wireless supplicant.

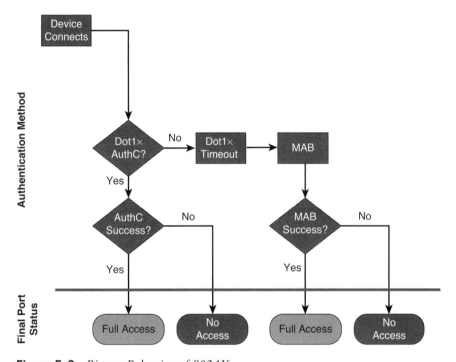

Figure 5-3   *Binary Behavior of 802.1X*

In the wired network world, there is no concept of an SSID. The client device does not "choose" to connect to a guest or to a corporate network. Therefore, configuring a single switch port to handle all possible use cases is much more complex.

As introduced earlier in the chapter, the two end-state modes are Low-Impact Mode and Closed Mode. It is key to the long-term success of your project to determine which mode works best for your organization, and then work toward that deployment. It's entirely possible that your organization may benefit from a hybrid approach, using different modes at different locations. We have worked with banking and retail customers, both of whom found it most beneficial to use Low-Impact Mode in the headquarters campus but Closed Mode in their bank branches and retail store locations, respectively.

End-State Choice 1: Low-Impact Mode

Low-Impact Mode builds on top of Monitor Mode. This mode is more desirable than Closed Mode in environments that have many nonauthenticating devices. Some examples of environments where Low-Impact Mode has been most successful include:

■ Preboot Execution Environment (PXE), commonly used for corporate workstation reimaging

■ Virtual desktop infrastructure (VDI) environments, in which thin clients are deployed into the campus or branch network and do not have configurable supplicants

■ Any environment with diskless workstations or thin clients

Low-Impact Mode is more desirable for these environments because it allows specific traffic to flow prior to authentication. Examples of protocols that would be allowed prior to authentication are DHCP, DNS, and TFTP. This permits a device to receive an IP address and even begin downloading its operating system from the server without worrying about timers.

Timers can wreak havoc in an 802.1X environment. There are many "race conditions" that may exist. For example, DHCP may time out before the authentication timer expires, causing the device to wind up without a valid IP address. Low-Impact Mode resolves these race conditions by allowing only a limited amount of traffic to enter the switch port prior to authentication.

Figure 5-4 illustrates the flows of Low-Impact Mode.

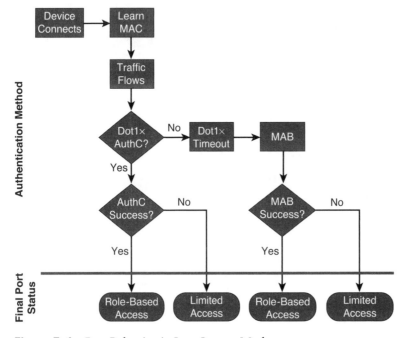

Figure 5-4   *Port Behavior in Low-Impact Mode*

If the device is successfully authenticated via 802.1X, MAB, or even web authentication, the authorization result should be configured to allow full network access, or very specific access that has been tailored for that user or device.

There is no limit to the authorization results (enforcement types) available in Low-Impact Mode. However, there are considerations. If the organization chooses to do VLAN assignment, only devices with supplicants will react predictably to the change from the default VLAN to the final VLAN. Any device without a supplicant may not recognize that there is a VLAN change, and therefore may not get the correct IP address for the final VLAN. This is related to the fact that the device's DHCP client may only request a new IP address based upon lease expiration parameters or the physical link being lost on the Ethernet interface.

Table 5-1 lists and describes the common wired enforcement options available in Low-Impact Mode.

Table 5-1   *Available Enforcement Types with Low-Impact Mode*

Enforcement Type	Description
Downloadable ACL (dACL)	dACLs are defined within the ISE GUI, and the entire ACL is downloaded to the switch as part of the authorization. This is a Cisco-proprietary option that allows the administrator to centrally define all ACLs without having to configure them on every Network Access Device (NAD).
Dynamic VLAN (dVLAN) assignment	dVLAN assignment is the ability of ISE to send a VLAN ID or VLAN name to the switch as part of the authorization. It ensures that the VLAN is assigned to the switch port for as long as the authentication session is still active.
Security Group Tag (SGT)	SGTs are used with Security Group Access (SGA). SGA is an advanced enforcement type that allows Tag to be assigned to an authentication session at the ingress NAD (the point where the device or user is entering the network) and applies enforcement based on that SGT elsewhere in the network (such as at firewalls or data center switches). SGA is also a Cisco-proprietary enhancement.
Filter-ID	Filter-ID is the industry-standard way of applying ACLs to a switch port after an authentication. ISE responds to the authentication request with a Filter-ID that identifies an ACL that is locally configured on the NAD.
URL-Redirection	URL-Redirection is a Cisco-proprietary enhancement that allows the NAD to redirect all HTTP/HTTPS traffic to a specific URL. This is commonly used in Secure Access deployments with Centralized Web Authentication (CWA).

Within the Low-Impact Mode end state, deploying these enforcement mechanisms slowly is still recommended. In other words: start simple and then get more specific.

One common way to accomplish this is to permit full access to all successful authentications first, and then tune the enforcements to be more specific later in the deployment. That way, determining exactly which ports or protocols need to be opened for each role type is does not stall the deployment.

End-State Choice 2: Closed Mode

Closed Mode is also known as the default 802.1X mode. Sometimes it is also called High-Security Mode. Don't be fooled by the names, though; this mode is not necessarily any more secure than Low-Impact Mode, as long as Low-Impact Mode is configured carefully. With Wi-Fi networks, Closed Mode is the only possible mode.

In Closed Mode, only 802.1X (EAPoL) traffic is permitted into the switch port prior to an authentication. That means that 802.1X timers will be a critical consideration for a successful Closed Mode deployment, to ensure that nonauthenticating devices will receive the appropriate access prior to DHCP timeouts.

Figure 5-5 illustrates the flow of Closed Mode.

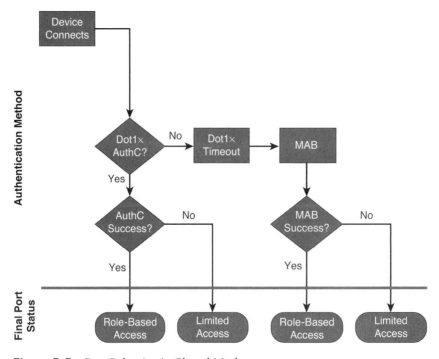

Figure 5-5 *Port Behavior in Closed Mode*

Just as with Low-Impact Mode, several authorization enforcements may be used with Closed Mode. Table 5-2 lists and describes the common wired enforcement options available in Closed Mode.

Table 5-2 *Available Enforcement Types with Closed Mode*

Enforcement Type	Description
Downloadable ACL (dACL)	dACLs are defined within the ISE GUI, and the entire ACL is downloaded to the switch as part of the authorization. This is a Cisco-proprietary option that allows the administrator to centrally define all ACLs, eliminating the need to configure them on every NAD.
Dynamic VLAN (dVLAN) assignment	dVLAN assignment is the ability of ISE to send a VLAN ID or VLAN name to the switch as part of the authorization. It ensures that the VLAN is assigned to the switch port for as long as the authentication session is still active.
Security Group TAG (SGT)	SGTs are used with Security Group Access (SGA). SGA is an advanced enforcement type that allows a Tag to be assigned to an authentication session at the ingress NAD (the point where the device or user is entering the network) and applies enforcement based on that SGT elsewhere in the network (such as at firewalls or data center switches). SGA is also a Cisco-proprietary enhancement.
Filter-ID	Filter-ID is the industry-standard way of applying ACLs to a switch port after an authentication. ISE will respond to the authentication request with a Filter-ID that identifies an ACL that is locally configured on the NAD.
URL-Redirection	URL-Redirection is a Cisco-proprietary enhancement that allows the NAD to redirect all HTTP/HTTPS traffic to a specific URL. This is commonly used in Secure Access deployments with Centralized Web Authentication (CWA).

Within the Closed Mode end state, deploying these enforcement mechanisms slowly is still recommended. In other words: start simple and then get more specific. One common way of doing this is to permit full access to all successful authentications at first, and then tune the enforcements to be more specific later in the deployment. That way, determining exactly which ports or protocols need to be opened for each role type does not stall the deployment.

Transitioning from Monitor Mode into an End-State Mode

Regardless of which end-state mode you choose for your organization, a staged approach is always the best way to transition gracefully from Monitor Mode to your chosen end-state mode. This is among the most critical concepts to ensure that there is little to no impact to the end users. Because Cisco ISE is a policy server for the entire deployment, the procedures created will affect every NAD. In other words, if care is not taken in the policy creation process, a single change may affect many or all end users connecting at all locations, not just at the location that is currently being deployed.

This book follows the best practice and uses Network Device Groups (NDGs) to dictate the mode of all the ports in a switch. Therefore, the authorization policy in ISE will send specific authorization results only to switches that are in an end-state NDG, and not to those that are in the Monitor Mode NDG. This practice is covered in detail in Chapter 22 and Chapter 23.

Figure 5-6 shows an example usage of a top-level NDG named Stage that has child groups named for each mode of deployment.

Figure 5-6   *Network Device Groups*

Summary

Implementing Secure Access with a phased approach to deployment is critical to the success of the project. Cisco provides three modes to assist with this phased approach: Monitor Mode, Low-Impact Mode, and Closed Mode.

The first phase should always be Monitor Mode, and upon completion of the project, the deployment should end up in either Low-Impact Mode or Closed Mode. Even within the end-state mode, it is recommended to slowly lock down the end user or device, and not to try to "boil the ocean."

Chapter 6

Building a Cisco ISE Network Access Security Policy

In order for any network-centric security solution to be successful, a solid network access security policy (NASP) must first be employed. Once a policy is in place, ISE will enforce the policy network wide. A network access security policy defines, in as much detail as is practical, the type of network access that will be given to users and device types. Because network and device security threats are constantly changing, a network access security policy must also be a living, changeable document. This book does not attempt to assemble an all-encompassing network access security policy; instead, it focuses on showing you how to build policies that are relevant to the Cisco ISE solution. Thus, this chapter guides you through the process of creating a comprehensive network access security policy that you can use in an environment that is safeguarded by Cisco ISE. Building a network access security policy is not always straightforward, and can even be frustrating at times, but stick with it; your hard work will be rewarded in the end.

What Makes Up a Cisco ISE Network Access Security Policy?

One of the hardest things about writing a comprehensive network access security policy is figuring out what should be included. This chapter guides you through the parts and pieces that, at a minimum, should be included in any network access security policy written for the Cisco ISE solution. In order for your ISE solution to be most effective, you first must determine exactly what an acceptable network access security posture is under different circumstances and contexts. After you do so, you can then translate your network access security policy into the proper checks, rules, and security requirements that ISE will use to determine the correct policy to apply to the network and/or device. For example, if the device is not a corporate asset and is connected to the corporate wireless network, then a strict network access security policy should be enforced. However, if a registered corporate asset of the same device type connects to the corporate wireless network, a less strict security policy should be enforced. You also need to determine what the network access security policy should be for different types of devices and their security posture. For example, if a contractor logs in to your network using a Windows 8 laptop, the security policy would differ from that applied to the same user logging in with a Mac OS X laptop.

An ISE NASP is made up of several different policy types. When combined inside ISE, these policy types provide you with the ultimate in flexibility for achieving a truly context-aware network access decision. The following are selected policy types for which ISE will obtain contextual information it can then use to build such policies:

- **Authentication Policy:** Verifies the user's and/or device's identity or provides unauthenticated guest access. For example: Authenticate all wireless users against the corporate Active Directory (AD).

- **Authorization Policy:** Describes both the contextual attributes used for authorization of the user and/or device and the enforcement method triggered once a policy rule is matched. For example: Users who are members of the AD group *Employees* and are using an approved company-owned device are allowed to use the wireless SSID corp.

- **Host Posture Assessment Policy:** Deals with the security level of the device itself and relies on a Cisco NAC Agent to gather this data for ISE. (Note: Different operating systems and device types offer different levels of posture assessment capability.) For example: All Windows 8 PCs must have all corporate patches and be running an approved up-to-date antimalware software package.

- **Device Profiling Policy:** Allows you to set policy based on the type of device that is trying to access your network. Profiling is an agentless method of passively watching the device's behavior and/or responses to determine what type of device it is. For example: If a user connects with an iPhone, it does not allow them access to any data center or HR resource.

The preceding list is not comprehensive but showcases the most popular policy types typically included in a comprehensive network access security policy.

Network Access Security Policy Checklist

The following is a checklist of the most common steps that are considered necessary to create an ISE network access security policy. Each checklist item will be explained in detail in the subsequent sections of this chapter. Use this checklist, along with the detailed explanations, to get a head start in the creation of your own unique network access security policy:

- ❐ Obtain senior management sponsors that will support you through the creation of the network access security policy and the deployment of the ISE solution.

- ❐ Determine which people and departments need to be involved in the creation of the network access security policy. Make sure they are included right from the start of the project.

❑ Determine what your high-level goals for network access security are.

❑ Break up your organization into security domains. The requirements of the network access security policy can then be customized for each security domain as necessary.

❑ Define authorization rules that are relevant for your organization.

❑ Establish an acceptable use policy (AUP) for your network.

❑ Define the ISE network access security checks, rules, and requirements for each authorization rule.

❑ Define the network access privileges that should be granted to each authorization rule.

❑ Define your guest access privileges, methods, and policies.

❑ Establish your security and access policy for Bring Your Own Device (BYOD).

❑ Establish a Network Access Security Policy life-cycle process that allows for the regular updating and changing of the network access security policy's checks, rules, and requirements.

Involving the Right People in the Creation of the Network Access Security Policy

At the very beginning of the planning for an ISE deployment or purchase, it is extremely important to obtain project sponsorship from senior-level management. Given that ISE will force a change on the user community's behavior and network access, this is a mandatory step. Without senior-level sponsorship, a few users who are not happy with or willing to accept the new policy changes could derail your ISE deployment. Having the endorsement of senior management grants you the power to push back on those users in a constructive way.

Too often the security group spends the time to develop sound security policies and practices only to be told that they are overly restrictive and need to be changed. This can be avoided by making sure that you keep your sponsors involved and up to date on the progress and content of your network access security policy. It is also critical that you have your final version approved by your sponsorship committee prior to releasing it to the public. Try to anticipate the type of reaction, resistance, and questions the user community will have. Be ready with solid rebuttals, facts, and collateral to combat their arguments, answer their questions, and make them feel more comfortable that the new network access security policy is the correct one.

While creating your network access security policy, keep in mind that Cisco ISE provides access control plus access enablement. Stress to your stakeholders and users that implementing network access controls via ISE enables IT to provide network access from more places and for more device types. Here are a few examples of the improved network access and less restrictive device type rules an ISE deployment can enable:

- The ISE Guest Server provides the ability for any employee to create a guest account for a visitor from anywhere on the network.

- ISE guest auto-provisioning of Ethernet ports and wireless access allows guests to connect to any available access method.

- ISE policy control allows your employees to use their own devices (BYOD) on your network securely (for example, personal iOS and Android devices).

- ISE policy control eliminates help desk calls to enable/disable or reprovision Ethernet ports. All ports can be kept enabled while ISE provisions them on-the-fly.

- ISE allows you to collapse the number of wireless SSIDs you need to advertise down to only one or two. ISE then provisions the access control dynamically for each device/user.

Focus your messaging on the benefits that are unlocked as a result of the increased network access control and security that ISE provides. Doing so will increase acceptance of the ISE solution by both the user community and the business stakeholders.

One of the first steps in the creation of any network access security policy (NASP) is the formation of the network access security policy committee. This committee should be made up of the principal persons whose groups or users will be most affected by or have some ownership in the new policy. It is a best practice to try to keep the committee small in the beginning phases of the policy creation. Once this core team has clear direction, some substance, and some content, then the NASP committee should be expanded to include more key persons.

When the NASP reaches a completed draft format, the NASP committee should again be expanded. This time the expansion is to include those principal persons who do not have any direct ownership or responsibility for the creation of the NASP but do have a sizeable user community that will be directly affected by the policy's proposed changes. This last group serves to scrutinize the policies in your NASP draft to make sure the policies do not inhibit business practices or workflow, are practical, and have achieved the proper balance of risk mitigation versus ease of network access for the organization.

Once a final NASP version has been created, the entire committee must agree to present a united front when the new policy begins to be enforced inside the organization. A nonunited, or splintered, NASP committee almost always will result in the splintering or haphazard adoption of the network access security policy within the organization.

The following is a list of the most common principal persons that should be a part of the creation of a network access security policy. Additionally, the CISO and CIO must be sponsors or core committee members. You should modify this list for your environment.

- Sponsors should include the following:
    - At least one CxO-level sponsor other than the CSO/CIO

- At least one company board member

- Someone from the legal department

■ Core NASP committee members should include key persons from the following groups:

- Security group

- Networking group

- Server group

- Desktop support group

- Operations group

- Security Incident Response team

■ Extended NASP committee members should include key persons from the following groups:

- Human Resources group

- Legal group

- Audit group

■ Final NASP committee members should include the following key persons:

- Managers of large end-user groups within the organization (such as division heads, department heads, and so on)

- Sampling of individuals from the end-user community, for feedback and impact analysis

This list should be used as a guideline and is not meant to be all-inclusive. The goal of committee member selection is to ensure the committee has adequate representation from all key stakeholders, budget holders, management, legal counsel, and technical staff. Each group will have a slightly different role to fulfill on the committee.

Determining the High-Level Goals for Network Access Security

Determining what your high-level goals are for network access security is a critical step toward the completion of a comprehensive network access security policy. These high-level goals will serve as your benchmarks and guides throughout the NASP creation process. The final NASP document should represent a detailed plan that achieves these high-level goals. It is important to periodically refer back to these high-level goals to ensure your NASP remains focused and on target to meet your stated security goals.

A definitive reference for creating a security policy is RFC 2196. The following comes from RFC 2196, *Site Security Handbook* (http://www.ietf.org/rfc/rfc2196.txt):

Your goals will be largely determined by the following key tradeoffs:

(1) services offered versus security provided –

Each service offered to users carries its own security risks. For some services, the risk outweighs the benefit of the service and the administrator may choose to eliminate the service rather than try to secure it.

(2) ease of use versus security –

The easiest system to use would allow access to any user and require no passwords; that is, there would be no security. Requiring passwords makes the system a little less convenient, but more secure. Requiring device-generated one-time passwords makes the system even more difficult to use, but much more secure.

(3) cost of security versus risk of loss –

There are many different costs to security: monetary (i.e., the cost of purchasing security hardware and software like firewalls and one-time password generators), performance (i.e., encryption and decryption take time), and ease of use (as mentioned above). There are also many levels of risk: loss of privacy (i.e., the reading of information by unauthorized individuals), loss of data (i.e., the corruption or erasure of information), and the loss of service (e.g., the filling of data storage space, usage of computational resources, and denial of network access). Each type of cost must be weighed against each type of loss.

Note   For more detailed information about the creation of network access security goals and security policies in general, reference IETF RFC 2196 at http://www.ietf.org/rfc/rfc2196.txt.

Your final high-level network access security goals will be the result of establishing a fine balance among the preceding trade-offs. The result of each trade-off will be different for each organization or division within an organization.

Common High-Level Network Access Security Goals

Here are some examples of network access security goals that are frequently instituted in organizations that deploy an ISE solution. These examples are meant to be a sampling and not a comprehensive list.

- Enforce a consistent context-based policy across the infrastructure for corporate governance.

- Obtain system-wide visibility showing who, what, and where a user or device is on the wired, wireless, or VPN network.

- Protect the network from unauthorized access, both internal and external, at all network access points.

- Authenticate all users attempting to gain access to the network.

- Authorize all users attempting to gain access to the network.

- Provide differentiated network access based on user and device attributes and context.

- All non-guest mobile devices must be enrolled in the corporate Mobile Device Management system.

- All users must periodically acknowledge an acceptable use policy before being granted network access.

- All PCs and Macs must be running an approved antimalware and personal firewall program that is up to date.

- All devices must be running an approved operating system that is up to date.

- Any device that is found to be running banned software applications will be denied network access.

- All guest devices must be segmented from non-guest devices and provided only Internet access.

- Corporate devices are not allowed to use the guest network.

It is common for an organization to modify its network access security goals based on a specific network location or access type. For example, an organization might have a policy that states that all devices connecting through wireless in the corporate headquarters must be corporate owned in order to gain network access.

Many organizations choose to deploy an ISE solution gradually by enforcing their network access security policies incrementally. Initially, network access security policy enforcement is instituted just for visibility into the users and device types that are on the network. Once this is done, the next popular step is mobile device provisioning, onboarding, and enrollment in a Mobile Device Management (MDM) system. Then, as the adoption of the ISE solution grows, the network access security policy enforcement is spread ubiquitously throughout the organization.

Figure 6-1 summarizes the process for determining the exact network access security policy that will be enforced for a given user, for a given device, or in a given network location.

The following list explains the device security policy decision steps shown in Figure 6-1. Following this list are several sections that describe these steps in greater detail.

1. The device connects to a location on the network.

2. The device is determined to be a member of a certain security domain. The NASP must define what the security domains are for the organization. The NASP must define one of three choices for each unique security domain:

■ Which security domains will not have ISE deployed, thus allowing unrestricted network access? The network access security policy for this security domain states that no network access security policies are to be enforced in this domain.

■ Which devices are exempt to ISE access control when they are seen on the network? In some cases, IP Phones would fall into this category.

■ Which security domains will force devices to comply fully with the ISE network access security policy?

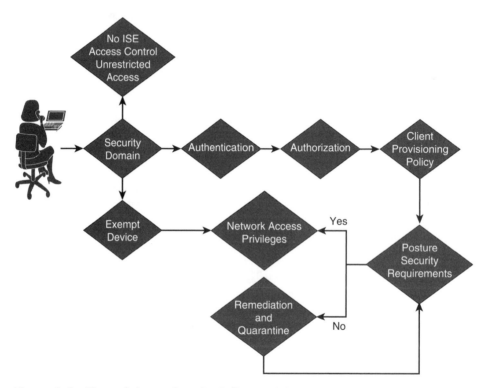

Figure 6-1   *Network Access Security Policy Decision Matrix*

3. If the device is a member of the exempt list, then it flows directly to the network access privileges. The remaining steps below are bypassed. The NASP must define exactly what the network access privileges will be for each type of exempt device. It is possible to have different network access security policies for different types of exempt devices. For example, you can have an exempt network access security policy that allows IP Phones to access the network unrestricted.

4. If the device is part of a security domain that requires full compliance with the ISE policy, then the client is forced to authenticate. The NASP should determine exactly how the user and/or device are authenticated and verified.

5. After successfully authenticating, the user and/or device is then authorized using points of context, including input from profiler, to determine their network access privileges.

6. The client provisioning rules are processed. These can configure the native 802.1X supplicant and deliver the Cisco NAC Agent to the client.

7. The posture of the device is checked to make sure it meets all the requirements defined for their assigned authorization rule. The NASP should define what the security requirements are.

8. If the posture requirements are met, the compiled access privileges are assigned to the network. The NASP should define the type of network access that should be granted to clients. The access requirements are produced from a combination of authentication, authorization, profiler, and posture rules combined.

9. If the device fails to meet its security requirements, it is moved into network quarantine. Typically, self-remediation functions are also provided here. The NASP should clearly specify what network access privileges, remediation functions, and time limits should be imposed on quarantined devices.

Defining the Security Domains

A security domain is used to group network areas, device types, and/or locations under a common network access security policy. The goal of creating security domains for an ISE solution is to define which networks and locations will require devices to use the ISE solution and which locations will not. It is also necessary to define the devices that will require exemption from the ISE solution within a given security domain. Figure 6-2 shows an example of security domains.

Most organizations will need to define the security domains that are depicted in Figure 6-2. Almost all organizations have an Internet connection, use VPN, have a WAN and Campus LAN, and use wireless. Because each of these network access types or locations usually requires its own unique network access security policy, each should be its own security domain. Many corporations also implement separate security domains for their data center areas and their Voice over IP (VoIP) segments. Separating these areas into unique security domains allows you to create unique network access security policies for each. The more compartmentalized your NASP is, the more granular and targeted it can be. This results in a more locked-down network access security policy for your organization. Using security domains is optional, of course, but makes a great way to segment your network access security policy. Above all, try to keep your policy short and concise; the keep it short and simple (KISS) principle applies here.

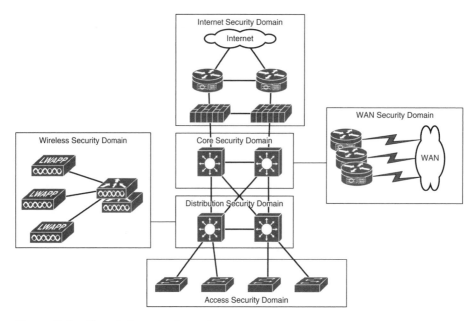

Figure 6-2   *Sample Security Domains*

Here are some commonly used security domains:

- **Remote Access:** This domain includes any device that is accessing the network remotely via VPN and/or dial-up modem.

- **OOB Management:** This domain includes any device that resides on the out-of-band network management network. This is typically a highly secured domain.

- **Internet:** This domain includes any device that accesses the Internet. An example policy for this domain could be: Before a device is allowed to access the Internet, its operating system and antivirus software must be up to date.

- **Guest:** This domain includes any device that is a guest on the network. This domain typically is segmented into access types as well (for example, guest wireless, guest VPN, and guest LAN domains). This allows for the creation of very granular network access security policies for guests.

- **Campus LAN:** This domain includes any device that connects to the network via a wired switch port. It is very common to separate security domains by VLAN or location at the LAN level. This allows the NASP to have policies for specific VLANs and locations instead of having one generic policy for all wired devices.

- **Wireless:** This domain includes any device that uses wireless to access the network. It is common for the wireless domain to be separated out by VLAN or location (for example, a guest wireless security domain or a Denver campus wireless security domain).

This list is by no means comprehensive, but it should serve to give you a good start in the creation of your own security domains.

Understanding and Defining ISE Authorization Rules

The effective use of authorization rules is a key component to any successful ISE deployment. ISE is very much rule based. An authorization rule defines the network access security policies that will be required for its members. The concept of authorization rules is the backbone of ISE.

The login information is used to gather attributes from an external identity server such as LDAP or RADIUS.

> **Tip**   It is a best practice to map attributes from an external authentication server (such as AD, LDAP, or RADIUS) to an authorization rule in ISE. A common attribute used is MemberOf in Windows AD. This allows authorization rules to be based on existing AD groups within your organization. For example, an LDAP user *Conor* is a MemberOf AD group *employee*.

ISE authorization rules have policies that determine which ISE functions will be performed on clients. All clients that match the authorization rule will be subjected to its security permissions. The common permissions that can be controlled by authorization rules are as follows:

- Access Type (Accept/Reject)
- Apply a security group tag to the client traffic
- Downloadable ACLs
- VLAN Assignment
- Voice Domain Permission
- Initiate Web Authentication
- Execute Switch Auto Smart Port
- Filter-ID—Sends ACL via RADIUS filter attribute
- Reauthentication—Decide if you want to maintain connectivity during reauthentication
- MACSec Policy—Sets 802.1AE encryption to must-secure, should-secure, or must-not-secure
- NEAT (Network Edge Authentication Topology)—Allows you to authenticate switches to other switches via 802.1X
- Web Authentication (Local Web Auth)

- Airespace ACL Name—Applies Named ACL to Cisco WLC

- ASA VPN

- Client posture assessment

- Network Scanner—NMAP

- Acceptable Use Policy

As you can see, authorization rules have a number of common permission controls available. ISE also has numerous advanced permissions via advanced attributes settings when defining your permissions.

Commonly Configured Rules and Their Purpose

This section focuses mostly on the rules that are commonly found in the network access security policies of organizations that use the ISE solution. The goal is to present you with a solid starting point from which to determine the authorization rule needs of your organization's network access security policy.

Let's explore some of the most commonly used rules. Remember, a rule defines the rights and privileges a client will have once they pass authentication, authorization, and posture assessment. All organizations must have their own customized rules. The number and purpose of these rules will vary according to your environment. Each of the rules you build should have a separate policy definition section in your network access security policy document. Here are some of the most commonly configured rules:

- Guest/Visitor Rule

- Employee Rule

- Corporate Authorization Rule

- Contractor/Temp Rule

- Student Rule

- Faculty Rule

- Authorization rule based on network location (such as a specific building)

- Admin Rule

- Staff Rule

- Wireless Authorization Rule

- VPN Authorization Rule

- Printers and other non-802.1X devices rule(s)

The non-802.1X-capable device rules, coupled with the ISE profiler, can be used to segment and limit access to/from the noninteractive network devices, such as some printers, faxes, IP Phones, and so on. This enables you to create very strict network access security policies for these devices. These policies should allow them to communicate only by using protocols that match the services they provide.

Establishing Acceptable Use Policies

A network acceptable use policy (AUP) is a clear and concise document that defines what users can and cannot do on a network. However, the primary focus of the AUP is to communicate to users what they cannot do. It also lays out the penalties for noncompliance and provides support contact information. Ideally, before a user/guest is granted network access for the first time, they must accept the organization's AUP. Thereafter, acceptance of the AUP can be requested periodically. The problem has always been how to enforce this requirement. Without some kind of network access control system, ubiquitous enforcement is not possible. The ISE solution supports the enforcement and auditing of network AUPs.

Before creating your AUP for ISE users and guests, determine who needs to be involved and what the approval process for a final policy will look like. Create an AUP committee that includes, at a minimum, persons from the legal and IT departments. Draft a flow chart of the expected approval process the AUP will have to go through. Next, determine which documents the committee needs to produce in order to successfully complete the AUP. For example, to have an AUP approved in the education space, it is customary to require the following documents:

- **Justification and purpose for creating an AUP:** This typically needs to be presented to the school board and must be approved in the beginning to allow for the creation of the AUP committee.

- **A high-level AUP specifically created for or by the school board to establish the framework from which the final detailed AUP will be crafted:** It establishes the major security goals and network use guidelines. This must be approved by the school board.

- **A parent letter and permission form informing them of the AUP and the use of ISE to enforce this AUP:** This must be approved by the school board.

- **The final Acceptable Use Policy document:** Typically, this is created by the committee and presented to the school board for approval. This is the document that will be used by the ISE solution.

In general, an acceptable use policy will include these sections:

- **AUP Overview or Purpose:** Serves as an introduction to the AUP.

- **AUP Scope or Coverage:** Defines who must comply with this acceptable use policy.

- **Acceptable Network Use Guidelines:** Conveys the appropriate use of the network.

- **Unacceptable or Prohibited Network Uses:** This section may have several subsections, such as a subsection each for email, copyrighted material, viruses and worms, unauthorized access, illegal activity, and so forth.

- **Violation or Enforcement Policy:** Communicates the penalties and/or legal action that could be taken against AUP violators.

- **Privacy Disclaimer:** Indicates that the organization assumes no responsibility or liability for a user's privacy while using the network.

- **Definitions:** Fully defines all acronyms and terms used in the document.

- **Legal Disclaimer:** Purpose is to release the organization from any and all legal liabilities resulting from the AUP itself or network use. Let the lawyers define this one.

- **Right to Modification:** A disclaimer communicating your right to modify this policy at any time without notice.

- **Contact Information:** Provides users with a point of contact for additional information, questions, or complaints.

Your AUP may include more or fewer sections than those listed above. The sections above should give you a general idea of what to include in your AUP.

Tip   To find additional information about AUPs, such as "How To" guides and examples, search Google using the keywords **network acceptable use policy**. For AUP samples, check out the SANS policy site at http://www.sans.org/resources/policies/.

The ISE solution has two methods for enforcing an AUP:

- **Via a guest portal login:** Used only by users that log in via web authentication.

- **Via the Cisco NAC Agent for Windows:** Used only by users that have the Cisco NAC Agent.

Both methods can, and typically do, use and enforce the same AUP. Both methods enforce the policy by denying users network access until they acknowledge or accept the network AUP. Once they accept the policy, they are granted network access.

The enforcement of an AUP is an optional feature. Enforcement can be selectively enabled as well. Enforcement can be turned on or off based on the client's identity group. Additionally, it can be enabled or disabled based on the use of web login or the Cisco NAC Agent. For example, you might want to enable AUP enforcement just for guest clients.

Defining Network Access Privileges

The ISE solution has several methods available to grant and restrict the network access privileges of clients. Most of these methods are defined per authorization rule. A network access security policy for ISE should include details on which network access privileges should be given to which authorization rules and devices. The authorization rules should take into consideration the posture status of a device (unknown, compliant, or noncompliant) to determine the access privileges given.

Note   Chapter 7, "Building a Device Security Policy," covers in detail Cisco ISE device security posture assessment and the creation of a device security policy.

Here is an example that uses access control rules in ISE: A client in the contractor authorization rule should be granted access to the Internet only on TCP ports 80 and 443, and should be denied all other network access. The following common and easily understandable syntax can be used for documenting ISE access control policies in the NASP. Typically, these rules are found under their corresponding authorization rule section in the NASP:

```
<line #> Permit|Deny <protocol> from <device(s) | network(s)> to <device(s) |
network(s)> equaling | not equaling port(s) <list of port numbers or names>
Description: <explanation of rule>
```

The previous example would be written in the NASP under the contractor authorization rule traffic control subsection as follows:

```
10 Deny IP from any to any internal network
Description: Block IP traffic from anyone to any internal subnet or device.
20 Permit tcp from guest authorization rule to any equaling ports 80 & 443
Description: Allow web traffic from clients in the guest authorization rule to the
internet
30 Permit DNS traffic for name resolution
40 Deny IP from guest authorization rule to any
Description: Block everything else
```

Formatting the rules in this way not only makes them unambiguous but allows them to be easily translated into the traffic control rules configured in the ISE Manager.

Enforcement Methods Available with ISE

ISE supports numerous types of permissions that can be applied to an authorization rule result. Not all enforcement methods supported by ISE are supported in all modes of operation. This issue applies mostly to limitations of the hardware the client is connected to, otherwise known as the network access device (NAD). For example, to support security group ACLs (SGACL), the wired switch or wireless controller NAD must be able to support SGACLs. Table 6-1 lists the different network access control permission methods available and provides a brief description for each.

Table 6-1   *ISE Authorization Rule Permissions*

Enforcement or Control Method	Description
Access control rules	The equivalent of network ACLs. They permit and deny traffic like a stateless firewall would.
VLAN segmentation	Dynamically changing the Layer 2 VLAN based on the authorization rule matched by the connected client.
SmartPort macro	Ability to run the macro that can affect just about anything on that switch port, including QoS settings.
Reauthentication	The timer serves as an absolute time limit for a client in a given authorization rule. Once the timer expires, the client is reauthenticated.
Security Group Tag	Cisco-proprietary tag that is applied to every frame sent from the client. Requires switch or WLC support.
MACSec encryption	Wire-speed Layer 2 encryption via 802.1ae. Requires switch or WLC support.
Web Authentication	Forces a URL redirect to a web authentication page.
Cisco RADIUS AV pair values	Almost any Cisco AV pair can be manipulated with ISE as part of authorization permissions.

Commonly Used Network Access Security Policies

In short, a network access security policy defines what a device can and cannot do on the network. Although the exact rules that make up any network access security policy will be customized for a particular environment, there are some commonalities shared between organizations. This section will focus on those common elements. The network access security policy defined in your NASP typically will cover all of the enforcement methods ISE supports (see Table 6-1). Access control lists are almost always tied to an authorization rule in ISE. Some authorization rules (such as guest) will usually have very restrictive network access policies, while others will be wide open (such as employee). Also, it is always a best practice to lock down the network access rule on any noncompliant posture authorization rule.

Here are some popular or mandatory authorization rules shown with a common example of their associated network access security policy. This is formatted for an ISE network access security policy. You can choose to use this NASP format or develop your own. It is important to ensure that your network access security policy is well documented. Note that these pick up where the earlier sample NASP left off, at Section IV.

Employee Authorization Rule

Table of Contents for Employee Security Policy:

I. Members pg. xxx

II. Acceptable Use Policy pg. xxx

III. Windows 7 Security Requirements pg. xxx

    1. Approved AV Installed & Up-to-date pg. xxx

        a. Security checks pg. xxx

        b. Security rules pg. xxx

IV. Network Access Permissions pg. xxx

    1. VLAN Segmentation pg. xxx

        a. Noncompliant Posture VLAN pg. xxx

        b. Access VLAN Name/ID pg. xxx

    2. Access Control List pg. xxx

    3. SmartPort Macro pg. xxx

    4. Security Group Tag number pg. xxx

...

IV. Network Access Permissions

1. VLAN Segmentation – Yes

    a. Noncompliant Posture VLAN = quarantine-vlan/100

    b. Access VLAN Name/ID = employees/10

2. Access Control List – Yes

    a. Compliant ACL = permit All IP

    b. Noncompliant ACL =

```
5 Permit TCP from any to "AUP web server" equaling 80
Description: Allow anyone to access the acceptable use policy link
```

```
10 Permit TCP from any to "Link based remediation resources" equaling 80 & 443
Description: Allow web traffic to the appropriate remediation resources
20 Permit TCP from any to "file based remediation" equaling 80 & 443
Description: Allow web traffic to the cam for remediation file distribution
30 Permit UDP from any to "dmz DNS Server" equaling DNS
Description: Allow DNS only to the dmz dns server
40 Deny IP from any to any
Description: Block everything else
```

3. SmartPort Macro – no

4. Security Group Tag number – 10

The subsequent partial example does not show the full network access security policy format. It shows only the "Network Access Permissions" section.

Guest Authorization Rule

1. VLAN Segmentation – Yes

   a. Noncompliant Posture VLAN = None, no posture required

   b. Access VLAN Name/ID = guest/20

2. Access Control List –

```
10 Permit UDP from any to "dmz DNS Server" equaling DNS
Description: Allow DNS but only to the dmz dns server
20 Deny IP from any to any internal network
Description: Block IP traffic from guests to any internal subnet or device.
30 permit IP from host to any external IP subnet
Description: Allow everything not internal
```

3. SmartPort Macro – no

4. SGT number – 20

Summary

This chapter examined the intricacies of creating a network access security policy for a Cisco ISE deployment. It included the following recommendations:

- Create and follow a NASP checklist.

- Make sure to obtain executive buy-in for the creation and subsequent enforcement of a NASP.

- Create a NASP committee. Be sure to involve the right people.

- Determine your organization's high-level network access security goals. Use these as guides when creating the detailed network access security policy.

- Break up your organization into security domains.

- Determine and create the authorization rules necessary for your organization.

- Create one or more acceptable use policies.

- Determine if host posture checks will be used. If so, decide which checks, rules, and requirements will be enforced for each posture rule.

- Establish and follow a method for adds, moves, and changes to authorization rules and posture rule checks, rules, and requirements.

- Determine a method for deploying the NAC Agent and/or remediation resources.

- Determine which network access permissions should be assigned to each authorization rule.

- Either use the network access security policy formatting shown throughout this chapter or pick your own formatting. It is important to document your network access security policy in a concise and easily understood manner.

Chapter 7

Building a Device Security Policy

The Cisco Identity Services Engine takes into account the security of the individual devices when determining the network access control policy to invoke. Chapter 6, "Building a Cisco ISE Network Access Security Policy," discussed the creation of a network access security policy, part of which took into account the device's security posture. Device posture assessment is one of two tools that Cisco ISE can use to determine the actual security of a network-connected device. ISE can use the following features to determine the device security policy to implement:

- Host security posture assessment
- Device profiling

This chapter explores these two features in some detail. The goal is to recognize the different ways in which ISE can identify devices types and determine their security posture.

Host Security Posture Assessment Rules to Consider

This section covers the process of how to include host posture criteria into an organization's network access security policy document and into Cisco ISE Posture Policy. One of the powerful features of ISE when using the Cisco NAC Agent is its ability to perform very granular device security posture assessments and remediation on Windows and Mac devices. Therefore, your network access security policy should contain the checks, rules, and requirements that ISE will use. This includes the discovery, enforcement, and remediation policies that ISE will employ on Windows and Mac devices. Because the agent is loaded on the device, it has the ability to read into the device's registry, applications, services, and file system. The Cisco NAC Agent can be installed directly onto the client or brought down as a temporary agent via a browser. The main difference between the two methods is that the temporary web agent doesn't have the rights to perform remediation actions for the user.

The full agent offers robust remediation capabilities for a device that fails a security requirement, such as an outdated AntiVirus definition. The remediation capabilities include file distribution, link distribution, delivery of instructions, and, most notably, an auto-update mechanism for AntiVirus, AntiSpyware, Windows OS patches, and client firewall rules. The network access security policy should include the details on how devices will be remediated under different circumstances.

All posture assessment and remediation configuration is done using the ISE GUI. It is here that you define the Posture Policy by configuring rules based on operating system and/or other conditions that will satisfy the policies contained in your corporate NASP document. Before you create your network access security policy for ISE, it is important to understand the ISE process for posture assessment. This technique uses a combination of policy checks, rules, and requirements. The ISE posture service checks the health (posture) of the clients for compliance with your corporate network security policies before the host gains privileged network access. The ISE Client Provisioning service deploys the NAC agent to any hosts that don't have it installed and set up.

An example of pre-configured Posture rules are shown in Figure 7-1.

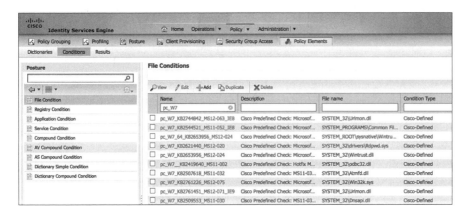

Figure 7-1 *File Condition Check Examples*

The ISE file condition checks shown in Figure 7-1 are the Cisco predefined checks that are downloaded from Cisco every two hours. Checks can be groups of several checks combined together using Boolean operators. They can also be operating system specific.

ISE then allows you to create posture rules that combine multiple checks into a compound condition. Figure 7-2 shows a sampling of the Cisco predefined rules in ISE.

ISE requirements, as shown in Figure 7-3, define what remediation action is offered to any noncompliant users. In this example, the Windows Server Update Services (WSUS) service is being turned on to ensure that all WSUS-enforced updates are installed on the PC.

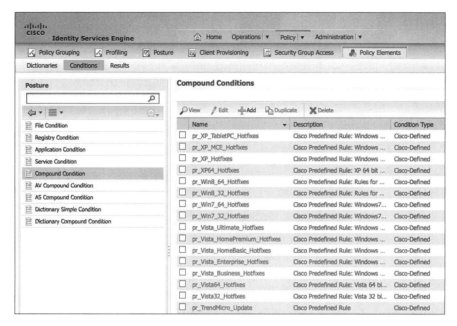

Figure 7-2 *Compound Condition Rules Example*

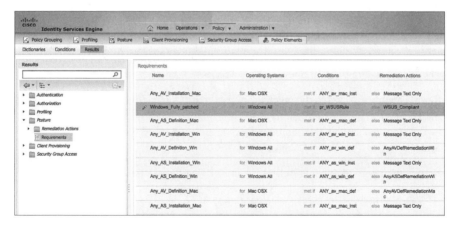

Figure 7-3 *Requirement Examples*

If all matching requirement rules are passed, then the client is marked as posture compliant. Otherwise, the client is marked as posture noncompliant. This overall status can then be used in authorization rules to properly adapt network access privileges. Figure 7-4 shows an example of restricting a noncompliant host using a downloadable access control list (DACL) that only allows hosts to get to remediation resources.

Figure 7-4 *Posture-Aware Authorization Rule Example*

Here is a summary of the rules and requirements structure in ISE:

- Rules are made up of one or more checks that can be combined into an expression using the Boolean operators and "&", or "|", not "!", and evaluation priority parentheses (). If the result is true, then the client passes the rule.

- Requirements are made up of one or more rules. A requirement can specify that a device must pass any selected rule, all selected rules, or no selected rules in order for the device to pass the requirement.

- Requirements also define the mechanism to use and the instructions that will allow the client to remediate any failed rules. For example: Distribute a file or link with the instructions "Click the link and download, install, and run the XYZVirus cleaning tool."

- Requirements are mapped to authorization rules and/or operating system types.

Table 7-1 shows the posture assessment options available in ISE when using the various Cisco NAC Agent software versions. You can see that the Windows NAC Agent has the most functionality of the three Agent types.

Table 7-1 *Posture Checks*

NAC Agent for Windows	Web Agent for Windows	NAC Agent for Mac OS X
Operating System/Service Packs/Hotfixes	Operating System/Service Packs/Hotfixes	—
Process Check	Process Check	Not supported

NAC Agent for Windows	Web Agent for Windows	NAC Agent for Mac OS X
Registry Check	Registry Check	—
File Check	File Check	Not supported
Application Check	Application Check	Not supported
Antivirus Installation	Antivirus Installation	Antivirus Installation
Antivirus Version/Antivirus Definition Date	Antivirus Version/Antivirus Definition Date	Antivirus Version/Antivirus Definition Date
Antispyware Installation	Antispyware Installation	Antispyware Installation
Antispyware Version/ Antispyware Definition Date	Antispyware Version/ Antispyware Definition Date	Antispyware Version/ Antispyware Definition Date
Windows Update Running	Windows Update Running	—
Windows Update Configuration	Windows Update Configuration	—
WSUS Compliance Settings	WSUS Compliance Settings	—

Table 7-2 displays all of the different remediation actions that the various NAC Agents can perform. Again, the Windows NAC Agent has the most functionality. These actions can be done for the user transparently or user interaction can be implemented.

Table 7-2 *Posture Remediation Actions*

NAC Agent for Windows	Web Agent for Windows	NAC Agent for Mac OS X
Message Text (Local Check)	Message Text (Local Check)	Message Text (Local Check)
URL Link (Link Distribution)	URL Link (Link Distribution)	URL Link (Link Distribution)
File Distribution	File Distribution	Not supported
Launch Program	Not supported	Not supported
Run Antivirus Definition Update	Not supported	Antivirus Live Update
Run Antispyware Definition Update	Not supported	Antispyware Live Update
Run Windows Update	Not supported	—
Run WSUS Update	Not supported	—

Now that we have explored all of the posture variables and features, let's take a look at a final summary flow of posture assessment in ISE. Figure 7-5 illustrates the order of operations ISE takes from checks to the final Posture Policy evaluation.

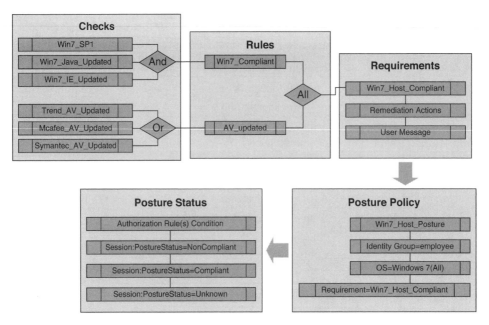

Figure 7-5   *ISE Posture Assessment Process*

Sample NASP Format for Documenting ISE Posture Requirements

As discussed, ISE uses several mechanisms to define what it should look for, or posture assess, on a given device. It also has several mechanisms for the proper remediation of any failed security requirements. Ultimately, the network access security privileges that a client receives are based on the posture status result (for example, compliant) of a matched policy rule, which in turn is used as an authorization rule condition that the client matches. With this in mind, your NASP should have sections for each Posture Policy rule, and under each you should have the checks, rules, and requirements that pertain to clients of that posture policy rule. Here is a nice example of a NASP formatted in this way:

Employee Posture Policy

Table of Contents for Employee Posture Policy:

I. Identity Group Criteria pg. xxx

II. Acceptable Use Policy pg. xxx

III. Windows 7 Security Requirements pg. xxx

    1. Approved AV Installed & Up-to-date pg. xxx

a. Security checks pg. xxx

b. Security rules pg. xxx

I. Identity Group Criteria – Any user that is a member of the employees group in Active Directory.

II. Acceptable Use Policy – Reference which AUP, if any, is to be enforced by ISE. For example, you might reference an AUP called Trusted_User_AUP. It is common that only a reference to an AUP name is put here and the actual AUP document lives in its own section within the NASP document. This allows for easy reuse of AUP policies across multiple roles.

III. Windows 7 Security Requirements

1. Approved AV Installed & Up-to-date

Trend_AV_Requirement – Link distribution that points to the Trend client download page on the corporate antivirus server.

Trend_AV_Requirement to Rule Mapping – Map requirement *Trend_AV_Installed* to rule *Trend_AV_Installed*. Requirement met if any rules succeed.

a. Security Rules –

Trend_AV_Installed rule – Rule expression only includes the Trend_AV_Installed check.

b. Security Checks –

Trend_AV_Installed check – Corporate Trend Micro antivirus client must be installed on all Windows devices.

The ISE solution has lots of predefined checks and rules that you can use to build your posture rules. All of the built-in predefined checks have pc_ preceding their name, such as pc_AutoUpdateCheck. All of the built-in predefined rules have pr_ preceding their name, such as pr_AutoUpdateCheck. These checks and rules are constantly updated by Cisco and are automatically downloaded by ISE. Also, ISE has auto-update support for Microsoft Windows, numerous antivirus vendors, and antispyware vendors out of the box. This means that ISE keeps up to date with the latest versions, DAT files, and hotfixes available for each of the supported vendors automatically. Keep this in mind when creating your ISE network access security policy.

Common Checks, Rules, and Requirements

The following are some of the most common checks, rules, and requirements implemented by administrators of the ISE solution. All of the examples shown have corresponding Cisco predefined checks and rules and are auto-updated by ISE.

■ An AntiVirus program must be installed, running, and up to date. Most organizations will specify particular AV programs for certain posture policy rules. For example, the employee posture rule may state that clients must use corporate Trend Micro AV, whereas the guest posture rule may state that clients are allowed to use any of the numerous ISE-supported AV vendors.

■ An antispyware program must be installed, running, and up to date. Most organizations will specify particular AS programs for certain authorization rules. For example, the employee posture rule may state that clients must use the corporate Webroot AS client, whereas the guest policy rule may state that clients are allowed to use any of the ISE-supported AS vendors.

■ All Windows 7 clients must be running Service Pack 1. The built-in check is called pc_W7_SP1.

■ All Windows clients must have the Windows auto-update service running. By default, ISE looks to make sure the wuauserv service is running. The built-in check is called pc_AutoUpdateCheck. The built-in rule is called pr_AutoUpdateCheck_Rule.

■ All 64-bit Windows 7 and 8 hosts must have installed the latest critical Microsoft security hotfixes as defined by the ISE rule pr_Win7_64_Hotfixes and pr_Win8_64_ Hotfixes, respectively. These rules, and their corresponding checks, are continuously updated by Cisco. They include the most critical security hotfixes for Windows 7 and Windows 8 operating systems. They do not, however, include every security update that Microsoft has ever released for each operating system. If you require additional hotfixes, you can duplicate the relevant pr_Win_64_Hotfixes predefined rule to include them.

■ All requirements dealing with the updating of antivirus and antispyware programs will use the built-in AV Definition Update type. These rules are preconfigured to map to the matrix of AV and AS vendors and products supported by ISE. These rules do not require you to configure any checks and are continuously updated by Cisco. If the user fails these requirements, the user can be presented with an Update button. When clicked, this Update button auto-launches the update program for the AV or AS program that failed the policy.

Method for Adding Posture Policy Rules

Many organizations do not have a process in place to determine if, when, and how a security update should be added to their network access security policy document. Organizations that lack this type of process, or method, are in greater danger of making bad decisions about the security updates they choose to install. For this reason, it is important for organizations to establish and follow a formal method for adding and updating their posture policy rules. This section deals with this topic as it pertains to the initial creation and subsequent revisions of the network access security policy document. Knowing which host security patches to enforce using ISE is a big job. The goal is to provide the information necessary for you to set up your own method, or process, for determining which posture rules you want to include in your initial network access security policy for ISE. A secondary goal is to provide the information necessary for you to set up your own method, or process, for determining when to add, change, and delete the checks, rules, and requirements that make up your host posture policy rules in ISE.

Research and Information

The ISE solution comes with many preconfigured checks and rules, as previously described. Simply implementing these built-in policies will go a long way toward increasing the security posture of most organizations' devices and networks. However, these are by no means the only security checks and rules that are available. In many cases, your organization may choose to implement checks, rules, and requirements that are beyond the scope of the predefined ones. When this occurs, it is vital that you are able to find the information and research needed to make the most informed decision possible. Regardless of whether or not the security fixes you put in place use the built-in policies, custom policies, or a combination of both, it is vital that you understand the purpose of the fixes, their impact, and their severity level. It is also necessary to remain informed about the emergence of new vulnerabilities, exploits, and viruses. Obtaining this information is not always trivial. Following are some of the commonly used security websites, blogs, and resources available online. Most are free but some also offer a paid service.

- **SecurityFocus** (http://www.securityfocus.com): Famous for its BugTraq list. This is one of the best places for obtaining the latest vulnerability information.

- **SecLists.Org Security Mailing List Archive** (http://seclists.org): This site is a mashup of the best security sites. It is your one-stop shop for staying in the know on the latest security news.

- **Microsoft TechNet Security Center** (www.microsoft.com/technet/security): This web portal serves as a good jumping-off point for investigating any Microsoft security vulnerabilities, updates, and exploits.

- **Microsoft Security Bulletins** (http://www.microsoft.com/technet/security/bulletin): This website has a nice search engine for locating Microsoft security bulletins. The site also has a link to sign up to receive security bulletins via email, RSS, or IM. The search engine allows you to search for vulnerabilities based on severity level and operating system type and version.

- **National Cyber Awareness System** (http://www.us-cert.gov/ncas/): The National Cyber Awareness System was created to ensure that you have access to timely information about security topics and threats. You can sign up here to receive alerts from the U.S. Computer Emergency Readiness Team (US-CERT).

- Government sites such as the National Vulnerability Database (http://nvd.nist.gov) and US-CERT (http://www.us-cert.gov) are filled with timely security alert information and are vendor agnostic.

- **Metasploit** (http://www.metasploit.com/): This site does not offer any security information but does provide a very easy-to-use security tool that will help you test the security of your devices.

- **Cisco Security Intelligence Operations** (http://www.cisco.com/go/sio): The Cisco SIO website serves as a security portal to find information regarding security bulletins from all the major application and operating system vendors. It also provides a wealth of cyber security reports and response bulletins.

These websites and others like them can be found throughout the Internet. They can be powerful tools for gathering the security information needed to make an informed decision on which security patches ISE should enforce.

Establishing Criteria to Determine the Validity of a Security Posture Check, Rule, or Requirement in Your Organization

Your organization's network access security policy should have a section that documents the criteria to be used to decide if a proposed security check, rule, or requirement needs to be added to ISE. The establishment of set criteria will serve to improve the accuracy of the decision process. The criteria used should be tailored for your specific environment and should refrain from using generalities whenever possible. The more fine-grained the criteria used, the more informed the decision process will be.

For every proposed and existing security fix in the NASP, and subsequently in ISE, you should be familiar with, or know where to obtain, the following information regarding security vulnerability:

- Which products, applications, and versions are affected?

- What is the severity level or Common Vulnerability Scoring System (CVSS) score?

- What is the potential impact or risk to the organization if the vulnerability is exploited? This point should be explored in detail, noting both a best- and worst-case scenario.

- Can the vulnerability be exploited remotely?

- Are exploits publicly available?

- Is the use of the affected software widespread in your organization?

- Are the ports, protocols, and devices in question being blocked using a firewall, IPS, personal firewall, or ISE already? If so, to what extent does this mitigate the exploit risk?

- Is a patch available for the vulnerability?

- If a patch is available, is it possible to test the patch to make sure it works as advertised?

- If no patch testing can be done, is the risk of deploying a faulty patch less than the risk of the vulnerability?

- If no patch is available, is it possible to use any of the security features in ISE to help mitigate this feature? If not, is it possible to use any other security products to do so?

Before taking action, it is important to understand what the expected overhead on the IT staff might be if the new patch or fix is implemented. This should be explored in detail, noting both a best- and worst-case scenario. Here are some of the topics for consideration:

- How stable is the new patch?

- Is additional help desk load necessary?

- Is additional IT staff load necessary?

- What is required of the end-user community?

- Was additional network load created due to deployment of new patches?

- If deploying patches over the WAN, what is the potential impact?

- Who will perform any testing needed? What resources are required to perform the testing?

- What is needed to set up the deployment method for distributing the patch or update?

- What is the expected impact on and reactions from the user community if the fix for the vulnerability is rolled out?

Method for Determining Which Posture Policy Rules a Particular Security Requirement Should Be Applied To

Once you have decided that a security fix or patch should be deployed in your environment, the next step is to decide which posture rules should receive the fix or if you should create a new rule. Additionally, it is important to determine whether the fix should be mandatory or optional. This might vary based on posture rule. It is a best practice to deploy new security requirements as optional first and then, after a set amount of time, make them mandatory. This results in the least impact possible on the user community. However, if a vulnerability poses significant risk to the organization, then the new security requirement should be rolled out as mandatory initially.

Here are some things to consider when deciding which posture rules should receive a new security requirement:

- Do all identity groups run the affected software?

- Do any of the identity groups pose a greater risk than others if the patch causes adverse affects on clients? In other words, do certain posture rules contain clients that, if debilitated due to a bad patch, would significantly affect the organization? If so, would starting with less risky rules first to further assess the robustness of the patch make sense?

- Do any posture rules have an elevated exposure to the vulnerability in question? If so, does this elevated exposure warrant mandatory enforcement of the new security requirement?

- Does the security requirement apply to the guest posture rule, if one exists?

Method for Deploying and Enforcing Security Requirements

Once you have decided that a security requirement should be added to the NASP and ISE, it is necessary to come up with a deployment strategy. As previously discussed in Table 7-2, a requirement remediation has the following options for resolution:

- File distribution

- Link distribution

- Launch executable

- Message only

- AV definition update

- AS definition update

- Windows update

The easiest options to deploy are the update types. They use the built-in deployment and updating mechanisms that are already configured on the local device. For example, the requirement type of windows update uses the Windows Update Service that is already present on and configured for the client that needs the updates.

Regardless of the requirement type chosen, the following deployment questions should be considered:

- Should the deployment method be the same for all posture rules?

- Which deployment method would be the most efficient at reaching the posture rules in question?

- Should the enforcement of the new security requirement be optional, audit, or mandatory in the beginning? Does this vary by posture rule or identity group?

- If optional, should the requirement be made mandatory at some point in time? If so, define the time period between optional and mandatory. Does this vary by posture rule?

- If audit only, what is the goal of the audit? What will be done with the data collected?

- Will it ensure that clients in quarantine have privileges to access the proposed remediation resources? For example, if you use a link to www.fixme.com as your deployment method, you need to ensure that access to this URL is not restricted.

ISE Device Profiling

In addition to its device security posture assessment feature, ISE includes a built-in device profiling function. Device profiling examines the behavior of a given node to determine what kind of device it is and how it is acting on the network. Profiling is also used for supplicant provisioning of clients. Cisco ISE profiler functionality requires the Advanced license to operate (the license options are described in Chapter 3). Cisco ISE includes over 280 built-in profiling rules and over 375 device profiler conditions. It uses multiple data sources from which to gather the information needed to make these determinations. This information is matched against the ISE profiler conditions until a best match is made. That condition is then used to match a profiler policy rule. Once a profiler policy rule is matched, the result can then be used as an ISE authorization rule condition. It is in this way that ISE can provide different network privileges based on a device profile.

Figure 7-6 depicts a sampling of the ISE profiler conditions that come preinstalled with ISE. ISE will also receive updated and new profiles through its profiler feed service. The feed service connects to Cisco.com to see if any new profile data is available for download. If so, it will download and update its profiling database accordingly.

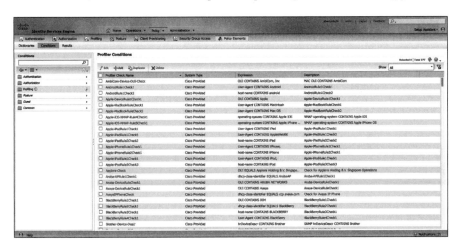

Figure 7-6 *ISE Profiler Conditions*

Each condition shown in Figure 7-6 contains logic that defines how the condition is met. As you can see, many of the conditions have multiple rules or multiple checks for the same device type. The Apple iPad conditions are a good example of this. Figure 7-7 shows just one of four checks that are used to determine if a device is an Apple iPad.

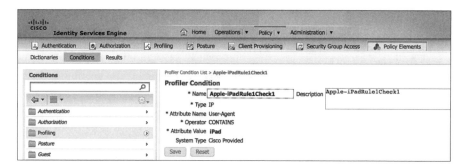

Figure 7-7 *ISE Apple iPad Profiler Conditions*

The example condition shown in Figure 7-7 matches the *user-agent string* from a web browser. There are several other built-in ISE profile conditions that can be used to identify an iPad. Figure 7-7 shows only one of the many available.

ISE Profiling Policies

The Cisco ISE conditions just discussed are used to create your ISE device profile policies. Sticking with the Apple iPad profile example, Figure 7-8 shows the profiler policy that uses the iPad condition shown in Figure 7-7.

The policy shown in Figure 7-8 uses two rules. Both rules, if matched, raise the certainty factor by 20 points. This profiler policy defines that the minimum certainty factor for this policy to be matched is 20. It is also important to note that in order for this policy to even be processed by ISE, the defined parent policy must have been matched first by the device being profiled. The parent policy in this Apple iPad policy is shown to be *Apple-Device*.

When you are creating your device security policy for Cisco ISE, be sure to include the logic that is used by ISE profiler in that policy. The policy should include the following for any custom-designed profiles needed:

- Device Profile Condition(s) Definition: Match criteria needed (that is, user-agent string, MAC OUI, DHCP hostname, and so on)
- Device Profile Policy
  - Rules definition of policy and amount to raise the certainty factor. Rules use the conditions above.
  - Define the minimum certainty factor for the policy.
  - Define any parent policies.

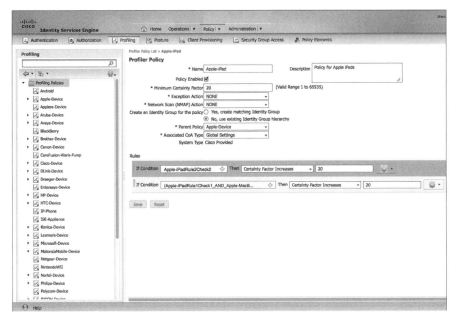

Figure 7-8 *ISE Apple iPad Profiler Policy*

ISE Profiler Data Sources

To create a profiler condition to match against, you first need to understand what match criteria is offered by Cisco ISE. Figure 7-9 shows the various types of conditions that can be used to match a device's behavior against.

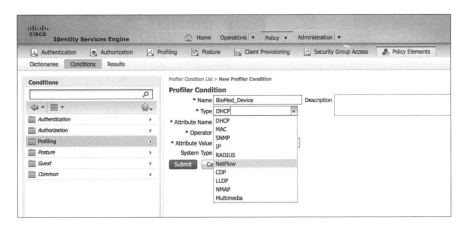

Figure 7-9 *Profiler Conditions*

Each of the ten condition types shown in the drop-down list has several subtypes to choose from as well. This allows you to create very specific conditions on which to match against. For example, the IP type can match against a specific browser user-agent string.

Note In an ISE distributed deployment, the Profiler Service runs as a part of the Policy Services Node.

Using Device Profiles in Authorization Rules

Once you have your profiler policies in place and matching correctly on devices, you need to configure ISE authorization rules to use your profiles. Figure 7-10 depicts an example of a rule that matches on Apple iPad devices that are accessing the network using wireless. The resulting permissions are to only allow Internet access to iPads.

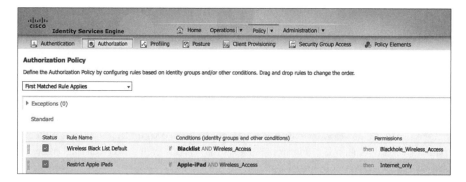

Figure 7-10 *ISE Apple iPad Authorization Policy*

Summary

This chapter covered the features and functionality that Cisco Identity Services Engine has for enforcing a device security policy. The two main features Cisco ISE employs are host posture assessment and device profiling. When writing a device security policy for your organization, you should follow a very similar logic structure to that Cisco ISE uses for device posture assessment and profiling.

Chapter 8

Building an ISE Accounting and Auditing Policy

Keeping track of what is happening inside the network and inside of ISE is critical to understanding how the ISE solution is behaving. It is also vital for compliance and internal audit reasons. For example, auditing the changes that each ISE administrator makes to the configuration is extremely important. ISE Accounting is the mechanism that absorbs the RADIUS accounting packets from network devices such as switches, Wireless LAN Controllers, and ASA VPN headends. ISE Auditing is the logging and reporting of everything that happens internal to ISE. This includes administrator configuration changes, ISE system health, processing of ISE rules, and full logging of authentication and authorization activities.

Note In a distributed ISE deployment, the Administration Node handles all ISE system-related configuration and configuration change auditing. The Policy Services Node handles all of the network access device (NAD) RADIUS accounting packets. All of the relevant information is also sent from each Admin and Policy services node to the Monitoring and Troubleshooting Node for purposes of creating accounting and auditing reports.

Why You Need Accounting and Auditing for ISE

Logging mechanisms, such as RADIUS accounting and ISE configuration auditing, provide the ability to track user and administrator activities. This is critical in preventing, detecting, or minimizing the impact of a security compromise. The presence of these logs in all environments allows thorough tracking, alerting, and analysis when something does go wrong. Determining the cause of a compromise or just a configuration mistake is very difficult, if not impossible, without accounting and auditing records.

Creating a comprehensive ISE audit trail is necessary for passing many of your compliance audits. The Payment Card Industry (PCI) Data Security Standard (DSS), a standard for the protection of credit card data, provides a robust framework for auditing requirements. It is highly likely that if you follow the auditing recommendations in PCI DSS, you will pass most other types of logging audits. It is for that reason that we are reusing much of the PCI DSS framework for the ISE accounting and auditing policy recommendations here.

Using PCI DSS as Your ISE Auditing Framework

PCI DSS Requirement 10 and its subrequirements lay out a nice framework you can use to build your own auditing policy for the Cisco Identity Services Engine. Table 8-1 depicts the relevant section from *Payment Card Industry (PCI) Data Security Standard Requirements and Security Assessment Procedures, Version 2.0* (available at https://www.pcisecuritystandards.org/documents/pci_dss_v2.pdf). The left column describes the requirement and the right column describes how you could audit that requirement to ensure it is being met.

Table 8-1   *PCI DSS 2.0 Requirement 10*

PCI DSS 2.0 Requirements	Audit Testing Procedures
Requirement 10: Track and monitor all access to network resources and cardholder data	
10.1 Establish a process for linking all access to system components (especially access done with administrative privileges such as root) to each individual user.	**10.1** Verify through observation and interviewing the system administrator, that audit trails are enabled and active for system components.
10.2 Implement automated audit trails for all system components to reconstruct the following events:	**10.2** Through interviews, examination of audit logs, and examination of audit log settings, perform the following:
10.2.1 All individual accesses to cardholder data.	**10.2.1** Verify all individual access to cardholder data is logged.
10.2.2 All actions taken by any individual with root or administrative privileges.	**10.2.2** Verify actions taken by any individual with root or administrative privileges are logged.
10.2.3 Access to all audit trails.	**10.2.3** Verify access to all audit trails is logged.
10.2.4 Invalid logical access attempts.	**10.2.4** Verify invalid logical access attempts are logged.
10.2 5 Use of identification and authentication mechanisms.	**10.2.5** Verify use of identification and authentication mechanisms is logged.
10.2.6 Initialization of the audit logs.	**10.2.6** Verify initialization of audit logs is logged.

PCI DSS 2.0 Requirements	Audit Testing Procedures
10.2.7 Creation and deletion of system-level objects.	**10.2.7** Verify creation and deletion of system level objects are logged.
10.3 Record at least the following audit trail entries for all system components for each event:	**10.3** Through interviews and observation, for each auditable event (from 10.2), perform the following:
10.3.1 User identification.	**10.3.1** Verify user identification is included in log entries.
10.3.2 Type of event.	**10.3.2** Verify type of event is included in log entries.
10.3.3 Date and time.	**10.3.3** Verify date and time stamp is included in log entries.
10.3.4 Success or failure indication.	**10.3.4** Verify success or failure indication is included in log entries.
10.3.5 Origination of event.	**10.3.5** Verify origination of event is included in log entries.
10.3.6 Identity or name of affected data, system component, or resource.	**10.3.6** Verify identity or name of affected data, system component, or resources is included in log entries.
10.4 Using time-synchronization technology, synchronize all critical system clocks and times and ensure that the following is implemented for acquiring, distributing, and storing time. *Note: One example of time synchronization technology is Network Time Protocol (NTP).*	**10.4.a** Verify that time-synchronization technology is implemented and kept current per PCI DSS Requirements 6.1 and 6.2.
	10.4.b Obtain and review the process for acquiring, distributing and storing the correct time within the organization, and review the time-related system-parameter settings for a sample of system components. Verify the following is included in the process and implemented:
10.4.1 Critical systems have the correct and consistent time.	**10.4.1.a** Verify that only designated central time servers receive time signals from external sources, and time signals from external sources are based on International Atomic Time or UTC.
	10.4.1.b Verify that the designated central time servers peer with each other to keep accurate time, and other internal servers only receive time from the central time servers.

PCI DSS 2.0 Requirements	Audit Testing Procedures
10.4.2 Time data is protected.	**10.4.2.a** Review system configurations and time-synchronization settings to verify that access to stored time data is restricted to only personnel with a business need to access time data.
	10.4.2.b Review system configurations and time synchronization settings and processes to verify that any changes to time settings on critical systems are logged, monitored, and reviewed.
10.4.3 Time settings are received from industry-accepted time sources.	**10.4.3** Verify that the time servers accept time updates from specific, industry-accepted external sources (to prevent a malicious individual from changing the clock). Optionally, those updates can be encrypted with a symmetric key, and access control lists can be created that specify the IP addresses of client machines that will be provided with the time updates (to prevent unauthorized use of internal time servers).
10.5 Secure audit trails so they cannot be altered.	**10.5** Interview system administrator and examine permissions to verify that audit trails are secured so that they cannot be altered, as follows:
10.5.1 Limit viewing of audit trails to those with a job-related need.	**10.5.1** Verify that only individuals who have a job-related need can view audit trail files.
10.5.2 Protect audit trail files from unauthorized modifications.	**10.5.2** Verify that current audit trail files are protected from unauthorized modifications via access control mechanisms, physical segregation, and/or network segregation.
10.5.3 Promptly back up audit trail files to a centralized log server or media that is difficult to alter.	**10.5.3** Verify that current audit trail files are promptly backed up to a centralized log server or media that is difficult to alter.
10.5.4 Write logs for external-facing technologies onto a log server on the internal LAN.	**10.5.4** Verify that logs for external-facing technologies (for example, wireless, firewalls, DNS, mail) are offloaded or copied onto a secure centralized internal log server or media.

PCI DSS 2.0 Requirements	Audit Testing Procedures
10.5.5 Use file-integrity monitoring or change-detection software on logs to ensure that existing log data cannot be changed without generating alerts (although new data being added should not cause an alert).	**10.5.5** Verify the use of file-integrity monitoring or change-detection software for logs by examining system settings and monitored files and results from monitoring activities.
10.6 Review logs for all system components at least daily. Log reviews must include those servers that perform security functions like intrusion-detection system (IDS) and authentication, authorization, and accounting protocol (AAA) servers (for example, RADIUS). *Note: Log harvesting, parsing, and alerting tools may be used to meet compliance with Requirement 10.6.*	**10.6.a** Obtain and examine security policies and procedures to verify that they include procedures to review security logs at least daily and that follow-up to exceptions is required. **10.6.b** Through observation and interviews, verify that regular log reviews are performed for all system components.
10.7 Retain audit trail history for at least one year, with a minimum of three months immediately available for analysis (for example, online, archived, or restorable from back-up).	**10.7.a** Obtain and examine security policies and procedures and verify that they include audit log retention policies and require audit log retention for at least one year. **10.7.b** Verify that audit logs are available for at least one year and processes are in place to immediately restore at least the last three months' logs for analysis.

The Cisco ISE solution is capable of meeting all of PCI DSS Requirement 10. The following sections depict some examples of how to configure ISE to meet a sampling of the requirements in Requirement 10.

ISE Policy for PCI 10.1: Ensuring Unique Usernames and Passwords

To ensure that each administrator of Cisco ISE has a unique username and password for auditing purposes, you must utilize role-based access control (RBAC) for administration users. Figure 8-1 shows an example of creating a local ISE super administrator account.

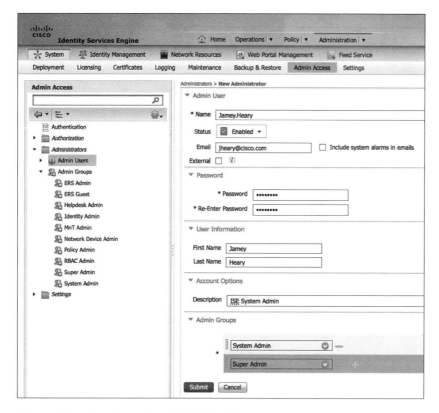

Figure 8-1   *Creating a Local ISE Administrator*

Each administrator should have their own account with the proper level of privileges
required for them to accomplish their job. Always exercise the concept of least privilege
when assigning administrators a privilege level. You want them to have only the bare
minimum privileges they require. You can use the built-in administrator authorization
permissions or create your own inside of ISE. The authorization permissions are broken
down into two types: Menu Access and Data Access. Menu Access permissions determine which menus the administrator can see. Data Access permissions allow you to grant
full or no access to the following data in the Cisco ISE interface:

- Admin Groups

- User Identity Groups

- Endpoint Identity Group

- Locations

- Device Types

Figure 8-2 depicts the Menu Access permissions screen in Cisco ISE.

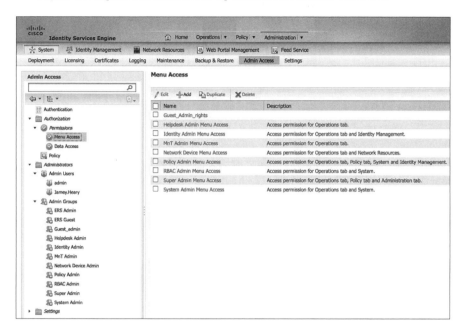

Figure 8-2   *Menu Access Permissions*

ISE Policy for PCI 10.2 and 10.3: Audit Log Collection

PCI Requirement 10.2 and its multiple subrequirements explain the types of audit logs that should be enabled on a system like ISE to ensure proper audit trails are created. Cisco ISE includes robust auditing controls and configuration options you can use to comply with PCI DSS 10.2 requirements. The requirements of PCI DSS 10.3 are met by the internals of the way ISE logs events and occur without you having to do any additional configuration.

The audit logs that ISE can create are broken into Logging categories, as shown in Figure 8-3. As a best practice, all of these categories should be enabled for local logging level (as shown in the Local Log Level column).

The Targets column indicates the logging servers to which the messages will be sent for logging and storage. Targets are typically syslog servers, but the various types will be explained next.

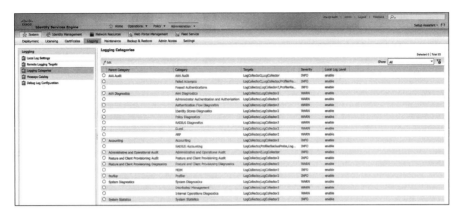

Figure 8-3   *ISE Audit/Logging Categories*

ISE Policy for PCI 10.5.3, 10.5.4, and 10.7: Ensure the Integrity and Confidentiality of Log Data

To ensure the integrity and confidentiality of audit log data, copying the logs to a non-ISE logging server is recommended. This ensures that in the event of an ISE compromise, administrator error, or system failure, the audit trail logs are not lost. You can also apply file integrity checking tools on the external log server data store for additional protection. Figure 8-4 illustrates the configuration options for configuring remote logging targets.

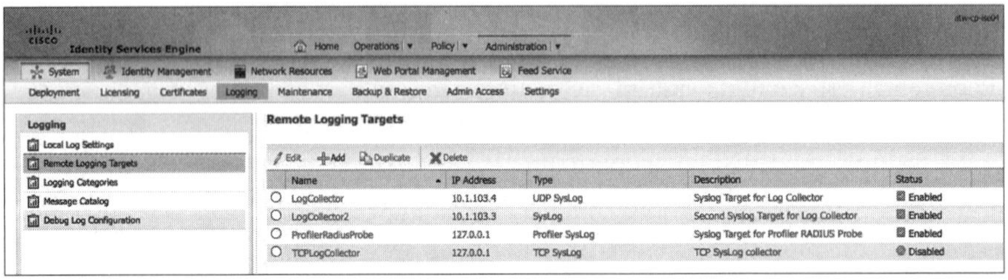

Figure 8-4   *Configuring ISE Remote Logging Targets*

The type of log server targets supported include UDP syslog, TCP syslog, and Secure syslog. You can assign multiple targets to a single audit category, as shown earlier in Figure 8-3.

PCI Requirement 10.7 necessitates that you keep audit logs for a period of one year, with at least 90 days' worth of logs kept readily available. To comply with 10.7, it is recommended that you configure ISE to hold 90 days of local audit logs and use your external logging target servers for the long-term, one-year storage. This allows Cisco ISE to operate without the burden of a large audit log data store. If 90 days' worth of audit data is too large to be stored locally on ISE, then use the external logging servers and reduce the number of days' worth of logs the ISE local log stores. Figure 8-5 shows the local log retention configuration options.

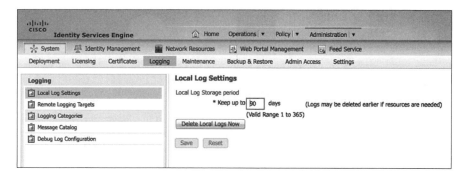

Figure 8-5 *ISE Local Log Data Retention Policy*

ISE Policy for PCI 10.6: Review Audit Data Regularly

Now that you have Cisco ISE set up to produce the proper audit trails, you need to review that data regularly. PCI requires that you review the logs of AAA servers such as Cisco ISE on a daily basis, which is a great best practice to follow. That, however, is a fairly tall order for today's overworked security analysts. Luckily, Cisco ISE has built-in reports and scheduled reports that can be created and, if desired, emailed to you every day or on a set interval. The Administrator Summary report, shown in Figure 8-6, is a good place to go to review all of the different administrator activity reports for ISE administrators.

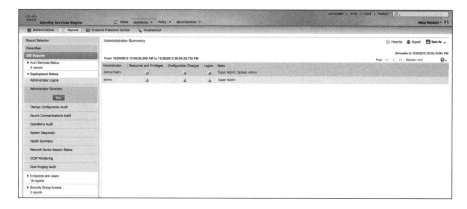

Figure 8-6 *ISE Administrator Summary Report*

Clicking any of the document magnifying-glass icons in the different columns will open and run a report for that column. Figure 8-7 depicts an example of an ISE administrator configuration change report.

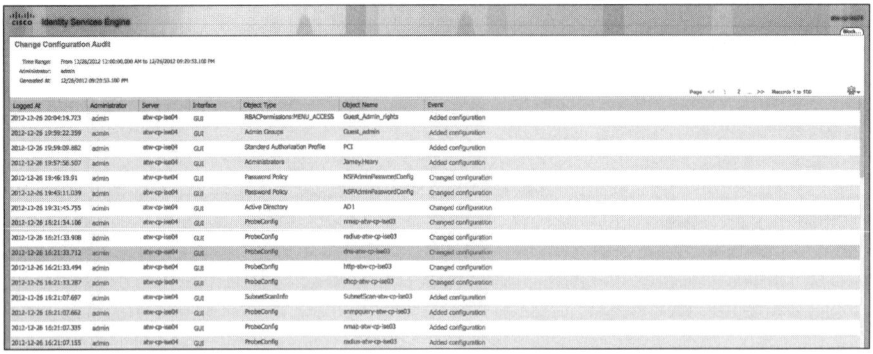

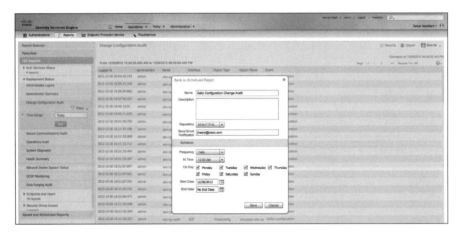

Figure 8-7   *ISE Administrator Change Configuration Audit Report*

Clicking any of the hyperlinks in the report will spawn another audit report with more details about the event.

Any ISE report that you run can be saved as a scheduled report. You can then input the relevant data, as shown in Figure 8-8, such as an email address to send the report to, frequency, and so forth.

Figure 8-8   *Scheduled Admin Change Configuration Report*

Cisco ISE User Accounting

In addition to auditing the administrators of ISE, it is also important to be able to audit the users authenticated via ISE. For this function, Cisco ISE offers the same user reporting structure that was just reviewed for administrators. It is found in the Operations > Reports > Auth Services Status section of the ISE GUI. The Authentication Summary report shown in Figure 8-9 is a good example of a user audit report.

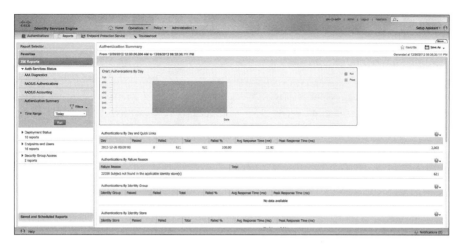

Figure 8-9 *User Authentication Summary Report*

For more user and device detailed reports, go to the Endpoint and Users report section under Operations > Reports > ISE Reports. Figure 8-10 depicts the Top Authorizations by User report.

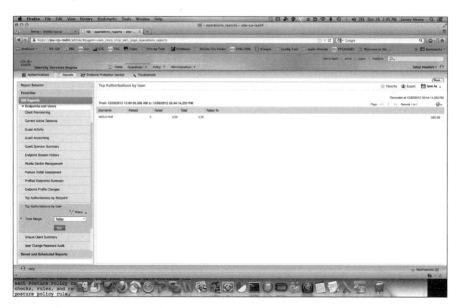

Figure 8-10 *Top Authorizations by User Report*

Summary

Proper auditing and accounting is instrumental in operating the ISE solution. It assists with troubleshooting tasks, compliance reporting, and locating configuration errors and security compromises. By using the PCI Requirement 10 as your guide, you will likely be able to pass audits against other security standards, including your own internal audit. Having said that, it is not a panacea, so be sure to check the regulations you will be audited against to ensure you configure Cisco ISE appropriately.

Chapter 9

The Basics: Principal Configuration Tasks for Cisco ISE

This chapter covers the initial installation and configuration of the Cisco Identity Services Engine. As discussed previously, Cisco ISE can be installed on a physical appliance or as a VMware appliance. Be sure to check the latest VMware requirements for ISE at http://www.cisco.com/go/ise. This chapter guides you through the initial setup steps for installing a standalone, non-high-availability mode, ISE deployment. It also covers the configuration of role-based access control (RBAC) for controlling administration of ISE.

Note If you are using the Cisco ISE 3400 Appliance, you can monitor the server inventory, health, and system event logs by using the built-in Cisco Integrated Management Controller (CIMC) GUI or the command-line interface (CLI). The default username for the CIMC server is *admin*. The default password is *password*.

Bootstrapping Cisco ISE

Follow these steps to perform the initial bootstrapping of ISE:

1. Install the Cisco ISE DVD.

2. When the Cisco ISE Installer boot options menu appears, as shown in Figure 9-1, enter 1 or 2, depending on your interface, and press Enter.

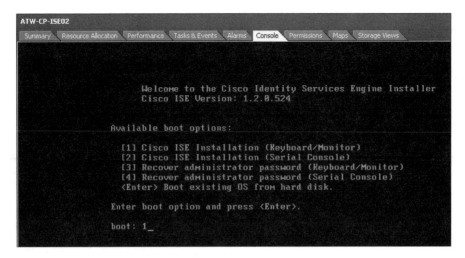

Figure 9-1   *ISE Boot Options Menu*

  3. Once the software installs, enter **Setup** at the prompt.

Note   It is recommended to ensure your ISE node is connected to the network before proceeding further.

  4. Enter the information requested in the prompts that follow.

Note   It is recommended that all ISE nodes be set for NTP and to the UTC time zone. This allows the time stamps on logs to remain consistent across the ISE deployment.

  5. ISE automatically reboots when you are finished. Expect this process to take several minutes.

  6. At the CLI login prompt, enter your username and password.

Note   While ISE is built on top of a purpose-built Linux platform known as the Application Development Environment Operating System (ADE-OS), it uses a CLI shell instead of a common Linux shell (such as Bash). The ISE CLI is very similar to the Cisco IOS CLI. There are two modes, exec and configuration mode. The ISE CLI has **show** commands (both **show run** and **show version** work, for example), and you can use **?** to get help. You can use the **do** command while in *configuration* mode to issue exec commands. This similarity should help you to navigate the ISE CLI quicker.

7. Check to ensure ISE is running properly by issuing the **show udi** and **show application status ise** commands. Write down The Unique Device Identifier (UDI), as it is important for licensing later on. When checking the application status, you should see something similar to Figure 9-2, which displays a message indicating that all services are running.

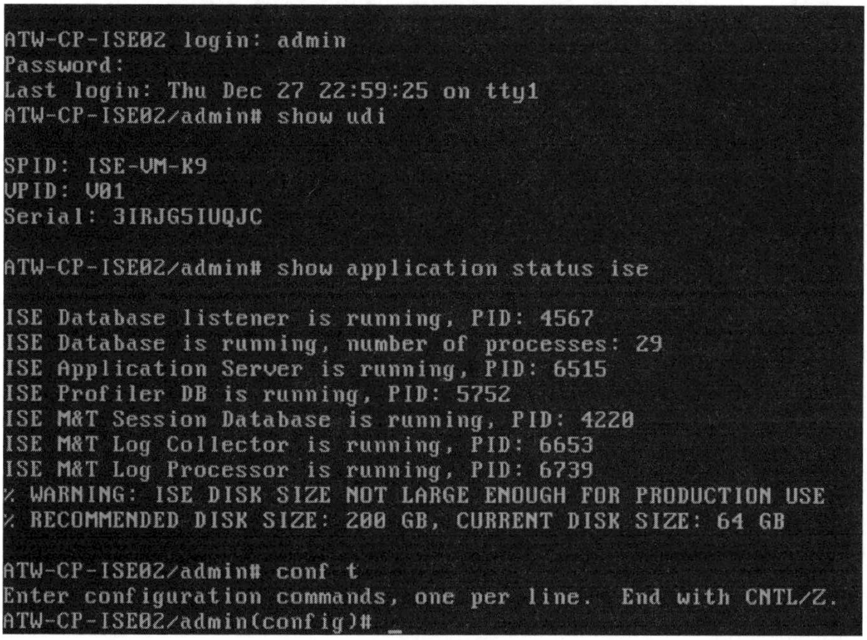

```
ATW-CP-ISE02 login: admin
Password:
Last login: Thu Dec 27 22:59:25 on tty1
ATW-CP-ISE02/admin# show udi

SPID: ISE-VM-K9
VPID: V01
Serial: 3IRJG5IUQJC

ATW-CP-ISE02/admin# show application status ise

ISE Database listener is running, PID: 4567
ISE Database is running, number of processes: 29
ISE Application Server is running, PID: 6515
ISE Profiler DB is running, PID: 5752
ISE M&T Session Database is running, PID: 4220
ISE M&T Log Collector is running, PID: 6653
ISE M&T Log Processor is running, PID: 6739
% WARNING: ISE DISK SIZE NOT LARGE ENOUGH FOR PRODUCTION USE
% RECOMMENDED DISK SIZE: 200 GB, CURRENT DISK SIZE: 64 GB

ATW-CP-ISE02/admin# conf t
Enter configuration commands, one per line.  End with CNTL/Z.
ATW-CP-ISE02/admin(config)#
```

Figure 9-2 *ISE CLI: Status Check*

8. Open your web browser to https://ISE/**admin** (replace ISE with the DNS name of your ISE node). Log in with your CLI credentials.

9. Select **Yes** to run the Cisco ISE Policy Setup Assistant wizard. This wizard speeds up the process of the initial configuration, described in the following section, and configures the most common initial features you will need. If you ever need to restart the wizard, just click **Setup Assistant** in the upper-right corner of the GUI (see Figure 9-3).

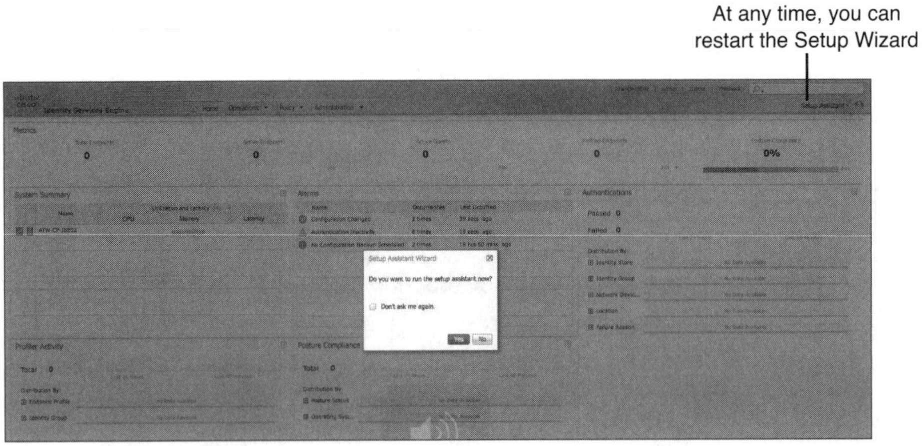

At any time, you can
restart the Setup Wizard

Figure 9-3 *Launching the ISE Policy Setup Assistant Wizard*

Using the Cisco ISE Setup Assistant Wizard

The Cisco ISE Setup Assistant wizard enables you to get your ISE server up and running quickly. It is not necessary to have your network devices preconfigured before starting this wizard. In fact, the wizard will provide you with the Cisco device configuration text at the end. You can use this wizard for the proof of concept phase of your ISE deployment. Your answers to the wizard's questions influence these Cisco ISE features:

■ Authentication

■ Authorization

■ Profiling

■ Posture

■ Client provisioning

■ Guest services and Web Portal management

■ Support for personal devices

Anything you configure during the wizard setup can be changed afterward by using the GUI.

Caution   Each time you complete the Setup Assistant wizard, it overwrites any previous ISE configuration! Anything not given values during the Setup Assistant wizard will be replaced with their default values. Because of this, you should run the wizard only upon initial setup or to erase and restart the ISE configuration process.

The ISE license type that you have will affect which options the Setup Assistant wizard displays to you. This section shows the options offered with the Basic and Advanced license installed.

If you will be using Active Directory, read the related Caution thoroughly before proceeding.

Caution   If you will be using Active Directory, the following requirements *must* be met to ensure that ISE can join the AD domain properly:

- Your ISE and AD clocks are time synchronized using NTP.
- The hostname of your ISE server is less than 15 characters in length.
- If you have a firewall between ISE and your AD domain server, the proper ports are allowed through: UDP\389, TCP\445, TCP\88, TCP\3268, TCP\3269, TCP\464, UDP\123, TCP\389, and TCP\636.
- If you have a multidomain AD forest, the domain to which ISE is connecting has a trust relationship with the other domains as necessary.
- DNS is configured and working properly in Cisco ISE. Be certain it can resolve the AD domain server name. You can use the CLI **ping** command for this.
- You have at least one AD global catalog in the AD domain that ISE is joining.
- The username employed to join the AD domain is either an Administrator user or has one of the following AD permissions:
  - Allowed to add workstations to the domain to which you are trying to connect.
  - Permitted to search users and groups in the directory that are required for authentication.

Here are the steps for completing the ISE Setup Assistant wizard:

1. On the Identity Policy Requirements page of the wizard, check either the **Wired** check box or the **Wireless** check box, or check both, to indicate the services for which you want to set up access. Fill in the required fields. For this exercise, click the **Monitor** radio button to indicate that you want to monitor user and endpoint access to your network. Monitor mode means that ISE will not enforce its policy yet on wired clients.At the bottom of the page, enter the internal networks that you do not want guest users to be able to access. This is also the initial list that non-posture-compliant PCs are restricted from accessing. You can modify both of these lists at a later time. Figure 9-4 shows the blocking of all RFC 1918 and multicast addresses. Click **Next**.

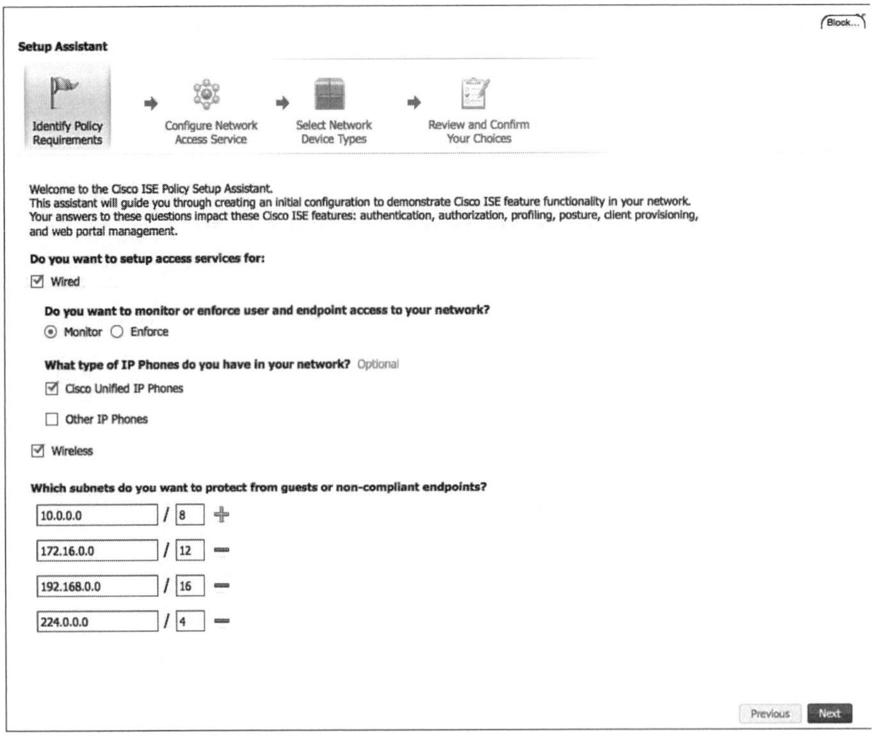

Figure 9-4   *ISE Setup Assistant Wizard: Identify Policy Requirements Page*

2. The first question on the Configure Network Access Service wizard page is Do You Want to Authenticate Users Using Cisco ISE? This is where you configure your identity store information. Most of you will use Microsoft Active Directory as your primary source for user authentication. If this is just an ISE guest server use case, then select the local ISE ID store. Figure 9-5 depicts the setup of AD and the selection of the group allowed to provision guest accounts and gain access to your network using 802.1X authentication.

    Once properly joined to the domain, you should see a **Connected to Domain: <your domain name>** message below the Join Domain button.

3. The second question on the Configure Network Access Service page is Do You Want to Evaluate Posture Compliance for Employees and Guests? In most cases, you should click the **No** radio button for posture assessment functionality (which, as indicated, is not applicable for wired access in monitor mode).

4. Scroll down the page (see Figure 9-6), and under the third question, Do You Want to Enable Endpoint Profiling?, click the **Yes** radio button to enable profiling. Enter your SNMP read-only community string. This will enable the following ISE profiler probes:

- DHCP

- RADIUS

- NMAP (Network Scan)

- SNMP Query

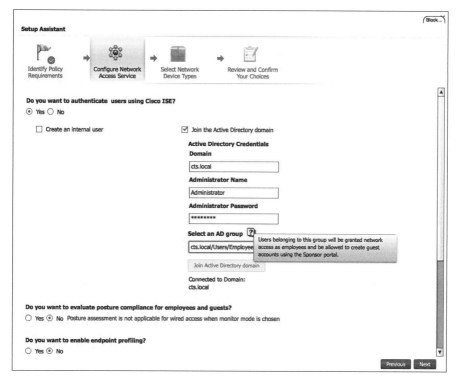

Figure 9-5 *ISE Setup Assistant Wizard: Configure Network Access Service Page (Top)*

5. If your ISE server requires the use of a proxy server to access the Internet, then click **Yes** under Do You Want to Configure Proxy Settings? and enter your proxy server details.

6. Under the fourth question, Do You Want to Allow Guests on Your Network, click **Yes** to enable the ISE guest server portal feature. In the Sponsor Name and Sponsor Password fields, enter a username and password for employees to use to create a guest account. You can add additional sponsor accounts later. You can also enter a simplified URL for the portal here and into your DNS server.

7. Under the last question, click **Yes** to enable the My Devices Portal for employees. Remember that employees are defined as those users who are members of the AD group you assigned earlier in the wizard. The My Devices Portal allows employees to self-register and control their own personal devices.

8. The final option on the Configure Network Access Service page is to customize the portal pages with your own company logo and so forth. Click the **Next** button when you are finished.

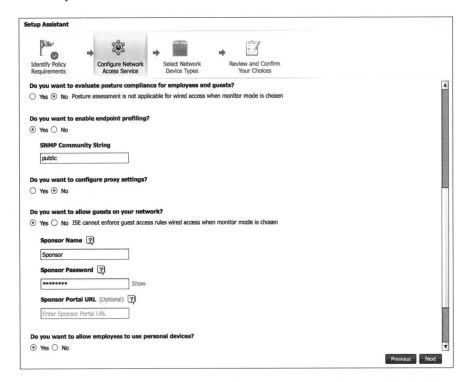

Figure 9-6 *ISE Setup Assistant Wizard: Configure Network Access Service Page (Bottom)*

9. The Select Network Device Types wizard page, shown in Figure 9-7, is where you can start to add your Cisco switches and/or Cisco Wireless LAN Controller to ISE. It is not necessary to have preconfigured your network devices before you complete this wizard. In fact, the wizard will provide you with the necessary device commands at the end.

   If you selected both wired and wireless modes, then you have to configure an item from each mode before you will be allowed to proceed to the next wizard page.

   In the Select Network Devices (Wired Network Diagram) section, check the box for your device model and then enter your device information (Figure 9-7 shows an example for Cisco Catalyst 3750 Series Switches):

   ■ Device hostname

   ■ Device management IP address and default gateway

- Employee VLAN ID and default gateway

- Voice VLAN ID and default gateway

- DHCP server IP address

- Uplink IP address that the switch uses to contact its default gateway. In a Layer 2 switched architecture, this is the same as the switch's IP address.

Figure 9-7 *ISE Setup Assistant Wizard: Wired Network Device Settings*

10. Scroll down the Select Network Device Types wizard page, and in the Select Wireless Network Device (Wireless Network Diagram) section, check the box for your device and then submit your wireless device information (Figure 9-8 shows an example for Cisco Wireless LAN Controller):

- Device hostname and IP address

- Employee SSID name

- Employee wired VLAN ID

- Employee default gateway (switched VLAN interface)

- Open Internet SSID name (guest SSID name)

- Guest wired VLAN ID

- Guest default gateway (switched VLAN interface)

- DHCP Server IP address

- WLC RADIUS shared secret

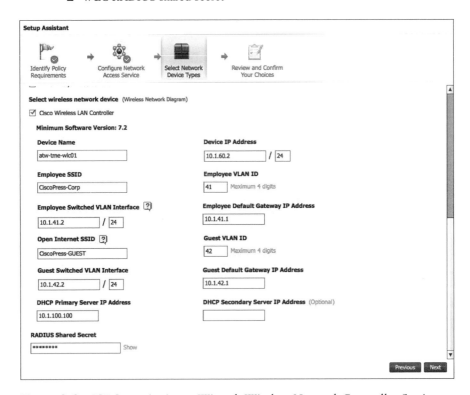

Figure 9-8   *ISE Setup Assistant Wizard: Wireless Network Controller Settings*

11. Click **Next**, review the settings, and then click the **Confirm Configuration Settings** button.

The wizard will now configure ISE according to your chosen settings. Once the configuration is complete, the wizard will provide you with both a wired device configuration and a wireless controller configuration. At this point, you can copy and paste the configuration text into your devices. Figure 9-9 shows the wireless controller configuration, and Figure 9-10 shows the wired switch configuration. In the event you need to see these configuration files after you close the wizard, choose **Setup Assistant > View Network Device Configuration**. The following section shows the complete configuration for each.

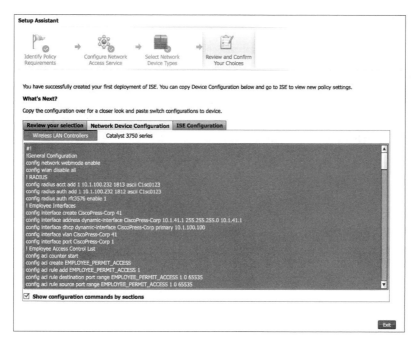

Figure 9-9   *ISE Setup Assistant Wizard: Wireless Device Configuration*

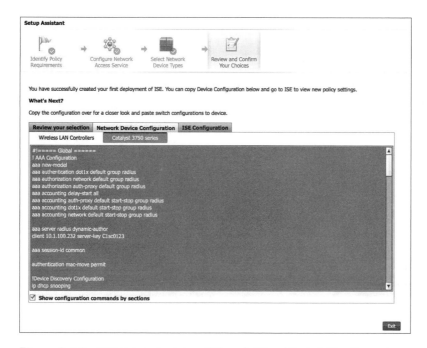

Figure 9-10   *ISE Setup Assistant Wizard: Wired Switch Configuration*

Configuring Network Devices for ISE

This section explores the basic configuration that must be added to your wired and wireless network devices. This is a not an exhaustive configuration review, but rather is meant as a review of the configuration that the ISE Policy Setup Assistant wizard produced in the previous section.

Wired Switch Configuration Basics

Example 9-1 shows the Cisco 3750X switch configuration output produced by the ISE Setup Assistant wizard. We have added comments throughout Example 9-1 to explain the configuration parts.

Example 9-1 *Cisco 3750X Switch Configuration*

```
#!===== Global Mode ======
! The AAA configuration enables AAA for 802.1X, web authentication, and radius to
ISE. This is very standard stuff you will want on your ISE controlled switches.
! AAA Configuration
aaa new-model
aaa authentication dot1x default group radius
aaa authorization network default group radius
aaa authorization auth-proxy default group radius
aaa accounting delay-start all
aaa accounting auth-proxy default start-stop group radius
aaa accounting dot1x default start-stop group radius
aaa accounting network default start-stop group radius
aaa server radius dynamic-author
client 10.1.100.232 server-key C1sc0123
aaa session-id common
authentication mac-move permit
! The Device discovery configuration enables probes that the ISE profiler will use
for profiling device types.
!Device Discovery Configuration
ip dhcp snooping
ip device tracking
! 802.1X configuration enables 802.1X globally on the switch and is required for all
dot1x enabled switches.
!802.1X Configuration
dot1x system-auth-control
! RADIUS configuration defines the radius attributes and radius servers (ISE) that
the switch will use.
!RADIUS Configuration
radius-server attribute 6 on-for-login-auth
radius-server attribute 8 include-in-access-req
```

```
radius-server attribute 25 access-request include
radius-server dead-criteria time 5 tries 3
radius-server host 10.1.100.232 auth-port 1812 acct-port 1813 key C1sc0123
radius-server vsa send accounting
radius-server vsa send authentication
! The next series of configuration sections set up the switch interfaces, http
server, logging, and routing you defined in the ISE Setup Assistant wizard. It also
enables DHCP forwarding (helper-address).
!VLAN Configuration
vlan 10
name DEFAULTVLAN
vlan 99
name VOICE
interface VLAN 10
ip address 10.1.10.1 255.255.255.0
ip helper-address 10.1.100.100
interface VLAN 99
ip address 10.1.99.1 255.255.255.0
ip helper-address 10.1.100.100
!Web interface Configuration
ip http server
ip http secure-server
!Routing Configuration
ip routing
ip route 0.0.0.0 0.0.0.0 10.1.48.1
!Logging Configuration
logging 10.1.100.232
! The access control list configuration defines the various ACLs needed to control
access properly in ISE monitor mode and given your wizard choices.
!Access Control List Configuration
ip access-list extended ACL-ALLOW
permit ip any any
ip access-list extended ACL-DEFAULT
remark Allow DHCP
permit udp any eq bootpc any eq bootps
remark Allow DNS
permit udp any any eq domain
permit icmp any any
permit tcp any host 10.1.100.232 eq 8443
permit tcp any host 10.1.100.232 eq 443
permit tcp any host 10.1.100.232 eq www
permit tcp any host 10.1.100.232 eq 8905
permit tcp any host 10.1.100.232 eq 8909
permit udp any host 10.1.100.232 eq 8906
```

```
permit udp any host 10.1.100.232 eq 8905
permit udp any host 10.1.100.232 eq 8909
deny ip any any
ip access-list extended ACL-WEBAUTH-REDIRECT
remark Pass through all non-web traffic including 443 to radius server
deny ip any host 10.1.100.232
remark Redirect all other web traffic
permit ip any any
! The Profiler configuration sets up SNMP and SNMP Trap to ISE.
!Profiler Configuration
access-list 20 remark ISE Profiling SNMP probe access
access-list 20 permit 10.1.100.232
snmp-server community public RW
snmp-server host 10.1.100.232 version 2c public
lldp run
! The Interface configuration should be copied to all interfaces that will be
controlled by ISE. In a full deployment this would be all non-trunk access ports
where clients could be connected.
#!===== Interface =====
switchport access vlan 10
switchport mode access
switchport voice vlan 99
ip access-group ACL-ALLOW in
authentication event fail action next-method
authentication event server dead action authorize vlan 10
authentication event server alive action reinitialize
authentication host-mode multi-domain
authentication open
authentication order dot1x mab
authentication priority dot1x mab
authentication port-control auto
authentication periodic
authentication timer reauthenticate server
authentication timer inactivity 180
authentication violation restrict
mab
dot1x pae authenticator
dot1x timeout tx-period 10
spanning-tree portfast
spanning-tree bpduguard enable
! The uplink interface command is used if you have a Layer 3 connection to the
upstream switch or router. This configures a switch port to be a routed port with an
IP address. If you are pure Layer 2 uplinks, then this configuration is not
necessary.
```

```
#!===== Uplink Interface =====
no switchport
ip address 10.1.48.2 255.255.255.0
```

Wireless Controller Configuration Basics

Example 9-2 presents the Cisco Wireless LAN Controller configuration output produced by the ISE Setup Assistant wizard. We have added comments throughout to explain the configuration parts. Most administrators choose to use the WLC GUI to configure their controllers. In that case, you can use the CLI configuration example as a guide to what you will need to configure in the GUI.

Example 9-2 *Cisco Wireless LAN Controller Configuration*

```
! The general configuration enables webmode and disables any currently configured
WLANs. This will be service impacting, so proceed with caution. Be sure to enter
config wlan enable all when you are done.
#!
!General Configuration
config network webmode enable
config wlan disable all
! RADIUS sets up authentication and accounting to ISE. It is very important to enable
rfc3576. Some versions of WLC do not allow this to be set from the CLI, in which
case you should enable it using the WLC GUI.
! RADIUS
config radius acct add 1 10.1.100.232 1813 ascii C1sc0123
config radius auth add 1 10.1.100.239 1812 ascii C1sc0123
config radius auth rfc3576 enable 1
! The next few sections configure the Employee Interface, ACL, and WLAN.
 ! Employee Interfaces
 config interface create CiscoPress-Corp 41
 config interface address dynamic-interface CiscoPress-Corp 10.1.41.2 255.255.255.0
10.1.41.1
 config interface dhcp dynamic-interface CiscoPress-Corp primary 10.1.100.100
 config interface vlan CiscoPress-Corp 41
 config interface port CiscoPress-Corp 1
 ! Employee Access Control List
 config acl counter start
 config acl create EMPLOYEE_PERMIT_ACCESS
 config acl rule add EMPLOYEE_PERMIT_ACCESS 1
 config acl rule destination port range EMPLOYEE_PERMIT_ACCESS 1 0 65535
 config acl rule source port range EMPLOYEE_PERMIT_ACCESS 1 0 65535
 config acl rule action EMPLOYEE_PERMIT_ACCESS 1 permit
```

```
config acl apply EMPLOYEE_PERMIT_ACCESS
! Employee WLAN
config wlan create 1 CiscoPress-Corp
config wlan security wpa enable 1
config wlan security web-auth server-precedence 1 radius local ldap
config wlan mfp client enable 1
config wlan aaa-override enable 1
config wlan nac radius enable 1
config wlan interface 1 CiscoPress-Corp
config wlan radius_server acct add 1 1
config wlan radius_server auth add 1 1
config wlan wmm allow 1
config wlan exclusionlist 1 60
config wlan broadcast-ssid enable 1
config wlan session-timeout 1 1800
config wlan enable 1
! The next few sections configure the Guest Interface, ACL, and WLAN.
! Internet Interfaces
config interface create CiscoPress-GUEST 42
config interface address dynamic-interface CiscoPress-GUEST 10.1.42.2 255.255.255.0
10.1.42.1
config interface dhcp dynamic-interface CiscoPress-GUEST primary 10.1.100.100
config interface vlan CiscoPress-GUEST 42
config interface port CiscoPress-GUEST 1

! Internet Access Control List
config acl create ANDROID_MARKETPLACE_REDIRECT
config acl rule add ANDROID_MARKETPLACE_REDIRECT 1
config acl rule destination address ANDROID_MARKETPLACE_REDIRECT 1 10.1.100.232
255.255.255.255
config acl rule destination port range ANDROID_MARKETPLACE_REDIRECT 1 0 65535
config acl rule source port range ANDROID_MARKETPLACE_REDIRECT 1 0 65535
config acl rule action ANDROID_MARKETPLACE_REDIRECT 1 permit
config acl rule add ANDROID_MARKETPLACE_REDIRECT 2
config acl rule destination port range ANDROID_MARKETPLACE_REDIRECT 2 0 65535
config acl rule source address ANDROID_MARKETPLACE_REDIRECT 2 10.1.100.232
255.255.255.255
config acl rule source port range ANDROID_MARKETPLACE_REDIRECT 2 0 65535
config acl rule action ANDROID_MARKETPLACE_REDIRECT 2 permit
config acl rule add ANDROID_MARKETPLACE_REDIRECT 3
config acl rule destination address ANDROID_MARKETPLACE_REDIRECT 3 10.1.42.1
255.255.255.0
config acl rule destination port range ANDROID_MARKETPLACE_REDIRECT 3 0 65535
config acl rule source port range ANDROID_MARKETPLACE_REDIRECT 3 0 65535
config acl rule direction ANDROID_MARKETPLACE_REDIRECT 3 in
config acl rule add ANDROID_MARKETPLACE_REDIRECT 4
```

```
  config acl rule destination port range ANDROID_MARKETPLACE_REDIRECT 4 0 65535
 config acl rule source port range ANDROID_MARKETPLACE_REDIRECT 4 0 65535
 config acl rule action ANDROID_MARKETPLACE_REDIRECT 4 permit
config acl create GUEST_PSP_ONLY
 config acl rule add GUEST_PSP_ONLY 1
 config acl rule destination port range GUEST_PSP_ONLY 1 53 53
 config acl rule source port range GUEST_PSP_ONLY 1 0 65535
 config acl rule protocol GUEST_PSP_ONLY 1 17
 config acl rule action GUEST_PSP_ONLY 1 permit
 config acl rule add GUEST_PSP_ONLY 2
 config acl rule destination address GUEST_PSP_ONLY 2 10.1.100.232 255.255.255.255
 config acl rule destination port range GUEST_PSP_ONLY 2 0 65535
 config acl rule source port range GUEST_PSP_ONLY 2 0 65535
 config acl rule action GUEST_PSP_ONLY 2 permit
 config acl rule add GUEST_PSP_ONLY 3
 config acl rule destination port range GUEST_PSP_ONLY 3 0 65535
 config acl rule source address GUEST_PSP_ONLY 3 10.1.100.232 255.255.255.255
 config acl rule source port range GUEST_PSP_ONLY 3 0 65535
 config acl rule action GUEST_PSP_ONLY 3 permit
 config acl rule add GUEST_PSP_ONLY 4
 config acl rule destination port range GUEST_PSP_ONLY 4 0 65535
 config acl rule source port range GUEST_PSP_ONLY 4 0 65535
 config acl rule protocol GUEST_PSP_ONLY 4 1
 config acl rule action GUEST_PSP_ONLY 4 permit
 config acl rule add GUEST_PSP_ONLY 5
 config acl rule destination port range GUEST_PSP_ONLY 5 67 67
 config acl rule source port range GUEST_PSP_ONLY 5 0 65535
 config acl rule protocol GUEST_PSP_ONLY 5 17
 config acl rule action GUEST_PSP_ONLY 5 permit
 config acl apply GUEST_PSP_ONLY
 config acl create ACL-GUEST-ACCESS
 config acl rule add ACL-GUEST-ACCESS 1
 config acl rule destination address ACL-GUEST-ACCESS 1 10.0.0.0 255.0.0.0
 config acl rule destination port range ACL-GUEST-ACCESS 1 0 65535
 config acl rule source port range ACL-GUEST-ACCESS 1 0 65535
 config acl rule add ACL-GUEST-ACCESS 2
 config acl rule destination address ACL-GUEST-ACCESS 2 172.16.0.0 255.240.0.0
 config acl rule destination port range ACL-GUEST-ACCESS 2 0 65535
 config acl rule source port range ACL-GUEST-ACCESS 2 0 65535
 config acl rule add ACL-GUEST-ACCESS 3
 config acl rule destination address ACL-GUEST-ACCESS 3 192.168.0.0 255.255.0.0
 config acl rule destination port range ACL-GUEST-ACCESS 3 0 65535
 config acl rule source port range ACL-GUEST-ACCESS 3 0 65535
 config acl rule add ACL-GUEST-ACCESS 4
 config acl rule destination address ACL-GUEST-ACCESS 4 224.0.0.0 240.0.0.0
```

```
config acl rule destination port range ACL-GUEST-ACCESS 4 0 65535
config acl rule source port range ACL-GUEST-ACCESS 4 0 65535
config acl rule add ACL-GUEST-ACCESS 5
config acl rule destination port range ACL-GUEST-ACCESS 5 0 65535
config acl rule source port range ACL-GUEST-ACCESS 5 0 65535
config acl rule action ACL-GUEST-ACCESS 5 permit
config acl apply ACL-GUEST-ACCESS

! Internet WLAN
config wlan create 2 CiscoPress-GUEST
config wlan security web-auth server-precedence 2 radius local ldap
config wlan security wpa wpa2 disable 2
config wlan security wpa akm 802.1X disable 2
config wlan security wpa disable 2
config wlan mac-filtering enable 2
config wlan aaa-override enable 2
config wlan nac radius enable 2
config wlan interface 2 CiscoPress-GUEST
config wlan radius_server acct add 2 1
config wlan radius_server auth add 2 1
config wlan exclusionlist 2 60
config wlan broadcast-ssid enable 2
config wlan session-timeout 2 1800
config wlan enable 2
! The blackhole ACL is used to restrict access to quarantined systems.
! Blackhole Access Control List
config acl create BLACKHOLE
config acl rule add BLACKHOLE 1
config acl rule destination port range BLACKHOLE 1 53 53
config acl rule source port range BLACKHOLE 1 0 65535
config acl rule protocol BLACKHOLE 1 17
config acl rule action BLACKHOLE 1 permit
config acl rule add BLACKHOLE 2
config acl rule destination address BLACKHOLE 2 10.1.100.232 255.255.255.255
config acl rule destination port range BLACKHOLE 2 0 65535
config acl rule source port range BLACKHOLE 2 0 65535
config acl rule action BLACKHOLE 2 permit
config acl rule add BLACKHOLE 3
config acl rule destination port range BLACKHOLE 3 0 65535
config acl rule source address BLACKHOLE 3 10.1.100.232 255.255.255.255
config acl rule source port range BLACKHOLE 3 0 65535
config acl rule action BLACKHOLE 3 permit
config acl rule add BLACKHOLE 4
config acl rule destination port range BLACKHOLE 4 0 65535
config acl rule source port range BLACKHOLE 4 0 65535
```

```
config acl rule protocol BLACKHOLE 4 1
config acl rule action BLACKHOLE 4 permit
config acl rule add BLACKHOLE 5
config acl rule destination port range BLACKHOLE 5 67 67
config acl rule source port range BLACKHOLE 5 0 65535
config acl rule protocol BLACKHOLE 5 17
config acl rule action BLACKHOLE 5 permit
config acl apply BLACKHOLE
```

Completing the Basic ISE Setup

With the Setup Assistant wizard complete, some basic setup still remains. The easiest way to complete this is to choose **Task Navigator > Setup**, as shown in the lower left corner of Figure 9-11. The Task Navigator provides you with step-by-step linear and interactive instructions for setting up different ISE features. The Setup task deals with the initial configuration tasks required by ISE.

Figure 9-11 shows the Setup Task menu, which is clickable. Click each one of the steps to complete them.

Figure 9-11   *ISE Setup Using Task Navigator*

First complete the Administration Password Policy, Network Access Password Policy, and Guest Access Password Policy Password Policy steps to comply with your standards, and then move on to the Licensing step, discussed next.

Install ISE Licenses

As described in Chapter 3, ISE has only a few license types: Basic, Advanced, and Wireless. The licenses include the user count, so if you run out, you can add another license to increase the count. Go to **Administration > System > Licensing** and click **Add Service**. Upload your Base license files and then your Advanced license files. Licenses come in Cisco PAK format. You should then see your license count change accordingly. See Figure 9-12 for details.

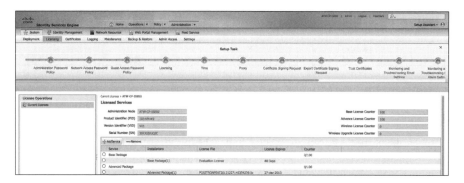

Figure 9-12   *ISE Licensing*

ISE Certificates

Once you are past the proof of concept phase, you'll want to install real certificates on your ISE server. For guest users, you will want to purchase from a certificate authority (CA) a certificate that is embedded in modern web browsers by default. For other use cases, like the My Devices Portal, you can use a certificate from your own CA if you wish. The key is to install a certificate that the clients will trust and for which they will not receive security alerts and such when using ISE resources. Just follow the Setup Task menu of the Task Navigator for the steps to install a non-self-signed certificate.

1. Generate the certificate-signing request. Figure 9-13 shows the fields that you need to fill in. Here is an example for the Certificate Subject field: CN=ATW-CP-ISE02. cisco.com, OU=Cisco O=security, C=US, S=CO, e=admin@cts.local. Click Submit when ready.

> **Note**   Ensure that the CN value in the Certificate Subject field is the fully qualified domain name (FQDN) of the ISE node. Otherwise, you will not be able to select the Management interface when binding the generated certificate.

2. Click **Certificate Signing Requests** in the Certificate Operations pane and export your CSR file.

3. Submit this CSR file to your CA server to obtain your ISE certificate. The obtained file must be in DER or PEM format. A PKCS#7 format is not fully supported.

4. Once you have the certificate, you need to bind it. Choose **Local Certificates > Add > Bind CA Certificate**, as shown in Figure 9-14.

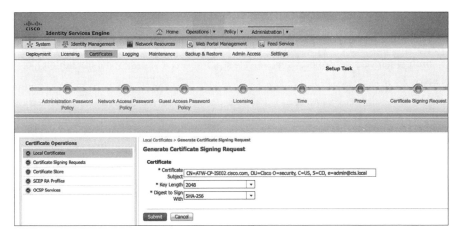

Figure 9-13 *Certificate Signing Request*

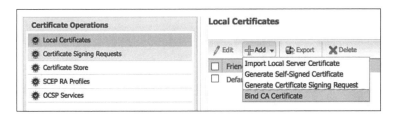

Figure 9-14 *Certificate Binding*

5. Enter the information shown in Figure 9-15 and click **Submit**. ISE will now restart services and log you out. Wait a few minutes before attempting to log back in. You should now see that ISE is using the new certificate you just added for your HTTPS GUI browser session.

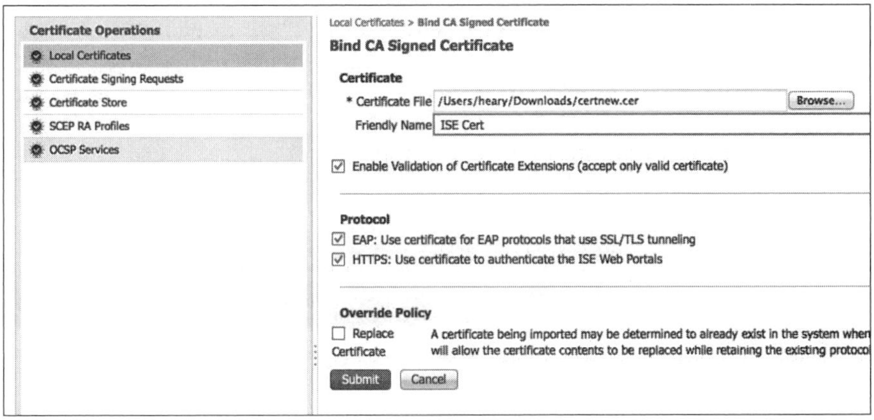

Figure 9-15 *Certificate Binding Upload*

6. Install the root certificate of the CA and any intermediate CA certificates into ISE. To do this, click **Certificate Store** in the Certificate Operations pane and then click **Import**. In most cases, you will want to check **Trust for Client Validation**. Click **Submit** when you are done. After a successful import, it should look something like Figure 9-16.

> **Note**   The ISE Certificate Store contains X.509 certificates that are used for trust and for the Simple Certificate Enrollment Protocol (SCEP). The certificates in the Certificate Store are managed on the primary administration node, and are replicated to every node in the ISE deployment automatically. Adding the SCEP server to ISE automatically installs the CA certificates in the Certificate Store.

Figure 9-16   *Import CA Certificate*

At this point you are done with the normal Certificate Store configuration options. Your users should no longer be using the original ISE self-signed certificate. In addition, all nodes in a distributed deployment will now be using the new certificates for node communications.

Installing ISE Behind a Firewall

In many cases, you will want to protect ISE by deploying a firewall in front of it. This is a fairly common practice when locating ISE inside of a data center that already has a firewall in place. In other cases, you might have a firewall in the traffic path between an ISE policy services node and the MnT or Admin nodes. In all of these cases, you will need to create rules in the firewall to permit ISE to operate.

ISE uses several services, ports, and protocols, and they vary based on the node type deployed. Table 9-1 lists the ISE communication ports and interfaces per node type. If you install a firewall between any of these nodes, you can reference Table 9-1 to determine which rules to write. Keep in mind that ISE Management is always hard-coded to nic0. All NICs can be IP addressed. Radius will listen on any NIC. Also consider that this services information could be used for building an ISE quality of service policy, particularly when communicating over long-distance or bandwidth-sensitive WAN links.

Table 9-1 *Cisco ISE 1.2 Services, Ports, and Protocols*

Role	Services	GE0	GE1	GE2	GE3
Administration Node	Administration	HTTP: TCP/80, HTTPS: TCP/443 (TCP/80 redirected to TCP/443) (not configurable) SSH Server: TCP/22 ERS (REST API): TCP/9060			
	Replication/Sync	HTTPS(SOAP): TCP/443 DB Listener/AQ: TCP/1521			
	Monitoring	SNMP Query: UDP/161			
Monitoring Node	Administration	HTTP: TCP/80, HTTPS: TCP/443 SSH Server: TCP/22			
	Replication/Sync	HTTPS (SOAP): TCP/443 DB Listener/AQ: TCP/1521 Oracle DB Listener (Secure JDBC): TCP/2484	DB Listener/AQ: TCP/1521 Oracle DB Listener (Secure JDBC): TCP/2484	DB Listener/AQ: TCP/1521 Oracle DB Listener (Secure JDBC): TCP/2484	DB Listener/AQ: TCP/1521 Oracle DB Listener (Secure JDBC): TCP/2484

Role	Services	GE0	GE1	GE2	GE3
	Logging	Syslog: UDP/20514, TCP1468 Secure Syslog: TCP/6514 (default ports configurable for ext log) Alarms: UDP/62627 (ISE 1.1)	Syslog: UDP/20514, TCP1468 Secure Syslog: TCP/6514 (default ports configurable for ext log) Alarms: UDP/62627 (ISE 1.1)	Syslog: UDP/20514, TCP1468 Secure Syslog: TCP/6514 (default ports configurable for ext log) Alarms: UDP/62627 (ISE 1.1)	Syslog: UDP/20514, TCP1468 Secure Syslog: TCP/6514 (default ports configurable for ext log) Alarms: UDP/62627 (ISE 1.1)
Policy Service Node	Administration	HTTP: TCP/80, HTTPS: TCP/443 SSH Server: TCP/22			
	Replication/Sync	HTTPS(SOAP): TCP/443; DB Listener/AQ: TCP/1521	DB Listener/AQ: TCP/1521	DB Listener/AQ: TCP/1521	DB Listener/AQ: TCP/1521
	Session	RADIUS Auth: UDP/1645, UDP/1812 RADIUS Accounting: UDP/1646, UDP/1813 RADIUS CoA: UDP/1700 (not configurable)	RADIUS Auth: UDP/1645, UDP/1812 RADIUS Accounting: UDP/1646, UDP/1813 RADIUS CoA: UDP/1700 (not configurable)	RADIUS Auth: UDP/1645, UDP/1812 RADIUS Accounting: UDP/1646, UDP/1813 RADIUS CoA: UDP/1700 (not configurable)	RADIUS Auth: UDP/1645, UDP/1812 RADIUS Accounting: UDP/1646, UDP/1813 RADIUS CoA: UDP/1700 (not configurable)
	Guest Services (Sponsor/Guest Portal/My Devices)	HTTPS: TCP/8443, TCP/8444 (default ports configurable)	HTTPS: TCP/8443, TCP/8444 (default ports configurable)	HTTPS: TCP/8443, TCP/8444 (default ports configurable)	HTTPS: TCP/8443, TCP/8444 (default ports configurable)

Role	Services	GE0	GE1	GE2	GE3
	Client Provisioning	Web/NAC Agent install: TCP/80, TCP/8443 (port setting follows Guest configuration) NAC Agent update: TCP/8905 Posture Agent and Supplicant install: UDP/8909, TCP/8909	Web/NAC Agent install: TCP/80, TCP/8443 (port setting follows Guest configuration) NAC Agent update: TCP/8905 Posture Agent and Supplicant install: UDP/8909, TCP/8909	Web/NAC Agent install: TCP/80, TCP/8443 (port setting follows Guest configuration) NAC Agent update: TCP/8905 Posture Agent and Supplicant install: UDP/8909, TCP/8909	Web/NAC Agent install: TCP/80, TCP/8443 (port setting follows Guest configuration) NAC Agent update: TCP/8905 Posture Agent and Supplicant install: UDP/8909, TCP/8909
	Posture/Heartbeat	Discovery (HTTPS): TCP/8905 Discovery (SWISS): UDP/8905 PRA/Keep-alive (SWISS): UDP/8905	Discovery (HTTPS): TCP/8905 Discovery (SWISS): UDP/8905 PRA/Keep-alive (SWISS): UDP/8905	Discovery (HTTPS): TCP/8905 Discovery (SWISS): UDP/8905 PRA/Keep-alive (SWISS): UDP/8905	Discovery (HTTPS): TCP/8905 Discovery (SWISS): UDP/8905 PRA/Keep-alive (SWISS): UDP/8905
	Profiling	Netflow: UDP/9996 (configurable) DHCP: UDP/67 (configurable), UDP/68 DHCPSPAN probe HTTP: TCP/80, TCP/8080 RADIUS logging: UDP/30514 DNS: UDP/53 (lookup) (Route table dependent) SNMPQUERY: UDP/161 (Route table dependent) SNMPTRAP: UDP/162 (configurable)	Netflow: UDP/9996 (configurable) DHCP: UDP/67 (configurable), UDP/68 DHCPSPAN probe HTTP: TCP/80, TCP/8080 RADIUS logging: UDP/30514 DNS: UDP/53 (lookup) (Route table dependent) SNMPQUERY: UDP/161 (Route table dependent) SNMPTRAP: UDP/162 (configurable)	Netflow: UDP/9996 (configurable) DHCP: UDP/67 (configurable), UDP/68 DHCPSPAN probe HTTP: TCP/80, TCP/8080 RADIUS logging: UDP/30514 DNS: UDP/53 (lookup) (Route table dependent) SNMPQUERY: UDP/161 (Route table dependent) SNMPTRAP: UDP/162 (configurable)	Netflow: UDP/9996 (configurable) DHCP: UDP/67 (configurable), UDP/68 DHCPSPAN probe HTTP: TCP/80, TCP/8080 RADIUS logging: UDP/30514 DNS: UDP/53 (lookup) (Route table dependent) SNMPQUERY: UDP/161 (Route table dependent) SNMPTRAP: UDP/162 (configurable)

Role	Services	GE0	GE1	GE2	GE3
	Clustering	UDP/45588, UDP/45590	UDP/45588, UDP/45590	UDP/45588, UDP/45590	UDP/45588, UDP/45590
	Administration	HTTPS (TCP/8443) (by Administration Node) SSH Server: TCP/22			
Inline Posture Node	Inline Posture	RADIUS Auth (proxy): UDP/1645, UDP/1812 RADIUS Accounting (proxy): UDP/1646, UDP/1813 RADIUS CoA: UDP/1700, UDP/3799 Redirect: TCP/9090	RADIUS Auth (proxy): UDP/1645, UDP/1812 RADIUS Accounting (proxy): UDP/1646, UDP/1813 RADIUS CoA: N/A Redirect: TCP/9090	—	—
	HA	—	—	Heartbeat: UDP/694	Heartbeat: UDP/694

Role-Based Access Control for Administrators

Having covered the basic setup of ISE, the next topic is controlling the administration of ISE. There are lots of features and functionality built into ISE to provide RBAC. In most environments, the concept of least privilege should be adopted when considering who, what, and where to allow ISE administration to. This section explores the functionality of RBAC in ISE and provides you with some best practices to consider for your environment.

There are two separate administrator accounts and privileges databases inside of ISE. One is for the ISE CLI access and the other is for ISE GUI. In the normal operation of ISE, the GUI is the only access method used to ISE. The CLI should rarely be accessed after initial setup of ISE, and therefore should be restricted accordingly based on that expectation.

RBAC for ISE GUI

RBAC is broken down into three main areas in ISE, all of which are under located **Administration > System > Admin Access:**

■ **Session and Access Settings and Restrictions:** This area enables you to define IP address access restrictions, concurrent sessions allowed, login banners, and idle time-outs.

■ **Authentication:** This area enables you to control the configuration of the authentication type and source used to authenticate administrators. It also enables you to control the password policy settings for admin accounts.

■ **Authorization:** This area is where the bulk of the control comes from. It enables you to control the permissions of each administrator or group of administrators. Permissions are broken up into Menu Access privileges and Data Access privileges. ISE has several built-in permission and admin groups for you to use.

RBAC: Session and Access Settings and Restrictions

To configure these settings, go to **Administration > System > Admin Access** and expand **Setting**s in the Admin Access pane on the left. You will see two submenus: Access and Session.

Choose **Access** first, as shown in Figure 9-17. On the Session tab, you can configure the Maximum Concurrent Sessions count for ISE. By default, ten administrators are allowed simultaneous access to the GUI and five are allowed simultaneous access to the CLI.

It is very important that you set up your pre-login banner for ISE. This displays any time an administrator opens the login page for ISE administration. This is an important step in ensuring your legal rights to prosecute abuse of the system.

Be sure to click **Save** to save any changes on this page before proceeding.

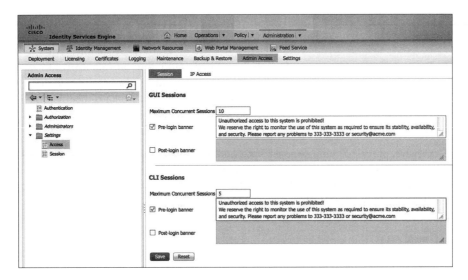

Figure 9-17 *RBAC: Access Session Settings*

Next, click the **IP Access** tab. As Figure 9-18 shows, you can create a list of IP addresses that are allowed to connect to ISE for the purpose of administration. It is highly recommended that you implement a restricted list in your environment.

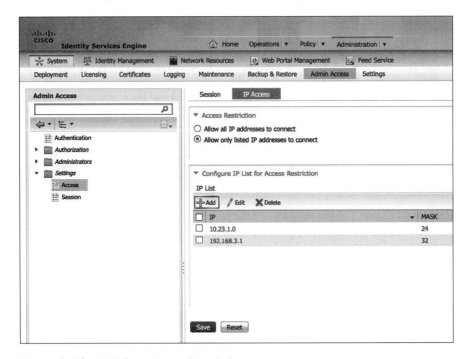

Figure 9-18 *RBAC: IP Access Restrictions*

Next, click **Session** under Settings in the Admin Access pane. Session menu. You will see two sections: Session Timeout and Session Info. It is highly recommended that you change the session timeout from the default of 60 minutes to 15 minutes. Most security best practice guides and security standards, such as PCI, recommend 15 minutes or less.

In the Session Info section, you will see a list of all the currently logged-in administrators. From here, you can kick them off ISE by clicking the Invalidate button.

RBAC: Authentication

To configure administrator authentication sources and features, go to **Administration > System > Admin Access** and click **Authentication** in the Admin Access pane. You will see two tabs : Authentication Method and Password Policy. As shown in Figure 9-19, you have two choices for authentication method. You can authenticate your administrators via traditional username/password (Password Based radio button) or you can use identity certificates (Client Certificate Based radio button), which provide a transparent and quick login to ISE. If you choose the Password Based radio button, then you can choose which identity source ISE should use. Common examples are

- Another radius server

- Microsoft Active Directory

- LDAP

- SecureID

- ISE Internal user database

Note   If you receive a password length error message from ISE, switch to the Password Policy tab and increase the minimum password length field for ISE; 8 is the recommended minimum.

Cisco ISE does not support administrator passwords with UTF-8 characters.

Figure 9-19   *RBAC: Authentication Method*

Cisco ISE is designed to "fall back" and attempt to perform authentication from the internal identity database, if communication with the external identity store has not been established or if it fails. In addition, an administrator can select Internal from the drop-down Identity Store selector on the Admin web login page for ISE.

Next you need to configure your password policy on the Password Policy tab. Figure 9-20 depicts the policy settings available to you. Choose the options according to your security standards.

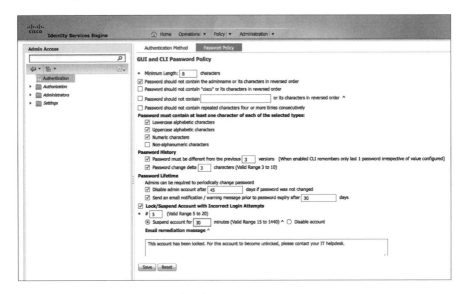

Figure 9-20   *RBAC: Password Policy*

RBAC: Authorization

ISE can use either the Internal database or an external database, such as Active Directory, for authorization of administrators. The Internal authorization tends to be easier to get up and running, but the external authorization allows you to use groups in your AD structure for ISE admin privilege level. Identity Services Engine includes several authorization policy settings and permission controls to support robust administrator role-based access control. To configure these, settings go to **Administration > System > Admin Access** and click **Authorization** in the Admin Access pane. You will see two submenus: **Permissions** and **Policy**. Permissions define the menu and data access privileges that are to be given to an administrator or admin group. There are several built-in access permissions to choose from, or you can create your own custom one. Figure 9-21 shows the built-in menu access permissions, while Figure 9-22 shows the built-in data access permissions. Each row includes a description of the access being granted.

Figure 9-21   *RBAC: Menu Access Permissions*

Figure 9-22   *RBAC: Data Access Permissions*

If you choose to use an external authorization database for ISE, then you need to modify or create new admin groups. Go to **Administration > System > Admin Access**, expand **Administrators** in the Admin Access pane, and click **Admin Groups.** You can either modify or duplicate/modify the existing admin groups or create just the ones you need. Figure 9-23 illustrates what an external enabled admin group looks like. This example shows modifying an existing admin group. A user's external group membership determines which ISE permission groups they will match.

The final step in RBAC is to set the RBAC policy. Figure 9-24 shows the list of built-in policy rules.

As you can see from Figure 9-24, a policy rule follows this logic: If you are a member of *Admin Group(S)*, then you receive these *permissions* for **Menu** and **Data** access. Each rule is processed and the admins privileges are an aggregate of all permissions with permit overriding deny. You cannot modify the built-in rules, but you can duplicate them and modify the duplicate. All custom rules must include both a Menu Access permission assignment and a Data Access permission assignment. You can only assign one of each per rule. However, if you create a custom rule with multiple admin group match criteria, the groups in the rule are OR'd, not AND'd, together. For example, you must be a member of admin groups: ise-admin or ise-mnt or ise-tra.

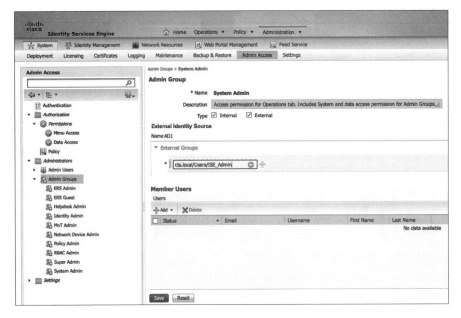

Figure 9-23   *External RBAC: Data Permissions*

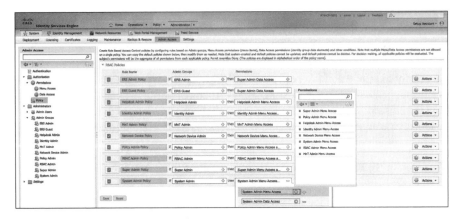

Figure 9-24   *RBAC: Policy Rules*

Summary

This chapter walked you through the initial configuration steps required to get the Cisco Identity Services Engine up and running quickly. It first showed you how to perform the initial bootstrapping of ISE, then guided you through the steps of the Cisco ISE Policy Setup Assistant wizard, and then explained how to use the Setup task of the Task Navigator to install ISE licenses and set up certificates. Finally, this chapter covered the role-based access control features for administration of ISE.

Chapter 10

Profiling Basics

This chapter examines

- Profiling concepts

- The importance of profiling to the context-aware policies necessary in today's business environment

- The multitude of ways that the Cisco Identity Services Engine (ISE) can glean the profiling data (probes)

- How to configure the infrastructure to efficiently use the ISE profiling probes, including virtual environments (VMware)

Understanding Profiling Concepts

The term *profiling* has been used a lot in today's society and can often have negative connotations. Police and security professionals may use a series of attributes about a human being, such as hair and eye color, the way they are dressed, and the way they behave to help "profile" them quickly as being a threat or a non-threat. However, this is ultimately guesswork that (hopefully) becomes more accurate with experience and practice.

Profiling, as it relates to network access, is very similar. However, the term should be thought of in a positive light as it relates to the Cisco Identity Services Engine (ISE) and Secure Unified Access solution.

The Cisco ISE Profiler is the component of the Cisco ISE platform that is responsible for endpoint detection and classification. It does so by using a probe or series of probes that collect attributes about an endpoint. The Profiler then compares the collected attributes to predefined device profiles to locate a match.

Why would profiling be an important technology for a company rolling out an identity solution? In the early days of identity-based networks and 802.1X, countless man hours were spent classifying all the devices that did not have supplicants. In other words, the devices that could not authenticate to the network using 802.1X, such as printers and fax machines. Your choices were to either identify the port connected to the printer and configure it to either

■ Not use 802.1X

■ Use MAC Authentication Bypass (MAB)

MAB is an extension to 802.1X that allows the switch to send the device's MAC address to the authentication server. If that MAC address is in the "approved list" of devices, the authentication server sends back an accept result, therefore allowing specific MAC addresses to bypass authentication.

Imagine just how many man hours were spent collecting and maintaining this list of MAC addresses. Additionally, an onboarding process had to be added, so that when a new printer was added to the network, its MAC address was added to the list prior to it being connected to the network for the first time, and so forth. Obviously, some enhancements to this onboarding were required. There had to be some way to build this list more dynamically and save all those man hours of prep and maintenance.

This is where profiling technology enters the picture. It allows you to collect attributes about devices from sources such as DHCP, NetFlow, HTTP user-agent-strings, and more. Those collected attributes are then compared to a set of signatures, similar to the way an Intrusion Prevention System (IPS) works. These signatures are commonly referred to as profiles.

An example would be collecting a MAC address that belongs to Apple, Inc.; seeing the HTTP user-agent-string contain the word "ipad," and therefore assigning that device to the profile of Apple-ipad.

Profiling technology has evolved, as technology often does. Now, your authentication server (ISE) has the ability to use that profiling data for much more than just building the MAB list.

The Cisco ISE uses the resulting collection and classification data from the profiler as conditions in the Authorization Policy. Now, you can build an Authorization Policy that looks at much more than your identity credentials. You can combine a user's identity with the classification result and invoke specific authorization results.

Figure 10-1 and Figure 10-2 are examples of a differentiated Authorization Policy based on profiling.

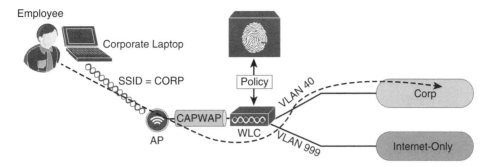

Figure 10-1   *Employee Using Corporate Laptop Gains Full Access*

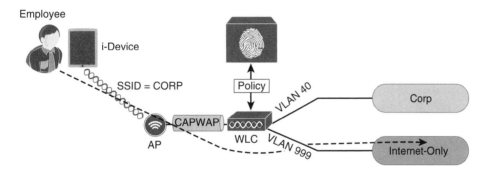

Figure 10-2   *Same Employee Credentials on an i-Device Gets Limited Access*

Users connecting to the same wireless SSID and the same credentials can be associated to different wired VLAN interfaces based on the device profile, such as

- Employees using corporate laptops with their Active Directory user ID are assigned to the corporate VLAN and given full access to the network.

- Employees using i-devices with their same Active-Directory user ID are assigned to a guest VLAN and provided only Internet access.

Although it may be intuitive to visualize the types of network access policies you are able to create based on the device's profile, the design of where and how the profiler collects the data in regard to the endpoints requires thought and planning.

Key Topic: One of the first questions a security team may ask when discovering profiling with any Network Access Control (NAC) solutions is, "Can we use this as an anti-spoofing solution?" Remember that MAB is a limited replacement for a strong authentication. It would be fairly easy for a malicious user to unplug a printer from the wall, configure his laptop to use the same MAC address as the printer (spoofing), and gain access to the network.

It is important to always keep in mind that profiling is a technology that compares collected attributes about an endpoint to a set of signatures called *profiling policies* to make the best guess of what a device is. Can this type of technology be used to prevent spoofing? Sure. However, it is difficult to accomplish anti-spoofing with this type of technology. It requires a lot of tuning, trial and error, and constant adjustment.

A best-practice approach is to use a defense-in-depth strategy. If the malicious user mentioned previously is successful in spoofing the MAC address of the printer and gains network access, what level of network access should that device have? In other words, the Authorization Policy for printers should not provide full network access, but provide a limited subset of access instead. For example, a printer should only be permitted to communicate using network ports critical to printer operations (such as TCP port 9100 or 9600).

Probes

As described, the Cisco ISE solution is capable of providing access policies where the decisions may be made based on who, what, where, when, how, and other. Profiling is focused on the "what" elements of the policy. For the policy engine to know what the device is, you must first collect that data.

The Cisco ISE solution uses a number of collection mechanisms known as *probes*. This probe is software designed to collect data to be used in a profiling decision. An example of this would be the HTTP Probe, which captures HTTP traffic and allows the profiler to examine attributes from the traffic, such as HTTP user-agent strings.

Without the probe enabled on the policy server, the data would never be collected.

Probe Configuration

You enable the probes on each Policy Service Node (PSN) where appropriate. In the Administration GUI of the PAN, navigate to **Administration > System > Deployment**. From here, select the PSN for which you are configuring the probes. Notice in the example lab, you have a Basic 2-node deployment. With this deployment, both nodes run all services, including profiling. Repeat these steps for each PSN in your deployment:

1. Select one of the Policy Services Nodes, as shown in Figure 10-3.

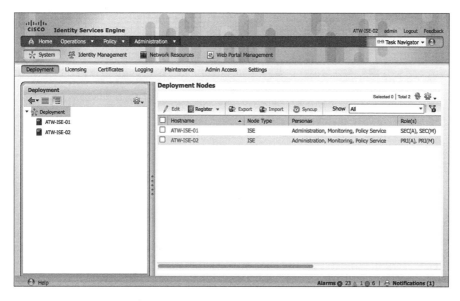

Figure 10-3 *ISE Deployment*

2. Ensure that the **Enable Profiling Service** check box is selected, as shown in Figure 10-4.

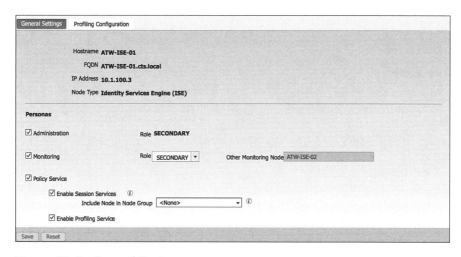

Figure 10-4 *General Settings*

3. Select the Profiling Configuration tab, as shown in Figure 10-5.

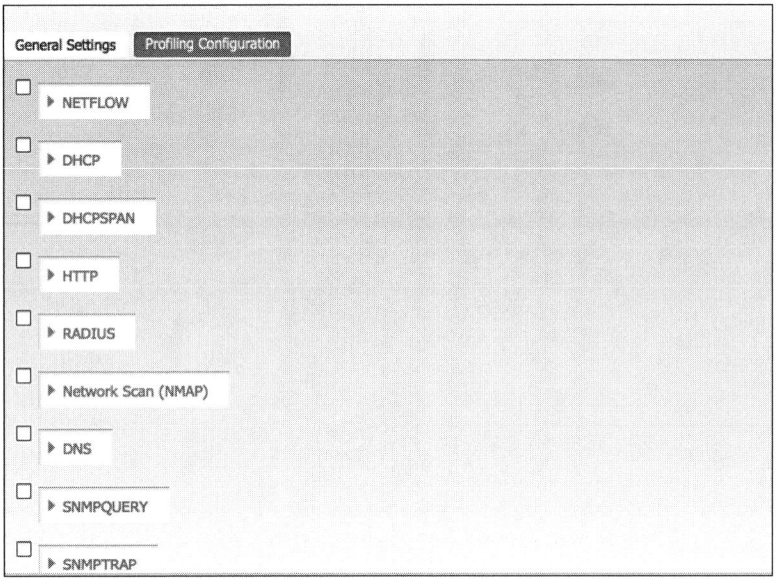

Figure 10-5   *Profiling Configuration*

Eight different probes are affected:

- HTTP probe
- DHCP
- NetFlow
- RADIUS
- Network Scan (NMAP)
- DNS
- SNMP
- IOS Device – Sensor

Each probe is described in further detail.

HTTP Probe

When applications use HTTP, such as a web browser or even software like Microsoft Outlook and Windows Update, it typically identifies itself, its application type, operating system, software vendor, and software revision by submitting an identification string to its operating peer. This information is transmitted in an HTTP Request-Header field called the User-Agent field.

The Cisco ISE uses the information in HTTP packets, especially the User-Agent field to help match signatures of what "profile" a device belongs in. Some common user-agent strings include

- **Dalvik/1.6.0 (Linux\; U\; Android 4.1.1\; GT-P3113 Build/JRO03C).** This user-agent string clearly calls out that the endpoint is running the Android OS.

- **Mozilla/5.0 (Linux; Android 4.2.2; Nexus 7 Build/JDQ39) AppleWebKit/535.19 (KHTML, like Gecko) Chrome/18.0.1025.166, Safari/535.19.** This user-agent also shows that it is an Android device, specifically a Google Nexus 7.

- **Mozilla/5.0 (iPhone; CPU iPhone OS 6_0_1, like Mac OS X) AppleWebKit/536.26 (KHTML, like Gecko) Version/6.0 Mobile/10A523, Safari/8536.25.** This user-agent string clearly comes from an iPhone.

Deployment Considerations

There are three primary mechanisms for the HTTP probe to collect the HTTP traffic:

- **Use a Switched Port Analyzer (SPAN) session in true promiscuous mode:** When using the SPAN method, consider the best location to create the SPAN session and gather the data. One recommended location is the Internet Edge, where a network organization typically deploys a Web Security Appliance, like the Cisco IronPort WSA.

  Figure 10-6 provides a logical representation of using SPAN in a network to capture HTTP traffic.

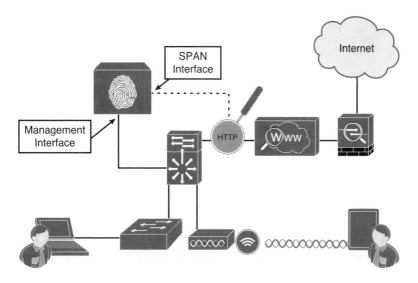

Figure 10-6 *HTTP SPAN Logical Design*

- **Use a SPAN session in conjunction with a filter to limit the traffic visible to ISE:** Another option to use with the SPAN design is VLAN ACLs (VACL) on a Catalyst

6500 or ACL-based SPAN sessions on a Nexus 7000. These options allow you to build an ACL that defines exactly what traffic you want to capture and send along to ISE instead of a pure promiscuous SPAN, where the ISE interface collects all traffic. This is a better way to manage the resource utilization on your ISE server when available.

- **Redirect devices' web traffic to the Guest or Client Provisioning Portal (CPP) on ISE:** To know which client to provision to the end system, the ISE CPP has a mechanism built into it to examine the user-agent strings to identify the client OS. Starting in ISE 1.1, the CPP and Guest portals automatically update the endpoint directory with user-agent data when a client connects to either portal.

  This saves the CPU cycles from having to run a promiscuous interface and examine all traffic, but you need to configure an Authorization Policy that sends all unknown devices to the CPP for OS recognition, which can cause an undesirable end-user experience when he is connecting with unknown devices.

As you can see, there are multiple ways to use the HTTP probe, and you must consider what works best for your environment and then deploy with that approach.

4. **Probe configuration:** Click the check box next to the HTTP probe to enable it, as shown in Figure 10-7. Select either the Gigabit 0 interface or all interfaces.

Multiple interfaces may not be individually selected. The choices will be a single interface or all interfaces.

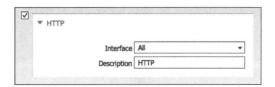

Figure 10-7   *HTTP Probe*

DHCP

DHCP can be one of the most useful data sources for an endpoint device. A primary use of DHCP in profiling is to capture the device MAC address; however, there are many other uses for the data. Much like HTTP, DHCP requests also carry a User-Agent field that helps to identify the OS of the device. Some organizations have been known to use a custom DHCP user-agent string, which helps identify the device as a corporate asset.

Not only the populated fields from the DHCP client, but other attributes, such as requested DHCP Options and DHCP Host-Name, are useful in classifying the device.

Here are some examples of dhcp-class-identifier:

- **dhcpcd-5.2.10:** Linux-3.0.16-gd0049f1:armv7l:vigor, which clearly calls out a Linux device. This one happens to be Android.

- **MSFT 5.0**, which is used by Windows 7 devices.

Deployment Considerations

Unlike HTTP, there are two DHCP probes:

- DHCP

- DHCP SPAN

Key Point: Although SPAN is possible, it is never the best practice. Use of more direct methods of capture are always preferred, such as the use of the ip-helper statement in Layer 3 Cisco routers and switches or the use of the RADIUS probe with IOS Device Sensor.

There are two primary methods for capturing DHCP data using the DHCP probes:

- Use a Switched Port Analyzer (SPAN) session in true promiscuous mode (see Figure 10-8).

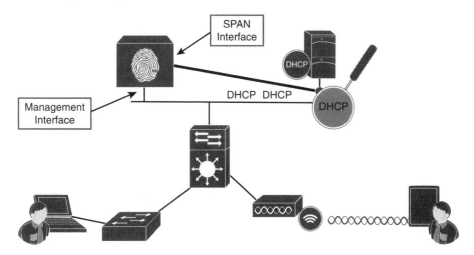

Figure 10-8 *DHCP SPAN Logical Design*

When using the SPAN method, consider the best location to create the SPAN session and gather the data. One recommended location is the DHCP server, where the DHCP probe examines both ends of the conversation (request and response). However, there are caveats to this method, such as, "What if the organization uses distributed DHCP servers?" This is why method 2 tends to be the most commonly deployed.

- Copy the DHCP requests to the ISE Policy Service Node(s) using the **ip helper-address** interface configuration command, as illustrated in Figure 10-9.

The **ip helper-address** command on a Layer 3 interface converts a DHCP broadcast (which is a Layer 2 broadcast) and converts it to a unicast or directed broadcast (which sends the broadcast to all hosts on a specific subnet). Simply add the IP address of your Policy Services Node(s) to the list of helper addresses, and it will be copied on all DHCP requests. Not to worry: The Cisco ISE server never responds to that request.

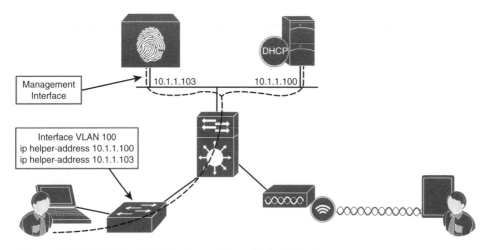

Figure 10-9   *DHCP with ip helper-address logical design*

Regardless of the SPAN or helper-address methods of using the DHCP probe(s), when using a Wireless LAN Controller (WLC), the WLC has a default configuration of acting as a RADIUS proxy, which is its own form of a helper-address, where the WLC acts as a middleman for all DHCP transactions. Unfortunately, this behavior has a negative affect on the DHCP probe and must be disabled on the WLC. Upon doing so, the DHCP requests from wireless endpoints appear as broadcast messages on the VLAN, and an IP helper-address statement must be configured on the Layer 3 interface of that VLAN (switch or router). This is covered in the Wireless LAN controller section of this book.

  5. **Probe configuration:** Click the check box next to the DHCP and/or DHCP SPAN Probe to enable them. Select either the Gigabit 0 interface or all interfaces. Multiple interfaces may not be individually selected. The choices will be a single interface or all interfaces, as illustrated in Figure 10-10.

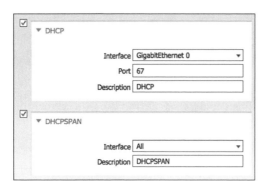

Figure 10-10   *DHCP Probes*

It's important to your overall deployment to only enable the profiling probes that you really need. The best practice is to enable DHCP SPAN only when you must, and use other probes when possible. As previously discussed, the PSN receives DHCP profiling data from Device-Sensor (if using Device-Sensor in the switch and/or WLC); or from the IP helper-address configuration on your Layer 3 devices.

NetFlow

NetFlow is an incredibly useful and under-valued security tool. Essentially, it is similar to a phone bill. A phone bill does not include recordings of all the conversations you had; instead, it is a detailed record of all calls sent and received.

Cisco routers and switches support NetFlow, sending a "record" of each packet that has been routed, including the ports used for the conversation between the endpoints, the number of packets and bytes sent during the conversation, and other useful information.

Deployment Considerations

Just enabling NetFlow in your infrastructure and forwarding it all to the Identity Services Engine can quickly over-subscribe your Policy Services Node. If you are planning to use the NetFlow probe, it is highly recommended that you have a third-party solution filter out any unnecessary data, and only send what you truly need to ISE. For that reason, this book does not focus on the NetFlow probe. It is recommended that you plan accordingly prior to its use.

6. **Probe configuration:** Click the check box next to the NetFlow Probe to enable it. Select either the Gigabit 0 interface or all interfaces.

    Multiple interfaces may not be individually selected. The choices are either a single interface or all interfaces, as shown in Figure 10-11.

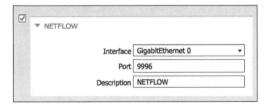

Figure 10-11 *NetFlow Probe*

As a general rule of thumb, it is not recommended to use this NetFlow probe. See the section, "Deployment Considerations," for details.

RADIUS

RADIUS is the primary communication mechanism from a network access device (NAD) to the authentication server (ISE). Within the RADIUS messages, there can be useful data to help classify a device.

Originally, the focus was on the MAC address and IP address of the device. By having this data conveyed in the RADIUS packet, ISE can build the all-important MAC ←→ IP address bindings. Because the endpoint database uses MAC addresses as the unique identifier for all endpoints, these bindings are absolutely critical. Without them, the Layer 3 probes, such as HTTP and endpoint scanning, would never work correctly.

The Calling-Station-ID field in the RADIUS packet provides the endpoint's MAC address, and the Framed-IP-Address field provides its IP address in the RADIUS accounting packet.

Additionally, the RADIUS probe can also trigger the SNMP probe to poll the NAD (see the following SNMP probe information).

Deployment Considerations

All NADs in the secure unified access deployment should be configured to send RADIUS accounting packets. It is also important to note that the Cisco switch must learn the endpoint's IP address via DHCP snooping or ip-device-tracking to fill in the Framed-IP-Address field.

7. **Probe configuration:** Click the check box next to the RADIUS probe to enable it, as shown in Figure 10-12. Notice that there is not really any configuration possible with this one. However, it is one of the most useful probes, especially when combined with device-sensor.

Figure 10-12 *RADIUS Probe*

Network Scan (NMAP)

A welcome improvement to ISE version 1.1 is the addition of the Endpoint Scanning (NMAP) probe. NMAP is a tool that uses port scans, SNMP, and other mechanisms to identify a device's OS or other attributes of the device. The NMAP probe may be manually run against a single IP address or subnet. More importantly, the profiler can be configured to react to a profiling event with a reactive NMAP probe.

For example, when an endpoint is discovered to be an Apple-Device, ISE launches an NMAP OS-Scan against that endpoint to determine if it is running MAC OS or iOS. From the results of that scan, ISE further classifies the device as a MAC or i-device.

Deployment Considerations

The NMAP probe is executed against an IP address or range of IP addresses. However, it is absolutely crucial to keep in mind that the endpoint database uses a MAC address as the unique identifier of any endpoint. As such, the Policy Services Node relies on the MAC address ←→ IP address binding to update an endpoint's attributes with the results of the NMAP scan. Therefore, it is critical that the PSN receive valid information from the other probes.

The NMAP probe can be manually run against a single IP address or subnet, or (more commonly) an NMAP scan may be triggered as an action of a profile.

8. **Probe configuration:** Click the check box next to the Network SCAN (NMAP) Probe to enable it. You may also run a manual scan from this screen, as shown in Figure 10-13.

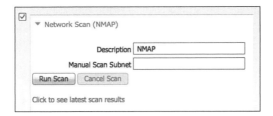

Figure 10-13 *NMAP Probe*

DNS

With the DNS probe enabled, ISE uses DNS to look up the endpoint's fully qualified domain name (FQDN).

Deployment Considerations

A reverse DNS lookup is completed only when an endpoint is detected by one of the DHCP, RADIUS, HTTP, and SNMP probes. A reverse lookup is when the IP address is checked in DNS, and the FQDN is returned for that IP address. In other words, the exact opposite of a normal DNS lookup.

9. **Probe configuration:** Click the check box next to the DNS probe to enable it, as shown in Figure 10-14. This probe uses the name-server configuration from the ISE node itself.

Figure 10-14 *DNS Probe*

SNMP

SNMP is used to query NADs that do not yet support Cisco IOS Device Sensor. After enabling the SNMPQUERY probe, ISE polls all the SNMP-enabled NADs at the configured polling interval.

Note It is recommended to remove SNMP settings from NADs that support the Cisco IOS Device Sensor to avoid double work.

Deployment Considerations

There are two SNMP probes:

- **SNMPTrap:** Receives information from the configured NAD(s) that support MAC notification, linkup, linkdown, and informs. The purpose of this probe is to trigger an SNMPQuery; so, in order for SNMPTrap to be functional, you must also enable the SNMPQuery probe.

  The SNMPTrap probe receives information from the specific NAD(s) when the MAC Address Table changes or when link state changes on a switch port. To make this feature functional, you must configure the NAD to send SNMP traps or informs (see the section, "Infrastructure Configuration"). Information received from the SNMP traps will not create a new endpoint in Cisco ISE, but it will potentially be used for profiling.

Note SNMPTrap-triggered queries are queued to same node for SNMPQuery probe. If local SNMPQuery probe is not enabled, those queries are dropped. Additionally, SNMPTraps should not be sent when using the RADIUS probe, because it will only trigger a duplicate SNMPQuery.

- **SNMPQuery:** Does the bulk of the work. There are actually two different kinds of SNMPQuery probes: The System Probe polls all NADs that are configured for SNMP at the configured interval, and the Interface Probe occurs in response to an SNMPTrap or RADIUS accounting "start" packet.

  The System probe queries the following MIBS at polling intervals (configured in the NAD definition):

  - system
  - cdpCacheEntry
  - cLApEntry (if device is WLC)
  - cldcClientEntry (if device is WLC)

The Interface probe runs after a RADIUS packet or SNMPTrap is received. It queries for the following data:

- Interface data (ifIndex, ifDesc, and so on)

- Port and VLAN data

- Session data (if interface type is Ethernet)

- Cisco Discovery Protocol data (if device is Cisco)

Note For distributed deployments, NAD polling is distributed among all Policy Services Nodes enabled for SNMPQuery probes.

10. **Probe configuration:** Click the check box next to the SNMPQUERY and SNMPTRAP Probes to enable them.

There is some configuration for these probes, such as the trap types to examine and the SNMP port. It is recommended to leave these at their default settings, as shown in Figure 10-15.

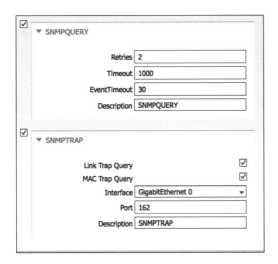

Figure 10-15 *SNMP Probes*

IOS Device-Sensor

As the Secure Unified Access system advances, more intelligence gets added not only the policy engine (ISE), but also to the NADs. The Cisco IOS Device Sensor (available beginning in IOS 15.0(2)) is one such enhancement. There is much valuable information about devices that get discovered and stored at the switch, such as CDP and LLDP data, which both describe a device and its capabilities, DHCP data that is captured and stored with DHCP snooping, and much more.

Distributing the profiling-sensor capabilities as close to the endpoint is a natural and welcome step in profiling evolution. This eliminates many of the design considerations that were already examined with the DHCP probes of having to configure ip helper-address statements or setting up the processor intensive SPAN sessions.

This technology was then added to the Cisco Wireless LAN Controller (WLC) in version 7.2.100.0. In WLC version 7.3, an HTTP probe was added. WLC version 7.4 has capabilities for DHCP, HTTP, and MDNS. Future versions of the Cisco WLC are road-mapped to supply more data.

With IOS 15.0(2), WLC 7.2.110.0 or above, and ISE 1.1, the Device-Sensors provide DHCP, CDP, LLDP, HTTP, and MAC OUI data via RADIUS accounting packets, and ISE consumes that data via the RADIUS probe. As Secure Unified Access continues to advance, more data should be added for communication through the Device-Sensors on Cisco NADs.

See the section, "Infrastructure Configuration," for configuration of these sensors.

Change of Authorization

The use of Change of Authorization (CoA) with profiling is critical to ensure a successful and smooth deployment. Through the normal process of profiling, an endpoint transitions from the unknown identity group to a more specific profile, such as Apple-Device. In many cases, it transitions another time to a more specific profile (for example, Apple-iPad).

When an endpoint policy (profile) changes, it is likely that the Authorization Policy rule also changes. For instance, you may not have provided access to a new endpoint until it was profiled as a workstation. The challenge is how to affect a new authorization for an endpoint that is already authenticated and authorized to the network.

To address this challenge Cisco helped to author the RFC Standards for Change of Authorization (CoA), defined in RFC 3576 and refined in RFC 5176.

CoA Message Types

As Cisco developed the secure access system, it became clear that the RFC standard CoA message types were not going to suffice for a positive end-user experience.

The only truly usable CoA message type was the CoA Disconnect Message (CoA-DM). Using the example previously described, where an Apple-iPad transitions profiles from unknown device to Apple-Device, then to Apple-iPad; the CoA-DM would cause the mobile device to lose its connection to the network upon each profile change if we wanted to immediately enforce the change in policy. That is not a positive user experience. In fact, it is the exact opposite: It is a hostile user experience.

Therefore, Cisco has advanced beyond the basic CoA's defined in the RFCs and added more intelligent ones for the Secure Unified Access system to ensure a positive end-user experience. Many other vendors will implement more advanced CoA types in their agents; however that does not enable itself well when a device does not have the agent (such as a printer). Cisco implements the advanced CoAs in the infrastructure itself, thereby eliminating the need for an agent to be resident. Some of the main CoA types are

- **Session Reauthentication (CoA-Reauth):** This is among the most common CoA messages used in the Secure Unified Access system. With this CoA message type, the session authentication will occur again, and the Authorization Policy may be re-evaluated. The user is oblivious to this.

- **Session Terminate (CoA-Terminate):** This is almost exactly like the standard CoA-DM message, only it ensures that the NAD clears the entire session out of its local Authentication Manager.

- **Session Terminate with Port-Bounce (CoA-PortBounce):** This CoA causes the interface to shut down and come alive again. This is commonly used when there is a non-authenticating device (an endpoint without a supplicant).

For example, you may have a printer that needs to be assigned a different VLAN. Without a supplicant, the printer would not recognize that the VLAN changed, and it may have the wrong IP address for the final VLAN. By using the Port-Bounce option, you cause the link-state of the network interface to drop and connect new, thereby triggering a DHCP refresh.

Note   As a safeguard, when multiple hosts are detected on a single port (such as with IP Telephony where the end user is behind the phone), ISE automatically switches from Port-Bounce to ReAuth.

Configuring Change of Authorization in ISE

There are two locations to set CoA message types in ISE. The first is the global setting that sets the default CoA message used throughout ISE. Secondly, a specific CoA type may be used per profile policy. An example of why both exist is to use Reauth as the global setting, but Port-Bounce for all printers.

In the following steps, you set the Global CoA type to ReAuth, and then view the setting for a printer profile.

From the ISE GUI, perform the following steps:

1. Navigate to **Administration > System > Settings > Profiling**.

2. Change the CoA Type drop-down to ReAuth, as shown in Figure 10-16.

3. Click **Save**.

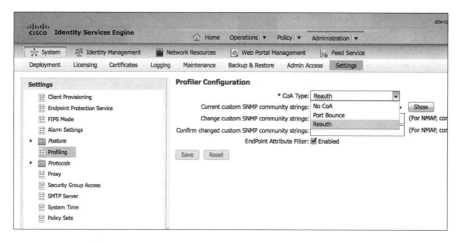

Figure 10-16   *Global CoA Type Setting*

4. Navigate to **Policy > Profiling > Brother-Device**.

5. Examine the Associated CoA Type drop-down, as shown in Figure 10-17.

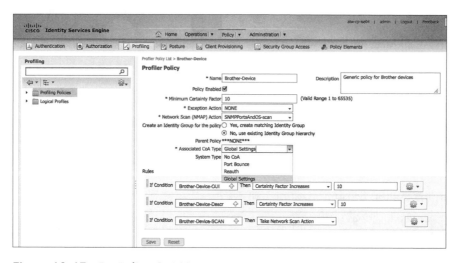

Figure 10-17   *Per Policy CoA Types*

Infrastructure Configuration

As an overall best practice, it is recommended to examine the cost-benefit analysis of using processor-intensive probes or probe designs. For example, it is often recommended to use DHCP-Helper instead of configuring a SPAN session and examining a multitude of traffic that may or may not be relevant.

Let's use HTTP traffic as an example. HTTP traffic is extremely useful for identifying the OS on a client endpoint; however, HTTP SPAN can consume a large amount of system resources on the Policy Services Node. Additionally, it may not be critical to have full visibility into the user-agent strings of all devices, such as corporate-managed Windows devices.

Some deployments will make use of VACL captures, which can limit what traffic is sent to the SPAN session. Other deployments will use the Authorization Policy in ISE to send unknown devices to the Client Provisioning Portal (CPP), allowing the CPP process to update the profiling data.

DHCP Helper

As shown in Example 10-1 and Figure 10-18, the **ip helper-address** commands are configured on the default gateway for each of the access-layer VLANs. To configure the destination address to copy DHCP requests to, enter interface configuration mode of the Layer 3 address for the VLAN and enter the **ip helper-address** [ip-address] command. Add the DHCP server and all applicable ISE Policy Service Nodes to the list of helper-address destinations.

Example 10-1   ip address-helper *Command Input*

```
C6K-DIST(config-if)#ip helper-address ?
  A.B.C.D    IP destination address?
```

```
C6K-DIST#sho run int VLAN41
Building configuration...

Current configuration : 152 bytes
!
interface Vlan41
  ip address 10.1.41.1 255.255.255.0
  ip helper-address 10.1.100.100
  ip helper-address 10.1.100.3
  ip helper-address 10.1.100.4
end

C6K-DIST#
```

DHCP Server

Policy Services Nodes

Figure 10-18   ip helper-address *Settings*

SPAN Configuration

A monitor session is configured in global-configuration mode and can be local (SPAN) or remote (RSPAN). Example 10-2 and Figure 10-19 show a SPAN configuration where an Internet-facing VLAN is the source of the session and an interface on the Policy Services

Node is the destination. For more on SPAN configuration, see www.cisco.com/en/US/products/hw/switches/ps708/products_tech_note09186a008015c612.shtml.

Example 10-2   monitor session *Command Input*

```
DC-4948(config)#monitor session [1-4] source [interface | vlan] [rx | tx]
DC-4948(config)#monitor session [1-4] destination interface [interface_name]
```

```
DC-4948#sho monitor session 1
Session 1
---------
Type              : Local Session          Source = VLAN 100
Source VLANs      :
    Both          : 100
Destination Ports : Gi1/47                 Source = VLAN 100
    Encapsulation : Native
          Ingress : Disabled
         Learning : Disabled
```

Figure 10-19   *Example Monitor Session (SPAN) Configuration*

VLAN Access Control Lists (VACL)

VACL configuration is a multi-step process:

1. Build an access list to classify the traffic you want to capture, as demonstrated in the following configuration:

   ```
   C6K-DIST(config)#ip access-list extended HTTP_TRAFFIC
   C6K-DIST(config-ext-nacl)#permit tcp any any eq www
   ```

2. Build an access list for all the rest of the traffic, as demonstrated in the following configuration:

   ```
   C6K-DIST(config)#ip access-list extended ALL_TRAFFIC
   C6K-DIST(config-ext-nacl)#permit ip any any
   ```

3. Create a VLAN access map sequence to "capture" HTTP traffic, as demonstrated in the following configuration:

   ```
   C6K-DIST(config)#vlan access-map HTTP_MAP 10
   C6K-DIST(config-access-map)#match ip address HTTP_TRAFFIC
   C6K-DIST(config-access-map)#action forward capture
   ```

4. Add a new sequence to the access map to forward all other traffic, as demonstrated in the following configuration:

   ```
   C6K-DIST(config)#vlan access-map HTTP_MAP 20
   C6K-DIST(config-access-map)#match ip address ALL_TRAFFIC
   C6K-DIST(config-access-map)#action forward
   ```

5. Apply the VLAN access map to the VLAN list, as demonstrated in the following configuration:

```
C6K-DIST(config)#vlan filter HTTP_MAP vlan-list 41,42
```

6. Configure the destination port for the PSN's SPAN interface, as demonstrated in the following configuration:

```
C6K-DIST(config)#switchport capture allowed vlan 41
C6K-DIST(config)#switchport capture allowed vlan add 42
C6K-DIST(config)#switchport capture
```

IOS Device-Sensor

IOS device-sensor requires a multi-part configuration. The first part is to configure the device-sensor filter-lists. These lists inform device-sensor of which items to focus on for the different protocols.

IOS device-sensor supports three protocols: DHCP, CDP, and LLDP. Create one list for each protocol:

1. Create a list for DHCP.

   There are three options you need to configure for ISE: host-name, class-identifier, and client-identifier, as demonstrated in the following configuration:

```
C3750X(config)#device-sensor filter-list dhcp list <dhcp_list_name>
C3750X(config-sensor-dhcplist)#option name host-name
C3750X(config-sensor-dhcplist)#option name class-identifier
C3750X(config-sensor-dhcplist)#option name client-identifier
```

2. Create a list for CDP.

   There are two CDP options you need to configure for ISE: device-name and platform-type, as demonstrated in the following configuration:

```
C3750X(config)#device-sensor filter-list cdp list <cdp_list_name>
C3750X(config-sensor-cdplist)#tlv name device-name
C3750X(config-sensor-cdplist)#tlv name platform-type
```

3. Create a list for LLDP.

   There are three LLDP options you need to configure for ISE: port-id, system-name, and system-description, as demonstrated in the following configuration:

```
C3750X(config)#device-sensor filter-list lldp list <lldp_list_name>
C3750X(config-sensor-lldplist)#tlv name port-id
C3750X(config-sensor-lldplist)#tlv name system-name
C3750X(config-sensor-lldplist)#tlv name system-description
```

4. Include the lists created in Steps 1–3 in the device-sensor.

In the previous steps, you defined what options that device-sensor should store. At this point, configure device-sensor to use those lists, as shown:

```
C3750X(config)#device-sensor filter-spec dhcp include list <dhcp_list_name>
C3750X(config)#device-sensor filter-spec lldp include list <cdp_list_name>
C3750X(config)#device-sensor filter-spec cdp include list <lldp_list_name>
```

5. Enable device-sensor.

Device-sensor is now configured. Now, enable the device-sensor service to run on the switch, and configure when it will send its updates, as shown:

```
C3750X(config)#device-sensor accounting
C3750X(config)#device-sensor notify all-changes
```

VMware Configurations to Allow Promiscuous Mode

As shown in Figure 10-20, VMware vSwitches reject promiscuous mode by default. To use SPAN type probes with ISE, configure the vSwitch to allow promiscuous connections.

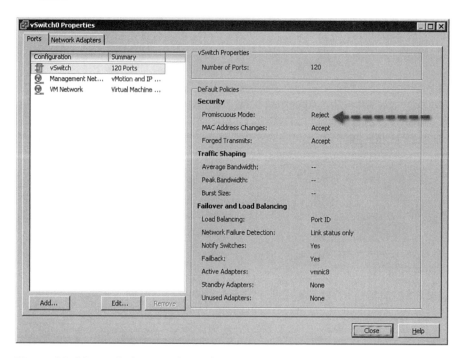

Figure 10-20   *Default vSwitch Configuration*

In the following steps, you configure a vSwitch to allow promiscuous traffic:

1. Highlight the vSwitch and click **Edit**.

2. Click the **Security Tab**.

3. Change the Promiscuous Mode drop-down to Accept, as shown in Figure 10-21.

Figure 10-21 *Promiscuous vSwitch Setting*

Best Practice Recommendations

There is a direct correlation between the difficulty to deploy a probe and its inherent value to your Secure Unified Access deployment. Tables 10-1, 10-2, and 10-3 summarize the best-practice recommendations for probes used in wired and wireless deployments.

These tables show a comparison of the Deployment Difficulty Index (DDI), Network Impact Index (NII), and a Probe Value Index (PVI). Each probe will receive a rating of 1 to 3 for each index.

Table 10-1 *Probe Comparison Chart Decoder Ring*

DDI	Deployment Difficulty Index	Easy	Medium	Difficult
NII	Network Impact Index	Low	Medium	High
PVI	Probe Value Index	High	Medium	Low

Table 10-2   *Wired Deployment Probe Comparison Chart*[1]

Probe	DDI	NII	PVI	Key Profiling Attributes	Notes
RADIUS	1	1	1	MAC address (OUI), IP address, user name, others	Fundamental probe for device detection and enabling other probes.
RADIUS w/ device-sensor	2	1	1	CDP/LLDP/DHCP attributes	If running 3k/4k access switches with device-sensor support, this is the ideal and optimized method to collect select attributes.
SNMPTrap	1	1	3	LinkUp/LinkDown and MAC notifications traps, informs	Detect endpoint connections/trigger SNMPQuery probe.
SNMPQuery	1	2	1	MAC address/ OUICDP/LLDP attributes, ARP tables	Polling of device ARP tables populates ISE MAC:IP bindings; be careful of high SNMP query traffic triggered by excessive RADIUS Accounting updates due to re-auth or interim updates.
DHCP (Helper)	2	1	1	DHCP attributes	Provides MAC:IP bindings; be wary of low DHCP lease timers.
DHCP SPAN	2	3	1	DHCP attributes	Provides MAC:IP bindings.
NMAP	1	2	2	Operating system, common ports, endpoint SNMP data	SNMP data assumes UDP/161 open and **public** string.
DNS	1	1	2	FQDN	Value depends on whether common naming conventions used.
HTTP (Redirect)	2	1	2	User agent	Value depends on relative importance of OS for wired access.

1. Comparison charts courtesy of Craig Hyps, Sr. Technical Marketing Engineer at Cisco.

Probe	DDI	NII	PVI	Key Profiling Attributes	Notes
HTTP (SPAN)	2	3	2	User agent	Consider SPAN of key HTTP chokepoints, like Internet edge; leverage smart SPAN solutions and VACL capture if possible.
NetFlow	3	3	2	Source/dest IP/ports/protocol	Recommended only for specific use cases, not general profiling.

Table 10-3   *Wireless Deployment Probe Comparison Chart*

Probe	EDI	NII	PVI	Key Profiling Attributes	Notes
RADIUS	1	1	1	MAC address (OUI), IP address, user name, others	Fundamental probe for device detection and enabling other probes.
RADIUS w/ device-sensor	2	1	1	CDP/LLDP/DHCP attributes	If running WLC 7.2MR1, sensor offers optimized delivery of DHCP attributes.
SNMPTrap					WLC traps not currently supported.
SNMPQuery	1	2	3	MAC address/OUI IP address; ARP tables	**Polling of device ARP tables populates ISE MAC:IP bindings**; be careful of high SNMP query traffic triggered by excessive RADIUS accounting updates due to re-auth or interim updates.
DHCP (Helper)	2	1	1	DHCP attributes	Provides MAC:IP bindings; be wary of low DHCP lease timers.
DHCP SPAN	2	3	1	DHCP Attributes	Provides MAC:IP bindings.

Probe	EDI	NII	PVI	Key Profiling Attributes	Notes
NMAP	1	2	2	Operating system, common ports	OS detection and common ports primary use case. SNMP not common for wireless clients.
DNS	1	1	2	FQDN	Value depends on whether common naming conventions used.
HTTP (Redirect)	2	1	1	User agent	Common requirement to distinguish mobile device types. HTTP often provides higher fidelity than other methods for OS detection.
HTTP (SPAN)	2	3	1	User agent	Consider SPAN of key HTTP chokepoints, like WLC connections and Internet edge; optionally, use intelligent SPAN/tap options or VACL capture where available.
NetFlow	3	3	2	Source/dest IP/ports/protocol	Recommended only for specific use cases, not general profiling.

Examining Profiling Policies

This book explores how to collect the profiling data that ISE uses to match an Endpoint Profiling Policy, including infrastructure configuration and the probe configuration on ISE. Now, let's look at the policies that examine the collected data and assign an endpoint to a specific profile called an Endpoint Profile Policy.

Endpoint Profile Policies

The profiling service collects attributes of endpoints, and the profile policies are similar to signatures, as they define the endpoint profiles themselves. For example, to match an Apple-Device profile, the endpoint must have a MAC address beginning with an OUI owned by Apple.

Each Endpoint Profile Policy defines a set of attributes that must be matched for a device to be classified as that endpoint type. ISE has a large number of pre-defined profile policies which may be viewed by navigating to **Policy > Profiling**, as shown in Figure 10-22.

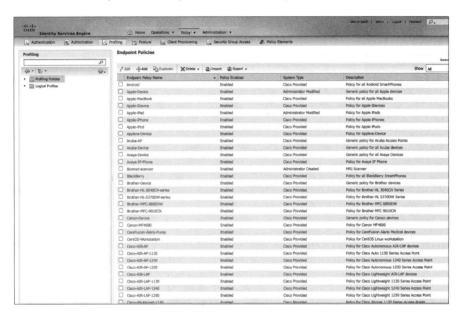

Figure 10-22   *Policy > Profiling*

Each profile is listed as Cisco provided or "Administrator Modified." This ensures that the feed service does not override one that has been changed by the administrator.

Profiles are hierarchical and inclusive in nature, and you can pick any level to use within your policies. Look at Figure 10-23, for example, and notice the existence of a Parent Policy named Cisco-Device with a child policy named Cisco-IP-Phone, and that has another child policy named Cisco-IP-Phone-7940 (Cisco-Device > Cisco-IP-Phone > Cisco-IP-Phone-7940).

An Authorization Policy may choose to use the profile at any point in that chain. If you select Cisco-Device, it applies to all devices classified as Cisco-Device and anything classified as a profile underneath Cisco-Device, as well as all their children.

Figure 10-24 displays the way a hierarchy is built within ISE.

Figure 10-23   *Cisco-Device Parent Profile*

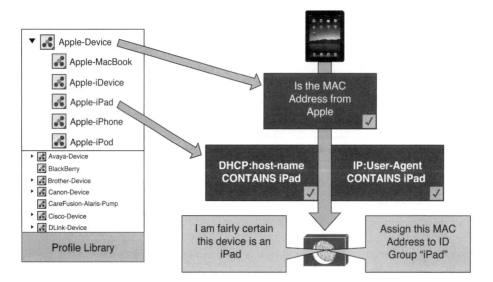

Figure 10-24   *Cisco-Device Parent Profile*

As another example, there is a predefined Authorization Rule named Profiled Cisco IP Phones that permits full access to the network and assigns permission to join the Voice VLAN—for all devices that meet the Cisco-IP-Phone profile. Figure 10-25 shows this rule.

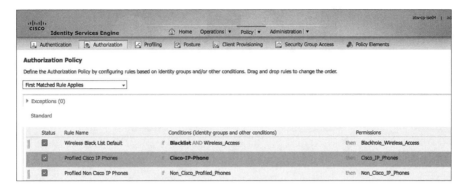

Figure 10-25 *Profiled Cisco IP Phone Authorization Rule*

Cisco IP Phone 7970 Example

To help explain the policy hierarchy and how it works, let's examine it more closely. This example uses a Cisco 7970 IP-Phone, which has been granted access from the Profiled Cisco IP Phones default authorization rule, which permits all devices matching a Cisco-IP-Phone profile Identity Group.

Start by examining the endpoint attributes and comparing them to the profiling policies:

1. Navigate to **Administration > Identity Management > Identities** and choose **Endpoints.**

2. Filter the list of endpoints to reduce the number displayed and make it easier to find the exact endpoint you want to examine, such as what's visible in Figure 10-26.

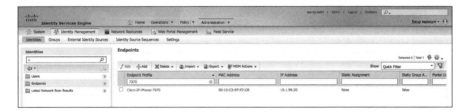

Figure 10-26 *Filtered Endpoint Identities*

3. Selecting this endpoint brings you into the endpoint details.

4. Immediately, notice that the Policy Assignment (profile of the device) is Cisco-IP-Phone-7970. However, the Identity Group Assignment is Cisco-IP-Phone, as shown in Figure 10-27.

Identity Services Engine
Home
Operations
Policy
Administration
System
Identity Management
Network Resources
Web Portal Management
Feed Service
Identities
Groups
External Identity Sources
Identity Source Sequences
Settings
Identities
Users
Endpoints
Latest Network Scan Results
Endpoint List > 00:13:C3:07:F2:C8
Endpoint
* MAC Address 00:13:C3:07:F2:C8
Static Assignment
* Policy Assignment Cisco-IP-Phone-7970
Static Group Assignment
* Identity Group Assignment Cisco-IP-Phone
Attribute List
22-tcp ssh
AuthenticationIdentityStore Internal Endpoints
AuthenticationMethod Lookup
AuthorizationPolicyMatchedRule Profiled Cisco IP Phones
BYODRegistration Unknown
CPMSessionID 0A01300200001602CBD5DE58
Called-Station-ID 1C-DF-0F-31-B0-01
Calling-Station-ID 00-13-C3-07-F2-C8
DestinationIPAddress 10.1.103.4
DestinationPort 1812
Device IP Address 192.168.254.1
Device Port 1645
Device Type Device Type#All Device Types#Swi
DeviceRegistrationStatus NotRegistered
EapAuthentication EAP-TLS
EndPointMACAddress 00-13-C3-07-F2-C8

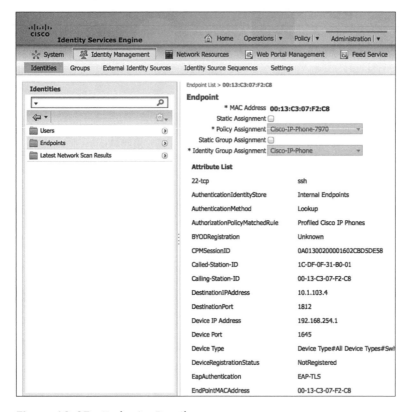

Figure 10-27 *Endpoint Details*

5. As you scroll down, notice that the EndPointSource is the RADIUS Probe. That means the RADIUS probe provided the most information needed to classify this device. This is pointed out in Figure 10-28.

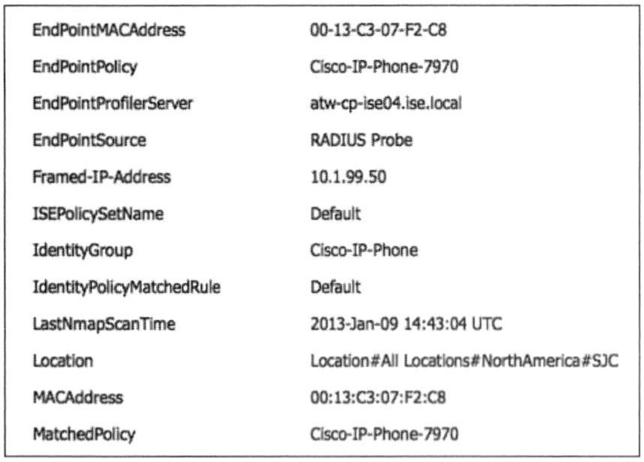

EndPointMACAddress 00-13-C3-07-F2-C8
EndPointPolicy Cisco-IP-Phone-7970
EndPointProfilerServer atw-cp-ise04.ise.local
EndPointSource RADIUS Probe
Framed-IP-Address 10.1.99.50
ISEPolicySetName Default
IdentityGroup Cisco-IP-Phone
IdentityPolicyMatchedRule Default
LastNmapScanTime 2013-Jan-09 14:43:04 UTC
Location Location#All Locations#NorthAmerica#SJC
MACAddress 00:13:C3:07:F2:C8
MatchedPolicy Cisco-IP-Phone-7970

Figure 10-28 *Endpoint Details: Endpoint Source*

6. Continuing down the list of attributes, notice the CDP and LLDP cached data from the switch, which was sent to ISE via the RADIUS probe, as displayed in Figure 10-29.

cdpCacheAddress	10.1.99.50
cdpCacheCapabilities	H;P;M
cdpCacheDeviceId	SEP0013C307F2C8
cdpCachePlatform	Cisco IP Phone 7970
cdpCacheVersion	SCCP70.9-1-1SR1S
dot1xAuthAuthControlledPortControl	2
dot1xAuthAuthControlledPortStatus	2
dot1xAuthSessionUserName	00-13-C3-07-F2-C8
ifDescr	GigabitEthernet1/0/1
ifIndex	10101
ifOperStatus	1
ip	10.1.99.50
lldpPortId	07:30:30:31:33:43:33:30:37:46:32:43:38:3a:50:31
lldpSystemDescription	Cisco IP Phone 7970G,V, SCCP70.9-1-1SR1S
lldpSystemName	SEP0013C307F2C8.cts.local
operating-system	Cisco embedded VoIP phone (accuracy 97%)

Figure 10-29 *Endpoint Details: CDP and LLDP Data*

Notice these attributes of the endpoint, but how is that used within the Profiling Policy? To answer that question, examine the profiling policy hierarchy for the endpoint.

7. Navigate to **Policy > Profiling**. Click **Cisco-Device**, which is the top-level of the profiling hierarchy for this endpoint, as shown in Figure 10-30.

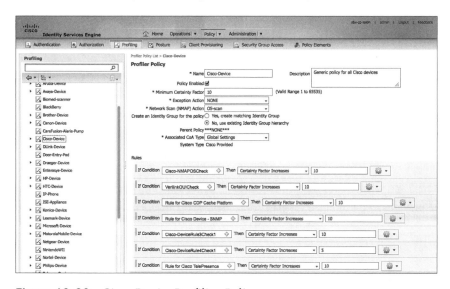

Figure 10-30 *Cisco-Device Profiling Policy*

Using Figure 10-30 as a reference point, note the following details:

■ The Minimum Certainty Factor of this profile is 10. Certainty Factor is an aggregate value between 1 and 65,535. Each of the conditions at the bottom of the policy may add more certainty to this profile, if they are matched.

■ Note that the OUI is Cisco Systems, as shown in Figure 10-31, and that matches the condition for Cisco-Device, as shown in Figure 10-32. This is one possible mapping that meets the minimum certainty value and should match the endpoint to this parent policy.

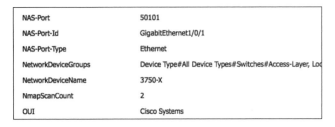

Figure 10-31 *OUI of the Endpoint*

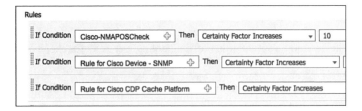

Figure 10-32 *OUI Condition in Cisco-Device Policy*

■ There is a Network Scan (NMAP) action set to OS-Scan. For this action to occur, there must be a condition below, whose result is to trigger the network scan. Figure 10-33 displays this mapping of the condition to the action. Figure 10-34 displays the contents of the condition, meaning that if the MAC OUI contains Cisco, then run the NMAP Scan type defined.

■ There are a tremendous number of conditions in this profiling policy, most of which add a certainty value of 5 to 10. The Certainty Value only needs to be a minimum of 10 to match the profile, so matching any one of these conditions will most likely equal a match.

The previous step examined the parent profile Cisco-Device, but what does it take to get one step further—to reach the Cisco-IP-Phone profile?

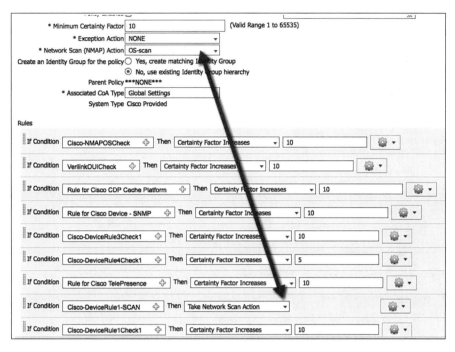

Figure 10-33 *Network Scan Action and Condition with Scan Result*

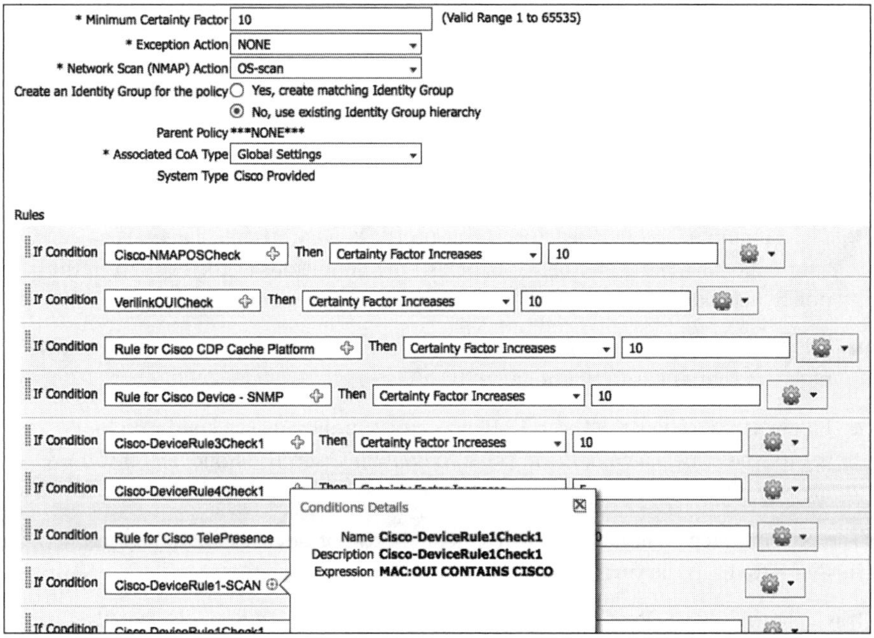

Figure 10-34 *Condition That Triggers the Scan Action*

8. Navigate to **Policy** > **Profiling** > **Cisco-Device** > **Cisco-IP-Phone**, as shown in Figure 10-35, and examine what conditions are used for this policy.

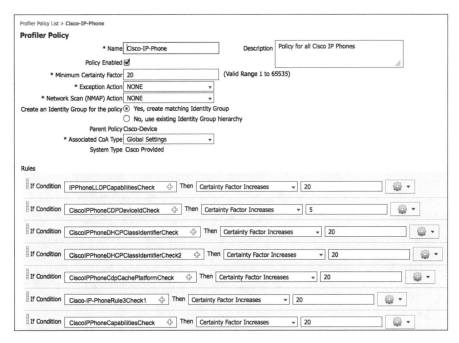

Figure 10-35   *Cisco-IP-Phone Profiling Policy*

Using Figure 10-35 as a reference, note the following details:

■ To even be compared to this profiling policy, the device must have first matched its parent policy. In this case, the device had to match the Cisco-Device policy before these conditions will ever be looked at.

■ The Minimum Certainty Factor of this profile is 20. Certainty Factor is an aggregate value between 1 and 65,535. Each of the conditions at the bottom of the policy may add more certainty to this profile if they are matched.

■ The CDP Cache, shown in Figure 10-36, shows that the cdpCachePlatform attribute was sent as Cisco IP Phone 7970.

■ Figure 10-37 shows the Cisco IP Phone profile policy uses a condition looking for the cdpChachePlatform value to contain Cisco IP Phone, and if it does, increase the certainty by 20.

The previous step examined Cisco-IP-Phone, but what does it take to get one step further—to reach the final Cisco-IP-Phone-7970 profile?

9. Navigate to **Policy** > **Profiling** > **Cisco-Device** > **Cisco-IP-Phone** > **Cisco-IP-Phone-7970** and examine what conditions are used for this policy.

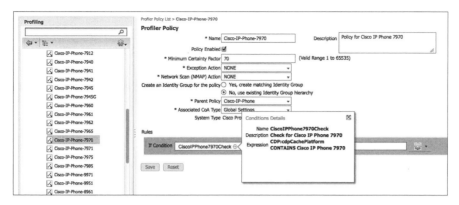

Figure 10-36 *Cisco-IP-Phone-7970 Profile*

Using Figure 10-36 as a reference point, note the following details:

- To even be compared to this profiling policy, the device must have first matched both its parent policies. In this case, the device had to match the Cisco-Device and Cisco-IP-Phone policy even before these conditions are looked at.

- The profile has only one condition, and that condition is that the cdpCachePlatform attribute is Cisco IP Phone 7970.

Rarely would you build an Authorization Policy that is specific to the point of the model number of the Cisco Phone; instead, you would just use the Cisco-IP-Phone parent policy in your Authorization Policies.

Using Profiles in Authorization Policies

As shown with the Profiled Cisco IP Phone authorization rule, the profile can be used as a condition of an authorization rule in the form of an Identity Group. Originally, ISE required an identity group in order to use any of the profiling policies in the rule; however, it evolved into having the ability to use the profile directly (called the EndPointPolicy).

Let's examine both Endpoint identity groups and the EndPointPolicy methods in this section.

Endpoint Identity Groups

Local identities within the ISE database may be in the form of User identities or Endpoint identities. There are also identity groups that may contain multiple identities, although an identity (user or endpoint) may be a member of only one identity group at a time.

To create an identity group based on the profile, simply select the option named "Yes, create matching Identity Group" on the profile, as displayed in Figure 10-37.

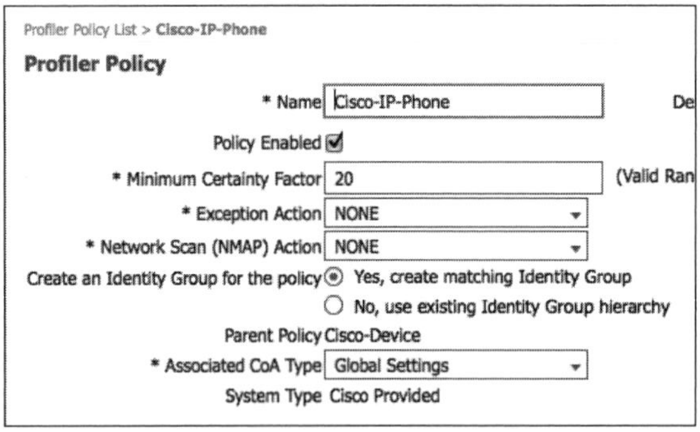

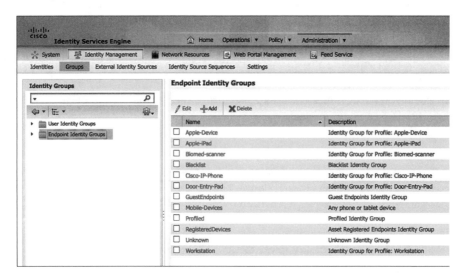

Figure 10-37   *Create Matching Identity Group*

If that option is selected, the matching identity group is found under **Administration > Identity Management > Groups > Endpoint Identity Groups** (as shown in Figure 10-38).

Figure 10-38   *Endpoint Identity Groups*

As you will read in the section, "EndPointPolicy," the use of profiling in authorization rules has been de-coupled from the Endpoint identity groups. Therefore, starting with ISE 1.2, you really use identity groups for a different purpose. They are employed more for a MAC Address Management (MAM) model, where you can create a static list of MAC addresses to be authorized specifically.

The Blacklist identity group is a perfect example of identity-group usage in this manner. If a user were to lose their personal device, he would be able to log in to the MyDevices portal and mark a device as Lost. This immediately adds the endpoint to the Blacklist group, which will be denied network access by default, as shown in Figure 10-39.

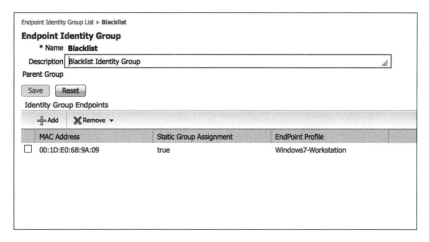

Figure 10-39 *Blacklisted Devices*

Selecting Reinstate moves the device from the Blacklist group to the RegisteredDevices group, as displayed in Figure 10-40.

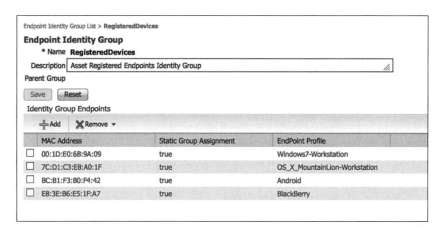

Figure 10-40 *RegisteredDevices Endpoint Identity Group*

The Profiled Cisco IP Phones default authorization rule depicted earlier in Figure 10-25 is a perfect example of using an identity group in an authorization rule.

Companies have started to use device groups to differentiate corporate-owned tablets from personally owned tablets.

EndPointPolicy

As mentioned, beginning with ISE 1.2, there is no longer a need to identify groups in order to apply policy based on the devices profile. You can now directly use the profile with the Endpoints:EndPointPolicy condition.

The easiest way to explain this concept is to show an example. In this example, let's create a new authorization rule that uses the Android profile, which does not have a corresponding identity group. The list of identity groups was shown in Figure 10-38.

Figure 10-41 shows an authorization rule where a device with the profile of Android (EndPoints:EndPointPolicy EQUALS Android) is denied access.

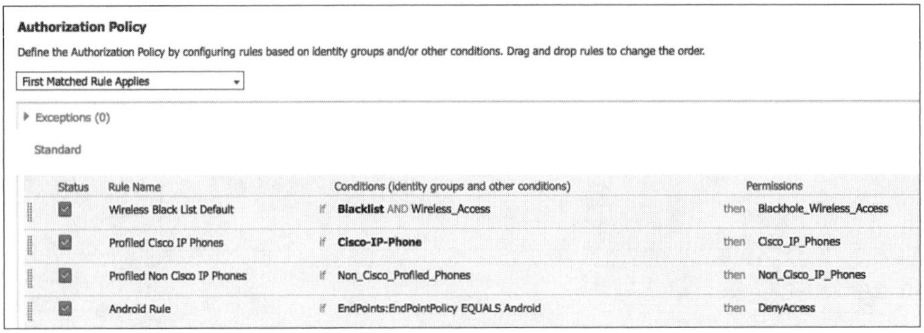

Figure 10-41 *Authorization Rule Using EndPointPolicy Condition*

Logical Profiles

Along with the ability to use profiles directly in an Authorization Policy, ISE 1.2 also adds the ability to create a logical grouping of profiles called Logical Profiles. This provides the ability to simplify the policy logic constructs. Let's use an example of wanting to deny access to all mobile platforms.

Figure 10-42 shows how the policy used to be created without logical profiles. Notice all the OR conditions that are required to build such a policy.

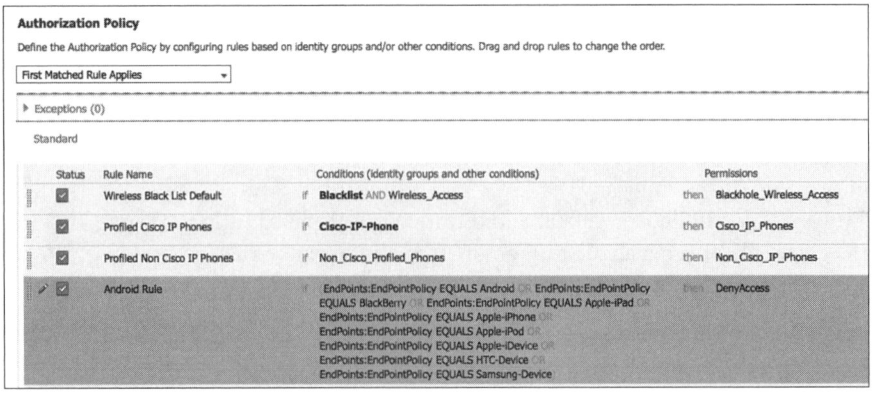

Figure 10-42 *Deny Access to Mobile Devices*

A simpler and cleaner way to create this policy is to add all these profiles into a single Logical Profile as shown in the following steps:

1. Navigate to **Policy > Profiling**.

2. Choose **Logical Profiles**.

3. You may select any number of existing profiles from the left side and add them to the logical profile on the right side, as shown in Figure 10-43.

4. Click **Submit** to save the Logical Profile.

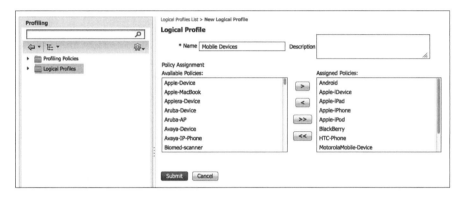

Figure 10-43   *Mobile Devices Logical Profile*

With the Logical Profile created, the authorization policy may use that single object, instead of all those individual objects. Figure 10-44 displays the same authorization rule using logical profiles.

Figure 10-44   *Deny Access to Mobile Devices with Logical Profile*

Comparing Figures 10-42 and 10-44, the benefits of logical profiles are evident. The policy is much cleaner, easier to read, and efficient with Logical Profiles.

Feed Service

Another new addition that comes with ISE 1.2 is the feed service. This service allows your ISE deployment to automatically download an updated OUI database, as well as profiler conditions, exception actions, and NMAP scan actions.

As visible earlier in Figure 10-22, each profile maintains a flag to state if it is

- Cisco provided
- Administrator created
- Administrator modified

These three states are maintained for all profile conditions, exception actions and NMAP scan actions. If you have modified one of the predefined profile conditions, there is no need to worry: The feed service will only overwrite Cisco Provided objects.

By default, the profiler feed service is disabled, and it requires an advanced license to enable the service. In addition to the automatic downloads, you may also provide subscriber information (such as an email address) to receive notifications of applied, success, and failures of updates.

When you enable the profiler feed service, ISE downloads the feed-service policies and the OUI database updates every day at 1 a.m. The updates are automatically applied, but ISE stores a set of changes so that you can revert these changes back to the previous state. If you revert from the set of changes that you last applied, profiling policies are returned to the previous state, and the profiler feed service is automatically disabled. OUI updates are made whenever the IEEE updates its vendor registration information for OUIs at the following location: http://standards.ieee.org/develop/regauth/oui/oui.txt. The profiling condition and other updates occur sporadically, after being validated by the ISE Quality Assurance team.

It is possible to revert any Administrator Modified Endpoint Profiling Policy back to the Cisco provided one; however, you must delete the modified policy.

Configuring the Feed Service

To enable the feed service, perform the following steps:

1. Navigate to **Administration > Feed Service > Profiler**.

2. Check Enable Profiler Feed Service to turn on the service.

3. A warning message displays that you are enabling the service, as shown in Figure 10-45.

4. Enter the email address for administrative updates for success and failures.

5. Sending information to Cisco will always be kept confidential.

Figure 10-46 displays the completed configuration of the feed service.

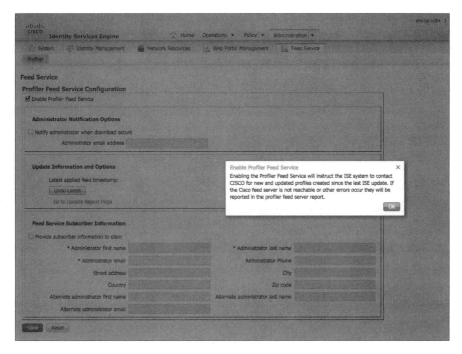

Figure 10-45 *Enable Profiler Feed Service*

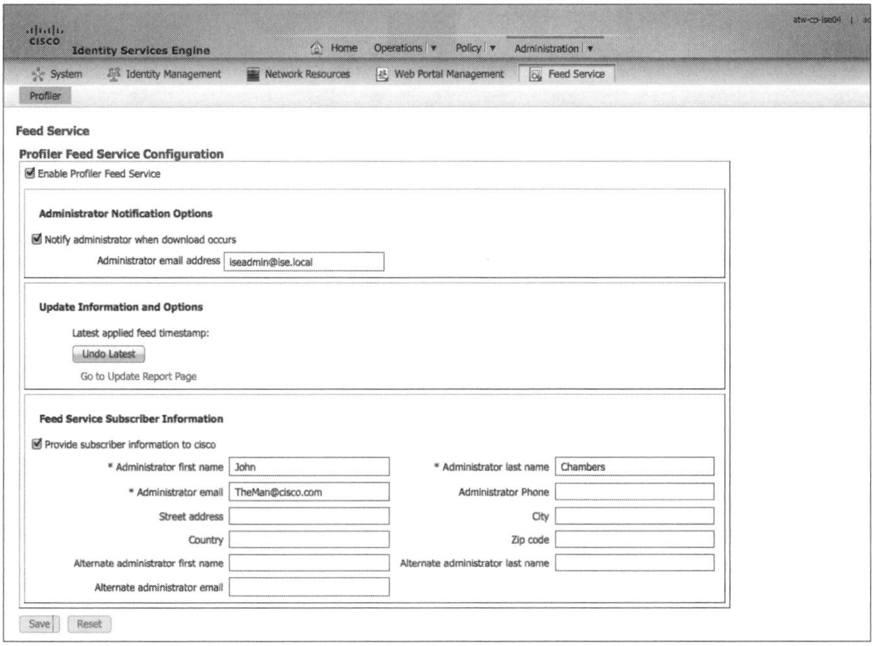

Figure 10-46 *Configured Profiler Feed Service*

Summary

This chapter examined the importance of device profiling for any network environment where identity is being enforced. There are many probes that the Cisco ISE can use, and the value of each probe is specific to your environment and needs. The configuration of profiling policies is covered in Chapter 24, "Advanced Profiling Configuration."

Chapter 11, "Bootstrapping Network Access Devices," covers the configuration of switches and wireless LAN controllers to enable communication with the Cisco ISE, and the best practices of this configuration.

Chapter 11

Bootstrapping Network Access Devices

I don't know about you, but when I go to put on my boots, I have to grab the bootstraps in order to pull the boots onto my feet. I can't wear them, or even begin to lace them up, without first pulling them on. So, "bootstrapping" is a critical step for me to be successful in wearing my chosen boots. This is where the metaphor "bootstrapping" came from. In the present context, it refers to configuring a device to work with Cisco ISE and the Secure Unified Access System. Before end users attempt to connect their devices to the network and have them be authenticated, the network access device (NAD) must be configured to authenticate those devices.

Two NAD types that are examined in this chapter, Cisco Catalyst Switches and Cisco Wireless LAN Controllers (WLC). For both, the focus is on establishing a predictable, repeatable configuration that follows Cisco best practices for most situations. Cisco ISE version 1.2 adds a new Bootstrap wizard that is designed to walk you through the bootstrap process for both Cisco switches and WLCs. This tool is terrific for getting up and running quickly. A more specific device configuration and explanation of the commands follows this section.

Bootstrap Wizard

As you saw in Chapter 9, there is a Cisco Setup Assistant Wizard that can generate the configurations for Cisco Network Access Devices, specifically Cisco Catalyst switches and Cisco Wireless LAN Controllers (WLC).

As stated in Chapter 9, the Setup Assistant can be very useful for quick setups, small environments, and proofs of concept. For most production deployments, the wizard will not prove very useful, as it does not lend itself to the numerous configuration variations that may exist in real-world environments. To that end, we are focusing on the specific configuration of the NADs in this chapter.

Cisco Catalyst Switches

Cisco switches are undergoing an evolution. Therefore, it is important to examine two different configuration types. We will examine configurations for Cisco IOS 12.2.x code and 15.x code. The big difference between them is in how profiling is handled.

Cisco IOS 15.x (Catalyst 3560, 3750, 4500) has Device Sensor capabilities. With these capabilities, the switch collects profiling attributes locally and sends them to ISE in a RADIUS accounting packet. With this capability, you should not configure the switch to allow SNMP polling to collect the profiling attributes; they will be received through the RADIUS probe instead, and there is no need to get the information twice.

Global Configuration Settings for All Cisco IOS 12.2 and 15.x Switches

This section covers the global configuration of all switches participating in the Secure Unified Access System. Specific sections for individual switch types or Cisco IOS versions are included in this chapter.

Configure Certificates on a Switch

Within the Cisco Secure Unified Access system, the switch performs the URL redirection for web authentication and the redirection of the discovery traffic from the posture to the Policy Service Node.

Performing URL redirection at the Layer 2 access (edge) device is a vast improvement over previous NAC solutions that require an appliance (such as the inline posture node) to capture web traffic and perform redirection to a web authentication page. This simplifies the deployment for both web authentication and the posture agent discovery process.

From global configuration mode on the switch, perform the following steps:

1. Set the DNS domain name on the switch.

   Cisco IOS does not allow for certificates, or even self-generated keys, to be created and installed without first defining a DNS domain name on the device.

   Type **ip domain-name** *domain-name* at the global configuration prompt.

2. Generate keys to be used for HTTPS.

   Type **crypto key generate rsa general-keys mod 2048** at the global configuration prompt.

Enable the Switch HTTP/HTTPS Server

The embedded HTTP/S server in Cisco IOS Software is employed to grab HTTP traffic from the user and redirect that user's browser to the Centralized Web Authentication Portal, or a Device Registration Portal, or even to the Mobile Device Management (MDM) onboarding portal. This same function is used for redirecting the Posture agent's traffic to the Policy Service Node.

1. Enable the HTTP server in global configuration mode.

   Type **ip http server** at the global configuration prompt.

2. Enable the HTTP Secure (HTTPS) server.

   Type **ip http secure-server** at the global configuration prompt.

Many organizations want to ensure that this redirection process using the switch's internal HTTP server is decoupled from the management of the switch itself, in order to limit the chances of an end user interacting with the management interface and control plane of a switch. This may be accomplished by running the following two commands from global configuration mode:

ip http active-session-modules none

ip http secure-active-session-modules none

Global AAA Commands

The previous section focused on some general commands that you are required to enter in global configuration mode. The following steps walk you through the essential authentication, authorization, and accounting (AAA) global configuration commands:

1. Enable AAA on the access switch(es).

   By default, the AAA "subsystem" of the Cisco switch is disabled. Prior to enabling the AAA subsystem, none of the required commands are available in the configuration. Enable AAA as follows:

   ```
   C3560X(config)# aaa new-model
   ```

2. Create an authentication method for 802.1X.

   An authentication method is required to instruct the switch to use a particular group of RADIUS servers for 802.1X authentication requests, as demonstrated in the following configuration:

   ```
   C3560X(config)# aaa authentication dot1x default group radius
   ```

3. Create an authorization method for 802.1X.

   The method created in Step 2 enables the user/device identity (username/password or certificate) to be validated by the RADIUS server. However, simply having valid credentials is not enough. There must also be an authorization. The authorization is what defines that the user or device is actually allowed to access the network, and what level of access is actually permitted, as demonstrated in the following configuration:

   ```
   C3560X(config)# aaa authorization network default group radius
   ```

4. Create an accounting method for 802.1X.

RADIUS accounting packets are extremely useful, and in many cases are required. These types of packets ensure that the RADIUS server (Cisco ISE) knows the exact state of the switch port and endpoint. Without the accounting packets, Cisco ISE would have knowledge only of the authentication and authorization communication. Accounting packets provide information on when to terminate a live session, as well as local decisions made by the switch (such as AuthFail VLAN assignment, etc.)

If the switch supports Device Sensor, the sensor data will be sent to ISE using the RADIUS accounting configuration.

```
C3560X(config)# aaa accounting dot1x default start-stop group radius
```

Global RADIUS Commands

A proactive method is configured to check the availability of the RADIUS server. With this practice, the switch sends periodic test authentication messages to the RADIUS server (Cisco ISE). It is looking for a RADIUS response from the server. A success message is not necessary—a failed authentication will suffice, because it shows that the server is alive.

The following steps walk you through adding the RADIUS server to your configuration and enabling the proactive RADIUS server health checks:

1. Within global configuration mode, add a username and password for the RADIUS keepalive, which is proactively checking the online status of the RADIUS server.

The username you create here (as demonstrated in the following configuration) will be added to the local user database in Cisco ISE at a later step. This account will be used in a later step where you define the RADIUS server.

```
C3560X(config)# username radius-test password password
```

2. Add the Cisco ISE servers to the RADIUS group.

In the following configuration, add each Cisco ISE Policy Service Node (PSN) to the switch configuration, using the test account you created previously. The server is proactively checked for responses one time per hour, in addition to any authentications or authorizations occurring through normal processes. Repeat for each PSN:

```
C3560X(config)# radius-server host ise_ip_address auth-port 1812 acct-port
1813 test username radius-test key shared_secret
```

3. Set the dead criteria.

The switch has been configured to proactively check the Cisco ISE server for RADIUS responses. Now, configure the counters on the switch to determine if the server is alive or dead. The following configuration settings are set to wait 5 seconds for a response from the RADIUS server and to attempt the test three times before marking the server dead. If a Cisco ISE server doesn't have a valid response within 15 seconds, it is marked as dead. High availability (HA) is covered in more detail in Chapter 18, "Setting Up a Distributed ISE Deployment."

```
C3560X(config)# radius-server dead-criteria time 5 tries 3
```

4. Enable Change of Authorization (CoA).

   Previously, you defined the IP address of a RADIUS server that the switch will send RADIUS messages to. However, you define the servers that are allowed to perform Change of Authorization (RFCs 3576 and 5176) operations in a different listing, also within global configuration mode:

```
C3560X(config)# aaa server radius dynamic-author
C3560X(config-locsvr-da-radius)# client ise_ip_address server-key shared_
secret
```

5. Configure the switch to use the Cisco vendor-specific attributes (VSA).

   Here you configure the switch to send any defined VSAs to Cisco ISE Policy Service Nodes (PSN) during authentication requests and accounting updates:

```
C3560X(config)# radius-server vsa send authentication
C3560X(config)# radius-server vsa send accounting
```

6. Enable the VSAs. These VSAs are Cisco-specific attributes used for a more advanced RADIUS session, as demonstrated in the following configuration:

```
C3560X(config)# radius-server attribute 6 on-for-login-auth
```

Note   This command ensures that the Service-Type attribute will be sent with all authentication requests. ISE will use that service-type to help distinguish between 802.1X login requests and MAC authentication Bypass requests.

```
C3560X(config)# radius-server attribute 8 include-in-access-req
```

Note   This command adds the ip-address of the endpoint to the authentication request. It carries the ip address in the "Framed-IP-Address" RADIUS field.

```
C3560X(config)# radius-server attribute 25 access-request include
```

Note   This command adds the RADIUS Class attribute to the authentication request.

7. Ensure that the switch always sends traffic from the correct interface.

Switches may often have multiple IP addresses associated to them. Therefore, it is a best practice to always force any management communications to occur through a specific interface. This interface IP address must match the IP address defined in the Cisco ISE network device object, as demonstrated in the following configuration:

```
C3560X(config)# ip radius source-interface interface_name
C3560X(config)# snmp-server trap-source interface_name
C3560X(config)# snmp-server source-interface informs interface_name
```

Create Local Access Control Lists

Certain functions on the switch that are related to your implementation, such as URL redirection, require the use of locally configured access control lists (ACL). Some of these ACLs that are created are used immediately, and some may not be used until a much later phase of your deployment. The goal of this section is to prepare the switches for all possible deployment models at one time, and limit the operational expense of repeated switch configuration.

You create these local ACLs in the following steps:

1. Add the following ACL to be used on switch ports in Monitor Mode:

```
C3560X(config)# ip access-list extended ACL-ALLOW
C3560X(config-ext-nacl)# permit ip any any
```

2. Add the following ACL to be used on switch ports in Low-Impact Mode:

```
C3560X(config)# ip access-list ext ACL-DEFAULT
C3560X(config-ext-nacl)# remark DHCP
C3560X(config-ext-nacl)# permit udp any eq bootpc any eq bootps
C3560X(config-ext-nacl)# remark DNS
C3560X(config-ext-nacl)# permit udp any any eq domain
C3560X(config-ext-nacl)# remark Ping
C3560X(config-ext-nacl)# permit icmp any any
C3560X(config-ext-nacl)# remark PXE / TFTP
C3560X(config-ext-nacl)# permit udp any any eq tftp
C3560X(config-ext-nacl)# remark Drop all the rest
C3560X(config-ext-nacl)# deny ip any any log
```

3. Add the following ACL to be used for URL redirection with Web Authentication:

```
C3560X(config)# ip access-list ext ACL-WEBAUTH-REDIRECT
C3560X(config-ext-nacl)# remark explicitly deny DNS from being redirected to
address a bug
C3560X(config-ext-nacl)# deny udp any any eq 53
```

```
C3560X(config-ext-nacl)# remark redirect all applicable traffic to the ISE
Server
C3560X(config-ext-nacl)# permit tcp any any eq 80
C3560X(config-ext-nacl)# permit tcp any any eq 443
C3560X(config-ext-nacl)# remark all other traffic will be implicitly denied
from the redirection
```

4. Add the following ACL to be used for URL redirection with the posture agent:

```
C3560X(config)# ip access-list ext ACL-AGENT-REDIRECT
C3560X(config-ext-nacl)#remark explicitly deny DNS and DHCP from being
redirected
C3560X(config-ext-nacl)# deny udp any any eq 53 bootps
C3560X(config-ext-nacl)# remark redirect HTTP traffic only
C3560X(config-ext-nacl)# permit tcp any any eq 80
C3560X(config-ext-nacl)# remark all other traffic will be implicitly denied
from the redirection
```

Global 802.1X Commands

You have enabled a number of RADIUS-related capabilities in the switch, but you have not yet enabled the software (commonly called an 802.1X supplicant) that understands how to communicate using EAP over LAN. In the following steps, you will enable the 802.1X supplicant on the switch and enable IP device tracking:

1. Enabling 802.1X globally on the switch does not actually enable authentication on any of the switch ports; it simply enables the 802.1X supplicant globally on the device. Authentication is configured, but it is not enabled until the later sections where you configure Monitor Mode. Enable the supplicant with the following configuration command:

```
C3560X(config)# dot1x system-auth-control
```

2. Enable IP device tracking in order for downloadable ACLs (DACL) to function. DACLs are a very common enforcement mechanism in a Cisco Secure Unified Access deployment. In order for DACLs to function properly on a switch, IP device tracking must be enabled globally, as demonstrated in the following configuration command:

```
C3560X(config)# ip device tracking
```

Global Logging Commands (Optional)

During a proof of concept or a limited pilot, it is often nice to have the switch's log messages correlated in the authentication reports. This provides you with a very nice centralized view of the success or failure of implementing your authorization results, such as

VLAN assignment, dACLs, and more. Configuring the switch to send its syslogs to ISE is an easy way to accomplish this goal.

While this feature is nice to have, it also has very real performance consequences and thus should only be enabled during limited pilots, proofs of concept, or times of trouble-shooting. During day-to-day operations of a Secure Access deployment, the logging messages should not be sent to ISE.

The following steps guide you through configuring this logging:

1. Enable syslog on the switch.

   Syslog may be generated on Cisco IOS Software in many events. Some of the syslog messages can be sent to the ISE Monitoring Node (MNT) to be used for trouble-shooting purposes. Enabling this across all NADs all the time is not recommended; instead, enable it when beginning your project and when troubleshooting.

   To ensure Cisco ISE is able to compile appropriate syslog messages from the switch, use the following commands:

   ```
   C3560X(config)# logging monitor informational
   C3560X(config)# logging origin-id ip
   C3560X(config)# logging source-interface <interface_id>
   C3560X(config)# logging host <ISE_MNT_PERSONA_IP_Address_x> transport udp
   port 20514
   ```

2. Set up standard logging functions on the switch to support possible troubleshoot-ing/recording for Cisco ISE functions.

   EPM is a part of the Cisco IOS Software module that is responsible for features such as web authentication and DACLs. Enabling EPM logging generates a syslog related to DACL authorization, and part of the log can be correlated inside Cisco ISE when such logs are sent to Cisco ISE.

   ```
   C3560X(config)# epm logging
   ```

Only the following NAD syslog messages are actually collected and used by Cisco ISE:

- AP-6-AUTH_PROXY_AUDIT_START

- AP-6-AUTH_PROXY_AUDIT_STOP

- AP-1-AUTH_PROXY_DOS_ATTACK

- AP-1-AUTH_PROXY_RETRIES_EXCEEDED

- AP-1-AUTH_PROXY_FALLBACK_REQ

- AP-1-AUTH_PROXY_AAA_DOWN

- AUTHMGR-5-MACMOVE

- AUTHMGR-5-MACREPLACE

- MKA-5-SESSION_START

- MKA-5-SESSION_STOP

- MKA-5-SESSION_REAUTH

- MKA-5-SESSION_UNSECURED

- MKA-5-SESSION_SECURED

- MKA-5-KEEPALIVE_TIMEOUT

- DOT1X-5-SUCCESS / FAIL

- MAB-5-SUCCESS / FAIL

- AUTHMGR-5-START / SUCCESS / FAIL

- AUTHMGR-SP-5-VLANASSIGN / VLANASSIGNERR

- EPM-6-POLICY_REQ

- EPM-6-POLICY_APP_SUCCESS / FAILURE

- EPM-6-IPEVENT:

- DOT1X_SWITCH-5-ERR_VLAN_NOT_FOUND

- RADIUS-4-RADIUS_DEAD

Global Profiling Commands

This section separates the configuration of devices that support Device Sensor capabilities and the configuration of devices that must rely on SNMP for profiling.

Switches with Device Sensor Capabilities

Cisco IOS Device Sensor requires a multipart configuration. The first part is to configure the device-sensor filter lists. These lists inform Device Sensor of which items to care about for the different protocols.

Cisco IOS Device Sensor supports three protocols: Dynamic Host Configuration Protocol (DHCP), Cisco Discovery Protocol, and Link Layer Discovery Protocol (LLDP). Create one list for each protocol by performing the following steps:

1. Create a list for DHCP.

   There are three options you need to configure for ISE—host-name, class-identifier, and client-identifier, as demonstrated in the following configuration:

   ```
   C3560X(config)# device-sensor filter-list dhcp list <dhcp_list_name>
   C3560X(config-sensor-dhcplist)# option name host-name
   C3560X(config-sensor-dhcplist)# option name class-identifier
   C3560X(config-sensor-dhcplist)# option name client-identifier
   ```

2. Create a list for CDP.

There are two CDP options you need to configure for ISE—device-name and platform-type, as follows:

```
C3560X(config)# device-sensor filter-list cdp list <cdp_list_name>
C3560X(config-sensor-cdplist)# tlv name device-name
C3560X(config-sensor-cdplist)# tlv name platform-type
```

3. Create a list for LLDP.

There are three LLDP options you need to configure for ISE—port-id, system-name and system-description, as follows:

```
C3560X(config)# device-sensor filter-list lldp list <lldp_list_name>
C3560X(config-sensor-lldplist)# tlv name port-id
C3560X(config-sensor-lldplist)# tlv name system-name
C3560X(config-sensor-lldplist)# tlv name system-description
```

4. Include the lists created in Steps 1–3 in the device-sensor.

In the previous steps, you defined which options that device-sensor should store. At this point, you configure device-sensor to use those lists:

```
C3560X(config)# device-sensor filter-spec dhcp include list <dhcp_list_name>
C3560X(config)# device-sensor filter-spec lldp include list <cdp_list_name>
C3560X(config)# device-sensor filter-spec cdp include list <lldp_list_name>
```

5. Enable Device Sensor.

Device-sensor is now configured. Now enable the device-sensor service to run on the switch, and configure when it will send its updates:

```
C3560X(config)# device-sensor accounting
C3560X(config)# device-sensor notify all-changes
```

Switches Without Device Sensor Capability

The ISE Policy Service Node uses SNMP to query the switch for certain attributes to help identify the devices that are connected to the switch. As such, configure an SNMP community for Cisco ISE to query.

1. Configure a read-only SNMP community.

ISE only requires read-only SNMP access. Ensure that this community string matches the one configured in the network device object in Cisco ISE, as demonstrated here:

```
C3560X(config)# snmp-server community community_string RO
```

Sample configurations are provided in Appendix E, "Sample Switch Configurations."

Interface Configuration Settings for All Cisco Switches

You have just completed the global configuration settings of the access layer switches, including RADIUS, SNMP, Profiling, and AAA methods.

This section focuses on building a single port configuration that can be used across your entire Secure Unified Access deployment, regardless of the switch type, the deployment stage, or which deployment model you choose.

Configure Interfaces as Switch Ports

One of the first things to do before configuring any of the authentication settings on the switch port is to ensure that the switch port is configured as a Layer 2 port, not a Layer 3 port. This command is a simple, one-word command that you run, and from that point the other commands you run will all take effect.

1. Enter interface configuration mode for the switch port range:

   ```
   C3560X(config)# interface range first_interface - last_interface
   ```

2. Ensure that the ports are Layer 2 switch ports:

   ```
   C3560X(config-if-range)# switchport
   ```

3. Configure the port for Layer 2 edge, using the host macro.

   The host macro automatically runs three commands for you. It configures the port to be an access port (nontrunk), disables channel groups, and configures spanning tree to be in portfast mode.

   ```
   C3560X(config-if-range)# switchport host
   switchport mode will be set to access
   spanning-tree portfast will be enabled
   channel group will be disabled
   ```

Configure Flexible Authentication and High Availability

The default behavior of 802.1X is to deny access to the network when an authentication fails. In many of the early customer deployments of 802.1X, this behavior was discovered to be undesirable because it does not allow for guest access and does not allow employees to remediate their computer systems and gain full network access.

The next phase in handling 802.1X authentication failures was to provide an "Auth-Fail VLAN" to allow a device/user that failed authentication to be granted access to a VLAN that provided limited resources. This was a step in the right direction, but it was still missing some practicality, especially in environments that must use MAC Authentication Bypass (MAB) for all the printers and other nonauthenticating devices. With the default behavior of 802.1X, an administrator has to configure ports for printers and other devices that do not have supplicants differently from the ports where they plan to do authentication.

In response to these issues, Cisco created Flexible Authentication (Flex-Auth). Flex-Auth allows a network administrator to set an authentication order and priority on the switch port, thereby allowing the port to attempt, in order, 802.1X, MAB, and then Web-based Authorization (WebAuth). All of these functions are provided while maintaining the same configuration on all access ports, thereby providing a much simpler operational model for customers than is provided by traditional 802.1X deployments.

As mentioned previously, there are multiple methods of authentication on a switch port: 802.1X (dot1x), MAB, and WebAuth. With 802.1X authentication, the switch sends an identity request (EAP-Identity-Request) periodically after the link state has changed to "up" (see the "Authentication Settings – Timers" section for recommended timer changes). Additionally, the endpoint supplicant should send a periodic EAP over LAN Start (EAPoL-Start) message into the switch port to speed up authentication. If a device is not able to authenticate, it merely waits until the dot1x timeout occurs, and then MAB occurs. Assuming the device MAC address is in the correct database, it is then authorized to access the network. Figure 11-1 illustrates this concept.

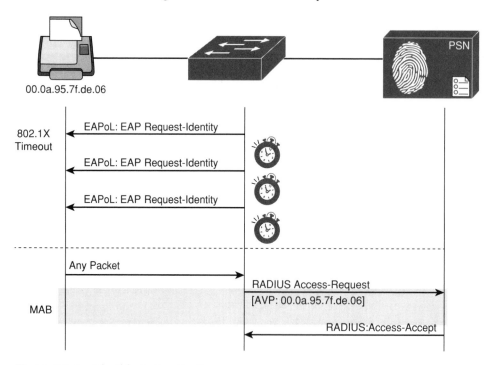

Figure 11-1   *Flexible Authentication*

The following steps walk you through the configuration of Flex-Auth and the configurable actions for authentication high availability:

1. Configure the authentication method priority on the switch ports.

   The best practice is to always prefer the stronger authentication method (dot1x). The dot1x method is also the default of all Cisco switches, as demonstrated in the following configuration:

   ```
   C3750X(config-if-range)# authentication priority dot1x mab
   ```

2. Configure the authentication method order on the switch ports.

   There are certain deployment methods where MAB should occur before 802.1X authentication, such as an environment that is primarily using MAB. For those corner cases, Cisco switches do allow for a network administrator to set a user-definable authentication order. However, the best practice is to maintain the order of dot1x and then MAB, as demonstrated in the following configuration:

   ```
   C3750X(config-if-range)# authentication order dot1x mab
   ```

3. Configure the port to use Flex-Auth:

   ```
   C3750X(config-if-range)# authentication event fail action next-method
   ```

4. Configure the port to use a local VLAN for voice and data when the RADIUS server is "dead" (when it stops responding), as demonstrated in the following configuration.

   In the "Global Configuration Settings for All Cisco IOS 12.2 and 15.x Switches" section, you configured the RADIUS server entry to use a test account that proactively alerts the switch when Cisco ISE has stopped responding to RADIUS requests. Now configure the switch port to locally authorize the port when that server is found to be "dead," and reinitialize authentication when the server becomes "alive" again, as demonstrated in the following configuration:

   ```
   C3750X(config-if-range)# authentication event server dead action authorize
   vlan vlan-id
   C3750X(config-if-range)# authentication event server dead action authorize
   voice
   C3750X(config-if-range)# authentication event server alive action reinitialize
   ```

5. Configure the port to use a local VLAN when the RADIUS server is "dead" and to allow existing and new hosts.

   This feature was introduced to resolve problems with multiple authenticating hosts on single port when some of them have already been authenticated while the RADIUS server was operational, and others (new hosts) are trying to authenticate when the RADIUS server is down.

   Prior to the introduction of this new feature, all authenticated hosts (when the RADIUS server is "up") get full access to the network and the others (the new hosts) do not get access to the network. With this new feature/CLI configuration, when new hosts try to access the network and the RADIUS server is down, that port is reinitialized immediately and all hosts (in this port) get the same VLAN.

```
C3750X(config-if-range)# authentication event server dead action reinitialize
vlan vlan-id
```

6. Set the host mode of the port.

The default behavior of an 802.1X-enabled port is to authorize only a single MAC address per port. There are other options, most notably Multi-Domain Authentication (MDA) and Multiple Authentication (Multi-Auth) modes. During the initial phases of any Cisco Secure Unified Access deployment, it is best practice to use Multi-Auth mode to ensure that there is no denial of service while deploying 802.1X.

Note   Port Security is not compatible with 802.1X, because 802.1X handles this function natively.

Multi-Auth mode allows virtually unlimited MAC addresses per switch port, and requires an authenticated session for every MAC address. When the deployment moves into the late stages of the authenticated phase, or into the enforcement phase, it is then recommended to use Multi-Domain mode. Multi-Domain Authentication allows a single MAC address in the Data Domain and a single MAC address in the Voice domain per port, as demonstrated in the following configuration:

```
C3750X(config-if-range)# authentication host-mode multi-auth
```

7. Configure the violation action.

When an authentication violation occurs, such as more MAC addresses than are allowed on the port, the default action is to put the port into an err-disabled state. Although this behavior may seem to be a nice, secure behavior, it can create an accidental denial of service, especially during the initial phases of deployment. Therefore, set the action to be **restrict**, as follows. This mode of operation allows the first authenticated device to continue with its authorization, and denies any additional devices.

```
C3750X(config-if-range)# authentication violation restrict
```

Configure Authentication Settings

802.1X is designed to be binary by default. Successful authentication means the user is authorized to access the network. Unsuccessful authentication means the user has no access to the network. This paradigm does not lend itself very well to a modern organization. Most organizations need to perform workstation imaging with Preboot Execution

Environments (PXE), or may have some thin clients that have to boot with DHCP and don't have any way to run a supplicant.

Additionally, when early adopters of 802.1X deployed authentication companywide, there were repercussions. Many issues arose. For example, supplicants were misconfigured; there were unknown devices that could not authenticate because of a lack of supplicant, and other reasons.

Cisco created open authentication to aid with deployments. Open authentication allows all traffic to flow through the switch port, even without the port being authorized. This feature permits authentication to be configured across the entire organization, but does not deny access to any device.

Figure 11-2 depicts the difference between a port with the default behavior of 802.1X and a port with Open Authentication configured. This is a key feature that enables the phased approach to deploying authentication.

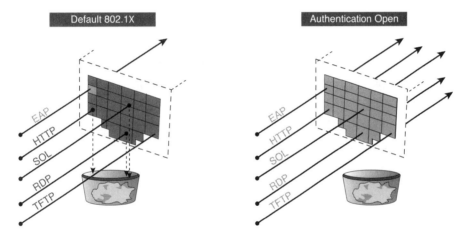

Figure 11-2   *Default 802.1X Versus Authentication Open*

Perform the following steps:

  1. Set the port for open authentication:

```
C3750X(config-if-range)# authentication open
```

  2. Enable MAB on the port:

```
C3750X(config-if-range)# mab
```

  3. Enable the port to perform IEEE 802.1X authentication:

```
C3750X(config-if-range)# dot1x pae authenticator
```

Configure Authentication Timers

Many timers can be modified as needed in a deployment. Unless you are experiencing a specific problem where adjusting the timer may correct unwanted behavior, it is recommended to leave all timers at their default values except the 802.1X Transmit timer (tx-period). The tx-period timer defaults to a value of 30 seconds. Leaving this value at 30 seconds provides a default wait of 90 seconds (3 × tx-period) before a switch port begins the next method of authentication, and activates the MAB process for nonauthenticating devices.

Based on numerous deployments, it is recommended that you set the tx-period value to 10 seconds to provide the most optimal time for MAB devices. Setting the value to less than 10 seconds may result in unwanted behavior; setting the value greater than 10 seconds may result in DHCP timeouts. To configure the tx-period timer value to 10 seconds, enter the following:

```
C3750X(config-if-range)# dot1x timeout tx-period 10
```

Apply the Initial ACL to the Port and Enable Authentication

The following steps prepare the port for Monitor Mode by applying a default ACL on the port without denying any traffic:

1. Apply the initial ACL (ACL-ALLOW):

```
C3750X(config-if-range)# ip access-group ACL-ALLOW in
```

2. (Optional) Enable authentication.

If you wish to enable authentication now, you may. However, it is recommended that you wait until after you configure your polices for Monitor Mode. See Chapter 21, "Monitor Mode," for more details.

```
C3750X(config-if-range)# authentication port-control auto
```

Note   The preceding command is required to enable authentication (802.1X, MAB, WebAuth). Without this command, everything appears to be working, but no authentication is sent to the RADIUS server.

Cisco Wireless LAN Controllers

This section reviews configuration for the Cisco Wireless LAN Controller. The focus is on version 7.3 and later, which includes integrated Device Sensor technology and support for FlexConnect access points.

As with the previous section covering configuration of Cisco Catalyst Switches, this section assumes you have established basic connectivity with the NAD and are now to the point of bootstrapping the WLC for use with ISE.

Configure the AAA Servers

The first step in bootstrapping the WLC is to add the ISE Policy Service Nodes to the WLC as RADIUS authentication and accounting servers.

Add the RADIUS Authentication Servers

In the following steps, you add the ISE PSNs as RADIUS servers in the WLC.

From the WLC GUI:

1. Choose **Security > RADIUS > Authentication**, as shown in Figure 11-3.

2. From the Call Station ID Type drop-down list, choose **System MAC Address**.

   This will ensure that the endpoint's MAC-Address is populated in the RADIUS "calling-station-id" field in all RADIUS packets.

3. From the MAC Delimiter drop-down list, choose **Hyphen**.

   This ensures that the format of the mac-address is aa-bb-cc-dd-ee-ff, which is the way ISE expects it to be.

4. Click **New** to add the ISE Policy Service Node.

Figure 11-3 *RADIUS Authentication Servers*

5. In the Server IP Address field, enter the IP address of the PSN (or the Virtual IP (VIP), if using a load balancer).

6. In the Shared Secret field, enter the shared secret. This *must* match what is configured in ISE for the Network Device.

7. In the Port Number field, enter **1812** for authentication.

8. From the Server Status drop-down list, choose **Enabled**.

9. From the Support for RFC 3576 (Change of Authorization) drop-down list, choose **Enabled.**

10. In the Server Timeout field, leave the default setting of **2** seconds for the default server timeout. You may need to make it longer if you are using load balancers or have some other unique situation like that.

11. For Network User, check the **Enable** check box. This simply indicates that the RADIUS server may be used for network authentications.

12. Click **Apply** in the upper-right corner.

13. Click Save Configuration in the upper-right corner.

Figure 11-4 shows a completed server configuration.

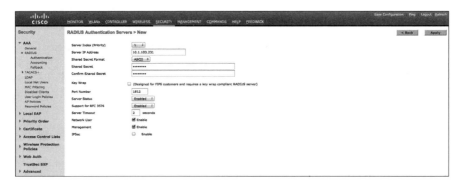

Figure 11-4   *Completed Server Configuration*

Repeat these steps for each Policy Service Node that you need to add.

Add the RADIUS Accounting Servers

Now that you have defined the ISE PSNs for authentication, you need to define them again for accounting.

From the WLC GUI, perform the following steps:

1. Choose **Security > RADIUS > Accounting,** as shown in Figure 11-5.

2. From the MAC Delimiter drop-down list, choose **Hyphen.**

3. Click **New** to add the ISE Policy Service Node.

4. In the Server IP Address field, enter the IP address of the PSN.

5. In the Shared Secret field, enter the shared secret to match what is configured on ISE.

6. In the Port Number field, enter **1813.**

7. From the Server Status drop-down list, choose **Enabled.**

Figure 11-5 *RADIUS Accounting Servers*

8. For Network User, check the **Enable** check box.

Figure 11-6 shows a completed server entry.

Figure 11-6 *Completed Accounting Server Configuration*

9. Click **Apply** in the upper-right corner.

10. Save Configuration.

Repeat these steps for each Policy Service Node that you need to add.

Configure RADIUS Fallback (High Availability)

The primary RADIUS server (the server with the lowest server index) is assumed to be the most preferable server for the Cisco WLC. If the primary server becomes unresponsive, the controller switches to the next active server (the server with the next lowest server index). The controller continues to use this backup server, unless you configure the controller either to fall back to the primary RADIUS server when it recovers and becomes responsive or to switch to a more preferable server from the available backup servers.

From the WLC GUI, perform the following steps:

1. Choose **Security > AAA > RADIUS > Fallback**, as shown in Figure 11-7.

2. From the Fallback Mode drop-down list, choose **Active**.

Selecting Active causes the Cisco WLC to revert to a server with a lower priority from the available backup servers by using RADIUS probe messages to proactively determine whether a server that has been marked inactive is back online.

3. In the Username field, enter the name to be sent in the inactive server probes.

We have been using radius-test as the username so far in the book. It's important to note that you do not need to enter a password for this test user account, because the system simply looks for a response from the RADIUS server; pass or fail does not matter.

4. In the Interval in Sec field, enter a value. The interval states the inactive time in passive mode and the probe interval in active mode. The valid range is 180 to 3600 seconds, and the default value is 300 seconds (as shown in Figure 11-7).

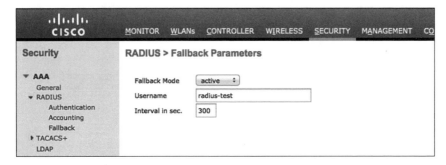

Figure 11-7   *Fallback Parameters*

Configure the Airespace ACLs

Earlier in the chapter, you pre-staged the Cisco Catalyst Switches with local ACLs; the requirement is the same for the WLC. You should pre-stage the WLC with some ACLs for the following:

■ Web Authentication (ACL-WEBAUTH-REDIRECT)

■ Posture Agent Redirection (ACL-AGENT-REDIRECT)

Notice that you are using the same ACL names that you used when configuring the Cisco Catalyst Switches. Although this is not required, it is preferred because it helps to ensure consistency and ease of support where possible.

Create the Web Authentication Redirection ACL

As with the Cisco Catalyst Switches, you need a local ACL on the WLC to redirect web traffic to the Centralized Web Authentication Portal. However, with the Catalyst Switch, a **permit** statement means that the traffic should be redirected, and a **deny** statement describes traffic that should not be redirected. With the switch, you need two ACLs: one to define what gets redirected, and a second one to filter traffic (permit or deny traffic flow).

The WLC has a single ACL, and it pulls double-duty. It permits and denies traffic flow, but at the same time it redirects the traffic that is denied to the Centralized Web Authentication Portal.

From the WLC GUI, perform the following steps:

1. Choose **Security > Access Control Lists > Access Control Lists**, as shown in Figure 11-8.

2. Click **New** to add a new ACL.

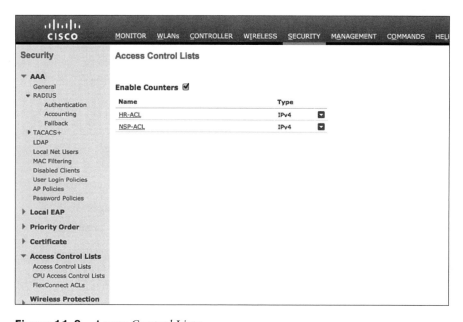

Figure 11-8   *Access Control Lists*

3. In the Access Control List Name field, enter the name **ACL-WEBAUTH-REDIRECT**, as shown in Figure 11-9.

4. Click **Apply.**

5. When you return to the main Access Control Lists screen, shown in Figure 11-10, click the new entry: ACL-WEBAUTH-REDIRECT.

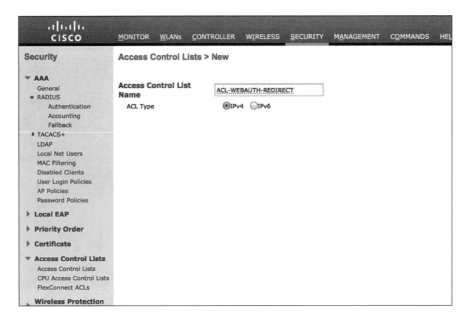

Figure 11-9   *Setting the ACL to ACL-WEBAUTH-REDIRECT*

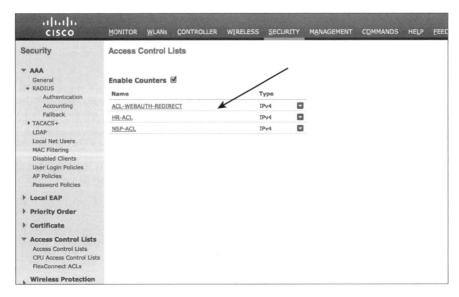

Figure 11-10   *Access Control Lists with New ACL*

6. Click **Add New Rule** in the upper-right corner.

A "rule" in the WLC is the equivalent of an access control entry (ACE) in the switch. It is a line in the ACL.

7. Create a set of rules for this ACL that does the following:

- Permits all traffic outbound (toward the client)

- Permits DHCP and DNS inbound

- Permits TCP port 8443 to the ISE servers

- Denies all other traffic—which will redirect all denied web traffic

Figure 11-11 shows you an example of a completed ACL.

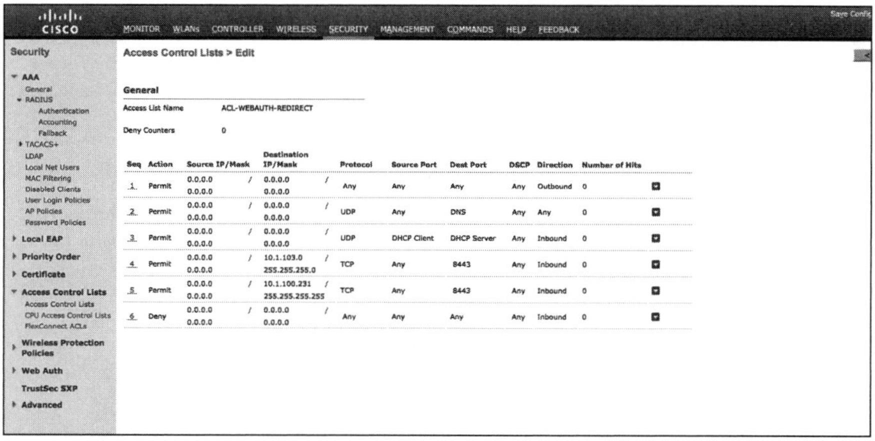

Figure 11-11 *ACL-WEBAUTH-REDIRECT Example*

Create the Posture Agent Redirection ACL

As with the Web Authentication traffic, you will want to have an ACL for Posture Assessments. When a client successfully authenticates to the network, but their posture is not known, the resulting authorization should be to put them in a Posture_Req state on the controller and use a URL-Redirection with an ACL to redirect traffic to ISE (just like with Web Authentication).

The difference here is that you must open some more ports to allow even more traffic to flow than with Web Authentication. Technically, there is nothing to prevent you from using a single ACL for both Web Authentication and Posture Agent Redirection, if you are willing to open up all that traffic in both use cases.

To maintain consistency throughout these deployment examples, we will create a separate ACL here.

From the WLC GUI, perform the following steps:

1. Choose **Security > Access Control Lists > Access Control Lists**.

2. Click **New** to add a new ACL.

3. In the Access Control List Name field, enter the name **ACL-AGENT-REDIRECT**.

4. Click **Apply**.

5. In the main Access Control Lists screen, click the new entry: ACL-AGENT-REDIRECT.

6. Click **Add New Rule** in the upper-right corner.

7. Build a rule set for this ACL that accomplishes the following:

- Permits all traffic outbound (toward the client)

- Permits DHCP and DNS inbound

- Permits TCP port 8443 to the ISE servers

- Permits TCP and UDP Port 8905 and 8909 to the ISE servers

- Permits applicable traffic to the remediation servers (the servers that will fix the client if it fails the posture assessment; could be patch-management systems, or even external websites)

- Denies all other traffic—which will redirect the denied traffic

Figure 11-12 shows an example of a completed ACL.

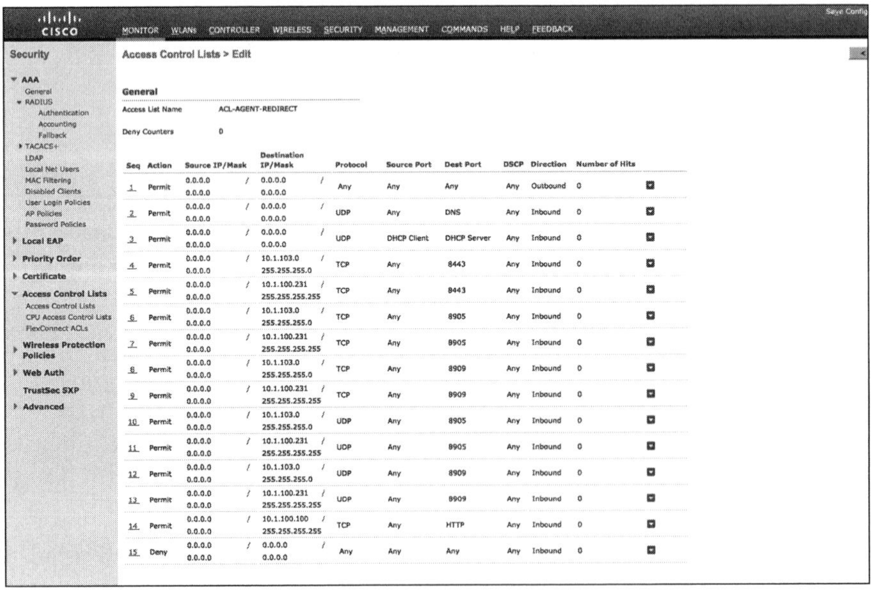

Figure 11-12   *ACL-AGENT-REDIRECT Example*

Create the Dynamic Interfaces for the Client VLANs

When you want to assign a user or device to a VLAN on a Catalyst Switch, just assign the VLAN to the port, and the entire switch port will now be assigned to that particular VLAN.

The WLC has only a few physical connections to the wired network, and it must bridge all wireless users from their RF network (Wi-Fi) to the physical wired network. The WLC must also have the ability to assign a different VLAN per authenticated session (if necessary). If you are thinking that the WLC just needs to be connected with a trunk, you are correct.

The WLC is configured to use 802.1Q to tag traffic for a specific VLAN as that traffic exits the controller. However, the controller calls this a "dynamic interface" because the WLC can either assign a physical interface to traffic, or assign an 802.1Q tag to the traffic.

You will create two dynamic interfaces in the following sections; one for employee traffic and one for guest traffic.

Create the Employee Dynamic Interface

This interface will be used for all successful authentications to the Corporate WLAN, providing full access to the entire network.

From the WLC GUI, perform the following steps:

1. Choose **Controller > Interfaces**.

2. Click **New**.

3. Name your interface. Use the name "employee" in this example.

4. In the VLAN identifier field, enter the VLAN ID to be used in the 802.1Q tag.

5. Click **Apply**.

6. Click the new interface named employee.

   You most likely will not need to change any settings until you reach the Physical Information section.

7. In the Interface Address section, provide an IP address, netmask, and gateway for the VLAN in the respective fields.

8. In the DHCP Information section, in the Primary DHCP Server field, enter the DHCP server address.

9. Click **Apply**.

Figure 11-13 shows an example employee dynamic interface configuration.

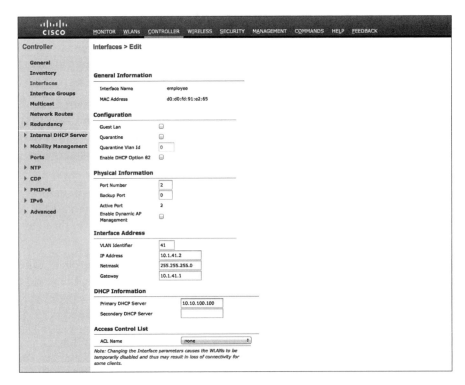

Figure 11-13   *Employee Dynamic Interface*

Create the Guest Dynamic Interface

This interface is used for all devices connecting to the GUEST WLAN, as well as for unsuccessful or unauthorized authentications to the Corporate WLAN. This interface has Internet access only.

From the WLC GUI, perform the following steps:

1. Choose **Controller > Interfaces**.

2. Click **New**.

3. Name your interface. Use the name "guest" in this example.

4. In the VLAN identifier field, enter the VLAN ID to be used in the 802.1Q tag.

5. Click **Apply**.

6. Click the new interface named guest.

   You most likely will not need to change any settings until you reach the Physical Information section. In the Configuration section, do not enable the Guest LAN check box. This is not for GUEST WLANs; rather, it is for providing guest access to directly connected wired LANs.

7. In the Interface Address section, provide an IP address, netmask, and gateway for the VLAN in the respective fields.

8. In the Primary DHCP Server field, enter the DHCP server address.

9. Click **Apply.**

Figure 11-14 shows an example guest dynamic interface configuration.

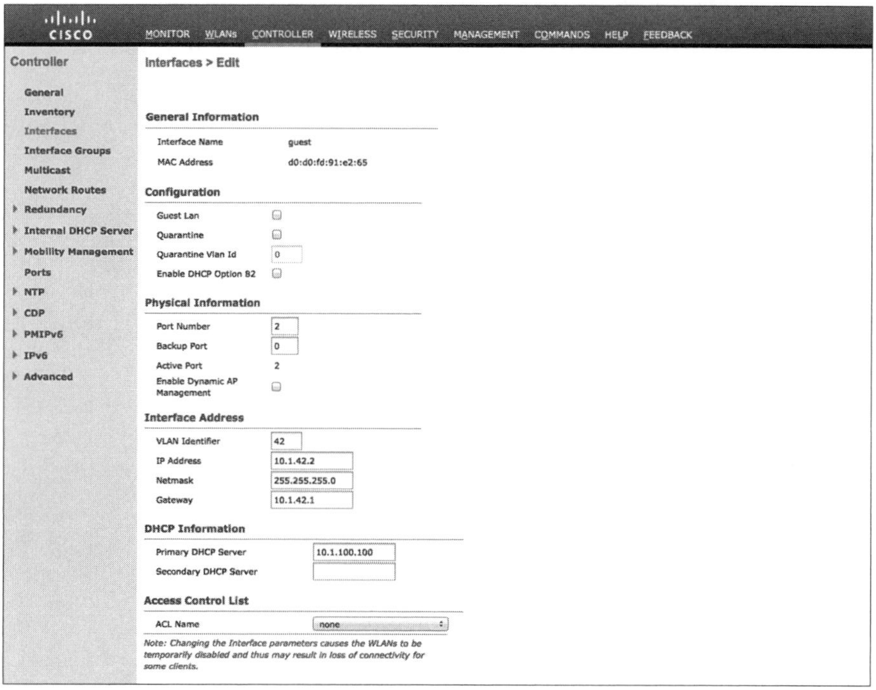

Figure 11-14   *Guest Dynamic Interface*

Create the Wireless LANs

Now that the RADIUS servers, ACLs, and dynamic interfaces are all created and configured, let's move on to creating two WLANs: GUEST and Corporate. The guest WLAN will be an "open" WLAN, while the corporate WLAN will be configured to use 802.1X to authenticate devices.

Create the Guest WLAN

The Guest WLAN will be created as an "open" SSID, but it will send the endpoint MAC addresses to ISE for MAB, just like the wired networks.

From the WLC GUI, perform the following steps:

1. Click the WLANs menu.

2. Click Create New.

3. Click **Go**.

4. From the Type drop-down list, choose **WLAN**.

5. In the Profile Name field, enter the WLAN profile name; use **CP-GUEST** in this example, as shown in Figure 11-15.

6. In the SSID field, enter an SSID name; use **CiscoPress-GUEST** in this example.

7. Click **Apply**.

   The Edit 'CP-GUEST' screen opens with the General tab displayed.

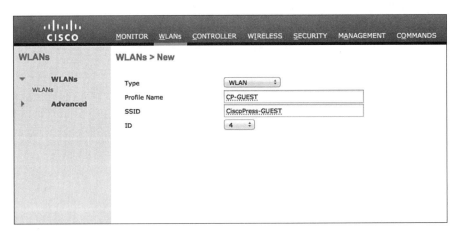

Figure 11-15   *Guest WLAN Creation*

8. If you are ready to work with this SSID, check the **Enabled** check box to the right of Status.

9. From the Interface/Interface Group(G) drop-down list, choose the **GUEST** interface that you created previously, as shown in Figure 11-16.

10. Click the **Security** tab.

11. On the Layer 2 subtab of the Security tab, shown in Figure 11-17, from the Layer 2 Security drop-down list, change from the default (WPA) to **None**.

12. Check the **MAC Filtering** check box (which is MAB).

13. Click the **Layer 3** subtab.

Figure 11-16   *General Tab for CP-GUEST*

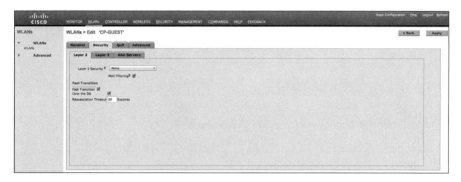

Figure 11-17   *Layer 2 Security Subtab for CP-GUEST*

14. From the Layer 3 Security drop-down list, choose **None**, as shown in Figure 11-18.

15. Click the **AAA Servers** subtab.

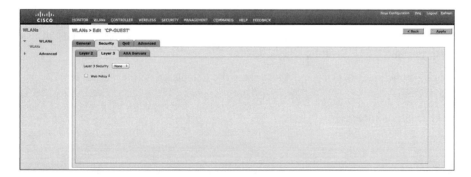

Figure 11-18   *Layer 3 Security Subtab for CP-GUEST*

16. Check the **Enabled** check box to the right of Radius Servers Overwrite Interface.

17. Select your ISE Policy Service Node(s) for both Authentication and Accounting, and ensure the Enabled check box is selected for both Authentication and Accounting columns.

18. Click **Apply**. Figure 11-19 shows a completed AAA Servers subtab.

19. Click the **Advanced** tab.

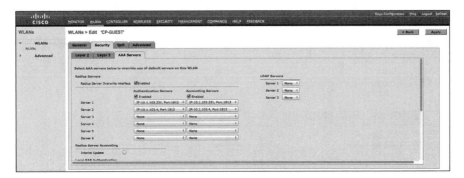

Figure 11-19 *AAA Servers Security Subtab for CP-GUEST*

20. Check the **Enable** check box for Allow AAA Override.

This enables ISE to assign a VLAN and ACL that are different from those that are configured on the WLAN by default.

21. Check the **Required** check box for DHCP Addr. Assignment.

This setting is required for the DHCP Device Sensor built into the WLC.

22. From the NAC State drop-down list, choose **Radius NAC**.

This setting is critical to allow for URL Redirection, Centralized Web Authentication, Posture Assessment, Native Supplicant Provisioning, and more.

23. Scroll down the Advanced tab and, under Client Profiling, check both the **DHCP Profiling** and **HTTP Profiling** check boxes.

24. Click **Apply**. Figures 11-20 and 11-21 show the completed Advanced tab for CP-GUEST.

25. Save Configuration.

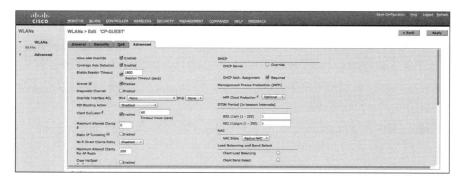

Figure 11-20 *Advanced Tab (Top) for CP-GUEST*

Figure 11-21 *Advanced Tab (Bottom) for CP-GUEST*

Create the Corporate SSID

The Corporate WLAN is created as a "closed" SSID and requires 802.1X authentication for an endpoint to associate to the WLAN. Unlike wired networks, wireless networks have the added benefit of truly rejecting all access without a successful authentication. Users are attuned to the requirement of configuring software in order to connect to a wireless network. The same is very much not true, inherently, when it comes to wired networks.

From the WLC GUI, perform the following steps:

1. Click the WLANs menu.

2. Click Create New.

3. Click **Go**.

4. From the Type drop-down list, choose **WLAN**.

5. In the Profile Name field, enter the WLAN profile name; use **CiscoPress** in this example.

6. In the SSID field, enter an SSID name; use **CiscoPress-Corp** in this example.

7. Click **Apply**.

    The Edit 'CiscoPress' screen opens with the General tab displayed.

8. If you are ready to work with this SSID, check the **Enabled** check box to the right of Status.

9. From the Interface/Interface Group(G) drop-down list, choose the **Employee** interface that you created previously, as shown in Figure 11-22.

10. Click the **Security** tab.

Figure 11-22   *General Tab for CiscoPress*

11. On the Layer 2 subtab of the Security tab, the default setting of WPA+WPA2 is correct for this sample configuration, as shown in Figure 11-23.

12. Do *not* check the MAC Filtering check box.

13. In the Authentication Key Management section, check the **Enable** check box for 802.1X.

14. Click the **Layer 3** subtab.

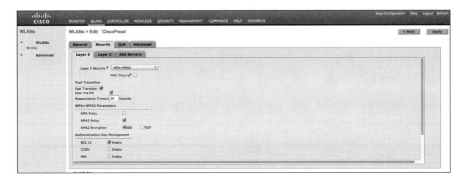

Figure 11-23   *Layer 2 Security Subtab for CiscoPress*

15. From the Layer 3 Security drop-down list, choose **None**, as shown in Figure 11-24.

16. Click the **AAA Servers** subtab.

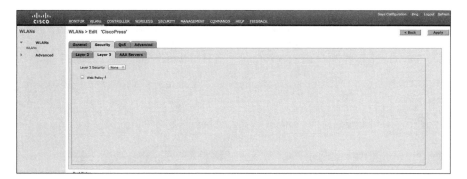

Figure 11-24   *Layer 3 Security Subtab for CiscoPress*

17. Check the **Enabled** check box to the right of Radius Servers Overwrite Interface.

18. Select your ISE Policy Service Node(s) for both Authentication and Accounting and ensure that the enabled checkbox is selected for both Authentication and Accounting columns, as displayed in Figure 11-25.

19. Click **Apply**.

20. Click the **Advanced** tab.

Figure 11-25   *AAA Servers Security Subtab for CiscoPress*

21. Check the **Enable** check box for Allow AAA Override.

This enables ISE to assign a VLAN and an ACL that are different from those that are configured on the WLAN by default.

22. Check the **Required** check box for DHCP Addr. Assignment.

This setting is required for the DHCP Device Sensor built into the WLC.

23. From the NAC State drop-down list, choose **Radius NAC**.

This setting is critical to allow for URL Redirection, Posture Assessment, Native Supplicant Provisioning, and more.

24. Scroll down the Advanced tab and, under Client Provisioning, enable both DHCP and HTTP Profiling options. Scroll down the Advanced tab and, under Client Profiling, check both the **DHCP Profiling** and **HTTP Profiling** check boxes.

25. Click **Apply**. Figures 11-26 and 11-27 illustrate the completed Advanced tab for CiscoPress.

26. Click the Save Configuration link in the upper-right corner.

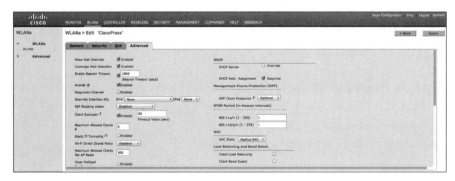

Figure 11-26 *Advanced Tab (Top) for CiscoPress*

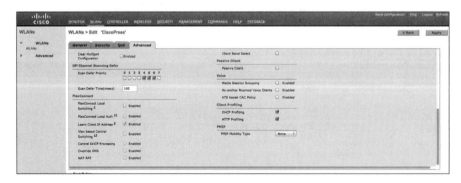

Figure 11-27 *Advanced Tab (Bottom) for CiscoPress*

Summary

This chapter reviewed the best practice configurations for Cisco Catalyst Switches and Cisco Wireless LAN Controllers. It walked you through the configuration of these network access devices for use in all scenarios and all deployment phases of the Secure Unified Access system.

An identity system like this one is so much more than just the Policy Server. The NADs themselves along with their advanced capabilities are absolutely critical to having a successful system. That is why this chapter and the NAD configurations it provides are absolutely mission critical to the success of your project.

Appendix E, "Sample Switch Configurations," includes configuration examples of various device types with multiple Cisco IOS versions, all designed to follow the guidelines and practices laid out in this chapter.

Chapter 12, "Authorization Policy Elements," examines another building block: roles within your organization. It shows how to create a logical security policy for those roles. Once the logical policy is created, it becomes much easier to translate that into an ISE Authentication and Authorization Policy.

Chapter 12

Authorization Policy Elements

This chapter focuses on exploring authorization policy elements, with emphasis on the authorization results policy elements. Cisco ISE policy elements are objects that are used in an authorization policy.

Cisco ISE policy elements are broken up into three high-level groups:

- **Dictionaries:** The dictionaries contain objects that are used throughout ISE to define conditions, policies, profiles, and more. A dictionary object's purpose is to "teach" ISE how to categorize external data that it either receives (syslog, snmp trap, RADIUS, and so on) or asks for (polling, AD query, RADIUS, and so on). ISE predefines hundreds of system dictionary objects for you. System-defined dictionaries are read-only. You cannot create, edit, or delete any system-defined attribute in a system dictionary. For example, ISE includes a predefined RADIUS dictionary. In that dictionary are hundreds of predefined RADIUS attributes. RADIUS class is one such attribute. This allows ISE to parse out and map a RADIUS message containing the attribute class. As shown in Figure 12-1, it will map the RADIUS *class* attribute to the ISE Internal attribute name of *class*.

- **Conditions:** Authorization Condition policy elements are objects that define a simple or compound expression to match against. Conditions are then used in Authorization policies. For example, see Figure 12-2: RADIUS:Service-Type=Outbound AND RADIUS:NAS-Port-Type=Ethernet can make a compound condition for Catalyst_Switch_Local_Web_Authentication. Other common conditions include things such as Active Directory Group membership, time of day, and much more.

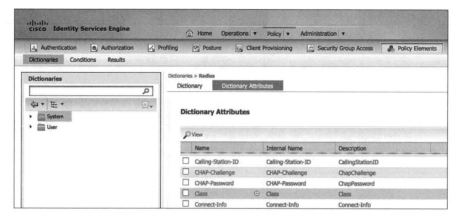

Figure 12-1   *ISE Dictionary Policy Element*

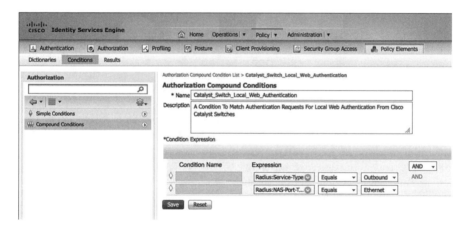

Figure 12-2   *ISE Condition Policy Element*

■ **Results:** Authorization Policy element *Results* are used to define and group Authorization permissions and are then used in an ISE authorization Policy Rule permissions column. Authorization Results are broken into three groups: Authorization Profiles, Downloadable ACLs, and Inline Posture Node Profiles. Results will be explained in detail in this chapter.

Authorization Results

Authorization Results are used to define the permissions that are eventually used in your authorization policy rules. They are, in general, the RADIUS attributes that will be sent to the Network Access Devices (NAD) to control some aspect of access control. Access Control Lists (ACL) that are downloaded from Identity Services Engine to the NAD, known as dACLS, are one of the more popular permissions used. This section explores dACLs and the other permission controls available in ISE. The basic idea is that you define Authorization profiles that contain permissions and then assign those profiles as permissions to an authorization policy rule. See Figure 12-3 for an example authorization policy rule showing permissions defined by authorization profiles.

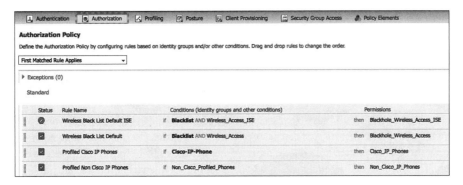

Figure 12-3   *ISE Authorization Policy Rule with Permissions*

Configuring Authorization Downloadable ACLs

An ACL is like a firewall policy. It contains a list of access control entries (ACE). ACLs may be downloaded from ISE to Cisco switches, and these special ACLs are known as downloadable ACLs (dACLs). Once you create a dACL on ISE, the dACL is then added to Authorization profiles and sent to the switch with the Access-Accept RADIUS result. Each access control entry (ACE) defines a traffic control rule that permit or deny packets. ACEs use the following attributes:

- **Source and destination protocols:** Authentication Header Protocol (**ahp**), Enhanced Interior Gateway Routing Protocol (**eigrp**), Encapsulation Security Payload (**esp**), generic routing encapsulation (**gre**), Internet Control Message Protocol (**icmp**), Internet Group Management Protocol (**igmp**), any Interior Protocol (**ip**), IP in IP tunneling (**ipinip**), KA9Q NOS-compatible IP over IP tunneling (**nos**), Open Shortest Path First routing (**ospf**), Payload Compression Protocol (**pcp**), Protocol-Independent Multicast (**pim**), Transmission Control Protocol (**tcp**), or User Datagram Protocol (**udp**).

- **Source and destination IP address:** The Source address must always be **any**. The NAD will replace **any** with the source IP address of the connected device. dACLs are only supported on switches; the Cisco Wireless LAN Controller (WLC) uses a different mechanism called Airespace ACLs.

- **Protocol source and destination ports:** Available ports are from 0 to 65535 for TCP and UDP.

- **Remark:** ACL comments.

- Cisco IOS syntax for a TCP ACL: access-list *access-list-number* {deny | permit}
  tcp *Any* [*operator port*] *destination destination-wildcard* [*operator port*] [estab-
  lished] [precedence *precedence*] [tos *tos*] [fragments] [log [log-input] | smartlog]
  [time-range *time-range-name*] [dscp *dscp*] [*flag*].

- All Access-Control Lists have an implicit **deny** at the end of them.

- If you use the **time-range** feature, you must manually configure the time range on
  the switch. ISE can then call the time-range in the ACL. Be sure to check that the
  naming matches exactly.

> **Note**   The **log** keyword should be used sparingly because logging is done in software
> on the switch. Also, the first packet that triggers the ACL causes a logging message right
> away, and subsequent packets are collected over 5-minute intervals before they appear
> as logged. The logging message includes the access list number, whether the packet was
> permitted or denied, the source IP address of the packet, and the number of packets from
> that source permitted or denied in the prior 5-minute interval.

Smartlog uses NetFlow records and therefore is more efficient on the switch.

To configure a dACL, go to **Policy > Policy Elements > Results > Authorization >
Downloadable ACLs** and click **Add**. You can also duplicate an existing ACL and edit the
duplicate.

Figure 12-4 shows an example of an ISE dACL configuration.

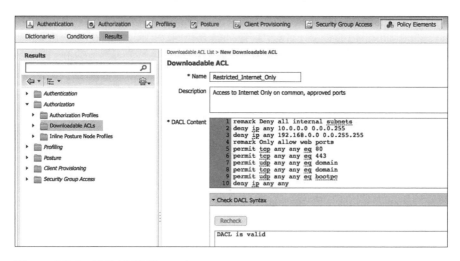

Figure 12-4   *ISE dACL Example*

Cisco ISE includes a basic dACL syntax checker to help to ensure your ACE statements
are correct. If you enter malformed syntax and click the Recheck button, it will show you

the error along with some assistance. The help is very similar to what you would receive at the command-line interface (CLI) of the switch itself.

The dACL syntax checker is able to check for basic ACL fields but does not support all the ACL commands that a particular Cisco switch might support. Therefore, if you use an unsupported ACE, the syntax checker will report an error even if your syntax is correct. At that point, it is up to you to ensure that your syntax is correct without the help of the syntax checker. If correct, the dACL will work just fine, regardless of the error shown in the syntax checker.

Figure 12-5 shows a dACL with a syntax error. Multiple ports are fine after the EQ, but the port 70000 is not a valid port.

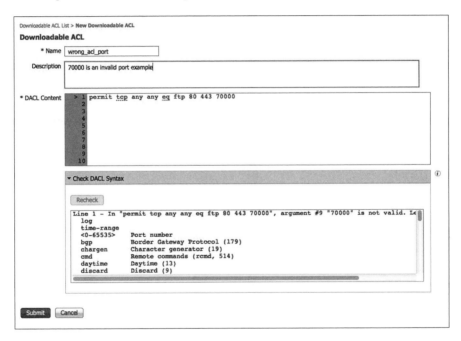

Figure 12-5 *ISE dACL Syntax Checker*

Configuring Authorization Profiles

An authorization profile acts as a container in which a number of specific permissions allow access to a set of network services. The authorization profile defines a set of permissions to be granted for a network access request. The Authorization Profile attributes are delivered via RADIUS. Figure 12-6 shows a RADIUS packet format. The RADIUS code is configured in the profile along with one or more attribute-value pairs (AVP). Figure 12-6 shows only a small handful of the hundreds of AVPs available, the most common of which are dACL, VLAN, and reauthentication timers.

Radius Code	Packet ID	Length	Authenticator	Attribute Value Pairs (AVPs)

Code	Assignment		Type	Assignment
1	Access-Request		4	NAS-IP-Address
2	Access-Accept		5	NAS-Port
3	Access-Reject		6	Service-Type
			7	Framed-Protocol
			8	Framed-IP-Address
			11	Filter-Id
			25	Class
			26	Vendor-Specific
			27	Session-Timeout
			28	Idle-Timeout
			61	NAS-Port-Type

Figure 12-6   *RADIUS Data Packet*

To configure an Authorization Profile, go to **Policy > Policy Elements > Results > Authorization > Authorization Profiles** and click **Add.** You can also duplicate an existing profile and then edit it. Figure 12-7 shows an example profile that uses the dACL created in Figure 12-4.

Figure 12-7 displays the following Authorization Profile fields:

■ **Name:** Enter a descriptive name; spaces are allowed here, as are ! # $ % & ' ( ) * + , - . / ; = ? @ _ {.

■ **Description:** Enter an explanatory description.

■ **Access Type:** The only two options are Access_Accept and Access_Reject. If you use Reject, the user is unconditionally denied access to all requested network resources. This field configures the RADIUS code value, as shown in Figure 12-6.

■ **Service Template:** Checking this check box tells ISE to use the profile name as the SA-NET profile name. SA-NET profiles are configured on newer Cisco switches. Ensure the naming matches exactly between ISE and the switch. Cisco ISE sends the name of the service template to the device, and the device downloads the content (RADIUS attributes) of the template if it does not already have a cached or statically defined version of it. In addition, Cisco ISE sends Change of Authorization (CoA) notifications to the device if a RADIUS attribute was added, removed, or changed in the service template.

The next section in the Authorization Profile is Common Tasks. This is a collection of the commonly used RADIUS AVPs. They are presented in plain English format to make it easy for the administrator to configure. Figure 12-8 depicts the Common Tasks list:

- An associated dACL

- An associated VLAN

- An associated security group ACL (SGACL)

- Any number of other dictionary-based attributes

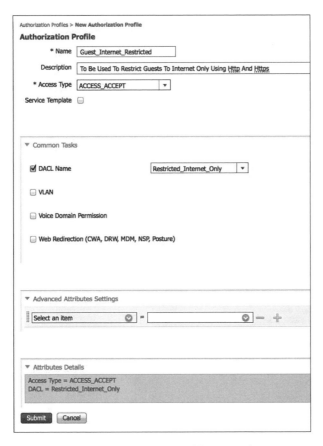

Figure 12-7   *Authorization Profile Example*

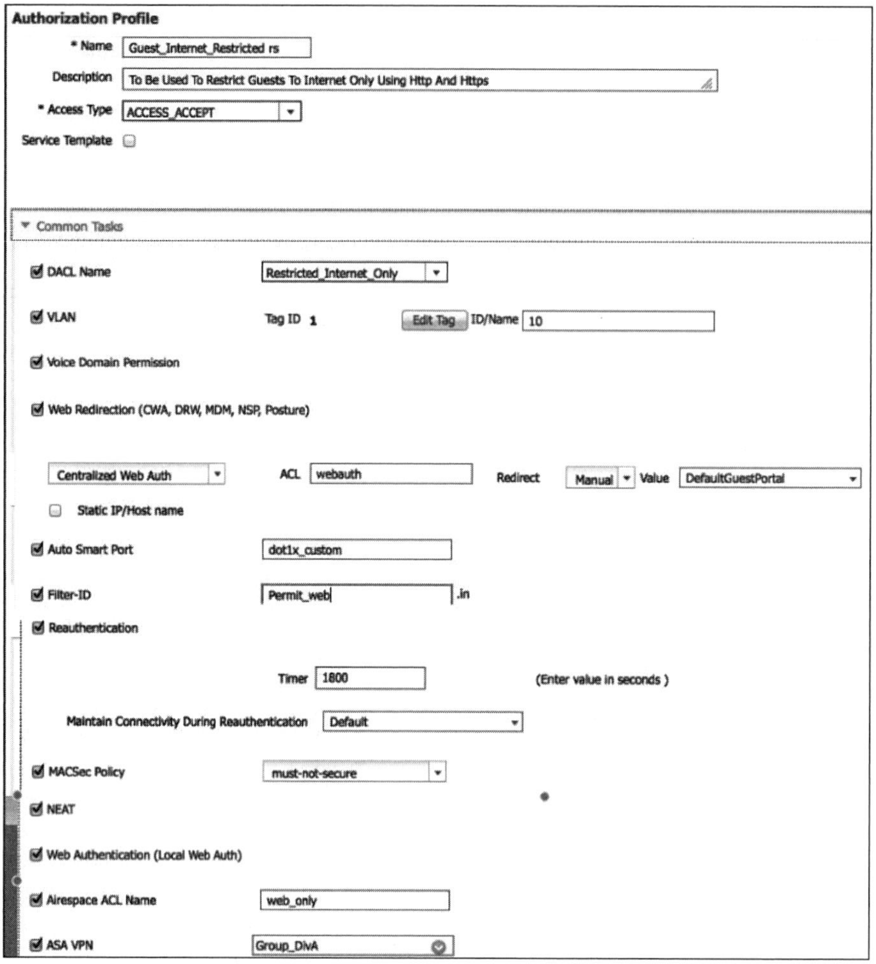

Authorization Profile

* Name   Guest_Internet_Restricted rs

Description   To Be Used To Restrict Guests To Internet Only Using Http And Https

* Access Type   ACCESS_ACCEPT ▼

Service Template ☐

▼ Common Tasks

☑ DACL Name   Restricted_Internet_Only ▼

☑ VLAN   Tag ID 1   Edit Tag   ID/Name 10

☑ Voice Domain Permission

☑ Web Redirection (CWA, DRW, MDM, NSP, Posture)

    Centralized Web Auth ▼   ACL webauth   Redirect Manual ▼ Value DefaultGuestPortal ▼
    ☐ Static IP/Host name

☑ Auto Smart Port   dot1x_custom

☑ Filter-ID   Permit_web   .in

☑ Reauthentication

        Timer 1800   (Enter value in seconds)

    Maintain Connectivity During Reauthentication   Default ▼

☑ MACSec Policy   must-not-secure ▼

☑ NEAT

☑ Web Authentication (Local Web Auth)

☑ Airespace ACL Name   web_only

☑ ASA VPN   Group_DivA ◉

Figure 12-8   *Authorization Profile Common Tasks List*

Summary

Authorization profiles let you choose the attributes to be returned when a RADIUS request is accepted. Cisco ISE provides a mechanism that enables you to configure Common Tasks settings to support commonly used attributes. You must enter the values for the Common Tasks attributes, which Cisco ISE translates to the underlying RADIUS values.

Policy elements are components that define the authorization policy. The policy elements are as follows:

- Dictionaries

- Condition(s)

- Results

These policy elements are referenced when you create policy rules, and your choice of conditions and attributes can create specific types of authorization profiles.

Chapter 13

Authentication and Authorization Policies

The previous chapter focused on the levels of authorization you should provide for users and devices based on your logical Security Policy. You will build policies in ISE that employ those authorization results, such as Downloadable Access Lists and Authorization Profiles to accommodate the enforcement of that "paper policy."

These authorization results are the end result; the final decision of a login session or a particular stage of a login session.

This chapter examines how to build the Authentication and Authorization Policies that will eventually assign those results that were created in Chapter 12. These policies can be equated to the rules in a firewall and are constructed in a similar fashion.

Relationship Between Authentication and Authorization

Many IT professionals, especially those with wireless backgrounds, tend to confuse these terms and what they actually do. Wireless is used as an example here, because it went through such tremendous growth over the last few years, and with that growth, appeared increased security. Wireless was the most prevalent use-case of 802.1X authentication, and in the vast majority of wireless environments, a user was given full network access as long as her username and password were correct (meaning that authentication was successful).

An authentication is simply put: "validating credentials." If you were to go into a bank and request a withdrawal from an account, it asks for ID. You pass your driver's license to the bank teller, and the teller inspects the driver's license, going through a checklist of sorts:

- Does the picture on the license look like the person in front of the teller's window?

- Is the license from a recognized authority (i.e., one of the United States or a Military ID)?

Let's say, for conversations sake, that you handed them a valid ID (authentication was successful); does that mean you are *entitled* to the money you asked for?

The next step of the bank teller is to check the account and ensure that the person requesting the withdrawal is entitled to complete that transaction. Perhaps you are allowed to withdraw up to $1,000, but no more. This is the process of authorization. Just having a successful authentication does not prove entitlement.

This is why most of the time working within a product like ISE is spent setting up and tuning the Authorization Policy. Authorization is where the bulk of the final decisions are made.

Authentication Policies

Authentication policies have a few goals, but the ultimate end goal of an Authentication Policy is to determine if the identity credential is valid or not.

Goals of an Authentication Policy

Authentication Policies have a few goals:

1. Drop traffic that isn't allowed and prevent it from taking up any more processing power.

2. Route authentication requests to the Correct Identity Store (sometimes called a Policy Information Point [PIP]).

3. Validate the identity.

4. Pass successful authentications over to the Authorization Policy.

Accept Only Allowed Protocols

By default, ISE allows nearly all supported authentication protocols. However, it would behoove the organization to lock this down to only the ones that are expected and supported. This serves a few purposes: keep the load on the Policy Service nodes down and use the Authentication Protocol to help choose the right identity store.

Route to the Correct Identity Store

Once the authentication is accepted, ISE makes a routing decision. The identity store that should be checked is based on the incoming authentication. Obviously, if a certificate is being presented, ISE should not try and validate that certificate against the internal users database.

If your company has multiple lines of business, it may also have more than one Active Directory domain or more than one LDAP store. Using attributes in the authentication request, you can pick the correct domain or LDAP store.

Validate the Identity

Once the correct identity store has been identified, ISE confirms the credentials are valid. If it's a username/password, do those match what is in the directory store? If it's a certificate, does ISE trust the certificate signer? Was that certificate revoked?

Pass the Request to the Authorization Policy

If the authentication failed, the policy can reject the request without wasting the CPU cycles comparing the request to the Authorization Policy. Also, if the request did not match any of the configured rules, should a reject message be sent? However, when the request passes authentication, it is now time for the hand-off to the Authorization Policy.

Understanding Authentication Policies

Now that you understand the four main responsibilities of the Authentication Policy, it will be easier to understand why you are doing the things that are introduced in this section. To understand Authentication Policies even more, let's examine a few.

From the ISE GUI, navigate to **Policy > Authentication**. Notice the default, as displayed in Figure 13-1.

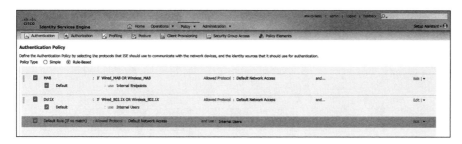

Figure 13-1 *Default Authentication Policy*

Basic Authentication Policy rules are logically organized in this manor:

> IF *conditions* THEN ALLOW PROTCOLS IN LIST *AllowedProtocolList*
>
> AND CHECK THE IDENTITY STORE IN LIST IdentityStore

Rules are processed in a top-down, first-match order; just like a firewall policy. So, if the conditions do not match, the authentication is compared to the next rule in the policy.

As shown in Figure 13-1, ISE is preconfigured with a default rule for MAC Authentication Bypass (MAB). Use this rule to dig into authentication rules and how they work. If you have a live ISE system, it may help to follow along with the text.

Figure 13-2 demonstrates the MAB rule in flowchart format.

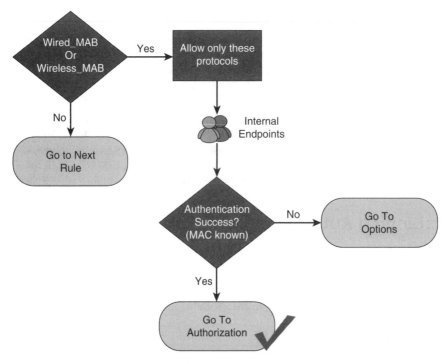

Figure 13-2   *MAB Rule Flow Chart*

Conditions

The conditions of this rule state, "If the authentication request is Wired_MAB or Wireless_MAB, it will match this rule." You can expand these conditions by mousing over the conditions and clicking the target icon that appears or by looking directly at the authentication conditions shown in the following steps:

1. Navigate to **Policy > Policy Elements > Conditions > Authentication > Compound Conditions**.

2. Select Wired_MAB.

   As you can see in Figure 13-3, Wired_MAB is looking for the RADIUS Service-Type to be Call-Check and the NAS-Port-Type to be Ethernet. This combination of attributes from the RADIUS authentication packet notifies ISE that it is a MAB request from a switch.

   Figure 13-4 highlights these key attributes in a packet capture of the MAB authentication request.

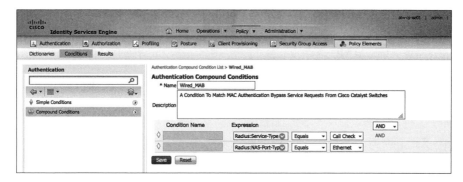

Figure 13-3 *Wired_MAB Condition*

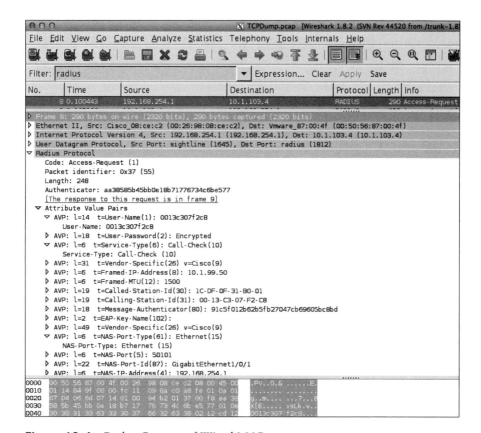

Figure 13-4 *Packet Capture of Wired MAB*

3. Navigate to **Policy > Policy Elements > Conditions > Authentication > Compound Conditions.**

4. Select **Wireless_MAB.**

As shown in Figure 13-5, wireless MAB is similar. However, it uses a NAS-Port-Type of Wireless - IEEE 802.11. This combination of attributes from the RADIUS authentication packet tells ISE that it is a MAB request from a wireless device.

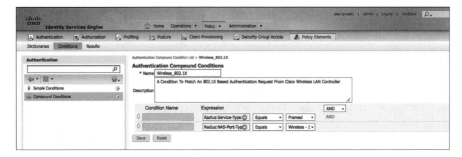

Figure 13-5   *Wireless_MAB Condition*

Allowed Protocols

After the conditions are matched, the rule now dictates what authentication protocols are permitted. Looking at the predefined MAB rule, this rule uses the Default Network Access list of allowed protocols (which is almost every supported authentication protocol).

Let's examine the default allowed protocols. From the ISE GUI, perform the following steps:

1. Navigate to **Policy > Policy Elements > Results > Authentication > Allowed Protocols.**

2. Select **Default Network Access.**

As you can see in Figure 13-6, the list of supported protocols and their options is extensive. This default list is inclusive with the intention of making deployments work easily for customers, but security best practice is to lock this down to only the protocols needed for that rule.

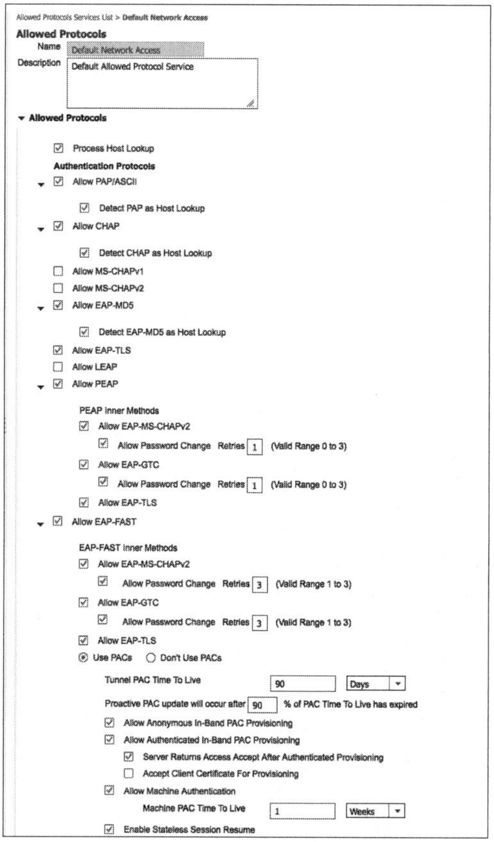

Figure 13-6 *Default Network Access*

Authentication Protocol Primer

This section examines the most common authentication protocols seen in most environments, so you can create a more specific list of allowed protocols for your deployment. Let's follow Figure 13-6, from top-down:

- **PAP:** Password Authentication Protocol. The username is sent in the clear, and the password is optionally encrypted. PAP is normally used with MAB, and some devices use PAP for Web authentications. We recommend you enable this for the MAB rule only and disable PAP for any authentication rules for real authentications.

  The check box for Detect PAP as Host Lookup allows PAP authentications to access the internal endpoints database. Without this check box selected, MAB would not work.

- **CHAP:** Challenge Handshake Authentication Protocol. The username and password are encrypted using a challenge sent from the server. CHAP is not often used with network access; however, some vendors send MAB using CHAP instead of PAP.

  The check box for Detect CHAP as Host Lookup allows CHAP authentications to access the internal endpoints database. Without this check box selected, MAB does not work.

Extensible Authentication Protocol (EAP) Types

EAP is an authentication framework providing for the transport and usage of identity credentials. EAP encapsulates the usernames, passwords, and certificates that a client is sending for purposes of authentication. There are many different EAP types, each one has its own benefit and downside. As an interesting sidenote, 802.1X defines EAP over LAN:

- **EAP-MD5:** Uses a Message Digest algorithm to hide the credentials in a HASH. The hash is sent to the server, where it is compared to a local hash to see if the credentials are accurate. However, EAP-MD5 does not have a mechanism for mutual authentication. That means the server is validating the client, but the client does not authenticate the server (i.e., does not check to see if it should trust the server). EAP-MD5 is common on some IP-Phones, and it is also possible that some switches send MAB requests within EAP-MD5. The check box for Detect EAP-MD5 as Host Lookup allows EAP-MD5 authentications to access the internal endpoints database. Without this check box selected, MAB does not work.

- **EAP-TLS:** Uses Transport Layer Security (TLS) to provide the secure identity transaction. This is similar to SSL and the way encryption is formed between your web browser and a secure website. EAP-TLS has the benefit of being an open IETF standard, and it is considered "universally supported." EAP-TLS uses X.509 certificates and provides the ability to support mutual authentication, where the client must trust the server's certificate, and vice versa. It is considered among the most secure EAP types, because password capture is not an option; the endpoint must still have the private key. EAP-TLS is quickly becoming the EAP type of choice when supporting BYOD in the enterprise.

Tunneled EAP Types

The EAP types previously described transmit their credentials immediately. These next two EAP types (see Figure 13-7) form encrypted tunnels first and then transmit the credentials within the tunnel:

- **PEAP:** Protected EAP. Originally proposed by Microsoft, this EAP tunnel type has quickly become the most popular and widely deployed EAP method in the world. PEAP forms a potentially encrypted TLS tunnel between the client and server, using the x.509 certificate on the server in much the same way the SSL tunnel is established between a web browser and a secure website. After the tunnel is formed,

PEAP uses another EAP type as an "inner method," authenticating the client using EAP within the outer tunnel.

- **EAP-MSCHAPv2:** When using this inner method, the client's credentials are sent to the server encrypted within an MSCHAPv2 session. This is the most common inner-method, as it allows for simply transmission of username and password, or even computer name and computer passwords to the RADIUS server, which in turn authenticates them to Active Directory.

- **EAP-GTC:** EAP-Generic Token Card (GTC). This inner method was created by Cisco as an alternative to MSCHAPv2 that allows generic authentications to virtually any identity store, including One-Time-Password (OTP) token servers, LDAP, Novell E-Directory and more.

- **EAP-TLS:** Although rarely used and not widely known, PEAP is capable of using EAP-TLS as an inner method.

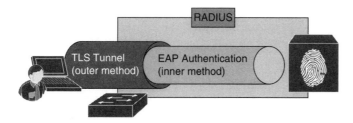

Figure 13-7   *Tunneled EAP Types (PEAP and FAST)*

- **EAP-FAST:** Flexible Authentication via Secure Tunnel (FAST) is similar to PEAP. FAST was created by Cisco as an alternative to PEAP that allows for faster re-authentications and supports faster wireless roaming. Just like PEAP, FAST forms a TLS outer tunnel and then transmits the client credentials within that TLS tunnel. Where FAST differs from the PEAP is the ability to use Protected Access Credentials (PAC). A PAC can be thought of like a secure cookie, stored locally on the host as "proof" of a successful authentication.

  - **EAP-MSCHAPv2:** When using this inner method, the client's credentials are sent to the server encrypted within an MSCHAPv2 session. This is the most common inner method, as it allows for simply transmission of username and password, or even computer name and computer passwords to the RADIUS server, which in turn authenticates them to Active Directory.

  - **EAP-GTC:** EAP-Generic Token Card (GTC). This inner method was created by Cisco as an alternative to MSCHAPv2 that allows generic authentications to virtually any identity store, including One-Time-Password (OTP) token servers, LDAP, Novell E-Directory, and more.

- **EAP-TLS:** EAP-FAST is capable of using EAP-TLS as an inner method. This became popular with EAP chaining.

- **EAP Chaining with EAP-FASTv2:** As an enhancement to EAP-FAST, a differentiation was made to have a user PAC and a machine PAC. After a successful machine authentication, ISE issues a machine-PAC to the client. Then, when processing a user authentication, ISE requests the machine-PAC to prove that the machine was successfully authenticated, too. This is the first time in 802.1X history that multiple credentials have been able to be authenticated within a single EAP transaction, and it is known as EAP chaining. The IETF is creating a new open standard based on EAP-FASTv2 and, at the time of publishing this book, it was to be referred to as EAP-TEAP (tunneled EAP), which should eventually be supported by all major vendors.

Identity Store

After processing the allowed protocols, the authentication request is then authenticated against the chosen identity store, or in this case with MAB, it is compared to the internal endpoints database (list of MAC addresses stored locally on ISE).

If the MAC address is known, it is considered to be a successful MAB (notice it was not termed successful *authentication*). MAB is exactly that, bypassing authentication, and it is not considered a secure authentication.

The selected identity source may also be an identity source sequence, which attempts a series of identity stores in order. This is covered in Chapter 21, "Monitor Mode."

Options

Every authentication rule has a set of options that are stored with the identity store selection. These options tell ISE what to do: if an authentication fails, if the user/device is unknown, or if the process fails. The options are Reject, Continue, and Drop:

- **Reject:** Send Access-Reject back to the NAD.

- **Continue:** Continue to the Authorization Policy regardless of authentication pass/fail. (Used with Web authentication.)

- **Drop:** Do not respond to the NAD; NAD will treat as if RADIUS server is dead.

See Chapters 20–23 for more details on when to use these options.

Common Authentication Policy Examples

This section considers a few quick examples of Authentication Policies, based on common use-case or simply because they were interesting.

Using the Wireless SSID

One of the most common Authentication Policy requests that I get is to treat authentications differently based on the SSID of the wireless network. Creating the policy is not difficult; what becomes challenging is the identification of the attribute to use, because Source-SSID is not a field in a RADIUS packet. The attribute you need to use is called-station-id. That is the field that describes the wireless SSID name.

For this example, let's build a rule for an SSID named CiscoPress. This rule will be configured to

- Only match authentications coming from that SSID

- Allow only EAP-FAST authentications

- Utilize EAP chaining

- Authenticate against Active Directory

From the ISE GUI, perform the following steps:

1. Navigate to **Policy > Authentication.**

2. Insert a new rule above the preconfigured Dot1X rule.

3. Provide a name for the rule. In this case, we named it CiscoPress SSID.

4. For the condition, choose **RADIUS > Called-Station-ID.**

5. Select **Contains.**

6. Type in the SSID Name in the text box. Figure 13-8 shows the condition.

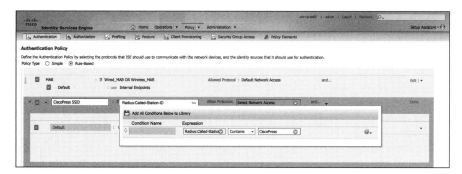

Figure 13-8 *Called-Station-ID Contains CiscoPress*

7. Create a new allowed protocol object that only allows EAP-FAST, as shown in Figure 13-9. Select the drop-down for Allowed Protocols.

8. Click the cog in the upper-right corner and choose Create a New Allowed Protocol.

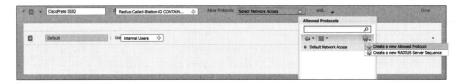

Figure 13-9   *Create a New Allowed Protocol*

9. Provide a name. In this case, it was named it EAP-FAST ONLY.

10. Optionally, provide a description.

11. Working top-down, ensure that all the check boxes are unchecked until you reach Allow EAP-FAST.

12. Confirm that Allow EAP-FAST is enabled.

13. For ease of use, enable EAP-MS-CHAPv2, EAP-GTC, and EAP-TLS for inner methods.

14. Select Use PACs for faster session re-establishment, and to allow EAP chaining.

    Figure 13-10 shows the EAP-FAST settings for the new Allowed Protocols definition.

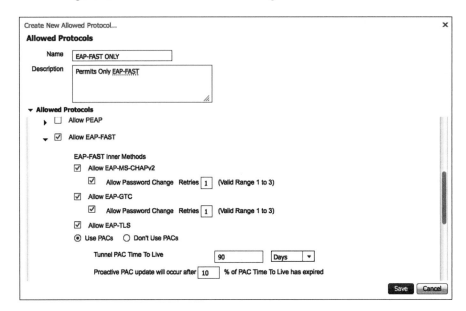

Figure 13-10   *Allowed Protocols*

15. For ease of deployment, select Allow Anonymous In-Band PAC Provisioning and Allow Authenticated In-Band PAC Provisioning.

16. Check the boxes for Server Sends Access-Accept After Authenticated Provisioning and Accept Client Certificate for Provisioning.

17. Enable Allow Machine Authentication.

18. Select Enable Stateless Session Resume.

19. Select Enable EAP chaining, as shown in Figure 13-11.

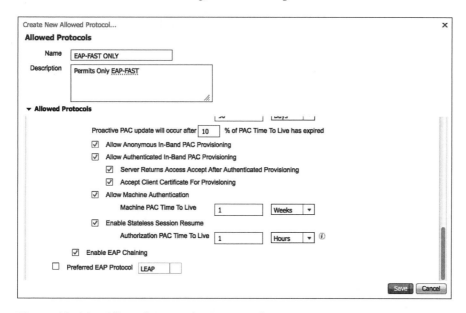

Figure 13-11   *Allowed Protocols, Continued*

20. Because you are only allowing one protocol, there is no need to set a preferred EAP Protocol.

21. Click **Save**.

22. Select the drop-down for the identity source (currently set for Internal Users), as shown in Figure 13-12.

23. Select your Active Directory source. In this case, the name is AD1.

24. Leave the default options.

25. Click **Done**.

26. Click **Save**.

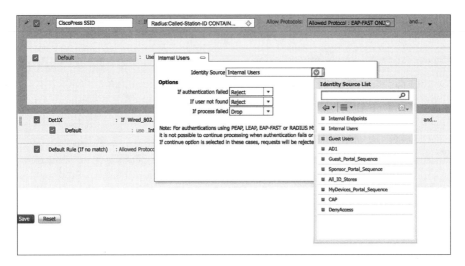

Figure 13-12 *Selecting the AD Identity Source*

Figure 13-13 shows the completed authentication rule.

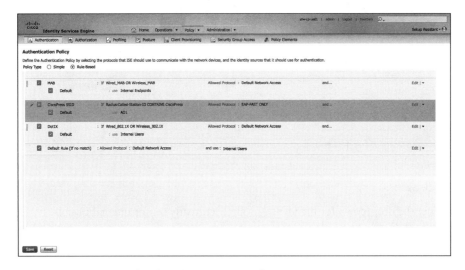

Figure 13-13 *Completed Authentication Rule*

This completes the creation of the authentication rule. Determining what actions to take for the authentications that passed is handled in the Authorization Policy.

Remote-Access VPN

Very often, authentications for a remote-access VPN connection get routed to an OTP server, like RSAs SecureID. For this example, let's build a rule for remote-access VPN authentications. This rule will be configured to

■ Only match authentications coming from the VPN device

■ Route that authentication to the OTP server

From the ISE GUI, perform the following steps:

1. Navigate to **Policy > Authentication**.

2. Insert a new rule above the preconfigured Dot1X rule.

3. Provide a name for the rule. In this case, it was named RA VPN.

4. For the condition, choose **DEVICE > Device Type**.

5. Set the operator to Equals.

6. Choose the Network Device Group VPN.

Figure 13-14 shows the selection of the conditions.

Figure 13-14   *Device Type Equals VPN*

7. For this example, just use the allowed protocol of Default Network Access.

8. For the identity store, the OTP server was selected that was previously configured in **Administration > Identity Management > External Identity Sources > RADIUS Token (ATWOTP)**.

9. Leave the default options.

10. Click **Done**.

11. Click **Save**.

Figure 13-15 shows the completed RA VPN rule.

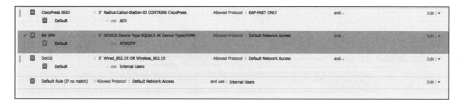

Figure 13-15   *Completed Authentication Rule*

Alternative ID Stores Based on EAP Type

In this modern day of BYOD and mobility, it is common to have multiple user and device types connecting to the same wireless SSID. In scenarios like this, often times, the corporate users with corporate laptops authenticate using EAP-FAST with EAP chaining while BYOD-type devices need to use certificates and EAP-TLS. Anyone authenticating with PEAP is recognized as a non-corporate and non-registered asset and sent to a device registration portal instead of being permitted network access.

For this example, let's modify the preconfigured Dot1X rule by creating subrules for each EAP type. This rule will be configured to

- Match wired or wireless 802.1X

- Route EAP-TLS authentications to a Certificate Authentication Profile (CAP)

- Route PEAP authentications to an LDAP server

- Route EAP-FAST to Active Directory

- Route EAP-MD5 to internal endpoints for host-lookup as a MAB request

From the ISE GUI, perform the following steps:

1. Navigate to **Policy > Authentication**.

2. Edit the preconfigured Dot1X rule.

3. Create a new allowed protocol object that only allows EAP authentications. Select the drop-down for allowed protocols.

4. Click the cog in the upper-right corner and choose Create a New Allowed Protocol.

5. Provide a name. In this case, it is named All EAP Types.

6. Optionally, provide a description.

7. Working top-down, ensure all EAP types are enabled, except for LEAP (unless you need LEAP for backward compatibility).

8. Enable EAP chaining, as done previously in the wireless SSID exercise.

9. Click **Save**.

10. Insert a new subrule above the Default Identity Store subrule and name it EAP-TLS.

11. For the condition, choose **Network Access > EapAuthentication equals EAP-TLS** (as shown in Figure 13-16).

Figure 13-16   *Network Access:EapAuthentication Equals EAP-TLS*

12. For the identity source, choose the preconfigured Certificate Authentication Profile
(CAP). This was configured at **Administration > Identity Management > External
Identity Sources > Certificate Authentication Profile.**

13. Insert a new row above the EAP-TLS row to insert EAP-FAST. Place EAP-FAST
above EAP-TLS, because EAP-TLS may be used as an inner-method of EAP-FAST.

14. Choose **Network Access > EapTunnel Equals EAP-FAST** for the condition.

15. Select the Active Directory object for the identity source.

16. Insert a new row above the EAP-TLS row to insert PEAP.

17. Choose **Network Access > EapTunnel Equals PEAP** for the condition.

18. Select the LDAP object for the identity source.

19. Insert a new row below the EAP-TLS row to insert EAP-MD5.

20. Choose **Network Access > EapAuthentication Equals EAP-MD5** for the condition.

21. Select internal endpoints for the identity source.

22. Change the default identity store (bottom row) to be Deny Access.

23. Click **Done.**

24. Click **Save.**

Figure 13-17 shows the completed rule and subrules.

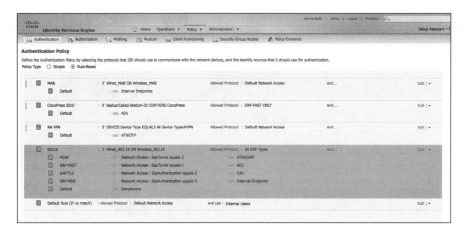

Figure 13-17   *Completed Authentication Rule and Sub Rules*

This completes the authentication section of this chapter. The next section takes an in-depth look at Authorization Policies and common authorization rules.

Authorization Policies

The ultimate goal of an Authentication Policy is to determine if the identity credential is valid or not. However, success or failure in the authentication policy may not necessarily determine whether the user or device is actually permitted access to the network. The authorization rules make that determination.

Goals of Authorization Policies

Authorization Policies have one main goal: to examine conditions in order to send an authorization result to the network access device (NAD). What conditions? Well, what did you have in mind?

Common conditions could include internal and external attributes, like Active Directory group membership or internal group membership within ISE. Policies can be built using attributes like location, time, if a device was registered, whether a mobile device has been jail-broken, nearly any attribute imaginable. Even the authentication is an attribute: was authentication successful; which authentication protocol was used; and what is the content of specific fields of the certificate that was used?

The policy compares these conditions with the explicit goal of providing an authorization result. The result may be a standard RADIUS access-accept or access-reject message, but it can also include more advanced items, like VLAN assignment, downloadable Access-Lists (dACL), Security Group Tag, URL redirection, and more.

The result allows or denies access to the network, and when it is allowed, it can include any and all restrictions for limiting network access for the user or endpoint.

Understanding Authorization Policies

Now that you understand the fundamental responsibilities of the Authorization Policy, it will be easier to understand the exercises in this section. To understand Authorization Policies even more, let's examine a few.

Basic Authorization Policy rules are logically organized in this manner:

IF *conditions* THEN *AssignThesePermissions*

Just like the Authentication Policy, Authorization Policy rules are processed in a top-down, first-match order. So, if the conditions do not match, the authentication is compared to the next rule in the policy.

ISE is preconfigured with a default rule for blacklisted devices, named Wireless Blacklist Default, Profiled Cisco IP-Phones, and Profiled Non Cisco IP-Phones. Let's examine the Cisco IP-Phone and blacklist rules in order to dig into authorization rules and how they work. If you have a live ISE system, it may help to follow along with the text.

From the ISE GUI, perform the following steps:

1. Navigate to **Policy > Authorization**.

    You should notice an immediate difference between the Authorization Policy and the Authentication Policy examined earlier in this chapter. The Authorization Policy attempts to display the rule logic in plain English. The bold text designates an identity group, while the standard font is a normal attribute. The operator is always AND when both identity group and other conditions are used in the same rule.

    Figure 13-18 displays the default Authorization Policy.

Figure 13-18 *Default Authorization Policy*

2. Edit the rule named Cisco IP-Phones.

    Notice the identity group is a separate list than the other conditions. In this rule, there is an identity group named Cisco-IP-Phones. The next field is where other conditions are selected.

    This particular rule is a prebuilt rule that permits any device that was profiled as a Cisco IP-Phone, sending an access-accept that also sends an attribute value pair

(AVP) that permits the phone into the voice VLAN. Figure 13-19 shows an identity group of Cisco-IP-Phone.

Figure 13-19   *Profiled Cisco IP Phones*

3. Examine the permissions (result) that is sent. Navigate to **Policy > Policy Elements > Results > Authorization > Authorization Profiles**.

Authorization Profiles are a set of authorization results that should be sent together. Notice that there are two other categories of authorization results: Downloadable ACLs and Inline Posture Node Profiles.

Figure 13-20 displays the default Authorization Profiles.

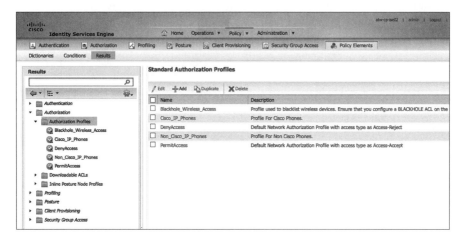

Figure 13-20   *Default Authorization Profiles*

4. Select the **Cisco_IP_Phones Authorization Profiles**.

The authorization result needs to be RADIUS attributes. To make that easier for the users of ISE, Cisco has included a Common Tasks section that presents the options in more of a "plain English" format. The Attributes Details section at the bottom displays the raw RADIUS result that is sent.

Figure 13-21 shows the common tasks, using the default Cisco_IP_Phones authorization profile as the example.

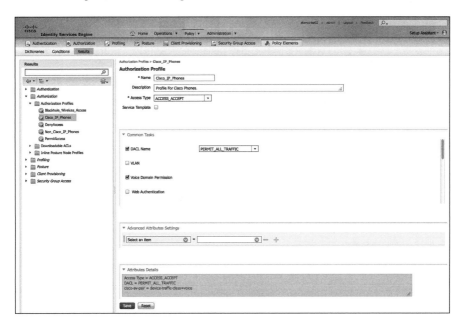

Figure 13-21   *Cisco_IP_Phones Authorization Profile*

In Figure 13-21, note the DACL name is a drop-down box where you select a downloadable access list that is created and stored in ISE. The Voice Domain Permission
check box is required for the switch to allow the phone into the voice VLAN on the
switch.

5. Notice in the Attributes Detail section, this authorization result sends a RADIUS
result with an access-accept, a dACL that permits all traffic, and the voice-domain
VSA to permit the phone to join the voice VLAN.

Next, examine the Wireless Blacklist Default Rule:

1. Navigate to **Policy > Authorization**.

2. Edit the rule named Wireless Black List Default.

Notice the Identity Group is a separate list than the other conditions. In this rule,
there is an Identity Group named "Blacklist". The next field is populated with a pre-
built condition specifying wireless connections. This particular rule is built to prevent devices that have been marked lost or stolen from accessing the network.

3. Examine the authorization condition being used. Navigate to **Policy > Policy
Elements > Conditions > Authorization > Compound Conditions**.

Figure 13-22 shows the default list of compound conditions.

Figure 13-22   *Pre-Built Authorization Compound Conditions*

4. Select **Wireless_Access.**

As shown in Figure 13-23, the Wireless_Access compound condition references the RADIUS attribute of NAS-Port-Type Equals Wireless – IEEE 802.11.

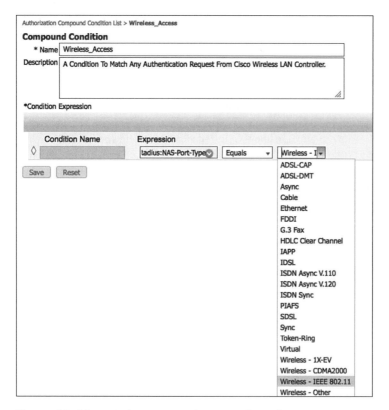

Figure 13-23   *Wireless_Access Compound Condition*

5. Examine the authorization result that is being sent for this Authorization Rule. Navigate to **Policy > Policy Elements > Results > Authorization > Authorization Profiles**.

6. Select **Blackhole_Wireless_Access**.

As shown in Figure 13-24, the Blackhole_Wireless_Access Authorization Profile does not use any of the common tasks. Instead, it employs the Advanced Attribute settings to send a URL-Redirect and URL-Redirect-ACL result to the WLC, along with an access-accept. So, this result allows the devices onto the network, but forces all traffic to redirect to a web page describing that the device was blacklisted.

Figure 13-24 *Blackhole_Wireless_Access Authorization Profile*

These two authorization rules demonstrate a variety of rules. This chapter examines a few common Authorization Policies in later sections.

Role-Specific Authorization Rules

The end goal of a Secure Access deployment is to provide very specific permissions to any authorization. In Chapter 6, "Building a Cisco ISE Network Access Security Policy," you learned all about the specific results and how to create those authorizations. However, that should always be handled in a staged approach in order to limit the impact to the end users.

Part V is dedicated to this phased approach.

Authorization Policy Example

This section provides an example of an Authorization Policy made up of numerous rules based on a common use case. This use case was selected to show multiple aspects of the Authorization Policy and help to solidify your working knowledge the parts/pieces of an Authorization Policy and the workflows associated with creating the policies.

For this example, let's configure three authorization rules: one that assigns full access to an employee that authenticated successfully with EAP chaining followed by a rule that assigns more limited access to the same employee authenticating with a non-corporate machine. The last rule created assigns Internet-only access to the same employee authenticating on a mobile device.

Employee and Corporate Machine Full-Access Rule

In this rule, assign full-access permissions to an employee that is authenticating from a valid corporate asset. From the ISE GUI, perform the following steps:

1. Navigate to **Policy > Authorization**.

2. Insert a new rule above the default rule.

3. Name the new rule Employee and CorpMachine.

4. For the other conditions drop-down, where it says Select Attribute, click the **+** and select **Create New Condition**.

5. Choose **Network Access > EapChainingResult**.

6. Choose **Equals**.

7. Select **User and Machine Both Succeeded**.

8. Click the cog on the right-hand side > **Add Attribute/Value**.

9. Select **AD1 > External Groups Equals "Employees"** (or another AD group of your choosing).

10. For the AuthZ Profiles, click the **+** sign.

11. Click the cog in the upper-right corner > **Add New Standard Profile**.

12. Name the new Authorization Profile Employee Full Access.

13. Optionally add a description.

14. Access Type = Access_Accept.

15. Select **DACL Name > Permit_ALL_TRAFFIC**.

    Figure 13-25 shows the Employee Full Access authorization profile.

16. Click **Save**.

17. Click **Done** to finish editing the rule.

18. Click **Save** to save the Authorization Policy.

    Figure 13-26 shows the completed authorization rule.

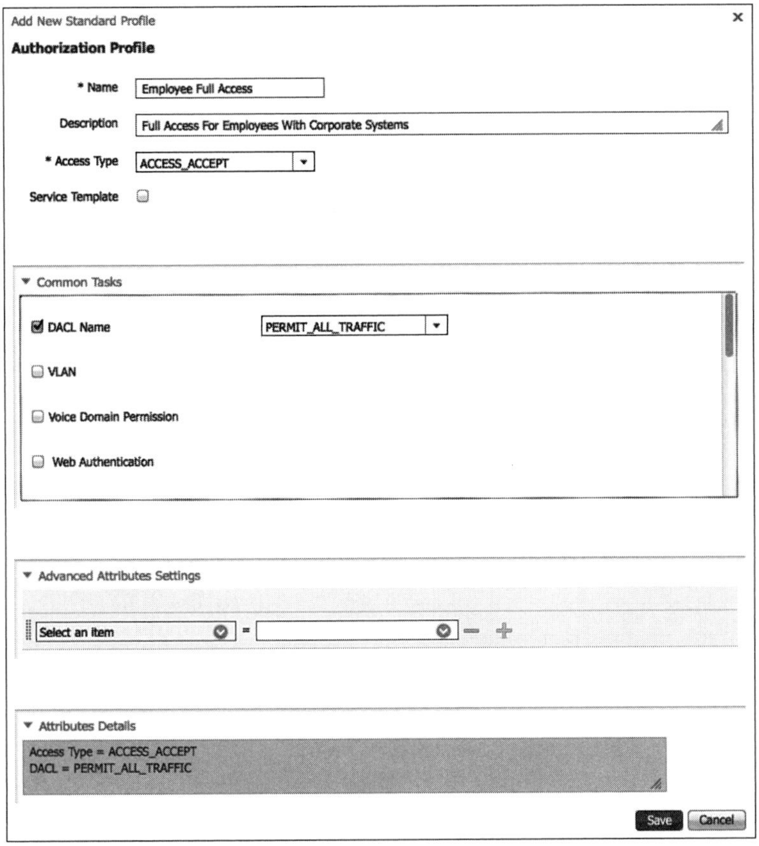

Figure 13-25   *Employee Full Access Authorization Profile*

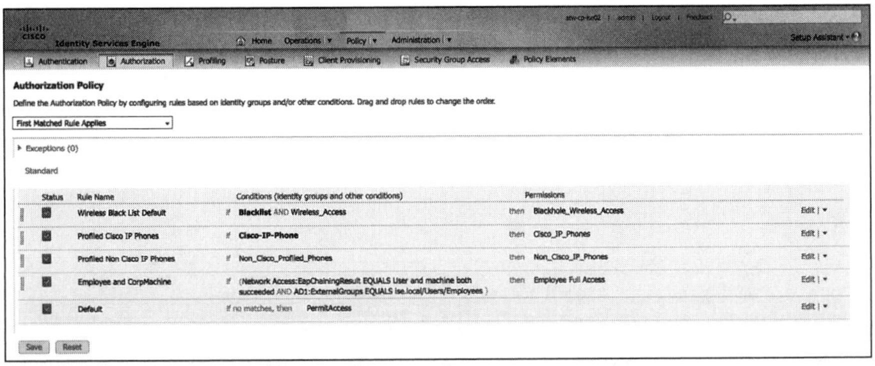

Figure 13-26   *Completed Employee and CorpMachine Rule*

Internet Only for iDevices

Now that the rule for employees with corporate devices has been created, you need to create the rule below it that provides Internet access only to employee authentications on mobile devices.

To begin this rule, first create a new DACL that is applied to switches, create the authorization result, and then go back into the Authorization Policy and build the rule:

1. Navigate to **Policy > Policy Elements > Results > Authorization > Downloadable ACLs**.

2. Click **Add**.

3. Name the ACL Internet Only.

4. Optionally provide a description.

5. Within DACL Content, provide an ACL that permits required traffic for Internet access and denies traffic destined to the corporate network.

   Figure 13-27 is just an example.

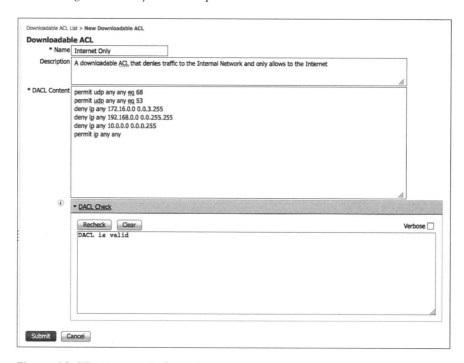

Figure 13-27   *Internet Only DACL*

6. Click **Submit**.

Now that the DACL is created, it's time to create the Authorization Profile:

1. Navigate to **Policy > Policy Elements > Results > Authorization > Authorization Profiles.**

2. Click **Add.**

3. Name the Authorization Profile Internet Only.

4. Optionally provide a description.

5. Access Type is ACCESS_ACCEPT.

6. Select **DACL Name** and select **Internet Only.**

7. Optionally provide a GUEST VLAN.

   Keep in mind this VLAN Name or ID is used for both wired and wireless devices. An alternative is to create separate rules for wired and wireless, so the user is assigned VLAN on wireless, but not wired.

8. Select **Airspace ACL Name** and fill in the name of the ACL on the controller that provides Internet Only Access.

9. Click **Submit.**

Figure 13-28 shows the completed Authorization Profile.

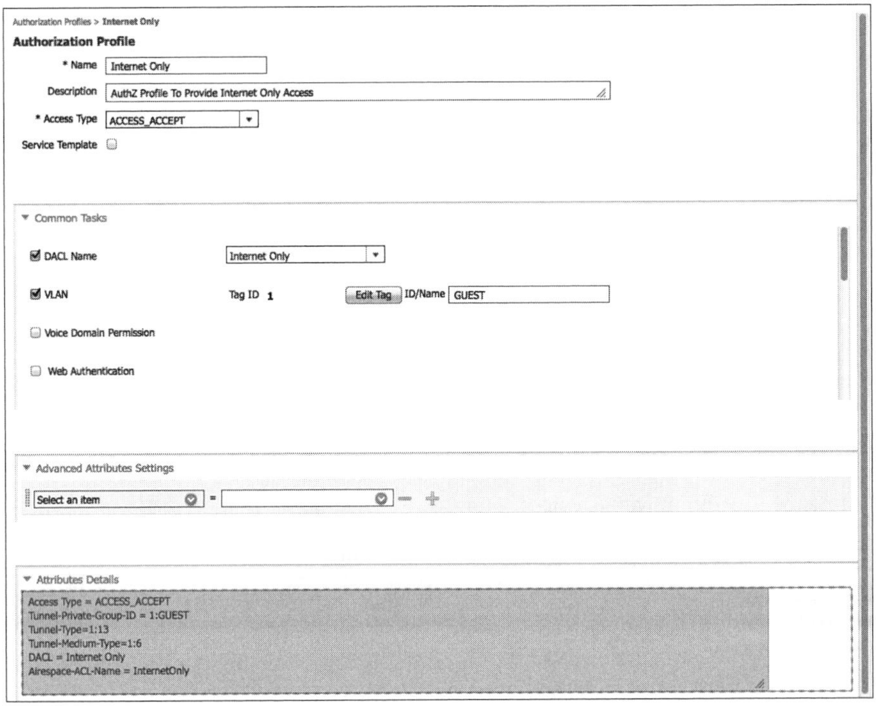

Figure 13-28 *Internet Only Authorization Profile*

Before you build the Authorization Policy, create a logical profiling policy that encompasses all mobile devices. This makes the policy building much easier and provides a reusable policy object:

1. Navigate to **Policy > Profiling > Logical Profiles**.

2. Click **Add**.

3. Name the Logical Policy iDevices.

4. Optionally provide a description.

5. Select all the mobile platforms from the Available Devices side, and click the **>** to move them to the Assigned Policies side.

6. Click **Submit**.

Figure 13-29 shows the iDevices Logical Profile.

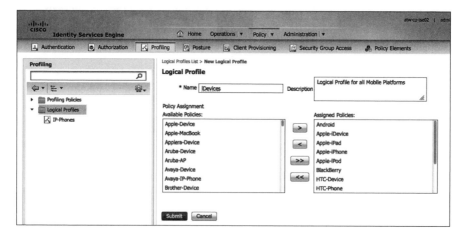

Figure 13-29   *iDevices Logical Profile*

Finally, it is now time to create the authorization rule:

1. Navigate to **Policy > Authorization**.

2. Insert a new rule above the default rule.

3. Name the Rule Employee iDevices.

4. Select the **+** sign for conditions, and select **Endpoints > LogicalProfile**.

5. Choose **Equals**.

6. Select **iDevices**.

7. Click the cog on the right-hand side > **Add Attribute/Value**.

8. Select **AD1 > External Groups Equals "Employees"** (or another AD group of your choosing).

9. For the AuthZ Profiles, click the **+** sign.

10. Select **Standard > Internet Only**.

11. Click **Done**.

12. Click **Save**.

The completed authorization rule is displayed in Figure 13-30.

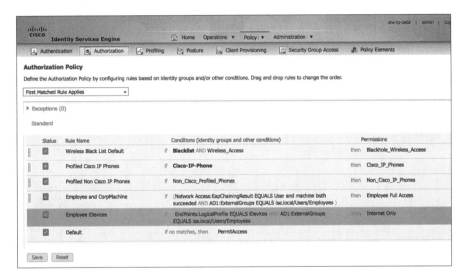

Figure 13-30   *Employee iDevices Authorization Rule*

Employee Limited Access Rule

Now the rule for employees connecting with mobile devices is created, you need to create the rule below it that provides limited access only to employee authentications on any other device.

To begin this rule, first create a new DACL that is applied to switches, create the authorization result, and then go back into the Authorization Policy and build the rule:

1. Navigate to **Policy > Policy Elements > Results > Authorization > Downloadable ACLs.**

2. Click **Add**.

3. Name the ACL Employee Limited.

4. Optionally provide a description.

5. Within DACL Content, provide an ACL that permits required traffic and denies traffic destined to the corporate network. For this example, allow traffic to reach our virtual desktop infrastructure and essential services, like DNS only.

Figure 13-31 shows the Employee Limited dACL.

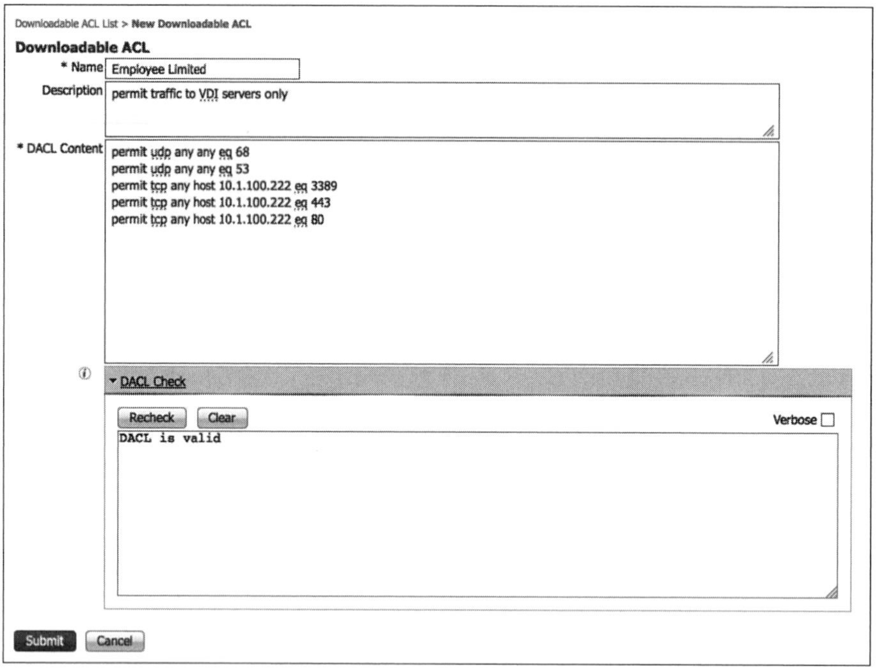

Figure 13-31 *Employee Limited DACL*

6. Click **Submit**.

Now that the DACL is created, build the Authorization Policy to permit network access and apply that DACL:

1. Navigate to **Policy > Policy Elements > Results > Authorization > Authorization Profiles**.

2. Click **Add**.

3. Name the Authorization Profile Employee Limited.

4. Optionally provide a description.

5. Access Type is ACCESS_ACCEPT.

6. Select **DACL Name** and select **Employee Limited**.

7. Do not assign a different VLAN for this authorization.

8. Select **Airspace ACL Name** and fill in the name of the ACL on the controller that provides Internet-only access.

9. Click **Submit**.

Figure 13-32 shows the completed Authorization Profile.

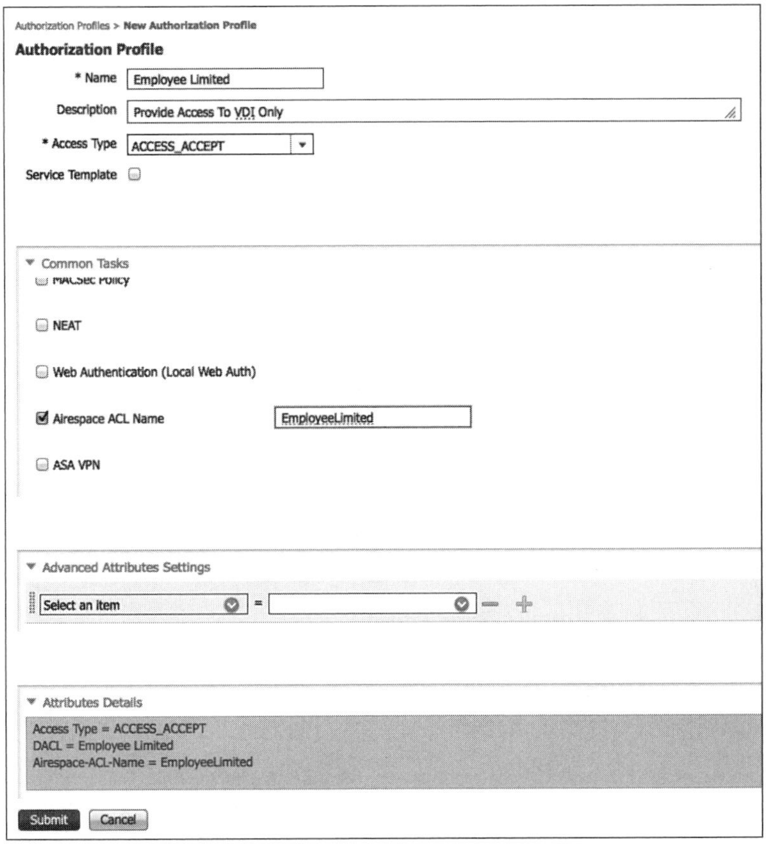

Figure 13-32   *Employee Limited Authorization Profile*

Now, create the Authorization Policy rule to assign that Authorization Profile:

1. Navigate to **Policy > Authorization**.

2. Insert a new rule above the default rule.

3. Name the Rule Employee Limited.

4. Select the **+** sign for conditions.

5. Select **AD1 > External Groups Equals "Employees"** (or another AD group of your choosing).

6. For the AuthZ Profiles, click the **+** sign.

7. Select **Standard > Employee Limited**.

8. Click **Done**.

9. Click **Save**.

Figure 13-33 shows the completed Employee Limited authorization rule.

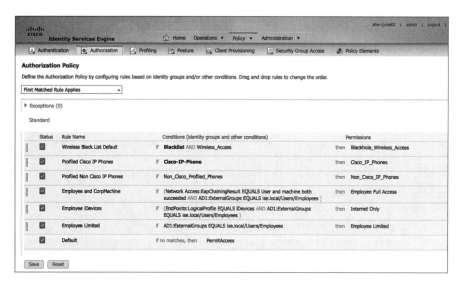

Figure 13-33   *Employee Limited Authorization Rule*

Saving Attributes for Re-Use

ISE offers the ability to save conditions to the library to make it much easier to reuse them in other policies. To show this, let's go back into your example Authorization Policy and save a few of the conditions.

From the ISE GUI, perform the following steps:

1. Navigate to **Policy > Authorization**.

2. Edit the Employee and CorpMachine rule.

3. Expand the conditions.

4. Click **Add All Conditions Below to Library**, as shown in Figure 13-34.

   This is adding the full set of conditions, including the AND operator.

Figure 13-34 *Add All Conditions Below to Library*

5. Provide a name for this new saved condition, such as EmployeeFullEAPChain.

6. Finish editing the rule.

7. Click **Save**.

As shown in Figure 13-35, the Authorization Policy text is simplified now with the name of the saved conditions instead of the raw attributes.

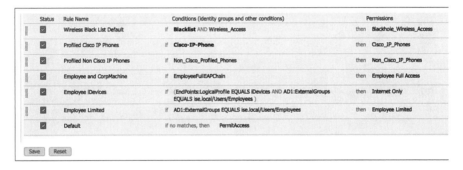

Figure 13-35 *Authorization Policy After Saving Conditions to Library*

Next, save the Employees group for AD as a condition:

1. Navigate to **Policy > Authorization**.

2. Edit the **Employee iDevices Rule**.

3. Expand the conditions.

4. Click the cog on the right-hand side of the Employees line.

5. Choose **Add Condition to Library**.

6. Name the condition Employees.

7. Click the green check mark.

Figure 13-36 displays the saving of Employees to the Conditions library.

Figure 13-36   *Saving Employees to Library*

  8. Click **Done** to finish editing the rule.

  9. Click **Save**.

  Figure 13-37 shows the final Authorization Policy.

	Status	Rule Name		Conditions (identity groups and other conditions)		Permissions
	☑	Wireless Black List Default	if	**Blacklist** AND Wireless_Access	then	Blackhole_Wireless_Access
	☑	Profiled Cisco IP Phones	if	**Cisco-IP-Phone**	then	Cisco_IP_Phones
	☑	Profiled Non Cisco IP Phones	if	Non_Cisco_Profiled_Phones	then	Non_Cisco_IP_Phones
	☑	Employee and CorpMachine	if	EmployeeFullEAPChain	then	Employee Full Access
	☑	Employee iDevices	if	(EndPoints:LogicalProfile EQUALS iDevices AND Employees)	then	Internet Only
	☑	Employee Limited	if	AD1:ExternalGroups EQUALS ise.local/Users/Employees	then	Employee Limited
	☑	Default	if no matches, then	PermitAccess		

Save   Reset

Figure 13-37   *Final Authorization Policy*

Summary

This chapter examined the relationship between authentication and authorization and how to build policies for each. It described a few common Authentication Policies and Authorization Policies to help solidify your knowledge of how to work with these policy constructs. Chapters 20 to 23 focus on specific configurations of these policies to help in the actual deployment of ISE and the Secure Unified Access Solution.

Chapter 14, "Guest Lifecycle Management," examines web authentication, guest access, and the full lifecycle management of guest users.

Chapter 14

Guest Lifecycle Management

Cisco Identity Services Engine (ISE) provides a complete solution for guest network access. A guest is defined as someone who needs temporary and restricted access to your network. This is usually a visitor or temporary contractor. The access provided to guests is usually limited to Internet access. But, as you will learn, this can be opened up or closed down as you see fit. Guest sponsors, employees that have the rights to create guest accounts, typically create and distribute guest username/passwords to their visitors. This is a common function of the front-desk receptionist who already has the job of checking in visitors. As visitors arrive, the receptionist checks them in and provides them with guest access while they are there if required.

ISE guest services support both wired and wireless access methods. Guest authentication takes two general forms: non-authenticated guest and authenticated guest. Non-authenticated guest provides just a web redirect to a guest portal page and allows the guest to click through to gain access. Authenticated guest requires the guest to enter a username and password on the guest portal page before allowing access to the network. Regardless, guest services are provided via a web authentication (auth) method that requires the guest use a browser to connect. ISE has two deployment modes available: Central Web Auth and Local Web Auth. Table 14-1 shows the differences.

Table 14-1 *Central Versus Local Web Authentication*

Local Web Auth (LWA)	Central Web Auth (CWA)
Web pages are delivered by the network device.	Web pages are redirected to ISE and delivered by ISE centrally.
Guest authentication is achieved by the network device.	Guest authentication is handled by ISE.
Does not allow/support CoA.	Allows/supports CoA. This allows posture and profiling services for guests. It also allows VLAN enforcement.

Local Web Auth (LWA)	Central Web Auth (CWA)
Authorization enforcement uses ACLs only.	Authorization enforcement uses ACLs and VLANs.
Requires complete local Web Auth configuration on each NAD (switch or WLC).	Configuration for Web Auth is achieved in ISE.
Each device has its own web portal files, web server, customization, etc.	Web portals and portal customization is achieved inside of ISE centrally.

As you have probably already deduced, Central Web Auth is by far the most popular and easiest method. In almost all cases, you want to deploy CWA. As a result, most of this chapter focuses on CWA with limited Local Web Authentication (LWA) discussion. The one drawback of CWA is that it requires certain minimum code versions to be deployed to participating Cisco switches and WLCs. Check the ISE release notes on Cisco.com for the latest versions required.

Figure 14-1 shows the local Web Authentication flow.

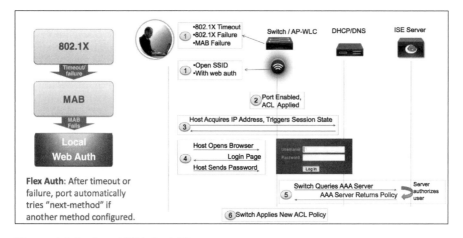

Figure 14-1   *Local Web Auth Flow*

Figure 14-2 shows the flow for central Web Authentication.

The ISE guest services are available using the basic ISE license. If you decide to use posture or profiling for guests, then standard additional licensing applies. The ISE policy services node type runs the guest services and web portal services.

Cisco ISE provides several methods of guest access. There are non-authenticated guest and authenticated guest options. Non-auth guest is useful when you just want to provide your visitors with a hassle free way to obtain access to the Internet. It typically involves a custom guest portal page that shows your acceptable use policy and provides a button they click to get on the network.

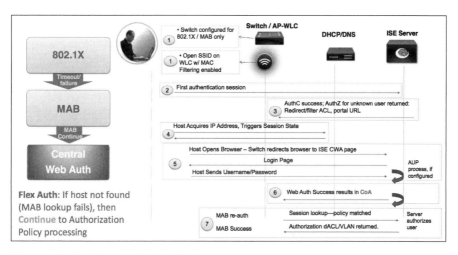

Figure 14-2 *Central Web Auth Flow*

Authenticated guest access requires all guests to have a username and password to gain access. These credentials are created by a guest sponsor who is typically an employee or receptionist of the company. The sponsor can select the access rights, time duration, and several other authorization guest privileges when creating the guest account. Cisco ISE also supports the creation of mass numbers of guest accounts quickly. This is useful for conferences, large meetings, and so on. In addition, ISE also supports self-service guest services similar to what you'd find at a café.

Guest Portal Configuration

Cisco ISE provides three types of guest end-user web portals that you can customize: Guest, Sponsor, and Device Registration Portals. These portals run on the ISE Policy Services nodes in your network. Here is a brief description of each portal type used for guests:

- **Guest Web Portal:** All visitors are redirected to this portal. ISE supports the creation of multiple guest portals that are selected based on criteria you specify. For example, a portal for long-term contractors is different from a visitor guest portal.

- **Sponsor Web Portal:** This is the location where your guest sponsors can create the accounts for guest users. From here, sponsors can send account details to their visitors via email, printing, or SMS. All guest account management is handled using the sponsor web portal.

- **Device Registration Portal:** This portal allows guests to obtain network access without a username or password. The guest is presented with a registration page which typically includes an AUP that they must accept. Once accepted, they are permitted access.

Configuring Identity Source(s)

The first step in configuring ISE for guest services is to define how ISE authenticates its users. ISE guest services includes two special kinds of user accounts: sponsors and guests. You define the access privileges and feature support for sponsors inside of ISE. Then, sponsors use the sponsor portal to create guest user accounts. Here are the steps to setup your identity sources:

1. If not already completed, create an Active Directory identity store. AD is the most popular ID store for sponsors, but it is possible to skip this step and use RADIUS or internal ISE users instead.

2. Go to **Administration** > **Identity Management** > **External Identity Sources** > **Active Directory**.

3. Configure and Join ISE to your Active Directory.

4. Choose or create a group in AD that will be used to specify who is a sponsor. For example, create a group called ISE Guest Sponsors and add the members you want to be sponsors. Select and add that group to ISE, as shown in Figure 14-3.

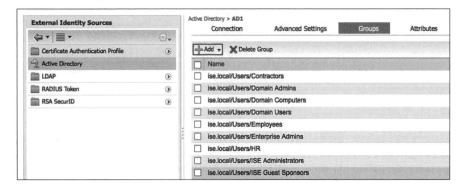

Figure 14-3   *AD Group for Sponsors*

5. Configure an Identity Source Sequence that includes AD. Go to **Administration** > **Identity Management** > **Identity Source Sequences**. Notice a built-in group called Sponsor_Portal_Sequence, as shown in Figure 14-4. Edit that group. Figure 14-5 depicts adding AD into the group and making it the first choice in the list followed by local ISE users. Local users can be used for sponsored guest accounts.

System
Identity Management
Network Resources
Web Portal Management
Feed Service
Identities
Groups
External Identity Sources
Identity Source Sequences
Settings
Identity Source Sequences
Edit
Add
Duplicate
Delete
Name
Description
Identity Stores
ALL_ID_Stores
CAP,Guest Users,Internal Users,AD1,Internal Endpoints
Guest_Portal_Sequence
A Built-in Identity Sequence For The Guest Portal
Internal Users,Guest Users,AD1
MyDevices_Portal_Sequence
A Built-in Identity Sequence For The My Devices Portal
AD1,Internal Users,Guest Users
Sponsor_Portal_Sequence
A built-in Identity Sequence for the Sponsor Portal
Internal Users,Guest Users

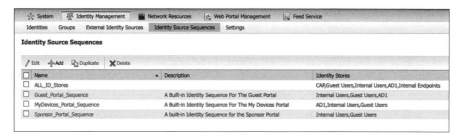

Figure 14-4 *Sponsor Portal Sequence List*

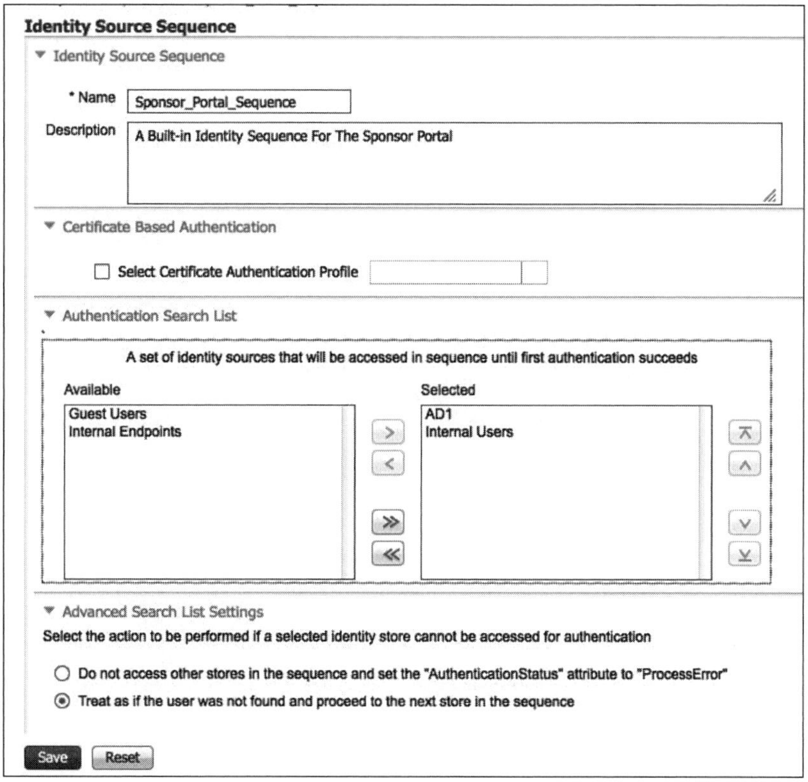

Identity Source Sequence
Identity Source Sequence
* Name
Sponsor_Portal_Sequence
Description
A Built-in Identity Sequence For The Sponsor Portal
Certificate Based Authentication
Select Certificate Authentication Profile
Authentication Search List
A set of identity sources that will be accessed in sequence until first authentication succeeds
Available
Guest Users
Internal Endpoints
Selected
AD1
Internal Users
Advanced Search List Settings
Select the action to be performed if a selected identity store cannot be accessed for authentication
Do not access other stores in the sequence and set the "AuthenticationStatus" attribute to "ProcessError"
Treat as if the user was not found and proceed to the next store in the sequence
Save
Reset

Figure 14-5 *Sponsor Portal Sequence Edit*

6. Apply the ID sequence as your sponsor authentication source. Go to **Administration > Web Portal Management > Settings > Sponsor > Authentication Source.** Select your sequence.

Guest Sponsor Configuration

This section covers the sponsored guest configuration of ISE.

Guest Time Profiles

If you are using time profiles for your guest accounts, you need to create them before your sponsor groups. Time profiles provide different levels of time access to different guest accounts. Sponsors must assign a time profile to a guest when creating an account, but they cannot make changes to the time profiles themselves. An ISE administrator does that. ISE has three built-in time profiles:

■ **DefaultEightHours:** Valid for 8 hours from guest account creation

■ **DefaultFirstLoginEight:** Valid for 8 hours from first guest login

■ **DefaultStartEnd:** Allows the sponsor to input the start and end time for the guest account

To add a custom time profile, go to **Administration > Web Portal Management > Settings > Guest > Time Profiles** and click **Add**. Fill out the desired information (see Figure 14-6 for an example).

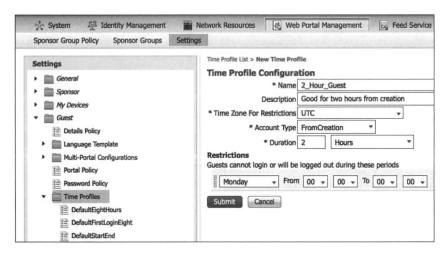

Figure 14-6   *Guest Time Profile*

There are three account types to choose from:

■ **StartEnd:** The sponsor specifies the start and end time upon guest account creation.

■ **FromCreation:** Sets a time period, such as 2 hours, that starts to count down as soon as the guest account is created. This is the most popular type.

- **FromFirstLogin:** Sets a time period, such as 2 hours, that starts to count down as soon as the guest users log in. This account type is less popular, given you could end up with a lot of active guest accounts that could be used at any moment or accumulated by visitors.

Time profiles also allow for **Restrictions.** Guests cannot log in or will be logged out during these restriction periods. You can have more than one line here; just click the gear icon to add more lines. A typical restriction would be disallowing weekends from Friday 6 to Monday 6. Another common use is to create restrictions that match allowed visitor hours or that match the receptionist hours.

Guest Sponsor Groups

Guest Sponsor configuration is accomplished in two parts. First, create the sponsor groups and then create the sponsor group policies. There are three built-in sponsor groups:

- **SponsorAllAccounts:** The super-admin group equivalent for sponsors. It allows a sponsor in this group to manage all guest accounts in the ISE network.

- **SponsorGroupGrpAccounts:** Sponsors can manage guest accounts from other sponsors in the same sponsor group.

- **SponsorGroupOwnAccounts:** Sponsors can manage only the guest accounts that they have created.

To create a new sponsor group, go to **Administration > Web Portal Management > Sponsor Groups** and click **Add.** Next, perform the following steps:

1. On the **General** tab, enter a descriptive name and description.

2. Set the Authorization Levels of the sponsor (see Figure 14-7). This list represents the options that will be available to the sponsor when he creates a guest account. Figure 14-7 shows the most common settings that would be given to a normal employee sponsor. Some of the bulk creation activities, time frames for account, ability to modify only their own guest accounts, etc., have been paired down to meet, but not exceed, the needs of most employees with visitors.

3. Assign the guest roles that the sponsor can set a guest account to. These roles are then used in ISE authorization rules to determine guest privileges on the network. Figure 14-8 shows guest and contractor roles allowed to be selected. You can create roles under **Administration > Identity Management > Groups.**

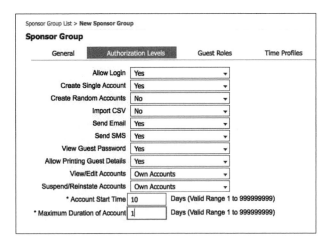

Figure 14-7   *Guest Sponsor Group: Authorization Levels*

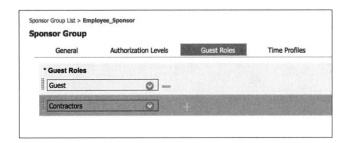

Figure 14-8   *Guest Sponsor Group: Guest Roles*

  4. Associate the time profiles that are available to sponsors creating guest accounts. Figure 14-9 shows an example where only 2-hour or 8-hour guest accounts can be created by these sponsors.

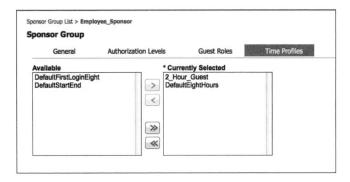

Figure 14-9   *Guest Sponsor Group – Time Profiles*

  5. Click **Save** when done.

Sponsor Group Policies

Sponsor group policies enable you to map identity groups to sponsor privilege groups you created in the previous section. Go to **Administration > Web Portal Management > Sponsor Group Policy**. Notice three default polices. All default policies rely on using the ISE internal user and group database. If you are using an external ID source, such as Active Directory, you need to create new policies. To add a new policy, click **Actions > Insert New Policy**. Follow these steps:

1. Configure a descriptive name for your policy, such as employee sponsors.

2. Leave identity group to the default of Any.

3. Select **other conditions** drop-down, and then select **Create New Condition**.

4. Select your Active Directory server from the list (for example, AD1).

5. Select **External Groups Equals <AD Group>**. Select an AD group you want to match on, such as ISE Guest Sponsors. Figure 14-10 shows an example condition.

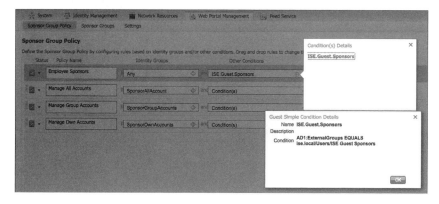

Figure 14-10   *Guest Sponsor Group Policies - Conditions*

6. If this is a condition you plan to use again, save it. Select the gear icon, and then **Add condition to library**. Provide a name, no spaces, for this condition. Select the green check mark to save and add it to the ISE library. You can now use this condition again under **Add Condition from Library**.

7. Select the sponsor group. Click **Save**. Figure 14-11 shows a final policy.

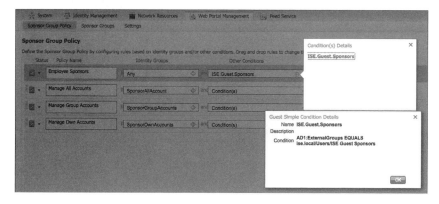

Figure 14-11   *Guest Sponsor Group Policy*

Authentication and Authorization Guest Policies

ISE now needs to be set up for guest Authentication and Authorization Policies. Given that Centralized Web Auth guest using MAC Authentication Bypass (MAB) to trigger the guest process, you need to ensure that it is configured correctly. Go to **Policy > Authentication**. You should see a MAB rule that is identical to the rule in Figure 14-12. If you don't see one, create one.

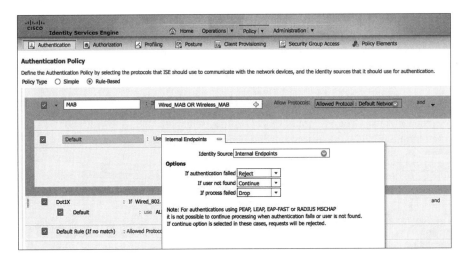

Figure 14-12   *Guest MAB Authentication Rule.*

One modification to the default rule, or your custom rule, is required for guest webauth to operate correctly. Edit the MAB rule and select **Internal Endpoints**. Now, set **If User Not Found** to **Continue**. Click **Done** and **Save**. Refer to Figure 14-12 for details.

Guest Pre-Authentication Authorization Policy

If needed, refer to Figure 14-2 for a refresher on the central Web Auth flow. After successful Web Authentication by the guest, ISE sends a CoA to the network access device. The endpoint is then re-authenticated. This authentication results in a session lookup that now matches a policy. That policy is matched in an authorization rule in ISE, and the configured permissions are then deployed to the NAD.

You need to configure an Authorization Policy that matches the first time a guest connects to the network and before he is authenticated. This is the unknown user or no matches catch all policy, as shown at the bottom of Figure 14-13. Its purpose is to initiate central Web Authentication via URL redirection of the guest to the ISE guest portal.

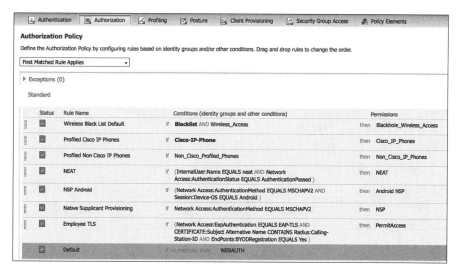

Figure 14-13 *Default Authorization Policy: Web Auth*

The group **WEBAUTH**, shown in Figure 14-13, is a custom Authorization Profile. Here is how you can create your own:

1. Go to **Policy > Policy Elements > Results > Authorization > Downloadable ACLs**. Click **Add**. Here, you will create a pre-auth ACL to limit network traffic that can flow during the guest authentication process. Create an ACL, as shown in Figure 14-14. Click **Submit**.

Note Downloadable ACLs (dACL) are not supported on Cisco Wireless LAN Controllers. Configure an Airespace ACL name instead and preposition the ACL on the WLC:

```
permit udp any any eq bootps
permit udp any any eq domain
permit tcp any any eq domain
remark ping for troubleshooting
permit icmp any any echo
permit icmp any any echo-reply
remark allow web traffic to kick off redirect
permit tcp any any eq www
permit tcp any any eq 443
remark VERY IMPORTANT: 10.1.100.232 is the ISE PSN for Guest Portal
permit tcp any host 10.1.100.232 eq 8443
permit tcp any host 10.1.100.232 eq 8905
permit tcp any host 10.1.100.232 eq 8909
permit udp any host 10.1.100.232 range 8905 8906
permit udp any host 10.1.100.232 eq 8909
```

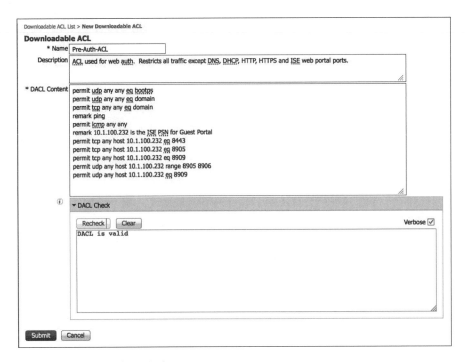

Figure 14-14 *Web Auth dACL*

Port 8443 is used by the ISE guest portal:

Ports 8905 and 8906 are used by NAC Agent Swiss protocol.

Port 8909 is used for client provisioning activity.

If deploying for wireless guest, be sure to enable the Airespace ACL Name as part of your policy. ISE will call the ACL that is configured on the WLC. It does not download the ACL. See Figure 14-15 for an example.

2. Go to **Policy** > **Policy Elements** > **Results** > **Authorization** > **Authorization Policies**. Click **Add**.

3. Provide a descriptive name and description. Under **Common Tasks**, select your DACL name, as shown in Figure 14-15. The DACL will be downloaded to the NAD by ISE.

4. Set up Web Authentication as shown in Figure 14-16. The ACL name needs to match perfectly with the ACL already on the switch/WLC. ISE will NOT download this ACL to the NAD.

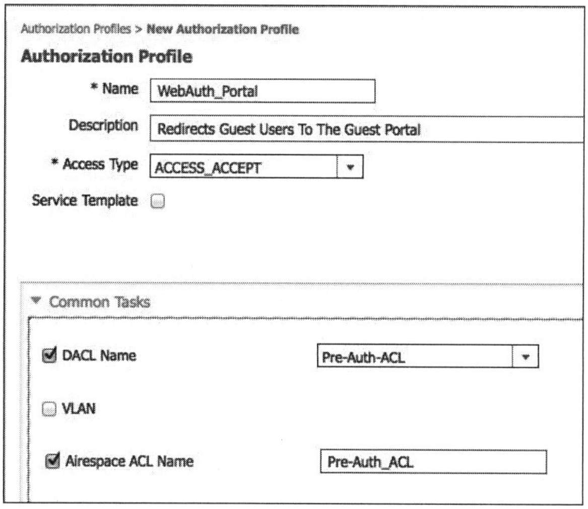

Figure 14-15 *WebAuth Authorization Profile: dACL and Airespace ACL*

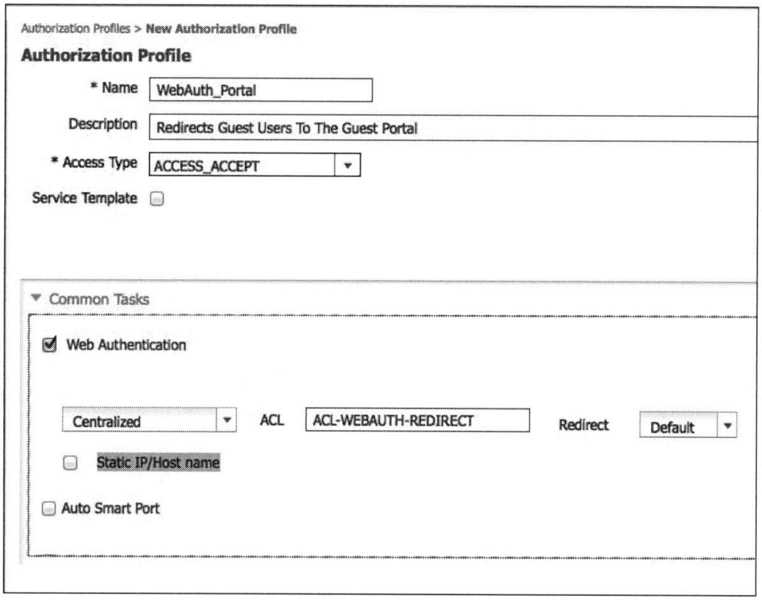

Figure 14-16 *WebAuth Authorization Profile: Web Authentication*

The contents of ACL-WEBAUTH-REDIRECT should include the following (10.1.100.232=ISE PSN):

```
ip access-list extended ACL-WEBAUTH-REDIRECT
    deny ip any host 10.1.100.232
    permit tcp any any eq www
```

```
     permit tcp any any eq 443
     permit tcp any any eq 8443
remark be sure to include any proxy ports you have enabled
     permit tcp any any eq 8080
```

Any ACL statement with a permit forces a URL redirect. This ACL does NOT permit and deny traffic, it only defines what ports kick off a URL redirect.

5. Add your newly created authorization profile to the default, if no matches, Authorization Policy rule. Go to **Policy > Authorization**. Click **Edit** on the last rule in the list called **Default**. Select your webauth_portal policy, like Figure 14-17. Click **Done** and **Save**.

Figure 14-17 *WebAuth Authorization Profile – Web Authentication*

Guest Post-Authentication Authorization Policy

Once the guest successfully authenticates using their guest account credentials, ISE issues a Change of Authorization (CoA) request to the NAD. This time, the MAB session lookup matches. You need to configure an Authorization Policy in ISE to set the guest permissions you want to allow. Go to **Policy > Authorization**, click the down-arrow icon Edit | ▼, as shown in Figure 14-18, select *insert new rule*, and follow these steps shown next.

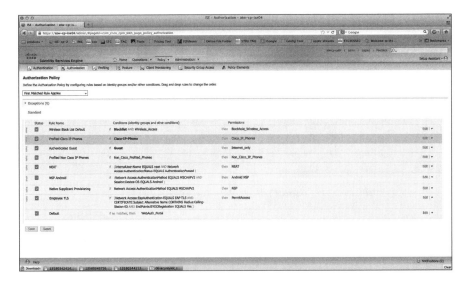

Figure 14-18 *Guest Authorization Policy Example*

Follow these steps to create an authorization rule:

1. Enter a descriptive rule name, such as Authenticated Guest.

2. Select the identity group **Guest**. Remember this identity group must match the Guest role that the sponsor assigned to the guest account upon its creation. If you have multiple guest roles, you need to create multiple authorization rules. Each rule provides different permissions to the guest.

3. Assign the permissions, such as Internet only. You can pick from your list of Authorization Profiles or create a new one by clicking the gear icon and selecting **Add new standard profile**. The most common permission elements are DACL and VLAN settings. Figure 14-19 shows an example.

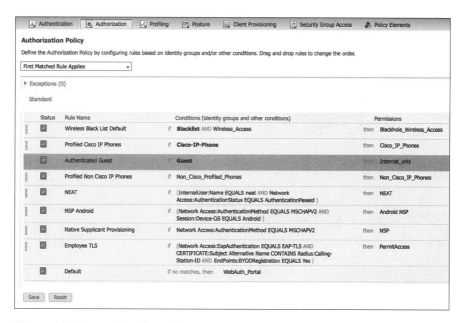

Figure 14-19 *WebAuth Authorization Profile: Guest*

Remember that authorization rules, by default, are processed top-down first match. Be sure that your guest rules are in the appropriate order. One of the most common issues with guest policies is ordering incorrectly.

Guest Sponsor Portal Configuration

It is the sponsor's obligation to create guest accounts for authorized visitors that need limited network or Internet-only connectivity while onsite. The sponsor portal is where sponsors can create, send, and manage guest accounts. You need to configure the sponsor portal to allow sponsors to create guest accounts.

Set up the method that you will use to authenticate your sponsors against. This was covered previously and is here for a refresher. In most cases, Active Directory is used. Go to **Administration > Web Portal Management > Settings > Sponsor > Authentication Source**.

Guest Portal Interface and IP Configuration

It is a best practice to configure your guest portal on its own ISE physical interface with its own IP address. This drastically reduces the security risk of an ISE compromise. Separating the Admin portal from the guest portal provides some of this added security. You can specify the port used for each web portal, allowing you to use different ports for the end-user portals, such as

- Sponsor
- Guest (also client provisioning)
- My Device
- Blacklist

The Blacklist portal should be kept all alone on its own interface with its own IP address. This is also true for the Admin configuration portal, which always uses Ethernet0 and a default port of https/443. Go to **Administration > Web Portal Management > Settings > General > Ports**.

Sponsor and Guest Portal Customization

The ISE sponsor portal can be completely customized to fit your organizations needs. Every button, label, icon, and text can be customized.

Customize the Sponsor Portal

You should customize the guest notifications that are available to the sponsors. There are three ways you can send guests their credentials: email, SMS, and printing. Go to **Administration > Web Portal Management > Settings > Sponsor > Language Template**. Choose the language you want to configure (for example, English). Notice the countless options that you can customize. They are broken up into sections; click a section to see the options. Click **Configure Email Notifications**. Here, you can customize the email template that is sent to guest users when their account is created by a sponsor. Figure 14-20 shows an example.

Configuring SMS text messaging is also straightforward; just click **Configure SMS Text Message Notification**. Enter a custom subject and enter the SMS server's destination address. This must be an SMS-equipped email server and email address.

You can also customize your printer template for printing guest accounts. Go to **Configure Print Notification** and customize the fields.

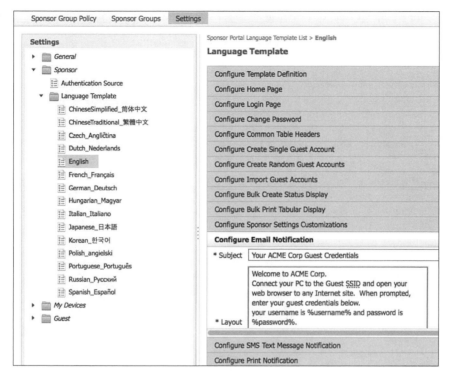

Figure 14-20 *Guest Email Notification*

Creating a Simple URL for Sponsor Portal

To make life easier, it is common to configure a simple URL for the Sponsor Portal page. You can specify a FQDN URL that automatically resolves to the sponsor portal. This is also available for the myDevices portal. To configure a simple URL, go to **Administration > Web Portal Management > Settings > General > Ports**. Check the portal you want and enter the simple URL. For example, https://sponsors.acme.com. Be sure to configure the network DNS server so that it resolves the FQDN to the sponsor portal IP address. Once you click **Save**, the node automatically restarts so the changes take effect.

Note Ensure that any ISE Policy Service node certificates you have also include this FQDN in their **Subject Alternative Name**. This prevents certificate-mismatch warnings from popping up on the sponsor's browser.

Guest Portal Customization

The customization for the guest portal is similar to the customization for the sponsor portal. Go to **Administration > Web Portal Management > Settings > Guest > Language Templates** and select the language to customize, that is, English. Almost every button, label, and text can be customized to meet your needs. Just select the portal section and customize the fields. Figure 14-21 shows an example of customizing the Guest Acceptable Use Policy.

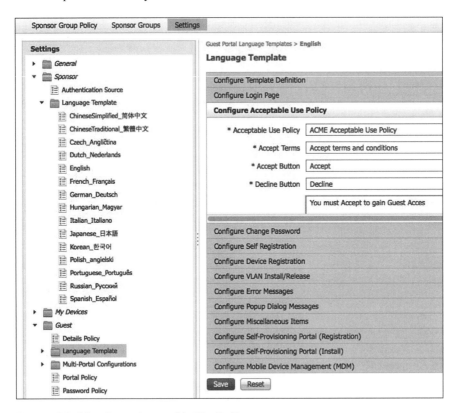

Figure 14-21   *Guest Acceptable Use Policy*

Customizing Portal Theme

The portal theme sets the colors and graphics for all the web portals inside of ISE: Guest portal, My Device portal, Sponsor portal, and so on. Only one theme is available inside of ISE.

Go to **Administration > Web Portal Management > Settings > General > Portal Theme**. Figure 14-22 shows the various options available.

As shown in Figure 14-22, you can upload your own logos and images. Just choose the drop-down and select **Upload New File**. It uploads files from your local PC. To view your changes, open your browser to https://<ip of ISE PSN>:8443/sponsorportal/. Here are some of the tips for getting your theme right:

■ Upload a .jpeg, .gif, or .png image file to use as the logo on the portal Login page for the Guest, Sponsor, and My Devices portals.

- When you upload an image, it is automatically resized to fit an image size required for that area. (See ISE help for details on image sizes.) To avoid distortion, resize your image to fit these dimensions:

  - Login logo and Banner logo image size of 86 pixels (width) by 45 pixels (height).

  - Login Background Image image size is 533 pixels (width) by 325 pixels (height).

  - Banner Background image size is 133 pixels (height). The width is not controlled, and the banner background color displays to fill the remaining area.

- The post-login banner displays for 15 seconds on the Sponsor and My Device portal and does not apply to the Guest portal.

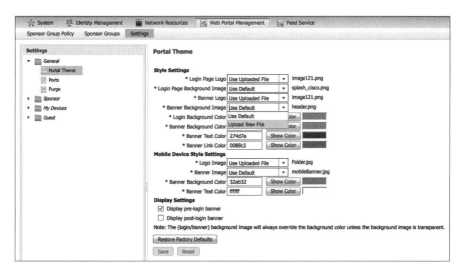

Figure 14-22 *Portal Theme*

At the bottom of Figure 14-22, you see two check boxes. These set the pre- and post-login banner messages. Each portal has its own banner message settings. To set them, perform the following:

1. Go to **Administration** > **Web Portal Management** > **Settings** > [replace with portal name, such as Sponsor] > **Language Template**.

2. Select your language.

   - **Sponsor Portal:** Go to Configure Common Items. Update the text in the Pre-Login Banner Text and Post-Login Banner.

   - **Guest or My Device Portal:** Go to Configure Login Page. Update the text in Pre-Login Banner Text and Post-Login Banner Text. Guest does not have a post-login banner.

3. Click **Save**.

Creating Multiple Portals

In some cases, you may want to create multiple portals for different uses. For example, you might have different business groups that each need their own name on the guest portal. Whatever the case might be, here is how you configure multiple portals:

1. Go to **Administration** > **Web Portal Management** > **Settings** > **Guest** > **Multi-Portal Configurations**. Click **Add**.

2. The name you enter becomes a part of your new portal's URL, so be sure to choose all lowercase and keep it short. This name also appears in the captive portal URL specified in the network access device (NAD) for wireless LAN controller (WLC) setups. For example, a portal with the name ClientPortal has the following case-sensitive access URL: https://ipaddress:portnumber/guestportal/portals/ClientPortal/portal.jsp.

3. Select a portal type. Remember that all non-custom portals share the same portal theme, including logos:

   ■ **Default Portal:** To customize, you choose a custom language template you have created. The easiest way to do this is to duplicate an existing language template and modify it for your use. Keep the browser local setting blank unless you are creating a language template that isn't built-in already.

   ■ **Device Web Authorization Portal:** Works the same as default portal type.

   ■ **Custom Default Portal:** Allows you to upload the complete HTML to create a customized Guest portal. You must create the complete site when you do this.

   ■ **Custom Device Web Authorization Portal:** Works the same as custom default portal.

4. Click **Operations**. As shown in Figure 14-23, you can set many options here. Select the ones you want for your new portal.

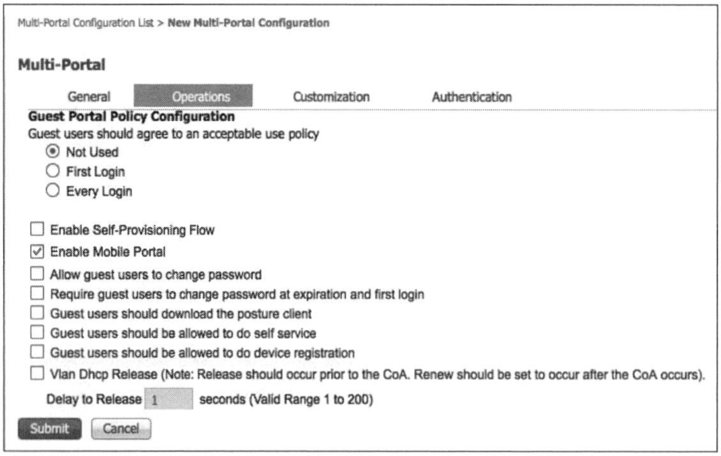

Figure 14-23   *Multi-Portal Operations*

5. As shown in Figure 14-24, select **Customization** and your customized language template.

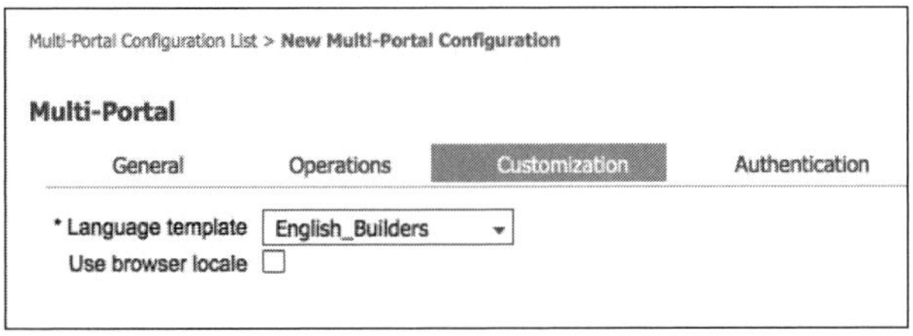

Figure 14-24 *Multi-Portal Customization*

6. Click the **Authentication** tab, as shown in Figure 14-25. Here, you set the type of user database you want to portal to authenticate against. If you choose guest, only the ISE internal guest user database will be used. If you choose Central Web Auth, the identity store sequence you choose will be followed. If you choose both, the internal guest DB will be used first and the identity store sequence next. If you plan to use the My Device portal as well, you must choose both.

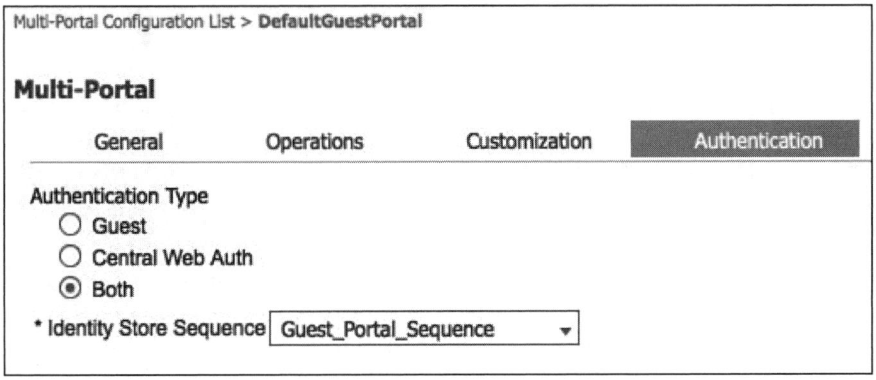

Figure 14-25 *Multi-Portal Authentication*

7. Click **Save**.

These steps show you how to use the new portal you just created:

1. Go to **Policy** > **Policy Elements** > **Results** > **Authorization** > **Authorization Profiles**. Click **Add**.

2. Under common tasks, assign a Web Authentication policy with a manual redirect to your new portal, as shown in Figure 14-26.

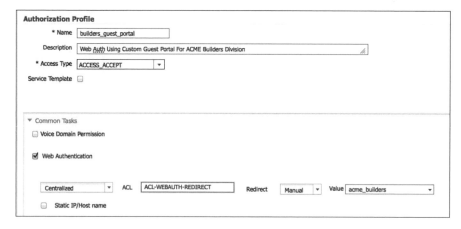

Figure 14-26   *Multi-Portal Authorization Element*

3. Fill in any other common tasks, like dACL or Airespace ACL. When done, click **Submit.**

4. Now you have to use it in an Authorization Policy rule. Go to **Policy > Authorization.** Add a new rule at the bottom, right above the default rule.

5. Select the conditions for which you want the new guest portal selected. Include a condition that matches MAB for wired and/or wireless. Also include a condition for endpoint=unknown. Then, add in other conditions where you want the portal to be used. Figure 14-27 shows an example using the location of the NAD device.

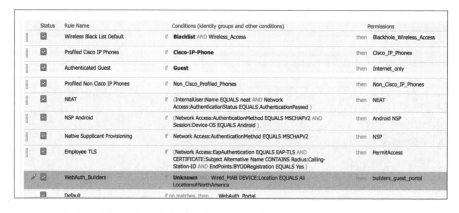

Figure 14-27   *Multi-Portal Authorization Rule*

Guest Sponsor Portal Usage

This section explains the usage of the Sponsor portal. The main topics addressed are

- Portal Layout
- Creating Guest Accounts
- Managing Guest Accounts

Sponsor Portal Layout

To access the ISE Sponsor portal, open your browser to https://ISE_guest_ip_address:8443/sponsorportal.

Notice the Sponsor login page, along with any customization you have made to the portal. Figure 14-28 shows an example sponsor login page.

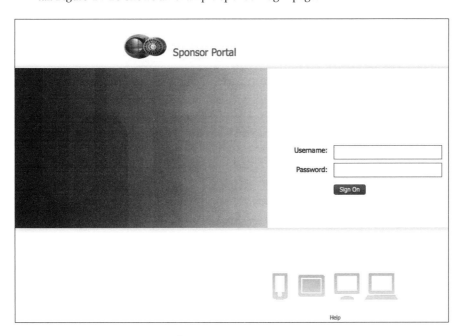

Figure 14-28   *Sponsor Portal Login*

At the bottom of the page is a link to help.

Once logged in, you notice a page similar to Figure 14-29. The options on your screen vary depending on the sponsor privileges you have. Figure 14-28 depicts an account with full sponsor privileges.

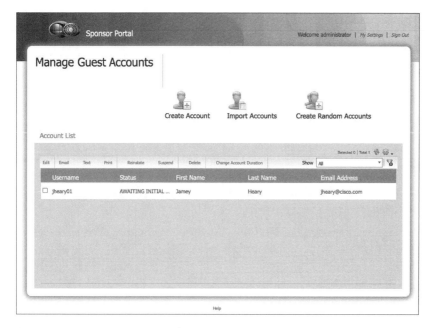

Figure 14-29   *Sponsor Portal*

Review/update your sponsor settings first. Click **My Settings** in the top-right corner.
Set up your email address as a minimum. Figure 14-30 shows the other options you can
change.

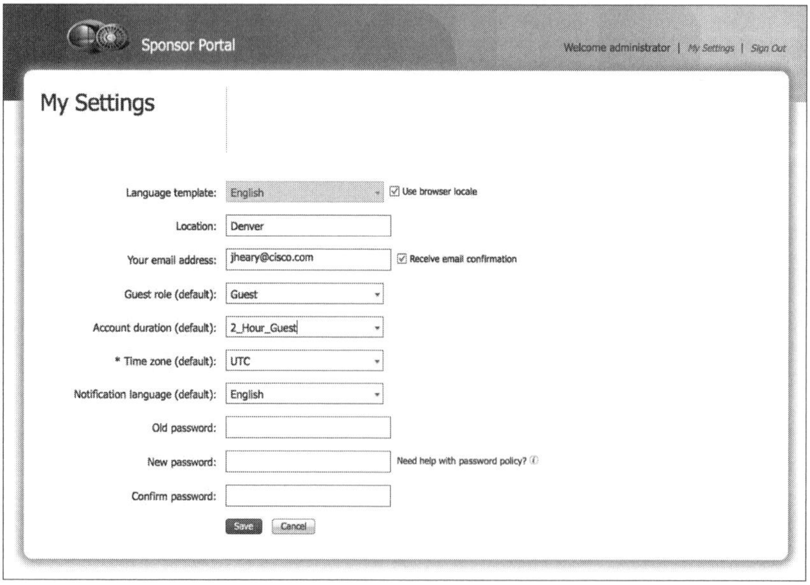

Figure 14-30   *Sponsor Portal: My Settings*

Creating Guest Accounts

There are three ways to create guest accounts:

- **Create Account:** Creates a single guest account.

- **Import Accounts:** Uses an Excel spreadsheet to import multiple accounts. From this option, the spreadsheet template is available for download.

- **Create Random Accounts:** Allows you to quickly generate many guest accounts at once.

To perform one of these options, just click its icon, as shown in Figure 14-31.

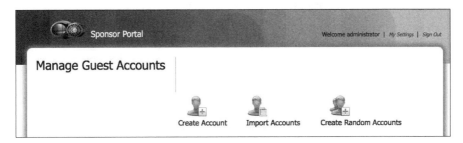

Figure 14-31   *Sponsor Portal: Guest Creation*

Next, fill out the required fields and submit. Finally, select the accounts; you can select multiple accounts by holding the Shift key, and then selecting the notification method of print, email, or text.

The Account list can be filtered by clicking the drop-down next to show and selecting **Advanced Filter**. You can then create a custom filter.

Managing Guest Accounts

Your ability to manage guest accounts depends on the privileges of your sponsor account. You can perform the following actions on an existing guest account:

- Edit

- Notify (email, text, print)

- Reinstate: Actives a previously suspended account

- Suspend

- Delete

- Change account duration

To perform one of the actions, select an account and click the action.

Configuration of Network Devices for Guest CWA

With ISE ready to serve as your centralized Web-Auth source, the next step is to configure your switches and WLCs. This process is straightforward and simple.

Wired Switches

This configuration assumes that you already have the switch configured to communicate with ISE. If not, see Chapter 9, "The Basics: Principal Configuration Tasks for ISE," for details. There are three steps to enabling CWA on your switches:

1. Configure a pre-authentication ACL on the switch. This determines what traffic is allowed to flow before authentication happens. Here is an example ACL:

```
permit udp any any eq bootps
permit udp any any eq domain
permit tcp any any eq domain
remark ping for troubleshooting
permit icmp any any echo
permit icmp any any echo-reply
remark allow web traffic to kick off redirect
permit tcp any any eq www
permit tcp any any eq 443
remark 10.1.100.232 is the ISE PSN for Guest Portal
permit tcp any host 10.1.100.232 eq 8443
permit tcp any host 10.1.100.232 eq 8905
permit tcp any host 10.1.100.232 eq 8909
permit udp any host 10.1.100.232 range 8905 8906
permit udp any host 10.1.100.232 eq 8909
```

2. Configure a redirect ACL on the switch. Any traffic that matches a permit statement is redirected to the guest URL. Here is a sample ACL:

```
ip access-list extended ACL-WEBAUTH-REDIRECT
    deny ip any host 10.1.100.232
    permit tcp any any eq www
    permit tcp any any eq 443
    permit tcp any any eq 8443
remark be sure to include any proxy ports you have enabled
    permit tcp any any eq 8080
```

3. Configure your switch ports for MAB and apply ACLs:

```
interface GigabitEthernet1/0/12
    description ISE1 - dot1x clients - UCS Eth0
    switchport access vlan 100
    switchport mode access
```

```
ip access-group webauth in
authentication order mab
authentication priority mab
authentication port-control auto
mab
spanning-tree portfast
```

You can use the **show auth sess int gi1/12** switch command to see the session information.

Wireless LAN Controllers

Configuring the Cisco WLC for central Web Auth is a three-step process. These steps assume that you already have the basic WLC 7.2+-to-ISE configuration completed. If not, refer to Chapter 9 for more details. Follow these steps to get up and running:

1. Ensure that the RADIUS server has RFC3576 (CoA) enabled, which is by default, as shown in Figure 14-32.

Figure 14-32 *WLC RFC3576*

2. Select or create your guest WLAN and SSID. Edit the WLAN and go to **Security > Layer 2**. Enable **MAC Filtering**, as shown in Figure 14-33.

3. Go to **Security > Layer 3**. Adjust the settings, as shown in Figure 14-34.

4. Go to **Security > AAA Servers**. Add ISE AAA, as shown in Figure 14-35.

5. Go to **Advanced** tab. Enable the settings highlighted, as shown in Figure 14-36.

6. Create the web-redirection ALC. Be sure to use the same name as you used in the ISE configuration authorization profile. Go to **Security > Access Control Lists > Access Control Lists.**

7. Click **Save.**

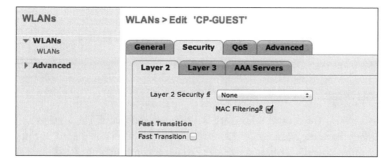

Figure 14-33 *WCL MAC Filtering*

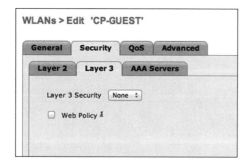

Figure 14-34 *WCL Layer 3*

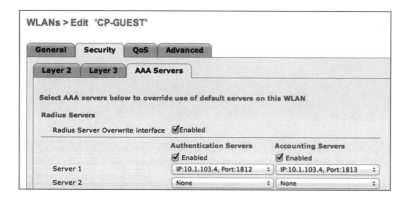

Figure 14-35 *WCL AAA Servers*

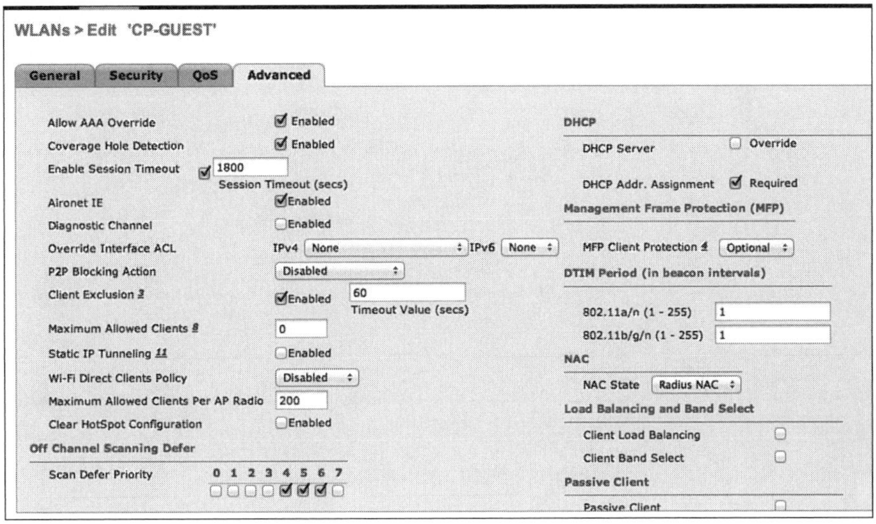

Figure 14-36 *WCL Advanced Tab*

Summary

This chapter focused on creating a robust guest user environment. It covered everything from basic setup to full portal customization. The majority use case covered was centralized Web Authentication. Topics explored in this chapter include

- Guest portals

- Sponsor portals

- Sponsor lifecycle

- Configuration of wired and wireless devices

- Guest authentication

- Portal customization

Chapter 15

Device Posture Assessment

The Cisco Identity Services Engine (ISE) supports posture assessment of clients. Posture assessment allows you to inspect the security "health" of your PC and MAC clients. This includes checking for the installation, running state, and last update for security software, such as anti-virus, anti-malware, personal firewall, and so on. It also ensures the operating systems (OS) are patched appropriately. In addition, ISE posture policies can check for additional custom attributes, like files, processes, registry settings, and applications just to name a few. Taken together, these features provide ISE with the ability to determine the security "health" of a client that is trying to access your network. ISE uses posture policies to determine the access rights and remediation options that should be provided to clients.

Note   ISE posture requires an advanced ISE license.

Here are the high-level steps required to set up the ISE posture assessment feature:

1. Configure global posture settings.

2. Configure the posture agent and client provisioning settings.

3. Configure posture conditions.

4. Configure posture remediation.

5. Configure posture requirements.

6. Configure posture policies.

7. Enable posture assessment in the network.

Figure 15-1 shows the Task Navigator for client provisioning and posture assessment. Use this navigator as a guide during this chapter.

Figure 15-1 *Posture Assessment Tasks*

> **Note**   Table 15-1 depicts a helpful comparison for those that are familiar with Cisco NAC Appliance and how posture assessment works there.

Table 15-1 *Posture Terms Comparison Between NACA and ISE*

NAC Appliance	Description	ISE Equivalent
Checks	AV/AS, file, registry, process, and so on	Conditions
Rules	Groups of checks put together to make a rule	Compound condition
Requirements	Groups of rules and remediation action by the OS	Requirements
Role requirements	Map requirements to roles/policy statements	Posture policy

ISE Posture Assessment Flow

It is important to understand where posture fits in the overall system flow of ISE. Figure 15-2 illustrates the flow that ISE goes through when posture assessment is enabled.

Figures 15-3 and 15-4 depict the flow ISE goes through for an 802.1X end user with posture assessment.

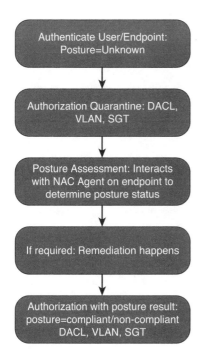

Figure 15-2 *ISE Flow When Posture Assessment Is Enabled*

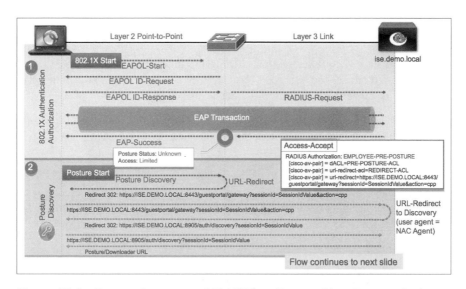

Figure 15-3 *Posture Assessment 802.1X Flow (Source: Cisco Systems, Inc.)*

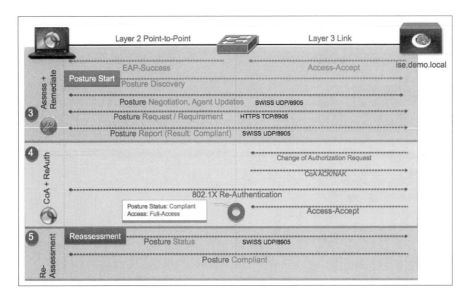

Figure 15-4   *Posture Assessment 802.1X Flow (Source: Cisco Systems, Inc.)*

Here is a brief description of what is happening at each stage (1–5) shown in Figures 15-3 and 15-4:

1. The client 802.1X supplicant talks to the access switch to start 802.1X. The EAP transaction takes place with the switch acting as the proxy between the client and ISE. If the authentication is successful, the posture status is set to *Unknown*.

2. ISE instructs the switch to redirect the client to ISE for downloading the posture NAC agent software or the dissolvable NAC web agent, depending on the policy. If the client already has the agent installed, Step 2 is skipped.

3. Now that the client has a NAC agent, posture assessment proceeds through its flow. The NAC agent uses the Swiss protocol to communicate with ISE. At the end, a posture result is created.

4. ISE sends a change of authorization request to the switch. This triggers an 802.1X re-authentication. A new authorization rule is matched given the new posture status of the client (compliant, non-compliant). The new access rights of the match authorization rule is downloaded to the switch.

5. If periodic reassessment is enabled, the client periodically goes through posture assessment to check for any changes. This happens without affecting the client communication. If the status changes, a CoA is issued and the steps begin anew.

Configure Global Posture and Client Provisioning Settings

In this section, you enable the global settings required to turn on posture assessment. There are two parts: client provisioning setup and posture setup. Client provisioning deals with the NAC agent software, its delivery, and other such settings. Posture setup is responsible for downloading the posture condition database, keeping it up to date, posture reassessment, and other general settings.

Posture Client Provisioning Global Setup

Here are the global steps to configure posture client provisioning. Go to **Administration > Settings > Client Provisioning**. Figure 15-5 shows the various settings available. Before making any changes, ensure that you have your ISE proxy settings configured, if required for your environment.

Figure 15-5 *Global Client Provisioning Settings*

1. Enable client provisioning.

2a. You can optionally enable automatic download. This downloads any and all client files from Cisco.com. Select the exact files you want. This is covered next.

2b. If you choose to enable automatic download, use the default feed URL or set up your own client repository site (covered next).

3. In most cases, keep the default setting for native supplicant policy unavailable.

4. Once you click Save, expect to wait a few minutes while ISE downloads the client files if you selected autodownload.

To select just the client files you need for your environment, go to **Policy > Policy Elements > Results > Client Provisioning > Resources**. This screen shows you all the agents previously downloaded. To add more, click **Add** and select either to add them from Cisco.com or from your local PC. If you select from Cisco.com, you will see a list of available agents and software. Select what you want and click **Save**. The software is downloaded; this can take several minutes, so be patient. Figure 15-6 shows the client provisioning resource screen, and Figure 15-7 shows the Cisco.com software select screen. To see the complete description filed, grab the column separator and drag it larger, similar to what you would do in Excel to make a column wider.

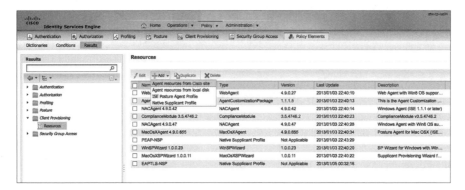

Figure 15-6   *Client Provisioning Resources*

	Name	Type	Version	Description
☑	AgentCustomizationPackage 1.1.1.5	AgentCustomizationPackage	1.1.1.5	This is the Agent Customization Packag
☑	ComplianceModule 3.5.4746.2	ComplianceModule	3.5.4746.2	ComplianceModule v3.5.4746.2
☐	MacOsXAgent 4.9.0.654	MacOsXAgent	4.9.0.654	Posture Agent for Mac OSX (ISE 1.1)
☑	MacOsXAgent 4.9.0.655	MacOsXAgent	4.9.0.655	Posture Agent for Mac OSX (ISE 1.1.1 c
☑	MacOsXSPWizard 1.0.0.11	MacOsXSPWizard	1.0.0.11	Supplicant Provisioning Wizard for Mac
☐	NACAgent 4.9.0.37	NACAgent	4.9.0.37	Windows Agent (ISE 1.0MR only)
☐	NACAgent 4.9.0.37	NACAgent	4.9.0.37	Windows Agent (ISE 1.1 release only)
☐	NACAgent 4.9.0.42	NACAgent	4.9.0.42	Windows Agent (ISE 1.1.1 or later)
☑	NACAgent 4.9.0.47	NACAgent	4.9.0.47	Windows Agent with Win8 OS support (I
☐	WebAgent 4.9.0.20	WebAgent	4.9.0.20	Web Agent (ISE 1.0MR only)
☐	WebAgent 4.9.0.24	WebAgent	4.9.0.24	Web Agent (ISE 1.1.1 or later)
☑	WebAgent 4.9.0.27	WebAgent	4.9.0.27	Web Agent with Win8 OS support (ISE 1
☐	WinSPWizard 1.0.0.22	WinSPWizard	1.0.0.22	Supplicant Provisioning Wizard for Wind
☑	WinSPWizard 1.0.0.23	WinSPWizard	1.0.0.23	SP Wizard for Windows with Win8 OS s

Figure 15-7   *Adding Client Provisioning Resources*

There are three major types of ISE agents for posture assessment:

- NAC agent for Windows
- NAC agent for Macs
- NAC web agent

The NAC web agent is temporal, meaning that it is downloaded temporarily and runs via the web browser ActiveX or Java applet. The NAC web agent is not permanent like the other NAC agents. The Windows and Mac NAC agents install permanently like any other agent software. Here is a list of all the client provisioning resource types:

- Persistent and temporal agents:
    - Windows and Mac OS X Cisco NAC agents
    - Cisco NAC web agent
- Agent profiles
- Agent compliance modules
- Agent customization packages

The following resources are also available, but are not used for ISE posture assessment. They are employed for the provisioning of the clients 802.1X supplicant and are covered in Chapter 16, "Supplicant Configuration."

- Native supplicant profiles
- Native supplicant provisioning/installation wizards

Posture Global Setup

This section steps through the global setup of host posture assessment using ISE.

General Settings

These global settings only take effect if there is not a more specific posture profile in effect.

Go to **Administration > System > Settings > Posture > General Settings**. Figure 15-8 shows the settings.

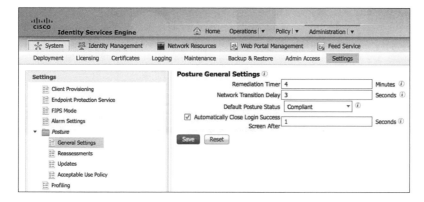

Figure 15-8 *General Posture Settings*

The default posture status provides posture status for non-agent devices (i.e., Linux-based operating systems) and endpoints for which no NAC agent installation policy applies. It is a best practice to enable **Automatically Close Login Success Screen**. This enhances the end-user experience.

Reassessments

If you want to periodically recheck the posture of your endpoints, you can enable it here. It works on a per-user identity group bases or is enabled for all. Figure 15-9 shows the reassessment settings.

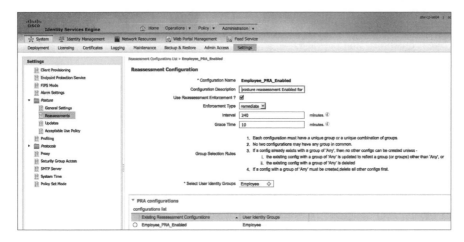

Figure 15-9   *Posture Reassessment*

Ensure that you consider the ramifications of enabling certain enforcement types in your configurations. Enforcement options include continue, logoff, and remediate. As you can see from Figure 15-9, ISE uses the following group selection rules:

1. Each configuration must have a unique group or combination of groups.

2. No two configurations should have any group in common.

3. If a configuration already exists with a group of Any, no other configurations can be created unless

   a. The existing configuration with a group of Any is updated to reflect a group (or groups) other than Any.

   or

   b. The existing configuration with a group of Any is deleted.

4. If a configuration with a group of Any must be created, delete all other configurations first.

Updates

Configure ISE to retrieve posture updates from either Cisco.com or from an internal server you maintain.

In most cases, you should enable **Automatically check for updates.** If this is your first time updating, click the **Update Now** button and ensure it is successful. Figure 15-10 shows the updates settings.

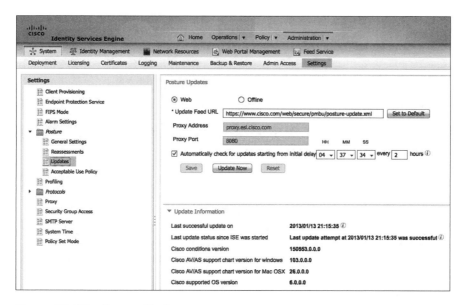

Figure 15-10   *Posture Updates*

Acceptable Use Policy

These settings apply to NAC agents. This Acceptable Use Policy (AUP) does not apply to guest users; use guest portal settings instead. The configuration is group based like the posture reassessment. If AUP is enabled for a group, users see a pop-up from their NAC agent each time they login.

The user must click Accept before being allow to login. Because this happens at each login, it is typically only enabled where required, such as contractors, non-employees, temporary workers, or other groups that haven't signed a corporate network AUP already. Another tactic is to enable the AUP for all network users once a year for a short period of time. This ensures that everyone is aware of your network AUP and accepts it yearly. Figure 15-11 depicts the AUP settings screen.

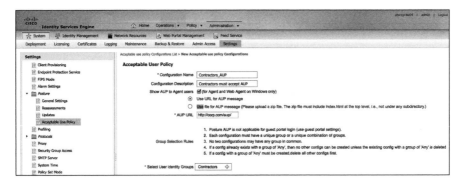

Figure 15-11   *Acceptable Use Policy Settings*

Configure the NAC Agent and NAC Client Provisioning Settings

Create a set of client provisioning policies. Client provisioning policy rules determine which users and endpoints receive certain resources (agents, agent compliance modules, and/or agent customization packages/profiles) from Cisco ISE after authentication. Go to **Policy > Client Provisioning.** Click **Actions > Insert New Policy.** There are two types of rules: native supplicant configuration and NAC agent configuration. Only NAC agent rules are covered here. Typically, you create at least one rule per OS. An example is shown in Figure 15-12.

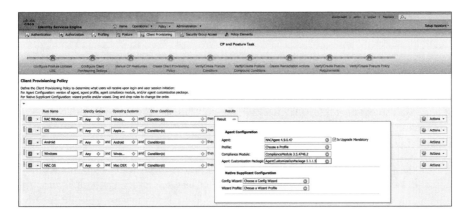

Figure 15-12   *NAC Client Provisioning Rule*

Each rule has the following settings:

- **Status: Enable, Disable, or Monitor:** Monitor disables the policy and just "watches" and logs the client provisioning requests.

- Rule name.

- Identity groups.

- **Operating Systems:** This is a requirement for a proper rule base. You should, at a minimum, have a Windows and a Mac policy.

- **Other Conditions:** Not typical.

- **Results:** Discussed previously. The only mandatory field is Agent. However, compliance module is almost always set.

Configure Posture Conditions

There are two types of posture conditions: simple conditions and compound conditions. Compound conditions are a collection of simple conditions.

To configure the conditions, go to **Policy > Policy Elements > Conditions.** Here are the various simple conditions (see Figure 15-13) available in ISE:

- File Condition

- Registry Condition

- Application Condition

- Service Condition

- Dictionary Simple Condition

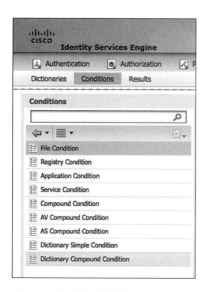

Figure 15-13 *ISE Posture Conditions*

Here is the list of the various compound conditions available in ISE:

- Compound Condition

- AV Compound Condition

- AS Compound Condition

- Dictionary Compound Condition

The good news is that many of these condition types are pre-populated from the Cisco.com posture update process that you configured earlier. Updates continue to flow in as they are available, always keeping your conditions up to date.

> **Note**   The NAC Agent for Macintosh OS X only supports the anti-virus (AV) and anti-spyware (AS) conditions. The other conditions do not apply to OS X. However, all conditions are supported by both the Windows web and NAC agent software.

Cisco-defined simple conditions have pc_ as their prefixes, and compound conditions have pr_ as their prefixes. You cannot delete or edit Cisco-defined posture conditions. However, you can duplicate them and edit the duplicate. Figure 15-14 shows an example file condition. This file condition checks for the existence of a file named nomalware.exe.

Figure 15-14   *File Condition Settings*

Figures 15-15 through 15-18 provide example screenshots of the other simple condition types.

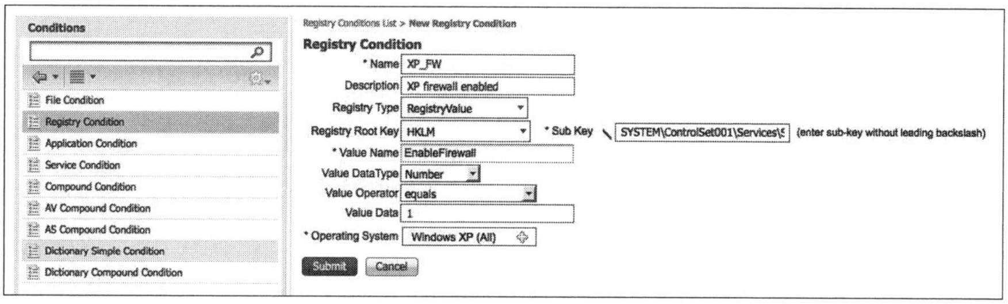

Figure 15-15 *Registry Condition Settings*

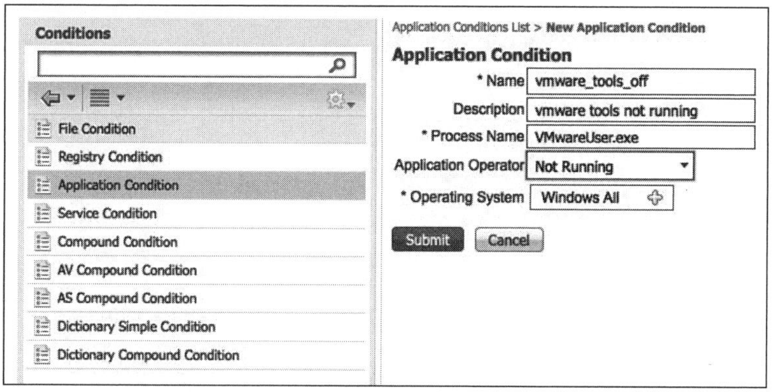

Figure 15-16 *Application Condition Settings*

Use the command-line tool, tasklist, to find all running Windows applications.

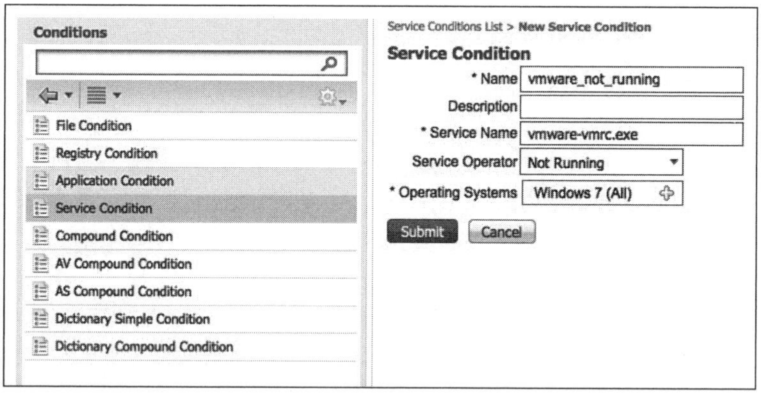

Figure 15-17 *Service Condition Settings*

Use the command-line tool, tasklist /svc, to find all running Windows services.

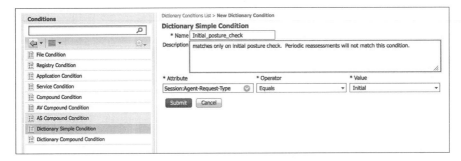

Figure 15-18 *Simple Dictionary Condition Settings*

The anti-virus and anti-spyware compound conditions are similar. By default, ISE provides a check for any AV or AS installed for Windows and Mac and a check for any AV or AS definition file that is five days or older than the latest file date for Windows and Mac. Figure 15-19 shows a custom AV condition.

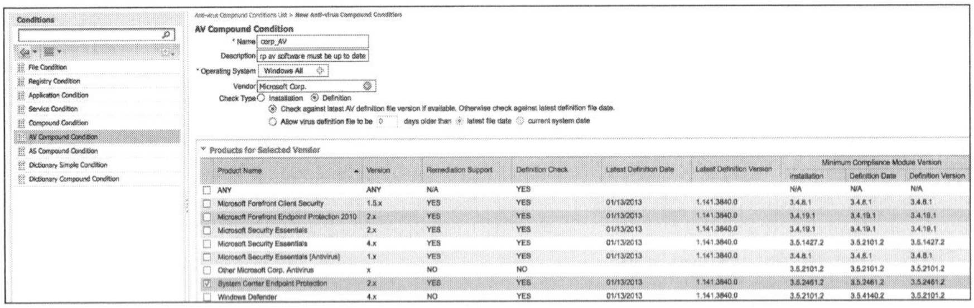

Figure 15-19 *Custom AV Condition*

Your custom AV or AS condition can check for either the definition, as shown in Figure 15-19, or the installation of the software.

Configure Posture Remediation

Now that you created your various conditions, the next step is to configure client remediation actions. These are actions that the NAC agent and/or end user can perform to fix any failed conditions and thus come into posture compliance. Table 15-3 lists the available remediation actions by supported agent type.

Table 15-3 *Supported Remediation Actions*

	Windows NAC Agent	Windows Web Agent	Mac OSX NAC Agent
Message Text (Local Check)	Supported	Supported	Supported

	Windows NAC Agent	Windows Web Agent	Mac OSX NAC Agent
URL Link (Link Distribution)	Supported (manual and automatic)	Supported (manual)	Supported (manual)
Launch Program	Supported (manual and automatic)	Supported (manual)	Supported (manual)
File Distribution	Supported	Supported	Not supported
Antivirus Definition Update	Supported (manual and automatic)	Not supported	Supported (manual)
Antispyware Definition Update	Supported (manual and automatic)	Not supported	Supported (manual)
Windows Update	Supported (manual and automatic)	Not supported	Not supported
WSUS	Supported (manual and automatic)	Not supported	Not supported

If a remediation action is manual, the end user sees a NAC agent popup with instructions to click it to perform the action, as shown in the following steps. If the action is automatic, the end user doesn't have to perform any action. The NAC agent performs the action automatically:

1. To create or edit remediation actions, go to **Policy > Policy Elements > Results > Posture > Remediation Actions**.

2. Select the type of remediation you want to create.

3. Fill in the fields.

Figure 15-20 provides an example of an AV remediation action.

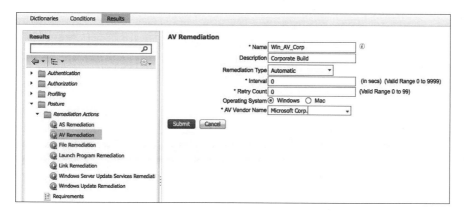

Figure 15-20 *AV Remediation Action*

In addition to creating a corporate AV remediation rule, it is also common to create a Windows Update rule. Figure 15-21 shows a typical Windows update rule example.

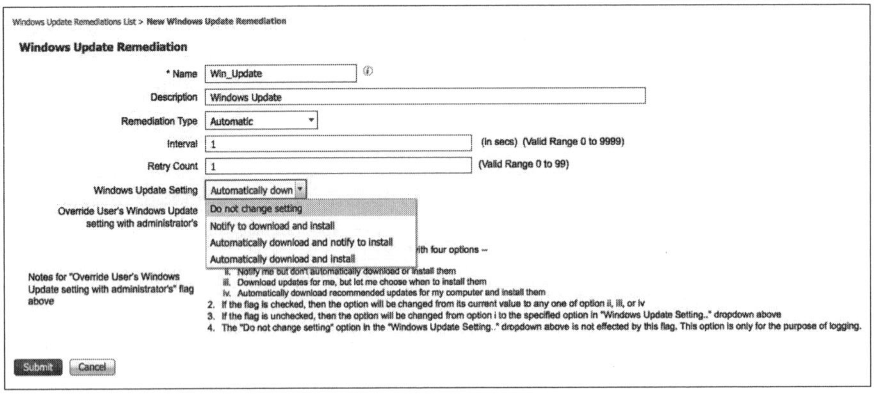

Figure 15-21 *Windows Update Remediation Action*

The instructions, as shown in Figure 15-21, are in the following steps:

1. The Windows Automatic Update feature comes with four options:

   i. Turn off automatic updates

   ii. Notify me but don't automatically download or install them

   iii. Download updates for me, but let me choose when to install them

   iv. Automatically download recommended updates for my computer and install them

2. If the flag is checked, the option changes from its current value to any one of option ii, iii, or iv.

3. If the flag is unchecked, the option changes from option i to the specified option in Windows Update Setting drop-down.

4. The Do Not Change Setting option in the Windows Update Setting drop-down is not affected by this flag. This option is only for the purpose of logging.

5. The Windows Update remediation action is usually taken upon a failure of the **pr_AutoUpdateCheck_Rule** that is built-in to ISE.

Another common Windows remediation rule is the WSUS rule. This remediation action allows the NAC agent to talk with the clients WSUS agent to ensure the client is patched correctly. You can choose to trust the severity settings on your WSUS server or trust the Cisco rules that are downloaded to ISE. If you choose the Cisco rules, select specific rules to check for in the corresponding posture requirement rule. These rules are ignored if you select the severity level option.

When using the severity level option, you must choose the pr_WSUSRule compound condition in the corresponding posture requirement rule. When the posture requirement fails, the NAC agent enforces the WSUS remediation action based on the severity level that you defined in the WSUS remediation action.

You also need to select the check box if you want to force a service pack update on the client if one is available. Use this with care, because Windows service pack upgrades can be time consuming and error prone.

Finally, you need to select the Windows update source type of either Microsoft server or managed server. A Microsoft server is hosted by Microsoft in the Internet, whereas a managed server is a WSUS that you administer internally. If you choose the show UI setting, your users must have administrator access to their Windows client for it to operate. The UI shows the WSUS update progress.

Figure 15-22 illustrates an example WSUS remediation action using severity level with a Microsoft server.

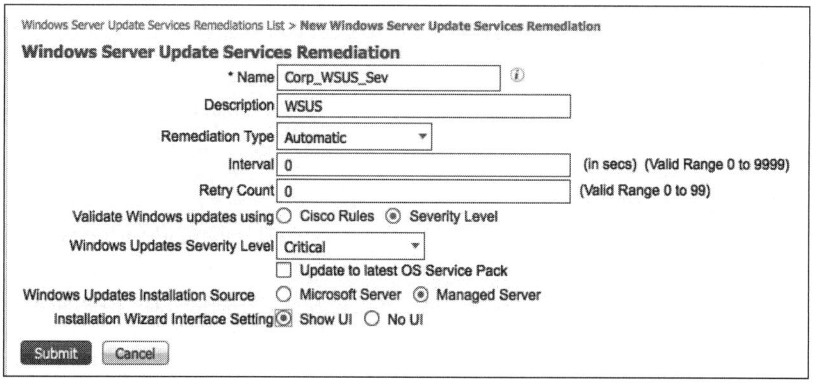

Figure 15-22 *WSUS Remediation Action*

Configure Posture Requirements

Now that you have configured or reviewed all the pieces, the next step is to put them together in a series of Posture Requirements. Several come predefined in ISE and cover the AV and AS use cases. In addition to these, you typically want to create a Windows update requirement or two. The requirements you create here are used as a part of your posture policies in the next section.

To create a posture requirement, go to **Policy > Policy Elements > Results > Posture > Requirements**.

1. Select the down arrow at the end of a row.

2. Select Insert New Requirement.

Figure 15-23 depicts an example requirement.

Figure 15-23   *Windows Update Posture Requirement*

The requirement in Figure 15-23 called *Windows Up-to-date* applies to all Windows 8 and Windows 7 endpoints and is met if the condition pr_AutoUpdateCheck_Rule is true. Otherwise, the remediation action of Win_update_service is executed.

Create the requirements that you need for your environment and host security policy. If you have not done so already, read Chapter 7, "Building a Device Security Policy," for more information on creating a strong host security policy for your organization.

Configure Posture Policy

Up to now, you configured items to support the policies you will create in this section. This section enacts the posture assessment process within ISE.

To configure posture policy, go to **Policy > Posture**. A posture policy maps posture requirements to selection criteria, such as OS, identity group, or other conditions. This allows you to define different posture requirement policies for the various client and user types. Each requirement listed as part of a posture policy has its own status setting of Mandatory, Optional, or Audit. Mandatory means the requirement must be met in order for the endpoint to be allowed on the network. Optional means that, if the endpoint fails the requirement, it will still pass onto the network, but any automatic remediation actions are executed. Audit only logs the requirement result and does not affect the client's ability to access the network nor execute any automatic remediation actions. Audit requirements are transparent to the end user.

Figure 15-24 shows the posture policy table along with an example policy. No policies are configured by default.

Figure 15-24   *Posture Policy Table*

The example policy shown in Figure 15-24 confirms that all Windows endpoints have an installed and up-to-date AV program. If the requirement fails, the assigned remediation action kicks off an AV client virus definition file that updates automatically. Let's step through the setup of this policy:

1. Set the status to Enabled (default) or Disabled.

2. Provide a descriptive name to the policy. It should describe the purpose of the policy.

3. Select the identity group you want the policy to match against. This can be set to **Any** or to a specific group like Employee or contractor. The example sets it to Employee.

4. Select the OS to match this policy against. The example selects Windows All, so any Windows OS matches it. You can select multiple OSs within the same type, but cannot mix operating systems of different types. For example, Windows 7(all) or Windows 8(all) is acceptable, but Windows 7(all) or Mac OS X does not work.

5. Setting other conditions is optional and not usually necessary. One other condition to consider is an "initial posture" condition. This means the policy only matches if the endpoint is going through its initial posture assessment and not a period reassessment. This condition was previously created in this chapter.

6. If all the conditions set are true, match the endpoint against requirements. In the example, there are two requirements: Any_AV_installation_Win and Any_AV_Definition_Win. You can use both of these built-in ISE requirements. What the policy doesn't show is the status of these requirements: Mandatory, Optional, or Audit. To edit or view the status, edit the policy and click the plus sign next to Requirements box. You see something similar to Figure 15-25.

Figure 15-25 *Posture Policy Requirements Status*

It is highly recommended that, in a production environment, all requirements start with a status of either Audit or Optional. This lessens the impact on your user community, helpdesk staff, and yourself. Because you already have a good idea of the impact your policies are having while in audit or optional status, you will know when the time is right to move them to Mandatory status. For example, you write a policy that requires AV to be installed and initially set it to Audit status. After a week, you check the ISE logs and determine that only 5% of your endpoints are failing the policy. At this time, you could move it to Optional status with automatic remediation. When you check back the following week, you see all endpoints are passing so you move the status to Mandatory.

Figure 15-26 depicts another common posture policy. This one is for monitoring the Windows update service.

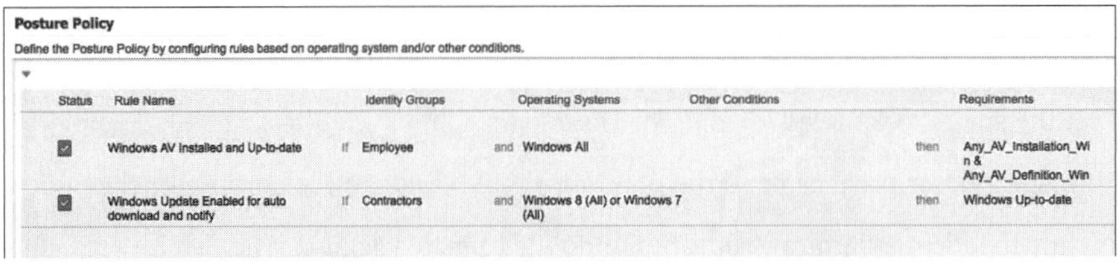

Figure 15-26 *Posture Policy Windows Update*

The policy checks to ensure that it is running and is set to automatically download updates and notify the user when there are new updates ready for them to install. This policy affects contractors and Windows 8(all) or Windows 7(all) endpoints. The Remediation action is to override the users settings with the requirements settings of auto download and notify.

It is a best practice not to burden clients with an excessive amount of posture policy requirements. Doing so can adversely affect the client's network experience and login times. Keep it to a handful of your top requirements per operating system.

Enabling Posture Assessment in the Network

You need to ensure that your endpoints are allowed the proper communication rights while in quarantine and performing posture assessment and remediation activities.

Confirm that the access switch pre-posture/limited access ACL allows Swiss communication between the Cisco ISE Policy Services node(s) and the endpoint. Example 15-1 illustrates an ACL showing the ports required for Posture to work.

Example 15-1 *Pre-Posture ACL*

```
remark Allow DHCP
permit udp any eq bootpc any eq bootps
remark Allow DNS
permit udp any any eq domain
remark Allow ping to ISE PSN and any other devices necessary
permit icmp any host <ISE PSN IP>
permit tcp any host <ISE PSN IP> eq 443 --> This is for URL redirect
permit tcp any host <ISE PSN IP> eq www --> This is for URL redirect
permit tcp any host <ISE PSN IP> eq 8443 --> This is for guest portal
permit tcp any host <ISE PSN IP> eq 8905 --> This is for posture
communication between NAC agent and ISE (Swiss ports)
permit udp any host <ISE PSN IP> eq 8905 --> This is for posture
communication between NAC agent and ISE (Swiss ports)
deny ip any any
```

Ensure that you create a similar quarantine ACL for the posture noncompliant endpoints with these rights plus rights to access the remediation IPs.

Finally, confirm that nothing in the traffic path—such as firewalls and ACLs—are preventing the traffic from flowing.

Summary

This chapter covered the details of configuring posture assessment on the Cisco Identity Services Engine ISE. Here are the high-level steps that were covered in this chapter:

- Configure global posture settings

- Configure the posture agent and client provisioning settings

- Configure posture conditions

- Configure posture remediation

- Configure posture requirements

- Configure posture policies

- Enabling posture assessment in the network

When used correctly, ISE posture assessment greatly increases the host security throughout your organization. Plus, you'll sleep better knowing only security-compliant endpoints are allowed to attach to your network.

Chapter 16

Supplicant Configuration

The client 802.1X supplicant is a critical part of any Identity Services deployment. What is a supplicant? A client supplicant is simply the piece of software that the operating system (OS) uses to connect to networks, both wired and wireless. All the major OSs, like Windows, Mac OS X, Android, iOS, Linux, and many network devices, like Cisco IP-Phones, IP cameras, and so on, include a built-in supplicant. The network access devices (NAD) interact with the client's supplicant upon connection to the wired or wireless network. The 802.1X transactions are performed between supplicant and the NAD. The NAD then talks RADIUS to the Cisco Identity Services Engine (ISE).

The Cisco ISE has a nice feature called native supplicant provisioning. This feature allows you to remove the burden from the end users to configure their own supplicant; instead, it does it automatically for them via an ISE-supplicant provisioning wizard. This feature is highly recommended because of its ability to simplify the deployment of ISE. It only works with the native built-in supplicants in the following OSs:

- Android

- Mac OS X (for Apple Mac computers)

- Apple iOS (for Apple iPhones and iPads)

- Microsoft Windows 7, Vista, and XP

Note If you use one of these, it is highly recommended that you skip this chapter and instead read Chapter 17, "BYOD: Self-Service Onboarding and Registration," which covers client provisioning in detail.

If you will not use the native supplicants or prefer not to use the ISE client provisioning wizards, this chapter is for you. It covers the configuration steps for the following client supplicants:

- Cisco AnyConnect Network Access Manager (NAM) for Windows

- Windows 7 Native Supplicant

- MAC OSX 10.8.2 Native Suppliant

The configuration steps focus solely on the wired network portion of their configuration. There is a lot of knowledge and readily available information for wireless configuration already out there, so including it here is redundant.

Comparison of Popular Supplicants

There are only a handful of popular supplicants on the market today and a bunch of niche supplicants. The most popular ones for wired are the following:

- Windows Native Supplicant

- MAC OS X Native Supplicant

- Android/iOS/Blackberry/other mobile OS native supplicants

- Cisco AnyConnect Secure Mobility NAM Client

- Linux Native Supplicants (wpa_supplicant)

When deciding which supplicant to use, answer these basic questions:

1. What is the dominant OS going to be in my ISE deployment?

2. Are most of my clients members of Active Directory?

3. What EAP type(s) will be required (PEAP, EAP-TLS, EAP-FAST, EAP-MSCHAPv2, and so on)?

4. Do I require an all-in-one client?

5. Will I be using the ISE native supplicant provisioning?

6. Is EAP-chaining required? EAP-chaining provides differentiated access based on enterprise and non-enterprise assets. It also has the ability to validate users and devices in a single EAP transaction. It can simultaneously perform both machine authentication and user authentication.

You must consider several other deciding factors, depending on the complexity of your ISE deployment, but these are the most common ones. After you answer these questions, you will be able to match your answers with the available supplicants and their requirements. It is space prohibitive, and highly susceptible to becoming quickly outdated, to list all the supplicants and their supported features here. Instead, check the websites of the supplicant vendors for these details.

Note   In general, the native OS supplicants are sufficient for your ISE deployment. If you are using either Microsoft Active Directory Group Policy or Cisco ISE Native Client Provisioning, you must choose the native supplicant.

Configuring Common Supplicants

This section deals with the manual configuration steps for some of the most common supplicants. Specifically, Windows 7 Native, MAC OS X Native, and Cisco AnyConnect NAM are covered. Only wired 802.1X configuration is covered.

Mac OS X 10.8.2 Native Supplicant Configuration

In versions 10.7 and 10.8 of OSX, Apple changed the wired 802.1X configuration steps. The good news is that it made it a zero configuration setup for the vast majority of wired 802.1X ISE deployments. Upon connecting to the Ethernet network, the 802.1X authentication process is automatically started, and the user is presented with a pop-up message to log in to the network.

Note   By default, OS X 10.8.2 requires that, during 802.1X authentication, the name in the server's certificate must match its DNS hostname. So, ensure that your ISE server-side certificate complies.

If the default setting for autoconnect, as shown in Figure 16-1, has been modified, it can be re-enabled by following the steps:

1. Click **System Preferences** and select **Network** under **Internet and Wireless**.

2. Click **Ethernet** and click **Advanced**.

3. Select the **802.1X** tab.

4. Select **Enable automatic connection**, as shown in Figure 16-2.

To access networks that cannot be joined with the method shown in Figure 16-2, or to use a login window mode or a system mode profile, you need to create and distribute a .mobileconfig file to clients that contains the correct network-configuration information. A .mobileconfig can be created by using the Profile Manager service provided in OS X Mountain Lion Server. See Apple's support site for detailed information.

Figure 16-1 *Network—Ethernet*

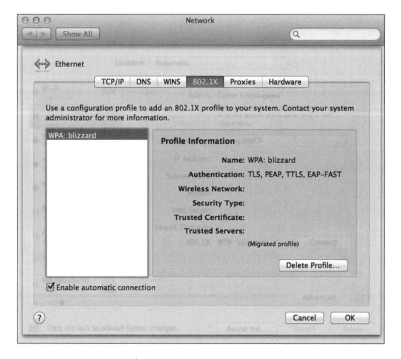

Figure 16-2 *Network—Ethernet*

Windows GPO Configuration for Wired Supplicant

Windows 2008r2 or better includes the ability to use group policy objects to configure clients' wired and wireless 802.1X settings. For complete instructions, go to http://tech-net.microsoft.com/en-us/library/cc733169.aspx.

Here are the common steps for configuring wired GPO 802.1X settings using EAP-TLS with certificates and single-sign on (SSO). This assumes you have already delivered the full certificate chain for your CA and machine and identity certificates to the client, hopefully using Group Policy Objects (GPO) for that.

Note   See Appendix C, "Configuring the Microsoft CA for BYOD," for details on how to provision certificates using a Microsoft CA server.

1. Open the Group Policy Management console (see Figure 16-3).

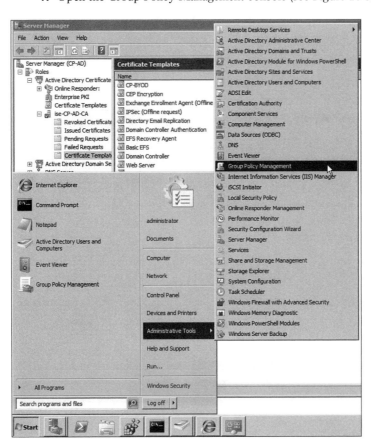

Figure 16-3   *GPO Management Console*

2. Select your domain. Either create a new Group Policy Object or select an existing one. Right-click > Edit. This opens the Group Policy Management Editor (see Figure 16-4).

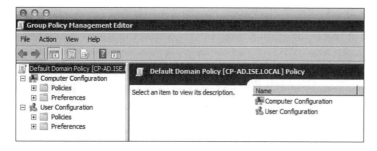

Figure 16-4 *Group Policy Management Editor*

3. Create a new wired network policy for Vista or later. To do this, go to **Computer Configuration > Policies> Windows Settings > Security Settings > Wired Network Policies.** Right-click and select Create a New Wired Policy (see Figure 16-5).

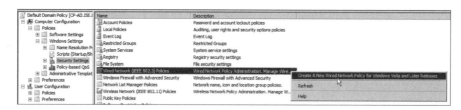

Figure 16-5 *Wired Network Policy Creation*

4. Fill in the policy name and description. Be sure to check **Use Windows Wired Auto Config service for clients.** Optionally, check **Don't allow shared user credentials.** See Figure 16-6 for an example.

5. Click the **Security** tab. Select **Enable use of IEEE 802.1X authentication** for network access.

6. For **Select a network authentication method,** select **Smart Card or other certificate.**

7. Select **Cache user information for subsequent connections to this network.** See Figure 16-7 for an example.

8. Click the **Advanced** button. Check **Enforce Advanced 802.1X settings.** You can leave the defaults or change for your environment.

9. Check **Enable Single Sign-On.** The most common setting is Perform Immediately Before User Logon. This allows the user to log on to the domain and run logon scripts.

10. Check Allow additional dialogs to be displayed during single sign-on.

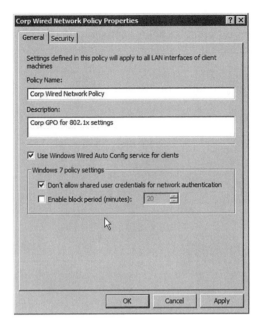

Figure 16-6 *Wired Network Policy—General Settings*

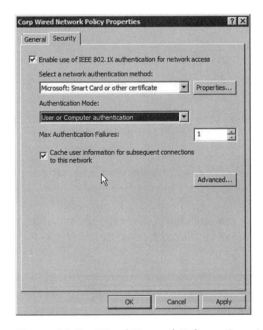

Figure 16-7 *Wired Network Policy—Security Settings*

11. If you will use ISE to change the wired switchport VLAN between machine logon and user logon, check **This network uses different VLAN for authentication with machine and user credentials**. This ensures that a change of IP address takes place smoothly.

12. Figure 16-8 shows an example of the Advanced Security Settings.

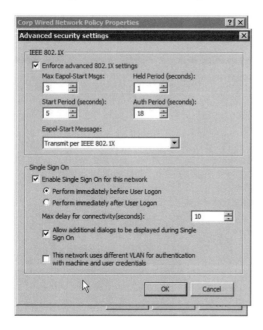

Figure 16-8   *Wired Network Policy—Advanced Security Settings*

13. Click **OK**. The Advanced Security Settings dialog box closes, returning you to the Security tab. On the Security tab, click **Properties**. The Smart Card or other Certificate Properties dialog box opens.

14. Select both **Use a certificate on this computer** and **Use simple certificate selection**.

15. Check **Validate server certificate**.

16. In Connect to these Servers, type the name of each ISE policy server, exactly as it appears in the subject field of the ISE server's certificate. Use semicolons to specify multiple ISE server names.

17. Leave everything else disabled. (For higher security settings, see the Microsoft documentation.) Click **OK** and **OK** to close this all out.

Figure 16-9 shows an example of certificate settings.

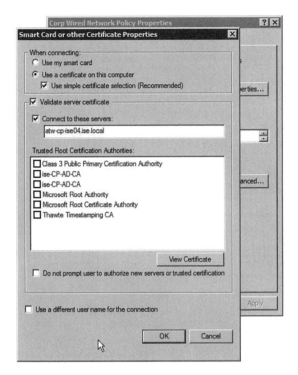

Figure 16-9 *Wired Network Policy—Certificate Settings*

18. Your new policy will be pushed out to your clients the next time they do a GPO update.

Windows 7 Native Supplicant Configuration

Microsoft disables 802.1X by default on Windows 7. The following steps show you how to enable and configure wired 802.1X. You must be logged in as an administrator to complete these steps:

1. Open Windows Services. Go to **Start > Search**. Type in **services** and select it. This opens the Services Management Console.

2. Select and double-click **Wired AutoConfig**. Change **Startup type** to **Automatic**. Click **Start** to start the service. Click **OK**. The 802.1X service is now enabled by default (see Figure 16-10).

3. Go to **Network Connections**, select your wired interface, right-click, and select **Properties**. See Figure 16-11 for details.

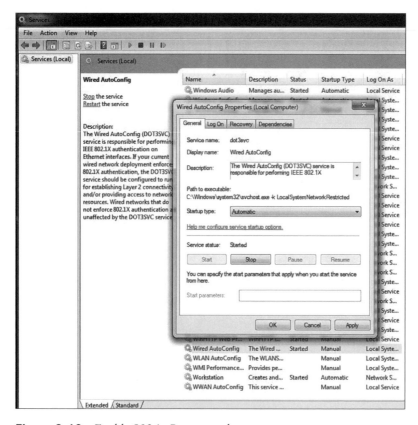

Figure 6-10   *Enable 802.1x Permanently*

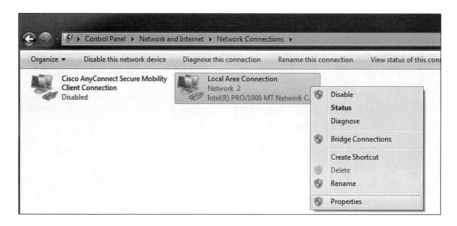

Figure 6-11   *Set Up Wired 802.1X*

4. Select the Authentication tab (this only shows up if you have enabled the Wired Autoconfig service). Check **Enable IEEE 802.1X.** Choose your authentication method; Protected Extensible Authentication Protocol (PEAP) is the most popular, because it uses your AD username and password by default. See Figure 16-12 for details.

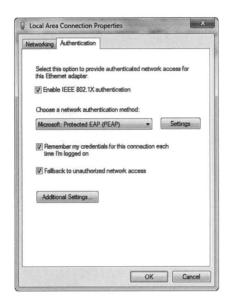

Figure 16-12   *Set Up Wired 802.1X Authentication*

5. Click **Additional Settings**. This brings you to the Advanced settings. Specify your authentication mode. Also, enable single sign-on. Click **OK**. See Figure 16-13 for an example.

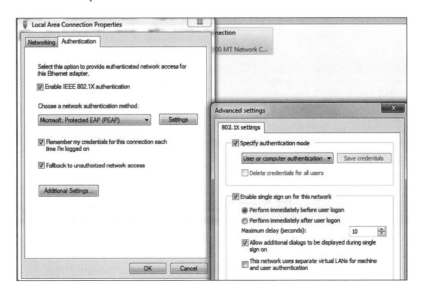

Figure 16-13   *Set Up Wired 802.1X Advanced Settings*

6. Optionally, click **Settings**. Depending on the authentication method you choose, you may or may not have to configure settings. If you chose PEAP, the defaults are fine in most cases. If you want to use PEAP, but not have it automatically, use your Windows logon name and password, and then click **Configure** next to EAP-MSCHAPv2 and uncheck the box. See Figure 16-14 for an example.

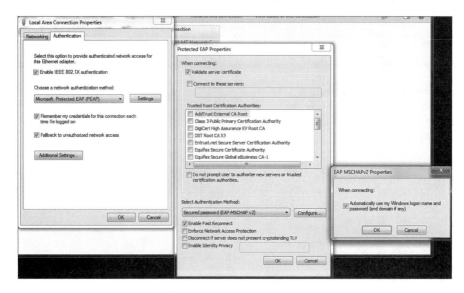

Figure 16-14   *Set Up Wired 802.1X PEAP Properties*

7. Click **OK** until you close out all the dialog boxes.

    Your Windows 7 Client is now ready to connect to a wired 802.1X protected network.

Cisco AnyConnect Secure Mobility Client NAM

This section walks you through the setup for the Cisco AnyConnect client for wired PEAP 802.1X authentication. To start, you must download the standalone AnyConnect Profile Editor from cisco.com or use the profile editor inside of ASDM or CSM. Once you have a profile editor installed, proceed with these steps:

1. Open AnyConnect Profile Editor and select **Networks**. Click **Add**. Provide a name. Change Group Membership to **In all groups**. Select **Wired** under Network Media. Click **Next**. See Figure 16-15.

2. Select **Authenticating Network**. Only if you are running in 802.1X open mode, do the following: Check **Enable Port Exceptions**. Select **Allow data traffic after authentication even if**. Select **EAP fails**. In open mode, ensure that your clients will still access the network even if they have a failure. This setting will accomplish that. Once you move away from open mode, you need to disable this setting. Click **Next**. See Figure 16-16.

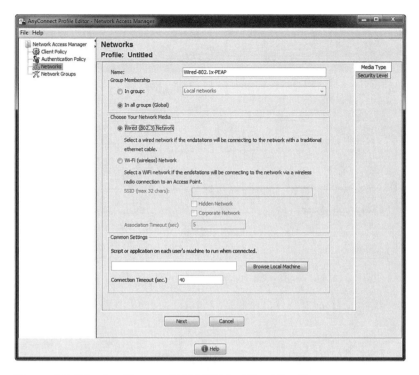

Figure 16-15 *AnyConnect NAM 802.1x Wired Profile*

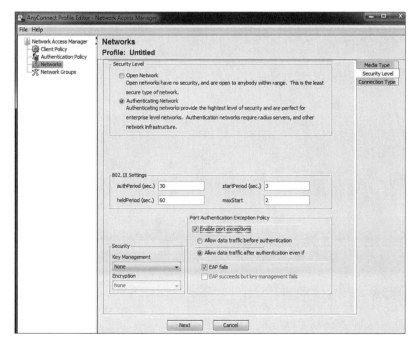

Figure 16-16 *AnyConnect NAM Profile Security Level*

3. Select **Machine and User Connection** or the setting of your choice. Click **Next**. See Figure 16-17.

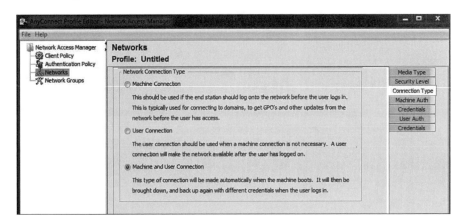

Figure 16-17 *AnyConnect NAM Profile Connection Type*

4. Enable PEAP. The default settings are usually not changed. Click **Next**. See Figure 16-18.

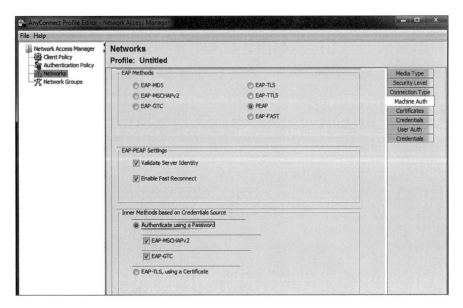

Figure 16-18 *AnyConnect NAM Profile Machine Auth*

5. This screen provides you with the ability to upload root certificates as part of the profile. If you need to do this (i.e., you are using your own CA server), add them here, as shown in Figure 16-19. Click **Next**.

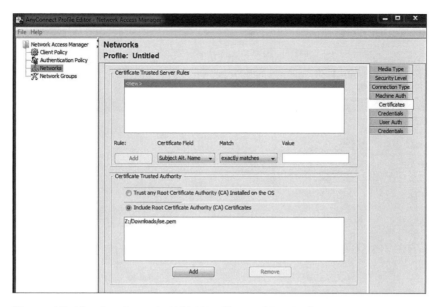

Figure 16-19 *AnyConnect NAM Profile Machine Auth Certs*

6. Set the credentials that the machine should use. Normally, the defaults are sufficient. Click **Next**.

7. For User Auth, select **PEAP** or your choice of authentication method. Normally, the defaults are fine. Click **Next**. See Figure 16-20 for an example.

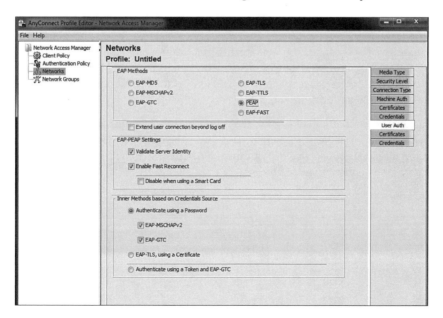

Figure 16-20 *AnyConnect NAM Profile User Auth*

8. The next screen is for user certificate checking. Repeat what you did for the machine certificates. Click **Next**.

9. For user credentials, select **Use Single Sign-On Credentials** or select the settings appropriate for your deployment. Click **Done**. See Figure 16-21.

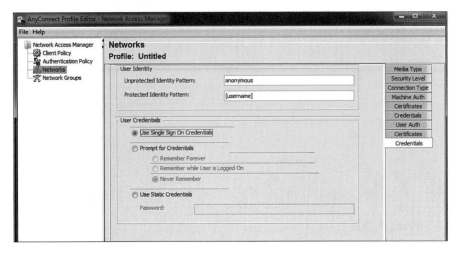

Figure 16-21   *AnyConnect NAM Profile User Credentials*

10. Go to the Network Groups tab. Under Global Networks: Wired, make sure that your policy is at the top of the list. Select it, and click the up-arrow button. See Figure 16-22.

11. Save the Profile file. On the top menu, click **File** and **Save As**.

12. You *must* save the configuration with the filename configuration.xml in the \ProgramData\Application Data\Cisco\Cisco AnyConnect Secure Mobility Client\Network Access Manager\newConfigFiles directory on Windows 7 or in the newConfigFiles directory on XP.

13. To apply this new configuration, go to the AnyConnect icon in the system tray. Right-click, and select **Network Repair**. This forces the Cisco AnyConnect NAM to restart its services. A service restart causes NAM to search the newConfigFiles directory for a configuration.xml file.

14. You're done!

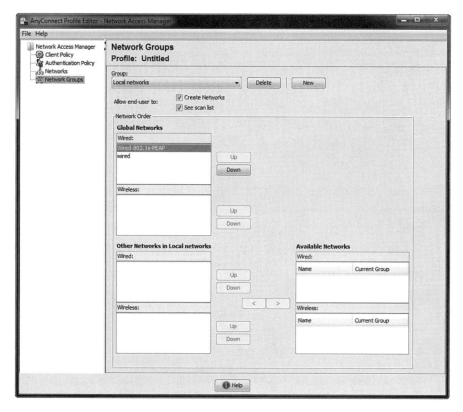

Figure 16-22 *AnyConnect NAM Profile Network Groups*

Summary

This chapter discussed 802.1X supplicants, with a particular focus on wired 802.1X
supplicant configuration. The setup of Windows 7, MAC OSX, and Cisco AnyConnect
supplicants were covered. The use of Microsoft Active Directory GPO as a supplicant
configuration tool was also discussed.

Chapter 17

BYOD: Self-Service Onboarding and Registration

Back in January 2007, Steve Jobs introduced the iPhone and suggested that Apple was shooting for 1% of the mobile device market. The device had a multi-touch screen interface, boasted a "real browser" instead of the cut-down versions on mobile devices to that point and arguably "changed the game" for the experience that users expected from their mobile devices from that point on. In January 2010, the iPad was released. In June 2010, I was at CiscoLive in Las Vegas presenting a session on Network Access Control (NAC).

In that session, I asked the audience if their company would allow users to bring in iPhones and iPad-type devices and connect to the corporate network for purposes of doing work from those devices. The few hundred people in my sample-size responded with about 90% no-way, and only a 10% affirmative response.

At that same conference, Cisco announced the CIUS, which was designed to be a "corporate tablet," a device to provide that wonderful user-experience along with the security and guarantees that IT departments required. Fast forward 18 months, and Cisco announced the end-of-sale of the CIUS, due to lack of adoption. In June 2012, when asked the same question about allowing personal devices, the result was 90% affirmative and only 10% said their organizations would not allow personal devices. What a difference two years makes! Bring Your Own Device (BYOD) has become an absolute reality.

As shown in Figure 17-1, we are moving into an era of Bring Your Own Device (BYOD), Choose Your Own Device (CYOD), and even moving into a Bring Your Own App (BYOA) type of model. Employees are demanding the use of the devices that make them most productive, with native applications running on those platforms that provide the user experience they have become accustomed to. This introduces a new paradigm for security, especially the identification of the user, device, the location of the user, and much more.

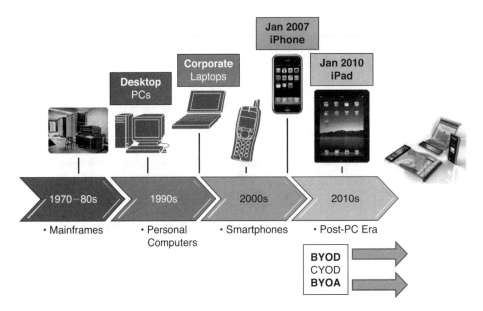

Figure 17-1   *BYOD Timeline*

BYOD Challenges

Because user identity is typically based on a single identity credential, IT does not possess the ability to create and enforce a rigorous secure access policy. Although the user might be authorized; the device, location, time, and access media can pose a company policy violation or even regulatory compliance violation that cannot be adequately detected or enforced.

This chapter focuses on the technical challenges of providing a secure BYOD access model. One of the most common challenges is referred to as *onboarding*. A user buys a new tablet or device and decides to connect it to the corporate WiFi and be productive on that consumer device. It has the challenge of identifying the device as a non-corporate device and provide a limited set of access to the device. This was originally what many companies used ISE to do. Figure 17-2 illustrates the flow of these original policies.

Then, mobile device management (MDM) solutions came into play. They were able to manage these mobile platforms to some extent. MDM policies ensured that devices had security enabled such as: encryption, remote wipe capabilities, screen lock (pin lock), and so forth. The MDM could provision certificates down to the device and supplicant profiles to preconfigure the device to have network access. Then, ISE would provide the correct level of access for the devices based on the certificate the device had.

Figure 17-3 illustrates a policy that uses certificates to differentiate access.

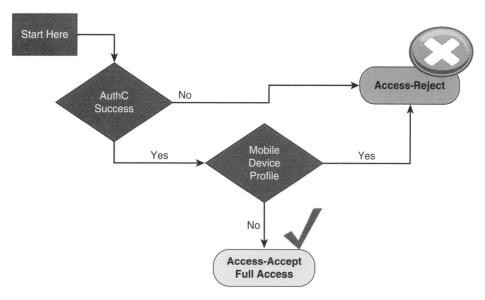

Figure 17-2   *Old Style Policy*

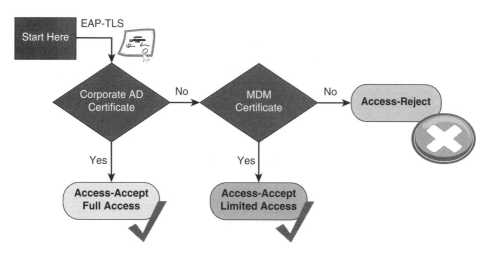

Figure 17-3   *Using Certificates to Differentiate Access*

MDMs typically cost money per device, and many companies were only looking for a good way to provision certificates and configure the device supplicant to use that certificate with 802.1X. The MDM cost was often prohibitive. The main objective was to provision the certificate and get the device on the network. Cisco customers were looking for a much easier and cheaper way to accomplish the onboarding aspect of network access.

Onboarding Process

This chapter focuses on two types of onboarding. The first is what Cisco calls BYOD onboarding, which includes registering the device with ISE, provisioning the certificate to the device, and configuring the device's supplicant. This uses the native supplicant within the operating system. It does not install a new one. The second is MDM onboarding, which is the process of registering the device with the MDM, installing the MDM client software, and enforcing the security policy on that device. The key to successful onboarding within a company is to make it self-service and not require involvement of IT.

BYOD Onboarding

ISE provides the My Devices portal, which allows users to register devices and manage those devices that have been registered. A device may simply be registered, which may provide one level of authorization, such as Internet-only access. Or the device may go through the full-blown onboarding and provisioning process where the supplicant configuration is installed into the device along with the optional certificate (for EAP-TLS connectivity).

Regardless of your choice to use device-registration only or to use the full onboarding process, there can be a single-SSID or dual-SSID approach to the onboarding, plus wired access (of course).

Figure 17-4 depicts the dual-SSID approach, while Figure 17-5 depicts the single-SSID approach. A quick comparison of the approaches follows.

Dual SSID

This section reviews the dual-SSID model of onboarding:

- Employee does not need to configure the supplicant on the device.
- Employee authenticates to a web form.
- Employee connects to the open SSID before the provisioning process, and the employee must connect to the corporate SSID after the process.

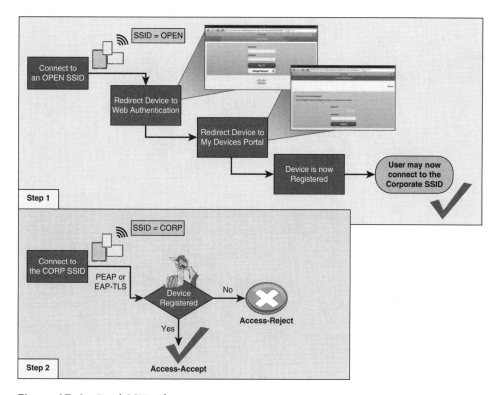

Figure 17-4 *Dual SSID Flow*

Single SSID

This section reviews the single-SSID model of onboarding (see Figure 17-5):

- Employee must configure the supplicant on the device to connect to the corporate SSID.

- The authentication used to connect to the corporate SSID is used for single sign-on to the onboarding and provisioning process.

- A Change of Authorization (CoA) is used to provide full access after the provisioning process without requiring the employee to reconnect to the network.

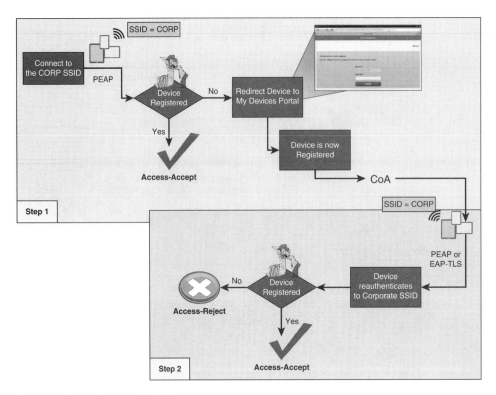

Figure 17-5   *Single-SSID Flow*

Configuring NADs for Onboarding

Dual SSID onboarding uses an open WLAN configured for NAC RADIUS, IEEE 3576 (CoA) and uses only MAC filtering for security (Wireless MAB). This network is most likely created already based on Chapter 14, "Guest Lifecycle Management," but this section briefly reviews the WLC settings.

Review of the WLC Configuration

This section briefly reviews the configuration for the Cisco wireless LAN controller.

The General tab of the WLAN should provide an SSID and profile name, as shown in Figure 17-6.

Under Security > Layer 2, Layer 2 security should be set to None. The MAC Filtering check box should be enabled, as displayed in Figure 17-7.

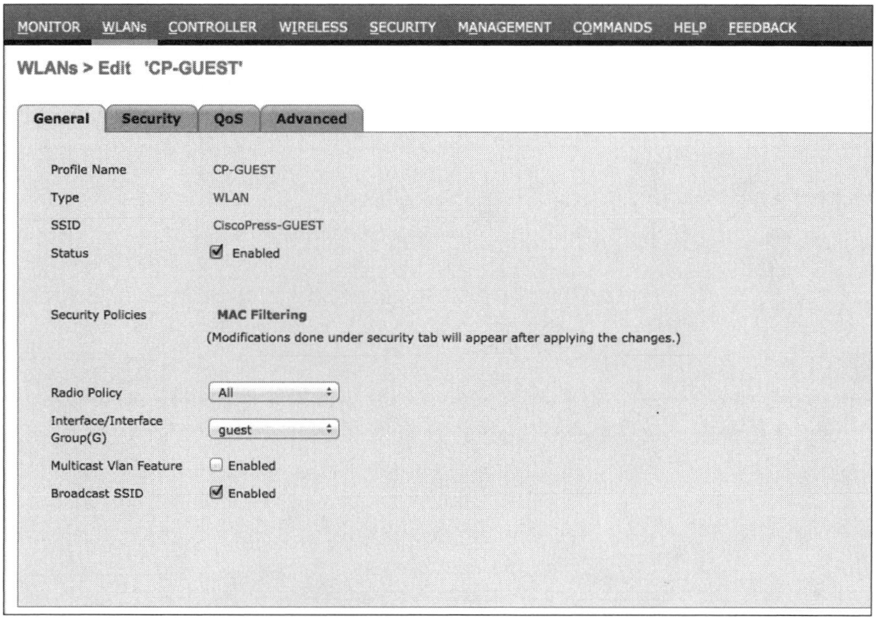

Figure 17-6   *Open WLAN General Tab*

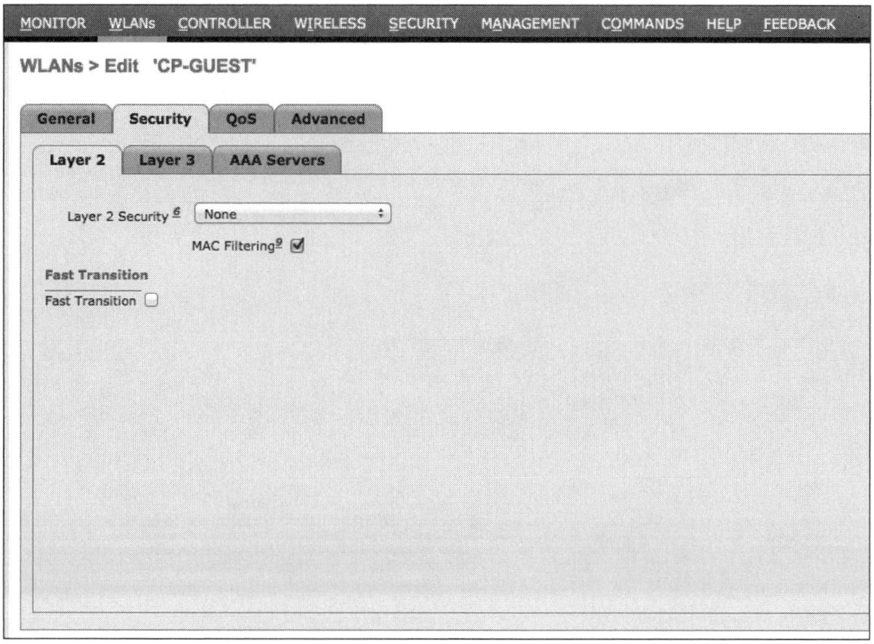

Figure 17-7   *Layer 2 Security Tab*

Under Security > Layer 3, Layer 3 security should be set to None, as shown in Figure 17-8.

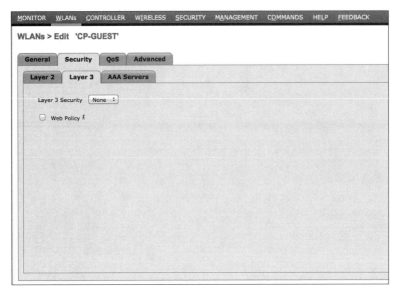

Figure 17-8   *Layer 3 Security Tab*

Under Security > AAA Servers, the ISE Policy Service mode(s) must be selected for authentication and accounting servers, as shown in Figure 17-9.

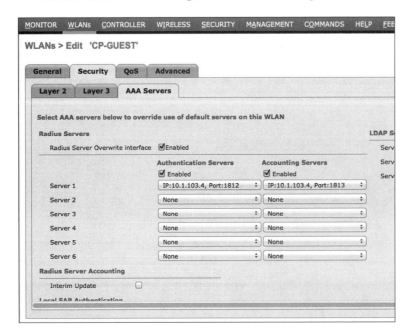

Figure 17-9   *AAA Servers Security Tab*

For the Advanced tab, configure the following: Allow AAA Override, and NAC State should be RADIUS NAC, as shown in Figure 17-10.

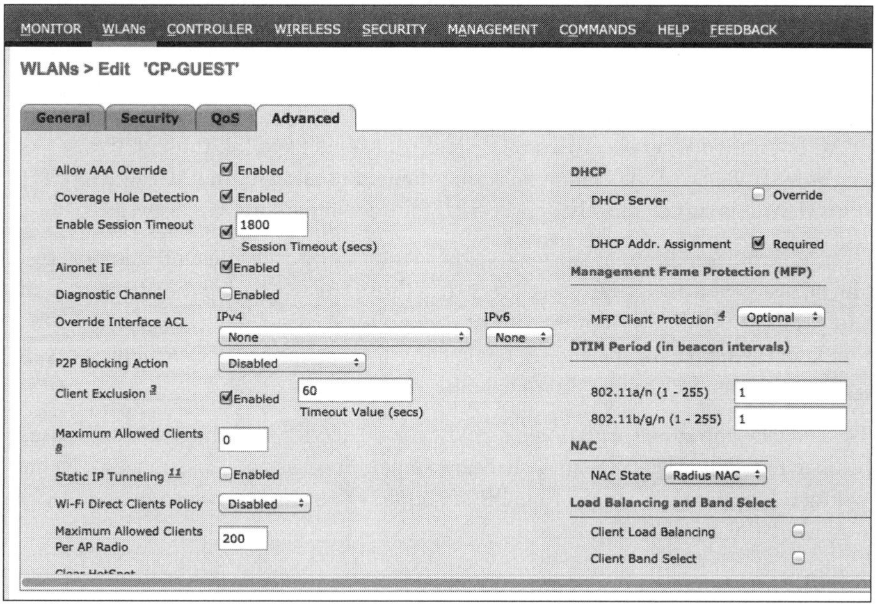

Figure 17-10   *Advanced Tab*

Double-check that the RADIUS Server Definition is configured to allow CoA, which is the RFC 3576 drop-down, as shown in Figure 17-11.

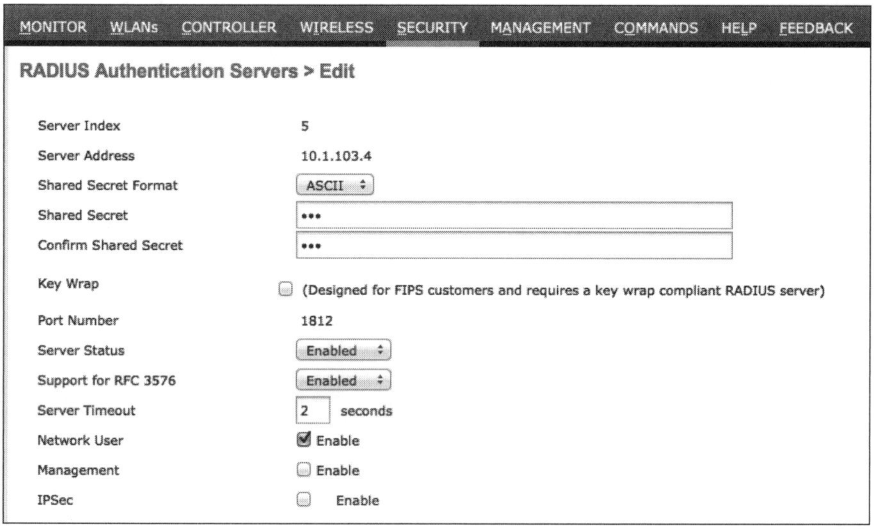

Figure 17-11   *RADIUS Authentication Servers Tab*

Required ACLs

You should have an ACL on the switches and the wireless controllers already named ACL-WEBAUTH-REDIRECT that permits DHCP, DNS, and traffic to ISE and denies most other traffic. This configuration was discussed and added in Chapter 14.

When onboarding with iOS, Windows and Mac OS, the endpoint need only communicate with ISE. iOS uses its native Over the Air (OTA) provisioning process. Windows and MAC both use a Java-based wizard that is downloaded from ISE through the devices browser. Because the communication is limited to just ISE, the ACL-WEBAUTH-REDIRECT ACL is sufficient to be repurposed for the onboarding ACL as well.

However, Android is a different story altogether. Android devices inherently do not trust apps being installed from an app store other than those trusted during the factory install. Therefore, ISE would not be allowed to host the app for Android devices by default. To keep the process simple for the end user, you have to open up the ACL to allow access to a range of addresses for Google Play.

The Google Play app store (play.google.com) is a cloud service, and the addresses it uses may change regularly. This presents a challenge to permit access to those ranges. The current solution is to permit a series of blocks of addresses that are known to be used by the Android Marketplace, as shown here:

- 74.125.0.0/16
- 173.194.0.0/16
- 173.227.0.0/16
- 206.111.0.0/16

These ACLs are used for both single and dual SSID onboarding. Here is a URL to a Google support thread, where Google discusses how to identify the current list of addresses: http://support.google.com/a/bin/answer.py?hl=en&answer=60764.

Create the ACL on the Wireless LAN Controller

From the WLC GUI, under Security > Access Control Lists, add a new ACL named Android-Marketplace, and configure the ACL as the one in Figure 17-12. The sample ACL is permitting all traffic from the inside network to speak to the client. It is allowing the client to communicate into the network for DNS and DHCP, as well as TCP traffic destined to the ISE servers. Next will be the lines that permit TCP traffic to the Android Market IP address ranges.

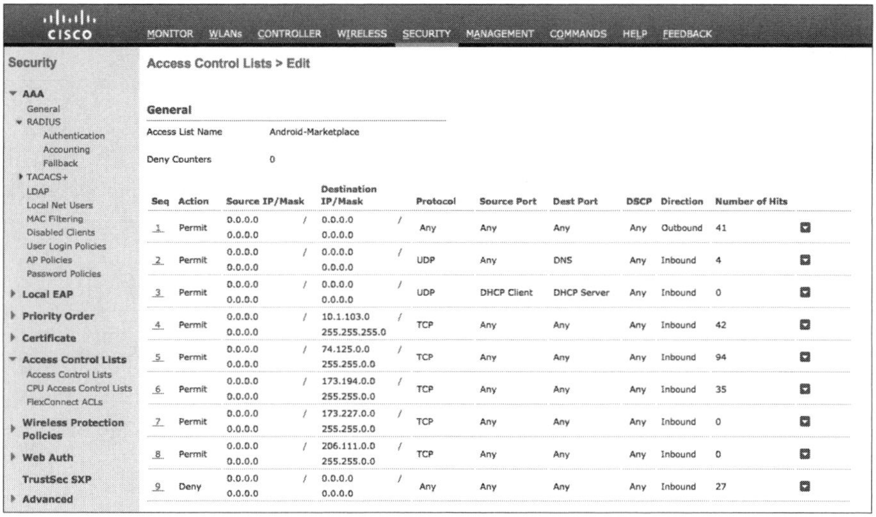

Figure 17-12 *Android Marketplace ACL*

Create the ACL on the Switch

From the WLC GUI, under Security > Access Control Lists, add a new ACL named Android-Marketplace, and configure the ACL as the one in Example 17-1. This ACL is allowing DNS to bypass redirection, along with all four of the known Android Marketplace address ranges; all other web traffic will be redirected to ISE.

Example 17-1 *Android-Marketplace ACL for Switches*

```
ip access-list extended Android-Marketplace
 deny    udp any any eq domain
 deny    tcp any 74.125.0.0 0.0.255.255
 deny    tcp any 173.194.0.0 0.0.255.255
 deny    tcp any 173.227.0.0 0.0.255.255
 deny    tcp any 206.111.0.0 0.0.255.255
 permit tcp any any eq www
 permit tcp any any eq 443
```

ISE Configuration for Onboarding

With the NADs prepared for the onboarding process, it's time to build the logic within the ISE Authorization Policy for both the dual and single SSID onboarding models.

The easier model to set up and understand first is the single SSID model. It assumes that, in order for a user or endpoint to be successfully admitted to the network, it must have authenticated with a certificate via EAP-TLS. If an authentication occurs with only a username and password (say, MsCHAPv2 inner method), you know the device must be onboarded.

For example, an employee shows up to work with their new mobile device. He decides to try and connect to the corporate WiFi, and it prompts him for a username and password. The employee enters his Active Directory credentials (as would be expected) and when he opens the browser on the mobile device, he is redirected to the My Devices portal, where he can begin the onboarding process. Simple, quick, and intuitive to most end users nowadays.

The first step is to configure the client provisioning portal so the correct profiles are sent for the appropriate operating systems. From there, configure the default action that should be taken when an unsupported device is sent to be provisioned.

End-User Experience

To fully understand the configuration of ISE, it is best that you experience the end-user experience for both single and dual SSID onboarding. That will aid you in your understanding of each policy that must be created, and each choice you will have to make. To demonstrate multiple user experiences, the following examples will use Apple iOS for one and Android for the other. However, each onboarding method could be used with any of the supported clients (iOS, Android, Mac OS X, and Windows).

Single-SSID with Apple iOS Example

The following steps are designed to follow the end-user experience with single-SSID onboarding, using an Apple iOS device:

1. You come in with your iOS device. Open Settings and connect to the corporate WiFi, such as what is shown in Figure 17-13.

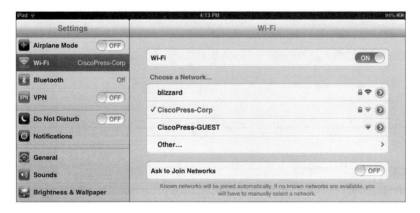

Figure 17-13   *iOS: Choose a WiFi Network*

2. You are prompted to input a username and password. Use your Active Directory username and password, as shown in Figure 17-14.

Figure 17-14   *iOS: Enter Credentials*

3. If the certificate used by ISE is not signed by a trusted root, you are prompted to accept (trust) the certificate used by ISE, as shown in Figure 17-15.

Figure 17-15   *iOS: Trust ISE Certificate*

4. Now you are successfully connected to the corporate network. Yet, you will not know that your access is actually limited, as shown in Figure 17-16.

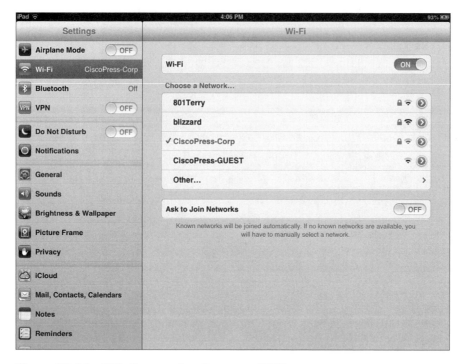

Figure 17-16 *iOS: Connected to Corporate WiFi*

5. Open a web browser, and you are redirected to the client provisioning portal, where OTA will begin.

6. The first step with OTA is to send the root CA's certificate to the iOS device to be trusted for OTA, as shown in Figure 17-17.

7. Click **Install.** A warning message is displayed about the root CA being added to the list of trusted certificates on the device, along with a warning about the profile itself (if the certificate was not in the trusted store already), as shown in Figure 17-18.

Figure 17-17   *iOS: OTA Trust the Root CA*

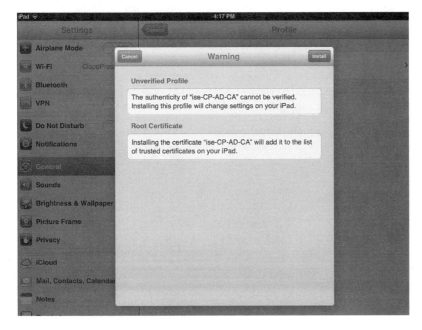

Figure 17-18   *iOS: OTA Warning Message*

8. The Certificate and Profile to allow OTA is successfully installed. Click **Done**, as shown in Figure 17-19.

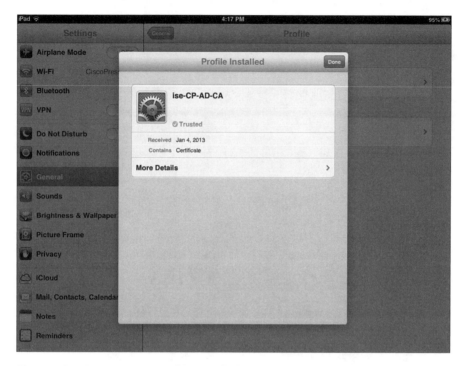

Figure 17-19   *iOS: OTA Profile Installed*

9. You are returned to your browser window, which displays the Device Registration page within the My Devices portal. The Device's MAC address will be prepopulated and noneditable. There is a description field for you to fill out, as shown in Figure 17-20.

10. Click **Register**. The screen immediately changes to the Install Profile Service, as shown in Figure 17-21.

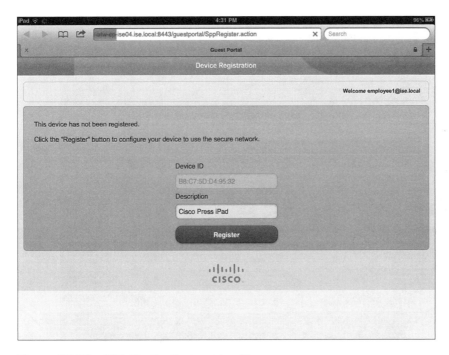

Figure 17-20 *iOS: Device Registration Page*

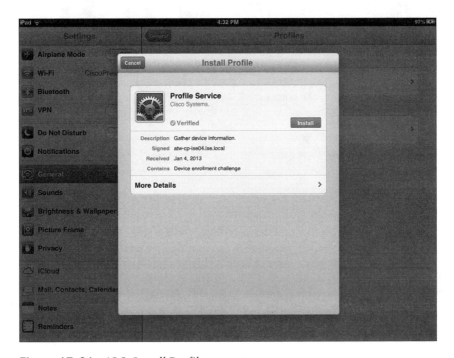

Figure 17-21 *iOS: Install Profile*

11. You are warned that clicking Install Profile will actually install a profile. Click **Install Now**, as shown in Figure 17-22.

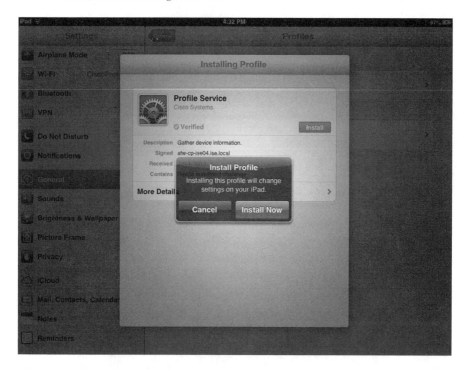

Figure 17-22 *iOS: Redundant Warning Message*

12. The profile begins to install, generates a certificate using SCEP, and prepares the device to be connected to the corporate SSID. The progression is shown in Figures 17-23 through 17-26.

Figure 17-23   *iOS: Gathering Device Information*

Figure 17-24   *iOS: Generating Certificate Request*

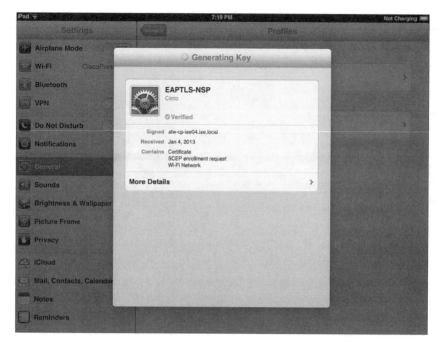

Figure 17-25   *iOS: Installing the Profile*

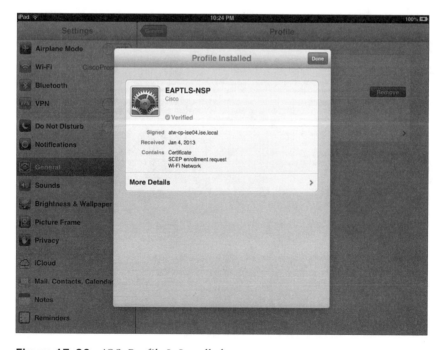

Figure 17-26   *iOS: Profile Is Installed*

13. When the profile is installed, click **Done** and return to your web browser where the success message is waiting for you, as shown in Figure 17-27.

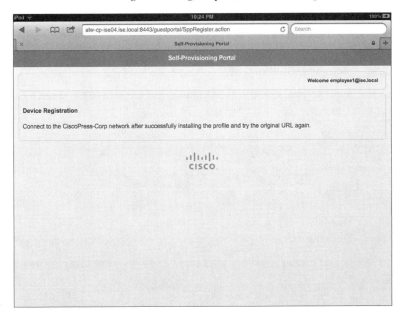

Figure 17-27 *iOS: Success Message*

14. You are now able to browse resources on the network, as shown in Figure 17-28.

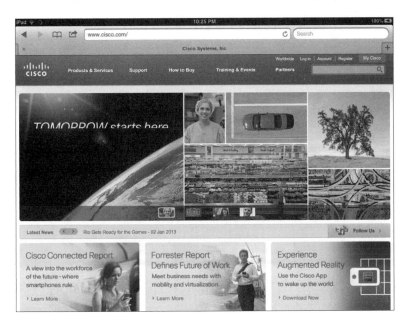

Figure 17-28 *iOS: Final Network Access*

That concludes the onboarding process for iOS with a single SSID. Next, let's examine the user experience with dual SSID by using an Android example.

Dual SSID with Android Example

The following steps are designed to follow the end-user experience with dual-SSID onboarding, using an Android-based device.

1. You come in with your Android device. Open Settings and connect to the Guest WiFi, as shown in Figure 17-29.

Figure 17-29   *Android: Choose a WiFi Network*

2. Because you protected the guest WiFi by requiring a login (Guest or Active Directory), you are redirected to the Web Authentication page, as shown in Figure 17-30.

3. After you log into the Web Auth portal, you are redirected to the device registration page. The device ID is predefined, as shown in Figure 17-31.

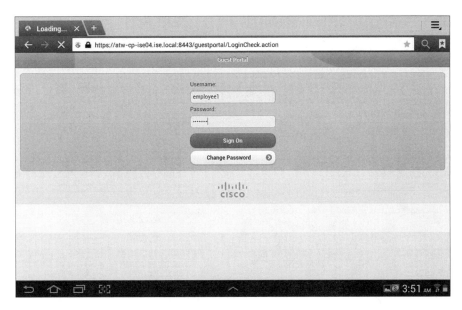

Figure 17-30   *Android: Web Auth Portal*

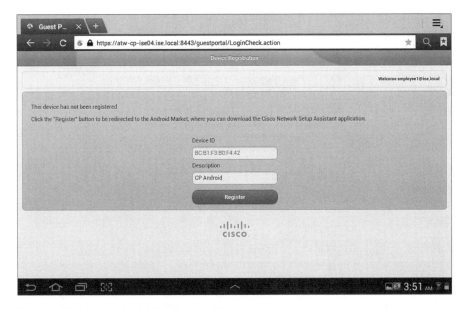

Figure 17-31   *Android: MyDevice Registration*

   4. Click **Register.** You are prompted to connect to the Android Marketplace
       (play.google.com) and given the choice between the Internet and the app, as
       shown in Figure 17-32.

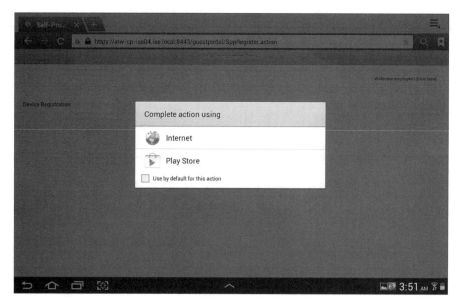

Figure 17-32 *Android: Connect to Android Marketplace*

5. Download the app from the marketplace, as shown in Figure 17-33.

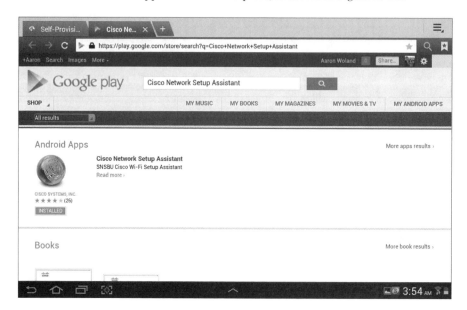

Figure 17-33 *Android: Download Cisco Network Setup Assistant*

6. Run the app and click **Start**, as shown in Figure 17-34.

Figure 17-34 *Android: Run the NSP App*

7. The NSP app downloads the profile from ISE, as shown in Figure 17-35.

Figure 17-35 *Android: NSP App Downloading Profile*

8. Name your certificate, as shown in Figure 17-36.

Figure 17-36   *Android: Name the Certificate*

9. Name the CA certificate, as shown in Figure 17-37.

Figure 17-37   *Android: Name the CA Certificate*

10. The NSP app automatically changes the network connection to the corporate SSID and authenticates with the new certificate using EAP-TLS, as shown in Figure 17-38.

Figure 17-38   *Android: Connects to the Corporate SSID*

11. Your Android device is now ready to be used regularly on the corporate network, as shown in Figure 17-39. The onboarding was a one-time thing.

Figure 17-39   *Android: Done*

Unsupported Mobile Device: Blackberry Example

You've seen both single and dual SSID onboarding with supported devices. Let's look at a brief example of a device that is not supported:

1. You bring your Blackberry mobile device to work and select the GUEST Wireless network, as shown in Figure 17-40.

Figure 17-40   *Blackberry: Selecting the Guest SSID*

2. The web browser is redirected to the Web Authentication page, where you enter your Active Directory credentials, as shown in Figure 17-41.

Figure 17-41   *Blackberry: Web Authentication*

3. If the global setting is Apply Defined Authorization Policy, you receive the message shown in Figure 17-42 and will not be able to gain network access. This is covered in more detail later in this chapter.

Figure 17-42   *Blackberry: Unable to Register*

4. If the global setting is Allow Network Access, you receive a notification that you may register the device through the My Devices portal, as shown in Figure 17-43. This is covered in detail later in this chapter.

Figure 17-43 *Blackberry: Registration Permitted*

5. You are now allowed to register the device and gain network access with manually configuring your supplicant, as shown in Figure 17-44.

Figure 17-44 *Blackberry: Registration the BlackBerry*

Configuring ISE for Onboarding

The end-user experience is designed to be straightforward and easy for a typical user to be able to follow without any interaction with the IT department. To keep things easy for the end user, there is some up-front work you will need to do on the configuration side. We will cover the entire configuration in this section.

Creating the Native Supplicant Profile

This subsection focuses on the creation of the native supplicant profile, which defines the network settings for the endpoints that will go through onboarding.

The native supplicant profile defines the following:

- Wireless SSID

- EAP type to use (PEAP or EAP-TLS)

- Key size for certificates

- Level of wireless security

- If it applies to wired, wireless, or both

The following steps guide you through adding the latest client provisioning resources from the Cisco site, and then creating the native supplicant profile.

1. Navigate to **Policy > Policy Elements > Results > Client Provisioning**.

2. Select **Resources**.

3. Click **Add > Agent Resources from Cisco site**.

4. Select the latest versions of the clients and wizards, as shown in Figure 17-45.

5. Click **Save**.

☑	Name ▲	Type	Version	Description
☑	AgentCustomizationPackage 1.1.1.5	AgentCustomizationPackage	1.1.1.5	This is the Agent Customization ...
☑	ComplianceModule 3.5.4746.2	ComplianceModule	3.5.4746.2	ComplianceModule v3.5.4746.2
☐	MacOsXAgent 4.9.0.654	MacOsXAgent	4.9.0.654	Posture Agent for Mac OSX (ISE...
☑	MacOsXAgent 4.9.0.655	MacOsXAgent	4.9.0.655	Posture Agent for Mac OSX (ISE...
☑	MacOsXSPWizard 1.0.0.11	MacOsXSPWizard	1.0.0.11	Supplicant Provisioning Wizard f...
☐	NACAgent 4.9.0.37	NACAgent	4.9.0.37	Windows Agent (ISE 1.0MR only)
☐	NACAgent 4.9.0.37	NACAgent	4.9.0.37	Windows Agent (ISE 1.1 release ...
☑	NACAgent 4.9.0.42	NACAgent	4.9.0.42	Windows Agent (ISE 1.1.1 or later)
☑	NACAgent 4.9.0.47	NACAgent	4.9.0.47	Windows Agent with Win8 OS su...
☐	WebAgent 4.9.0.20	WebAgent	4.9.0.20	Web Agent (ISE 1.0MR only)
☐	WebAgent 4.9.0.24	WebAgent	4.9.0.24	Web Agent (ISE 1.1.1 or later)
☑	WebAgent 4.9.0.27	WebAgent	4.9.0.27	Web Agent with Win8 OS suppor...
☐	WinSPWizard 1.0.0.22	WinSPWizard	1.0.0.22	Supplicant Provisioning Wizard f...
☑	WinSPWizard 1.0.0.23	WinSPWizard	1.0.0.23	SP Wizard for Windows with Win...

Download Remote Resources

Save   Cancel

Figure 17-45 *Agent Resources from Cisco Site*

6. Click **Add > Native Supplicant Profile**.

7. Name the native supplicant profile EAPTLS-NSP.

8. Operating system may remain the default of ALL.

9. Ensure that Wireless is checked.

10. Wired is optional.

11. Provide the SSID for the corporate wireless network.

12. Select the security level (such as WPA2).

13. Choose TLS for the allowed protocol.

14. Select the certificate size (such as 2048).

15. Click **Submit**.

Figure 17-46 shows the completed native supplicant profile.

Native Supplicant Profile > **New Supplicant Profile**

Native Supplicant Profile

* Name	EAPTLS-NSP
Description	
* Operating System	ALL
* Connection Type	☐ Wired
	☑ Wireless
*SSID	CiscoPressCorp
Security	WPA2 Enterprise
* Allowed Protocol	TLS
* Key Size	2048

Submit   Cancel

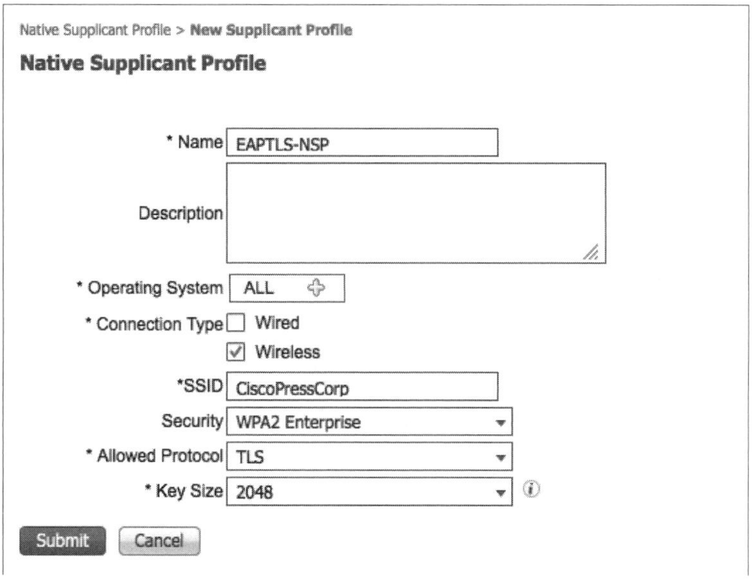

Figure 17-46   *Native Supplicant Profile for EAP-TLS*

Configure the Client Provisioning Policy

You configure a Client Provisioning Policy to dictate the software and profiles that should be downloaded and installed based on the operating system of the endpoint and a multitude of other possible attributes. For example, you might configure a policy for Android to be provisioned for the CORP-SSID wireless network when an employee is going through the provisioning process while configuring the CONTRACTOR-SSID for all vendors and contractors who are also working through the provisioning process.

For our example, let's create one client provisioning policy per OS using the following steps:

1. Navigate to **Policy > Client Provisioning**.

2. Name a new rule iOS.

3. Set the operating system as Apple iOS Al.l.

4. Set the result to be the EAPTLS-NSP supplicant profile.

> **Note**   The ISE client provisioning portal automatically uses the Over the Air (OTA) provisioning process that is native to iOS for Apple iOS. There is no need to specify that here.

5. Insert a new rule below the iOS rule; name that rule Android.

6. Set the operating system as Android.

7. Set the result to be the EAPTLS-NSP supplicant profile.

> **Note**   The ISE client provisioning portal automatically redirects Android devices to play.google.com to download the supplicant-provisioning app. There is no ability to specify a different app store.

8. Insert a new rule below the Android rule; name that rule Windows.

9. Set the operating system as Windows All.

10. Configure the results to use the WinSPWizard AND EAPTLS-NSP, as shown in Figure 17-47.

    The drop-down provides many more possibilities for Windows, because we also have the ability to provision the NAC agent or web agent to the Windows operating system. Windows uses the Cisco Supplicant Provisioning wizard (a Java applet) to implement the provisioning, and that must be specified here.

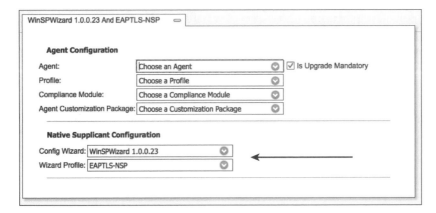

Figure 17-47   *CPP Results for Windows Operating Systems*

11. Insert a new rule below the Windows rule; name that rule MAC OS.

12. Set the operating system as Mac OS X.

13. Configure the results to use the MacSPWizard AND EAPTLS-NSP.

Like Windows, the drop-down choices for Mac OSX provide many more possibilities, because you have the ability to also provision the NAC agent to the Mac OS X
operating system. MAC OS will use the Cisco Supplicant Provisioning wizard (a Java
applet) to implement the provisioning, and that must be specified here.

Figure 17-48 shows the final client provisioning policy.

Figure 17-48 *Client Provisioning Policy*

Configure the WebAuth

The client provisioning policy is now created, and it will be used with both dual-SSID
and single-SSID provisioning. However, you must ensure that the Web Auth Portal page is
ready for the dual-SSID flow.

There is a plethora of options when it comes to Web Authentication and supplicant provisioning. For instance, it is absolutely possible to configure different web portals based
on a number of attributes available from the authentication request (such as source SSID).
This way, you can enable the device registration and supplicant provisioning to occur per
use case, if you so choose.

For simplicity, use the DefaultGuestPortal for your example:

1. Navigate to **Administration > Web Portal Management > Guest**.

2. Choose **Multi-Portal Configuration > DefaultGuestPortal**.

3. Click **Operations**.

4. Ensure the Enable Self-Provisioning Flow check box is selected, as shown in Figure
17-49.

5. Click **Save**.

Figure 17-49 *Web Portal Configuration*

Verify Default Unavailable Client Provisioning Policy Action

ISE supports iOS, Android, Windows, and Mac OS X. However, it is possible for an end user to attempt access with a client that is not supported by ISE native supplicant provisioning (such as attempting with a BlackBerry or Windows Mobile device). ISE offers two options for that situation:

- **Allow Network Access:** With this option, users are allowed to register their device through the My Devices Portal and gain network access without having to install and launch a native supplicant wizard. This assumes the user will have to interact and configure the supplicant independently. This option may be attractive if the end users are capable of requesting and installing their own certificates.

- **Apply Defined Authorization Policy:** Basically, this option leaves the client in the current state, which is a state of limited access. This is also the default setting.

Figure 17-50 shows the setting for Native Supplicant Provisioning Policy Unavailable.

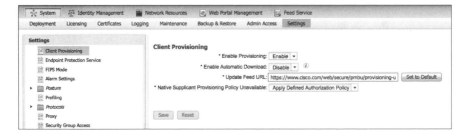

Figure 17-50 *Default Unavailable Client Provisioning Policy Action*

Create the Authorization Profiles

Although having the client provisioning policy is required, the Authorization Policy is still mission-critical. Without the properly configured Authorization Policy, there is no "call to action" that sends the endpoint over to the client provisioning portal. Of course, an authorization rule needs an Authorization Policy that includes that call to action.

Create two authorization profiles, one for Android and another for the remaining devices:

1. Navigate to **Policy > Policy Elements > Results > Authorization > Authorization Profiles.**

2. Add a new authorization profile, named Android NSP.

3. Select a dACL to permit traffic when doing wired onboarding.

4. Select **Web Authentication.**

5. From the drop-down, choose **Supplicant Provisioning.**

6. Enter the Android Marketplace ACL.

7. Click **Submit.**

   Figure 17-51 shows the Android NSP authorization profile.

Authorization Profiles > **NSP**
Authorization Profile

* Name	Android NSP
Description	Send To Native Supplicant Provisioning
* Access Type	ACCESS_ACCEPT
Service Template	☐

▼ Common Tasks

☑ Web Authentication

    Supplicant Provisioning ▼   ACL   Android-Marketplace
        ☐ Static IP/Host name

☐ Auto Smart Port

▼ Advanced Attributes Settings

Select an item ⊘ = ⊘ — ✛

▼ Attributes Details

Access Type = ACCESS_ACCEPT
DACL = PERMIT_ALL_TRAFFIC
cisco-av-pair = url-redirect-acl=Android-Marketplace
cisco-av-pair = url-redirect=https://ip:port/guestportal/gateway?sessionId=SessionIdValue&action=nsp

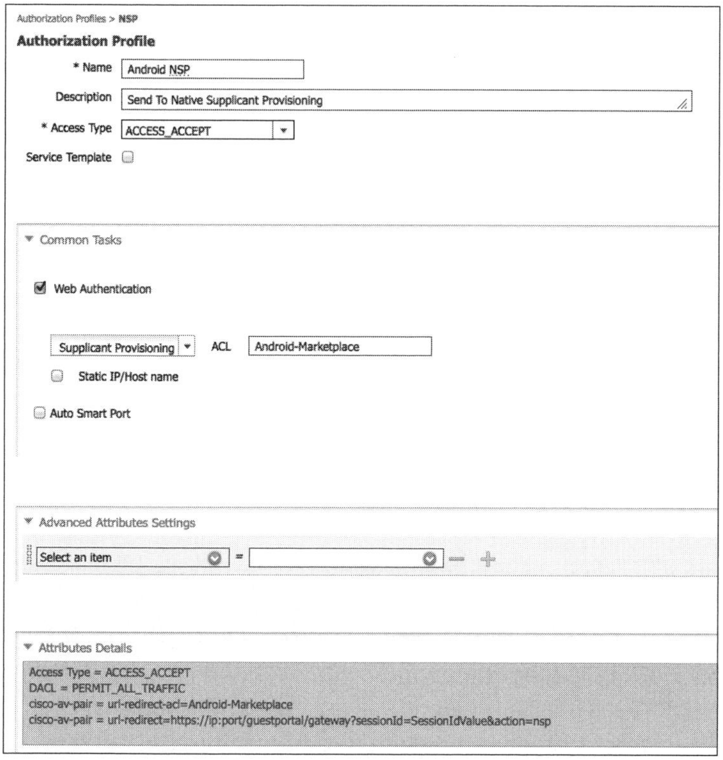

Figure 17-51 *Android NSP Authorization Profile*

8. Add a new authorization profile, named NSP.

9. Select a dACL to permit traffic when doing wired onboarding.

10. Select Web Authentication.

11. From the drop-down, choose Supplicant Provisioning.

12. Enter the ACL-WEBAUTH-REDIRECT ACL.

13. Click **Submit**.

Figure 17-52 shows the NSP authorization profile.

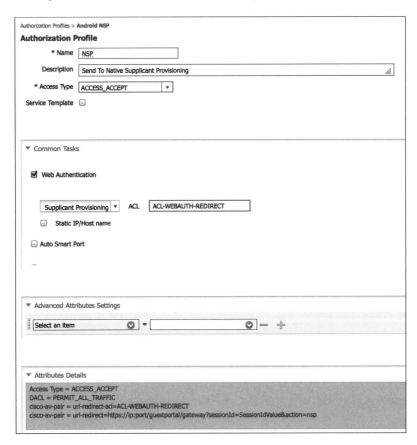

Figure 17-52 *NSP Authorization Profile*

Create the Authorization Policy Rules

Now you have the authorization profiles, you need to create the authorization rules that use those profiles for results. Create two authorization rules that result in a client provisioning action: one for Android and another for the remaining devices. Lastly, create an authorization rule that permits the devices that have already been provisioned.

The following steps create the Android NSP authorization rule:

1. Navigate to **Policy > Authorization.**

2. Add a new rule, just above the default rule.

3. Name the rule Android NSP.

4. Set the conditions as

   Network Access:AuthenticationMethod EQUALS MSCHAPV2

   And

   Session:Device-OS EQUALS Android

5. Set the authorization result to be the Android NSP created earlier.

6. Click **Done.**

Now you've created the Android NSP Rule is created. What is remaining is to create the non-Android (all other devices) rule, and rule for any devices that have already been onboarded. The following steps configure the non-Android provisioning rule:

1. Add a new rule, just above the default rule and below the Android rule.

2. Name the rule Native Supplicant Provisioning.

3. Set the conditions as

   Network Access:AuthenticationMethod EQUALS MSCHAPV2

4. Set the authorization result to be the NSP Authorization profiler created earlier.

5. Click **Done.**

Now you have created both provisioning rules in the authorization table, all that remains is to add the EAP-TLS rule for successful authentications. The following steps create a rule that matches authentications using certificates and ensures that the MAC address of the endpoint matches the MAC address burned into the certificate during the onboarding process:

1. Add a new rule, just above the default rule and below the NSP rule.

2. Name the rule Employee TLS.

3. Set the conditions as

   Network Access:AuthenticationMethod EQUALS x509_PKI

   And

   CERTIFICATE:Subject Alternative Name CONTAINS Radius:Calling-Station-ID

And

Endpoints:BYODRegistration EQUALS Yes

4. Set the authorization result to be Permit Access.

5. Click **Done**.

6. Click **Save**.

Figure 17-53 shows the completed authorization policy with all three of the new rules.

☑	Native Supplicant Provisioning	if	Network Access:AuthenticationMethod EQUALS MSCHAPV2	then	NSP
☑	Employee TLS	if	(Network Access:EapAuthentication EQUALS EAP-TLS AND CERTIFICATE:Subject Alternative Name CONTAINS Radius:Calling-Station-ID AND EndPoints:BYODRegistration EQUALS Yes)	then	PermitAccess
☑	Default		if no matches, then	WEBAUTH	

Figure 17-53 *Authorization Policy with the NSP Rules*

Configure SCEP

ISE acts as a registration authority (RA) for the certificate enrollment and provisioning of the devices that are being onboarded. So, with ISE 1.2, ISE is not the certificate authority (CA); instead it is a "broker" of sorts that uses Simple Certificate Enrollment Protocol (SCEP) to request and provision a certificate to the client from the CA of your choice.

Multiple CAs could be used. Although it is not commonly deployed, Cisco offers CA functionality in the higher-end routers, like the 7200, 7300, and 7600 series routers, as well as integrated services routers (ISR). At the time of this publishing, no CA function is available for the aggregated services router (ASR).

At present, the most common CA seems to be the Microsoft Certificate Authority. The Microsoft CA has support for SCEP and it is called Network Device Enrollment Services (NDES). It requires Windows 2008 R2 Enterprise or newer and that server must be part of a domain.

Note   There are companies who have created a brand-new Active Directory domain with only the one server in it, just for the CA and NDES functionality to be separate from their production AD. This is not necessarily recommended, just noting the example to show the level of flexibility you might have, if needed. For more details on the configuration of a Microsoft CA, refer to Appendix C, "Configuring the Microsoft CA for BYOD."

You may use any CA of your choosing, as long as it meets the requirements:

■ Must support SCEP

■ Must support an automated or automatic issuing of the requested certificates

The configuration of ISE to use the CA is simple. There is really just one setting to configure by using the following steps:

1. Navigate to **Administration > System > Certificates**.

2. Click **SCEP RA Profiles**.

3. Click **Add**.

4. Name the CA (example is CP_AD_CA).

5. Add the URL, such as http://*ip-address-of-ca*/certsrv/mscep/

6. Click **Test Connectivity**.

7. Click **Submit**.

Figure 17-54 shows the completed SCEP RA profile.

Figure 17-54 *Completed SCEP RA Profile*

Assuming your CA configuration was complete, your deployment is now ready to do BYOD onboarding.

BYOD Onboarding Process Detailed

Yes, this chapter is getting very long. However, it is my hope that you will find all this information useful if you ever find yourself in a spot where you need to do troubleshooting of this process. You have seen that the user experience is simple and straightforward, but the process behind the scenes is complex.

iOS Onboarding Flow

We examine, in detail, the experience with iOS devices and onboarding. To do so, we are focusing on a single SSID onboarding experience. The end user should only have to complete four actions, as noted in Figure 17-55. However, we look at all the items that occur behind the scenes.

Phase 1: Device Registration

1. User joins the corporate SSID and the iOS device prompts the user for credentials.

2. The user enters his AD username and password.

3. The EAP login request is sent to the wireless controller, which wraps the request in a RADIUS access-accept request to ISE

4. The authorization result from ISE will include a URL-redirection to the NSP portal.

5. The user opens his web browser, which is redirected to the NSP portal on ISE, displaying the device-registration page with the device-ID pre-populated with the MAC address.

6. The user clicks register, which immediately triggers three events:

    ■ Sets the BYODRegistration flag for the endpoint identity to Yes.

    ■ Adds the endpoint to the RegisteredDevices identity group.

    ■ Sends the CA's certificate to the IOS device for it to trust for OTA.

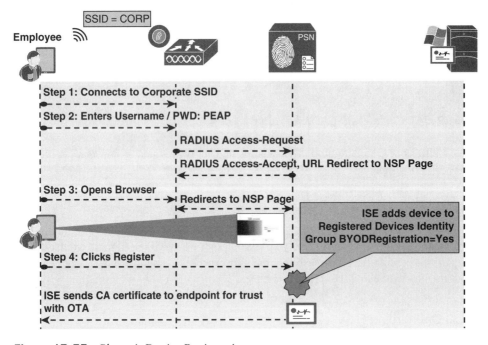

Figure 17-55 *Phase 1: Device Registration*

Phase 2: Device Enrollment

1. ISE sends a profile service to ISE via Over the Air Provisioning (OTA).

2. The profile instructs iOS to generate a Certificate Signing Request (CSR) using the Unique Device Identifier (UDID) as the certificate's subject, and the MAC address as the Subject Alternative Name (SAN) field:

   ■ CN=device-UDID

   ■ SAN=MAC-Address

3. The device CSR is sent to ISE, which uses SCEP to proxy the certificate enrollment request to the CA.

4. The CA automatically issues the certificate.

5. The certificate is sent back to ISE, which sends it to the device through the OTA service.

Phase 2 is illustrated in Figure 17-56.

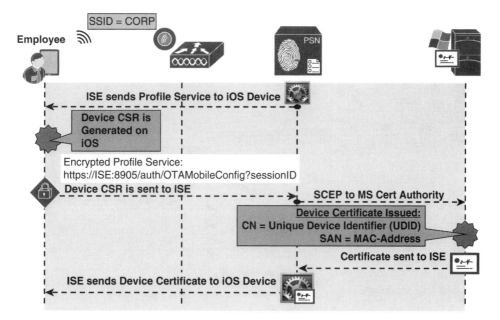

Figure 17-56 *Phase 2: Device Enrollment*

Phase 3: Device Provisioning

1. The iOS device generates another CSR, using the employee's credentials (given to iOS by ISE via the OTA service) as the certificate's subject, and the MAC address as the Subject Alternative Name (SAN) field:

- CN=Username

- SAN=MAC-Address

2. The user CSR is sent to ISE, which uses SCEP to proxy the certificate enrollment request to the CA.

3. The CA automatically issues the certificate.

4. The certificate is sent back to ISE, which sends it to the device through the OTA service. Included in that profile is the WiFi configuration, which details the SSID and to use EAP-TLS.

5. ISE sends a CoA to the NAD of the type ReAuth, which causes a new authentication.

6. The endpoint now authenticates to the corporate SSID using the certificate via EAP-TLS.

Phase 3 is illustrated in Figure 17-57.

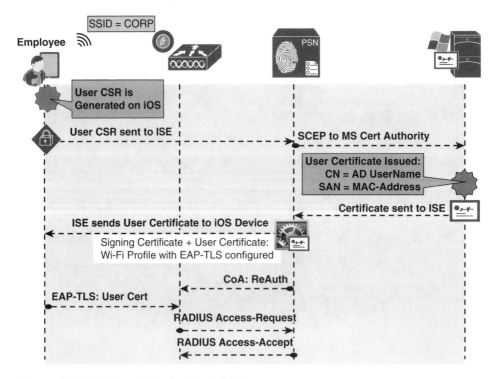

Figure 17-57   *Phase 3: Device Provisioning*

Android Flow

To detail the flow of onboarding with Android, we will use the dual-SSID approach. Android is certainly capable of doing a single-SSID approach as well. The end-user should only have to complete four actions, as noted in Figure 17-55. However, let's take a look at all the items that occur behind the scenes.

Phase 1: Device Registration

1. User joins the open SSID, and ISE sends a redirection to the Centralized Web Authentication portal.

2. The WLC sends a MAC Authentication Bypass (MAB) request to ISE.

3. The authorization result from ISE will include a URL-redirection to the Centralized Web Authentication (CWA) portal.

4. The user opens a browser, and is redirected to the CWA portal.

5. The user enters his AD username and password.

6. The successful Web Auth triggers two events:

   ■ The web page changes to the native supplicant provisioning portal.

   ■ A CoA is sent to the WLC, which includes a redirection to the NSP portal.

7. The NSP portal displays the device-registration page with the device-ID pre-populated with the MAC address of the endpoint.

8. User click Register, which immediately triggers five events:

   ■ Sets the BYODRegistration flag for the endpoint identity to Yes.

   ■ Adds the endpoint to the RegisteredDevices identity group.

   ■ Sets the Session:Device-OS attribute to Android. (This is a temporary attribute and only used for the provisioning process.)

   ■ Sends a CoA to the WLC to apply the correct ACL, allowing Google Marketplace access for the Android device.

   ■ The web page sends the browser to Google Play Store.

Phase 1 is illustrated in Figure 17-58.

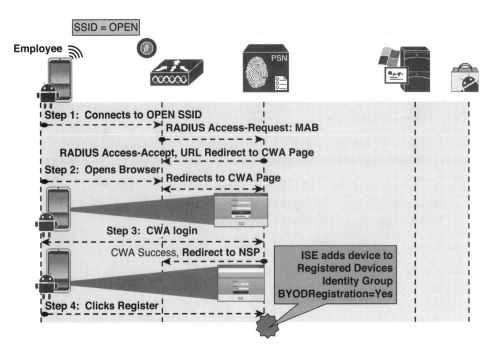

Figure 17-58   *Phase 1: Device Registration*

Phase 2: Download SPW

1. The CoA from phase 1 applied an ACL that permits traffic to the Google Play Store (Android Marketplace).

2. The browser was automatically sent to the Google Play Store and the Android device prompts the user to choose the Internet or Play Store to complete the request.

3. The user may be prompted to login to the Google Play Store.

4. The user clicks to install the Cisco Network Setup Assistant app.

Phase 2 is illustrated in Figure 17-59.

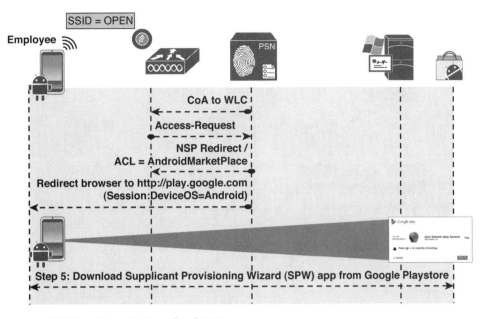

Figure 17-59 *Phase 2: Download NSA*

Phase 3: Device Provisioning

1. The Network Setup Assistant installs, and the user runs it.

2. The NSA sends a discovery message to http://*default-gateway*/auth/discovery

3. The WLC redirects that HTTP message to the ISE native supplicant provisioning portal based on the URL-REDIRECT result within the authorization from ISE.

4. ISE sends the Android profile based on the EAPTLS-NSP supplicant profile to the endpoint.

5. NSA generates the Certificate Signing Request (CSR), using the employee's credentials as the certificate's subject, and the MAC address as the Subject Alternative Name (SAN) field:

   ■ CN=Username

   ■ SAN=MAC-Address

6. The CSR is sent to ISE, which uses SCEP to proxy the certificate enrollment request to the CA.

7. The CA automatically issues the certificate.

8. The certificate is sent back to ISE, which sends it to NSA app. Included in that profile is the WiFi configuration, which details the SSID and to use EAP-TLS.

9. The NSA app connects the endpoint to the corporate SSID and ISE sends a CoA to the NAD of the type ReAuth, which also causes a new authentication.

10. The endpoint now authenticates to the corporate SSID using the certificate via EAP-TLS.

Phase 3 is illustrated in Figure 17-60.

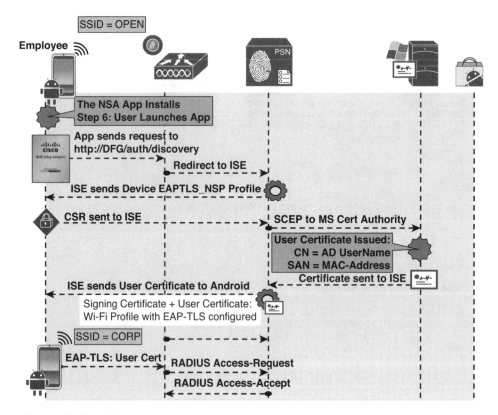

Figure 17-60 *Phase 3: Device Provisioning*

Windows and Mac-OSX Flow

Mac OS X and Windows both use a wizard to accomplish the onboarding and provisioning. It is a Java-based applet called the Cisco native supplicant provisioning wizard. The wizard takes care of triggering the CSR from the OS and installing the supplicant profile. This is only a two-phase process.

Phase 1: Device Registration

1. User joins the corporate SSID, and the iOS device prompts the user for credentials.

2. The user enters his AD username and password.

3. The EAP login request is sent to the wireless controller, which wraps the request in a RADIUS access-accept request to ISE.

4. The authorization result from ISE includes a URL-redirection to the NSP portal.

5. The user opens his web browser, which is redirected to the NSP portal on ISE, displaying the device-registration page with the device-ID pre-populated with the MAC address.

6. The user clicks register, which immediately triggers two events:

   ■ Sets the BYODRegistration flag for the endpoint identity to Yes.

   ■ Adds the endpoint to the RegisteredDevices identity group.

Phase 1 is illustrated in Figure 17-61.

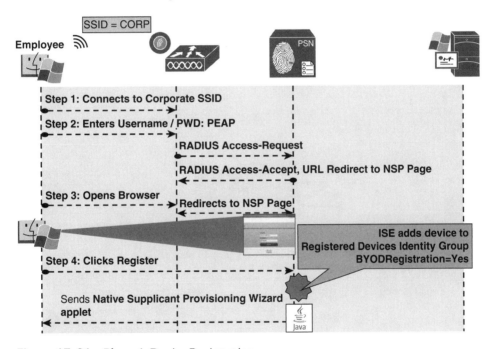

Figure 17-61   *Phase 1: Device Registration*

Phase 2: Device Provisioning

1. The native supplicant provisioning wizard is downloaded and runs.

2. The NSP wizard sends a discovery message to http://default-gateway/auth/discovery.

3. The WLC redirects that HTTP message to the ISE native supplicant provisioning portal based on the URL-REDIRECT result within the authorization from ISE.

4. ISE sends the NSP profile based on the EAPTLS-NSP supplicant profile to the endpoint.

5. The NSP wizard generates the Certificate Signing Request (CSR), using the employee's credentials as the certificate's subject, and the MAC address as the Subject Alternative Name (SAN) field:

- CN=Username

- SAN=MAC-Address

6. The CSR is sent to ISE, which uses SCEP to proxy the certificate enrollment request to the CA.

7. The CA automatically issues the certificate.

8. The certificate is sent back to ISE and is sent down to the NSP wizard. Included in that profile is the WiFi configuration, which details the SSID and to use EAP-TLS.

9. The NSP wizard connects the endpoint to the corporate SSID, and ISE sends a CoA to the NAD of the type ReAuth, which also causes a new authentication.

10. The endpoint now authenticates to the corporate SSID using the certificate via EAP-TLS.

Phase 2 is illustrated in Figure 17-62.

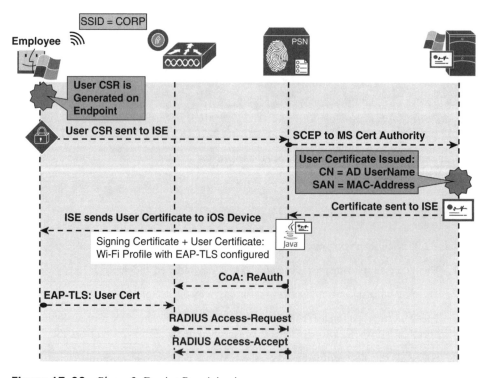

Figure 17-62 *Phase 2: Device Provisioning*

MDM Onboarding

Many organizations use MDM solutions. These solutions provide endpoint management for a plethora of devices. They help enforce specific security requirements, such as endpoint encryption, PIN lock, jail-break detection, remote wipe capabilities, and more. Many MDMs will even provision supplicants and certificates to devices as part of their management package.

What would typically occur is that a user would bring in a mobile device, and to gain access to the network, he had to call the helpdesk and receive instructions on how to onboard the device with the MDM, so he could gain access to the network. There are some significant downsides to this process, such as

- Users are required to manually connect to the MDM solution to begin the onboarding process.

- There was no enforcement to help "steer" the user toward that solution.

- An MDM license was required for every device the organization would provision and allow to have network access, which can be cost prohibitive.

However, this presented a beneficial and strategic opportunity for Cisco and the MDM vendors. The MDM vendors possessed the mobile device-management capabilities, and Cisco had the onboarding, network access policy, and enforcement mechanisms.

ISE 1.2 adds the integration of five of the industries top MDM vendors:

- AirWatch

- Mobile Iron

- ZenPrise (acquired by Citrix)

- Good Technologies

- SAP Afaria

These five vendors have implemented an Application Programming Interface (API) written by Cisco to enable scalable bidirectional communication between their solution and ISE.

Integration Points

The API provides ISE with the ability to use MDM attributes in the authorization policies. The authorization may use a macro-level attribute stating that the device is in compliance with the MDM policy or Micro level attributes, such as jail break status, PIN lock, or even endpoint encryption.

Table 17-1 documents the possible MDM attribute values, provides a definition of each value, and lists the possible values for each attribute.

Table 17-1 *MDM Attributes*

MDM Attribute	Definition	Possible Values
DeviceRegisterStatus	Is the device registered with the MDM?	Unregistered Registered
DeviceComplianceStatus	Macro-level attribute stating if the device meets the security policy of the MDM.	NonCompliant Compliant
DiskEncryptionStatus	Is encryption enabled on the storage of the device?	On Off
PinLockStatus	Does the device have an automatic lock, requiring a PIN or password to unlock the device?	On Off
JailBrokenStatus	Has the device been jail broken?	Unbroken Broken
Manufacturer	What is the manufacturer of the device?	Text field or can be compared to attribute from AD/LDAP
Model	Model of the device	Text field or can be compared to attribute from AD/LDAP
IMEI	Unique ID	Text field or can be compared to attribute from AD/LDAP
SerialNumber	Self-explanatory	Text field or can be compared to attribute from AD/LDAP
OSVersion	Version of the operating system	Text field or can be compared to attribute from AD/LDAP
PhoneNumber	Self-explanatory	Text field, or can be compared to attribute from AD/LDAP

Configuring MDM Integration

Before you configure ISE to communicate with the MDM, ISE needs to trust the certificate of the MDM for the SSL-encrypted communications. You can accomplish this by using the following steps:

1. Navigate to **Administration > Certificates**.

2. Choose **Certificate Store**.

3. Import the Certificate of the MDM as a trusted certificate.

Now that the certificate is trusted, add the MDM Server to ISE. ISE may be configured with the knowledge of many MDMs, but only one may be active at a time:

4. Navigate to **Administration > Network Resources > MDM**.

5. Click **Add**.

6. Input a name for the connection to the MDM.

7. Add an optional description.

8. Input the hostname of the server.

9. The port should be 443, unless otherwise instructed by your MDM vendor.

10. Instance name is usually not used, but may be used in some cases when the vendor is multi-tenant aware.

11. Use the administrator name that will enroll all the mobile devices and its password.

12. Click **Verify** to test the connectivity.

13. Click **Save**.

Figure 17-63 shows the successful addition of the MDM.

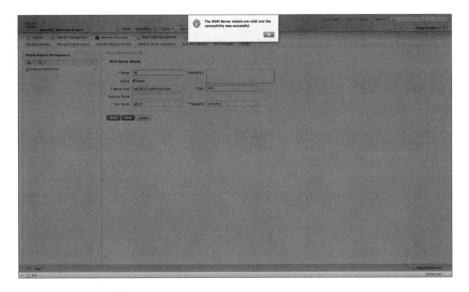

Figure 17-63 *Add MDM*

Configuring MDM Onboarding Policies

The MDM onboarding is configured much like the ISE BYOD onboarding. The authorization rules need to be configured to redirect the endpoint to MDM onboarding if it meets specific requirements.

One example of where to place an MDM onboarding policy is just below the BYOD onboarding rules, but above the rule that would permit final access. Some organizations would not want to send all devices to the MDM, but would prefer that specific devices be included. One way to achieve this is to maintain a separate list of MAC addresses belonging to corporate owned assets, and add that list to an endpoint identity group. The example shown in Figure 17-64 does not use identity groups, but it represents a policy that has been used in production at a number of installs.

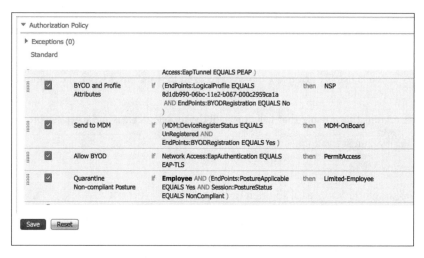

Figure 17-64   *MDM Authorization Rule Example*

The first step is to create the authorization profile that redirects the endpoint to the MDM for onboarding:

1. Navigate to **Policy** > **Policy Elements** > **Results** > **Authorization**.

2. Select **Authorization Profiles**.

3. Add a new authorization profile named MDM Onboard.

4. Access type set to Access-Accept.

5. Set Web Authentication to MDM Redirect.

6. The Web Authentication ACL should reference an ACL that permits access to the MDM and ISE, but denies access to the rest of the Internet.

7. Click **Submit**.

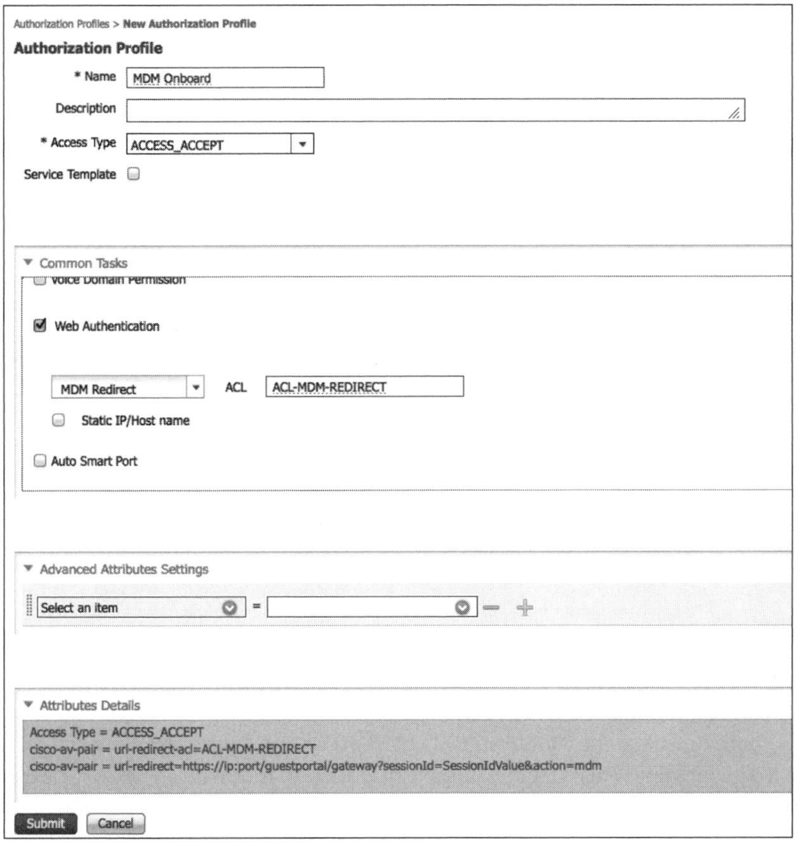

Figure 17-65 *MDM Onboard Authorization Profile*

Now, create an authorization rule to send devices to the MDM for onboarding:

1. Navigate to **Policy > Authorization**.

2. Insert a new rule where it makes sense in your policy.

3. Name the rule MDM Onboard.

4. Add the conditions, as follows:

   Endpoints:BYODRegistration EQUALS Yes

   And

   MDM:DeviceRegistrationStatus EQUALS Unregistered

5. Set the result to the MDM Onboard Authorization Profile.

6. Click **Done**.

Add another rule below it that permits access to devices that are registered and meet the MDM Compliance:

7. Navigate to **Policy** > **Authorization**.

8. Insert a new rule below the MDM Onboard Rule.

9. Name the rule MDM Permit.

10. Add the conditions, as follows:

    Endpoints:BYODRegistration EQUALS Yes

    And

    MDM:DeviceRegistrationStatus EQUALS Registered

    And

    MDM:DeviceComplianceStatus EQUAL Compliant

11. Set the Result to Permit Access.

12. Click **Done**.

13. Click **Save**.

When using MDM attributes as part of the authorization policy, ISE checks with the MDM at every authorization. So, if the MDM is unavailable, the rule will never match. There is also a bulk download of data from the MDM every four hours, detailing endpoint status. If an endpoint is marked non-compliant during that download, a CoA is sent and the device is forced to reauthenticate, providing a different result (such as quarantine).

Managing Endpoints

Each user may manage the devices they have personally onboarded from the My Devices portal, or the administrator may manage the devices from the endpoints screen.

Table 17-2 lists the options available with registered devices and provides a description of each option.

Table 17-2   *Registered Device Options*

Registered Device Option	Description
Lost	When marking a device as lost, it will be added to the black-list endpoint identity group and denied further access to the network until reinstated.
Reinstate	When the device is reinstated, it will be moved from the blacklist identity group to the RegisteredDevices identity group, so it may be permitted access to the network again.

Registered Device Option	Description
Delete	Remove the endpoint from the endpoint directory.
Full Wipe	An MDM action to wipe the entire endpoint.
Corporate Wipe	An MDM action to remove only the containerized data on the endpoint considered corporate.
PIN Lock	An MDM action to initiate a remote lock on the device.

Self Management

The end users self-manage the devices they have registered via the MyDevices portal. Navigate to https://ISE:8443/mydevices/ or the friendly URL configured at Administration > Web Portal Management > Settings > General > Ports.

After logging in to the My Devices portal, the list of registered devices is displayed. As shown in Figure 17-66, the end user may select his device and initiate one of the options, such as Corporate Wipe.

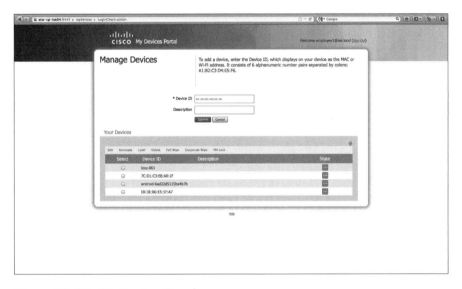

Figure 17-66 *MyDevices Portal*

Administrative Management

From an administrative perspective, the endpoints are administered just like any other endpoint at Administration > Identity Management > Identities > Endpoints. From here, an administrator may initiate actions against the registered devices, as shown in Figure 17-67.

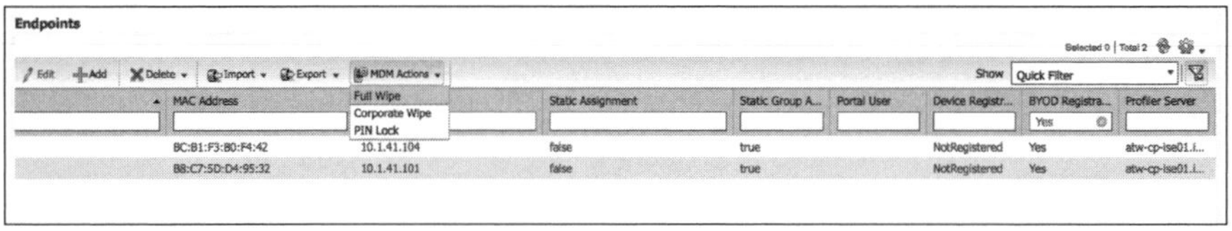

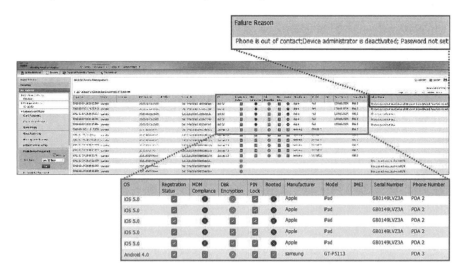

Figure 17-67   *Endpoint Identities*

You may also run a report to get a list of all registered devices and their current status (Operations > Reports > Endpoints and Users > Mobile Device Management Report). Figure 17-68 shows the MDM report with specific entries called out.

Figure 17-68   *Mobile Device Management Report*

The Opposite of BYOD: Identify Corporate Systems

For many years, customers have voiced their business need to identify the machine as an authorized asset, in addition to the user being an authorized user. Given that Microsoft Windows has both a user and a machine state, it allows the device to be authenticated to the network with what is commonly known as machine auth, as well as the ability to have the interactive user authenticated to the network.

The issue is that EAP was always designed to transport a single credential. The machine authentication occurs when there is no interactive user or if the supplicant profile is configured to only issue the machine's credentials. When the user logs into the system, it changes to a user-state and issues the credentials associated to the user. With standard RADIUS and standard EAP, there was no way to join those authentications together.

To answer the issue, Cisco enhanced EAP-FAST with the ability to do EAP chaining. EAP chaining is the ability to authenticate both the machine and the user within the same authentication session. EAP-FASTv2 is being standardized on and should be known as EAP-TEAP when it finalizes standardization.

EAP Chaining

With EAP-FASTv2 and EAP-chaining, both the machine and the user are issued a Protected Access Credential (PAC), similar to secure cookie. So, ISE may request the machine PAC during the user authentication process, and the authorization policy is capable of using the results of either or both authentications.

The authorization condition is NetworkAccess:EAPChainingResult, and the options are

- No chaining
- User and machine both failed
- User and machine both succeeded
- User failed and machine succeeded
- User succeeded and machine failed

With that level of flexibility and authorization, a result may be provided that permits limited access to remediate a single failure, no access if neither succeeds, and full access if both succeed.

Figure 17-69 shows an example authorization rule that uses EAP chaining.

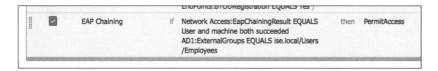

Figure 17-69 *EAP Chaining Authorization Rule Example*

A practical example from a customer was to use EAP chaining to identify corporate owned and managed devices. The authorization rule acted like this:

If

the device and user authentication both succeed

and the endpoint posture is compliant

and the user is a member of the PCI group in Active Directory

and the location of the endpoint is on a corporate campus

Then

permit full access

and assign the PCI Security Group Tag (SGT)

That authorization rule allowed only those devices to communicate to the servers housing credit card data.

Summary

This chapter took an in-depth look at BYOD onboarding and MDM integration. It provided a brief look at identifying corporate assets and users with EAP chaining. The next chapter focuses on distributed ISE deployments.

Chapter 18

Setting Up a Distributed Deployment

Chapter 4, "Making Sense of All the ISE Deployment Design Options," discussed the many options within ISE design. At this point, you should have an idea of which type of deployment will be the best fit for your environment, based on the number of concurrent endpoints and the number of policy services nodes that will be used in the deployment. This chapter focuses on the configuration steps required to deploy ISE in a distributed design.

Configuring ISE Nodes in a Distributed Environment

All ISE nodes are installed in a standalone mode by default. When in a standalone mode, the ISE node is configured to run all personas by default. That means that the standalone node runs Administration, Monitoring, and Policy Service personas.

It is up to you, the ISE administrator, to promote the first node to be a "Primary" Administration node and then join the additional nodes to this new deployment. At the time of joining, you will also determine which services will run on which nodes; in other words, you will determine which persona the node will have.

Make the Policy Administration Node a Primary Device

Because all ISE nodes are standalone by default, you must first promote the ISE node that will become the Primary Policy Administration node to be a "Primary" device instead of a standalone.

From the ISE GUI, perform the following steps:

1. Choose **Administration > System > Deployment**. Figure 18-1 shows an example of the Deployment screen.

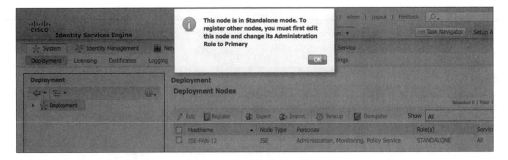

Figure 18-1 *Deployment Screen*

2. Select the ISE node (there should only be one at this point).

3. Click the **Make Primary** button, as shown in Figure 18-2.

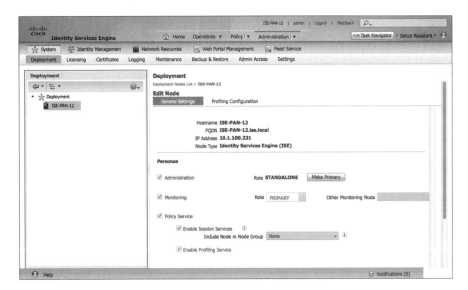

Figure 18-2 *Make Primary Button*

4. At this point, the Monitoring and Policy Service check boxes have become select-able. If the Primary node will not also be providing any of these services, uncheck them now. (You can always return later and make changes.)

5. Click Save.

Register an ISE Node to the Deployment

Now that there is a primary PAN, you can now implement a multinode deployment. From the GUI on the primary admin node, you will register and assign personas to all ISE nodes.

From the ISE GUI on the primary PAN, perform the following steps:

1. Choose **Administration > System > Deployment**.

2. Choose **Register > Register an ISE Node**, as shown in Figure 18-3.

Note   As with all other operations with ISE, DNS is a critical component.

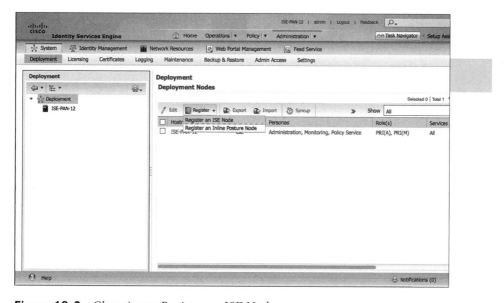

Figure 18-3   *Choosing to Register an ISE Node*

3. In the Hostname or IP Address field, enter the IP address or DNS name of the first ISE node you will be joining to the deployment, as shown in Figure 18-4.

4. In the User Name and Password fields, enter the administrator name (admin by default) and password.

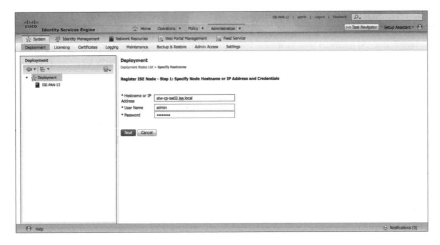

Figure 18-4   *Specifying Hostname and Credentials*

5. Click **Next**.

> **Note**   If you have not installed valid certificates from a trusted root, you will receive an error. You'll be required to install the certificate of each ISE node as a trusted root, because they are all self-signed certificates. Best practice is to always use certificates issued from a trusted source. (See Chapter 9, "The Basics: Principle Configuration Tasks for Cisco ISE," for more information.)

6. On the Configure Node screen, shown in Figure 18-5, you can pick the main persona of the ISE node, including enabling of profiling services. However, you cannot configure which probes to enable yet. Choose the persona for this node.

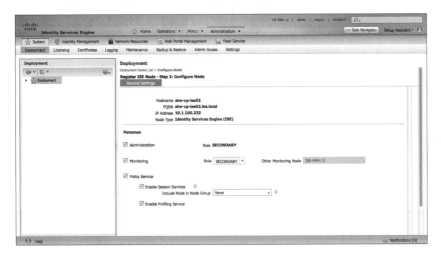

Figure 18-5   *Configure Node Screen*

7. Click **Next**. At this point, the Policy Administrative Node will sync the entire database to the newly joined ISE node, as you can see in Figure 18-6.

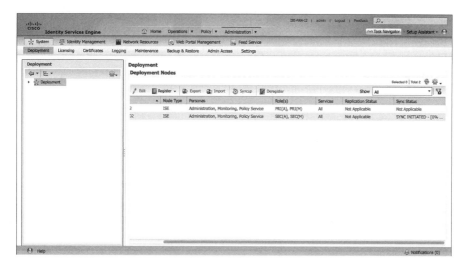

Figure 18-6   *Sync Initiated*

8. Repeat these steps for all the ISE nodes that should be joined to the same deployment.

Ensure the Persona of All Nodes Is Accurate

Now that all of your ISE nodes are joined to the deployment, you can ensure that the correct personas are assigned to the appropriate ISE nodes. Table 18-1 shows the ISE nodes in the sample deployment, and the associated persona that will be assigned. Figure 18-7 shows the final Deployment screen, after the synchronization has completed for all nodes.

Note   This is also a good time to double-check that all the desired probes are enabled on the PSNs. We have personally experienced a number of customers who called with problems of "database not replicating" and things like that, but it actually turned out to be that the probes were not enabled.

Table 18-1   *ISE Nodes and Personas*

ISE Node	Persona
ATW-ISE-12	Administration, Monitoring
atw-cp-ise02	Administration, Monitoring

ISE Node	Persona
atw-cp-ise03	Policy Service
atw-cp-ise04	Policy Service

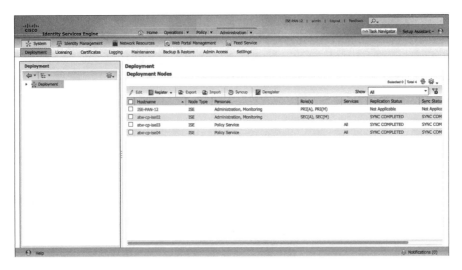

Figure 18-7   *Final Personas and Roles*

Understanding the HA Options Available

There are many different items to note when it comes to high availability (HA) within a Secure Unified Access deployment. There are the concerns of communication between the Policy Administration Nodes (PAN) and the other ISE nodes for database replications and synchronization. There is also the issue of authentication sessions reaching the PSNs in the event of a WAN outage, as well as a NAD recognizing that a PSN may no longer be active, and sending authentication requests to the active PSN instead.

Primary and Secondary Nodes

PANs and Monitoring and Troubleshooting (MnT) nodes both have a concept of Primary and Secondary nodes, but they operate very differently. Let's start with the easiest one first, the MnT node.

Monitoring and Troubleshooting Nodes

As you know, the MnT node is responsible for the logging and reporting functions of ISE. All Policy Service Nodes (PSN) will send their logging data to the MnT node as syslog messages (UDP/20514).

When there are two Monitoring nodes in an ISE deployment, all ISE nodes will send their audit data to both Monitoring nodes at the same time. Figure 18-8 displays this logging flow.

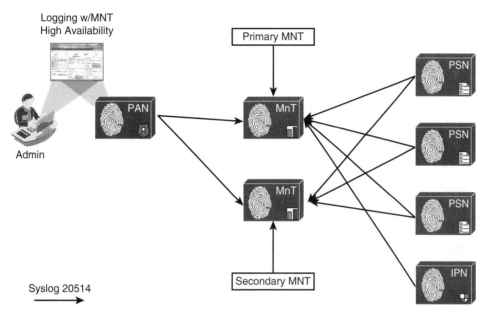

Figure 18-8 *Logging Flows*

Note Inline Posture Nodes (IPN) will send syslog only to a single target.

The active/active nature of the MnT nodes can be viewed easily in the administrative console, as the two MnTs get defined as LogCollector and LogCollector2. Figures 18-9 and 18-10 display the log collector definitions and the log settings, respectively.

Upon MnT failure, all nodes continue to send logs to the remaining MnT node. Therefore, no logs are lost. The PAN retrieves all log and report data from the Secondary MnT node, so there is no administrative function loss, either. However, the log database is not synchronized between the Primary and Secondary MnT nodes. Therefore, when the MnT node returns to service, a backup and restore of the monitoring node is required to keep the two MnT nodes in complete sync.

Note The best practice for logging is to also send logging data to a Security Information Manger (SIM) tool, for long-term data archiving and reporting.

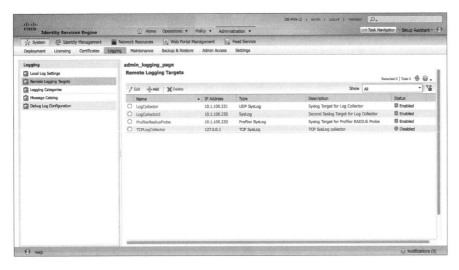

Figure 18-9 *Logging Targets*

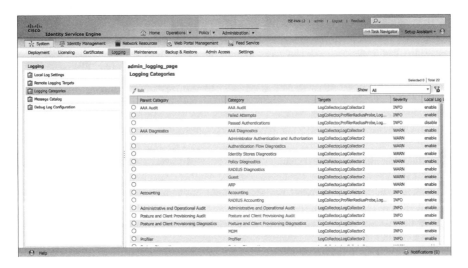

Figure 18-10 *Logging Categories*

Policy Administration Nodes

The PAN is responsible for providing not only an administrative GUI for ISE but also the critical function of database synchronization of all ISE nodes. All ISE nodes maintain a full copy of the database, with the master database existing on the Primary PAN.

A PSN may get new data about an endpoint, and when that occurs it must sync that data to the Primary PAN. The Primary PAN then synchronizes that data out to all the ISE nodes in the deployment. As the PAN may have many updates to send to each node, those nodes must acknowledge the last update before they may be sent a new update.

Because the functionality is so arduous, and having only a single source of truth for the data in the database is so critical, failing over to the Secondary PAN is a manual process. In the event of the Primary PAN going offline, no synchronizations occur until the Secondary PAN is promoted to Primary. Once it becomes the Primary, it takes over all synchronization responsibility. This is sometimes referred to as a "warm spare" type of HA.

Promoting the Secondary PAN to Primary

To promote the Secondary PAN to Primary, connect to the GUI on the Secondary PAN and perform the following steps:

1. Choose **Administration > System > Deployment**.

2. Select the Secondary PAN.

3. Click **Promote to Primary**. Figure 18-11 illustrates the Promote to Primary option available on the Secondary node.

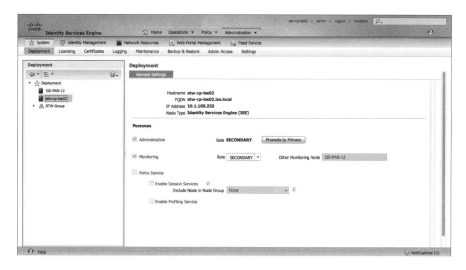

Figure 18-11   *Promoting a Secondary PAN to Primary*

Node Groups

Policy Services Nodes do not necessarily need to have an HA type of configuration. Every ISE node maintains a full copy of the database, and the NADs have their own detection of a "dead" RADIUS server, which triggers the NAD to send AAA communication to the next RADIUS server in the list.

However, ISE has the concept of a *node group*. Node groups are made up of Layer 2 adjacent (same VLAN) PSNs, where the PSNs maintain a heartbeat with each other. If a PSN goes down while a session is being authenticated, one of the other PSNs in the node group sends a Change of Authorization (CoA) to the NAD so that the endpoint can restart the session establishment with a new PSN.

Node groups are most commonly used when deploying the PSNs behind a load balancer. However, there is no reason node groups could not be used with any Layer 2 adjacent PSNs.

Create a Node Group

To create a node group, from the ISE GUI, perform the following steps:

1. Choose **Administration > System > Deployment**.

2. In the Deployment pane on the left side of the screen, click the cog icon and choose **Create Node Group**, as shown in Figure 18-12.

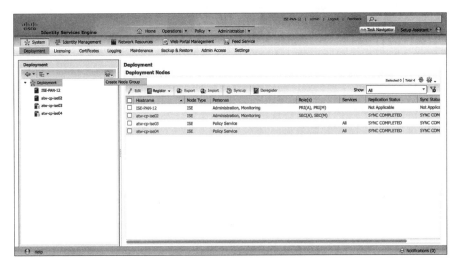

Figure 18-12   *Choosing to Create a Node Group*

3. On the Create Node Group screen, shown in Figure 18-13, enter in the Node Group Name field a name for the node group. Use a name that also helps describe the location of the group.

4. In the Description field, enter a more detailed description that helps to identify exactly where the node group is (for example, NodeGroup for DataCenter 1).

5. In the Multicast Address field, enter a multicast address for keep-alive communication. As indicated below the field, make sure you do not enter a multicast address that is already in use.

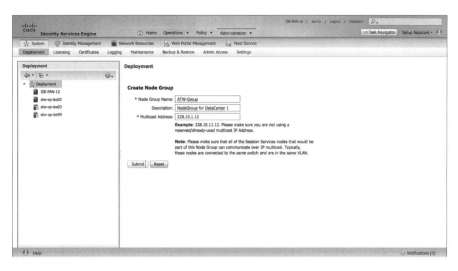

Figure 18-13 *Node Group Creation*

6. Click **OK** in the success popup window, as shown in Figure 18-14. Also notice the appearance of the node group in the left pane.

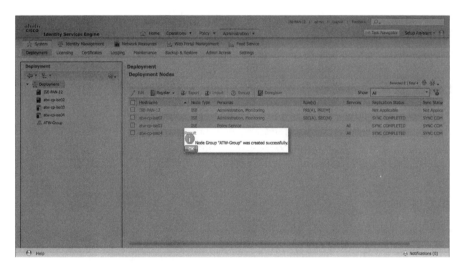

Figure 18-14 *Success Popup*

Add the Policy Services Nodes to the Node Group

To add the PSNs to the node group, from the ISE GUI, perform the following steps:

1. Choose **Administration > System > Deployment**.

2. Select one of the PSNs to add to the node group.

3. Click **node group drop-down** and select the newly created group, as shown in Figure 18-15.

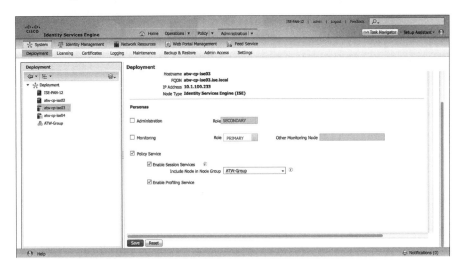

Figure 18-15   *Assigning a Node Group*

4. Click **Save**.

5. Repeat the preceding steps for each PSN that should be part of the node group.

Using Load Balancers

One high-availability option that is growing in popularity for Cisco ISE deployments is the use of load balancers, such as the Cisco ACE Load Balancer. This section is not a complete guide to using load balancers; instead, it provides basic guidelines to aid you in your understanding of load balancer usage with ISE and its constraints.

General Guidelines

When using a load balancer, you must ensure the following:

■ Each PSN must be reachable by the PAN/MnT directly, without having to go through Network Address Translation (NAT). This sometimes is referred to as *routed mode* or *pass-through mode*.

■ Each PSN must also be reachable directly from the endpoint.

  ■ When the PSN sends a URL-Redirection to the NAD, it will use the address embedded in its certificate CN= field, not the virtual IP (VIP) address.

- You may want to "hack" the certificates to include the VIP fully qualified domain name (FQDN) in the Subject Alternative Name (SAN) field.

- The same PSN is used for the entire session. User persistence, sometimes called "sticky" needs to be based on Calling-Station-ID and Framed-IP-address.

- The VIP gets listed as the RADIUS server of each NAD for all 802.1X-related AAA.

  - Includes both authentication and accounting packets.

  - Some load balancers will use a separate VIP for each protocol type.

- The list of RADIUS servers allowed to perform Dynamic-Authorizations (also known as Change of Authorization (CoA)) on the NAD should use the real IP addresses of the PSNs, not the VIP.

- The load balancer(s) will also get listed as NADs in ISE so their test authentications may be answered.

- ISE uses the device's Layer-3 Address to Identity the NAD, not the NAS-IP-Address in the RADIUS packet...this is another reason to avoid Source NAT (SNAT).

- Load balancers should be configured to use test probes to ensure the PSNs are still "alive and well."

  - A probe should be configured to ensure RADIUS is responding.

  - HTTPS should also be checked.

  - If either probe fails, the PSN should be taken out of service.

  - A PSN must be marked dead and taken out of service in the load balancer before the NAD's built-in failover occurs.

Failure Scenarios

If a single PSN fails, the load balancer takes that PSN out of service and spreads the load over the remaining PSNs. When the failed PSN is returned to service, the load balancer adds it back into the rotation. By using node groups along with a load balancer, another of the node group members issues a CoA-reauth for any sessions that were establishing. This CoA causes the session to begin again. At this point, the load balancer directs the new authentication to a different PSN.

NADs have some built-in capabilities to detect when the configured RADIUS server is "dead" and automatically fail over to the next RADIUS server configured. When using a load balancer, the RADIUS server IP address is actually the VIP address. So, if the entire VIP is unreachable (for example, the load balancer has died), the NAD should quickly fail over to the next RADIUS server in the list. That RADIUS server could be another VIP in a second data center or another backup RADIUS server.

Summary

This chapter discussed the following:

- Distributing the ISE personas onto separate ISE nodes
- The manual promotion from Secondary PAN to take over the synchronization duties of a PAN
- The active/active nature of the MnT nodes, node groups
- The use of load balancers for the Policy Services Nodes (PSNs)

Chapter 19

Inline Posture Node

The Secure Unified Access system is built around the premise that it must work for Cisco customers first, and everyone else second. Or at least that would be our interpretation of it. As stated previously in the book, Cisco has developed enhancements to identity networking to bring functionality beyond what the industry standards can provide today.

One example of these enhancement is session-aware networking (*sessionization*), where the network access device (NAD) and the RADIUS server (ISE) share a common session ID per authentication, which, for the first time ever, allows both the policy server and the NAD to have a clear understanding of the current state of an authentication. Another example is the use of multiple Change of Authorization (CoA) messages, not just the Packet of Disconnect to end a session.

However, not all Cisco equipment supports these enhancements. As of version 9.0, Cisco's own ASA VPN solution does not support CoAs yet. Older Cisco Wireless controllers, and possibly even third-party RADIUS-capable NADs, may also be deployed without these capabilities. To still provide similar levels of service to devices that are not capable of sessionization or CoA, Cisco created the Inline Posture Node (IPN).

This chapter takes a brief look at the Cisco Inline Posture Node.

Use Cases for the Inline Posture Node

It is important to note that the Inline Posture Node will not provide full functionality to equipment that cannot participate in the Secure Access system natively. It is a solution that allows the posture assessment and enforcement flows to function for RADIUS clients that cannot work with Cisco's CoA or web redirection results.

Overview of IPN Functionality

The Inline Posture Node acts as a RADIUS proxy and an inline traffic enforcement device for use cases involving posture assessment combined with RADIUS authentication. An IPN functions in the following manner:

1. The IPN sits inline between the NAD and the PSN.

2. The NAD is configured to send RADIUS requests to the IPN.

3. The IPN uses RADIUS proxy to forward those requests to the PSN.

4. The PSN responds to the IPN.

5. The IPN sends Access-Accept or Access-Reject to the NAD.

The NAD typically understands only the basic Access-Accept and Access-Reject messages. Once it receives an Access-Accept, it permits full access to the client that is making the authentication request. The IPN executes the more specific Authorization results, such as ACLs and URL Redirection, to perform posture assessment, client provisioning, and discovery. Figure 19-1 shows this logical flow.

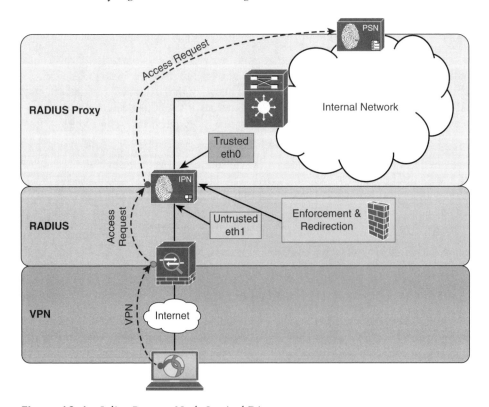

Figure 19-1 *Inline Posture Node Logical Diagram*

IPN Configuration

Inline Posture Nodes do not have a GUI of their own. Once the device has been boot-strapped and added to the deployment, all configuration will occur through the normal ISE GUI on the Primary Policy Administration Node (PAN). Figure 19-2 shows an example of the user interface.

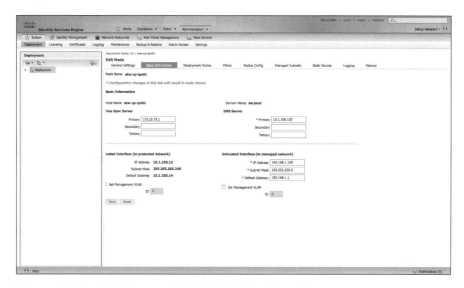

Figure 19-2   *Inline Posture Node in PAN User Interface*

IPN Modes of Operation

As stated, the IPN is an inline enforcement device (like a firewall of sorts). So traffic will physically flow through an IPN after leaving the inside interface of the VPN or WLC. The IPN has an untrusted interface (closest to the endpoint) and a trusted interface (facing the inside of the corporate network).

The IPN may be configured for inline operation in either of two main modes:

- **Bridged mode:** This mode is typically used when the IPN is Layer 2 adjacent to the NAD. In this mode, the IPN acts as a bridge between a trusted VLAN and an untrusted VLAN and is not involved in the routing decision of the network traffic. This is a very common way to deploy the IPN, and is often referred to as the "bump-in-the-wire" mode.

- **Routed mode:** In this mode, each interface is assigned an IP address, and traffic must be routed through the IPN. This requires you to configure some static routes (route summarizations), because the IPN does not support any dynamic routing protocols. You must ensure that all traffic that is destined for the client subnets (or VPN pools) is directed to the trusted interface of the IPN. The IPN will then route that traffic through to the client subnets.

Summary

This chapter briefly examined the Inline Posture Node (IPN). You have learned that it has limited use cases, where the NAD does not support the Change of Authorization commands necessary to perform RADIUS authentication with posture assessment.

The IPN has limited usability, and a limited life expectancy. It is Cisco's stated direction to eventually incorporate all of this functionality into a different inline device, such as a router or ASA.

For more on the Inline Posture Node, refer to the *Cisco ISE User Guide*: http://www.cisco.com/en/US/docs/security/ise/1.1/user_guide/ise_ipep_deploy.html.

Chapter 20

Deployment Phases

This book has already examined quite a bit of configuration detail about ISE and the network access devices. It has covered the technical merit of policy creation, guest lifecycle management, posture assessment, and much more. There is obviously a great deal to consider when you deploy a system such as this one. It is not something you should just enable overnight with the "flip of a switch."

This chapter focuses on the recommended approach to deploying the Secure Unified Access system. It reviews some of the challenges that were encountered in the past, and why certain technologies were enhanced to provide a more prescriptive approach to deployment.

Why Use a Phased Approach?

As described in Chapter 5, back in the early 2000s a, new technology was emerging that would revolutionize networking as we knew it. This technology was IEEE 802.1X, which enabled authentication of a network access port prior to allowing devices onto the network. The concept was simple, and some predicted that within 5 years there would not be any "hot ports" in the world that wouldn't first authenticate the user, and that unauthorized users would no longer be able to access networks.

802.1X was originally created to be very binary in nature. A device either is authenticated and gets access or fails authentication and is denied. Figure 20-1 graphically represents the logical process of 802.1X authentication.

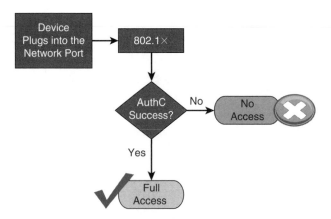

Figure 20-1 *802.1X Intended Behavior*

However, as you already know from reading the previous chapters in this book, this authentication process has many different moving parts that must all be aligned properly if you want to avoid causing denial of service (DoS) on your own user population. This can be accomplished with the following:

- Supplicants must be configured on devices.

- Lists of MAC addresses must be created in order to properly MAB devices.

- Profiling probes must be enabled and have the ability to collect data regarding endpoints to help build that list of MAC addresses.

- Certificates must be trusted.

- Guest accounts must be created.

If you were to just "flip the switch" and enable 802.1X on all access-layer switch ports all at once, you would most likely have a swarm of angry users converging on the IT department threatening to terminate their jobs. That is called a "career-limiting event," or CLE for short.

We're reminded of one implementation at a financial organization with 2000 switch ports in its campus building. Due to an audit requirement, the organization had to enable network authentication by a certain date to avoid being subject to fines. The mandate came down from management, the project received its funding, and away we went. We lab tested everything and proved it all would work using our Cisco Catalyst 6513 Switches and the native Windows XP (Service Pack 3) supplicant configured for EAP-TLS machine authentication with the Active Directory–issued machine certificate.

It was beautiful. Everything was working perfectly on our test systems in the lab, the desktop team assured us that the Group Policy Object (GPO) was sent out properly and all the Windows XP systems were ready to authenticate. All we had to do was turn on the authentication on the switch ports (theoretically).

Our advice was still to deploy in Monitor Mode first, and then change over to Closed Mode (the end state). This meant that the **authentication open** command needed to be applied to the switch port, but Monitor Mode would allow us to validate that authentications would all be successful before we truly enforced access to the network.

The security oversight committee nixed the idea immediately, because the word "open" was in the command. We were simply not allowed to use it—ever. Never mind that all 2000 ports were currently wide open and that using the command would not make matters worse at all. We simply were not allowed to use that command.

So, the big day arrived. At 10 p.m. on a Sunday night, we had our change-control window to run our scripts and enable Closed Mode authentication across 2000 switch ports in a matter of minutes. Of those 2000 ports, only 10 were authenticating successfully, and we had accomplished exactly what I feared: a denial of service for all other systems.

Why did this occur? The policies were all correct. The certificates had all been pushed out to the desktops. The supplicants were configured. However, no one had realized that the supplicant configuration would not take effect prior to rebooting the Windows systems! We did not figure that out until the next afternoon, after the desktop team had researched the issue further; meanwhile, we had created a DoS problem for all the users that morning.

The story has a happy ending. After the desktop team pushed out a job to reboot all the systems, we re-enabled authentication at the next change-control window and were able to get 99 percent of the systems to authenticate successfully.

However, not all deployments are that lucky, or that well planned out in advance. This is why a phased approach to deploying identity solutions is always a good idea.

A Phased Approach

Using a phased deployment approach, you start off in Monitor Mode and gradually transition into your end state of either Low-Impact Mode or Closed Mode. By doing so, you can avoid DoS scenarios such as the one described in the previous section. With a monitoring phase, you have time to build your list of endpoints with profiling. You can manually import the MAC addresses that will be MAB'd without profiling and ensure that you know exactly what will happen, before it happens.

Then, you can gradually move into a final state of enforcement. Figure 20-2 shows how you logically start with Monitor Mode in Phase 1 and then move to either Low-Impact Mode or Closed Mode.

Note   The end state of your deployment does not necessarily need to be either Low-Impact Mode or Closed Mode; you can blend the two. We have worked with a number of customers who use Low-Impact Mode in campus environments, and Closed Mode in their branches. It is up to you to determine what works best for your environment, and then deploy accordingly.

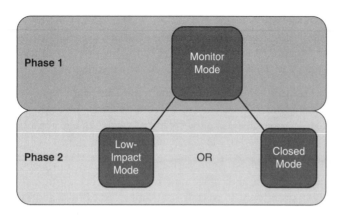

Figure 20-2   *Phased Deployments*

Authentication Open Versus Standard 802.1X

As previously described, a port that is protected with 802.1X will not allow network traffic to flow without a successful authentication. Figure 20-3 illustrates that an 802.1X-controlled port normally only allows EAP, CDP, and LLDP traffic to enter the port (all three are Layer 2 protocols) and denies all other traffic. When 802.1X is enabled on a port, the port is said to be a *supplicant authenticator*. That is a fancy way of stating that the port will communicate with EAP at Layer 2; the switch will broker that authentication to the RADIUS server.

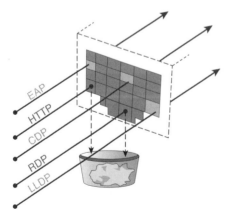

Figure 20-3   *Default Port Behavior with 802.1X*

Cisco created an enhancement to standard 802.1X ports that allows the port to be a supplicant authenticator. However, it permits all traffic to flow normally through the switch port even without an authentication occurring. This allows the supplicant to authenticate correctly if it is configured, but if the device does not have a supplicant configured or the switch receives an Access-Reject message from the RADIUS server, the Reject message is ignored.

Figure 20-4 illustrates that, regardless of authentication, the switch port allows all traffic to flow, but it also authenticates the supplicant and performs MAB just like a standard 802.1X-enabled switch port.

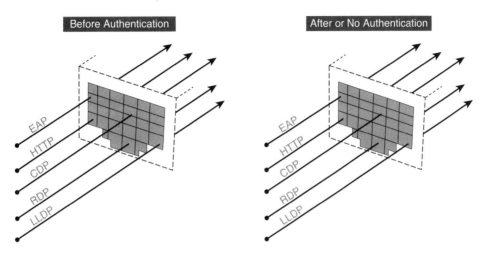

Figure 20-4   *Port Behavior with Open Authentication*

It is the creation of this authenticator enhancement that truly made Monitor Mode possible. It is, of course, not the only necessary component of Monitor Mode, but it is certainly the catalyst (pardon the pun).

Monitor Mode

Monitor Mode is a process, not just a command on a switch. The process is to enable authentication (with **authentication open**) to see exactly what devices fail and which ones succeed.

Figure 20-5 shows a high-level flow diagram describing Monitor Mode.

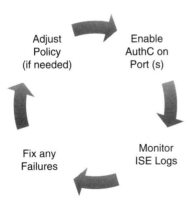

Figure 20-5   *Monitor Mode Operational Flow*

One key point to understand about Monitor Mode is that it is applicable to wired environments only. If you have ever configured a device to connect to a wireless network, you are familiar with the concept of a service set identifier (SSID). When using Wi-Fi, configuring a client (supplicant) is expected behavior. You must tell the Wi-Fi-capable endpoint which network to connect to by identifying its SSID, and then you provide credentials for that network. It's common, it's expected, and it's well known.

A wired network, however, does not have the concept of an SSID, so there is no popup window on the endpoint asking which network you would like to connect with. It's just assumed that your device is physically connected and therefore you are attached to the correct network. With wireless, if you don't have a supplicant, you cannot connect. Wired environments are expected to always work, supplicant or not. The wired port must be able to handle the following:

- A device that has a supplicant (802.1X)

- A corporate device that doesn't have a supplicant but belongs on the network (such as an IP-Phone or printer)

- Guest users

So, there is quite a bit to audit when in Monitor Mode.

Another very important thing to understand about Monitor Mode is that authorization results from the RADIUS server will absolutely be honored (Access-Reject is the only command that is ignored). So, if your authorization result from ISE includes dynamic VLAN (dVLAN) assignment or downloadable ACLs (dACL), those will absolutely be honored and applied to the port.

For a phased deployment approach, it is highly recommended to use Network Device Groups (NDG) in ISE. Using these NDGs, you can build specific policies that only send the basic authorization results (Access-Accept and Access-Reject) to switches that are part of a Monitor Mode NDG.

Figure 20-6 shows a high-level flow diagram describing Monitor Mode.

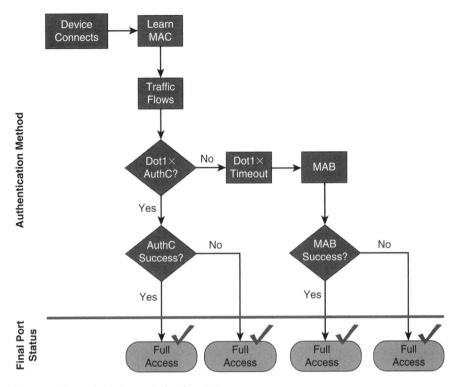

Figure 20-6 *Monitor Mode Flow Diagram*

Prepare ISE for a Staged Deployment

One of the primary ways to differentiate modes within your ISE policies is to use NDGs. In this section, you will configure the NDGs to have a top-level group of Stage, and then subgroups for Monitor Mode, Low-Impact Mode, and Closed Mode. With these NDGs, the authorization policies may look for the particular stage of deployment. For purposes of keeping the policies nice and clean, use separate Policy Sets for each stage of deployment.

Note The following exercises assume that Policy Sets have been enabled already under Administration > Settings > Policy.

Create the Network Device Groups

A Network Device Group may be a top-level group, such as Location or Type. The NDG may also be created as a child (aka subgroup) of an existing top-level group, such as Switch (which would be a subgroup of the Type NDG). The following steps guide you through the creation of both a new top-level group, named Stage, and subgroups.

From the ISE GUI, perform the following steps:

1. Navigate to **Administration > Network Resources > Network Device Groups**.

2. Click **Add**.

3. In the Name field, name the Network Device Group **Stage**, as shown in Figure 20-7.

4. In the Type field, enter **Stage** again.

5. Click **Submit**.

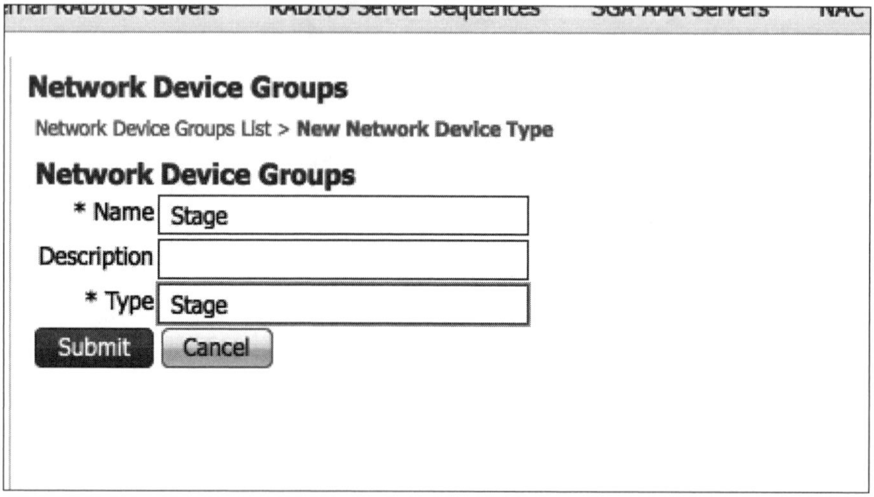

Figure 20-7   *Add a Stage NDG*

6. Click **New Stage Group** in the left pane.

7. Repeat Steps 2 through 5 and create the following three new subgroups (as shown in Figure 20-8):

   ■ Monitor Mode

   ■ Low Impact Mode

   ■ Closed Mode

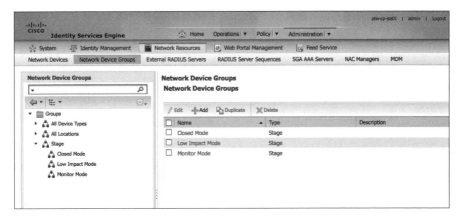

Figure 20-8   *Final Stage Network Device Groups*

Create the Policy Sets

Now that you have the NDGs configured for the different stages of the deployment, you can move on to creating the policies themselves. From the ISE GUI, perform the following steps:

1. Navigate to **Policy > Policy Set**.

2. Ensure that your default policy is selected on the left side (as shown in Figure 20-9) and click the **+** icon in the upper-left corner.

3. Choose **Create Above**.

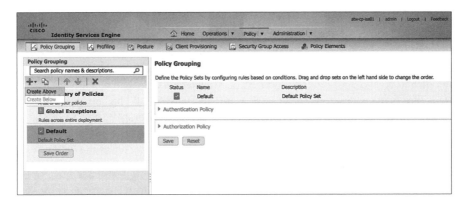

Figure 20-9   *Default Policy Set Selected*

4. Name the new Policy Set **MonitorMode** and provide a description, as shown in Figure 20-10.

5. Add a new condition of **DEVICE > Stage Equals Monitor Mode**.

6. Click **Done**.

Figure 20-10   *Monitor Mode Policy Set*

At this point, any network device that is a member of the NDG named MonitorMode will use this Policy Set. All authentications and authorizations occur with this set of policies.

It is up to you, the administrator of ISE policies, to ensure that any authorization results for Monitor Mode switches are only Access-Accept and Access-Reject. Always remember that other authorization results will be accepted and applied to the switch port, so you must ensure that web authentication, ACLs, and VLAN assignments do not occur for these switches.

Low-Impact Mode

As described previously in this chapter, Low-Impact Mode is one of the end-state choices for your deployment. Closed Mode is the other final stage. There is no specific best practice for which mode is better to deploy; it is entirely dependent on the organization and its needs.

For example, we have worked with a number of large organizations that use a variety of technologies to reimage desktop systems that make use of the Preboot Execution Environment (PXE) to boot into a pseudo OS and then connect to an imaging server that reimages the company desktop. Those PXEs were time sensitive and had no ability to authenticate to the network infrastructure. Yet they had to seamlessly be able to boot, connect to the reimaging server, and update the desktop to the latest corporate image, and do so without any additional user interaction. Low-Impact Mode was the only way to make this work feasibly in those environments.

Another example is a retail organization that uses thin clients in its retail stores. These thin clients must be able to boot using PXE, gain limited access to the network, download their OS from the local store server, and have that access before their local DHCP timers expire. Once that OS is loaded into memory and takes the system over, its supplicant sends an EAPoL Start message into the network and authenticates with 802.1X. Low-Impact Mode allows the thin client to boot automatically and have the appropriate levels of access to the store server to download the OS.

Low-Impact Mode adds security on top of the framework that was built in Monitor Mode. It continues to use the **authentication open** capabilities of the switch port, which allows traffic to enter the switch prior to an authorization result. This permits the DHCP clients to be assigned an IP address before their DHCP timers run out (for example).

With Low-Impact Mode, you are adding security right from the start by putting a port-based ACL (pACL) on the switch port interface. This is a traffic-filtering ACL that gets applied to the port as part of the switch configuration and is then overridden by the dACL sent down from ISE.

Figure 20-11 shows the operational flow intended for Low-Impact Mode. As one of the two possible end states (Closed Mode being the second), it provides very specific access per user, per device, or other condition that you wish to use in the ISE Authorization Policies. Remember, the goal of Low-Impact Mode is to administer very limited network access to devices without authentication, and then provide very specific access to those that have been authorized. As with any other security solution, tuning the authorization results is something that can take a lot of operational man-hours. So, it is always recommended to deploy authorization results in stages. For example, begin with a policy that permits full access to any device that has authenticated successfully. Ensure that the environment is fully functional, and then begin to "ratchet down" the security. Make the dACLs more specific, and so on.

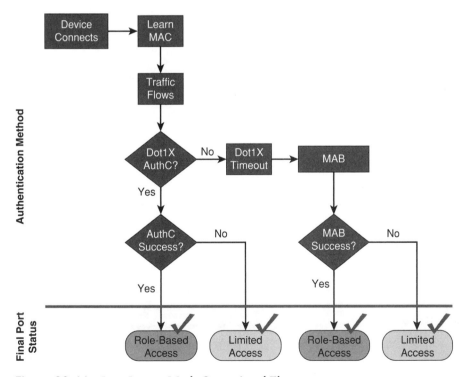

Figure 20-11 *Low-Impact Mode Operational Flow*

Figure 20-12 shows that the Port ACL is applied prior to authentication, which only allows specific traffic into the port. Once the authentication occurs, the authorization needs to include a dACL that selectively permits or denies traffic. Other authorization results may also be applied at the port, such as:

■ URL Redirection

■ VLAN assignment

■ MACSec encryption

■ Security Group Tagging

Note   VLAN assignment should be used only on devices that use supplicants. Without a supplicant, the device will most likely not be able to identify the VLAN change, and may end up with the wrong IP address for its final VLAN assignment.

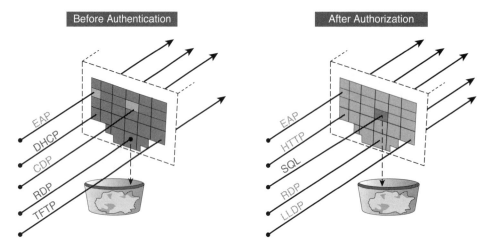

Figure 20-12   *Low-Impact Mode Port Behavior*

Closed Mode

Closed Mode is similar to the default behavior of 802.1X. As shown earlier in Figure 20-3, the port does not allow any traffic before the authentication (except for EAP, CDP, and LLDP), and then the port will be assigned to specific authorization results after the authentication.

Note   Closed Mode was once called High-Security Mode. It was renamed to discourage the perception that it is more secure than Low-Impact Mode. In truth, both modes are equally protected. The security level of either end state is truly dependent on the configuration of the devices and the policies on ISE, not the mode of operation. In other words, an administrator can make Closed Mode very insecure or very secure, depending on their implementation.

As shown in Figure 20-1 earlier in the chapter, the operational model of 802.1X was always designed to deny access to any device that does not authenticate successfully. This is a perfectly understandable model for wireless network access, where a human is required to interact with the device and configure a wireless client (supplicant) to connect to a specific SSID with specific credentials.

However, in a wired world, there are many devices that require network access without any user interaction, such as IP cameras, IP-Phones, printers, fax machines, badge readers, and so much more. So, MAC Authentication Bypass (MAB) had to be added to the process flow.

The concept of completely denying access to the network if authentication fails, or if a supplicant is not configured, proved to have operational difficulties. Some level of access was needed. Originally, the switch itself would have a "Failed Authentication VLAN," where the switch makes a local decision to authorize access to a specific VLAN when a device failed authentication. Additionally, if authentication were to time out (meaning there was no supplicant on the endpoint), then it would authorize access to a locally configured guest VLAN.

One of the problems with that original logic was the lack of centralized knowledge and control. As far as the policy server was concerned, the access was denied. Yet the device was still on the network because the NAD made a local decision in spite of what the policy server said.

Figure 20-13 shows the operational flow of Closed Mode. Notice that it is nearly exactly the same as Low-Impact Mode. All the same authorization results are available for use, but Closed Mode does not allow any of the PXE-type traffic into the port prior to the authorization result, unlike Low-Impact Mode.

Figure 20-14 shows the port behavior in Closed Mode. Virtually zero traffic is allowed into the port before the authentication. Once the session is authorized, very specific authorization results may be applied to the port, such as:

- VLAN assignment
- dACL
- URL Redirection
- MACSec encryption
- Security Group Tags

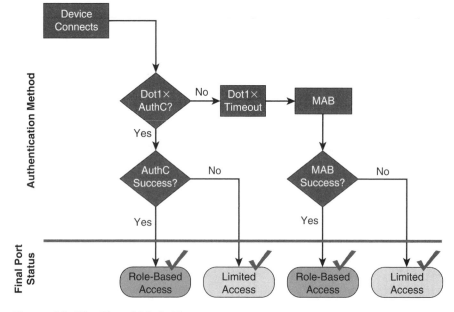

Figure 20-13   *Closed Mode Flow*

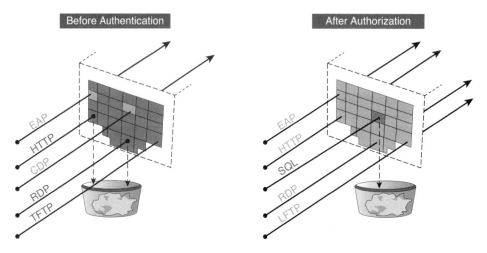

Figure 20-14   *Closed Mode Port Behavior*

Transitioning from Monitor Mode to Your End State

The key to using a phased deployment approach successfully is to understand how to transition from Monitor Mode to the end state chosen (Low-Impact Mode or Closed Mode). This is why you built out NDGs and Policy Sets previously in this chapter.

With Monitor Mode, you must ensure that only Access-Accept and Access-Reject authorizations are used. With Low-Impact Mode and Closed Mode, you are able to send the other authorization results, such as sending a URL Redirection for Centralized Web Authentication (CWA).

The purpose of Monitor Mode is to ensure that the endpoints are all authenticating correctly, either via 802.1X with their supplicants or via MAB with profiling or even statically. You could get the first pilot switch ready, prepare all the devices for authentication, and, seeing that everything looks good, flip the switch and change the default Authorization Policy to send a CWA result instead of just the basic accept or reject message. That first switch will be fine, all the devices will work correctly, and life will look easy.

However, you wouldn't want to push the CWA result to the switch port if you have not fully prepared the supplicants and educated the users on a possible change of experience when logging in to the network. That would be another career-limiting event.

That is why you use NDGs. You ensure with the NAD's membership of the "Stage" NDG that you are sending the correct results to the correct network devices.

Imagine rolling out ISE to thousands of branch locations. You prepare a branch by putting it into Monitor Mode. When you are certain that that branch is fully ready and all the devices are recognized and authenticating successfully, you then can simply move the switch from the MonitorMode NDG to the end-state NDG, and make a few command modifications to the switches.

See Chapters 21 through 23 for configuration specifics for each mode.

Wireless Networks

Wireless networks behave differently than wired networks. With the creation of a WLAN, you must define the security for that WLAN. When using 802.1X, set the security to use WPA+WPA2 for key management. This setting cannot be mixed with an open authentication, and there are no "fallback" options.

For a guest authentication, the guest needs to connect to a different SSID. This is fundamentally a much different model from that used for a wired network.

Even though wireless behaves differently, the authorization results in ISE may be configured to send the responses to wired devices and wireless devices, providing a unified access strategy. This permits wireless networks to be managed as part of your Low-Impact Mode or Closed Mode deployments.

Summary

This chapter provided an overview of the phased deployment approach to deploying ISE and 802.1X. It covered the importance of Monitor Mode for wired environments, with an emphasis on using only basic authorization results while in Monitor Mode.

This chapter showed you how to configure Policy Sets differently for NADs based on their "Stage" NDG membership. It also discussed methods for how to use those NDG memberships to transition one switch at a time from Monitor Mode to the end-state mode of your choice.

The next few chapters detail the configurations of Monitor Mode, Low-Impact Mode, and Closed Mode.

Chapter 21

Monitor Mode

As discussed in Chapter 20, "Deployment Phases," Monitor Mode is the first phase of the deployment. This is where you will do the bulk of the preparation work. During the Monitor Mode phase of an ISE deployment, you will

- Utilize profiling to pre-populate the endpoint database.

- Test out the device configurations, ensuring that all devices can successfully authenticate to the network.

- Prepare your Authentication and Authorization Policies.

All this testing is completed prior to enabling any levels of enforcement, which prevents the impending required authentication from becoming a denial of service to your user population.

As detailed in Chapter 20, Monitor Mode is a process that involves combining the "authentication open" command on a Cisco switch and policies on ISE that will only send basic authorization results. The process is to enable authentication (with authentication open), and monitor what devices fail and which ones succeed.

Figure 21-1 shows a high-level flow diagram that describes Monitor Mode.

Monitor Mode allows you to enable authentication without any impact to user or endpoint access to the network. Monitor Mode is, in essence, like placing a security camera at an unlocked door to monitor and record who enters and leaves without any means to enforce or prevent access.

With RADIUS accounting enabled, you can log authentication attempts (successful or not) and gain visibility into who and what is connecting to your network with an audit trail. You will know which endpoints (PCs, printer, camera, and so on) are connecting to your network, where they connected, and whether they are 802.1X capable or not, as well as whether they have valid credentials. Additionally, you will know if the endpoints have known valid MAC addresses via the failed MAB attempts.

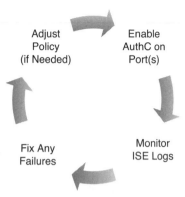

Figure 21-1   *Monitor Mode Operational Flow*

Key Point   Monitor Mode is applicable to wired environments only.

If you ever configured a device to connect to a wireless network, you recognize that configuring a client (supplicant) is expected behavior when using Wi-Fi. You must tell the Wi-Fi capable endpoint which network to connect to (SSID) and provide credentials for that network. It's common, it's expected, and it's well known.

This is not expected behavior on a wired network. Printer administrators expect to be able to plug their new printer into the wall and have it work (for example). No extra network configuration required.

Endpoint Discovery

One of the goals of Monitor Mode is to get the endpoint database (the local database of MAC addresses) populated in order to tune and build authentication policies to allow devices to gain access to the network. This process is commonly referred to as *Endpoint Discovery*.

One customer with hundreds of remote locations enabled NetFlow at that remote location and pointed the NetFlow to ISE. Using the NetFlow probe, the endpoint database was built quickly, and this met their needs—right up until the problems started. Remember what was covered in Chapter 10, "Profiling Basics," about the NetFlow probe being used sparingly, because it is easy to overload a server with all those flows. It is recommended that you filter NetFlow for de-duplication of flows and only send required flows to ISE.

The concept of performing endpoint discovery before enabling authentication at a location is a very sound one. This way, the operations team is ready with device classification before enabling authentication on the ports. This makes the process of identifying misconfigured endpoints even easier.

An easier way to build this database is using one of the following three methods:

- **SNMP Trap Method:** Enable Mac-Notification traps on the switch with the SNMP Trap, SNMP Query, DNS, and DHCP probes enabled on ISE.

- **RADIUS with SNMP Query Method:** Enable authentication on the switch, but in Monitor Mode, with the SNMP Query, DHCP, DNS, and RADIUS Probes enabled on ISE.

- **Device Sensor Method:** Enable device sensor on the switch with the RADIUS and DNS probes enabled on ISE.

These three different approaches were listed as such because of the way that profiling probes work. Remember that SNMP Traps are only sent to ISE to trigger an SNMP Query when a new MAC address is added/changed on the switch. There is no need to use SNMP Traps once RADIUS packets are being sent for authentications, because the RADIUS probe will also trigger the SNMP Query to occur.

There is also no need for SNMP or DHCP when using device sensor, because the switch sends that information directly to ISE in a RADIUS Accounting packet.

Refer to Chapter 10, "Profiling Basics," for a more detailed overview of the different probes and how they operate.

SNMP Trap Method

If you are not ready to enable Monitor Mode on the switch for authentications, you can still populate the endpoint database "passively" with this combination of SNMP Trap, SNMP Query, and DHCP probes.

Note   Keep in mind that this is a temporary endpoint discovery mode, and you need to switch to one of the other two modes for the long-term when you fully deploy. SNMP trap should be disabled once you begin processing network authentications.

For this method, configure the switch to send an SNMP trap to ISE whenever there is a MAC address inserted or changed in the mac-address-table on the switch. This in turn triggers ISE to use the SNMP Query probe to pull data from the switch. Concurrently enable the DHCP and DNS probes on ISE to capture the all-important DHCP data, as well as attributes, such as FQDN, to help identify corporate assets. Figure 21-2 illustrates this process.

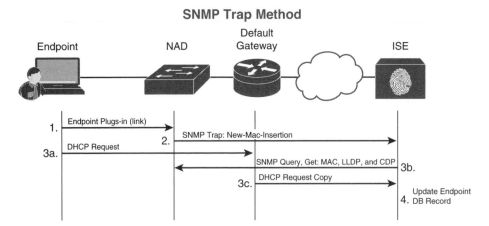

Figure 21-2 *SNMP Trap Method*

Configuring the ISE Probes

It is assumed that the ISE probes are already configured from Chapter 10. However, go back into the GUI and ensure the probes are enabled on all the Policy Services Nodes in the following steps.

From the ISE GUI, perform the following steps:

1. Navigate to **Administration > System > Deployment**.

2. Select an ISE node running Policy Services. (You need to repeat for all PSNs.)

3. Ensure that the DNS, SNMP Query, and SNMP Trap probes are enabled, as shown in Figure 21-3.

4. Ensure the DHCP, RADIUS, and (optionally) the NMAP probes are enabled, as shown in Figure 21-4.

5. Repeat Steps 1 through 4 for all ISE nodes in the deployment (such as ISE CUBE) running policy services.

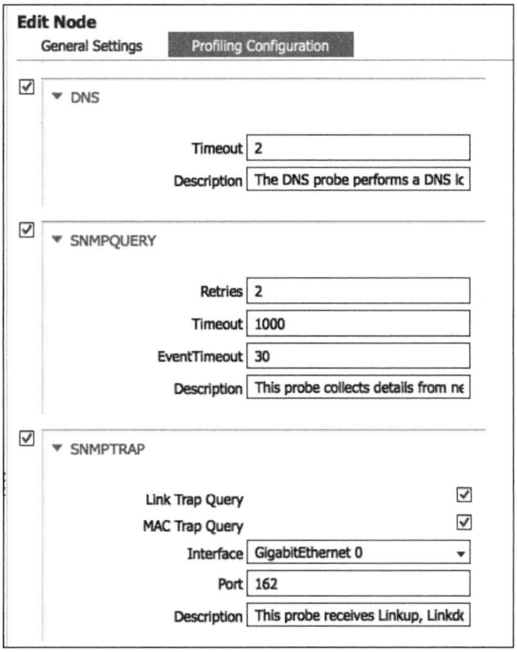

Figure 21-3   *DNS, SNMP Query, and SNMP Trap Probes*

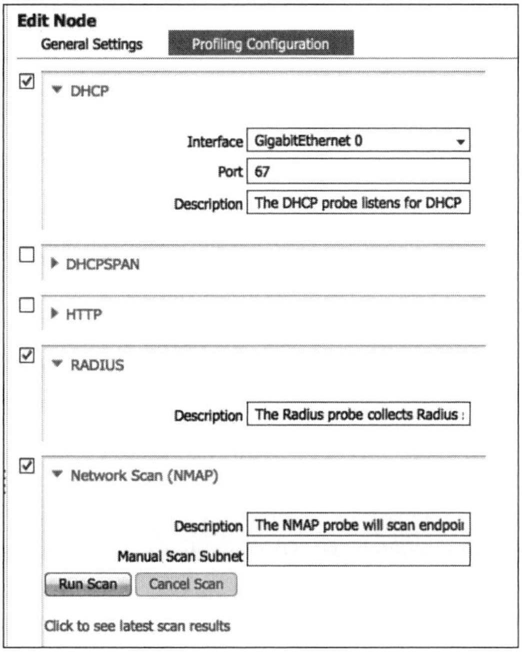

Figure 21-4   *DHCP, RADIUS, and NMAP Probes*

Adding the Network Device to ISE

Based on previous chapters, ISE may already be configured for these network devices. However, ensuring the proper configuration of the Network Device definition in ISE is critical to this pre-population of the endpoint database. It's crucial because ISE must have knowledge of the switch and its SNMP community configuration in order to use SNMP to query the switch.

From the ISE GUI, perform the following steps:

1. Navigate to **Administration > Network Resources > Network Devices**.

2. If the network device is already in the list, click the check box and choose Edit. If the Network Device is not already in the list, choose Add.

   Figure 21-5 displays the network devices list.

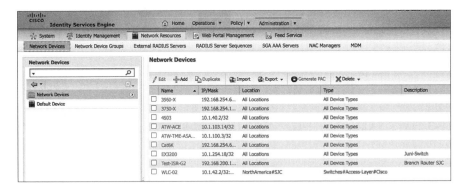

Figure 21-5 *Network Devices*

3. Ensure the correct IP Address is configured.

   This should match the ip radius source-interface command configured on the switch.

4. Set the Network Devices Groups correctly. While all NDG assignment is important, pay especially close attention to use the MonitorMode Stage, as shown in Figure 21-6.

   Even though RADIUS is not needed for this discovery method, it is best to configure it now to ensure that it is configured correctly later.

5. Ensure that the check box next to Authentication Settings is enabled.

6. Fill in the shared secret.

   This should match the key configured in the **radius-server host** command on the switch.

7. Ensure that the check box is enabled for SNMP-Settings.

8. Configure the SNMP information for ISE to query the NAD.

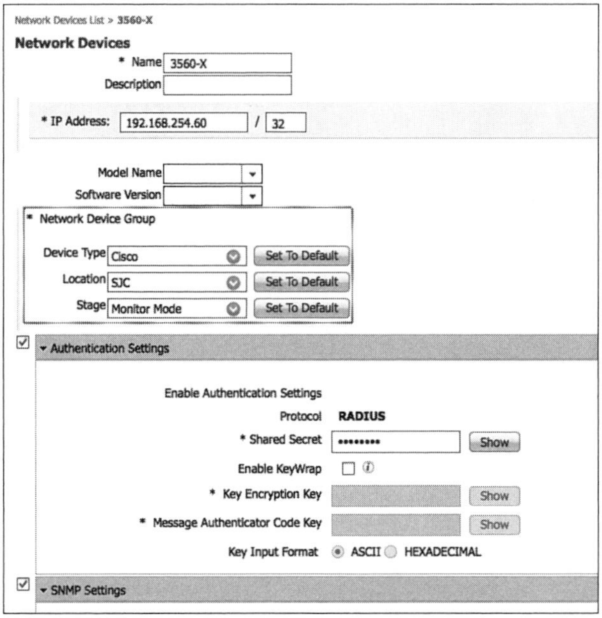

Figure 21-6 *Network Device Configuration*

This should match the SNMP configuration in the switch configured with the **snmp-server community** *community-string* **RO** command on the switch.

Figure 21-7 highlights the SNMP configuration section of the network device settings.

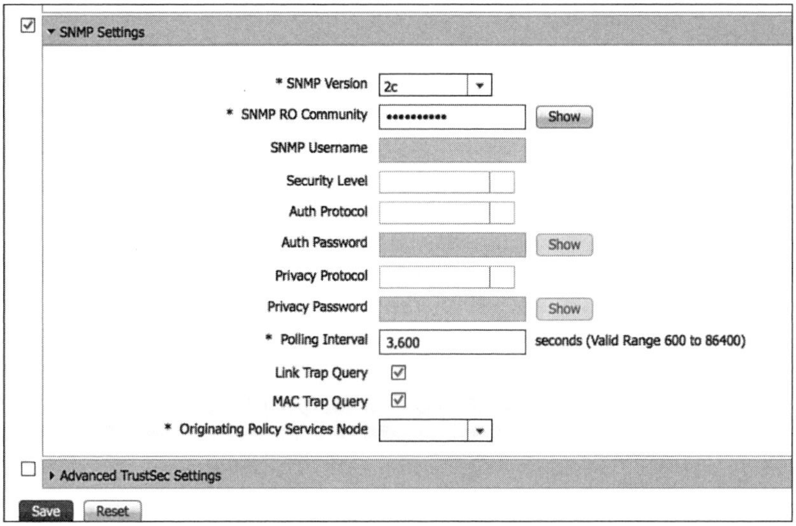

Figure 21-7 *Network Device Configuration - SNMP*

9. Repeat Steps 2 through 8 for all remaining network devices to be used with the SNMP Trap method.

Configuring the Switches

Based on previous chapters, the switches may already be configured for this method, except for the SNMP Traps (most likely). However, go back into the Switches CLI and ensure that the appropriate pieces of the configuration are in place.

You must set the Global Configuration settings to enable the MAC address change notifications and send traps to ISE. From the Switch CLI Global Configuration, perform the following steps:

1. Enter **mac address-table notification change.**

2. Enter **mac address-table notification mac-move.**

3. Enter **snmp-server trap-source** *interface-name.*

4. Enter **snmp-server enable traps snmp linkdown lnkup.**

5. Enter **snmp-server enable traps mac-notification change move.**

6. Enter **snmp-server host** *ISE-IP-Address* **version** [2c | 3] *community-name.*

7. Enter **interface range** *interface-name first-interface last-interface.*

8. Type **snmp trap mac-notification change added.**

9. Type **snmp trap mac-notification change removed.**

10. Enter **snmp-server community** *community-name* [RO | RW].

Figure 21-8 shows the topology in use for this example. Example 21-1 shows the configuration of a 3560-X.

Example 21-1   *SNMP Configuration on a 3560-X*

```
3560-X(config)#mac address-table notification change
3560-X(config)#mac address-table notification mac-move
3560-X(config)#snmp-server trap-source Loopback 0
3560-X(config)#snmp-server enable traps snmp linkdown linkup
3560-X(config)#snmp-server enable traps mac-notification change move
3560-X(config)#snmp-server host 10.1.100.231 version 2c CiscoPressRO
3560-X(config)#int range g0/1 - 12
3560-X(config-if-range)#snmp trap mac-notification change added
3560-X(config-if-range)#snmp trap mac-notification change removed
3560-X(config-if-range)#exit
3560-X(config)#snmp-server community CiscoPressRO RO
3560-X(config)#end
```

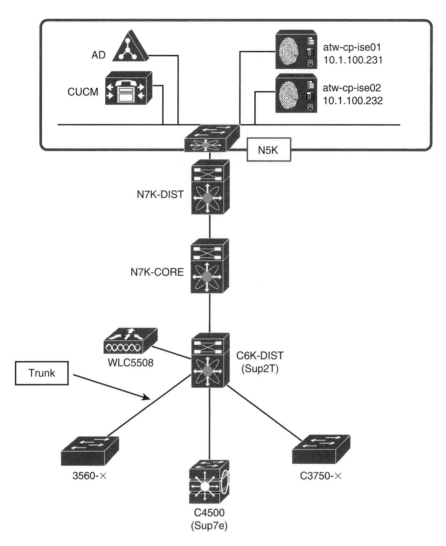

Figure 21-8 *Example Network Topology*

SNMP Query and SNMP Trap are not the only probes to be employed in this mode. The DHCP (dhcp-helper) probe is also used, and the default-gateway of the data VLAN should be configured to copy ISE on DHCP requests.

Enter interface configuration mode for the VLAN interface (SVI) or other Layer 3 interface for that VLAN:

1. Type **ip helper-address** *ISE-IP-Address*.

2. Repeat Step 1 for all Layer 3 interfaces (such as voice and data VLANS).

In the example depicted in Figure 21-8, the 3560-X is a Layer 2 switch that has a trunk configured to the Catalyst 6500 distribution layer switch. The Catalyst 6500 must be configured to copy ISE with DHCP requests. Example 21-2 displays the commands that would be added on the distribution switch.

Example 21-2   *IP Helper Configuration on the 6500 Distribution*

```
C6K-DIST(config)#int vlan 41
C6K-DIST(config-if)#ip helper-address 10.1.100.231
```

At this point, ISE receives SNMP Traps from the Layer 2 switch whenever there is a change in the MAC address table. That triggers ISE to query the switch via SNMP and gather data from the LLDP and CDP tables. Additionally, the distribution switch copies ISE on all DHCP requests, which provides ISE with the IP addressing information for the endpoints. From there, ISE does a reverse lookup in DNS and, if the device does Dynamic DNS Updates, as all Active Directory members should do, the device name is gathered to aid in the identification of endpoints.

RADIUS with SNMP Query Method

Unlike using SNMP Traps, this method uses the actual RADIUS packets from the switch. That means the switch configuration all have the AAA commands. This is illustrated in Figure 21-9. Ensure the SNMP Traps are not being sent to ISE.

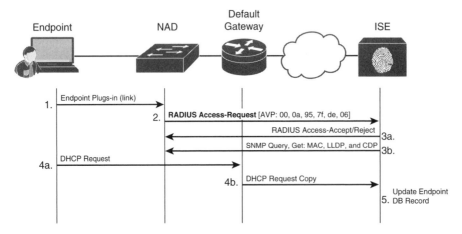

Figure 21-9   *RADIUS with SNMP Query Method*

Configuring the ISE Probes

It is assumed that the ISE probes are already configured (from Chapter 10 or even from the previous section). However, go back into the GUI and ensure that the probes are enabled on all the Policy Services Nodes in the following steps.

From the ISE GUI:

1. Navigate to **Administration > System > Deployment**.

2. Select an ISE node running Policy Services. (You need to repeat for all PSNs.)

3. Ensure that the DNS, SNMP Query, and SNMP Trap probes are enabled (refer to Figure 21-3).

4. Ensure the DHCP, RADIUS, and optionally the NMAP probes are enabled (refer to Figure 21-4).

5. Repeat Steps 1 through 4 for all ISE nodes in the deployment (such as ISE CUBE) that are running the Policy Services persona.

Adding the Network Device to ISE

Based on the previous chapters and sections, ISE may already be configured for these network devices. However, ensuring the proper configuration of the network device definition in ISE is critical to this endpoint discovery process. It's important because ISE must have knowledge of the switch, its SNMP community, and RADIUS shared secret in order to accept the RADIUS packets and then run the SNMP query against the switch.

From the ISE GUI, perform the following steps:

1. Navigate to **Administration** > Network **Resources** > **Network Devices**.

2. If the network device is already in the list, click the check box and choose Edit. If the network device is not already in the list, choose Add.

3. Ensure the correct IP address is in configured.

   This should match the **ip radius source-interface** command configured on the switch.

4. Set the Network Devices Groups correct. Pay close attention to use the MonitorMode Stage, as shown in Figure 21-6.

5. Ensure that the check box next to Authentication Settings is enabled.

6. Fill in the shared secret.

7. Ensure that the check box is enabled for SNMP-Settings.

8. Configure the SNMP information for ISE to query the NAD.

   This should match the SNMP configuration in the switch configured with the **snmp-server community** *community-string* **RO** command on the switch.

9. Repeat Steps 2 through 8 for all remaining network devices to be used with the RADIUS with SNMP Query method.

Configuring the Switches

Based on the previous chapters, the switches may already be configured for this method, except for the SNMP Traps (most likely). However, go back into the Switches CLI and ensure the appropriate pieces of the configuration are in place.

Unlike the SNMP Trap method, this approach requires the switches to be configured for authentication, including 802.1X and MAC Authentication Bypass (MAB). For more details on the configuration of network access devices, see Chapter 11, "Bootstrapping Network Access Devices." It is important to note that this configuration is not only for endpoint discovery and Monitor Mode, but continues to be used throughout the additional modes of operation.

From the Switch CLI Global Configuration, perform the following steps:

1. Set the Global Configuration settings to enable RADIUS Authentication, Authorization, and Accounting.

2. Enter **aaa new-model** to enable AAA globally on the switch.

3. Type **aaa authentication dot1x default group** [*group-name* | **radius**].

4. Type **aaa authorization network default group** [*group-name* | **radius**].

5. Enter **aaa accounting dot1x default start-stop group** [*group-name* | **radius**].

6. Ensure that device tracking is enabled by typing **ip device tracking**.

7. Globally enable 802.1X with the **dot1x system-auth-control** command.

8. Ensure the correct interface is used to source the RADIUS traffic using the **ip radius source-interface** *interface-name* command.

    Ensure the correct attributes are being sent in the radius communications. See Chapter 11 for more details on these commands.

9. Enter **radius-server attribute 6 on-for-login-auth**.

10. Enter **radius-server attribute 8 include-in-access-req**.

11. Enter **radius-server attribute 25 access-request include**.

12. Enter **radius-server vsa send accounting**.

13. Enter **radius-server vsa send authentication**.

14. Enter **radius-server dead-criteria time** [value] **tries** [value].

    Add the ISE Policy Service Nodes as RADIUS server hosts.

15. Enter **radius-server host** *ISE-IP-Address* **auth-port 1812 acct-port 1813 key** *Shared-Secret*.

16. Repeat Step 15 for all ISE Policy service nodes.

    Add the ISE Nodes for change of authorization (CoA).

17. Type **aaa server radius dynamic-author** to enter into that sub-mode.

18. Enter **client** *ISE-IP-Address* **server-key** *Shared-Secret*.

19. Repeat Step 18 for all ISE Policy service nodes.

Enter Interface Configuration mode and configure the interfaces for 802.1X in Open Mode by performing the following steps:

1. Enter **interface range** interface-name *first-interface - last-interface*.

2. Use the built-in macro **switchport host** to set the port as an access port with spanning-tree portfast.

3. Type **ip access-group** *Your-Permit-All-ACL* **in**.

4. Type **authentication event fail action next-method**.

5. Type **authentication event server dead action authorize vlan** *VLAN*.

6. Type **authentication event server alive action reinitialize**.

7. Type **authentication host-mode multi-auth**.

8. Type **authentication open**.

9. Type **authentication order mab dot1x**.

10. Type **authentication priority dot1x mab**.

11. Type **authentication port-control auto**.

12. Type **authentication violation restrict**.

13. Type **mab**.

14. Type **dot1x pae authenticator**.

15. Enter **dot1x timeout tx-period** *time*.

Add the SNMP configuration to the switch:

1. Enter **mac address-table notification change**.

2. Enter **mac address-table notification mac-move**.

3. Enter **snmp-server trap-source** *interface-name*.

4. Enter **snmp-server enable traps snmp linkdown lnkup**.

5. Enter **snmp-server enable traps mac-notification change move**.

6. Enter **snmp-server host** *ISE-IP-Address* **version [2c | 3]** *community-name*.

Enter Interface Configuration mode and configure the interfaces for the SNMP Traps:

1. Enter **interface range** interface-name *first-interface last-interface*.

2. Type **snmp trap mac-notification change added**.

3. Type **snmp trap mac-notification change removed**.

   Create the Read-Only SNMP Community for ISE to query the switch.

4. Enter **snmp-server community** *community-name* [**RO** | **RW**].

Appendix E, "Sample Switch Configurations," contains complete configurations for multiple switch models.

RADIUS and SNMP Query are not the only probes used in this mode. The DHCP (dhcp-helper) probe is also employed, and the default-gateway of the data VLAN should be configured to copy ISE on DHCP requests.

Enter interface configuration mode for the VLAN interface (SVI) or other Layer 3 interface for that VLAN by performing the following steps:

1. Type **ip helper-address** *ISE-IP-Address*.

2. Repeat Step 1 for all Layer 3 interfaces (such as voice and data VLANS).

In the example depicted in Figure 21-7, the 3560-X is a Layer 2 switch that has a trunk configured to the Catalyst 6500 distribution layer switch. The Catalyst 6500 must be configured to copy ISE with DHCP requests. Example 21-3 shows what the configuration would have been on that Catalyst 6500.

Example 21-3   *IP Helper Configuration on the 6500 Distribution*

```
C6K-DIST(config)#int vlan 41
C6K-DIST(config-if)#ip helper-address 10.1.100.231
```

At this point, ISE receives RADIUS authentication requests either from configured supplicants attempting to authenticate via 802.1X, or requests from MAC Authentication Bypass (MAB). Those RADIUS requests identify the endpoint's MAC address from the Calling-Station-ID field and triggers ISE to perform an SNMP Query against the switch. Additionally, ISE learns information about the endpoint from the DHCP traffic that has been copied to ISE, and possibly even DNS names of the endpoints, if they are configured for Dynamic DNS.

Device Sensor Method

As discussed in Chapter 10, the newer Cisco switches may have the IOS Device Sensor capability, which entirely eliminates the need for the SNMP and the DHCP probes. Just like the previous RADIUS method, this method also requires the switch to be configured for authentication. All the device sensor data is then sent to ISE inside of RADIUS accounting packets, as shown in Figure 21-10.

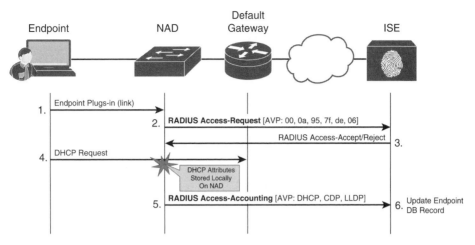

Figure 21-10 *Device Sensor Method*

Configuring the ISE Probes

It is assumed that the ISE probes are already configured (from Chapter 10 or even the previous section). However, go back into the ISE GUI and ensure that the probes are enabled on all the Policy Services nodes.

From the ISE GUI, perform the following steps:

1. Navigate to **Administration > System > Deployment**.

2. Select an ISE node running Policy Services. (You need to repeat for all PSNs.)

3. Ensure that the DNS probe is enabled. You may choose to disable the SNMP Query and SNMP Trap probes if all of your switches support device sensor.

4. Ensure that the RADIUS and (optionally) the NMAP probes are enabled, as shown in Figure 21-3. You may choose to disable the DHCP probe if all the switches support Device Sensor.

5. Repeat Steps 1 through 4 for all ISE nodes in the deployment (such as ISE CUBE) that are running the Policy Services persona.

Adding the Network Device to ISE

Based on the configuration sections in previous chapters, your ISE may already be configured for these network devices. However, ensuring the proper configuration of the network device definition in ISE is critical to this endpoint discovery process. It's important because ISE must have knowledge of the switch, its SNMP community, and the RADIUS shared secret in order to accept the RADIUS packets and then run the SNMP query against the switch.

From the ISE GUI, perform the following steps:

1. Navigate to **Administration** > **Network Resources** > **Network Devices**.

2. If the network device is already in the list, click the check box and choose Edit. If the network device is not already in the list, choose Add.

3. Ensure the correct IP address is in configured.

   This should match the **ip radius source-interface** command configured on the switch.

4. Set the Network Devices Groups correct. Pay close attention to use the MonitorMode Stage, as shown in Figure 21-6.

5. Ensure that the check box next to Authentication Settings is enabled.

6. Fill in the shared secret.

7. Repeat Steps 2 through 6 for all remaining network devices to be used with the Device Sensor method. Notice, with this method, there is no need to configure any information under SNMP; RADIUS is all we need to know about the device.

Configuring the Switches

Based on the configuration sections of previous chapters, your switches may already be configured for this method, except for the SNMP Traps (most likely). However, go back into the Switches CLI and ensure the appropriate pieces of the configuration are in place.

This approach requires the switches to be configured for authentication, including 802.1X and MAB. For more details on the configuration of network access devices, refer to Chapter 11. It is important to note that this configuration is not only for endpoint discovery and Monitor Mode, but continues to be used throughout the additional modes of operation.

From the Switch CLI Global Configuration:

Set the Global Configuration settings to enable RADIUS Authentication, Authorization, and Accounting.

1. Enter **aaa new-model** to enable AAA globally on the switch.

2. Type **aaa authentication dot1x default group** [*group-name* | **radius**].

3. Type **aaa authorization network default group** [*group-name* | **radius**].

4. Enter **aaa accounting dot1x default start-stop group** [*group-name* | **radius**].

5. Ensure that device tracking is enabled by typing **ip device tracking**.

6. Globally enable 802.1X with the **dot1x system-auth-control** command.

7. Ensure the correct interface is used to source the RADIUS traffic using the **ip radius source-interface** *interface-name* command.

Ensure the correct attributes are being sent in the radius communications. See Chapter 11 for more details on these commands.

8. Enter **radius-server attribute 6 on-for-login-auth**.

9. Enter **radius-server attribute 8 include-in-access-req**.

10. Enter **radius-server attribute 25 access-request include**.

11. Enter **radius-server vsa send accounting**.

12. Enter **radius-server vsa send authentication**.

radius-server dead-criteria time [*value*] **tries** [*value*]

13. **radius-server host** *ISE-IP-Address* **auth-port 1812 acct-port 1813 key** *Shared-Secret*

14. Repeat Step 13 for all ISE Policy Service nodes.

15. Type **aaa server radius dynamic-author** to enter into that sub-mode.

16. Enter **client** *ISE-IP-Address* **server-key** *shared-secret*.

17. Repeat Step 16 for all ISE Policy Service nodes.

Enter Interface Configuration mode and configure the interfaces for 802.1X in open mode.

18. Enter **interface range** interface-name *first-interface - last-interface*.

19. Use the built-in macro **switchport host** to set the port as an access port with spanning-tree portfast.

20. Type **ip access-group** *Your-Permit-All-ACL* **in**.

21. Type **authentication event fail action next-method**.

22. Type **authentication event server dead action authorize vlan** *VLAN*.

23. Type **authentication event server alive action reinitialize**.

24. Type **authentication host-mode multi-auth**.

25. Type **authentication open**.

26. Type **authentication order mab dot1x**.

27. Type **authentication priority dot1x mab**.

28. Type **authentication port-control auto**.

29. Type **authentication violation restrict**.

30. Type **mab**.

31. Type **dot1x pae authenticator**.

32. Enter **dot1x timeout tx-period** *time*.

Appendix E contains complete configurations for multiple switch models.

Unlike the previous two methods, RADIUS may be the only probe necessary for this model. So, there is no need to configure the **ip helper-address** commands on the default gateway for the access VLANs.

Using Monitoring to Identify Misconfigured Devices

Now that you have built the endpoint database through the device discovery process, it is time to look at the results and tune your Profiling Policies so that you are accurately profiling endpoints. Although ISE comes with a tremendous number of preconfigured profiles, it is often necessary to tune those—or even create custom ones. See Chapter 24, "Advanced Profiling Configuration," for details on creating custom profiles.

Tuning the Profiling Policies

There are a number of ways to investigate the list of endpoints, but the easiest method is to list the endpoints themselves from Administration > Identity Management > Identities > Endpoints. From this screen, create a quick filter and look for the endpoint profiles that are non-specific, like "unknown" and "workstation," as shown in Figure 21-11.

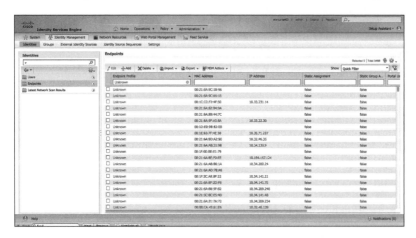

Figure 21-11   *Filtering Endpoint Identities List*

The next step is to work through the list of endpoints in these generic endpoint profiles to find the common attributes and more accurately profile these devices. This enables you to more adequately prepare your authentication and authorization policies for network access, while preventing a denial of service.

The tuning of endpoint profiles can be as much art as it is science. Ultimately, start by looking into the endpoint details. Examine what information was gathered and what may be missing. Using Figures 21-12 and 21-13 as examples, you can see that this unknown device has authenticated by EAP-FAST and the endpoint profiling source was the

RADIUS probe. Ultimately, you can identify that this device appears to actually be a Cisco Office Extend Access Point (OEAP), but you need to create a new profile policy that can uniquely identify these correctly.

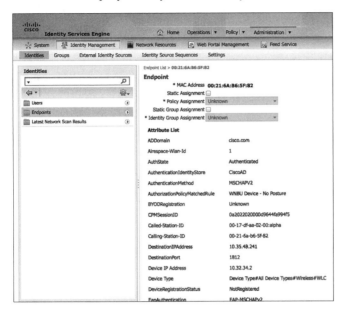

Figure 21-12 *Endpoint Details: Part I*

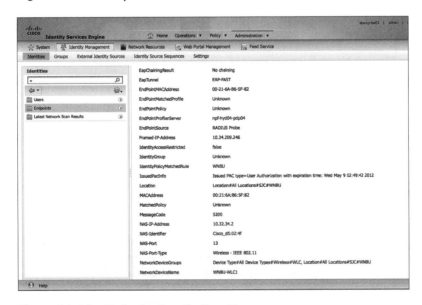

Figure 21-13 *Endpoint Details: Part II*

See Chapter 24, "Advanced Profiling Configuration," for more detail on creating custom profiles.

Creating the Authentication Policies for Monitor Mode

There is a default Authentication Policy for MAB, as shown in Figure 21-14. This policy looks for a RADIUS Service-Type equal to Call-Check and NAS-Port-Type is equal to Ethernet (Wired_MAB). This default Authentication Rule compares the MAC address sent in the calling-station-id field of the RADIUS packet to entries within the internal endpoint identity store.

If the MAC address exists, then the authentication succeeds. But remember, just because an authentication is successful does not mean the device is permitted access. That is the responsibility of the Authorization Policy, not the Authentication Policy. Passing the Authentication Policy simply means that the session proceeds to the Authorization Policy for further analysis.

One of the most fundamental changes that must be made in preparation of Low-Impact or Closed Mode is to change the setting for MAB to "continue" when a MAC Address is not found in the Internal Endpoints store. The default setting is to reject. This sends an Access-Reject message back to the NAD, by changing "reject" to "continue" the authentication proceeds to the authorization table, even though the mac address was not found.

Let's continue our configuration following the Policy Sets that was built in Chapter 20. In that chapter, you created a Policy Set for Monitor Mode. The criteria to use that group instead of the default group is RADIUS traffic being sourced from a switch in the MonitorMode network device group.

First, duplicate the MAB rule from the default policy set. From the ISE GUI, perform the following steps:

1. Navigate to **Policy > Policy Sets.**

2. Select the **Monitor Mode Policy Set** from the left-hand side.

3. Expand the **Authentication Policy.**

4. Insert a new rule above the default authentication rule.

5. Name the rule **MAB.**

6. Click the **+** sign for Condition > Choose existing condition.

7. Select **Compound Condition > Wired_MAB.**

8. Click the drop-down next to **select network access.**

9. Choose **Allowed Protocols > Default Network Access.**

10. Click the **+** sign for the "use" drop-down, and select **Internal Endpoints.**

11. Under **Options,** change **If user not found** to **Continue.** See Figure 21-14 for a graphical representation of this setting.

12. Click **Done.**

13. Click **Save.**

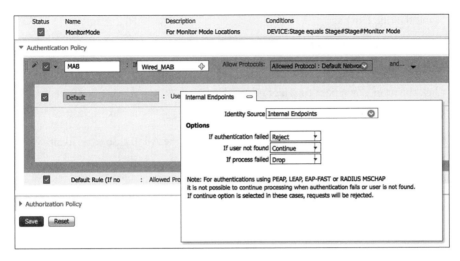

Figure 21-14   *Identity Store Options.*

The resulting MAB rule should look like Figure 21-15.

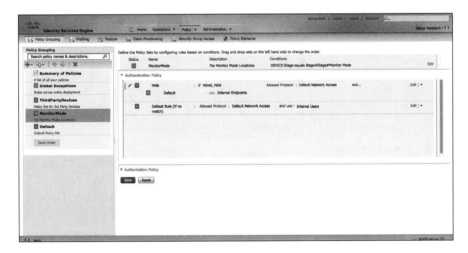

Figure 21-15   *Final MAB Rule*

Now, duplicate the Dot1X rule from the default policy set. This allows those devices that do have configured supplicants to authenticate successfully. From the ISE GUI, perform the following steps:

1. Navigate to **Policy > Policy Sets**.

2. Select the **Monitor Mode Policy Set** from the left-hand side.

3. Expand the **Authentication Policy**.

4. Insert a new rule above the default authentication rule.

  5. Name the rule **Dot1X**.

  6. Click the **+** sign for Condition > Choose Existing Condition.

  7. Select **Compound Condition > Wired_802.1X**.

  8. Click the drop-down next to **select network access**.

  9. Choose **Allowed Protocols > Default Network Access**.

  10. Click the **+** sign for the "use" drop-down, and select the **All_ID_Sources** identity source sequence that we created in Chapter 9.

  11. Click **Done**.

  12. Click **Save**.

The resulting 802.1X rule should look like Figure 21-16.

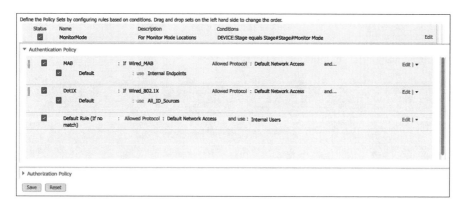

Figure 21-16   *Final Dot1X Rule*

Finally, change the Default Authentication Rule. By default, it is to check the internal users identity store only. Also, change that one to the All_ID_Sources sequence. Figure 21-17 shows the final Authentication Policy for Monitor Mode.

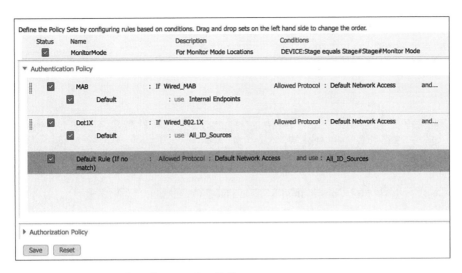

Define the Policy Sets by configuring rules based on conditions. Drag and drop sets on the left hand side to change the order.

Status	Name	Description	Conditions
☑	MonitorMode	For Monitor Mode Locations	DEVICE:Stage equals Stage#Stage#Monitor Mode

▼ Authentication Policy

		Name		Description	Conditions	
⋮	☑	MAB	: If Wired_MAB		Allowed Protocol : Default Network Access	and...
	☑	Default	: use Internal Endpoints			
⋮	☑	Dot1X	: If Wired_802.1X		Allowed Protocol : Default Network Access	and...
	☑	Default	: use All_ID_Sources			
	☑	Default Rule (If no match)	: Allowed Protocol : Default Network Access	and use : All_ID_Sources		

▶ Authorization Policy

[Save] [Reset]

Figure 21-17 *Final Authentication Policy*

Creating Authorization Policies for Non-Authenticating Devices

The Authentication Policy was the first step of policy creation. The Authorization Policies are where the bulk of the work is completed and where the ultimate decisions need to be made. At this point, devices that need to use MAB reach the Authorization Policy table—either by existing in the Internal Endpoint store or by landing on the Continue option if they are not in the database.

The Authorization Policy needs to be designed to allow specific devices based on their endpoint profile. Configure the default rule in the Monitor Mode table to send Access-Reject messages (such as deny access). As you recall, a key fundamental orientation of Monitor Mode is to ensure that only Access-Accept, Access-Reject, and Voice permissions are returned to the network access devices.

IP-Phones

IP-Phones are a special case and require additional configuration. In addition to requiring the RADIUS Access-Accept response, they also need the response to include a Cisco Attribute Value (AV) pair named device-traffic-class=voice. This response permits the phone to use the Voice VLAN that is configured on the switch port.

Cisco has pre-built Authorization Policies for IP-Phones. These results may be re-used for Monitor Mode, as well as your end-state mode of operation.

From the ISE GUI, perform the following steps:

1. Navigate to **Policy > Policy Sets**.

2. Select the Monitor Mode Policy Set from the left-hand side.

3. Expand the Authorization Policy.

4. Insert a new rule above the default authorization rule.

5. Name the rule IP Phones.

Note Ignore the Identity Groups picker, because these are legacy configuration options from early ISE versions and are only utilized now for MAC Address Management (MAM) groups.

1. Click the + sign for **Condition(s) > Create New Condition**.

2. Click the drop-down for **Select Attribute**.

3. Choose **Endpoint > Logical Policy > Equals > IP-Phones**.

4. Click the + for AuthZ Profiles.

5. Choose **Standard > Cisco IP Phones**.

Note This result sends an Access-Accept, a dACL that permits all traffic, and the device-traffic-class=voice AV pair. There is another Authorization Result option named Non_Cisco_IP_Phones, but the result is exactly the same.

6. Click **Done**.

7. Click **Save**.

The resulting IP-Phone Authorization Rule should look like Figure 21-18.

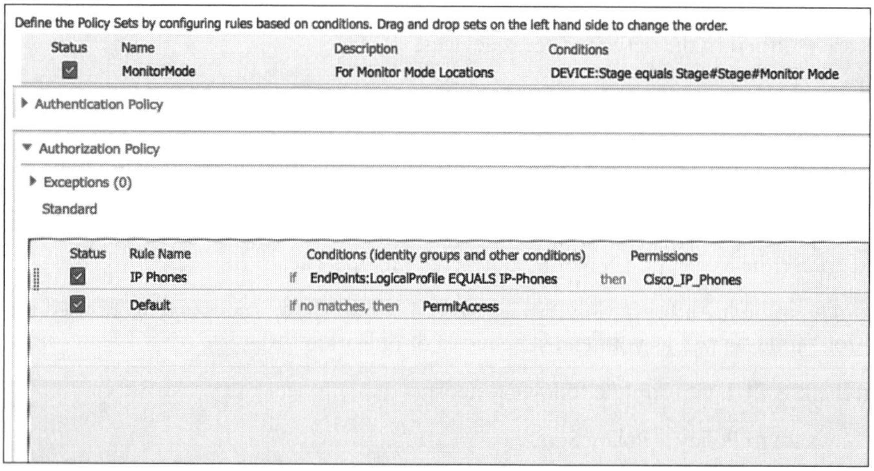

Figure 21-18 *IP-Phone Authorization Rule*

Wireless APs

Now that you have an Authorization Policy for the Cisco IP Phones, you need one for the Wireless Access Points (AP) that may exist in the environment. Cisco Wireless APs can join the wired network in a few ways. They can use MAC Authentication Bypass, or you may configure the APs to authenticate to the network using EAP-FAST.

To keep things simple in Monitor Mode, create a rule that permits access to devices matching the AP profile. This accommodates both MAB and 802.1X authentications of APs.

From the ISE GUI, perform the following steps:

1. Navigate to **Policy > Policy Sets.**

2. Select the **Monitor Mode Policy Set** from the left-hand side.

3. Expand the **Authorization Policy.**

4. Insert a new rule above the default authorization rule (will place rule between the default rule and the IP-Phones rule).

5. Name the new rule **Wireless AP.**

6. Click the **+** next to **Conditions.**

7. Click **Create New Condition.**

8. Configure it as **Endpoint > EndpointPolicy equals Cisco-Access-Point.**

9. Click the **+** next to AuthZ Profile(s).

10. Choose **Standard > Permit Access.**

11. Click **Done.**

12. Click **Save.**

Figure 21-19 displays the Wireless AP Authorization Rule.

You built this Authorization Rule without specific access, because you are in Monitor Mode. In Low-Impact or Closed Mode, you want to use a more specific level of access control, such as only permitting CAPWAP protocols or assigning a Security Group Tag.

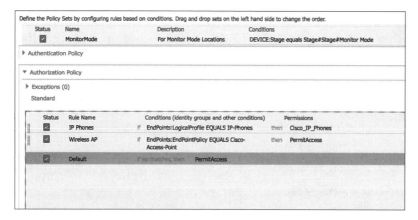

Figure 21-19   *Wireless AP Authorization Rule*

Printers

For printers, it makes sense to build a logical profile that consists of all the many pre-built endpoint profiles for printers. Then, you can use that local profile in your authorization policies.

From the ISE GUI, perform the following steps:

1. Navigate to **Policy > Profiling > Logical Profiles**.

2. Click **Add**.

3. Name the Logical Profile **Printers**.

4. Add all the applicable Printer Endpoint Profiles from the left side to be members of the logical group. Figure 21-20 shows an example.

5. Click **Submit**.

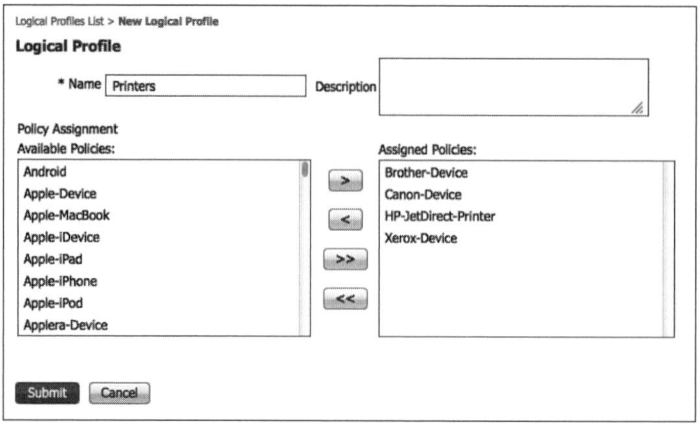

Figure 21-20   *Printers Logical Profile*

Now that the logical profile is built, use it in the Authorization Policy. From the ISE GUI, perform the following steps:

1. Navigate to **Policy > Policy Sets**.

2. Select the **Monitor Mode Policy Set** from the left-hand side.

3. Expand the **Authorization Policy**.

4. Insert a new rule above the default authorization rule (will place rule between the default rule and the Wireless AP rule).

5. Name the new rule **Printers**.

6. Click the **+** next to **Conditions**.

7. Click **Create New Condition**.

8. Configure it as **Endpoint > Logical Profile equals Printers**.

9. Click the **+** next to AuthZ Profile(s).

10. Choose **Standard > Permit Access**.

11. Click **Done**.

12. Click **Save**

Figure 21-21 shows the Printers Authorization Rule.

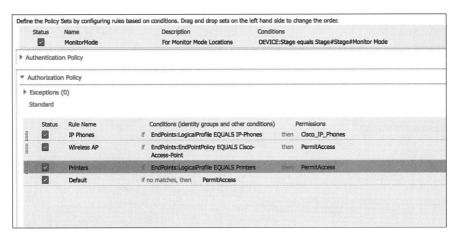

Figure 21-21 *Authorization Rule for Printers*

What you accomplished in this short section can be repeated for all other non-authenticating devices that you encounter in your environment.

Creating Authorization Policies for Authenticating Devices

You now have the Authorization Policies in place for the non-authenticating devices. Now, build specific policies for devices that do use 802.1X authentication. This section focuses on two main authorizations: Machine and User.

Machine Authentication (Machine Auth)

With an Active Directory environment, the machines that are managed by the domain require ongoing communication to and from the domain controllers. This communication is needed to keep machines up to date with machine policy (GPO), software updates, and other important communication.

To achieve that communication on a network with 802.1X enabled, Microsoft created Machine Auth. This allows a Windows workstation without an interactive user to still authenticate to the network, using the machine's credentials (instead of user credentials). This is known as the machine state.

Let's create an Authorization Rule that permits access to machines that authenticate successfully. Depending on the configuration of the supplicant configuration, the machine will either authenticate with its machine name and password or with the machine's domain-issued certificate.

From the ISE GUI, perform the following steps:

1. Navigate to **Policy > Policy Sets**.

2. Select the **Monitor Mode Policy Set** from the left-hand side.

3. Expand the **Authorization Policy**.

4. Insert a new rule above the default authorization rule (will place rule between the default rule and the Printers rule).

5. Name the new rule **Machine Auth**.

6. Click the **+** next to **Conditions**.

7. Click **Create New Condition**.

8. Configure it as **AD1 > External Groups EQUALS Domain Computers**.

9. Click the **+** next to **AuthZ Profile(s)**.

10. Choose **Standard > Permit Access**.

    That ensures the authenticated machine is a member of the domain computers group. Now, check that machine authentication was formatted correctly.

11. Add an **Attribute/Value**.

12. Configure it as **Network Access > Hostname > Starts With**.

13. Type **host/**.

14. Click **Done.**

15. Click **Save.**

Figure 21-22 shows the resulting Authorization Rule.

Status	Name	Description	Conditions
☑	MonitorMode	For Monitor Mode Locations	DEVICE:Stage equals Stage#Stage#Monitor Mode

Define the Policy Sets by configuring rules based on conditions. Drag and drop sets on the left hand side to change the order.

▶ Authentication Policy

▼ Authorization Policy

▶ Exceptions (0)

Standard

Status	Rule Name	Conditions (identity groups and other conditions)	Permissions
☑	IP Phones	if EndPoints:LogicalProfile EQUALS IP-Phones	then Cisco_IP_Phones
☑	Wireless AP	if EndPoints:EndPointPolicy EQUALS Cisco-Access-Point	then PermitAccess
☑	Printers	if EndPoints:LogicalProfile EQUALS Printers	then PermitAccess
☑	Machine Auth	if AD1:ExternalGroups EQUALS ise.local/Users /Domain Computers AND Network Access:UserName STARTS_WITH host/	then PermitAccess
☑	Default	if no matches, then PermitAccess	

Figure 21-22 *Authorization Rule for Machine Auth*

User Authentications

Let's create an Authorization Rule that permits access to those possessing valid Active Directory usernames and passwords. If the supplicant presents a valid username and password, the rule will permit access.

From the ISE GUI, perform the following steps:

1. Navigate to **Policy > Policy Sets.**

2. Select the **Monitor Mode Policy Set** from the left-hand side.

3. Expand the **Authorization Policy.**

4. Insert a new rule above the default authorization rule (will place rule between the default rule and the Machine Auth rule).

5. Name the new rule **Domain Users.**

6. Click the **+** next to **Conditions.**

7. Click **Create New Condition.**

8. Configure it as **AD1 > External Groups EQUALS Domain Users.**

9. Click the **+** next to **AuthZ Profile(s).**

10. Choose **Standard > Permit Access.**

11. Click **Done**.

12. Click **Save**.

Figure 21-23 shows the resulting Authorization Rule.

Define the Policy Sets by configuring rules based on conditions. Drag and drop sets on the left hand side to change the order.

Status	Name	Description	Conditions
☑	MonitorMode	For Monitor Mode Locations	DEVICE:Stage equals Stage#Stage#Monitor Mode

▶ Authentication Policy

▼ Authorization Policy

▶ Exceptions (0)

Standard

	Status	Rule Name		Conditions (identity groups and other conditions)		Permissions
	☑	IP Phones	if	EndPoints:LogicalProfile EQUALS IP-Phones	then	Cisco_IP_Phones
	☑	Wireless AP	if	EndPoints:EndPointPolicy EQUALS Cisco-Access-Point	then	PermitAccess
	☑	Printers	if	EndPoints:LogicalProfile EQUALS Printers	then	PermitAccess
	☑	Machine Auth	if	(AD1:ExternalGroups EQUALS ise.local/Users /Domain Computers AND Network Access:UserName STARTS_WITH host/)	then	PermitAccess
	☑	Domain Users	if	AD1:ExternalGroups EQUALS ise.local/Users /Domain Users	then	PermitAccess
	☑	Default		if no matches, then	PermitAccess	

Figure 21-23   *Authorization Rule for Users*

Default Authorization Rule

The Monitor Mode policy set has a default authorization rule. When no more specific rule is matched, the authorization uses the default rule. That rule is currently set to Permit Access, so change it to Deny Access, which sends an Access-Reject RADIUS response. Remember that this affects switches that should be configured for Monitor Mode only, and therefore, the Access-Reject message will be ignored by the switch. Even though the switch ignores the reject message, ISE still logs it as a failed authorization, and you may use live log and the AAA Reports to identify all devices that are failing authentication/authorization and identify why.

From the ISE GUI, perform the following steps:

1. Navigate to **Policy > Policy Sets**.

2. Select the **Monitor Mode Policy Set** from the left-hand side.

3. Expand the **Authorization Policy**.

4. Edit the **Default Authorization Rule**.

5. Click the **+** next to **Permit Access**.

6. Choose **Standard > Deny Access**.

7. Click **Done**.

8. Click **Save**.

Figure 21-24 shows the resulting default rule.

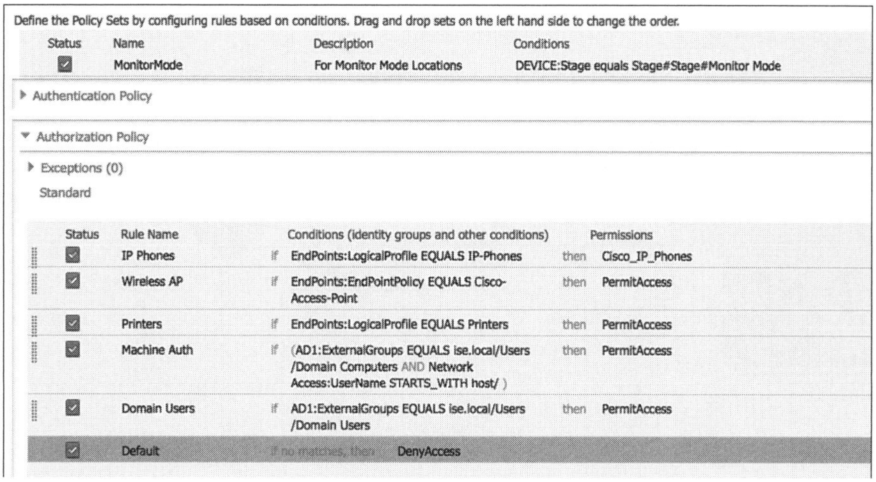

Figure 21-24   *Default Authorization Rule*

Summary

Your ISE deployment is now ready for Monitor Mode. You learned the three main methods of endpoint discovery that may be used prior to implementing authentication at a location. You also learned how to create an Authentication Policy that allows devices that have properly configured supplicants to authenticate successfully, while still providing access to those devices that are not yet configured, or have no configurable supplicant.

You configured an Authorization Policy that provides access to those devices who have been properly profiled and are allowed to access the network, as well as providing access to successful machine and user authentications.

With Monitor Mode, when an Access-Reject message is sent as the authorization result, the switch ignores the reject message and ISE logs it as a failed authorization. You may then use Live Log and the AAA Reports to identify all devices that are failing authentication/authorization, identify why, and make the necessary corrections. Once you are rid of the unwanted failures, you will be ready to transition from Monitor Mode to either Low-Impact or Closed Mode.

Chapter 22 focuses on Low-Impact Mode. One of the major differences between the modes is how to handle devices or users that do not pass authentication. Monitor Mode still allows them to have access, but in Low-Impact Mode, all failed authentications are directed to a centralized web Authentication page.

Low-Impact Mode

As previously described in Chapter 20, "Deployment Phases," Low-Impact Mode is one of the end-state choices for your deployment. Closed Mode is the other final stage. There is no specific best practice for which mode is better to deploy; it entirely depends on your organization and its specific needs.

Figure 22-1 shows the operational flow intended for Low-Impact Mode. This mode is one of the two possible end-states (closed mode being the second) and, as such, specific access may be provide per user, device, or other condition that you want to use in the ISE Authorization Policies. Remember, the end goal of Low-Impact Mode is to provide limited network access to devices without authentication, and then provide specific access to those who have been authorized.

As with any other security solution, tuning the Authorization Results is something that can take a lot of operational man hours. It is also always recommended to deploy authorization results in stages. For example, begin with a policy that permits full-access to any device that has authenticated successfully. Ensure that the environment is fully functional and then begin to "ratchet down" the security. Make the dACLs more specific, assign specific VLANs, add Security Group Tags, and so on.

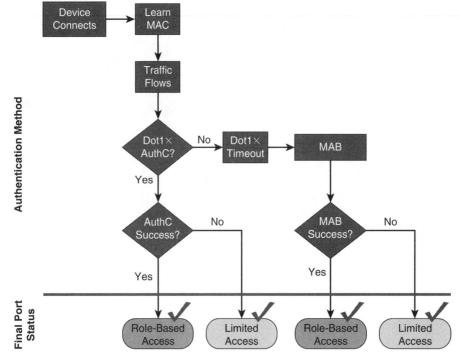

Figure 22-1   *Low-Impact Mode Operational Flow*

Figure 22-2 shows that the Port ACL is applied prior to authentication, which only allows specific traffic into the port. Once the authentication occurs, authorization must include a dACL that selectively permits and/or denies traffic. Other authorization results may also be applied at the port, such as URL redirection, VLAN assignment, MACSec encryption, Security Group Tagging, and more.

Note   VLAN assignment should only be used on devices that use supplicants. Without a supplicant, the device will most likely not be able to identify the VLAN change and may end up with the wrong IP address for its final VLAN assignment.

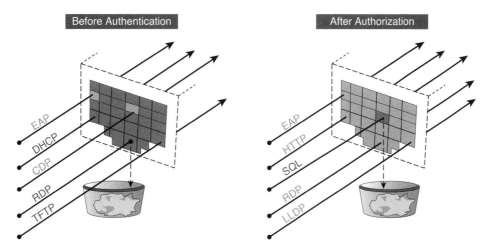

Figure 22-2   *Low-Impact Mode Port Behavior*

Transitioning from Monitor Mode to Low-Impact Mode

Low-Impact is a natural transition from Monitor Mode. Both modes use the Open Authentication technology in Cisco Switches.

When you are ready to transition a location from Monitor Mode to an end-state mode, like Low-Impact, it only requires some minor changes. The first change is to replace the default port ACL that is permitting all traffic with one that permits only the bare minimum of traffic for your organization. Things like DNS, DHCP, and TFTP are usually considered must haves. This type of ACL on the port allows things like PXE boot, thin clients, and workstation re-imaging to continue to function, even though they have not successfully authenticated.

Meanwhile, when a device does successfully authenticate, either via MAB or through true 802.1X authentication, the Authorization Result includes a dACL that permits much more traffic for the endpoint.

A second difference between Monitor Mode and Low-Impact is the default rule in ISE. When in Monitor Mode, the default rule sends an Access-Reject (which the switch promptly ignores). The default rule in Low-Impact Mode changes to a Web Authentication result. In other words, if a user or device does not receive a specific authorization, it is redirected to a Web Authentication Portal. This allows the misconfigured users to enter their AD credentials and gain some limited access to the network, as well provides the Portal for GUEST users to authenticate and be provided with some form of Internet access.

Always keep in mind that this creates a change in user experience. In Monitor Mode, anything that did not authenticate successfully was still permitted full access to the network, and the user experience was unchanged as compared to a network without any authentication. With Low-Impact Mode, those users no longer receive full network access; they will only be able to access the Centralized Web Portal. Therefore, it is critical that you do not transition a site from Monitor Mode to Low-Impact Mode before the user population is ready.

Configuring ISE for Low-Impact Mode

Typically, it is recommended that you configure the initial Low-Impact results to permit all traffic once a device has successfully authenticated. Then, after a "break-in" period, begin to lock the results down and be more specific per user/device. This helps limit the impact to the end-user population even more.

Set Up the Low-Impact Mode Policy Set in ISE

The first step of Low-Impact Mode is to build out the Policy Set in ISE. For this, simply duplicate the Monitor Mode Policy Set. That saves some operational expense by not duplicating the effort already put forth building the Monitor Mode policies.

Duplicate the Monitor Mode Policy Set

In the following steps, you duplicate the Monitor Mode Policy Set and name the resulting copy "LowImpact."

From the ISE GUI, perform the following steps:

1. Navigate to **Policy > Policy Set**.

2. On the left-hand side, highlight the **MonitorMode Policy Set**.

3. Click the **Duplicate** button and choose **Duplicate Below**, as shown in Figure 22-3.

   A New Policy Set named "MonitorMode_copy" appears beneath the MonitorMode Policy Set and populates the right-hand side of the screen, as shown in Figure 22-4.

4. Select **Edit** for the new MonitorMode_copy Policy Set.

5. Rename the Policy Set to **LowImpactMode**.

6. Change the description.

7. Modify the condition to be **Stage equals Low Impact Mode**.

8. Click **Done**.

9. Click **Submit**.

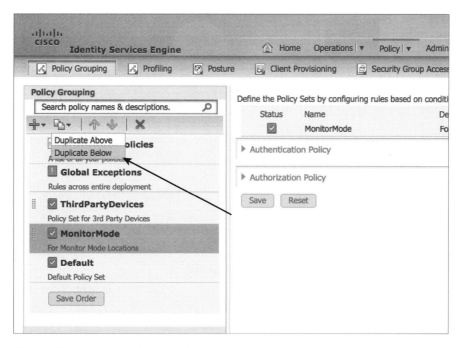

Figure 22-3   *Duplicating the MonitorMode Policy Set*

Figure 22-4   *MonitorMode_copy Policy Set*

Figure 22-5 shows the duplicated Policy Set.

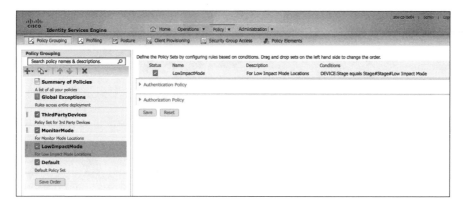

Figure 22-5 *Duplicated Policy Set*

Create the Web Authentication Authorization Result

Next, create an authorization result that sends any failed or unknown authentications to the Centralized Web Portal:

1. Navigate to **Policy > Policy Elements > Results**.

2. Choose **Authorization > Downloadable ACLs**.

3. Click **Add**.

4. Permit only specific traffic that would be required.

    For example, DNS will be necessary, as will web traffic to the ISE Policy Service Nodes (PSN). Figure 22-6 shows a sample dACL that permits web traffic to the ISE subnet, as well as DNS and DHCP.

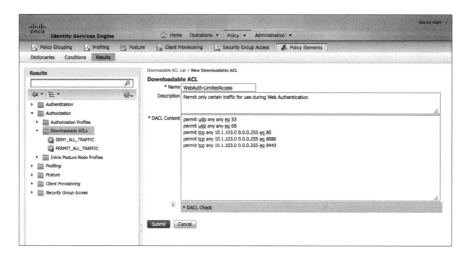

Figure 22-6 *Sample WebAuth dACL*

  5. Click **Submit**.

  6. Choose **Authorization > Authorization Profiles**.

  7. Click **Add**.

  8. Provide this Authorization Profile a name, such as "Web Auth."

  9. Provide a description, such as "Centralized WebAuth for Wired and Wireless."

  10. Under Common Tasks, check the box for **DACL NAME**.

  11. Use the drop down and choose the **dACL** that you created in Step 4.

Note dACLs only affect wired deployments. The Wireless LAN Controller simply ignores the dACL that is sent to it, thereby allowing us to use single Authorization Policy for Wired and Wireless.

  12. Check the box for Web Authentication.

  13. Ensure that Centralized is selected with the drop-down.

  14. In the ACL text box, enter the name of the Redirection ACL that is configured locally on the switch and WLC (configured in Chapter 11, "Bootstrapping Network Access Devices").

Note This ACL defines the "interesting traffic" on the switch. In other words, the traffic that is permitted is redirected; traffic that is denied is not redirected. It is not a traffic-filtering ACL on the switch. However, on the WLC, the ACL with this name does traffic filtering and redirection. Traffic that is permitted bypasses redirection and is permitted through the WLC. Traffic that is denied is redirected to ISE.

  This ACL must exist locally on both the WLC and the switches, as shown in Figure 22-7.

  15. In the Redirect drop-down, ensure that Default is selected. If you configured a custom portal for this authorization result, select Manual and then choose that custom portal.

  16. Click **Submit**.

Figure 22-8 illustrates the final WebAuth Authorization Profile.

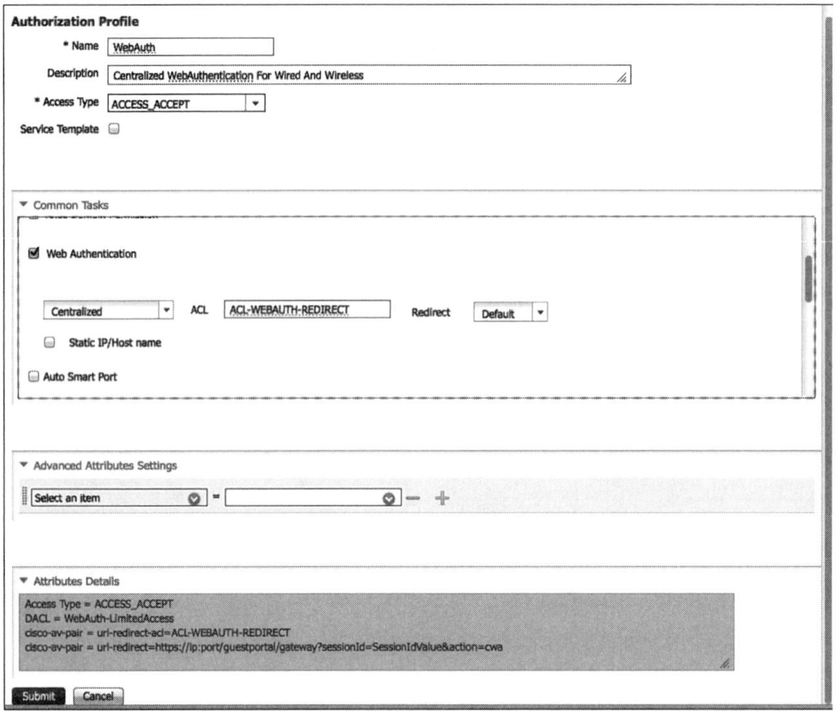

Authorization Profile
* Name WebAuth
Description Centralized WebAuthentication For Wired And Wireless
* Access Type ACCESS_ACCEPT
Service Template
Common Tasks
Web Authentication
Centralized
ACL ACL-WEBAUTH-REDIRECT
Redirect Default
Static IP/Host name
Auto Smart Port
Advanced Attributes Settings
Select an item
Attributes Details
Access Type = ACCESS_ACCEPT
DACL = WebAuth-LimitedAccess
cisco-av-pair = url-redirect-acl=ACL-WEBAUTH-REDIRECT
cisco-av-pair = url-redirect=https://ip:port/guestportal/gateway?sessionId=SessionIdValue&action=cwa
Submit
Cancel

Figure 22-7 *Local Redirection ACL on WLC and Switches*

Common Tasks
Voice Domain Permission
Web Authentication
Centralized
ACL ACL-WEBAUTH-REDIRECT
Redirect Default
Static IP/Host name
C3750X#show ip access-list
Extended IP access list ACL-AGENT-REDIRECT
10 deny udp any any eq domain
20 permit tcp any any eq www
Extended IP access list ACL-ALLOW
Extended IP access list ACL-WEBAUTH-REDIRECT
20 permit tcp any any eq www (29398 matches)
30 permit tcp any any eq 443 (12 matches)
Extended IP access list AGENT-REDIRECT
10 deny udp any any eq domain
20 permit tcp any any eq www
Extended IP access list xACSACLx-IP-PERMIT_ALL_TRAFFIC-505c03a1 (per-user)
10 permit ip any any
C3750X#
MONITOR
WLANs
CONTROLLER
WIRELESS
SECURITY
MANAGEMENT
Security
Access Control Lists
Name
Type
ACL-POSTURE-REDIRECT
HR-ACL
ACL-WEBAUTH-REDIRECT
Local EAP
Priority Order
Certificate
Access Control Lists

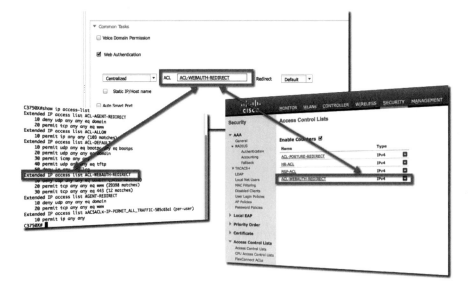

Figure 22-8 *WebAuth Authorization Profile*

Configure the Web Authentication Identity Source Sequence

You also must ensure the Web Portal authenticates both guest users and Active Directory users (assuming that matches your company's policy). From the ISE GUI, perform the following steps:

1. Navigate to **Administration > Identity Management > Identity Source Sequences**.

2. Edit the **Guest_Portal_Sequence**.

3. Ensure that all needed Identity Sources are in the **Selected** list, as shown in Figure 22-9.

4. Click **Save**.

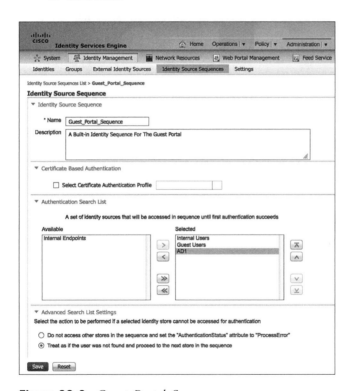

Figure 22-9   *Guest_Portal_Sequence*

Modify the Default Rule in the Low-Impact Policy Set

Finally, change the default rule in Low-Impact Mode to use the Centralized Web Authentication result that you configured:

1. Navigate to **Policy > Policy Set**.

2. Choose the **LowImpactMode Policy Set** on the left side.

3. Expand the **Authorization Policy**.

4. Edit the Default rule at the bottom of the policy.

5. Click the **+** sign next to **DenyAccess**.

6. Choose **Standard > WebAuth**.

7. Click **Done**.

8. Click **Save**.

Figure 22-10 shows the completed Low-Impact Mode Default rule being set to WebAuth.

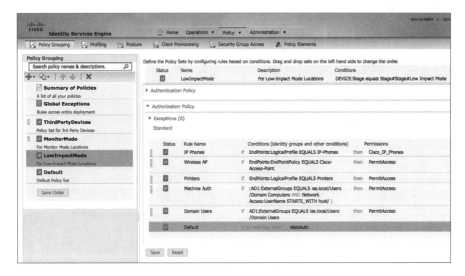

Figure 22-10   *Default Rule Set to WebAuth*

Assign the WLCs and Switches to the Low-Impact Stage NDG

For the WLCs and the switches authentication traffic to use the Low-Impact Mode Policy Set, add those network access devices to the Low-Impact Stage Network Device Group (NDG), as shown in the following steps:

1. Navigate to **Administration > Network Resources > Network Devices**.

2. Edit one of the network devices that should be in Low-Impact Mode.

3. In the Network Device Group section, change the Stage to **Low Impact Mode**, as shown in Figure 22-11.

4. Click **Save**.

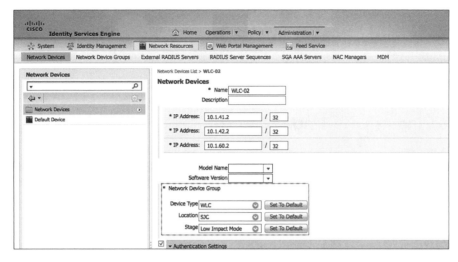

Figure 22-11 *Network Device Group set to 'Low Impact Mode'*

5. Repeat Steps 1–4 for all network devices that should use the Low-Impact Mode Policy Set.

Modify the Default Port ACL on the Switches That Will Be Part of Low-Impact Mode

Currently, the switch should have an ACL on each port that permits all traffic. As discussed in Chapter 20, and previously in this chapter, a more restrictive port ACL should be used to provide less access to devices that have not successfully authenticated.

Let's assign the ACL named ACL-DEFAULT that you configured on each switch in Chapter 11. Figure 22-11 shows the contents of ACL-DEFAULT.

From the switch CLI, perform the following steps:

1. Enter global configuration mode by typing **configure terminal**.

2. Configure the access-layer interfaces by typing **interface range** *interface-name first-interface last-interface*.

3. Type **ip access-group** *access-list-name* **in**.

4. Type **end**.

5. Enter **copy running-config startup-config** to save the configuration:

```
C3750X#conf t
Enter configuration commands, one per line. End with CNTL/Z.
C3750X(config)#int range g1/0/1 - 12
C3750X(config-if-range)#ip access-group ACL-DEFAULT in
C3750X(config-if-range)#end
```

```
C3750X# copy running-config startup-config
Destination filename [startup-config]?
Building configuration...
[OK]
```

Monitoring in Low-Impact Mode

Keep an eye on the Live Authentication Log and the AAA reports, just like you did in Monitor Mode. Additionally, be aware of user experience complaints or feedback. There can sometimes be applications that slow down the users' login experience when they are denied access to the server. Tweaking the ACL-DEFAULT ACL may be required.

Tightening Security

At this point, any device that authenticates receives the Permit Access Authorization result. That authorization result uses a Permit-All-Traffic downloadable ACL (dACL).

Creating AuthZ Policies for the Specific Roles

To tighten security, use a separate authorization result for each role type. The result may contain a specific VLAN, a dACL, or even a Security Group Tag. This should be part of your defense-in-depth strategy—especially when using profiling with MAB, which is really a bypass of authentication.

For example, a printer should not have full access to the network. It only needs a few ports to be open. TCP ports 9100–9103 (JetDirect ports), TCP, and UDP 161 (SNMP) are required for an HP JetDirect printer. So, let's create that dACL and authorization result.

From the ISE GUI, perform the following steps:

1. Navigate to **Policy > Policy Elements > Results**.

2. Choose **Authorization > Downloadable ACLs**.

3. Click **Add**.

4. Name the new dACL **HP Printers**.

5. Enter the following into the text box:

   ```
   permit udp any any eq 68
   permit udp any any eq 53
   permit tcp any any range 9100 9102
   permit tcp any any eq 161
   permit udp any any eq 161
   ```

6. Click **Submit**.

7. Navigate to **Authorization Profiles.**

8. Click **Add.**

9. Name the new Authorization Profile **HP Printers.**

10. Ensure Access Type is **Access_Accept.**

11. Under Common Tasks, select **dACL NAME.** Choose the **HP Printers dACL.**

12. Click **Submit.**

13. Navigate to **Policy > Policy Set.**

14. Choose the **LowImpactMode Policy Set.**

15. Expand the **Authorization Policy.**

16. Edit the rule for printers.

17. Change the permissions result from Permit Access to **HP Printers.**

18. Click **Done.**

19. Click **Save.**

Figure 22-12 and Figure 22-13 display the creation of the dACL and the authorization profile for printers.

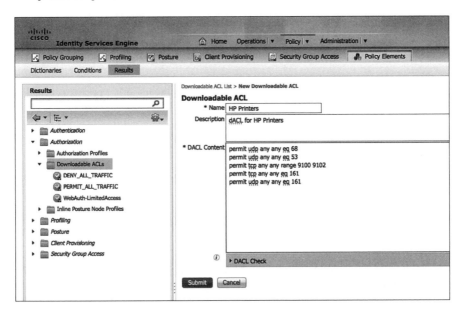

Figure 22-12 *Printers dACL*

Figure 22-13   *Printers Authorization Profile*

This authorization result may need to be tweaked if you are using other printer types, but it provides a useful example of specific authorization results in Low-Impact Mode. Repeat these steps for the other device types and roles that were defined as part of your authorization policy in Chapter 6, "Building a Cisco ISE Network Access Security Policy," and Chapter 7, "Building a Device Security Policy."

Change Default Authentication Rule to Deny Access

As you tighten security, you want to lock down a default authentication rule in the authentication policy by changing the default result to deny access. That means that any device that has not successfully authenticated or been successfully MAB'd (which includes WebAuth) is sent an Access-Reject, so it will not waste the CPU cycles of processing the Authorization Policy.

From the ISE GUI, perform the following steps:

1. Navigate to **Policy > Policy Set.**

2. Choose the **LowImpactMode Policy Set.**

3. Expand the **Authentication Policy**.

4. Edit the Default Rule at the bottom of the Authentication Policy.

5. Change Internal Users to **Deny Access**.

6. Click **Done**.

7. Click **Save**.

Figure 22-14 shows a sample Low-Impact Mode Policy Set.

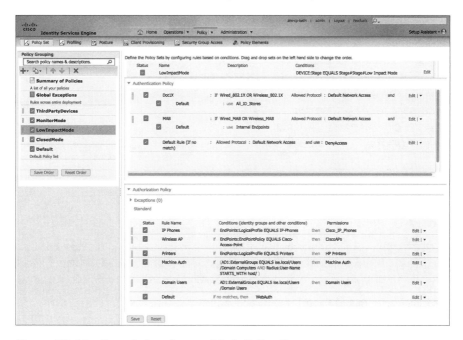

Figure 22-14   *Sample Low-Impact Mode Policy Set*

Moving Switch Ports from Multi-Auth to Multi-Domain

It is generally considered a best practice to limit the number of devices on any particular switch port to the smallest number possible. 802.1X was inherently designed to permit a single MAC address per port. This was modified to allow one device on the data VLAN and another device on the voice VLAN with Multi-Domain Authentication (MDA). However, with Monitor Mode, you most often deploy with Multi-Authentication (Multi-Auth) Mode instead. That mode allows for a virtually unlimited number of devices per port, each one requiring its own authentication.

Your organization and security policy should be factors when you determine which mode is truly best. However, to support technology such as MACSec (802.1AE) encryption, MDA or Single Mode is a requirement. Multi-Auth will not permit the encryption.

Example 22-1 shows the available host modes and changing the host mode on a range of interface to be multi-domain mode.

Example 22-1   *Changing from Multi-Auth to Multi-Domain*

```
C3750X#conf t
Enter configuration commands, one per line. End with CNTL/Z.
C3750X(config)#int range g1/0/1 - 12
C3750X(config-if-range)#authentication host-mode ?
  multi-auth     Multiple Authentication Mode
  multi-domain   Multiple Domain Mode
  multi-host     Multiple Host Mode
  single-host    SINGLE HOST Mode
C3750X(config-if-range)#authentication host-mode multi-domain
C3750X(config-if-range)#end
C3750X# copy running-config startup-config
Destination filename [startup-config]?
Building configuration...
[OK]
```

Summary

In this chapter, you learned about the transition from Monitor Mode to the Low-Impact Mode end state. You configured the policies. This chapter also examined the importance of tuning the security to be specific to the authorization and other best practices.

The next chapter examines the other end-state mode.

Chapter 23

Closed Mode

As previously described in Chapter 20, "Deployment Phases," Low-Impact Mode and Closed Mode are the end-state choices for your deployment. There is no specific best practice for which mode is better to deploy; it entirely depends on your organization and its specific needs.

One of the benefits of deploying in Closed Mode is the ability to easily assign VLANs to any authorization. Unlike Monitor and Low-Impact Modes, where devices are provided network access before the authentication request is sent to ISE, Closed Mode provides zero access before receiving a response from ISE or a timeout occurs. (See Chapter 18, "Setting Up a Distributed ISE Deployment," for more on timeouts and High Availability.) Because no access was provided, no IP address was obtained, and a VLAN may be assigned alongside of the Access-Accept message, without the concerns of the endpoint needing to refresh its IP address.

Figure 23-1 shows the operational flow intended for Closed Mode. Remember that the end goal of Closed Mode is to provide zero network access to devices without authentication, and then provide specific access to those who have been authorized. Closed Mode is based on the default behavior of 802.1X, but adds on some Cisco-specific capabilities that make 802.1X more easily deployable.

As with any other security solution, tuning the Authorization Results is something that can take a lot of operational man hours. As such, it is also always recommended to deploy authorization results in stages. For example, begin with a policy that permits full access to any device that has successfully authenticated. Ensure that the environment is fully functional and then begin to "ratchet down" the security. Add role- or device-specific dACLs and a Security Group Tag to the authorization result, not just VLAN assignment.

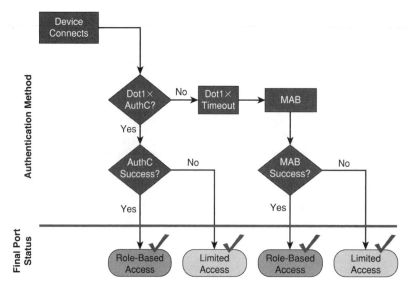

Figure 23-1   *Closed Mode Operational Flow*

Figure 23-2 shows the port behavior in Closed Mode. Virtually zero traffic is allowed into the port before authentication. Once the session is authorized, specific authorization results may be applied to the port, such as

- VLAN assignment

- dACL

- URL redirection

- MACSec encryption

- Security Group Tags

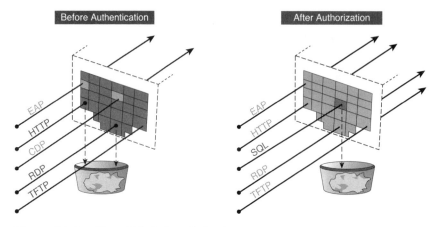

Figure 23-2   *Closed Mode Port Behavior*

Transitioning from Monitor Mode to Closed Mode

When you are ready to transition a location from Monitor Mode to an end-state mode like Closed Mode, it requires some minor changes. The first change is to remove the default port ACL that permits all traffic and the authentication open command that is applied to the port.

802.1X authentication occurs relatively quickly, and therefore, traffic such as DHCP is not normally affected by the lack of traffic flow. However, a device that does not have a configured 802.1X supplicant must then fall back to MAC authentication bypass.

The default timeout for 802.1X is 30 seconds, with two retries, thereby providing a 90-second timeout before MAB begins. This is typically too long for many DHCP timers and causes problems for those devices. Therefore, the best practice is to change the default tx-timer from 30 seconds to 10 seconds, reducing the total time from 90 seconds to 30 seconds. Of course, this timer may be tuned per environment, but typically, this 10-second tx-timer works well in the majority of environments.

A second difference between Monitor Mode and Closed Mode is the default rule in ISE. When in Monitor Mode, the default rule is to send an Access-Reject (which the switch promptly ignores). The default rule in Closed Mode is changed to a Web Authentication result. In other words, if a user or device does not receive a specific authorization, they are permitted limited access and redirected to a Web Authentication Portal. This allows the misconfigured users to enter their AD credentials and gain some limited access to the network, as well as provide the portal for GUEST users to authenticate and have some form of Internet access.

Always keep in mind that this now changes user experience. In Monitor Mode, anything that did not authenticate successfully was still permitted full access to the network, and the user experience was unchanged as compared to a network without any authentication. With Closed Mode, those users no longer receive full network access; they will only be able to access the Centralized Web Portal. Therefore, it is critical that you do not transition a site from Monitor Mode to Closed Mode before the user population is ready.

Configuring ISE for Closed Mode

Typically, it is recommended that you configure the initial Closed Mode results to permit all traffic once a device has successfully authenticated. Then, after a "break-in" period begin to lock the results down and be more specific per user/device. This helps limit the impact to the end-user population even more.

Set Up the Closed Mode Policy Set in ISE

The first step of Closed Mode is to build out the Policy Set in ISE. For this, simply duplicate the Monitor Mode Policy Set. That saves you some operational expense by not duplicating the effort already put forth building the Monitor Mode policies.

Duplicate the Monitor Mode Policy Set

The following steps duplicate the monitor mode policy set.

From the ISE GUI, perform the following steps:

1. Navigate to **Policy > Policy Set.**

2. On the left-hand side, highlight the MonitorMode Policy Set.

3. Click the **Duplicate** button and choose **Duplicate Below**, as shown in Figure 23-3.

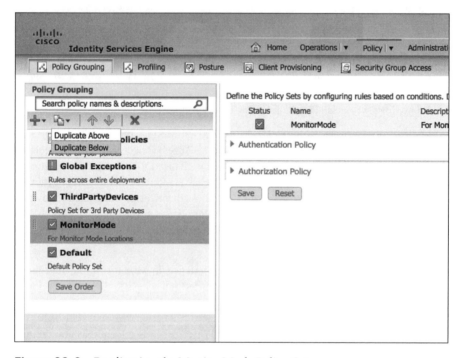

Figure 23-3   *Duplicating the MonitorMode Policy Set*

A New Policy Set named MonitorMode_copy appears beneath the MonitorMode Policy Set and populates the right-hand side of the screen, as shown in Figure 23-4.

4. Select **Edit** for the new MonitorMode_copy Policy Set.

5. Rename the Policy Set to **ClosedMode.**

6. Change the description.

7. Modify the Condition to be **Stage equals Closed Mode.**

8. Click **Done.**

9. Click **Submit.**

Figure 23-5 shows the duplicated Policy Set.

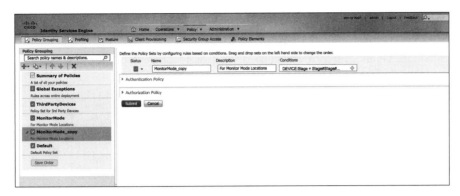

Figure 23-4 *MonitorMode_copy Policy Set*

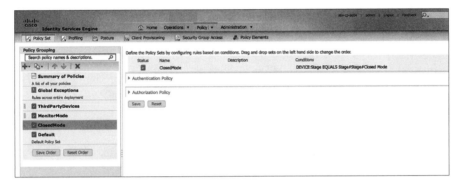

Figure 23-5 *Duplicated Policy Set*

Create the Web Authentication Authorization Result

Next, you need to create an authorization result that sends any failed or unknown authentications to the Centralized Web Portal. Note: You may have completed this already if you followed the procedures from Chapter 22, "Low-Impact Mode."

This authorization result consists of a RADIUS Access-Accept, a URL redirection, and the name of a local ACL that defines what traffic should be redirected. Additionally, because this is Closed Mode, a VLAN assignment and dACL may also be included in the Authorization Result. The choice between assigning a specific VLAN or using a dACL to limit the allowed traffic while in the WebAuthentication state (or a combination of the two) is entirely subjective to the customer environment. Let's do both VLAN assignment and dACL restriction in this example, which is shown in the following steps:

1. Navigate to **Policy > Policy Elements > Results**.

2. Choose **Authorization > Downloadable ACLs**.

3. Click **Add**.

4. Permit only specific traffic that would be required.

    For example, DNS and web traffic to the ISE Policy Service Nodes (PSN) are both
    necessary. Figure 23-6 shows a sample dACL that permits web traffic to the ISE sub-
    net, as well as DNS and DHCP.

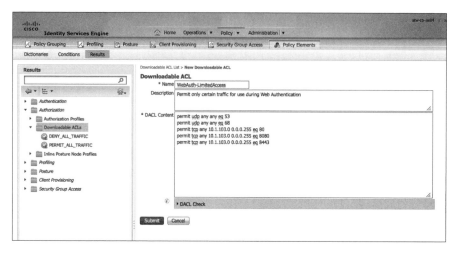

Figure 23-6   *Sample WebAuth dACL*

5. Click **Submit**.

6. Choose **Authorization > Authorization Profiles**.

7. Click **Add**.

8. Provide this Authorization Profile a name, such as WebAuth.

9. Provide a description, such as "Centralized WebAuth for Wired and Wireless."

10. Under Common Tasks, check the box for **DACL NAME**.

11. Use the drop-down and choose the dACL that you created in Step 4.

Note   dACLs only affect wired deployments. The Wireless LAN Controller simply
ignores the dACL that is sent to it, thereby allowing you to use single Authorization Policy
for Wired and Wireless.

12. Check the box for VLAN and enter the GUEST VLAN ID.

Note   This VLAN ID is used for both Wired and Wireless VLAN assignment. An
alternative is to use a name and ensure that the name matches the correct VLAN at the
different Network Access Devices.

13. Check the box for Web Authentication.

14. Ensure that **Centralized** is selected with the drop-down.

15. In the ACL text box, enter the name of the Redirection ACL that is configured locally on the switch and WLC (configured in Chapter 11, "Bootstrapping Network Access Devices").

> **Note**   This ACL defines the "interesting traffic" on the switch. In other words, the traffic that is permitted is redirected; traffic that is denied is not redirected. It is not a traffic-filtering ACL on the switch. However, on the WLC, the ACL with this name does both traffic filtering and redirection. Traffic that is permitted bypasses redirection and is permitted through the WLC. Traffic that is denied is redirected to ISE.

This ACL must exist locally on both the WLC and the switches, as shown in Figure 23-7.

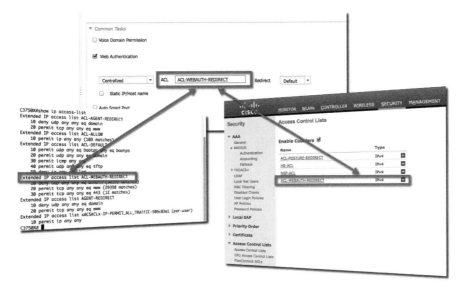

Figure 23-7   *Local Redirection ACL on WLC and Switches*

16. In the Redirect drop-down, ensure that Default is selected. If you have configured a custom portal for this authorization result, select Manual and then choose that custom portal.

17. Click **Submit**.

Figure 23-8 illustrates the final WebAuth Authorization Profile.

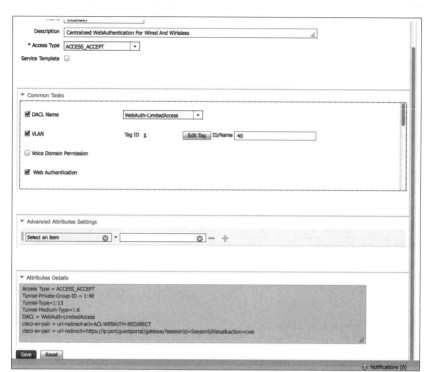

Figure 23-8   *WebAuth Authorization Profile*

Configure the Web Authentication Identity Source Sequence

You need to ensure that the Web Portal authenticates both guest users and Active Directory users (assuming that matches your company's policy). From the ISE GUI, perform the following steps:

1. Navigate to **Administration > Identity Management > Identity Source Sequences**.

2. Edit the Guest_Portal_Sequence.

3. Ensure that all needed Identity Sources are in the Selected list, as shown in Figure 23-9.

4. Click **Save**.

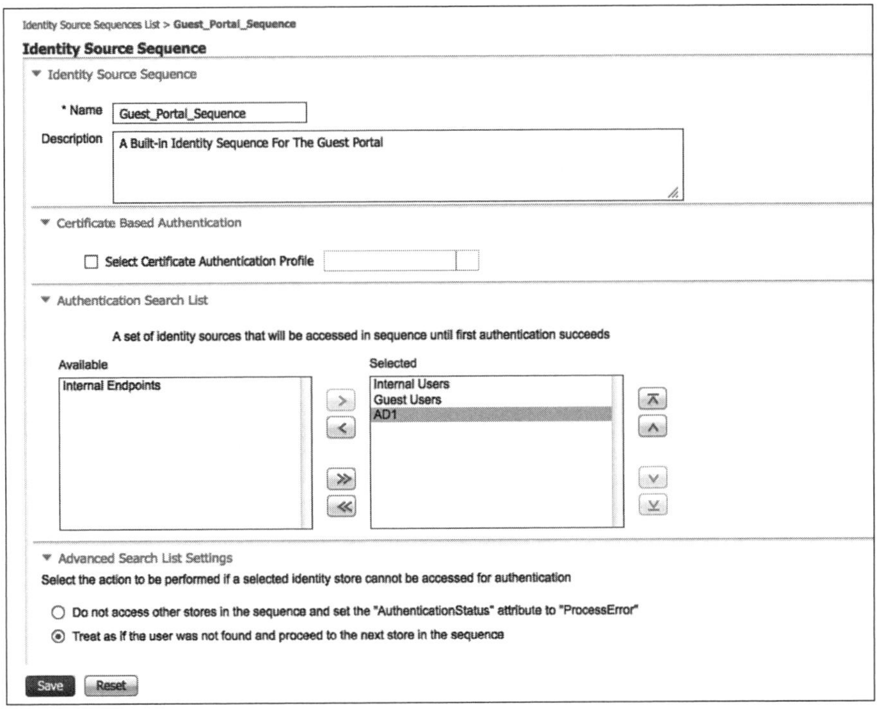

Identity Source Sequences List > **Guest_Portal_Sequence**

Identity Source Sequence

▼ Identity Source Sequence

* Name   Guest_Portal_Sequence

Description   A Built-in Identity Sequence For The Guest Portal

▼ Certificate Based Authentication

☐ Select Certificate Authentication Profile

▼ Authentication Search List

A set of identity sources that will be accessed in sequence until first authentication succeeds

Available

Internal Endpoints

Selected

Internal Users
Guest Users
AD1

▼ Advanced Search List Settings

Select the action to be performed if a selected identity store cannot be accessed for authentication

○ Do not access other stores in the sequence and set the "AuthenticationStatus" attribute to "ProcessError"

◉ Treat as if the user was not found and proceed to the next store in the sequence

Save   Reset

Figure 23-9   *Guest_Portal_Sequence*

Modify the Default Rule in the Closed Policy Set

Finally, change the default rule in Closed Mode to use the Centralized Web Authentication result that you configured with the following steps:

1. Navigate to **Policy > Policy Set.**

2. Choose the **ClosedMode Policy Set** on the left side.

3. Expand the **Authorization Policy.**

4. Edit the **Default** rule at the bottom of the policy.

5. Click the **+** sign next to DenyAccess.

6. Choose **Standard > WebAuth.**

7. Click **Done.**

8. Click **Save.**

Figure 23-10 shows the default rule being set to WebAuth.

Figure 23-10 *Default Rule Set to WebAuth*

Assign the WLCs and Switches to the Closed Stage NDG

For the WLCs and the switches authentication traffic to use the Closed Mode Policy Set, add those network access devices to the Closed Stage Network Device Group (NDG) with the following steps:

1. Navigate to **Administration > Network Resources > Network Devices**.

2. Edit one of the network devices that should be in Closed Mode.

3. In the Network Device Group section, change the Stage to **Closed Mode**, as shown in Figure 23-11.

4. Click **Save**.

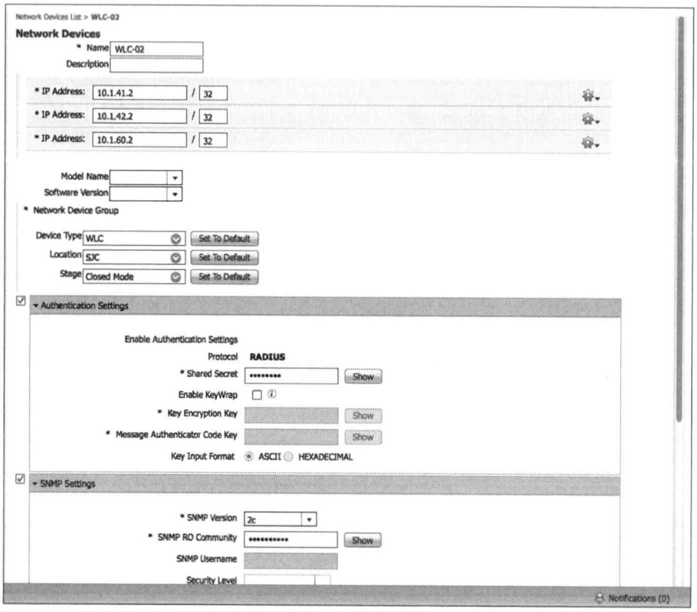

Figure 23-11 *Network Device Group Set to 'Closed Mode'*

5. Repeat Steps 1–4 for all network devices that should use the Closed Mode Policy Set.

Modify the Default Port ACL on the Switches That Will Be Part of Closed Mode

Currently, the switch should have an ACL on each port that permits all traffic. As discussed in Chapter 20 and previously in this chapter, the default port ACL and the Authentication Open commands are removed for Closed Mode.

From the switch CLI, perform the following steps:

1. Enter global configuration mode by typing **configure terminal.**

2. Configure the access-layer interfaces by typing **interface range** *interface-name first-interface last-interface.*

3. Type **no ip access-group** *access-list-name* **in.**

4. Type **no authentication open.**

5. Type **end.**

6. Enter **copy running-config startup-config** as shown to save the configuration:

```
C3750X#conf t
Enter configuration commands, one per line. End with CNTL/Z.
C3750X(config)#int range g1/0/1 - 12
C3750X(config-if-range)#no ip access-group ACL-ALLOW in
C3750X(config-if-range)#no authentication open
C3750X(config-if-range)#end
C3750X# copy running-config startup-config
Destination filename [startup-config]?
Building configuration...
[OK]
```

Monitoring in Closed Mode

Pay close attention to the Live Authentication Log and the AAA reports, just like you did in Monitor Mode. Additionally, listen for user-experience complaints or feedback.

Tightening Security

At this point, any device that authenticates receives the Permit Access Authorization result. That authorization result uses a Permit-All-Traffic downloadable ACL (dACL) and provides an Access-Accept, assigning the device to the default VLAN configured on the interface or the WLAN.

Creating Authorization Policies for the Specific Roles

To tighten security, a separate authorization result should be used for each role type. The result may contain a specific VLAN, a dACL, or even a Security Group Tag. This should be part of your defense-in-depth strategy—especially when using profiling with MAB, which is really a bypass of authentication.

For example, a printer should not have full access to the network. It only needs a few ports to be open. TCP ports 9100–9103 (JetDirect ports), TCP, and UDP 161 (SNMP) are required for an HP JetDirect printer. So, let's create that dACL and authorization result.

From the ISE GUI, perform the following steps:

1. Navigate to **Policy > Policy Elements > Results**.

2. Choose **Authorization > Downloadable ACLs**.

3. Click **Add**.

4. Name the new dACL **HP Printers**.

5. Enter the following into the text box:

   ```
   permit udp any any eq 68
   permit udp any any eq 53
   permit tcp any any range 9100 9102
   permit tcp any any eq 161
   permit udp any any eq 161
   ```

   Figure 23-12 shows the completed dACL.

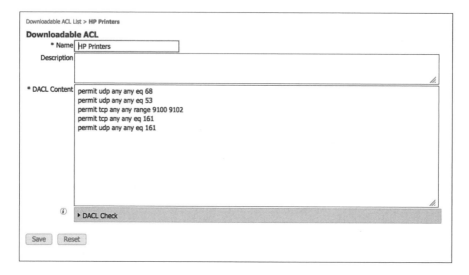

Figure 23-12   *HP Printers dACL*

6. Click **Submit**.

7. Navigate to Authorization Profiles.

8. Click **Add**.

9. Name the new Authorization Profile **HP Printers**.

10. Ensure Access Type is **Access_Accept**.

11. Under Common Tasks, select **DACL NAME**. Choose the **HP Printers dACL**.

> **Note**   Because this is Closed Mode, you can also choose to assign this printer to a VLAN dedicated for printers.

Figure 23-13 shows the completed authorization profile.

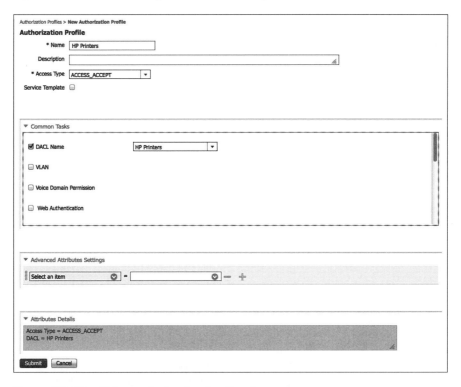

Figure 23-13   *Printers Authorization Result*

12. Click **Submit**.

13. Navigate to **Policy > Policy Set**.

14. Choose the **ClosedMode Policy Set**.

15. Expand the **Authorization Policy**.

16. Edit the rule for **Printers**.

17. Change the **Permissions** result from Permit Access to **HP Printers**.

18. Click **Done**.

19. Click **Save**.

Figure 23-14 shows a sample Closed Mode policy that has been locked down with specific authorization results.

This authorization result may need to be tweaked if you are using other printer types, but it provides a useful example of specific authorization results in Closed Mode. You should repeat these steps for the other device types and roles that were defined as part of your Authorization Policy in Chapter 6, "Building a Cisco ISE Network Access Security Policy," and Chapter 7, "Building a Device Security Policy."

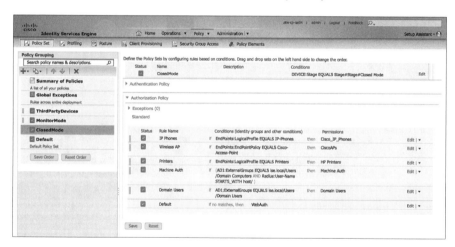

Figure 23-14   *Sample Closed Mode Authorization Policy*

Change Default Authentication Rule to Deny Access

As you tighten security, there is a default authentication rule in the Authentication Policy that you will want to lock down by changing the default result to deny access. That means that any device that has not successfully authenticated or been successfully MAB'd (which includes WebAuth) is sent an Access-Reject and doesn't waste the CPU cycles of processing the Authorization Policy.

From the ISE GUI, perform the following steps:

1. Navigate to **Policy > Policy Set**.

2. Choose the **ClosedMode Policy Set**.

3. Expand the **Authentication Policy**.

4. Edit the Default Rule at the bottom of the Authentication Policy.

5. Change Internal Users to **Deny Access**.

6. Click **Done**.

7. Click **Save**.

Figure 23-15 shows a sample Closed Mode Policy Set.

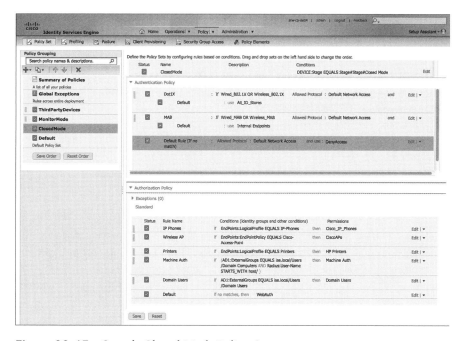

Figure 23-15 *Sample Closed Mode Policy Set*

Moving Switch Ports from Multi-Auth to MDA

It is generally considered a best practice to limit the number of devices on any particular switch port to the smallest number possible. 802.1X was inherently designed to permit a single MAC address per port. This was modified to allow one device on the data VLAN and another device on the voice VLAN with Multi-Domain Authentication (MDA). However, with Monitor Mode, you most often deploy with Multi-Authentication (Multi-Auth) Mode instead. That mode allows for a virtually unlimited number of devices per port, each one requiring its own authentication.

Your organization and your security policy should be the determining factors as to which mode is truly best. However, to support technology such as MACSec (802.1AE) encryption, MDA, or Single Mode is a requirement. Multi-Auth does not permit the encryption.

Example 23-1 shows the command sets to convert interfaces from Multi-Auth to Multi-Domain Mode.

Example 23-1   *Changing from Multi-Auth to Multi-Domain*

```
C3750X#conf t
Enter configuration commands, one per line. End with CNTL/Z.
C3750X(config)#int range g1/0/1 - 12
C3750X(config-if-range)#authentication host-mode ?
  multi-auth     Multiple Authentication Mode
  multi-domain   Multiple Domain Mode
  multi-host     Multiple Host Mode
  single-host    SINGLE HOST Mode
C3750X(config-if-range)#authentication host-mode multi-domain
C3750X(config-if-range)#end
C3750X# copy running-config startup-config
Destination filename [startup-config]?
Building configuration...
[OK]
```

Summary

In this chapter, you learned about the transition from Monitor Mode to the Closed Mode end state and configured the policies. This chapter also discussed the importance of tuning the security to be specific per authorization and other best practices.

Chapter 24

Advanced Profiling Configuration

This chapter explores the intricacies of the Identity Services Engine (ISE) profiling service. The profiling service is designed to help corporations correctly identify various device types that are attaching to their network. Chapter 10, "Profiling Basics," explained the basic configuration of the ISE profiling service and its different profiling probes. This chapter explains how to create basic and complex profile policies, custom profile rules, and how to use profile data in authorization policies. By the end of this chapter, you will have a firm grasp of the advanced capabilities and configuration of the Cisco ISE profiling service.

Creating Custom Profiles for Unknown Endpoints

Cisco ISE profiler includes hundreds of device profiles out of the box. However, given the thousands of network device types available, it is inevitable that you will need to create a few custom profiles for your environment. When ISE cannot identify a device, it marks it as unknown and adds it to the Unknown Device Identity Group. ISE also saves all the attributes and their values it has collected on the device's behavior. You can then use these values to assist in creating your custom profile for this device type.

The key to creating a reliable custom device profile is to find profiler probe values that are unique to your custom device. If the values are too generic, you will have false-positive results matching your new device profile. Therefore, it is imperative that you choose unique profiler probe values or a combination of values that become unique when combined into a profiler rule set.

As a review, here is the list of profiler probes that ISE provides. For more info on these probes, see Chapter 10:

- NetFlow
- DHCP

- DHCP SPAN

- HTTP

- Radius and IOS Sensor

- NMAP

- DNS

- SNMP Query and Trap

Identifying Unique Values for an Unknown Device

To identity the values that ISE profiler has collected on a device, go to Administration > Identity Management > Identities > Endpoints. Click the Filter icon to bring up the search dialog boxes, as shown in Figure 24-1. You can then filter to find your device.

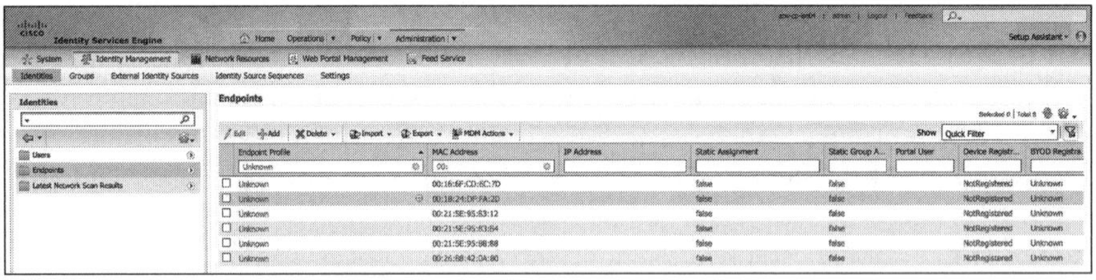

Figure 24-1   *Filtering Endpoints in ISE*

Once you find your unknown device, click it. You are shown a list of all the attributes and their values that ISE recognized from that device so far. Hopefully, this list is populated with enough unique information that you can now create your custom device profile. If this is not the case, you can do two things: create different traffic from this device and/or enable additional ISE profiler probes to capture more information types from this device. By nature of the way profiling is used, make sure that the types of attributes and their values you use to create your device profile are

- Sent from the device every time it connects to the network

- Happens very, very early after the device is connected to the network

Figure 24-2 and Figure 24-3 depict an example device showing its various attributes/values that ISE has collected. You can use any of these in the creation of your new custom device profile.

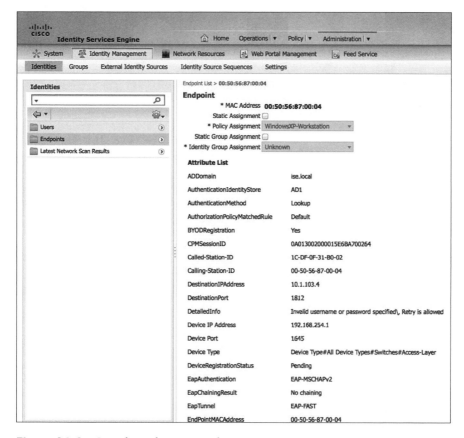

Figure 24-2   *Sample Endpoint Attributes*

Some of the more useful attributes, shown in Figure 24-2 and Figure 24-3, for creating custom device profilers include

- **User-Agent:** Mozilla/4.0 (compatible; MSIE 6.0; Windows NT 5.1; SV1)

- **dhcp-class-identifier:** MSFT 5.0

- **host-name:** ssu-xp

- **ip:** 10.1.10.50

- **OUI:** VMware, Inc.

The user-agent string is populated with information gathered from packets sent from a web browser. All web browsers send a user-agent string in the HTML requests and responses to identify the type of browser and operating system being used.

The dhcp-class-identifier is populated by either the manufacturer of the device or by the operating system that is running on the device. In the case of embedded systems, it is almost always populated by the manufacturer and thus can be a helpful profiling attribute.

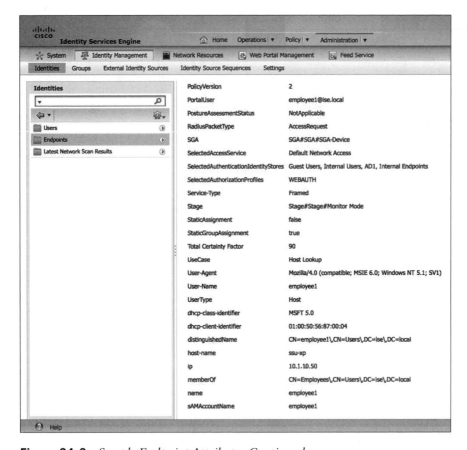

Figure 24-3   *Sample Endpoint Attributes Continued*

Hostname is beneficial as a supporting attribute. For example, if the hostname contains a string, such as "iPad," you can use that as part of a larger profiler policy with other rules. The other rules might be OUI vendor equaling "apple" and user-agent string containing "iPad." Each rule adds something to the certainty value of the policy when matched. But alone, neither could add enough certainty to cause a match of the whole device profile policy. This helps to cut down on false positives with your custom profile policies.

Collecting Information for Custom Profiles

Table 24-1 depicts an example worksheet that you could create to collect the information needed for your custom ISE device profiles.

Table 24-1 *Device Profile Information Worksheet*

Device Type	Attribute Type	Attribute Name	Condition	Attribute Value	Collection Method
MRI	DHCP	Host-name	Contains	TS34D	DHCP SPAN of corp dhcp server ports
	MAC	OUI	Equals	Drier-ACME	RADIUS authentication
A/C unit	DHCP	Vendor Class	Contains	GE	DHCP SPAN
	DHCP	Host-name	Contains	GE	DHCP SPAN

Seeing as there are so many network-connected medical devices these days, let's walk through creating a theoretical profile policy to identify a medical device.

Here are the high-level steps:

1. (Optional) Create one or more profiler conditions using attributes and values collected by ISE.

2. Create an endpoint profiler policy using the conditions created.

3. (Optional) Create a logical profiler policy to group similar profiling policies under a single logical name. For example IP-Phones would include all IP-Phone-related profiler policies.

Creating Custom Profiler Conditions

Creating a profiler condition is not a required step, but it is definitely a common one. Instead of creating a condition, you could just create the conditions within the profile policy ruleset. In most cases, however, you will want to create a condition for anything that you may use again, use in multiple policies, or have to change the value periodically. Here are the steps to creating a profiler condition:

1. Connect the new device to your ISE profiler monitored network. Try to log on to the network with this device and then perform any typical startup activities that this device or operator would normally complete. This allows ISE to collect information about the device.

2. Look up the MAC address of your test device in the ISE endpoint identities list. Examine what was captured and look for values that are unique either by themselves or would be unique when combined. Write these down.

3. Create a set of profiler conditions using the unique values that were captured. Go to **Policy > Policy Elements > Conditions > Profiling.** You should see a screen like Figure 24-4.

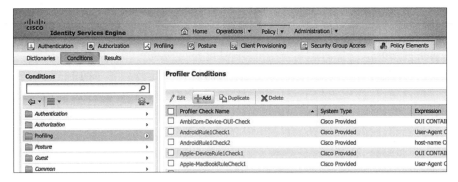

Figure 24-4 *Profiler Conditions List*

4. To create a new condition, click **Add**.

> **Tip**   Each condition can only contain a single attribute and value. This makes it critical that your naming of the condition be descriptive of the device type, but also the type of condition it is checking. Names are case sensitive and should usually start with a capital letter. A good name would be something like "Biomed-scanner-dhcp." The condition name communicates that it is a biomed device of type scanner that is keying off a DHCP attribute.

5. Create your condition using the attributes and values you obtained from the endpoints list. Figure 24-5 depicts an example profiler condition for an MRI scanner.

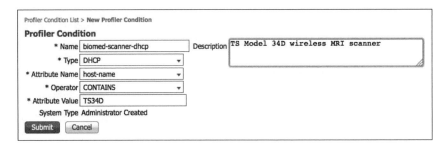

Figure 24-5 *Example Profiler Condition*

6. Create as many additional profiler conditions as required for your device.

Creating Custom Profiler Policies

1. Go to **Policy** > **Profiling** > **Profiling Policies**. Click **Add**.

2. Fill in the policy information with a descriptive name and description.

Tip   It is a best practice to start with a minimum certainty value of at least 1000 for all custom profiler policies. This makes sure that they will not be undermined by current or future Cisco provided policies.

If multiple profiler policies match a device, the one with the highest certainty value is used. Ties are handled through first alphabetical match of the policy name.

3. Fill in the minimum certainty value for the policy; leave everything else to their default values.

4. Add your rules. Insert a rule, using the ⚙️ ▾ icon for each condition that you built previously for this device. Ensure that, when you add your certainty values, they equal or exceed the minimum certainty value you set for the device policy. See Figure 24-6 for an example.

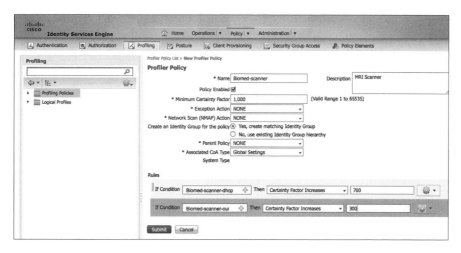

Figure 24-6   *Example Profiler Policy*

5. Click **Save** when complete.

6. Profiler will re-profiles all devices. Any matches to your new profile policy will immediately take effect.

These simple steps allow you to create all sorts of custom profiles. You can choose to group some of your policies into logical policies (refer to Chapter 10). Some custom policies may be simple; others might be extremely complex. Be sure to use a consistent naming scheme and always fill in the Description field on conditions and policies.

Advanced NetFlow Probe Configuration

Cisco NetFlow data for profiling is beneficial when the other ISE probes are not able to capture enough unique data from a device to be used in a custom device policy. In most cases, you will not need to enable the NetFlow probe. But if you do, here are some of the best practices for setting it up.

> **Note** The NetFlow probe should be used with caution, given its ability to overwhelm an ISE Policy Services Node with millions of NetFlow records if not properly deployed.

Cisco NetFlow captures IP session data for network traffic flows. A NetFlow record can contain lots of useful information, but at a minimum, it contains the SRC/DST IP address and SRC/DST port/protocol of a flow. NetFlow is supported on all Cisco router platforms and some Cisco switching and wireless platforms. NetFlow is collected from NetFlow-capable Cisco devices that export the flow data to an ISE Policy Services Node. The default port that Cisco ISE listens on for NetFlow is 9996.

NetFlow is a Cisco-proprietary messaging protocol that comes in several versions. The only version that is useful to ISE is NetFlow v9, because it also carries the host MAC address. Don't bother sending ISE the other versions; it's just not worth it. Cisco IOS NetFlow version 5 packets do not contain MAC addresses of endpoints. The attributes that are collected from NetFlow version 5 cannot be directly added to the Cisco ISE database. The following is a partial list of Cisco devices that support NetFlow:

- Cisco 7.4+ WLC
- Cisco ISR G1
- Cisco ISR G2
- Cisco 7200/7300
- Cisco ASR1000
- Cisco ASR9000
- Cisco 3750X and 3560X
- Cisco 4500 and 4500X with Sup 7
- Cisco 6500 with SUP2T
- Cisco 6500 with Sup 32 and Sup 720
- Cisco 7600
- Cisco C3KX-SM-10G
- Cisco 10000
- Cisco XR12000/12000 series routers
- Cisco CRS-1
- Cisco Nexus 7000
- Cisco Nexus 1000V

In addition to the NetFlow probe's ability to match a device to a device type based on its traffic flow characteristics, it can also identify a device that sends anomalous traffic. Here is an example: A certain biomed device should only ever talk to two IP addresses and only on two TCP ports, 5454 and 4533. If NetFlow recognizes traffic other than that profiler, it can issue a change of authorization or start a NMAP scan of the device to see if the device type for that MAC address has changed. Perhaps someone is trying to spoof the MAC address of a known device with his or her own device. Or perhaps the device itself has been compromised with malware and is being used as part of a botnet. Whatever the case might be for the anomalous traffic, NetFlow can detect it, and ISE profiler can take additional action because of it.

Commonly Used NetFlow Attributes

Cisco NetFlow offers a multitude of field types, called attributes by ISE. However, only a handful are commonly used for developing ISE device profiles. Here is a list and description of the most favored ISE NetFlow attributes:

- **IPv4_SRC_ADDR:** Source IP address of the flow

- **IPv4_DST_ADDR:** Destination IP address of the flow

- **L4_SRC_PORT:** TCP/UDP source port

- **L4_DST_PORT:** TCP/UDP destination port

- **DIRECTION - Flow direction:** 0 - ingress flow, 1 - egress flow

Example Profiler Policy Using NetFlow

Typically, NetFlow attributes are used in conjunction with other ISE probe data, such as OUI and DHCP rules. Figure 24-7 depicts a sample profiler policy that is just pure NetFlow rules.

The policy shown in Figure 24-7 has one rule. But, that rule is made up of three conditions that all must be true, as well as the operator between them:

1. IPv4 source address contains 192.168.45. This effectively would mean the src addr needs to be in the 192.168.45.0/24 subnet.

2. IPv4 destination address must be 192.168.45.10. The source must be talking to this destination.

3. Layer 4 destination UDP/TCP port must equal 443.

Also, notice that the policy does not use defined conditions, but creates new conditions within the policy itself. To accomplish this, click the Create New Condition button, as shown in Figure 24-8.

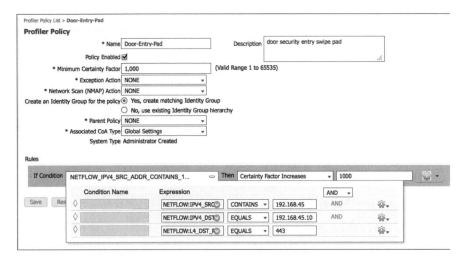

Figure 24-7   *NetFlow-Based Profiler Policy*

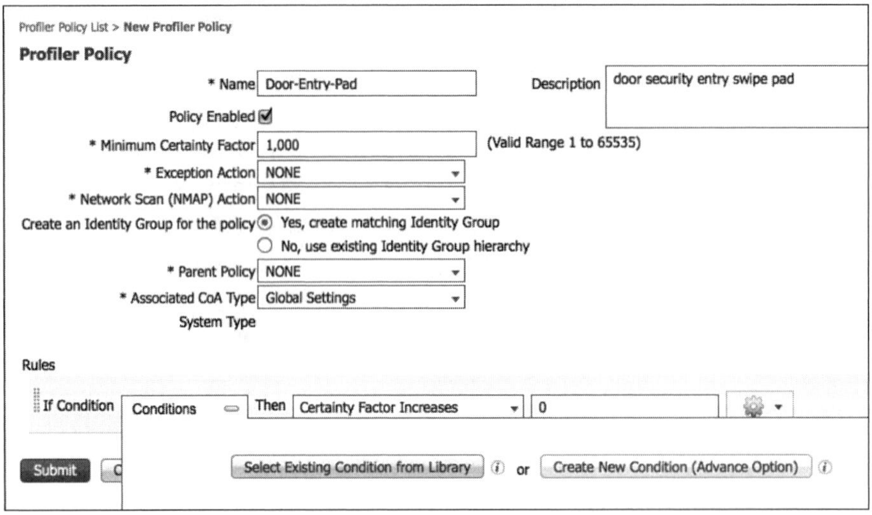

Figure 24-8   *NetFlow-Based Profiler Policy Continued*

Designing for Efficient Collection of NetFlow Data

As stated earlier, the collection of NetFlow data, if not done properly, can saturate the
ISE, causing a sort of denial of service condition. By using some best practices, you can
alleviate much of that risk. The following best practices should be considered in your
deployment:

- Only export an IP flow once and from a single direction (ingress or egress) to the ISE profiler.

- Use a dedicated ISE network interface for NetFlow collection. It will have its own IP address.

- Only export flows to ISE from parts of the network that are needed in ISE device profile policies.

- Position your policy services nodes as close to the NetFlow collectors as is practical. Avoid collection over a long-distance or low-speed WAN link.

- Use flexible NetFlow to reduce the amount of data that is exported to the ISE Policy Services Node profiler.

- Implement a third-party NetFlow collector and forwarder that allows you to filter the exported NetFlow data to the bare minimum required for your ISE NetFlow policies.

- Regularly monitor the health of your policy services nodes to ensure that NetFlow is not causing a problem.

Configuration of NetFlow on Cisco Devices

There are many ways to configure NetFlow on the various Cisco devices. This section focuses on the best practices and tips for configuring NetFlow to work properly with ISE. There are four steps to configuring flexible NetFlow v9 on a Cisco device:

1. Create customized flow records. These records define what attributes you want to store for the flow. Keep these to the minimum needed for your profiler policies.

2. Configure a flow exporter. The exporter destination is the closest ISE Policy Services Node running profiler. Remember to export to a dedicated IP/interface on the ISE Policy Services Node. This interface is created using the ISE CLI.

3. Configure a flow monitor. A flow monitor defines the records, exporters, and cache to use. The flow monitor is assigned to interfaces for flow collection.

4. Apply a flow monitor to an interface(s). This starts the flexible NetFlow process. You're done!

Examples 24-1 through 24-4 depict some of the best practice configurations for each step.

Example 24-1 *Flexible NetFlow Record Configuration*

```
flow record ise-flows
 description export only flows needed by ise
 match datalink mac source-address
 match ipv4 protocol
 match ipv4 source address
```

```
 match ipv4 destination address
 match transport source-port
 match transport destination-port
 collect transport tcp flags
C3750X#show flow record
flow record ise-flows:
  Description:        export only flows needed by ise
  No. of users:       0
  Total field space:  20 bytes
  Fields:
    match datalink mac source-address
    match ipv4 protocol
    match ipv4 source address
    match ipv4 destination address
    match transport source-port
    match transport destination-port
    collect transport tcp flags
```

Example 24-2   *Flexible NetFlow Exporter Configuration*

```
flow exporter ISE
 description Export to ISE PSN1
 destination 10.1.103.4
 source TenGigabitEthernet1/1/1
 transport udp 9996
C3750X#show flow exporter
Flow Exporter ISE:
  Description:          Export to ISE PSN1
  Export protocol:      NetFlow Version 9
  Transport Configuration:
    Destination IP address: 10.1.103.4
    Source IP address:    10.1.48.2
    Source Interface:     TenGigabitEthernet1/1/1
    Transport Protocol:   UDP
    Destination Port:     9996
    Source Port:          49736
    DSCP:                 0x0
    TTL:                  255
    Output Features:      Not Used
```

Example 24-3   *Flexible NetFlow Monitor Configuration*

```
flow monitor ISE-Flows
 description Used for ISE Profiler
```

```
 record ise-flows
 exporter ISE
 cache timeout active 60


C3750X#show flow monitor
Flow Monitor ISE-Flows:
  Description:          Used for ISE Profiler
  Flow Record:         ise-flows
  Flow Exporter:       ISE
  Cache:
    Type:              normal
    Status:            not allocated
    Size:              128 entries / 0 bytes
  Cache:
    Type:              normal (Platform cache)
    Status:            not allocated
    Size:              Unknown
  Timers:
                       Local        Global
    Inactive Timeout:  15 secs
    Active Timeout:    60 secs      1800 secs
    Update Timeout:    1800 secs
```

Example 24-4   *Flexible NetFlow Interface Configuration*

```
interface TenGigabitEthernet1/1/1
 description Cat6K Ten1/5
 no switchport
 ip flow monitor ISE-Flows input
 ip flow monitor ISE-Flows output
 ip address 10.1.48.2 255.255.255.252
 ip authentication mode eigrp 1 md5
 ip authentication key-chain eigrp 1 EIGRP
 load-interval 60
C3750X#show flow interface te1/1/1
Interface TenGigabitEthernet1/1/1
  FNF:  monitor:          ISE-Flows
        direction:        Input
        traffic(ip):      on
  FNF:  monitor:          ISE-Flows
        direction:        Output
        traffic(ip):      on
```

Profiler COA and Exceptions

If you want ISE profiler to take a more proactive action based on a device profile rule match or network activity, use Profiler Change of Authorization (CoA) and exception rules. By default, profiler is passive and doesn't perform CoA actions. You may want to change this default behavior globally and/or based on certain profiler conditions and exceptions. A profiler policy-based CoA action overrides the global CoA settings for profiler.

Here are some of the conditions when ISE profiler issues a CoA request to a NAD:

- Endpoint is deleted from the Endpoints page.

- A profile policy exception is triggered.

- An endpoint is profiled for the first time.

- The profiling service issues a CoA when there is any change in an endpoint identity group, and the endpoint identity group is used in the authorization policy for the following:

  - The endpoint identity group changes for endpoints when they are dynamically profiled.

  - The endpoint identity group changes when the static assignment flag is set to true for a dynamic endpoint.

- An endpoint profiling policy has changed, and the policy is used in an authorization policy

- If you have profiler policies that trigger a re-authentication based on anomalous device behavior.

- CoA sent when a device changes to a new profile that results in a change to the endpoints access rights. These access rights are defined in the Authorization Policies that use Device Identity Groups.

It is also important to know what conditions do not produce a CoA event. Here are many of them:

- An endpoint disconnects from the network.

- When a wired endpoint that is EAP capable connects to the network. For example, an 802.1X supplicant-enabled client.

- When there are multiple hosts connected to a single port, a CoA with reauth is always issued if you configure port bounce.

- For wireless clients, a packet-of-disconnect is sent to the WLC instead of a port bounce.

- CoA is disabled for any device going through the Guest Device Registration portal/flow.

■ If the global profiler CoA setting in ISE is set to No CoA, all profiler policy CoA actions are ignored. In effect, a global No CoA setting disables the ability of ISE profiler to issue any CoA.

Types of CoA

CoA is used by ISE to force an update on switches. This ensures that any new policies take effect on the switch and the client connected to the switchport.

There are three types of CoA settings:

■ No CoA (default)

■ Port Bounce

■ Re-Authentication

To use CoA inside profiler, you must enable it globally. Go to **Administration** > **System** > **Settings** > **Profiling**. In most cases, you will select the Re-Authentication option, as shown in Figure 24-9.

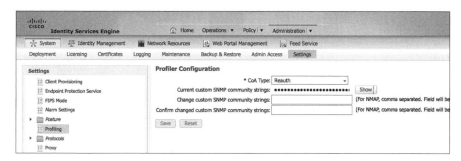

Figure 24-9   *Global Profiler CoA Setting*

Creating Exceptions Actions

Exception actions allow ISE to trigger in a profiling policy, such as an nmap scan or CoA. The default action triggers CoA.

A custom exception action does two things:

■ Forces a CoA or prevents a CoA from happening

■ Statically assigns the device to a profiler policy

To create an exception action, go to **Policy** > **Policy Elements** > **Results** > **Profiling** > **Exception Actions**. The CoA option either forces a CoA if checked or prevents a CoA if unchecked. See Figure 24-10 for an example.

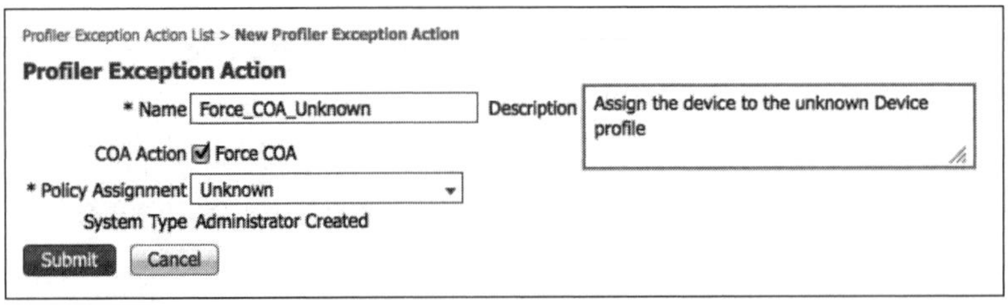

Profiler Exception Action List > **New Profiler Exception Action**

Profiler Exception Action

* Name Force_COA_Unknown   Description Assign the device to the unknown Device profile

COA Action ☑ Force COA

* Policy Assignment Unknown

System Type Administrator Created

Submit   Cancel

Figure 24-10 *Exception Action*

The action shown in Figure 24-10 forces a CoA and assigns the unknown profile to the device.

Configuring CoA and Exceptions in Profiler Policies

Now that you created a few exception actions, you can use them in your profiler policies. It is also in the profile policy that you can change the CoA action from the global default. Changing the CoA action, known as the Associated CoA Type, is trivial. As shown in Figure 24-11, use the drop down and select the type you want to use for this profiler profile.

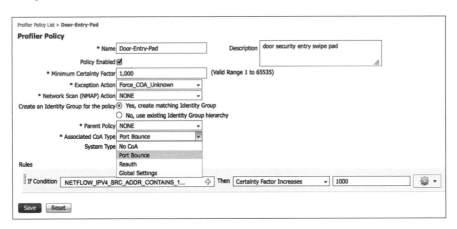

Profiler Policy List > **Door-Entry-Pad**

Profiler Policy

* Name Door-Entry-Pad   Description door security entry swipe pad

Policy Enabled ☑

* Minimum Certainty Factor 1,000   (Valid Range 1 to 65535)

* Exception Action Force_COA_Unknown

* Network Scan (NMAP) Action NONE

Create an Identity Group for the policy ⦿ Yes, create matching Identity Group
                                        ○ No, use existing Identity Group hierarchy

* Parent Policy NONE

* Associated CoA Type Port Bounce

System Type No CoA
             Port Bounce
Rules   Reauth
             Global Settings

If Condition NETFLOW_IPV4_SRC_ADDR_CONTAINS_1... ⊹ Then Certainty Factor Increases   1000   ⚙ ▾

Save   Reset

Figure 24-11 *Per Profiler Policy CoA Action*

To configure an exception rule, you need to define what the condition is that triggers an exception action. In Figure 24-12, the exception condition defined is this: If device communicates with any IP destination address except for 192.168.45.10, issue the exception action.

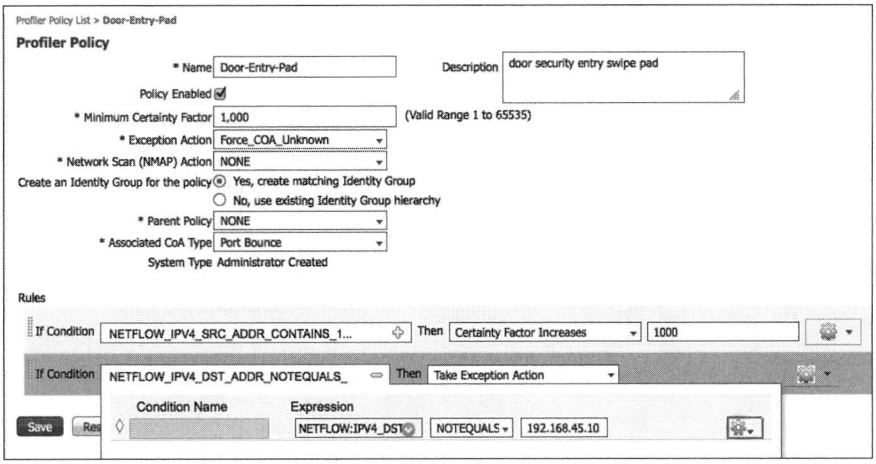

Figure 24-12   *Exception Profiler Policy Rule*

Profiler Monitoring and Reporting

ISE includes several reports that specifically deal with the profiler function. These reports can be used to

■ Audit what devices are on your network

■ Provide you with a device inventory

■ Help you troubleshoot profiler issues and so on

This section covers the most useful reports and monitoring tools available in ISE.

The first place you can quickly see profiler results in the ISE Home Dashboard screen. Figure 24-13 shows the multiple profiler portlets.

This dashboard provides you with a live snapshot of the profiled endpoints on the network and profiler activity over the last 24 hours.

A useful troubleshooting tool for device profiling is the Live Authentications screen, as shown in Figure 24-14.

Figure 24-13 *Home Dashboard*

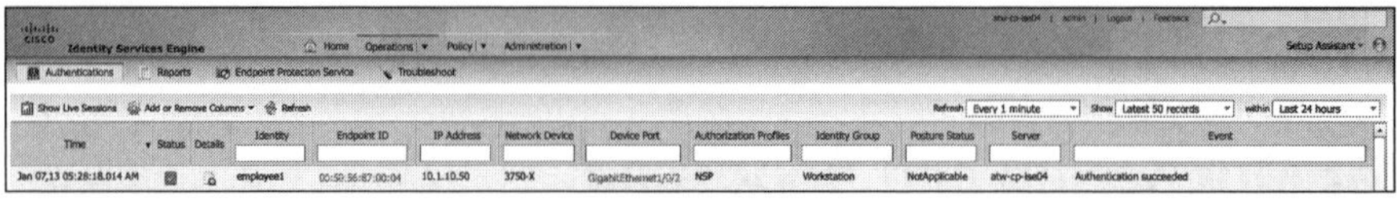

Figure 24-14 *Live Authentications Screen*

The identity group column shows the profile group that the device matched. This value doesn't necessarily pair the exact profile policy that was a match. It shows the closest identity group that is part of the profile policy hierarchy. To see the actual match profile for the device, click the Details icon in the row of the device. This opens the Details screen. As shown in Figure 24-15, if you scroll down, you see the EndPointMatchedProfile attribute with a value. This value shows the exact profile policy matched.

SelectedAuthenticationIdentityStores	AD1
SelectedAuthenticationIdentityStores	Internal Endpoints
ServiceSelectionMatchedRule	Dot1X
IdentityPolicyMatchedRule	Default
ADDomain	ise.local
IssuedPacInfo	Issued PAC type=User Authorization with expiration time: Mon Jan 7 06:28:17 2013
CPMSessionID	0A013002000015E7BD39CAE2
EndPointMACAddress	00-50-56-87-00-04
EndPointMatchedProfile	Microsoft-Workstation
EapChainingResult	No chaining
ISEPolicySetName	Default
HostIdentityGroup	Endpoint Identity Groups:Profiled:Workstation
Device Type	Device Type#All Device Types#Switches#Access-Layer
Location	Location#All Locations#NorthAmerica#SJC

Figure 24-15 *Live Auth Details*

Under **Operations > Reports > Endpoints and Users,** you see several profiler reports. Figure 24-16 shows them.

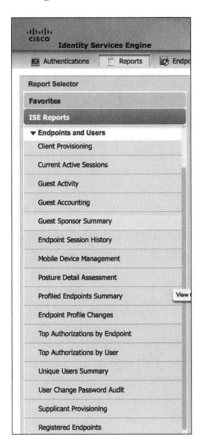

Figure 24-16   *Profiler Reports*

Two of the most helpful reports include

■ **Endpoint Profile Changes Report:** This report shows endpoints that have changed from one profile match to a different profile match.

■ **Profiled Endpoints Summary Report:** Clicking Details next to a device provides you with all sorts of useful information for reporting and troubleshooting profiler. This screen also shows you the profile history of a particular device over time, as shown in Figure 24-17.

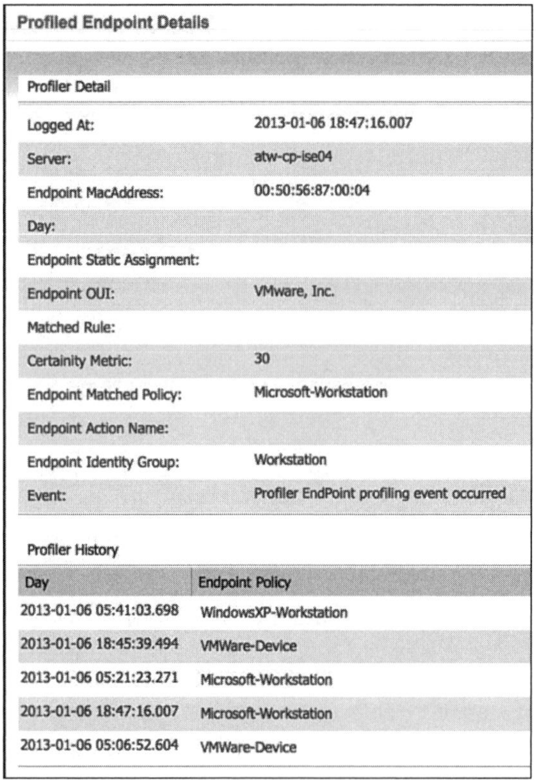

Profiled Endpoint Details

Profiler Detail	
Logged At:	2013-01-06 18:47:16.007
Server:	atw-cp-ise04
Endpoint MacAddress:	00:50:56:87:00:04
Day:	
Endpoint Static Assignment:	
Endpoint OUI:	VMware, Inc.
Matched Rule:	
Certainty Metric:	30
Endpoint Matched Policy:	Microsoft-Workstation
Endpoint Action Name:	
Endpoint Identity Group:	Workstation
Event:	Profiler EndPoint profiling event occurred

Profiler History

Day	Endpoint Policy
2013-01-06 05:41:03.698	WindowsXP-Workstation
2013-01-06 18:45:39.494	VMWare-Device
2013-01-06 05:21:23.271	Microsoft-Workstation
2013-01-06 18:47:16.007	Microsoft-Workstation
2013-01-06 05:06:52.604	VMWare-Device

Figure 24-17 *Profiler Reports*

Summary

This chapter covered several advanced profiler concepts, configuration, and best practices. These include creating custom profiles, advanced NetFlow, Change of Authorization (COA), profiler exceptions, profiler monitoring, and reports. It discussed that, when implemented correctly, NetFlow can be used as an effective profiler probe—just be careful with the amount of NetFlow you send to ISE. This chapter also showed you how to create your own custom and complex profile conditions and policies. Using these ensures that you are able to correctly identify all the devices on your network.

Chapter 25

Security Group Access

Throughout this book, you have been exposed to many different ways of controlling network access based on the context of a user and device. There is VLAN assignment, in which access is controlled at the Layer 3 edge, or by isolating that VLAN into a segmented virtual network (VRF). Additionally, there is ACL assignment, which can be a local ACL, called into action by a RADIUS attribute, or a downloaded ACL (dACL). These ACLs are applied ingress at the switchport or virtual port in the case of the Wireless LAN Controller (WLC).

These are all good access-control methods, but regulating passage only at the point of network ingress can leave room for a more desirable and scalable solution. This chapter discusses one such Cisco enhancement to make access control more scalable and powerful: Security Group Access (SGA).

This chapter focuses on the fundamentals of SGA as well as the configuration of the many different devices available for use in an SGA environment. Basic use cases are presented for Security Group ACL and security group firewalls.

Ingress Access Control Challenges

VLAN assignment and downloadable ACLs (dACL) are fantastic ways of controlling access to a network. However, when a network grows, so do the challenges of keeping up with the ingress access controls. Let's look at each one of these standard use cases individually and discuss the challenges.

VLAN Assignment

VLAN assignment based on the context of a user or device is a common way to control access to the network. Let's use a hypothetical scenario of controlling access to servers that contain credit-card data, which falls under Payment Card Industry (PCI) compliance.

1. A user is a member of the Retail-Managers group in Active Directory.

2. The posture of the system is compliant.

3. Therefore, ISE assigns the user into the PCI Allowed VLAN on the switch or WLC.

   Now, to use that VLAN assignment to control access to the servers that house that PCI data, an ACL must be applied somewhere. Let's assume the ACL is applied at a firewall between the campus/branch networks and the data center.

4. The ACL on the data center firewall must be updated to include the entire source IP address range of PCI Allowed VLANs throughout the entire network infrastructure, as shown in Figure 25-1.

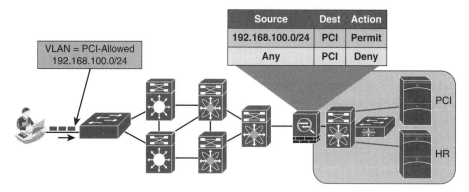

Figure 25-1   *Controlling Access with VLANs on Single Switch*

Next, the company decided to control access to the HR server, so that only members of the HR department may talk to HR servers. Another set of rules must be built that assign the HR VLAN, and another set of entries in the access list, as shown in Figure 25-2.

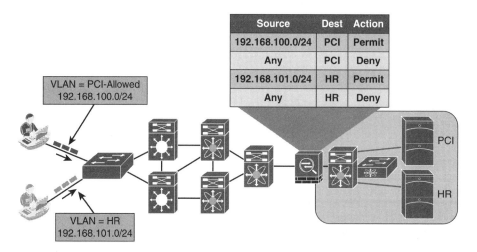

Figure 25-2   *Controlling Access with 2 VLANs on Single Switch*

Now, consider how this can scale as you continue to add VLANs and switches and WLCs to the equation. One of your large customers has over 50,000 switches in their access-layer. That is a tremendous number of VLANs to create, and addresses to maintain in an access list on a firewall. That same customer had 15 full-time employees managing the firewall rules. It needed to find some better mechanism to control access that would lower its OPEX tremendously.

What if you had 100 remote sites? That is 100 new IP subnets and that can easily modify your existing route summarization strategy. When that is the case, the route summarization alone can cause a network redesign, which will add even more operational cost, as shown in Figure 25-3.

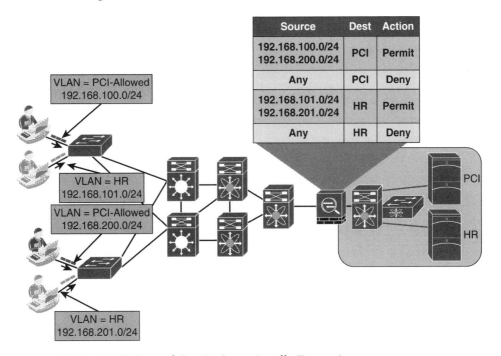

Source	Dest	Action
192.168.100.0/24 192.168.200.0/24	PCI	Permit
Any	PCI	Deny
192.168.101.0/24 192.168.201.0/24	HR	Permit
Any	HR	Deny

Figure 25-3 *VLAN Control Can Be Operationally Expensive*

There is a formula to determine the number of access control entries (ACE) in an access control list (ACL). The formula takes the number of sources multiplied by the number of destinations multiplied by the permissions of the ACL:

(# of sources) * (# of destinations) * permissions = # of ACE's

With the environment depicted in Figure 25-3, only 4 sources * 2 destinations * 4 permissions you would need 32 ACEs. This is obviously just a small example. This is examined more in the following sections.

Ingress Access Control Lists

Another way to control access is to use access lists applied ingress (inbound) at the port (or virtual port) that the user or device is using to access the network. This could be locally defined ACLs that are called by using the filter-ID RADIUS attribute, or they could be dACLs, where the entire ACL is defined on ISE and downloaded to the port.

Obviously, dACLs provide a better operational model, because there is only one place to update an ACL when a change needs to be made. Additionally, the number of ACEs required is lower when applying the ACL to a switchport than it would be to apply the ACL to a centralized location. Because the ACL is being applied at the point of ingress, there would only be a single source IP address (theoretically). Cisco switches perform source-substitution on these ACLs to make it even easier. With source substitution, the any keyword in the source field of an ACL is replaced with the actual IP address of the host on the switchport.

Using the same formula for six destinations and four permissions, you would have

1 source * 6 destinations * 4 permissions = 24 ACEs

However, there are a few complications with using ACLs on access layer devices. Two major drawbacks that exist are the regular maintenance of the access lists and the size of the access lists.

If ACLs are being used to explicitly defend hosts, they must be updated regularly for all new destinations that get added to the network. This can cause an exorbitant amount of operational expense maintaining the lists and ensuring they get updated correctly. Additionally, there is a limited number of ACEs that a switch will be able to apply.

ACLs get loaded into and executed from Ternary CAM (TCAM). Access layer switches have a limited amount of TCAM, which is usually assigned per ASIC. Therefore, the number of ACEs that can be loaded depends on various factors, such as the number of hosts per ASIC and the amount of free TCAM space.

Because of that limited amount of TCAM, ACLs cannot be overly large, especially when the access layer may be a mixture of different switches; each switch having a different level of TCAM per ASIC. The best practice recommendation is to keep the ACEs less than 64 per dACL. This may need to be adjusted for your specific environment, but it is a good place to start.

Figure 25-4 shows ingress ACLs in the network.

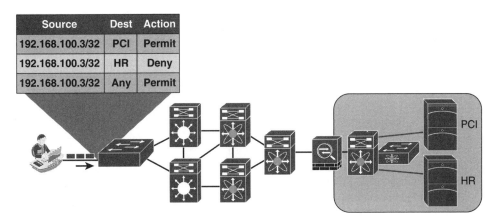

Source	Dest	Action
192.168.100.3/32	PCI	Permit
192.168.100.3/32	HR	Deny
192.168.100.3/32	Any	Permit

Figure 25-4 *Ingress ACLs*

What Is Security Group Access?

Security Group Access (SGA) is a next-generation of access control enforcement that was created to address the growing operational expenses with maintaining firewall rules and access lists. SGA is a complimentary enforcement technology that removes the concerns of TCAM space and ACE explosion.

The ultimate goal of SGA is to assign a TAG (known as a Security Group Tag, or SGT) to the user/device's traffic at ingress (inbound into the network), and then enforce the access elsewhere in the infrastructure (in the data center, for example). So, SGA assigns a TAG at login and enforces that TAG elsewhere in the network (egress enforcement).

The SGT should be representative of some overarching roles within the company. For instance, an SGT may be assigned to a GUEST user, so that GUEST traffic may be isolated from non-GUEST traffic throughout the infrastructure. Here is a list of some common security groups:

- **Network Infrastructure:** This SGT gets assigned to all the switches, routers, WLCs, and firewalls within the organization.

- **Network Services:** This SGT is assigned to the servers providing common services that most everyone should be able to reach (DNS, DHCP, NTP, and so on).

- **Executive:** Many organizations may classify their executives into their own SGT, simply to ensure that executives will never be denied access to anything.

- **Sales:** This SGT would signify a member of the sales organization.

- **Finance:** This SGT would signify a member of the finance organization.

- **HR:** Used to signify a member of the Human Resources department.

- **Line-of-Business-1:** SGTs are used often when an umbrella company has many different lines of business, and those lines of business cannot have access to each others data.

- **Line-of-Business-2:** *See previous.*

The trick with SGTs is to use them for bulk access control, and do your fine-grain access control within the application security itself. Additionally, each end user or end device may only be assigned a single SGT. You do not want to create too many roles, or you will spend too much operational time mapping users to the correct tags.

So, What Is a Security Group Tag?

A Security Group Tag (SGT) is a 16-bit value that ISE assigns to the user or endpoint's session upon login. The network infrastructure views the SGT as another attribute to assign to the session, and inserts the Layer 2 tag to all traffic from that session. The SGT can represent the context of the user and device. Let's look at the following example.

This is one of my favorite examples from a client that I worked with directly. It is a retail organization, and therefore, it accepts credit cards from customers, which places it under the domain of Payment Card Industry (PCI) compliance. Access to any server housing credit-card data must be protected as strictly as any technology will allow.

In this client's case, we defined a rule in ISE that looked for machine and user authentication (EAP chaining) *and* verified the user was a member of a PCI group in Active Directory *and* the machine's posture was compliant. If the user and machine met all these conditions, an SGT named PCI was assigned. No access was granted to PCI servers without the PCI SGT.

So, as you can see, SGTs can be applied based on the full context of the authentication or simply based on a single condition, such as Guest.

Note The endpoint itself is not aware of the tag. It is known in the network infrastructure. Figure 25-5 illustrates the SGT being assigned to an authentication session.

```
C3750X#sho authentication sess int g1/0/2
            Interface: GigabitEthernet1/0/2
          MAC Address: 0050.5687.0004
           IP Address: 10.1.10.50
            User-Name: employee1
               Status: Authz Success
               Domain: DATA
      Security Policy: Should Secure
      Security Status: Unsecure
       Oper host mode: multi-auth
     Oper control dir: both
        Authorized By: Authentication Server
           Vlan Group: N/A
              ACS ACL: xACSACLx-IP-Employee-ACL-
                  SGT: 0002-0
      Session timeout: N/A
         Idle timeout: N/A
    Common Session ID: 0A01300200000022DC6C328F
      Acct Session ID: 0x00000033
               Handle: 0xCC000022

Runnable methods list:
        Method State
        dot1x  Authc Success
```

Figure 25-5 *SGT Applied to Session*

See the section, "Making the SGT Ubiquitous," for more information on SGT transport.

Defining the SGTs

ISE serves as the single-source-of-truth for what SGTs exist and considers an SGT a policy result. Therefore, create one SGT result for each SGT you want to define in the environment.

Create the SGTs in ISE. From within the ISE GUI, perform the following steps:

1. Navigate to **Policy > Policy Elements > Results**.

2. Select **Security Group Access > Security Groups**.

   Notice in Figure 25-6 how there is a default SGT of 0, unknown. This tag will be used if traffic arrives that is untagged. In other words, even the lack of an SGT can be used in the security policy.

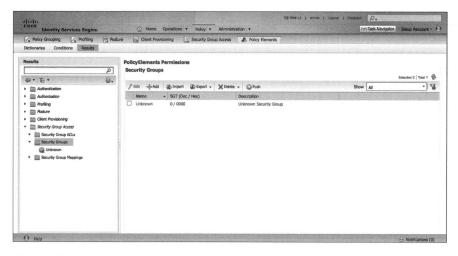

Figure 25-6   *Security Groups*

3. Click **Add**.

4. Provide the new SGT a name of "NADs."

Let's begin by creating a security group for network access devices. A dedicated security group is required for network devices that use native tagging, but notice in Figure 25-7 that the SGT value is predetermined. ISE automatically assigns the value in order from 1 to 65,535.

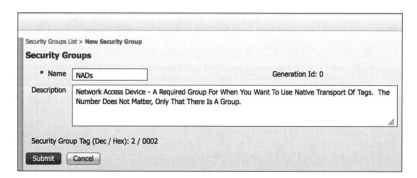

Figure 25-7   *Adding a Security Group for NADs*

5. Click **Submit** to save.

It is considered a best-practice to also have a security group for all the common network services that will exist on a network. These services should always be accessible by any device, services like DNS and DHCP.

6. Click **Add**.

7. Name the new group CommonServices.

8. Click **Submit** to save.

9. Repeat Steps 6–8 until you have the appropriate groups created.

Figure 25-8 shows an example set of security groups.

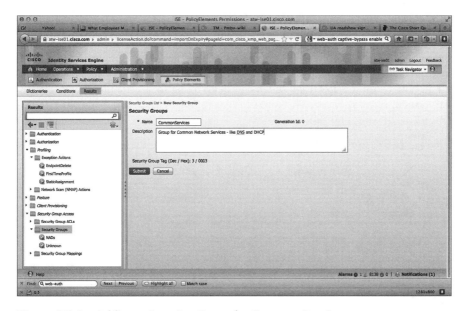

Figure 25-8   *Adding a Security Group for Common Services*

Figure 25-9 shows a sample list of security groups.

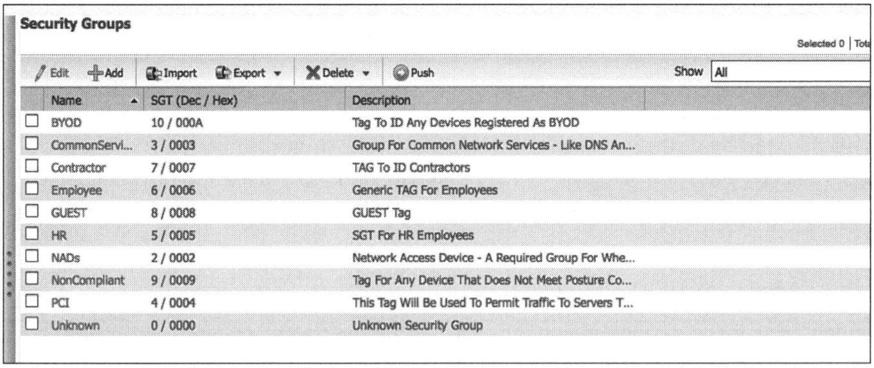

Name	SGT (Dec / Hex)	Description
BYOD	10 / 000A	Tag To ID Any Devices Registered As BYOD
CommonServi...	3 / 0003	Group For Common Network Services - Like DNS An...
Contractor	7 / 0007	TAG To ID Contractors
Employee	6 / 0006	Generic TAG For Employees
GUEST	8 / 0008	GUEST Tag
HR	5 / 0005	SGT For HR Employees
NADs	2 / 0002	Network Access Device - A Required Group For Whe...
NonCompliant	9 / 0009	Tag For Any Device That Does Not Meet Posture Co...
PCI	4 / 0004	This Tag Will Be Used To Permit Traffic To Servers T...
Unknown	0 / 0000	Unknown Security Group

Figure 25-9   *Example Security Groups*

Classification

This should not come as a surprise to you, but to use SGTs within your infrastructure, your devices must support SGTs. All Secure Unified Access supported Cisco switches and wireless controllers do support the assignment of the SGT. This is defined as classification. The process of communicating that assigned SGT upstream into the network can either occur via native tagging or via a peering-protocol, and this process is defined as transport.

Figure 25-10 shows an example of one access switch that has native tagging, and the packets get tagged on the uplink port and through the infrastructure. It also shows a non-native-tagging capable switch, which uses a peering protocol to update the upstream switch. In both cases, the upstream switch continues to tag the traffic throughout the infrastructure.

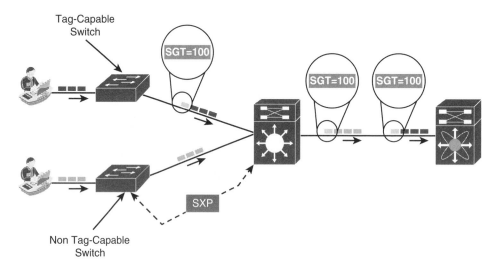

Figure 25-10 *Security Group Tagging*

In order to use the Security Group Tag, the tag needs to be assigned. This may happen dynamically, and be downloaded as the result of an ISE Authorization; they may be assigned manually at the port level; or even mapped to IP addresses and downloaded to SGT capable devices.

Dynamically Assigning SGT via 802.1X

Assigning a tag is as simple as adding it as another permission or result of an authorization in an Authorization Policy. When viewing the Authorization Policy, perform the following steps:

1. Edit your existing authorization rule.

2. Click the + sign under permissions.

3. Click the + sign next to the authorization profile.

4. Choose Security Group.

5. Select the Appropriate Security Group to apply, as shown in Figures 25-11 and 25-12.

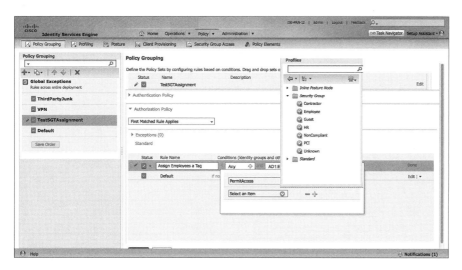

Figure 25-11 *Adding the Security Group to the Results*

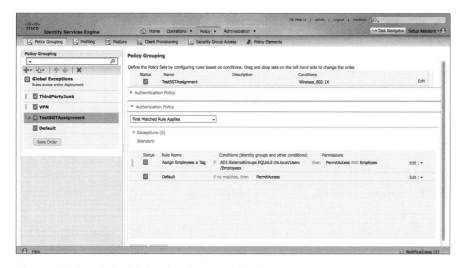

Figure 25-12 *Final Rule Showing SGT Assignment*

Manually Assigning SGT at the Port

In most cases, 802.1X is not used in the data center. Servers are not usually required to authenticate themselves to the data center switch, as the DC is normally considered physically secure, and there is no network access control applied there. However, the servers themselves will be the destination of traffic coming from the campus and from within the data center itself.

Because 802.1X is not typically used in the data center, you need a manual way to apply the SGT. This is configured at the interface level of the Nexus configuration and is manually applied to the port itself:

```
NX7K-DIST(config)# int eth1/3
NX7K-DIST(config-if)# cts manual
NX7K-DIST(config-if-cts-manual)# policy static sgt 0x3
```

This has manually assigned the SGT 3 to the port on the Nexus 7000. This is also available on the Nexus 5000 and 1000v.

Manually Binding IP Addresses to SGTs

As an alternative to assigning the SGT to the port itself, ISE added the ability to centrally configure a database of IP addresses and their corresponding SGTs. Then, SGT-capable devices may download that list from ISE, as shown in Figures 25-13 and 25-14.

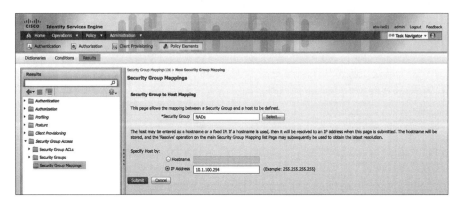

Figure 25-13   *Mapping an SGT to an IP Address in ISE*

Now that the mappings exist on ISE, you can download them to the other devices, such as a Nexus7000 DataCenter switch.

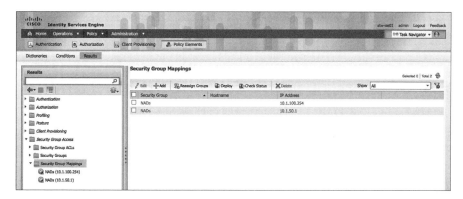

Figure 25-14 *Final Rule Showing SGT Assignment*

Access Layer Devices That Do Not Support SGTs

Because it isn't a perfect world, and not all the equipment on the network will be the latest and greatest, you need another way to classify the endpoint traffic. For example, an older Cisco Wireless LAN Controller (like the 4400) that does not support version 7.2 or newer therefore cannot accept the SGT classification from ISE nor send the update via SXP.

Additionally, this could be a VPN Ccncentrator, or some third-party equipment that found its way into the deployment. Although that gear may not support the classification and transport natively, it may be capable of assigning different VLANs or IP addresses per authorization result.

With the Catalyst 6500, you have the ability to map subnets and VLANs and assign all source IP addresses from the subnet or VLAN to a specific tag.

Mapping a Subnet to an SGT

Use the **cts role-based sgt-map** [*ipv4-subnet* | *ipv6-subnet*] **sgt** *tag-value* command to enable this binding. When used, the device-tracking feature in the Catalyst 6500 Supervisor 2T will be used to identify matches and assign the SGT. Example 25-1 shows an example of this mapping.

Example 25-1 *Enabling SGT to Subnet Mapping*

```
C6K-DIST(config)#cts role-based sgt-map 192.168.26.0/24 sgt 4
```

Mapping a VLAN to an SGT

Use the **cts role-based sgt-map vlan-list** *vlans* **sgt** *tag-value* commands to enable this binding. When used, the device-tracking feature in the Catalyst 6500 Supervisor 2T will be used to identify matches and assign the SGT. Example 25-2 shows an example of this mapping.

Example 25-2   *Enabling SGT to Subnet Mapping*

```
C6K-DIST(config)#cts role-based sgt-map vlan-list 40 sgt 4
```

Transport: Security Group eXchange Protocol (SXP)

In a perfect world, all of your access layer devices will support tagging the users traffic natively. Not all devices support native tagging. However, all supported Cisco switches support the assignment of the SGT to the authentication session (known as classification).

Cisco developed a peering protocol (like BGP) to allow devices to communicate their database of IP address to SGT mappings to one another. This peering protocol is called Security Group eXchange Protocol (SXP). Because this is a peering protocol, it is possible to be specific and deterministic as to which devices send updates and which ones receive updates.

An SXP peer may be a speaker or a listener. The definition of a speaker is a device that sends the IP address to SGT bindings. The definition of a 'listener' is a device that receives the IP address to SGT bindings.

SXP Design

Because SXP uses TCP as its transport, the peer may be Layer 2 adjacent or multiple hops away. A network device may peer directly to the enforcement device (the data center switch or security group firewall), as shown in Figure 25-15.

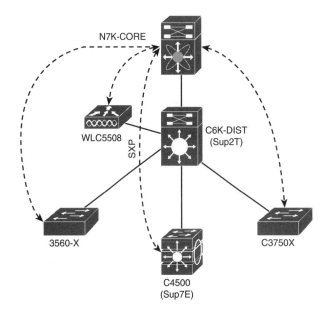

Figure 25-15   *SXP Peering*

Routing protocols have a limitation for the number of neighbors they can scale to, and so does SXP. Because of the limitations of scale for the number of peers, SXP design may be architected to be multi-hop, which allows for aggregation points, as shown in Figure 25-16. Devices like the Catalyst 6500 with a Supervisor 2T engine or the Aggregation Services Router (ASR) are solid choices for SXP aggregation.

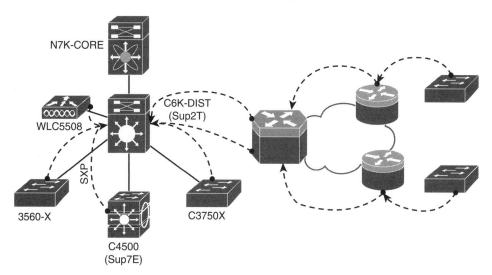

Figure 25-16 *SXP Multi-Hop*

There are numerous benefits to this design. Not only does it not require SXP-aware infrastructure along every hop in the network path, but it also provides a deterministic scalable design.

Configuring SXP on IOS Devices

The following steps walk you through the SXP configuration on IOS-based devices.

From global configuration, perform the following steps:

1. Enter **cts sxp enable**.

   This has turned SXP on globally. Each peer needs to be added individually, as well as setting a global default SXP password.

2. Enter **cts sxp connection peer** [*peer-ip-address*] password [default | none] mode [local | peer] [listener | speaker].

   This command is used to define the SXP peer. The options are as follows:

   ■ **password default:** States to use the password defined globally for all SXP connections. At the current time, it is not possible to have different SXP passwords per peer.

   ■ **password none:** Do not use a password with this SXP peer.

- **mode local:** States that the following SXP argument is defining the local side of the connection.

- **mode peer:** States that the following SXP argument is defining the peer's side of the connection.

- **listener:** Defines that the specified device (local or peer) will receive SXP updates through this connection.

- **speaker:** Defines that the specified device (local or peer) will send SXP updates through this connection.

3. (optional) **cts sxp default password** *password*

Step 3 is an optional step for when your connections will use the globally defined password, instead of no password.

Examples 25-3 and 25-4 display the steps for setting up the SXP connection between a 4500 (access layer device that does not support native tagging) and a 6500 with a Supervisor 2T (distribution layer device that supports native tagging), as shown in Figure 25-17.

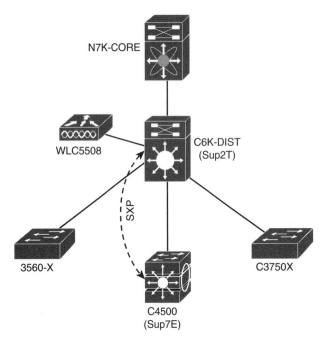

Figure 25-17 *SXP Between 4500 and 6500*

Example 25-3 *Enabling SXP on the 4500*

```
4503(config)#cts sxp enable
4503(config)#
*Aug  9 06:51:04.000: %CTS-5-SXP_STATE_CHANGE: CTS SXP enabled
4503(config)#cts sxp connection peer 10.1.40.1 password default mode peer listener
4503(config)#
*Aug 10 09:15:15.564: %CTS-6-SXP_TIMER_START: Connection <0.0.0.0, 0.0.0.0> retry
open timer started.
*Aug 10 09:15:15.565: %CTS-6-SXP_CONN_STATE_CHG: Connection <10.1.40.1, 10.1.40.2>-1
state changed from Off to Pending_On.
4503(config)#
*Aug 10 09:15:15.566: %CTS-3-SXP_CONN_STATE_CHG_OFF: Connection <10.1.40.1,
10.1.40.2>-1 state changed from Pending_On to Off.
4503(config)#cts sxp default password TrustSec123
4503(config)#
*Aug 10 09:17:20.936: %CTS-5-SXP_DFT_PASSWORD_CHANGE: CTS SXP password changed.
```

Example 25-4 *Enabling SXP on the 6500*

```
C6K-DIST(config)#cts sxp enable
C6K-DIST(config)#
Aug 10 16:16:25.719: %CTS-6-SXP_TIMER_START: Connection <0.0.0.0, 0.0.0.0> retry
open timer started.
C6K-DIST(config)#cts sxp default password TrustSec123
C6K-DIST(config)#cts sxp connection peer 10.1.40.2 password default mode peer speaker
C6K-DIST(config)#
Aug 10 16:17:26.687: %CTS-6-SXP_CONN_STATE_CHG: Connection <10.1.40.2, 10.1.40.1>-1
state changed from Off to Pending_On.
Aug 10 16:17:26.687: %CTS-6-SXP_CONN_STATE_CHG: Connection <10.1.40.2, 10.1.40.1>-1
state changed from Pending_On to On.
```

Configuring SXP on Wireless LAN Controllers

Cisco's Wireless LAN Controller (WLC) added support for SGT classification and SXP transport in the 7.2 release.

From the WLC user interface, perform the following steps:

1. Using the top-menu navigation, select **Security**.

2. Along the left-hand side, choose TrustSec SXP (second from the bottom), as shown in Figure 25-18.

Configure the settings on this page to be:

3. SXP State = Enabled.

4. Default Password = the same default password you configured on the switches. All passwords in the SXP domain need to be the same.

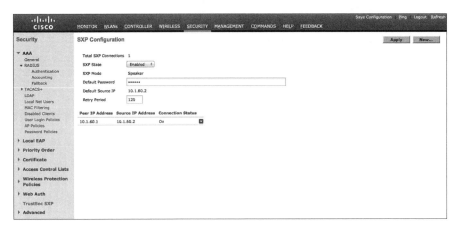

Figure 25-18   *WLC Global SXP Settings*

This has turned SXP on globally. Each peer must be added individually. To add a new SXP peer (a listener), follow these steps:

5. Click **New...** (button in the upper-right corner).

6. Enter the IP address of the listener peer.

7. Click **Apply** (upper-right corner), as shown in Figure 25-19.

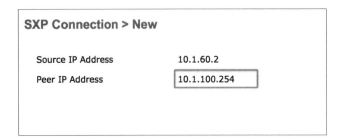

Figure 25-19   *New SXP Connection on WLC*

The added peers are displayed on the TrustSec SXP page. Their status is listed next to their IP address. Once the peer is configured on the other side, the status changes from "off" to "on," as shown in Figure 25-20.

It is also possible to verify the SXP connection from the other side, as shown in Example 25-5.

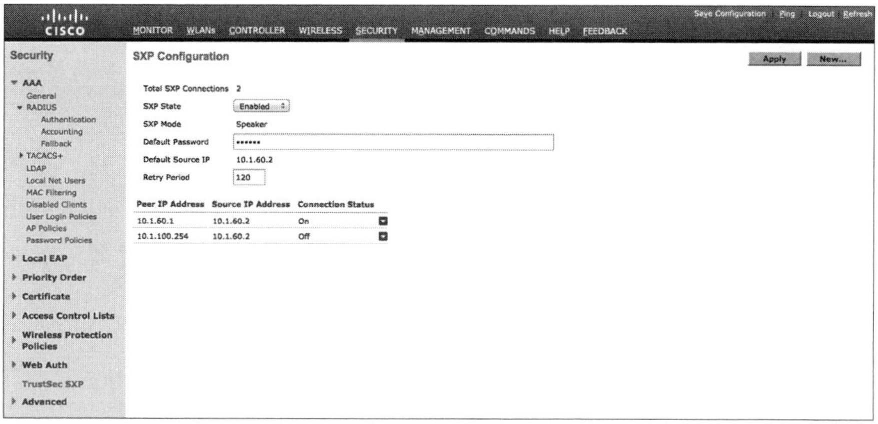

Figure 25-20   *TrustSec SXP Page: Peer Status*

Example 25-5   *Verifying the Connection Between the WLC and 6500*

```
C6K-DIST#sho cts sxp connections brief
 SXP            : Enabled
 Default Password : Set
 Default Source IP: Not Set
Connection retry open period: 120 secs
Reconcile period: 120 secs
Retry open timer is not running
-------------------------------------------------------------------------------
Peer_IP          Source_IP        Conn Status      Duration
-------------------------------------------------------------------------------
10.1.40.2        10.1.40.1        On               4:06:36:24 (dd:hr:mm:sec)
10.1.60.2        10.1.60.1        On               0:00:03:31 (dd:hr:mm:sec)
Total num of SXP Connections = 2
```

Configuring SXP on Cisco ASA

The Cisco Adaptive Security Appliance (ASA) added support for SGT enforcement (known commonly as SG-Firewall). Although the ASA does not currently support native tagging, it does support SXP for the transport of IP to TAG bindings.

It is important to note that the ASA has multiple functions. These functions include Deep Packet Inspection Firewalling and Remote Access VPN (among many others). At the time this book was written, it is only the firewalling functions of SGTs that are supported in ASA 9.0, not the remote-access VPN. So the ASA will **enforce** SGTs, it will receive SGTs (**transport**), but it will not assign SGTs (**classification**).

From the ASA Device Manager (ASDM), perform the following steps:

1. Navigate to **Configuration > Firewall > Identity by TrustSec**, as shown in Figure 25-21.

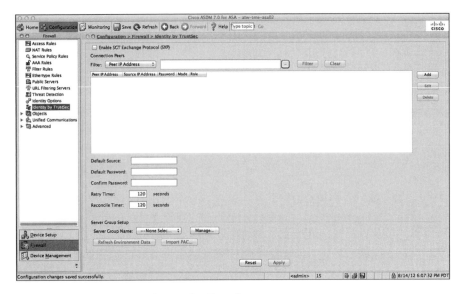

Figure 25-21   *ASDM: Identity by TrustSec*

2. Globally enable SXP by checking the Enable SGT Exchange Protocol (SXP) check box in the upper left.

3. Click **Add** to add a new SXP peer.

4. In the Add Connection Peer pop-up window, add the IP address of the remote peer.

5. Choose Default for the Password (unless you will not be using passwords).

6. Set the mode to Peer.

7. Set the role to Speaker.

8. Click **OK**.

   Figure 25-22 illustrates the global SXP settings on the ASA.

   After clicking OK, you are returned to the main Identity by TrustSec page. At this point, you have SXP enabled and a single peer defined, but no default password yet.

9. (Optional) If you will be specifying the source IP address of the ASA, you may configure that source in the Default Source field.

10. Enter the default password for your entire SXP deployment.

    Verifying SXP connections in ASDM is done through the Monitoring > Properties > Identity by TrustSec pages.

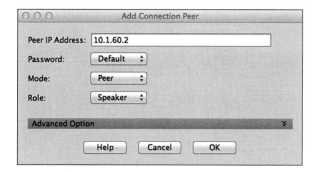

Figure 25-22 *Configuring SXP Connections in ASDM*

11. Click **SXP Connections** to see the configured peers and their status, as shown in Figure 25-23.

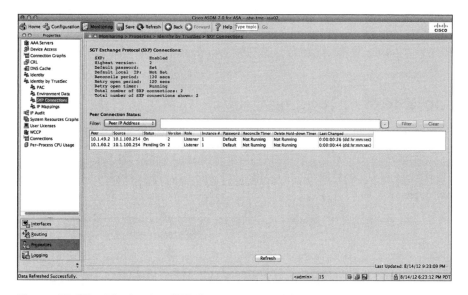

Figure 25-23 *Monitoring SXP Connections in ASDM*

12. Click IP Mappings to see any IP address to SGT mappings that the ASA has learned about, as shown in Figure 25-24.

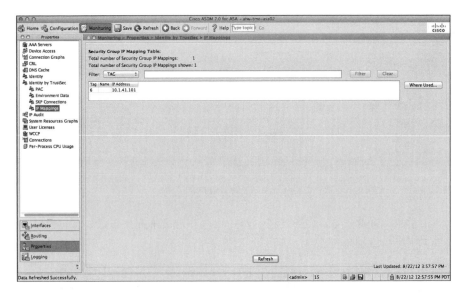

Figure 25-24 *Monitoring IP Address to SGT Mappings in ASDM*

Transport: Native Tagging

Native tagging is the ultimate goal. With this approach, the access layer is capable of applying the Security Group Tag (SGT) to the Layer 2 frame, as it is sent across the wire to the upstream host. The upstream host continues that and ensures the tag is applied. So, the tag is always present throughout the entire infrastructure, as shown in Figure 25-25.

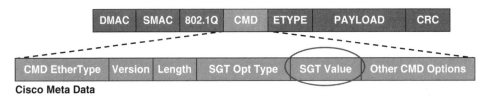

Figure 25-25 *Layer 2 Frame Format with SGT*

Native tagging allows the technology to scale virtually endlessly, and it remains completely independent of any Layer 3 protocol. In other words, architecturally speaking: If the traffic is IPv4 or IPv6, it does not matter. The tag is completely independent.

As shown in Figure 25-11, when native tags are supported pervasively within the infra-structure, the SGT is communicated hop-by-hop. This provides for end-to-end segmenta-tion and tremendous scale. With the tag being applied to the traffic at every Layer 2 link, we are able to enforce policy at any point in the infrastructure, and there are no limita-tions to the size of an IP-to-SGT mapping database, because the database is not being used at all.

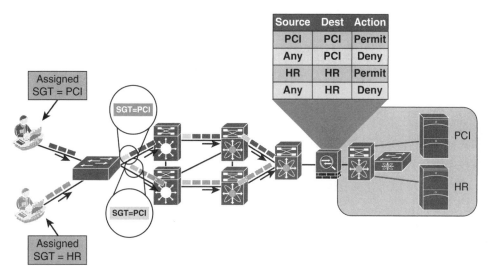

Source	Dest	Action
PCI	PCI	Permit
Any	PCI	Deny
HR	HR	Permit
Any	HR	Deny

Figure 25-26 *Pervasive Tagging*

For added security, the tag may be encrypted with MACSec or IPsec, and the network infrastructure may be authenticated prior to sending or receiving tags (NDAC). Those technologies are discussed in Chapter 26, "MACSec and NDAC."

Configuring Native SGT Propogation (Tagging)

The next few configuration exercises show the enabling of native security group tagging on three different types of switches: a 3000 series access layer switch, a 6500 series dis-tribution layer switch, and Nexus DataCenter switches. Figure 25-27 shows the logical network layout used in the configuration examples to follow.

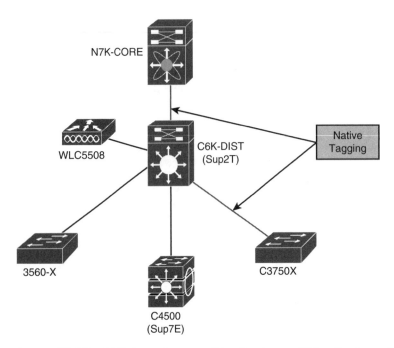

Figure 25-27   *SGTs from Access to Distribution and Distribution to DataCenter*

Configuring SGT Propagation on Cisco IOS Switches

This section discusses the configuration of SGT propagation on access layer switches, such as the 3560-X and 3750-X, that have the ability to use native tags. The Catalyst 6500 and Nexus series switches are covered in a different section.

When it comes to inserting the TAG into Layer 2 traffic, there is a fundamental choice to make: to use encryption or not to use encryption. For simplicity, this chapter focuses on the easy one: without encryption. Encrypting the tag is discussed in Chapter 26 when you review Network Device Access Control (NDAC) and MACSec (IEEE 802.1AE).

From global configuration, perform the following steps:

1. Enter **cts role-based enforcement.**This globally enables the tagging of SGTs. It also enables the ability to enforce SGACLs (discussed in a future section). However, without this command in the global configuration, the switch will not tag the Layer 2 traffic.

2. Enter into interface configuration mode of the tagging-capable port by typing **interface** *interface-name.*

3. Enter **cts manual.**

   You are using cts manual, because you are not utilizing NDAC at this point. The cts manual mode of operation allows you to apply the tag to the Layer 2 frame without having to negotiate encryption or requiring a fully trusted domain of Cisco switches (as you would need with NDAC).

4. Enter **policy static** sgt *sgt-value* **trusted**.

When you developed your security groups earlier in this chapter, you created a special group for network access devices. We called that security group NADs, and the value of that group was 2 (0x02). That is the value you are applying here with this **policy static sgt 2 trusted** command. The trusted keyword in this command ensures that no changes are made to the incoming tags, as they are from a trusted source.

Example 25-6 displays the configuration to enable tagging, while Example 25-7 shows the monitoring output.

Example 25-6   *Enabling Tagging on a 3750-X Series Access Switch*

```
C3750X(config)#cts role-based enforcement
C3750X(config)#interface Ten 1/1/1
C3750X(config-if)#cts manual
C3750X(config-if-cts-manual)#policy static sgt 2 trusted
```

Example 25-7   *Verifying Tagging on a 3750-X Series Access Switch*

```
C3750X#sho cts interface Ten 1/1/1
Global Dot1x feature is Enabled
Interface TenGigabitEthernet1/1/1:
    CTS is enabled, mode:      MANUAL
    IFC state:                 OPEN
    Authentication Status:     NOT APPLICABLE
        Peer identity:         "unknown"
        Peer's advertised capabilities: ""
    Authorization Status:      SUCCEEDED
        Peer SGT:              2
        Peer SGT assignment: Trusted
    SAP Status:                NOT APPLICABLE
        Configured pairwise ciphers:
            gcm-encrypt
            null
        Replay protection:        enabled
        Replay protection mode: STRICT
        Selected cipher:
    Propagate SGT:             Enabled
    Cache Info:
        Cache applied to link : NONE
    Statistics:
        authc success:            0
```

```
        authc reject:            0
        authc failure:           0
        authc no response:       0
        authc logoff:            0
        sap success:             0
        sap fail:                0
        authz success:           3
        authz fail:              0
        port auth fail:          0
   L3 IPM:    disabled.
```

Configuring SGT Propagation on a Catalyst 6500

The Catalyst 6500 is a special case. This switch is sometimes used in the access layer, but it's most often used in the distribution layer or even in the data center. There are also a tremendous number of line cards possible for this chassis based switch, some of which can support native tagging and some cannot. Because of the possibility of multiple locations and multiple line-card possibilities, the catalyst 6500 requires the administrator to set whether the switch should be used for egress (receiving the tag from other devices) or ingress, which would place it at the access layer. These modes are referred to as reflector modes.

Note   This switch is unable to be configured for both ingress and egress mode simultaneously.

Ingress reflector mode should only be used in the access layer. This mode allows the use of non-SGA capable line cards along with an SGA capable supervisor. (An example of this would be a Catalyst 6504-E chassis populated with a Supervisor 2T and a 6148 series line card.) With this mode, all packet forwarding occurs on the Supervisor 2T PFC. Line cards that use distributed forwarding are not supported in ingress reflector mode (such as the 6748-GE-TX).

With this mode of operation, ISE is able to assign an SGT to a device entering the access layer via any supported line card, but that tag is only applied to network traffic leaving one of the ports physically on the Supervisor 2T. In other words, the switch applies the tag on an uplink port, but not any of the downlink ports. Additionally, the switch cannot read the incoming tag on any ports except the ones physically on the Supervisor 2T module itself.

Note   Using a Supervisor 2T in the access layer is not normally recommended and is not part of Secure Unified Access systems testing.

Egress reflector mode is normally associated with the 6500 being deployed in the distribution layer or data center. With this mode, SGA propagation and encryption (MACSec) may be enabled on the Supervisor 2T and 6900 series line cards. These are the model of line card most often seen in the distribution layer, and as such, this provides for a nice SGA aggregation design. The switch can read all incoming SGT tagged packets and apply that tag to the traffic leaving the switch as well. This is the model of SGT that one normally thinks of when discussing the topic. Additionally, if the Catalyst 6500 is a SXP peer, it is capable of applying the SGT to Layer 2 traffic based on the IP to SGT bindings learned via SXP.

From global configuration on the Catalyast 6500, perform the following steps:

1. Choose the CTS reflector mode by typing **platform cts** {**egress** | **ingress**}.

   Because this is a distribution layer deployment of the catalyst 6500, choose egress mode. If this were an access layer deployment, where end users would be authenticated, you would have chosen ingress mode.

2. Enter **cts role-based enforcement**.

   This globally enables the tagging of SGTs. It also has the ability to enforce SGACLs (discussed in a future section). However, without this command in the global configuration, the switch will not tag the Layer 2 traffic.

3. Enter into interface configuration mode of the tagging-capable port by typing **interface** *interface-name*.

4. Enter **cts manual**.

   You are using cts manual, because you are not utilizing NDAC at this point. The cts manual mode of operation allows us to apply the tag to the Layer 2 frame without having to negotiate encryption or require a fully trusted domain of Cisco switches (as would be necessary with NDAC).

5. Enter **policy static** sgt *sgt-value* **trusted**.

When you created your security groups earlier in this chapter, you developed a special group for network access devices. You called that security group NADs, and the value of that group was 2 (0x02). That is the value you are applying here with this **policy static sgt 2 trusted** command. The trusted keyword in this command ensures that no changes are made to the incoming tags, as they are from a trusted source.

Examples 25-8 and 25-9 display the enabling and verifying of tagging with the Catalyst 6500 Supervisor 2T.

Example 25-8   *Enabling Tagging on Catalyst 6500 Supervisor 2T*

```
C6K-DIST(config)#platform cts egress
C6K-DIST(config)#cts role-based enforcement
C6K-DIST(config)#interface Ten1/5
C6K-DIST(config-if)#cts manual
C6K-DIST(config-if-cts-manual)#policy static sgt 2 trusted
```

Example 25-9   *Verifying Tagging on the Catalyst 6500 Supervisor 2T*

```
C6K-DIST#show cts interface Ten1/5
Global Dot1x feature is Enabled
Interface TenGigabitEthernet1/5:
    CTS is enabled, mode:      MANUAL
    IFC state:                 OPEN
    Authentication Status:     NOT APPLICABLE
        Peer identity:         "unknown"
        Peer's advertised capabilities: ""
    Authorization Status:      SUCCEEDED
        Peer SGT:              2
        Peer SGT assignment: Trusted
    SAP Status:                NOT APPLICABLE
        Configured pairwise ciphers:
            gcm-encrypt
            null
        Replay protection:     enabled
        Replay protection mode: STRICT
        Selected cipher:
    Propagate SGT:             Enabled
    Cache Info:
        Cache applied to link : NONE

    Statistics:
        authc success:              0
        authc reject:               0
        authc failure:              0
        authc no response:          0
        authc logoff:               0
        sap success:                0
        sap fail:                   0
        authz success:              1
        authz fail:                 0
        port auth fail:             0
    L3 IPM:    disabled.
```

Configuring SGT Propagation on a Nexus Series Switch

The following steps guide you through the configuration of SGT propagation on the Nexus series switch.

From global configuration on the Nexus Series switch, perform the following steps:

1. Type **feature dot1x** at global configuration mode.

   The Nexus series requires the feature dot1x to be enabled before enabling CTS features.

2. Type **cts enable** at global configuration mode.

   This command enables Security Group Access, MACSec, and NDAC features to be enabled and configured.

3. Enter **cts role-based enforcement**.

   This globally enables the tagging of SGTs. It also provides the ability to enforce SGACLs (discussed in a future section). However, without this command in the global configuration, the switch will not tag the Layer 2 traffic.

4. Enter into interface configuration mode of the tagging-capable port by typing **interface** *interface-name*.

5. Enter **cts manual**.

   You are using cts manual because you are not utilizing NDAC at this point. The cts manual mode of operation allows you to send the apply the tag to the Layer 2 frame, without having to negotiate encryption or requiring a fully trusted domain of Cisco switches (such as we would need with NDAC).

6. Enter **policy static** sgt *sgt-value* **trusted**.

When you created your security groups earlier in this chapter, you developed a special group for network access devices. You called that Security Group NADs, and the value of that group was 2 (0x02). That is the value you are applying here with the **policy static sgt 2 trusted** command. The trusted keyword in this command ensures that no changes are made to the incoming tags, as they are from a trusted source.

Example 25-10 walks through the enabling of tagging on a Nexus 7000 series switch.

Example 25-10   *Enabling Tagging on Nexus 7000*

```
NX7K-CORE(config)# feature dot1x
NX7K-CORE(config)# cts enable
NX7K-CORE(config)# cts role-based enforcement
NX7K-CORE(config)# int eth1/26
NX7K-CORE(config-if)# cts manual
NX7K-CORE(config-if-cts-manual)# policy static sgt 0x2 trusted
```

Enforcement

Now that you have security groups being assigned (Classification) and they are being transmitted across the network (Transportation), it is time to focus on the third staple of Security Group Access: enforcement.

There are multiple ways to enforce traffic based on the tag, but can ultimately be summarized into two major types:

- Enforcement on a switch (SGACL)

- Enforcement on a firewall (SG-FW)

SGACL

Historically, enforcement with SGACL was the only option available. It started with the Nexus 7000 Series and has expanded to the Nexus 5000 Series, Catalyst 6500 (Supervisor 2T), and the 3000-X Series switches. A major benefit to SGACL usage is the consolidation of access control entries (ACE) and the operational savings involved with maintenance of those traditional access lists.

An SGACL can be visualized in a format similar to a spreadsheet. It is always based on a source tag to a destination tag. Figure 25-28 shows an example SGACL policy on ISE, which represents the SGACLs in a columns and rows presentation. The box highlighted in gray shows that, when traffic with a source of the Employee SGT (6) attempts to reach a destination with the HR SGT (5), an SGACL named Permit_WEB will be applied and a catch-all of Deny IP. The contents of the Permit_WEB ACL are displayed in Figure 25-29, where you can see only HTTP and HTTPS are permitted.

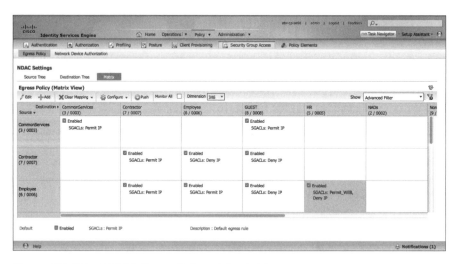

Figure 25-28   *SGACL Egress Policy: Matrix View*

As you can see with Figures 25-28 and 25-29, the resulting ACL would be to permit HTTP (tcp/80) and HTTP (tcp/443) and deny all other traffic. This traffic is applied egress of the switch where the SGACL is configured. In this case, it is applied at the Nexus 7000 in the DataCenter, as traffic attempts to reach the HR server.

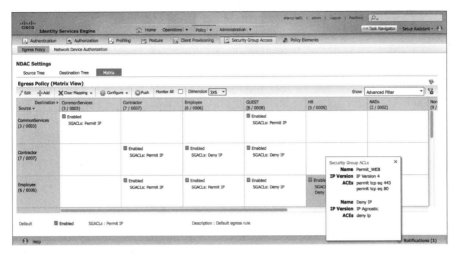

Figure 25-29 *Permit_WEB SGACL Contents*

This form of traffic enforcement can provide a tremendous savings on the complexity and number of ACEs to maintain. There is a general formula to see the savings:

(# of sources) * (# of destinations) * permissions = # of ACEs

With a traditional ACL on firewall:

4 VLANs (src) * 30 (dst) * 4 permission = 480 ACEs

Per source IP on port using dACL:

1 group (source) * 30 (dst) * 4 permission = 120 ACEs

With SGACLs, the number of ACEs are a magnitude smaller:

4 SGT (src) * 3 SGT (dst) * 4 permission = 48 ACEs

There are two main ways to deploy SGACLs: North-South and East-West, as shown in Figure 25-30. North-South refers to the use-case of a user or device being classified at the access layer, but enforcement with the SGACL occurring at the DataCenter. For example, a guest entering the access layer is assigned a GUEST SGT. Traffic with a GUEST SGT is dropped if it tries to reach a server with financial data.

East-West refers to the use-case of an SGACL protecting resources that exist on the same switch. For example, a development server and a production server on the same Nexus 5000 series switch in the DataCenter, an SGACL may be deployed to prevent the development server from ever communicating with the production server. Another East-West example is a guest and an employee both using the same access layer switch. Traffic may be filtered between these two devices so the guest cannot communicate to the employee who is in the same VLAN on the same switch.

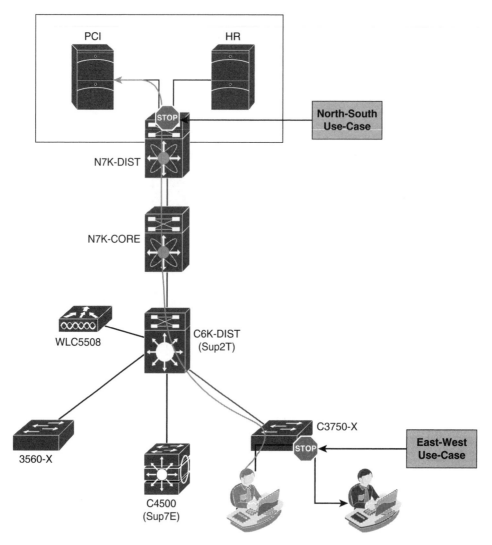

Figure 25-30   *North-South Versus East-West Visually Explained*

Creating the SG-ACL in ISE

ISE provides three different views to create Security Group ACLs (SGACL). There are two tree views (Source Tree and Destination Tree), and there is a Matrix View. The Matrix View is the one that looks and acts more like a spreadsheet. That view is the focus in this book.

From the ISE Administration GUI, perform the following steps:

1. Navigate to **Policy > Security Group Access > Egress Policy**, as shown in Figure 25-31.

Figure 25-31   *Policy > Security Group Access > Egress Policy*

As shown in Figure 25-32, ISE's default view is the Source Tree view.

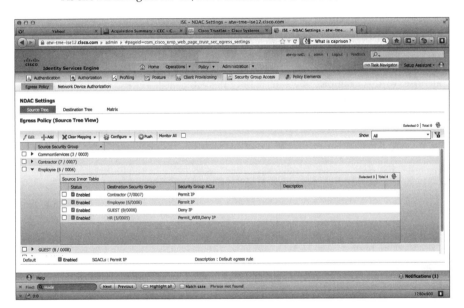

Figure 25-32   *Egress Policy: Source Tree View*

2. Click the **Matrix** button.

3. Click the square that represents the intersection of a source SGT and a destination SGT.

   This example uses the square where the contractor SGT is trying to reach a device with the HR SGT and is shown in Figure 25-33.

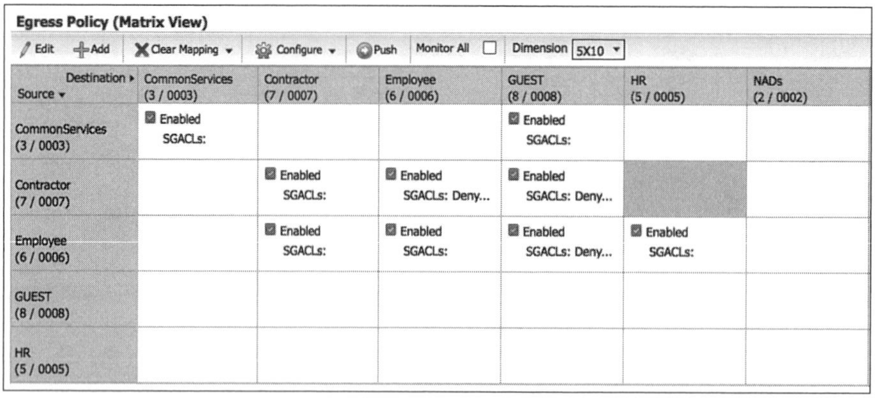

Egress Policy (Matrix View)

Edit	Add	Clear Mapping ▾		Configure ▾	Push	Monitor All ☐	Dimension 5X10 ▾	

Destination ▸ Source ▾	CommonServices (3 / 0003)	Contractor (7 / 0007)	Employee (6 / 0006)	GUEST (8 / 0008)	HR (5 / 0005)	NADs (2 / 0002)
CommonServices (3 / 0003)	☑ Enabled SGACLs:			☑ Enabled SGACLs:		
Contractor (7 / 0007)		☑ Enabled SGACLs:	☑ Enabled SGACLs: Deny...	☑ Enabled SGACLs: Deny...		
Employee (6 / 0006)		☑ Enabled SGACLs:	☑ Enabled SGACLs:	☑ Enabled SGACLs: Deny...	☑ Enabled SGACLs:	
GUEST (8 / 0008)						
HR (5 / 0005)						

Figure 25-33   *Matrix View, Selecting Contractor (7) to HR (5)*

4. Double-click the square.

5. The Edit Permissions screen is displayed.

   From this screen, you can select an SGACL and pick a final Catch All rule. For the purposes of this example, you simply only deny all traffic from contractor (7) to HR (5), as shown in Figure 25-34.

6. Click the drop-down for Final Catch All Rule, and choose Deny IP.

7. Click Save.

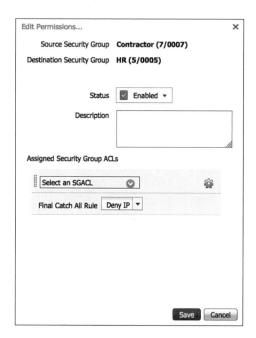

Figure 25-34   *Deny IP from Contractor to HR*

Next, follow similar steps, but create an SGACL that permits common services, like DNS and DHCP from Employees to Common Services. This is normally handled by a default permit-traffic rule for any undefined boxes, but you are performing this as an example.

8. Double-click the box where the two SGTs "intersect."

9. Click the drop-down for Select and SGACL.

10. Click the silver cog in the upper-right corner and select **Create New Security Group ACL**, as shown in Figure 25-35.

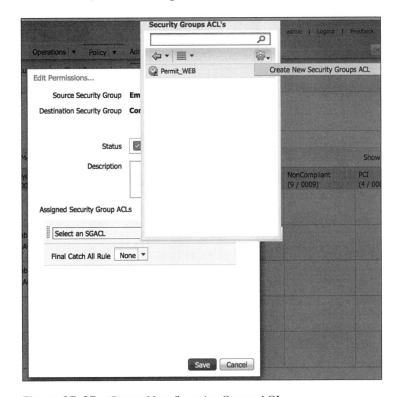

Figure 25-35   *Create New Security Group ACL*

11. The Create New Security Group ACL dialog box appears.

12. Provide the ACL a name and description.

13. The IP version may be IPv4, IPv6, or Agnostic.

14. The Security Group ACL Content is where the ACEs belong.

Notice the Security Group ACL contents in Figure 25-36. These ACLs are egress only, so you are only building an ACE for the traffic going to the destination tag. (There is no source in the ACL at all, only the destination.)

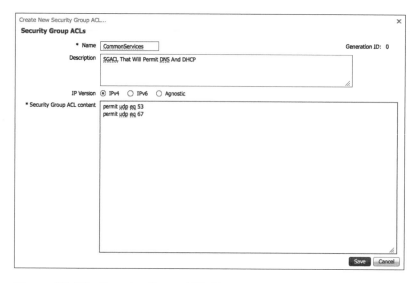

Figure 25-36 *Security Group ACL Contents*

15. Click **Save**.

16. Ensure the new SGACL is selected in the Edit Permissions window.

17. Choose the Final Catch All. In this example, we are setting the final catch all to Deny IP, as shown in Figure 25-37.

18. Click **Save**.

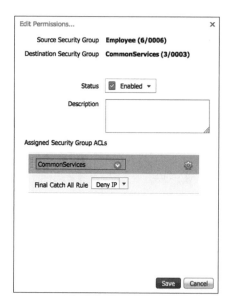

Figure 25-37 *Final Settings in Edit Permissions Window*

Configure ISE to Allow the SGACLs to Be Downloaded

Now that the SGACLs are created in ISE, you still need download them to the switches that will be performing enforcement. This is the first time in this book that you needed the DataCenter switches to communicate directly to ISE. You are adding them to ISE so you can download the IP-SGT bindings that you created earlier, so it can download the SGACLs that you created and the egress policies.

The configuration of this should be familiar to you at this point, with a few minor differences. Let's look from the ISE GUI:

1. Navigate to **Administration** > **Network Resources** > **Network Devices**.

2. Click **Add**.

3. Enter the device name, IP address, and any network device groups, as you have done in previous chapters.

4. Add the RADIUS shared secret under the Authentication settings.

   Now begins the new part. Most likely, you have never clicked the Advanced TrustSec Settings section, unless it was just to look at what might be there. Every device that will download SGACLs will perform a mutual authentication with ISE. As you can see in Figure 25-38, there is a device ID and password that must match on both sides.

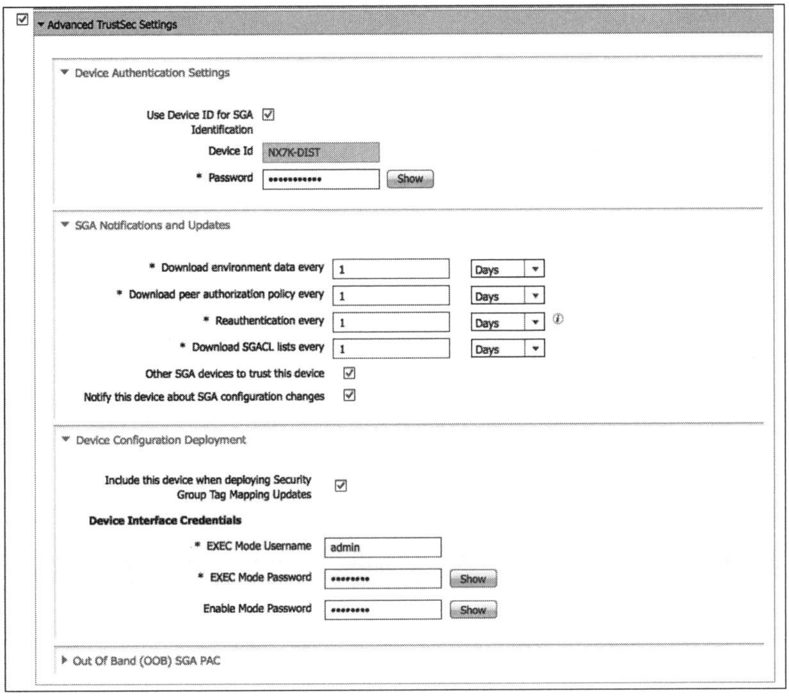

Figure 25-38   *Network Device Settings*

5. Expand Advanced TrustSec Settings.

6. Enter the device name and password to match what is configured on the SGA-capable switch.

7. Under the SGA Notifications and Updates section, the default settings will most likely suffice, but can be tuned for your environment.

8. Under Device Configuration Deployment, enter the EXEC mode username and passwords as requested.

   This setting pushes IP to SGT bindings defined on ISE to the switch.

9. Click **Save**.

Repeat steps 1–9 for all SGACL capable switches that need to download the environment data.

Configure the Switches to Download SGACLs from ISE

Now that ISE is configured to allow the switch to download the SGA environment data, you must configure the switch to allow the same.

From global configuration, perform the following steps:

1. Configure the device ID and password to match what is configured on ISE with the **cts device-id** *name* **password** *password* command.

2. Add ISE as a RADIUS server by typing **radius-server host** *ip-address* **key** *shared-secret-key* **pac** command.

> **Note**   The **pac** keyword is needed to have the device request a protected credential from ISE.

3. Create a RADIUS server group using the **aaa group server radius** *group-name* command.

4. Add the server to the group by entering **server** *ip-address*.

5. If there are VRFs in use, configure which VRF to use to communicate to ISE with the **use-vrf** *vrf-name* command.

6. Type **exit** to return to global configuration mode.

7. Configure AAA authentication for 802.1X using the command: **aaa authentication dot1x default group** *group-name*.

8. Configure AAA accounting for 802.1X using the command: **aaa accounting dot1x default group** *group-name*.

9. Do same for CTS authorization: **aaa authorization cts default group** *group-name*.

10. Enter the cts device ID and password again to immediately kick-start the pac file download: **cts device-id** *name* **password** *password*.

Example 25-11 shows the configuration required for the Nexus 7000 and ISE to communicate.

Example 25-11   *Configuring the Nexus7000 to Communicate with ISE*

```
NX7K-DIST(config)# cts device-id NX7K-DIST password TrustSec123
NX7K-DIST(config)# radius-server host 10.1.100.231 key TrustSec123 pac
NX7K-DIST(config)# aaa group server radius ise-radius
NX7K-DIST(config-radius)# server 10.1.100.231
NX7K-DIST(config-radius)# use-vrf default
NX7K-DIST(config-radius)# exit
NX7K-DIST(config)# aaa authentication dot1x default group ise-radius
NX7K-DIST(config)# aaa accounting dot1x default group ise-radius
NX7K-DIST(config)# aaa authorization cts default group ise-radius
NX7K-DIST(config)# cts device-id NX7K-DIST password TrustSec123
```

Validating the PAC File and CTS Data Downloads

This section reviews how to validate the pac file and CTS data downloads from ISE. Example 25-12 shows how to validate that the Protected Access Credential (PAC) file is correctly downloaded from ISE.

Example 25-12   show cts pac

```
NX7K-DIST(config)# sho cts pac
PAC Info :
==============================
  PAC Type           : Trustsec
  AID                : e9e44428fc9c3fc6be59d35784bb285f
  I-ID               : NX7K-DIST
  AID Info           : Identity Services Engine
  Credential Lifetime : Mon Nov 26 22:57:21 2012
  PAC Opaque         : 000200b80003000100040010e9e44428fc9c3fc6be59d35784bb285f
0006009c00030100d068ae1f1d873e923e2c317e9852bd91000000135034e4aa00093a807e635ba2
e5ae451bdddbd9b17cdcf000dd4516f55324eca75a8dae4786d5e33d669a19d41a62fc9116962c58
b208cac2537eccd2aff08e4b6de47965e69d76e5b16d214030c91f5ebc15ac23e9d5356d60e69cbe
90e9cfa9ee756d259c200dd1afd7abe66c694e0649475665cad145191ac140234d78158e7ceca829
```

Example 25-13 shows the use of the **show cts environment-data** command to validate that the environment data has successfully downloaded from ISE.

Example 25-13   show cts environment-data

```
NX7K-DIST(config)# sho cts environment-data
CTS Environment Data
==============================
  Current State           : CTS_ENV_DNLD_ST_ENV_DOWNLOAD_DONE
  Last Status             : CTS_ENV_SUCCESS
  Local Device SGT        : 0x0000
  Transport Type          : CTS_ENV_TRANSPORT_DIRECT
  Data loaded from cache  : FALSE
  Env Data Lifetime       : 86400 seconds after last update
  Last Update Time        : Tue Aug 28 22:22:52 2012
  Server List             : CTSServerList1
     AID:e9e44428fc9c3fc6be59d35784bb285f IP:10.1.100.231 Port:1812
```

Example 25-14 shows the use of the **show cts role-based access-list** command to view and validate the RBACLs that exist on the switch.

Example 25-14   show cts role-based access-list

```
NX7K-DIST(config)# sho cts role-based access-list
rbacl:Deny IP
        deny ip
rbacl:Permit IP
        permit ip
rbacl:CommonServices
```

Example 25-15 shows the use of the **show cts role-based policy** command to view and validate the RBACLs that are applied to the SGT pairs.

Example 25-15   show cts role-based policy

```
NX7K-DIST(config)# sho cts role-based policy
sgt:3
dgt:3    rbacl:Permit IP
        permit ip
sgt:6
dgt:3    rbacl:Deny IP
        deny ip
sgt:any
dgt:any rbacl:Permit IP
        permit ip
```

Example 25-16 shows the use of the **show cts role-based sgt-map** command to view and validate any ip to SGT bindings.

Example 25-16   show cts role-based sgt-map

```
NX7K-DIST(config)# sho cts role-based sgt-map
IP ADDRESS          SGT       VRF/VLAN       SGT CONFIGURATION
10.1.100.254        3         vlan:100       Learned on interface:Ethernet1/3
10.1.50.2           2         vrf:1          Learned on interface:Ethernet1/1
```

Figure 25-39 shows the successful downloads of CTS data and PAC files through Live Log in ISE.

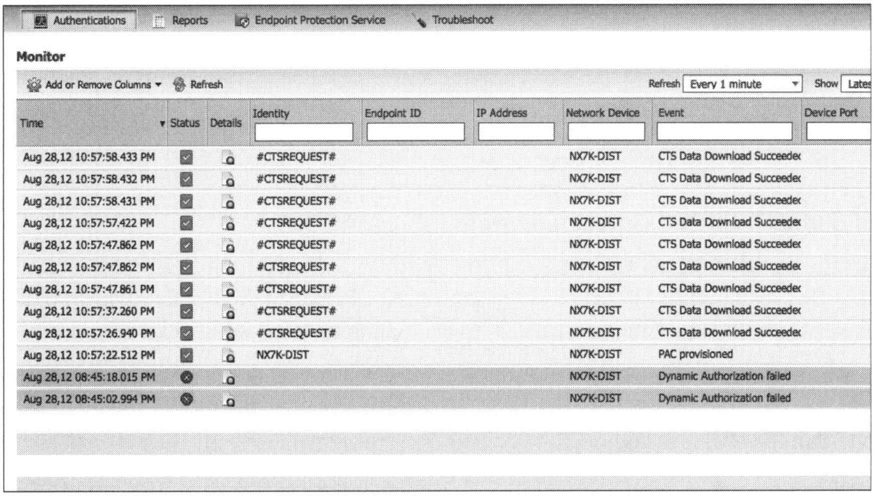

Figure 25-39   *ISE Live Log Showing PAC and CTS Download*

Security Group Firewalls

Some organizations prefer to do the traffic enforcement on the switching infrastructure, on a device that was purpose-built to do traffic filtering, a firewall. Cisco has added the ability to enforce traffic on firewalls by implementing the Security Group Firewall (SG-FW). There are two different types of Security Group Firewalls that exist: the ASA-based SG-FW and the router-based SG-FW. This makes sense, because the routers use a Zone-Based Firewall (ZBF) and the ASA does not.

Security Group Firewall on the ASA

Beginning with ASA version 9.0, the ASA firewall gains SG-FW functionality. ASDM supports the full configuration, and therefore, the ASA is the only SG-FW that has a GUI (as of the writing of this book).

The SG-FW in the ASA is a simple concept. The powerful firewall policy in the firewall has been expanded to include source and destination security groups into the decision. As you can see in Figure 25-40, there is a new Security Group column in the Source and Destination Criteria sections.

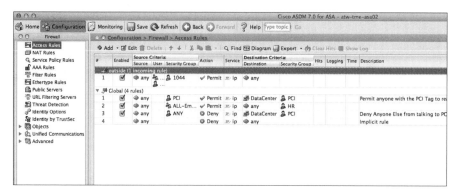

Figure 25-40   *ASDM Firewall Policy*

Configuring TrustSec Downloads from ISE via ASDM

Unlike the switches, an SG-FW does not download the SGACLs from ISE. Firewalls tend to have their own security policies. However, the SG-FW must still be able to download the list of SGTs that exist and the static IP to SGT mappings that were created from ISE.

From within the Configuration > Firewall section of ASDM, there is a new option called Identity by TrustSec. This is the primary location for any and all TrustSec configuration from within the GUI (see Figure 25-41).

The following steps configure the SGA server groups in ASDM:

1. To start, we need to add ISE an authentication server. At the bottom of the screen, in the Sever Group Setup section, click **Manage**.

2. The Configure AAA Server Groups pop-up window appears, as shown in Figure 25-42.

3. Click **Add** at the top right to create a new server group.

4. Provide a name for the new group.

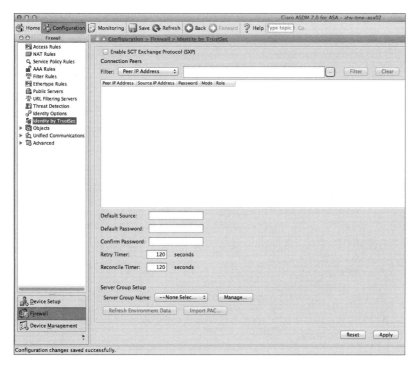

Figure 25-41 *Identity by TrustSec*

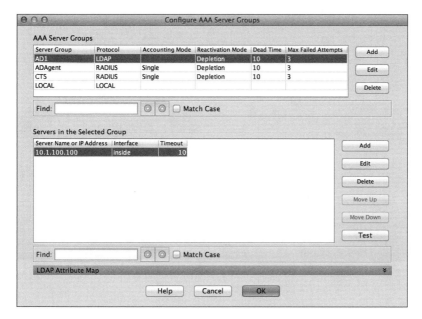

Figure 25-42 *Configure AAA Server Groups*

5. Ensure that the protocol chosen is RADIUS, as shown in Figure 25-43.

6. Click **OK**.

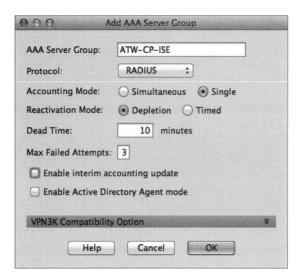

Figure 25-43 *Add AAA Server Group*

7. On the Configure AAA Server Groups screen, ensure that the new server group is highlighted, as shown in Figure 25-44.

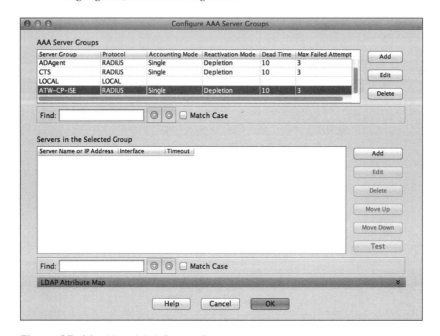

Figure 25-44 *New AAA Server Group*

8. Click **Add** on the lower half to add a new authentication server to the group, as shown in Figure 25-45.

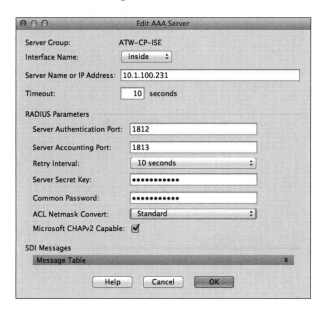

Server Group:	ATW-CP-ISE
Interface Name:	inside
Server Name or IP Address:	10.1.100.231
Timeout:	10 seconds

RADIUS Parameters

Server Authentication Port:	1812
Server Accounting Port:	1813
Retry Interval:	10 seconds
Server Secret Key:	••••••••••
Common Password:	••••••••••
ACL Netmask Convert:	Standard
Microsoft CHAPv2 Capable:	☑

Figure 25-45 *The New AAA Server*

9. Choose the correct interface to reach ISE.

10. Add the IP address of the ISE.

11. ISE uses port 1812 for authentication and 1813 for accounting. (ASDM default values are 1645 and 1646.)

12. Enter the Shared Secret key for the RADIUS communication.

13. Click **OK** to save the server.

14. Click **OK** to save the server group.

15. Ensure your new server group is selected in the Server Group Setup section and click **Apply**.

Now that the ASA is configured to communicate with ISE, you must ensure that ISE has the ASA added as a network device. Unlike the Nexus series, the ASA does not automatically download the pac file; it must be manually generated in the ISE GUI and imported via ASDM.

16. From within the Advanced TrustSec Features section of the Network Device, click **Generate PAC**.

17. The Generate PAC pop-up screen appears, with the Identity field already populated, as shown in Figure 25-46.

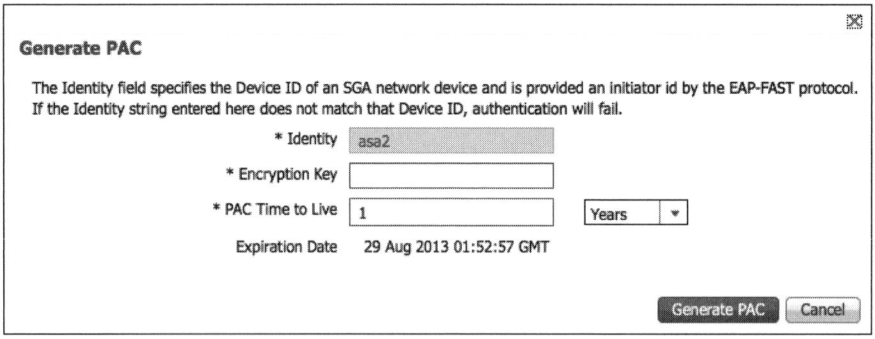

Generate PAC
The Identity field specifies the Device ID of an SGA network device and is provided an initiator id by the EAP-FAST protocol. If the Identity string entered here does not match that Device ID, authentication will fail.
* Identity
asa2
* Encryption Key
* PAC Time to Live
1
Years
Expiration Date
29 Aug 2013 01:52:57 GMT
Generate PAC
Cancel

Figure 25-46 *Generate PAC*

18. Enter in an encryption key that you will remember and click **Generate PAC.**
19. The download should begin automatically, as shown in Figure 25-47.

Opening asa2.pac
You have chosen to open
asa2.pac
which is a: Binary File
from: https://atw-tme-ise12.cisco.com
Would you like to save this file?
Cancel
Save File

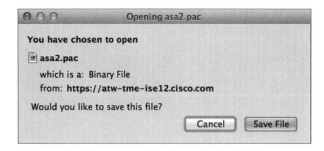

Figure 25-47 *Save the PAC File*

20. Save the file to a location that you will remember.
21. In ASDM, Identity by TrustSec, click **Import PAC**, as shown in Figure 25-48.

Import PAC
Filename:
/Users/aawoland/Downloads/asa2.pac
Browse...
Password:
Confirm Password:
Help
Cancel
Import

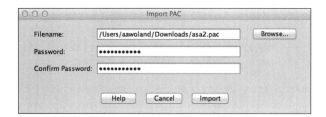

Figure 25-48 *Import PAC*

22. Click **Browse** and choose the saved pac file.

23. Enter the encryption key into the Password and Confirm Password fields.

24. Click **Import**.

25. You should receive a PAC Imported Successfully message.

Validating the TrustSec Communication

The following steps allow you to validate that TrustSec communication is working with the ASA.

Within ASDM, perform the following steps:

1. Navigate to **Monitoring > Identity by TrustSec**.

2. Choose Environment data.

Figure 25-49 shows the screen that notifies you of the status of your communication with ISE, the last successful download, and the Table of Security Group.

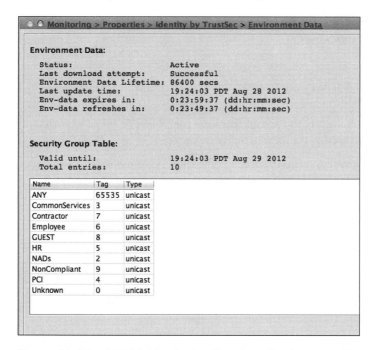

Figure 25-49   *ASDM: Identity by TrustSec > Environment Data*

3. To verify the imported PAC file, navigate to **Identity by TrustSec > PAC**, as shown in Figure 25-50.

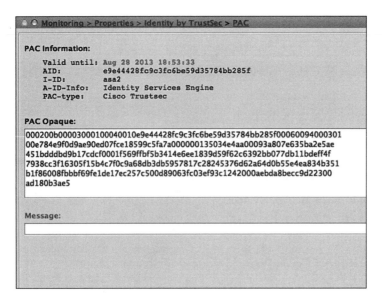

Figure 25-50 *ASDM: Identity by TrustSec > PAC*

Configuring SG-FW Policies via ASDM

Now that all the communication between the ASA and ISE is configured and working, the ASA knows about all the security groups that were configured on ISE. Those security groups may now be used in the firewall policy on the ASA.

From within the Configuration > Firewall section of ASDM, perform the following steps:

1. Select **Access Rules**.

2. Click **Add** to add a new rule or **Edit** to modify an existing rule.

3. Configure a source IP (if needed). In the example shown in Figure 25-51, you are only basing the rule on the source tag, not source IP or AD user.

4. Choose the source security group.

5. Configure a destination IP (if needed). In the example shown in Figure 25-51, you are choosing a destination of your DataCenter subnets.

6. Choose a destination security group. In the example in Figure 25-51, notice the destination Security Group of PCI.

   This rule has been created to allow any source with an SGT of PCI to reach any server in the DataCenter that also has the PCI tag. The next rule in the firewall policy is to deny all other traffic to any server with the PCI tag, as shown in Figure 25-52.

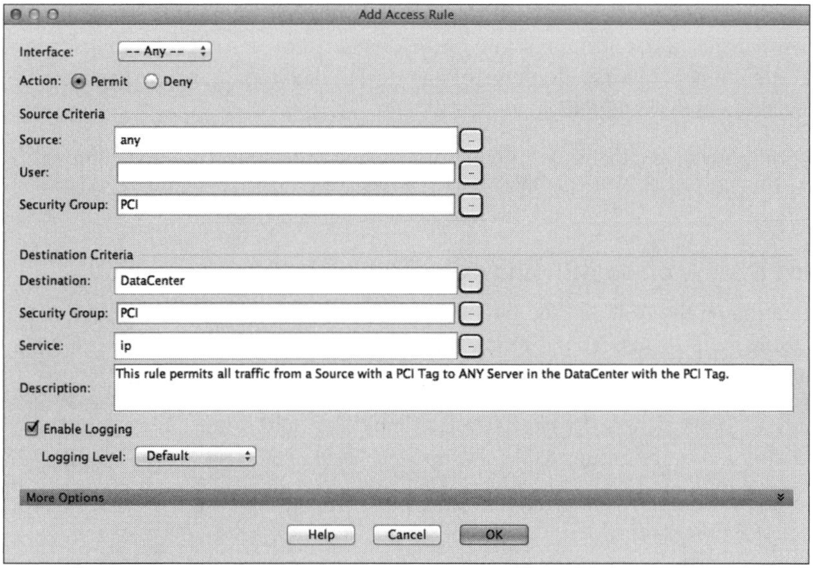

Figure 25-51   *Adding a FW Rule to Permit Traffic to PCI Servers*

7. Click **OK**.

Repeat Steps 2 through 7 for the remainder of your rules. Figure 25-52 shows a sample firewall policy.

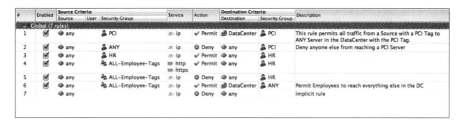

Figure 25-52   *Sample Firewall Policy*

Security Group Firewall on the ISR and ASR

The ASA is not the only security group firewall on the market. Both the Integrated Services Router Generation 2 (ISR-G2) and the Aggregation Services Router (ASR) have a powerful ZBF capability.

The Cisco ISR Gen2 (c3900, c3900e, c2900, c2901, c1941, c890) began support of SG-FW as of version 15.2(2)T. The Cisco ASR 1000 added support of the SG-FW as of IOS-XE version 3.4.

As of the time this book was written, neither the ISR or the ASR support the downloading of the environmental data from ISE yet, or the download of IP to SGT bindings from
ISE. So they are not able to take advantage of any of that data today, and all tags must be
created manually within the IOS CLI.

However, both routers are capable of running the SXP, and the ASR has native tagging
capabilities.

Configuring SG-FW on an ASR and ISR

The configuration on the ASR and the ISR is identical with one exception. The ASR is
capable of using the SGT in both the source and destination of the ZBF, while at the time
that this chapter was written, the ISR is only capable of using the source SGT.

For this configuration example, let's keep things simple and only create a few security
groups, and then add those groups to the ZBF policy. Figure 25-53 shows the sample
topology for this example.

Note   With IOS ZBF, any traffic not explicitly permitted with a **pass** or **inspect**
command is dropped.

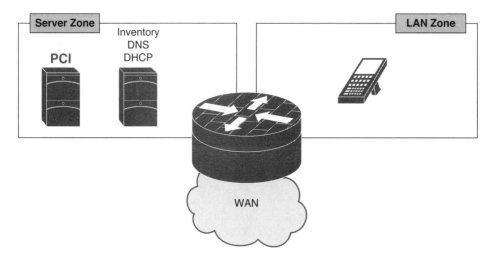

Figure 25-53   *Simple Branch ZBF w/ SG-FW Example Layout*

With the following steps, you create a few security groups, and then add those groups to
the ZBF policy:

1. Add the Security Groups at Global Configuration mode, as demonstrated in the following configuration:

```
atw-asr1k(config)#object-group security PCI
atw-asr1k(config-security-group)#description SGT for PCI users and servers
```

```
atw-asr1k(config-security-group)#security-group tag 4
Example 25-x          Adding the NADs Security Group
atw-asr1k(config)#object-group security NADs
atw-asr1k(config-security-group)#description Network Devices
atw-asr1k(config-security-group)#security-group tag 2
Example 25-x          Adding the CommonServices Security Group
atw-asr1k(config)#object-group security CommonServices
atw-asr1k(config-security-group)#description Group for things like DNS
atw-asr1k(config-security-group)#security-group tag 3
```

2. Add an inspection class-map for the security groups, as demonstrated in the following configuration:

```
atw-asr1k(config)#class-map type inspect match-all pci-sgt
atw-asr1k(config-cmap)#match group-object security source PCI
atw-asr1k(config-cmap)#match group-object security destination PCI
! - this has configured a class-map that looks for
! - traffic with ssgt=pci and dsgt=pci only.
Example 25-x                Creating class-map for only Destination SGT = PCI
atw-asr1k(config)#class-map type inspect match-all pci-sgt-dest
atw-asr1k(config-cmap)#match group-object security destination PCI
! - this has configured a class-map that looks for
! - traffic with a dsgt=pci, and is not looking for the ssgt at all
```

3. Create the policy-map to inspect, pass, or drop traffic, as demonstrated in the following configuration. This example allows only PCI tagged traffic to reach PCI servers and permit all other traffic:

```
atw-asr1k(config)#policy-map type inspect branch-policy
atw-asr1k(config-pmap)#class type inspect pci-sgt
atw-asr1k(config-pmap-c)#inspect
! - Configures deep packet inspection for all traffic with ssgt=pci to
dsgt=pci
atw-asr1k(config-pmap)#class type inspect pci-sgt-dest
atw-asr1k(config-pmap-c)#drop
! - Configures deep packet inspection for all traffic from all else to
dsgt=pci
atw-asr1k(config-pmap)#class class-default
atw-asr1k(config-pmap-c)#pass
! - Allows all other traffic into the server zone
```

4. This next set of commands is optional and would only be configured if you did not already have the security zones and service policy:

```
atw-asr1k(config)#zone security lan
atw-asr1k(config)#zone security servers
atw-asr1k(config)#zone security lan-servers source lan destination servers
atw-asr1k(config-sec-zone-pair)#service-policy type inspect branch-policy
```

5. This next set of commands is optional and would only be configured if you did not already have the interfaces assigned to the security zones:

```
atw-asr1k(config)#int g0/0/2
atw-asr1k(config-if)#zone-member security lan
atw-asr1k(config)#int g0/0/3
atw-asr1k(config-if)#zone-member security servers
```

Summary

This chapter explained Security Group Access, and at this point, you should be able to articulate why it is so valuable and how much operational expense it can save your organization.

You learned that there are three foundational pillars of security group access: classification, transport, and enforcement. Where classification is the ability to accept the tag for a particular network authentication session, transport is the ability to send that assigned tag to upstream neighbors either via native tagging or Security group eXchange Protocol (SXP); and that enforcement may be on switches using Security Group ACLs (SGACL) or on a Security Group Firewall (SG-FW).

Additionally, this chapter covered the basic configuration of all these features across the many different supported platforms.

Chapter 26 introduces Network Device Admission Control (NDAC) and IEEE 802.1AE (MACSec), where all the Cisco devices in the network are able to form a trusted domain, where all traffic (including the SGT) is encrypted across network links.

MACSec and NDAC

In years long passed, when WiFi was first being introduced into the consumer and corporate space, security concerns were raised. The concerns focused on sensitive data being transmitted through the air, without any level of confidentiality. The temporary answer to this was to use Wired Equivalency Protection (WEP). WEP was not very secure (as history has confirmed), but it provided an extra level of protection designed to bring wireless connections to the same security-level as a wired network.

Well, the fun part (for geeks like me) is that wireless networks quickly became even more secure than wired networks. As described many times in this book so far, 802.1X authentication took off like a rocket in wireless networks, and enhancements were made to the encryption and keying mechanisms (such as WiFi Protected Access [WPA/WPA2] using AES encryption). So, wireless networks had full encryption mechanisms to provide the confidentiality and integrity of data traversing the Layer 2 hop from the endpoint into the network infrastructure, in addition to the strong identity capabilities of 802.1X.

Wireless Equivalency was necessary for wired networks to provide equivalent confidentiality and integrity. What was the answer? Should IPSec be employed on every endpoint to every other endpoint, encrypting the entire communication from end-to-end? If that was done, how could you provide strong levels of quality of service (QoS) if you couldn't see the content of a packet, and how could you glean into the packet to ensure security with all the Security tooling that you invested in? If you used end-to-end IPsec, you would simply be encrypting both good and bad traffic across the network.

The answer was to provide Wireless Equivalency. A viable alternative to end-to-end IPsec was to layer on the confidentiality and integrity using IEEE 802.1AE (a.k.a. MACSec). MACSec provides Layer 2 encryption on the LAN between endpoints and the switch, as well as between the switches themselves. Figure 26-1 provides a logical representation of MACSec.

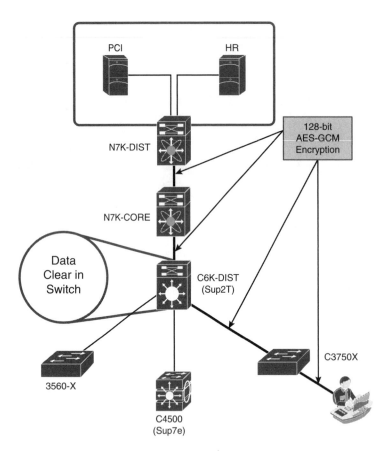

Figure 26-1   *MACSec Layer 2 Hop-by-Hop Encryption*

MACSec

As described in this chapter's introduction, MACSec (IEEE 802.1AE) provides Layer 2 encryption on the LAN. The encryption also encapsulates and protects the Cisco Meta Data (CMD) field, which carries the Security Group Tag (SGT), which is described in Chapter 25, "Secure Group Access."

Currently, two keying mechanisms are available, both using 128-bit AES-GCM (Galois/Counter Mode) symmetric encryption that is capable of line-rate encryption and decryption for both 1Gb- and 10Gb-Ethernet interfaces and provides replay attack protection of each and every frame.

The keying mechanisms are Security Association Protocol (SAP) and MAC Security Key Agreement (MKA). SAP is a Cisco-proprietary keying protocol used between Cisco switches, while MKA is going to be the industry standard and is currently used between endpoints and Cisco switches.

Downlink MACSec

Downlink MACSec is the term used to describe the encrypted link between an end-point and the switch. The encryption between the endpoint and the switch is handled by the MKA keying protocol. This requires a MACSec-capable switch (such as a Cisco Catalyst 3750-X), and a MACSec-capable supplicant on the endpoint (such as the Cisco AnyConnect Network Access Manager). The encryption on the endpoint may be handled in hardware (if the endpoint possesses the correct hardware) or in software using the main CPU for the encryption and decryption.

The Cisco switch has the ability to force encryption, make it optional, or force non-encryption; that setting may be configured manually per port (not common) or dynamically as an authorization result from ISE (more common). If ISE returns an encryption policy with the authorization result, the policy issued by ISE overrides anything set using the switch CLI.

Figure 26-2 shows the MACSec Policy within an Authorization Profile on ISE. Notice at the bottom that the attribute sent to the switch is cisco-av-pair=subscriber:linksec-policy, followed by the policy itself. The choices are Must-Secure, Should-Secure, and Must-Not-Secure. Example 26-1 shows these options on the switch CLI, and Table 26-1 displays the resulting policy based on the Supplicant Policy and Switch Policy.

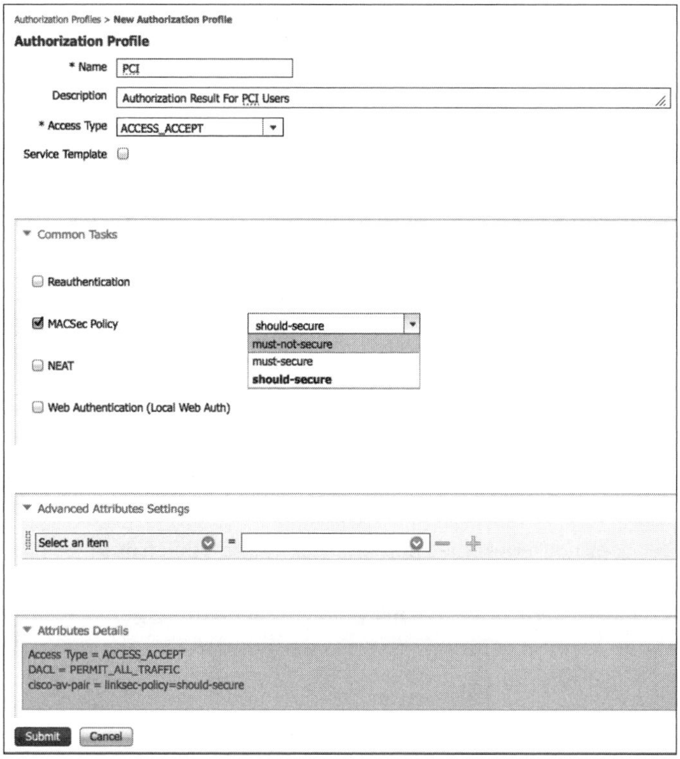

Figure 26-2 *Authorization Profile*

Example 26-1   *MACSec Policy Switch CLI*

```
C3750X(config-if)#authentication linksec policy ?
  must-not-secure  Never secure sessions
  must-secure      Always secure sessions
  should-secure    OPTIONALLY secure sessions
```

Table 26-1   *Resulting MACSec Policies*

Supplicant Policy	Switch Policy	Resulting Policy
Client Supplicant Not Capable of MACSec		
Not MACSec Capable	Not MACSec Capable	Not Secured
Not MACSec Capable	Must-Not-Secure	Not Secured
Not MACSec Capable	Should-Secure	Not Secured
Not MACSec Capable	Must-Secure	Blocked or Fallback
Client Supplicant Configured as "Must-Not-Secure"		
Must-Not-Secure	Not MACSec Capable	Not Secured
Must-Not-Secure	Must-Not-Secure	Not Secured
Must-Not-Secure	Should-Secure	Not Secured
Must-Not-Secure	Must-Secure	Blocked or Fallback
Client Supplicant Configured as "Should-Secure"		
Should-Secure	Not MACSec Capable	Not Secured
Should-Secure	Must-Not-Secure	Not Secured
Should-Secure	Should-Secure	Secured
Should-Secure	Must-Secure	Secured
Client Supplicant Configured as "Must-Secure"		
Must-Secure	Not MACSec Capable	Blocked
Must-Secure	Must-Not-Secure	Blocked
Must-Secure	Should-Secure	Secured
Must-Secure	Must-Secure	Secured

If the authentication server does not return the appropriate attribute-value pair to set the policy, the switch uses the configured policy on the port. If no policy is specified in the switch configuration, the switch reverts to the default policy of Should-Secure.

Switch Configuration Modes

Only a few configurations on the switch interface have implications for a MACSec deployment, such as the authentication host-mode. The host-mode plays an important role, because it determines the number of endpoints that may be connected to a single switch interface:

- **Single Mode:** MACSec is a fully supported in single-host-mode. In single-host-mode, only a single MAC or IP address can be authenticated and secured with MACSec. If a different MAC address is detected on the port after an endpoint has authenticated, a security violation will be triggered on the port.

- **Multi-Domain Authentication (MDA) Mode:** With this mode, a single endpoint may be on the Data domain, and another endpoint may be on the Voice domain. MACSec is fully supported in multi-domain authentication host mode. If both endpoints are MACSec capable, each is secured by its own independent MACSec session. If only one endpoint is MACSec capable, that endpoint is secured while the other endpoint sends traffic in the clear.

- **Multi-Authentication Mode:** With this mode, a virtually unlimited number of endpoints may be authenticated to a single switch port. MACSec is not supported in this mode.

- **Multi-Host Mode:** Although MACSec usage with this mode may technically be possible, it is not recommended. With Multi-Host Mode, the first endpoint on the port authenticates, and then any additional endpoints are permitted onto the network via the first authorization. So, MACSec works with the first connected host, but no other endpoint's traffic actually passes, because it isn't encrypted traffic.

Example 26-2 shows a switch interface configuration for MACSec-enabled endpoints. The example uses the default MACSec policy of Should-Secure and, therefore, the default setting is not displayed.

Example 26-2 *Switch Interface Configuration for MACSec*

```
interface X
 switchport access vlan 10
 switchport mode access
 switchport voice vlan 99
 ip access-group ACL-ALLOW in
 authentication event fail action next-method
 authentication event server dead action authorize vlan 2274
 authentication event server alive action reinitialize
```

```
authentication event linksec fail action next-method
authentication host-mode multi-domain
authentication open
authentication order dot1x mab
authentication priority dot1x mab
authentication port-control auto
authentication violation restrict
macsec
mka default-policy
mab
dot1x pae authenticator
dot1x timeout tx-period 10
spanning-tree portfast
end
```

ISE Configuration

Downlink MACSec is configured as attribute within the Authorization Profile (the result of an authorization). To add this result to an Authorization Profile, perform the following steps:

1. Navigate to **Policy > Policy Elements > Results.**

2. Choose **Authorization Profiles.**

3. Edit an Authorization Profile to which you want to add MACSec. (PCI was used in our example.)

4. Under Common Tasks, scroll to MACSec Policy.

5. Select must-secure, should-secure, or must-not-secure.

6. Click Submit or Save to save the change.

Figure 26-3 shows a MACSec policy being added to an Authorization Profile.

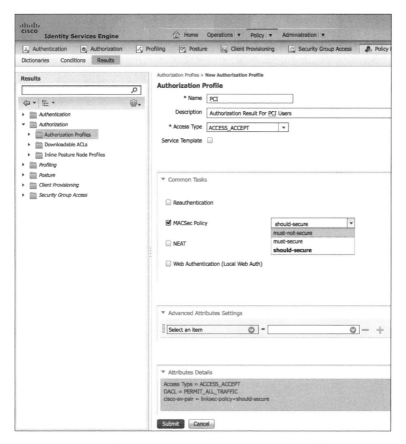

Figure 26-3   *Adding MACSec to an Authorization Profile*

Uplink MACSec

Uplink MACSec describes encrypting the link between the switches with 802.1AE. At the time this book was written, the switch-to-switch encryption used Cisco's proprietary Security Association Protocol (SAP) instead of MKA, which is used with the downlink MACSec. The encryption is still the same AES-GCM-128 encryption used with both Uplink and Downlink MACSec.

Uplink MACSec may be achieved manually or dynamically. Dynamic MACSec requires 802.1X between the switches and is covered in the section, "Network Device Admission Control (NDAC)." This section focuses on manual mode.

Manually Configuring Uplink MACSec

This method of MACSec is perfect to layer on top of the Manual SGT's configured as part of Chapter 25. It encrypts the inter-switch links without requiring the entire domain of trust (the way that NDAC does). It also removes the dependency on ISE for the link keying, similar to how an IPSEC tunnel is built using pre-shared keys.

Let's start by re-examining the configuration of your uplink interface as you had it configured at the end of Chapter 25.

With the configuration shown in Example 26-3, the uplink between the 3750-X and the 6500-Sup2T is set up to use manual keying, without any encryption at all, to apply Security Group Tags (SGT) to the frames. Now, layer encryption on top of this to provide confidentiality and integrity of the SGTs and the data. Figure 26-4 depicts the relevant infrastructure configuration used for this example.

Example 26-3 *Uplink Configuration from Chapter 25*

```
C3750X# show run int Ten 1/1/1
Building configuration...
Current configuration : 286 bytes
!
interface TenGigabitEthernet1/1/1
 description Cat6K Ten1/5
 no switchport
 ip address 10.1.48.2 255.255.255.252
 ip authentication mode eigrp 1 md5
 ip authentication key-chain eigrp 1 EIGRP
 load-interval 60
 cts manual
  policy static sgt 2 trusted
 no macro auto processing
end
```

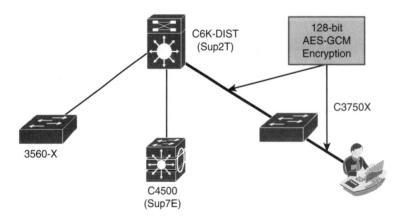

Figure 26-4 *Adding MACSec to the Uplink*

The following steps guide you through adding encryption to the interface:

1. From interface configuration mode, enter **cts manual**.

2. Enable encryption with the **sap pmk** *pairwise-master-key* **mode-list gcm-encrypt** command.

   The Pairwise Master Key (PMK) should be a hexadecimal value configured to be the same on both sides of the link. This master key can be compared to a RADIUS shared-secret between a NAD and ISE, or even the pre-shared key used with IPsec encryption. For the added security of dynamic keying, you must use NDAC.

3. Add the **sap pmk** *pairwise-master-key* **mode-list gcm-encrypt** command to the other side of the link.

Example 26-4 displays the example configuration steps, while Example 26-5 shows the final configuration for the uplink port on the 3750-X.

Example 26-4 *Adding Encryption to the Uplink Interface*

```
C3750X#conf t
Enter configuration commands, one per line. End with CNTL/Z.
C3750X(config)#int Ten1/1/1
C3750X(config-if)#cts manual
C3750X(config-if-cts-manual)#sap pmk 26 mode-list gcm-encrypt
C3750X(config-if-cts-manual)#end
C3750X#
```

Example 26-5 *Final Configuration for Uplink Interface*

```
C3750X#sho run int ten1/1/1
Building configuration...
Current configuration : 386 bytes
!
interface TenGigabitEthernet1/1/1
 description Cat6K Ten1/5
 no switchport
 ip address 10.1.48.2 255.255.255.252
 ip authentication mode eigrp 1 md5
 ip authentication key-chain eigrp 1 EIGRP
 load-interval 60
 cts manual
  policy static sgt 2 trusted
  sap pmk 00000000000000000000000000000000000000000000000000000000000000026 mode-list
gcm-encrypt
 no macro auto processing
end
```

Verifying the Manual Configuration

Validate that the manual encryption on the uplink was successful with the **show cts interface** command, as shown in Example 26-6. SAP status is the status of the encryption; in the example, notice that SAP succeeded, the pairwise cypher is using gcm-encrypt, and that replay protection is enabled.

Example 26-6   *Output of* **show cts interface** *Command*

```
C3750X#show cts interface TenGigabitEthernet 1/1/1
Global Dot1x feature is Enabled
Interface TenGigabitEthernet1/1/1:
    CTS is enabled, mode:    MANUAL
    IFC state:               OPEN
    Authentication Status:   NOT APPLICABLE
        Peer identity:       "unknown"
        Peer's advertised capabilities: "sap"
    Authorization Status:    SUCCEEDED
        Peer SGT:            2
        Peer SGT assignment: Trusted
    SAP Status:              SUCCEEDED
        Version:             2
        Configured pairwise ciphers:
            gcm-encrypt
        Replay protection:      enabled
        Replay protection mode: STRICT
        Selected cipher:        gcm-encrypt
    Propagate SGT:           Enabled
    Cache Info:
        Cache applied to link : NONE
    Statistics:
        authc success:            0
        authc reject:             0
        authc failure:            0
        authc no response:        0
        authc logoff:             0
        sap success:              2
        sap fail:                 0
        authz success:            5
        authz fail:               0
        port auth fail:           0
    L3 IPM:   disabled.
C3750X#
```

As you can see from this section, there is not much configuration necessary to use manual Uplink MACSec, assuming that you are using MACSec-capable hardware. However, there is still this concept of a "domain of trust" with the Secure Access solution—where you can authenticate and authorize any network devices before they participate in your infrastructure. To examine that domain of trust further, let's discuss Network Device Admission Control (NDAC).

Network Device Admission Control

The Secure Unified Access architecture builds secure networks by establishing domains of trusted network devices. The days of someone grabbing a rogue off-the-shelf switch and connecting it to your enterprise network infrastructure and possibly wreaking havoc are a thing of the past.

For a network device to be part of the network infrastructure and pass traffic, its peer(s) must first authenticate it. You are authenticating the switch via 802.1X, much like you are now authenticating the endpoints and users with 802.1X. However, once the device is allowed to join the network infrastructure, the communication on the links between devices is secured with MACSec. This process is known as Network Device Admission Control (NDAC).

There are three main roles within NDAC:

- **Supplicant:** The role of an unauthenticated switch connected to a peer within the trusted domain, and attempting to join that domain.

- **Authentication server:** The server that validates the identity of the supplicant and issues the policies to allow the device onto the network as well as being responsible for the encryption keys. This is the Cisco ISE server.

- **Authenticator:** An authenticated device that is already part of the trusted domain and can authenticate new peer supplicants on behalf of authentication server.

There is another role: seed device. There must be at least one seed device. This device has knowledge of at least one ISE Policy Service Node. The seed device begins or creates the NDAC-trusted domain. When a new switch is added to the network, a switch that's already a member of the NDAC domain authenticates it, as shown in Figure 26-5.

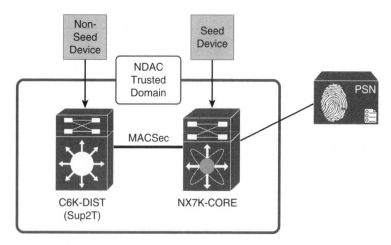

Figure 26-5   *NDAC Seed Device*

Creating an NDAC Domain

An NDAC domain is created when the first switch (known as the seed device) is authenticated and authorized by ISE.

Configuring ISE

The following steps prepare ISE for NDAC and SGA.

Perform the following steps from the ISE GUI:

1. Navigate to **Administration > Network Resources > Network Device Groups**.

2. Add a new Top-Level Device Group.

3. Name the Group and the Type SGA.

4. Create a new NDG named SGA-Device; the type should be SGA.

5. Create a new NDG named Non-SGA-Device; the type should be SGA.

Figure 26-6 shows the final Network Device Groups.

Now, add the switch to ISE as a NAD. This procedure may have been completed during Chapter 25; however, go through the screens in ISE and ensure it all configured correctly.

From the ISE GUI, perform the following steps:

1. Navigate to **Administration > Network Resources > Network Devices**.

2. If the switch is already in the device list, edit it. If not, add a new device.

3. Ensure that the RADIUS shared secret is configured.

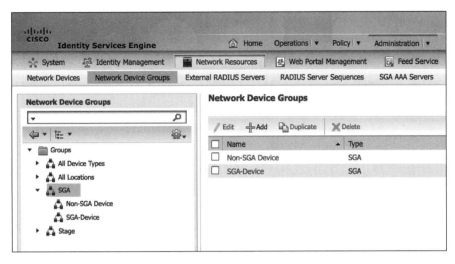

Figure 26-6   *SGA Network Device Groups*

4. Set the Network Device Groups. Specifically, assign the NAD to the SGA-Device NDG.

5. Enable the Advanced TrustSec Settings section of the NAD definition.

6. Here, you may use either the device-id for SGA Identification or configure a new name.

> **Note**   This name must match what you configure on the switch in later steps.

7. The Device Configuration Deployment section allows ISE to push SGT-to-IP mappings to the switch. This is optional, but if you want that functionality, add the exec and enable passwords.

8. Click **Save**.

9. Repeat Steps 1 through 8 for all network devices that participate in the NDAC trusted domain.

Figure 26-7 displays the completed Advanced TrustSec settings for a Nexus switch.

Once you submit a network device with the Advanced TrustSec Settings configured, the device name and password are added to a special internal identity store, known as Internal CTS Devices. This identity store is what will be used for the NDAC authentications.

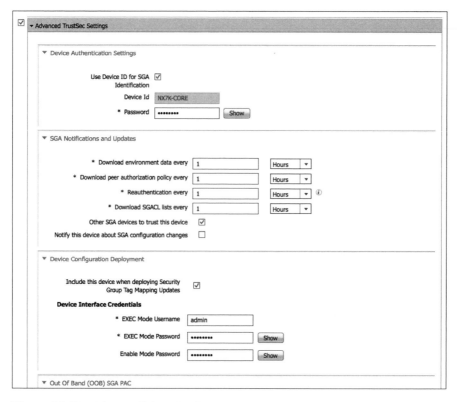

Figure 26-7   *Advanced TrustSec Settings*

The big difference between seed and non-seed devices is whether the device is configured with the list of AAA servers for NDAC. Instead, it gets the list of AAA servers from
the seed device. To build the list of AAA servers to be sent to non-seed devices, add it to
the SGA AAA Servers list within ISE:

1. Navigate to **Administration > Network Resources > SGA AAA Servers**.

2. Click **Add**.

3. Enter the PSN name.

4. Enter the PSN IP address.

5. Click **Submit**.

6. Repeat Steps 2 through 5 for all PSNs that will be involved with NDAC.

Figure 26-8 shows an example list of two AAA servers to be sent to the non-seed
devices.

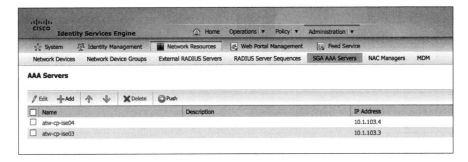

Figure 26-8 *SGA AAA Servers*

Create a Network Authorization Policy for the switches to be assigned an SGT and permitted to join the NDAC Trusted Domain:

1. Navigate to **Policy > Security Group Access > Network Device Authorization**.

2. Insert a rule above the default rule.

3. Name the rule SGA Devices.

4. Set the condition to be SGA equals SGA-Device. This is using the Network Device Group you created earlier in this chapter.

5. Set the resulting security group to be the NADs group created in Chapter 25 (SGT = 2).

6. Click **Done**.

7. Click **Save**.

Figure 26-9 shows a simple NDAC policy.

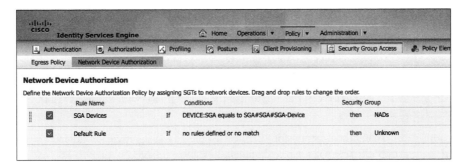

Figure 26-9 *Network Device Authorization Policy*

Configuring the Seed Device

Now that ISE is prepared, it is time to configure the first switch of the NDAC trusted domain, the seed device. For this example, let's use the Nexus core switch as the seed device, shown in Figure 26-5. All switches may be configured as seed devices, if that is your choice.

From the switch CLI, perform the following steps:

1. Enter **show dot1x** to see if the feature is enabled from Chapter 25. If it is not, type **feature dot1x** from global configuration mode.

2. Enter **show cts** and validate that the feature is enabled from Chapter 25. If not, type **feature cts** from global configuration mode.

3. Set the CTS device-id at global configuration mode using the **cts device-id** *device-id* **password** *password* command.

> **Note** This device-id and password must match exactly what was configured in the network device definition within ISE.

4. Add ISE to the configuration with the **radius-server host** *ip-address* **key** *shared-secret* **pac**.

> **Note** The **pac** keyword is used to configure the Nexus switch to download a Protected Access Credential (PAC) that will be used to secure the RADIUS transactions.

5. Repeat Step 4 for all applicable RADIUS servers.

6. Create a RADIUS server group with the **aaa group server radius** *group-name* command.

7. Add the servers to the group with the **server** *ip-address* command.

8. Repeat Step 7 for all applicable servers.

9. Configure the RADIUS server group to use the correct VRF with the **use-vrf** *vrf-name* command.

10. Configure AAA authentication for 802.1X with the **aaa authentication dot1x default group** *radius-group-name* command.

11. Configure AAA accounting for 802.1X with the **aaa accounting dot1x default group** *radius-group-name* command.

12. Configure CTS authorization for 802.1X with the **aaa authorization cts default group** *radius-group-name* command.

13. Re-enter the **cts device-id** *device-id* **password** *password* command to trigger an immediate download of the PAC file.

Example 26-7 shows an example configuration on the Nexus 7000 Core switch.

Example 26-7 *Configuring the Nexus 7000 Seed Device*

```
NX7K-CORE(config)# cts device-id NX7K-CORE password Cisco123
NX7K-CORE(config)# radius-server host 10.1.103.4 key Cisco123 pac
NX7K-CORE(config)# radius-server host 10.1.103.3 key Cisco123 pac
NX7K-CORE(config)# aaa group server radius ise
NX7K-CORE(config-radius)# server 10.1.103.4
NX7K-CORE(config-radius)# server 10.1.103.3
NX7K-CORE(config-radius)# use-vrf default
NX7K-CORE(config)# aaa authentication dot1x default group ise
NX7K-CORE(config)# aaa accounting dot1x default group ise
NX7K-CORE(config)# aaa authorization cts default group ise
NX7K-CORE(config)# cts device-id NX7K-CORE password Cisco123
NX7K-CORE(config)#
NX7K-CORE(config)# sho cts pac
PAC Info :
===============================
  PAC Type           : Trustsec
  AID                : 01ecb966907841dd6af9cfdc810c3d4e
  I-ID               : NX7K-CORE
  AID Info           : Identity Services Engine
  Credential Lifetime : Wed Mar 27 14:51:01 2013
  PAC Opaque         : 000200b8000300010004001001ecb966907841dd6af9cfdc810c3d4e
0006009c00030100eb281feae6759891966c609335bb71930000001350d502f300093a805f1acdce
863015e76decbd96e98d628146738491ef414d34d5c4685d09fdec04dbfbb46ebee17174e4b75403
a10e29014032189c3c1cba408261f5862dbaee1e9c275bcc264267bdce1333baeaa370aa7e49f97e
0c353b620badb4ca00a185af6fb1b7e0c5a12407c7ecfd2284f2aa50e168640040eeefe8ca9c4e7d

NX7K-CORE(config)#
NX7K-CORE(config)# sho cts environment-data
CTS Environment Data
===============================
  Current State      : CTS_ENV_DNLD_ST_ENV_DOWNLOAD_DONE
  Last Status        : CTS_ENV_SUCCESS
  Local Device SGT    : 0x0002
  Transport Type      : CTS_ENV_TRANSPORT_DIRECT
  Data loaded from cache : FALSE
  Env Data Lifetime   : 600 seconds after last update
  Last Update Time    : Thu Dec 27 14:09:43 2012
  Server List         : CTSServerList1
```

```
AID:01ecb966907841dd6af9cfdc810c3d4e IP:10.1.103.4 Port:1812
AID:01ecb966907841dd6af9cfdc810c3d4e IP:10.1.103.3 Port:1812
```

Example 26-8 shows an example configuration on the Catalyst 6500 Sup2T Distribution switch.

Example 26-8   *Configuration of a Catalyst 6500 Seed Device*

```
C6K-DIST#cts credentials id C6K-DIST password Cisco123
CTS device ID and password have been inserted in the local keystore.
Please make sure that the same ID and password are configured in the
server database.
C6K-DIST(config)#cts authorization list default
C6K-DIST(config)#radius-server host 10.1.103.3 auth-port 1812 acct-
port 1813 test username radius-test pac key Cisco123
Request successfully sent to PAC Provisioning driver.
C6K-DIST(config)#radius-server host 10.1.103.4 auth-port 1812 acct-
port 1813 test username radius-test pac key Cisco123
Request successfully sent to PAC Provisioning driver.
Note: the pac keyword in the radius-server configuration is
essential, to ensure the RADIUS communication between the switch and
ISE is secured for NDAC.
C6K-DIST(config)#radius-server vsa send authentication !(this will
most likely be configured already)
C6K-DIST(config)#dot1x system-auth-control !(this will most likely be
configured already)
```

Adding Non-Seed Switches

A non-seed device does not have a configuration to locate the AAA servers to use with NDAC. Instead, the list is downloaded from the seed device. However, the device still needs to be added to ISE as a network device, which was accomplished in an earlier procedure.

It is not required to use any non-seed devices, but it is a viable option and, therefore, is covered in this chapter. For these examples, let's configure the 3750X as a non-seed device, and all other switches will be configured as seed devices.

Figure 26-10 displays the example NDAC environment.

The majority of the configuration required to be a non-seed device has been accomplished when bootstrapping the device to work with ISE in Chapter 11, "Bootstrapping Network Access Devices."

The CTS credentials must be entered into the device, just as with the seed device, as shown in Example 26-9.

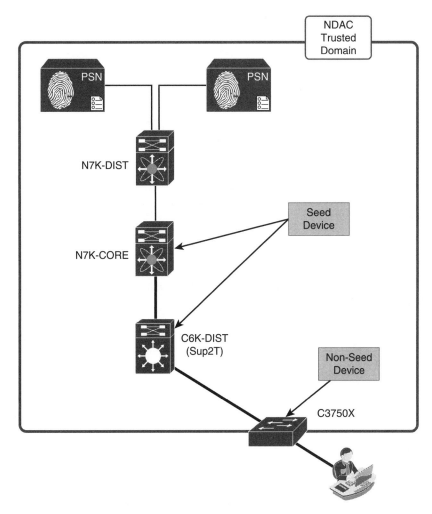

Figure 26-10 *Example NDAC Environment*

Example 26-9 *3750-X Non-Seed Device Configuration*

```
C3750X#cts credentials id C3750X password Cisco123
CTS device ID and password have been inserted in the local keystore.
Please make sure that the same ID and password are configured in the
server database.
```

The next set of commands should already be configured in the switch from Chapter 11:

```
C3750X(config)#aaa new-model
C3750X(config)#aaa authentication dot1x default group radius
C3750X(config)#aaa authorization network default group radius
```

```
C3750X(config)#aaa accounting dot1x default start-stop group radius
C3750X(config)#radius-server vsa send authentication
C3750X(config)#dot1x system-auth-control
```

Configuring the Switch Interfaces for Both Seed and Non-Seed

Once the global configuration is complete, all that is truly needed for the switch interfaces is to enter the **cts dot1x** command on the interfaces that are to be trusted in NDAC, as shown in Example 26-10.

Example 26-10   *Enabling NDAC on the Interface*

```
C3750X(config)#int Ten1/1/1
C3750X(config-if)#cts dot1x
C3750X(config-if-cts-dot1x)#
```

To verify the interface activities, use the **show cts interface** *interface-name* command as shown in Example 26-11.

Example 26-11   *Verifying Interface Activities with* **show cts interface**

```
C6K-DIST#sho cts interface
Global Dot1x feature is Enabled
Interface TenGigabitEthernet1/5:
    CTS is enabled, mode:    DOT1X
    IFC state:               OPEN
    Authentication Status:   SUCCEEDED
        Peer identity:        "C3750X"
        Peer's advertised capabilities: "sap"
        802.1X role:          Authenticator
        Reauth period configured:     86400 (default)
        Reauth period per policy:     86400 (server configured)
        Reauth period applied to link: 86400 (server configured)
        Reauth starts in approx. 0:14:11:09 (dd:hr:mm:sec)
    Authorization Status:    SUCCEEDED
        Peer SGT:             2:NADs
        Peer SGT assignment: Trusted
    SAP Status:              SUCCEEDED
        Version:              2
        Configured pairwise ciphers:
            gcm-encrypt
            null
        Replay protection:      enabled
        Replay protection mode: STRICT
```

```
    Selected cipher:        gcm-encrypt
  Propagate SGT:        Enabled
  Cache Info:
    Cache applied to link : NONE
  Statistics:
    authc success:            4890
    authc reject:             40
    authc failure:            11
    authc no response:        0
    authc logoff:             31
    sap success:              2
    sap fail:                 0
    authz success:            19
    authz fail:               4871
    port auth fail:           0
  L3 IPM:   disabled.
Dot1x Info for TenGigabitEthernet1/5
----------------------------------
PAE                      = AUTHENTICATOR
QuietPeriod              = 60
ServerTimeout            = 0
SuppTimeout              = 30
ReAuthMax                = 2
MaxReq                   = 2
TxPeriod                 = 30
```

MACSec Sequence in an NDAC Domain

When the link between a supplicant and an authenticator first appears, the following sequence of events typically occurs:

1. **Authentication:** Using Network Device Admission Control (NDAC), ISE authenticates a device using EAP-FAST before allowing it to join the network. During the EAP-FAST exchange, ISE creates and sends a unique protected access credential (PAC) to the supplicant switch (the switch attempting to join the NDAC domain). That PAC contains a shared key and an encrypted token for future secure communications with the authentication server.

2. **Authorization:** Based on the identity information of the supplicant switch, ISE provides authorization policies to each of the linked peers. The authentication server provides the identity of each peer to the other, and each peer then applies the appropriate policy for the link.

3. **SAP negotiation:** When both sides of a link support encryption, the supplicant and the authenticator negotiate the necessary parameters to establish a security association (SA) and encrypt the traffic.

4. When all three steps are complete, the authenticator changes the state of the link from the unauthorized (blocking) state to the authorized state, and the supplicant switch becomes a member of the NDAC trusted domain.

Summary

In Chapter 25, you learned about Security Group Access (SGA) and the ability to apply a tag to traffic based on the contextual identity of the endpoint or user; you also learned how to apply this traffic manually, and without the inherent security associated with a domain of trusted devices, using strong encryption between them.

In this chapter, you learned about Network Device Admission Control (NDAC) and IEEE 802.1AE (MACSec), where all the Cisco devices in the network are authorized before being added to the network, and all devices can form a trusted domain, which encrypts all traffic (including the SGT) across network links between those trusted devices.

Chapter 27, "Network Edge Access Topology," briefly focuses on another addition to this trusted-domain approach, meant for conference rooms where wired connectivity is a requirement. This technology is known as Network Edge Access Topology (NEAT).

Chapter 27

Network Edge Authentication Topology

A friend of ours, Chuck Parker, is a systems engineer at Cisco who was responsible for one of the largest deployments of 802.1X in the world. Chuck has this wonderful expression that I want to share with you: "When it comes to network security, if it's not everywhere, it's nowhere."

Let's look at a specific example of a business problem: conference room network access. Most conference rooms have few network drops in them, where a guest or an employee may be able to plug in and gain access to the network or the Internet. These conference rooms may often need more connections than exist. If wireless is not an option, how does a company securely permit this access? Many organizations would want to put unmanaged switches in the conference room, similar to a hub. However, that most likely will not meet the security requirements of the organization.

Another option might be to physically place a switch in each conference room and configure the ports at the wall to be trunk ports using NDAC to authenticate any switches that plug into that port. However, that is not cost-effective. It also has ramifications where endpoints would not be able to plug directly into the wall, because the port was configured to be a trunk port.

What is needed is the ability to have portable switches that can be placed on the conference room table and authenticate to the network in a fashion similar to an endpoint. It should have the ability to trunk to the network and apply a multitude of authorization results, such as assigning different VLANs to each endpoint in the conference room to provide the maximum flexibility and cost-effectiveness.

Enter the Network Edge Authentication Topology (NEAT) solution. This solution allows the conference room port on the access switch to be configured to support either an endpoint or another switch.

NEAT Explained

The NEAT solution extends secure access into areas beyond the wiring closet (such as conference rooms). As illustrated in Figure 27-1, NEAT allows you to configure a switch to act as a supplicant to another switch. Thus, with NEAT enabled, the desktop switch can authenticate itself to the access switch.

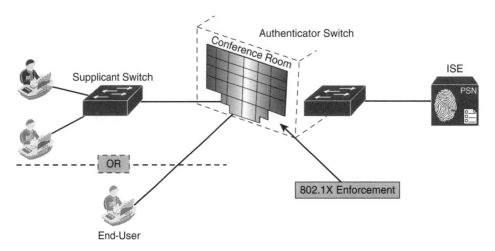

Figure 27-1   *NEAT Illustrated*

The pieces of the NEAT puzzle include

- **Client Information Signaling Protocol (CISP):** Developed for switch-to-switch communications. CISP is used for the access layer switch (authenticator switch) to recognize the supplicant as a switch and not an endpoint.

- **802.1X supplicant switch:** The "desktop" switch that connects to the access layer switch. The switch configured with the 802.1X switch supplicant feature authenticates with the upstream switch for secure connectivity. Once the supplicant switch authenticates successfully, the port mode changes from access to trunk.

- **Authenticator switch:** The authenticator switch is the access layer switch. Its ports are configured like all the other ports in the access layer, with one exception: CISP is enabled.

You can configure NEAT ports with the same configurations as the other authentication ports. When the supplicant switch successfully authenticates, ISE must be configured to return the switch vendor-specific attributes (VSA) (device-traffic-class=switch) along with the authorization result.

Receiving that VSA in the RADIUS result changes the authenticator switch port mode from an access port to a trunk port and enables 802.1X trunk encapsulation. The access VLAN (if any) is converted to a native trunk VLAN. The VSA result does not change any of the port configurations on the supplicant.

Configuring NEAT

The configuration of the NEAT solution requires an authorization policy on ISE, and some basic configuration on the authenticator and supplicant switches.

Preparing ISE for NEAT

The NEAT authentication uses a username and password combination. To keep this simple, first create a new user identity group called service accounts, and then a new internal user named neat. After that is prepared, create a new authorization profile for NEAT authentications that sends the correct VSA, followed by a new authorization rule for these authentications.

Create the User Identity Group and Identity

The following steps walk through adding a local user identity group for service accounts. This group may already exist if you have created one for wireless access points or other network devices. You then create a local user for the authentication and authorization of NEAT switches:

1. Navigate to **Administrator > Identity Management > Groups**.

2. Add a new user identity group named **Service Accounts**.

3. Navigate to **Administration > Identity Management > Identities**.

4. Add a new User named **neat**.

5. Provide a strong password for the user account.

6. Add the user to the Service Accounts user group.

7. Click **Submit**.

Figure 27-2 shows the completed neat user account to be used for the authentications.

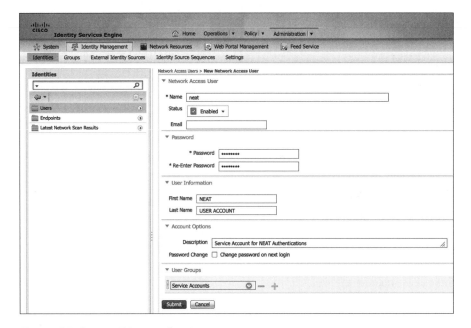

Figure 27-2   *NEAT User Identity*

Create the Authorization Profile

The following steps walk through adding an authorization profile for successful NEAT authentications that includes a RADIUS access-accept and the appropriate Cisco Attribute Value Pairs (AVP):

1. Navigate to **Policy > Policy Elements > Results**.

2. Choose **Authorization > Authorization Profiles**.

3. Click **Add**.

4. Name the Authorization Profile **NEAT**.

5. Access type should be **Access-Accept**.

6. In the Common Tasks, scroll down and select **NEAT**. Notice the Attribute Details section; the VSA of cisco-av-pairs = device-traffic-class=switch will be sent in the authorization result.

7. Click **Submit**.

Figure 27-3 shows the completed NEAT authorization profile.

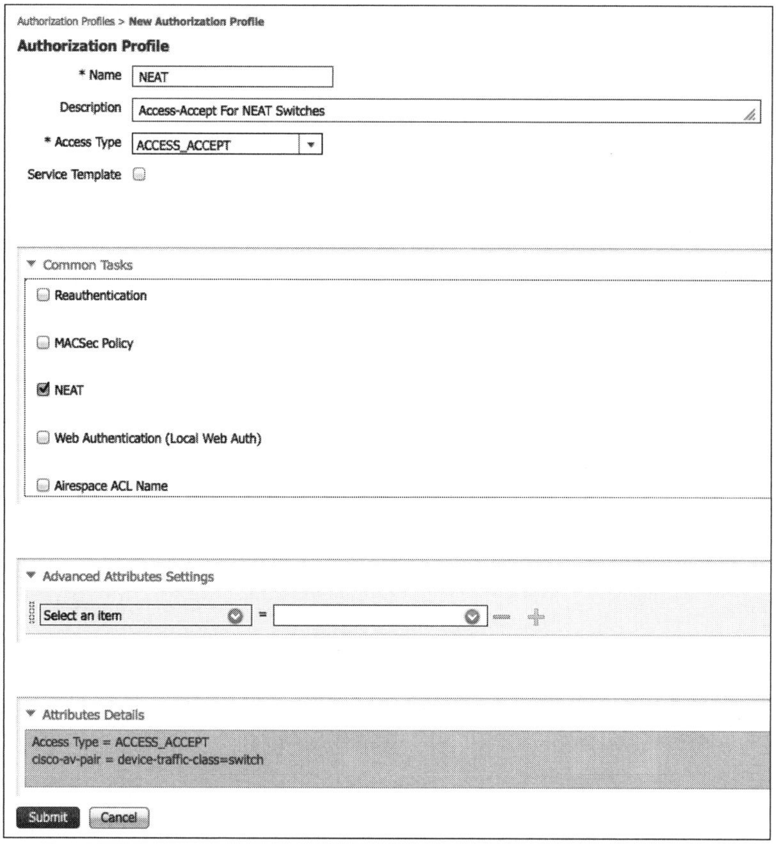

Figure 27-3 *NEAT Authorization Profile*

Create the Authorization Rule

The following steps walk through adding a rule in the authorization table for NEAT authentications that assigns the newly created NEAT authorization profile:

1. Navigate to **Policy > Authorization**.

2. Insert a new authorization rule named NEAT.

3. Set the condition to be

   a. InternalUser:Name EQUALS neat

   And

   b. NetworkAccess:AuthenticationStatus EQUALS AuthenticationPassed

4. Set the result to be the authorization profile we created named NEAT.

5. Click **Done** and **Save**.

Figure 27-4 displays an authorization policy that includes the NEAT authorization rule.

Figure 27-4 *NEAT Authorization Rule*

Access Switch (Authenticator) Configuration

The access switch is also known as the authenticator switch. This device is configured to authenticate endpoints at the access layer, which you connect a desktop switch to. Figure 27-1 illustrates the difference between the switches.

The only difference between a normal access switch and one that is used as an authenticator for NEAT is the enabling of CISP at global configuration mode, as shown in Example 27-1. Otherwise, your switch should be configured as described in Chapter 11, "Bootstrapping Network Access Devices."

Example 27-1 *Enabling NEAT on the Authenticator Switch*

```
C3750X#conf t
Enter configuration commands, one per line. End with CNTL/Z.
C3750X(config)#cisp enable
C3750X(config)#end
C3750X#
```

Desktop Switch (Supplicant) Configuration

The desktop switch is also known as the supplicant switch. This is usually a compact switch (like a Catalyst 3560-CG) and is the device that is placed in the conference room to authenticate to the network and, in turn, allow the end users to authenticate. Figure 27-1 illustrates the difference between the switches.

Unlike a normal access layer switch, notice that the desktop switch is not added to ISE a NAD, nor is a RADIUS server configured on the NEAT desktop switch. Example 27-2 displays the configuration of a supplicant switch.

Example 27-2 *Enabling NEAT on the Supplicant Switch*

```
C3560CG#conf t
Enter configuration commands, one per line. End with CNTL/Z.
C3560CG(config)#username neat password Cisco123
C3560CG(config)#cisp enable
```

```
C3560CG(config)#dot1x credentials neat
C3560CG(config-dot1x-creden)#username neat
C3560CG(config-dot1x-creden)#password Cisco123
C3560CG(config-dot1x-creden)#exit
C3560CG(config)#dot1x supplicant force-multicast
C3560CG(config)#interface gig0/24
C3560CG(config-if)#switchport trunk encap dot1q
C3560CG(config-if)#switchport mode trunk
C3560CG(config-if)#dot1x pae supplicant
C3560CG(config-if)#dot1x credentials neat
C3560CG(config-if)#end
```

Summary

This chapter introduced and explained the configuration for Network Edge Authentication Topology (NEAT), which is a technology created to allow for switch-to-switch authentication and provisioning. NEAT and NDAC are mutually exclusive, meaning you either perform NEAT or NDAC (for the desktop switch).

NEAT was developed for mini-switches that are dynamically connected to the access layer ports without the need to configure the access layer port any differently.

Chapter 28

Understanding Monitoring and Alerting

This chapter introduces you to the monitoring, reporting, and alerting functions inside of the Identity Services Engine (ISE). Monitoring provides you with real-time or close-to-real-time data depicting the various activities, functions, and processes that ISE performs. Monitoring gives you an important operational tool for the daily usage of ISE and is key to the long-term success of an ISE deployment. Reporting provides you with non-real-time information that is typically based on either a time frame or number of events. Examples of reports are top-client authentication, all authentications yesterday, administrator changes last month, and so on. The catalog of reports that ISE provides are meant to assist with analyzing trends, performance, and activities over time. Reports can also be run periodically or scheduled and then emailed and/or stored on completion. ISE-alerting functions are handled by alarms. ISE alarms notify you when critical events occur or thresholds are met/crossed. Alarms are also sent when ISE completes some system functions, like database purge, so you know it has been completed. ISE alarms are divided into multiple categories and are sent real-time when an alert is triggered. Let's look at monitoring first.

ISE Monitoring

ISE displays monitoring information in many places, but the most prominent is the ISE dashboard. As shown in Figure 28-1, the dashboard provides a live snapshot of many different activities. Unless otherwise noted, the information shown is for a 24-hour period. Each one of these is called a *dashlet*.

Figure 28-1 also shows the elements within the dashboard. For more information on an element, hover your mouse over it. Additionally, many of the elements are clickable and provide you with a drill-down view. You should explore the drill-down views of the dashboard elements and become familiar with them. The description of each element is shown in Table 28-1.

Figure 28-1   *ISE Dashboard*

Table 28-1   *ISE Dashboard Elements*

ISE Dashboard Element	Name	Description
1	Metrics	This dashlet summarizes the most important live information on the state of ISE.
2	System Summary	Provides system-health information for each ISE node. Hover over the green check box to see a status of each service.
3	Alarms	List of current alarms. Click them for more detail and a description of the alarm.
4	Authentications	Passed/failed auths and a distribution of auths by type.
5	Profiler Activity	Profiled devices in the last 24 hours and last 60 minutes.
6	Posture Compliance	Security posture of devices by status and OS type over last 24 hours and 60 minutes.

Live Authentications Log

This is perhaps the most useful monitoring tool that the ISE has. It can be used for monitoring and for troubleshooting. This section covers just the monitoring aspects of the Live Authentication page. Figure 28-2 displays the live authentications.

The filtering options with this list are extensive. At the top of every column, you have a filter box. This filter box allows for complete or partial matches but not compound conditions. For example, you could input 00:13 in the endpoint ID filter, and it shows you all devices with 00:13 anywhere in their MAC address. You can also sort by time or status by clicking the column headers. In the top right, notice a few additional fields you can change: refresh rate, show number of records, and within a timeframe. On active networks, setting the refresh rate to fast causes the page to hang. On the top left, you can change the view style of the Live Authentication page. Just click the **Show Live Authentication** button.

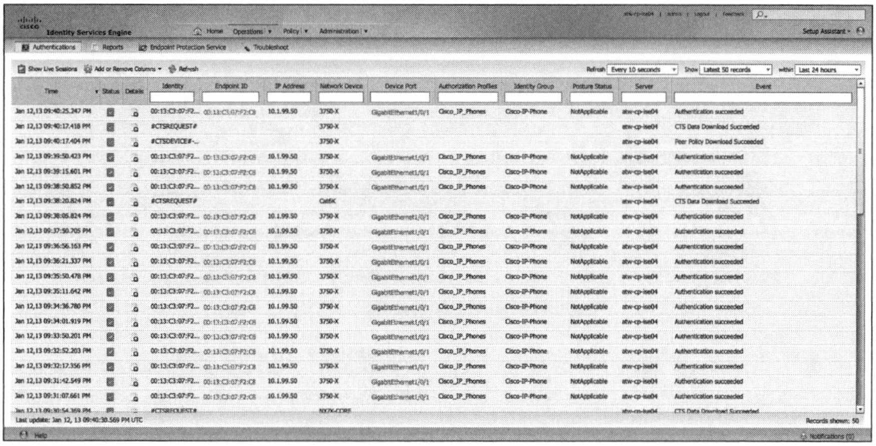

Figure 28-2 *ISE Live Authentications*

This alternate view also provides you with additional options. In Figure 28-3, this view creates a folder like hierarchy-based NAS IP address and port number. The folders are then default sorted by last authentication initiated.

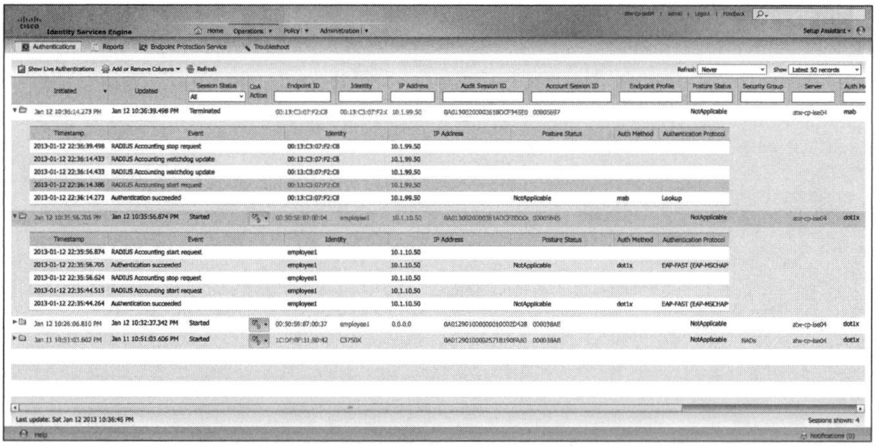

Figure 28-3 *ISE Live Authentications Alternate View*

Also, notice on the view that you can initiate a Change of Authentication (CoA) action. Figure 28-4 shows the various CoA actions that can be taken. These actions affect the switch port and, depending on the action taken, one or more devices attached to the switch port. Use this with care so you don't affect unintended hosts.

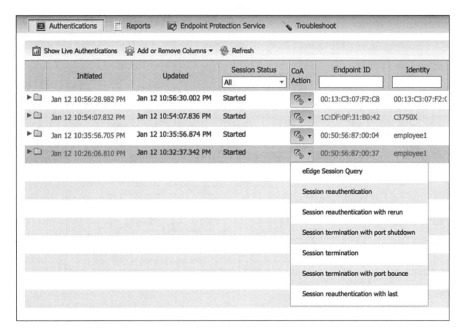

Figure 28-4   *ISE Live Authentications CoA Action*

Monitoring Endpoints

ISE includes an endpoint identity monitoring tool. This is updated real-time. Figure 28-5 shows the list of devices. This list is default sorted by endpoint profile, but can be searched using the show quick or advanced filters. In the top right, it also provides you with a count of all devices ISE has ever seen since its last database purge.

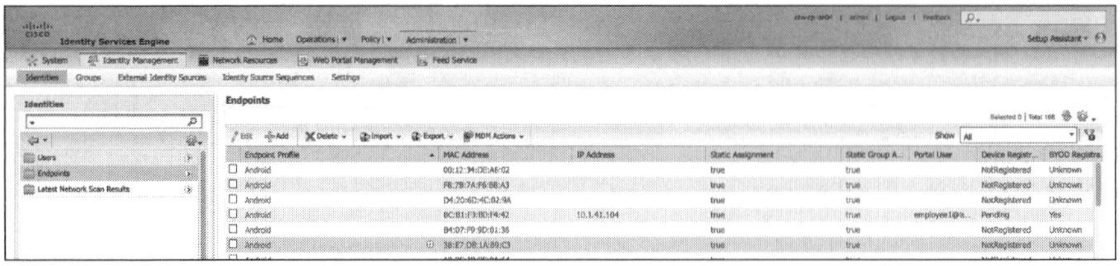

Figure 28-5   *ISE Endpoint List*

You can also delete and add endpoints from here. Clicking an endpoint shows you all the profile, location, and attribute information ISE has on that MAC address.

In addition, if you have attached a compatible third-party mobile device management (MDM) system to ISE, you can assess MDM features from this page. Clicking the MDM Actions button reveals three actions:

- Full Wipe
- Corporate Wipe
- Pin Lock

ISE then notifies the MDM to initiate the action you choose for the devices selected.

Global Search

The Global Search function, positioned at the top of the ISE GUI, enables you to find endpoints. Here is a list of search criteria you can enter into global search:

- User name
- MAC address
- IP address
- Authorization profile
- Endpoint profile
- Failure reason
- Identity group
- Identity store
- Network device name
- Network device type
- Operating system
- Posture status
- Location
- Security group
- User Type

With global search, the most popular search criteria are username, device name, IP address, and failure reason.

Figure 28-6 shows the results of searching for a switch device name containing 3750-x. As you can see, a lot of information is broken down by distribution.

Figure 28-6 *ISE Global Search*

The search result shows a detailed current status of the device. At the top, notice live statistics on connection status. Clicking a device shows you the latest session trace (see Figure 28-7).

From here, click the **Endpoint Details** button or go back to the **search results** by clicking that button. The endpoint details displays a wealth of information on the selected device. It shows authentication, accounting, and profiler data. Figure 28-8 presents an example of authentication detail. Notice that there are several other buttons (Result | Other attributes | Steps) to see more info. All this data can be exported as a formatted text file.

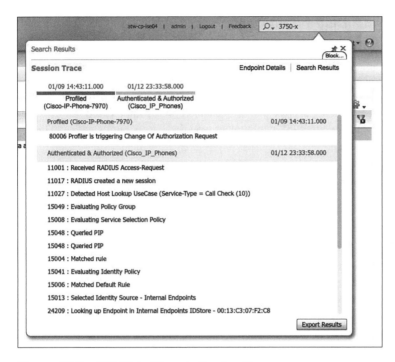

Figure 28-7   *ISE Global Search: Session Trace*

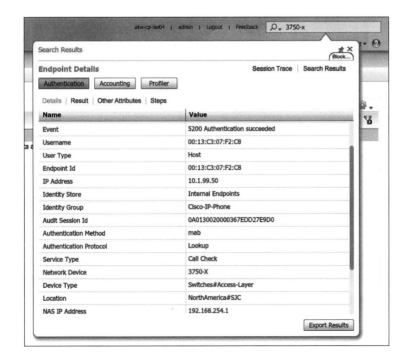

Figure 28-8   *ISE Global Search: Endpoint Details*

Monitoring Node in a Distributed Deployment

In larger deployments, it is required to set up a dedicated ISE monitoring node. A Cisco ISE node with this persona functions as the log collector and stores log messages from all the administration and Policy Service ISE nodes in your network. At least one node in your distributed setup must assume the monitoring persona. It is a best practice to not have the Monitoring and Policy Service personas enabled on the same Cisco ISE node. It is recommended that, in a larger ISE deployment, you dedicate a pair of nodes to be monitoring nodes.

Device Configuration for Monitoring

For ISE to properly monitor your system, it must receive the appropriate information from network access devices (NAD). This requires that the NADs be configured properly. This section provides some examples of proper NAD configuration.

Cisco ISE monitoring requires that the logging source-interface of a NAD be the same as the network access server (NAS) IP address configured in ISE. This allows ISE to correctly associate log messages with the proper NAD source. To accomplish this, configure the source-interface command on the NAD devices. The value of source-interface should be the same as the NAS IP address configured in ISE. Here is the command syntax for iOS:

```
logging source-interface type number
!sets the IP address associated with fastethernet 0/1 as the syslog message
source.
logging source-interface fastethernet 0/1
```

The next command you want to have on your Cisco access switches is the global command **epm logging**. EPM is short for Policy Enforced Module. EPM logging messages are displayed during the following switch events:

- **POLICY_APP_SUCCESS:** Policy application success events on named ACLs, proxy ACLs, service policies, and URL redirect policies.

- **POLICY_APP_FAILURE:** Policy application failure conditions similar to unconfigured policies, wrong policies, download request failures, and download failures from AAA.

- **IPEVENT:** IP assignment, IP release, and IP wait events for clients.

- **AAA:** AAA events (similar to download requests or download successes from AAA)

Finally, you need to send switch syslog messages over to the ISE monitoring node. Again, the source interface must be the ISE NAS IP. This configuration is straight forward:

```
logging monitor informational
logging origin-id ip
logging source-interface interface_id
logging host ISE Monitoring Node IP transport udp port 20514
```

For a complete list of the NAD syslogs that ISE collects, see the ISE user guide on cisco.com/go/ise.

ISE Reporting

The log data that the ISE collects are organized and available in reports. The reports aggregate the data in useful ways so that you can get a longer term view of ISE's operations. ISE provides a set of reports for you to use. Some customization is possible in these reports, but as of ISE version 1.2, fully customized reports are not available. To see the ISE reports, go to **Operations > Reports**. As shown in Figure 28-9, the ISE reports are grouped into four categories.

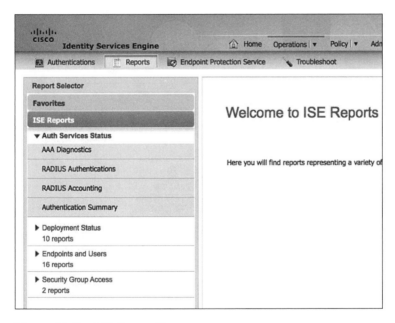

Figure 28-9 *ISE Report Groups*

Click any report to run it. As shown in Figure 28-10, you must select a time range and, if needed, filters.

You can then use these filters to customize the contents of the report.

In the upper right of the report screen, you see a few options. The first is **Favorite**; just click this button to put this report into your favorites. The second is **Export**; just click to export a CSV version of the currently run report. The third button is **Save As**. This has two options: **Report** and **Schedule Report**. Any saved or scheduled reports will show up in your left-hand pane under **Saved and Scheduled Reports**.

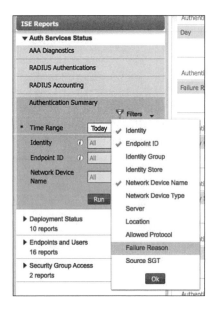

Figure 28-10   *Running Reports*

Data Repository Setup

If you don't already have a data repository set up or need to set up a new one, go to **Administration > System > Maintenance > Repository**. Click **Add**. Figure 28-11 shows the repository setup.

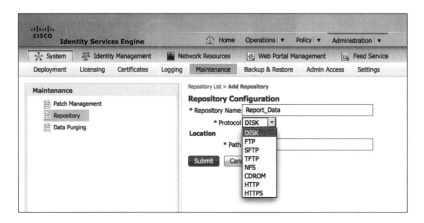

Figure 28-11   *Creating a Data Repository*

As you can see, there are many protocols you can use for data storage. Be careful when using **DISK**, as you may quickly run out of disk space on your ISE nodes. Any local repositories created on the Admin node are replicated to all other nodes.

ISE Alarms

ISE uses alarms to alert you to critical events or important system events. To customize alarms, go to **Administration > System > Settings > Alarm Settings**. As of ISE 1.2, you cannot create new alarms, but you can customize the default alarms. Some alarms allow more customization than others, but all alarms allow you to enable or disable them. To customize an alarm, select the alarm and click **Edit**. The settings shown in Figure 28-12 come from the **Excessive failed attempts** alarm.

Figure 28-12   *Editing Alarms*

In most cases, you do not need to customize the default alarms.

When an alarm fires, it shows up in a couple places in the ISE GUI. The first place is on the dashboard dashlet **Alarms**. Clicking an alarm brings up the alarm details, as shown in Figure 28-13.

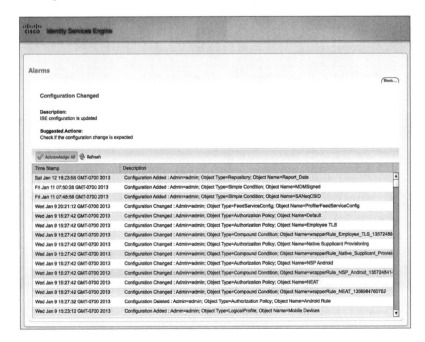

Figure 28-13   *Showing Alarm Details*

Click **Acknowledge** to remove the alarm from the active alarms. At any given point in time, only the latest 15,000 alarms are retained. If you want to send alarms to an email address or to a syslog server, you must configure these. For syslog setup, go to **Administration > System > Logging > Remote Logging Targets** and click **Add**. For email, go to **Administration > System > Settings > SMTP Server** and fill in the email server details.

Summary

This chapter explored the various monitoring, reporting, and alarms that the ISE offers. Key monitoring features, like the ISE dashboard, dashlets, and the useful Live Authentications page, were discussed. Key reporting and alarm configuration settings and their usage were also reviewed. A firm understanding of the features and their operations will help ensure the successful operation of your ISE deployment.

Chapter 29

Troubleshooting

Troubleshooting a product can sometimes get fairly complex. Troubleshooting a solution made up of multiple products is bound to get down-right difficult. The biggest tip we can give you is this: always stay calm, take your time, and think through the flows. Once you are comfortable with the Secure Unified Access solution and how the parts work together, troubleshooting it really is not bad at all.

This chapter attempts to provide you with a strong foundation by introducing proven troubleshooting methodologies for the Secure Unified Access solution and examining some of the built-in tools and tricks that have assisted us in the field.

We'll start off by introducing some of the tools that are provided within ISE.

Diagnostics Tools

Cisco ISE provides the following built-in tools to aid in your troubleshooting efforts:

- RADIUS Authentication Troubleshooting
- Evaluate Configuration Validator
- TCP Dump

We'll look at each in turn.

RADIUS Authentication Troubleshooting

The RADIUS Authentication Troubleshooting tool examines different aspects of a session and provides some additional details that may not have been available in the detailed authentication report. It also provides some suggestions for items to check next. To use this tool, follow these steps:

1. Navigate to **Operations > Troubleshoot > Diagnostic Tools > General Tools > RADIUS Authentication Troubleshooting,** as shown in Figure 29-1.

2. From here you may select any number of specifics to limit your search, such as a specific username, failed or passed authentication status, and more.

3. Select one of the entries presented as the result of the search, scroll to the bottom, and click **Troubleshoot.**

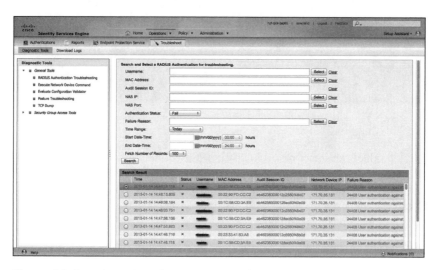

Figure 29-1   *RADIUS Authentication Troubleshooting Tool*

ISE will examine aspects of the session details, look for possible causes of an issue, and offer suggestions on possible fixes, as shown in Figure 29-2.

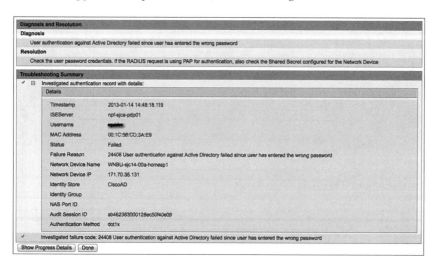

Figure 29-2   *RADIUS Authentication Troubleshooting Tool - Result*

In this simple example, either the user has mistyped their password or the Shared Secret is incorrect between the NAD and ISE. Differentiating which is truly the cause is impossible because the Shared Secret is used to encrypt the password between the endpoint and the RADIUS server, and the result of a mismatched Shared Secret is the same as the result of an incorrect password.

Evaluate Configuration Validator

This is a great tool...with a terrible name. This tool connects to a switch via Telnet, Secure Shell (SSH), or even through a console server. It examines the configuration, compares it to a "template" configuration built into ISE, and then reports any differences between the configurations. At the time of writing, the tool was overdue for an update, as explained next, but it still may provide a lot of value.

The following list explains why Evaluate Configuration Validator may misdiagnose as missing or incorrect a few of the common configurations:

- Evaluate Configuration Validator does not currently understand Device Sensor, and expects the use of SNMP for the SNMP probe(s).

- Evaluate Configuration Validator does not recognize the active test options when defining a RADIUS server, and therefore may think the RADIUS server definition is incorrect.

- WebAuth is Local WebAuth only, and the tool does not recognize that MAB is used for Centralized WebAuth instead.

Even with the limitations listed, this tool is still recognized by Cisco Technical Assistance Center (TAC) as being useful for quickly identifying a high number of misconfigurations, and in many cases would have prevented a customer from opening the TAC case.

The following steps show you how to run the Evaluate Configuration Validator tool:

1. Navigate to **Operations > Troubleshoot > Diagnostic Tools > General Tools > Evaluate Configuration Validator**, as shown in Figure 29-3.

2. From this screen, enter the IP address of the NAD, and choose which options you would like the tool to examine.

   In Figure 29-3, the check box for Web Authentication is unchecked because the tool is hard-coded to look for Local WebAuth (LWA), and not Centralized WebAuth (CWA).

3. Click **Run** to begin the evaluation.

4. ISE connects to the switch, and prompts for your interaction if the switch asks for user authentication or other interactive prompts, as shown in Figure 29-4. If prompted, click the **User Input Required** button, enter your credentials in the dialog box shown in Figure 29-5, and then click **Submit**.

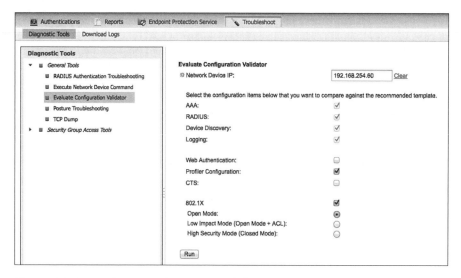

Figure 29-3   *Evaluate Configuration Validator*

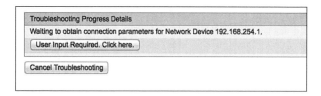

Figure 29-4   *User Input Required*

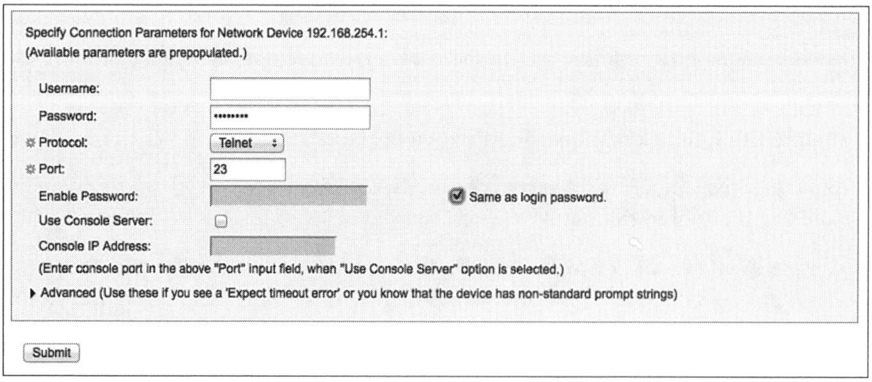

Figure 29-5   *Entering Credentials*

5. You should be prompted to select which interfaces you wish to compare, as shown in Figure 29-6. If you have followed the guidelines set forth in this book, nearly every interface will have the exact same configuration, so you should only select one interface to compare, and then scroll to the bottom and click **Submit**.

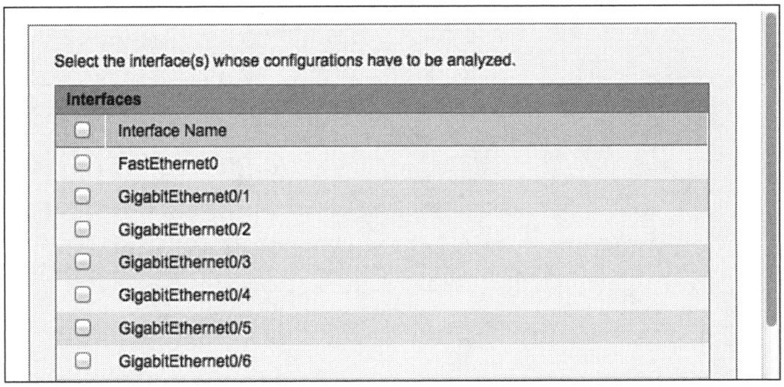

Select the interface(s) whose configurations have to be analyzed.

Interfaces
☐ Interface Name
☐ FastEthernet0
☐ GigabitEthernet0/1
☐ GigabitEthernet0/2
☐ GigabitEthernet0/3
☐ GigabitEthernet0/4
☐ GigabitEthernet0/5
☐ GigabitEthernet0/6

Figure 29-6 *Select an Interface*

6. After the comparison is completed, click **Show Results Summary** to see the results, as shown in Figure 29-7.

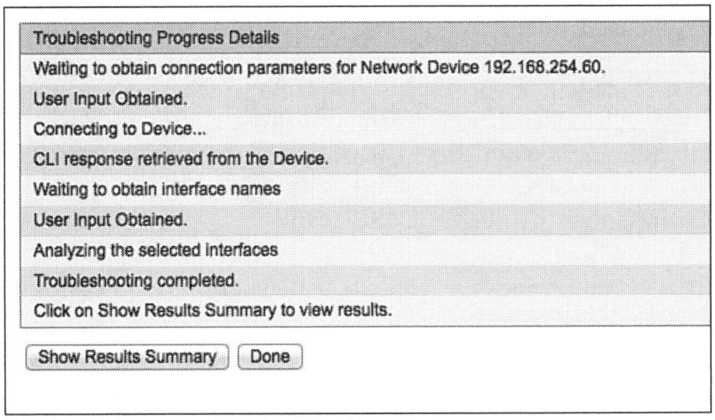

Troubleshooting Progress Details
Waiting to obtain connection parameters for Network Device 192.168.254.60.
User Input Obtained.
Connecting to Device...
CLI response retrieved from the Device.
Waiting to obtain interface names
User Input Obtained.
Analyzing the selected interfaces
Troubleshooting completed.
Click on Show Results Summary to view results.

[Show Results Summary] [Done]

Figure 29-7 *Comparison Complete*

The report will be broken down into sections, as shown in Figure 29-8, and anything found to be missing or incorrect will be displayed in red. At this point, it is up to you to be familiar with your own deployment. For instance, you should know whether you truly need the SNMP community strings or are using Device Sensor instead.

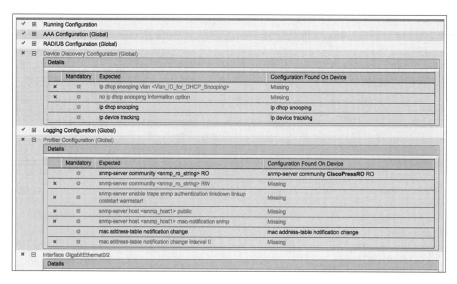

Figure 29-8   *Results Summary*

TCP Dump

When troubleshooting 802.1X, in order to get a better understanding of what is transpiring, it is often necessary to go deeper than the GUI and live log would normally allow you to do. This is where Packet Captures come in very handy. We have personally used Wireshark more times than we can count to get a deep view of what is transpiring, such as whether ISE is even receiving the RADIUS message; what the Certificate Signing Request of the client actually looks like; and much more.

Cisco includes TCP Dump in ISE and even provides a fantastic way to grab TCP Dumps from any ISE node on the deployment, right from the main Admin GUI! TCP Dump also enables you to filter the capture, such as by specifying ip host 10.1.40.60 (as shown in Figure 29-9). We use this filter all the time so that we can limit the traffic to just the NAD that we are troubleshooting with.

To set a TCP Dump capture, perform the following steps:

1. Navigate to **Operations > Troubleshoot > Diagnostic Tools > General Tools > TCP Dump**.

2. From the Host Name drop-down list, choose which ISE node to grab the TCP Dump from.

3. From the Network Interface drop-down list, choose which interface on that ISE node should be used.

4. Click the **On** radio button for Promiscuous Mode if you want to grab all traffic seen on the interface, even if it's not destined for ISE. So, if you have a Switched Port

Analyzer (SPAN) set up for one of the ISE interfaces, you could capture all traffic seen on that SPAN interface.

5. In the Filter field, you can accept any standard TCP Dump filter, and limit the traffic captured.

Here is a link for TCP Dump Filters: http://bit.ly/Va243S.

6. From the Format drop-down list, choose the file format:

   ■ **Human Readable:** Choosing this option will format the file as XLM, which can be used when a sniffer tool (such as Wireshark) is unavailable.

   ■ **Raw Packet Data:** This will save the file as a pcap (common packet capture format) and can be opened in the sniffer tool of your choice.

7. Click **Start** to begin the capture.

8. Click **Stop** to end the capture.

9. Click the **Download** button to initiate a download of the pcap file.

10. Click Delete if you want to delete the pcap file from ISE. Only one capture may be stored at a time, and starting a new capture will automatically overwrite the existing one.

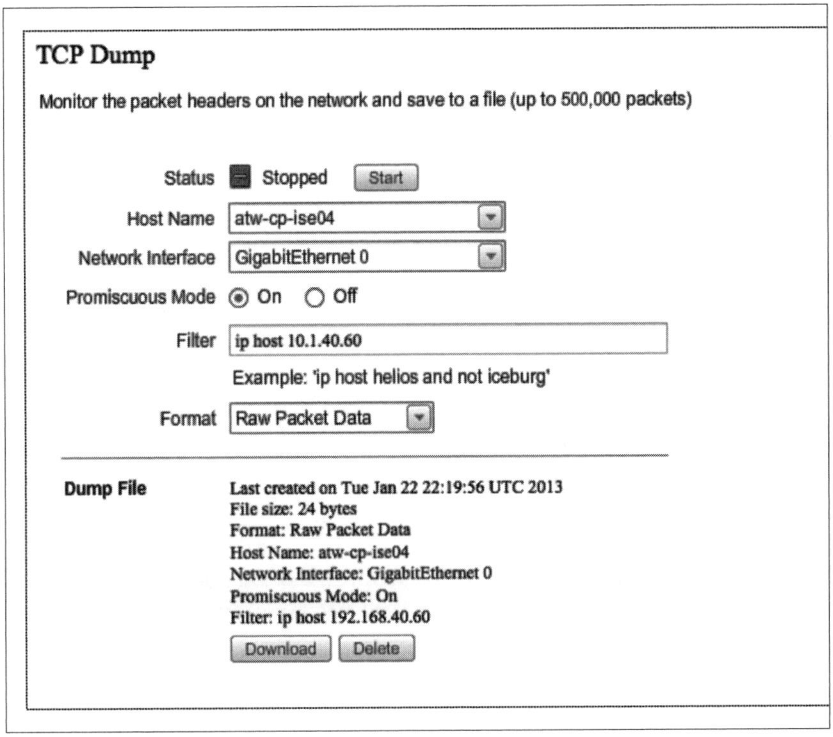

Figure 29-9 *TCP Dump*

Troubleshooting Methodology

As you read this section, keep in mind the tip from the beginning of the chapter: always stay calm, take your time, and think about how the solution works. Taking your time may sound counterproductive, but when you rush to fix a problem, you often end up taking much longer. There have been many situations where we were asked to help when "it just isn't working," and by staying calm, taking our time, and thinking through the flows, we came to the solution very quickly.

This section examines some common troubleshooting exercises and how to resolve the problems.

Troubleshooting Authentication and Authorization

This section offers some possible options and solutions to a common complaint that a help desk or IT administrator may hear: "I plugged into the network, but my system is not granted access." As you read this section, your focus should be on understanding the methodology and the secure access flow. Always keep the authentication and authorization flows in mind, as shown in Figure 29-10.

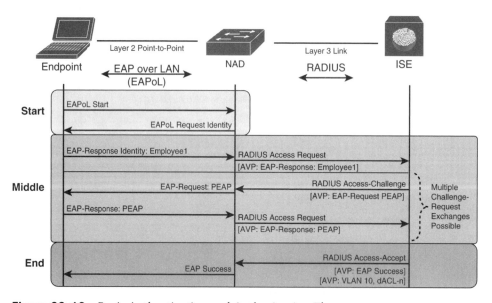

Figure 29-10 *Basic Authentication and Authorization Flows*

The first action you should take after being contacted with this kind of problem is to gather as much data as you can about the client machine and then examine the Live Log on ISE, as described in the following steps:

1. Collect as many of the following data points about the client machine as you can, if not all of them:

- Username (good)

- Machine name (good)

- Switch or Wireless LAN Controller name (better)

- Switch interface (even better)

- MAC address of the machine (best)

2. Go to the Live Log by navigating to **Operations > Authentications**.

3. Filter the log using the data that you gathered, until you find the attempted authentication. Figure 29-11 shows the Live Log being filtered by Endpoint ID (MAC address).

Your next action depends on what you find in the Live Log:

- If the log contains no entry at all for that MAC address, then you must determine whether ISE is even receiving an authentication request, as described in the following section.

- If the log contains an entry for the MAC address, proceed as described in the subsequent section, "Option 2: An Entry Exists in the Live Log."

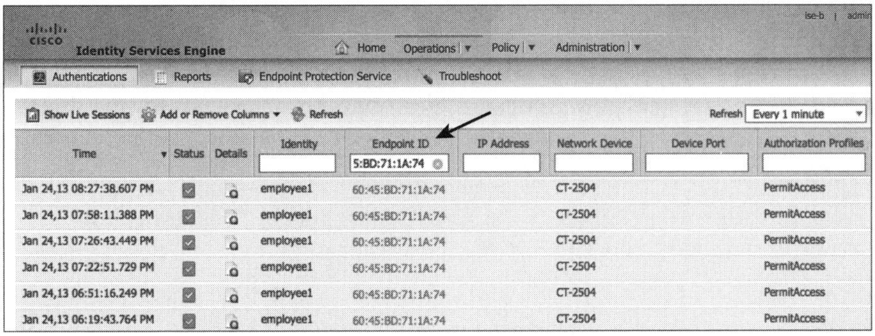

Figure 29-11 *Live Log Filtered by MAC Address*

Option 1: No Live Log Entry Exists

If there is no entry at all in the Live Log, you need to examine the communication between the NAD and ISE. Always keep the flows in mind, as shown in Figure 29-12.

Remember that there must be an EAP communication occurring locally between the NAD and the endpoint first, which gets "wrapped" inside of RADIUS from the NAD to ISE. If EAP is not present (that is, no supplicant is present), then there should be a MAB request from the switch to ISE.

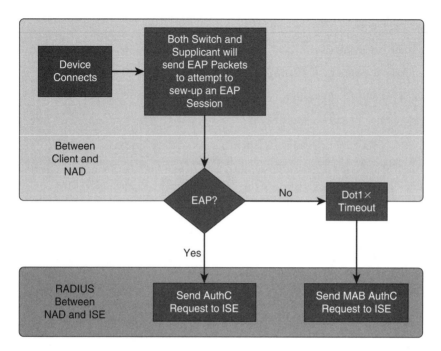

Figure 29-12 *Authentication Flow*

At this point, you need to verify that ISE is receiving the authentication requests. There are a few ways to accomplish this. Normally, either one of these methods would suffice, but for the purposes of completeness in this chapter, you will be shown both options in the steps that follow:

1. From the dashboard in ISE, check the alarms section for any "Unknown NAD" alarms, as shown in Figure 29-13. If you see this alarm, there are two possible reasons:

   a. ISE does not have the switch configured as a Network Device.

   b. The switch is sending the request from an IP address that is not defined in the network device object within ISE.

2. Ensure that the request is reaching ISE with TCP Dump. Run the TCP Dump utility, with a filter of **ip host** *ip-address-of-nad*.

In this case, you will see that the issue is actually Step 1b. The **ip radius source-interface** command is missing on the switch. How we made the determination that it was Step 1b is described next.

The two alarms of interest in Figure 29-13 are RADIUS Request Dropped and Unknown NAD. Double-click the first alarm to drill into it, and you see the source of these alarms is 10.1.40.60, as shown in Figure 29-14.

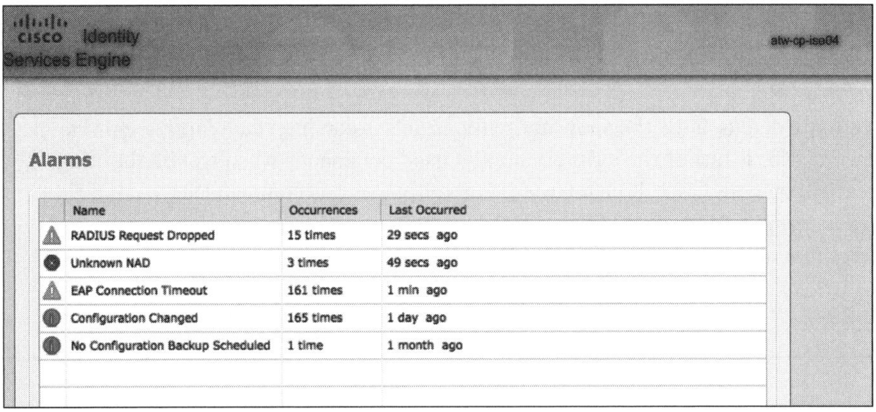

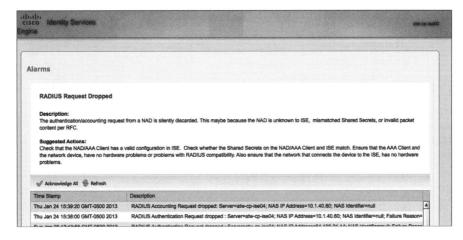

Figure 29-13 *Alarms*

Figure 29-14 *Alarm Details*

The device with the IP address of 10.1.40.60 is the 3560-X switch, and you connect to it via SSH or the console. Upon doing so, notice immediately that authentication-related failures exist, as displayed in Example 29-1.

Example 29-1 *Failures Shown in the Switch Logs*

```
*Sep 13 19:26:39.634: %MAB-5-FAIL: Authentication failed for client
(0050.5687.0039) on Interface Gi0/1 AuditSessionID
0A01283C0000001517B7584B

*Sep 13 19:26:39.634: %AUTHMGR-7-RESULT: Authentication result
'server dead' from 'mab' for client (0050.5687.0039) on Interface
Gi0/1 AuditSessionID 0A01283C0000001517B7584B

*Sep 13 19:26:39.634: %AUTHMGR-5-FAIL: Authorization failed for
```

```
client (0050.5687.0039) on Interface Gi0/1 AuditSessionID
0A01283C0000001517B7584B
```

To see more details, issue the **show authentication session interface** *interface-name* command. This is one of the most commonly used commands when troubleshooting authentication with Cisco IOS Software. The output of this command shows that the switch is trying to do both MAB and 802.1X, and neither is successful. Example 29-2 displays that output.

Example 29-2   *Output of the* **show authentication session interface** *Command*

```
3560-X# sho authen sess int g0/1


            Interface:  GigabitEthernet0/1
          MAC Address:  0050.5687.0039
           IP Address:  10.1.41.102
            User-Name:  005056870039
               Status:  Running
               Domain:  UNKNOWN
      Security Policy:  Should Secure
      Security Status:  Unsecure
       Oper host mode:  multi-auth
       Oper control dir: both
      Session timeout:  N/A
         Idle timeout:  N/A
    Common Session ID:  0A01283C00000018F595EC0B
      Acct Session ID:  0x00000049
               Handle:  0x41000018
Runnable methods list:
      Method    State
       mab      Failed over
       dot1x    Running
```

To verify which IP addresses the switch may be sending the RADIUS messages from, issue the **show ip interface brief** command, with the **| include up** option to limit your display, as shown in Example 29-3.

Example 29-3   *Output of the* **show ip int brief | include up** *Command*

```
3560-X# sho ip int brief | include up

Vlan1                 unassigned      YES NVRAM  up                    up
Vlan40                10.1.40.60      YES NVRAM  up                    up
GigabitEthernet0/1    unassigned      YES unset  up                    up
```

```
GigabitEthernet0/24     unassigned      YES unset  up              up
Loopback0               192.168.254.60  YES NVRAM  up              up
3560-X#
```

Next, verify the NAD definition in ISE by navigating to **Administration > Network Resources > Network Devices** and then editing the 3560-X object, as shown in Figure 29-15. Within this object, notice that the expected IP address is 192.168.254.60, which is the loopback interface.

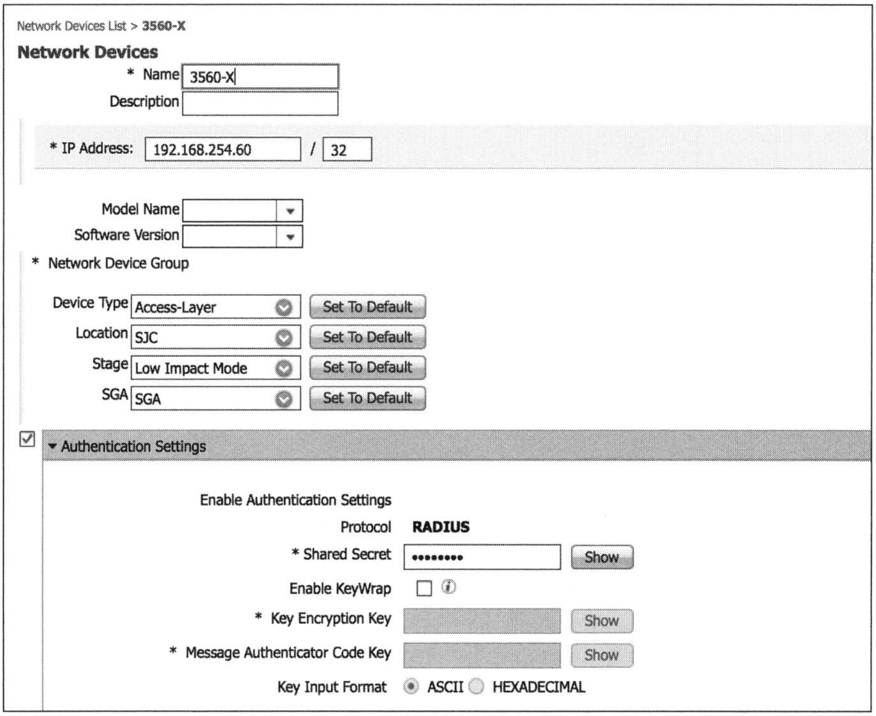

Figure 29-15 *NAD Object Definition*

In order to correct this, add the **ip radius source-interface** *interface-name* command into the configuration, as shown in Example 29-4.

This should have been part of your configuration already, based on Chapter 11, "Bootstrapping Network Access Devices," but obviously something must have happened. This occurs quite often in customer environments; an admin might not fully know what the command was used for and could have removed it from the configuration, or the switch might have been added without the appropriate command. The reason behind the interface not being set is not the purpose of this exercise; the purpose is to enable the users to authenticate again.

Example 29-4   *Output of the* ip radius source-interface *Command*

```
3560-X(config)# ip radius source-interface Loopback0
3560-X(config)#
```

Verify that everything works now by reissuing the **show authentication session interface** *interface-name* command, or by checking the Live Log on ISE.

Example 29-5 shows the working authentication on the switch, which happens to be a Centralized Web Authentication result.

Example 29-5   *Output of the* show authentication session interface *Command*

```
3560-X# sho authen sess int g0/1

            Interface:  GigabitEthernet0/1
           MAC Address:  0050.5687.0039
            IP Address:  10.1.41.102
             User-Name:  00-50-56-87-00-39
                Status:  Authz Success
                Domain:  DATA
       Security Policy:  Should Secure
       Security Status:  Unsecure
        Oper host mode:  multi-auth
       Oper control dir:  both
          Authorized By:  Authentication Server
            Vlan Group:  N/A
               ACS ACL:  xACSACLx-IP-Pre-Auth-ACL-50fc97ba
       URL Redirect ACL:  ACL-WEBAUTH-REDIRECT
          URL Redirect:  https://atw-cp-
ise04.ise.local:8443/guestportal/gateway?sessionId=0A01283C0000001AF5
  9D671A&action=cwa
       Session timeout:  N/A
          Idle timeout:  N/A
     Common Session ID:  0A01283C0000001AF59D671A
        Acct Session ID:  0x0000004B
                Handle:  0xAC00001A
Runnable methods list:


        Method    State
        mab       Authc Success
        dot1x     Not run
3560-X#
```

Option 2: An Entry Exists in the Live Log

If there is an entry for the MAC address in the Live Log, you are in luck, because you can troubleshoot this almost entirely from the ISE GUI, as described in the following steps:

1. Starting with the Live Log, as shown in Figure 29-16, in the Details column, click the icon (which looks like a magnifying glass on a piece of paper) to view the details of the failure.

Figure 29-16 *Live Log with a Failure*

2. Review the Authentication Details that open in the new window (shown in Figure 29-17), and you can see almost instantly that the authentication failed because the user's AD account is disabled.

Figure 29-17 *Authentication Details*

3. Access your Active Directory management console and check the account; reenable the account if it really is disabled by selecting "unlock account," as displayed in Figure 29-18.

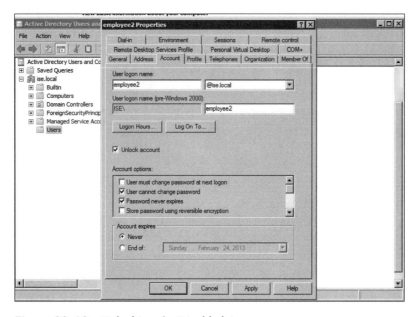

Figure 29-18 *Unlocking the Disabled Account*

Now, the authentications are succeeding for Employee2, as shown in Figure 29-19.

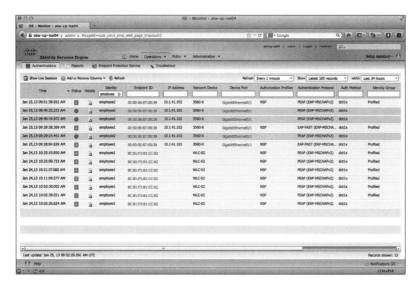

Figure 29-19 *Success*

General High-Level Troubleshooting Flowchart

One of our colleagues, Hosuk Won, put together the flowchart shown in Figure 29-20 to aid in the troubleshooting of the Secure Unified Access system. This is an excellent flowchart to follow for general high-level troubleshooting.

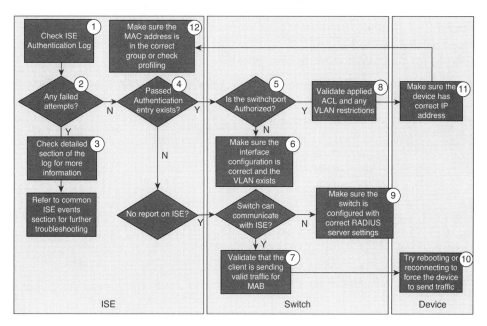

Figure 29-20 *High-Level Troubleshooting Flowchart*

Troubleshooting WebAuth and URL Redirection

The URL Redirection employed by CWA—as well as by both BYOD and MDM onboarding—is one of those things that can be confusing to folks who are new to it. One of the most common troubleshooting exercises that our team(s) will get involved in is helping someone when they report "WebAuth isn't working." Of course, they will also report "nothing was missed" and "nothing has changed." You know, the normal cliché statements that you hear from someone who is asking for assistance. Ninety-nine times out of a hundred, staying calm and remembering to always "follow the flows" is what enabled us to solve their problem.

The following is an example series of steps to follow:

1. Check the Live Log. Ensure that the authorization result includes the URL Redirection, as displayed in Figure 29-21. If so, make note of the url-redirect-acl name.

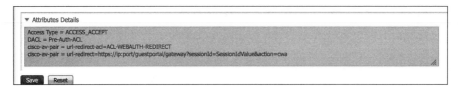

Figure 29-21 *Attribute Details from the Authorization Result*

2. Gather information about the client session.

    a. For wired URL Redirection, execute the **show authentication session interface** *interface-name* command:

```
3560-X# sho authen sess int g0/1

              Interface:  GigabitEthernet0/1
            MAC Address:  0050.5687.0039
             IP Address:  10.1.41.102
              User-Name:  00-50-56-87-00-39
                 Status:  Authz Success
                 Domain:  DATA
        Security Policy:  Should Secure
        Security Status:  Unsecure
         Oper host mode:  multi-auth
        Oper control dir:  both
          Authorized By:  Authentication Server
             Vlan Group:  N/A
               ACS ACL:  xACSACLx-IP-Pre-Auth-ACL-50fc97ba
       URL Redirect ACL:  ACL-WEBAUTH-REDIRECT
           URL Redirect:  https://atw-cp-
ise04.ise.local:8443/guestportal/gateway?sessionId=0A01283C0000001D05931
   7CE&action=cwa
        Session timeout:  N/A
           Idle timeout:  N/A
       Common Session ID:  0A01283C0000001D059317CE
        Acct Session ID:  0x00000055
                 Handle:  0x7500001D
Runnable methods list:

         Method   State
         dot1x    Failed over
         mab      Authc Success
```

The preceding output highlights the most important fields for this exercise. The ACS-ACL field is displaying the downloadable ACL (dACL) name that was downloaded from ISE and applied to the sessions' IP traffic. This ACL is examined further in step 4.

The URL Redirect ACL describes the name of a *local* ACL that must preexist on the switch for it to be used. That ACL determines which traffic is redirected and which is not. This ACL is examined in a further in step 4.

Lastly, the session ID from ISE will be present in the URL Redirect field, and it must match the Common Session ID displayed below it. If by chance these IDs do not match, you should open a TAC case to receive further assistance.

b. For Wireless Redirection, choose **Monitor > Clients**, as shown in Figure 29-22.

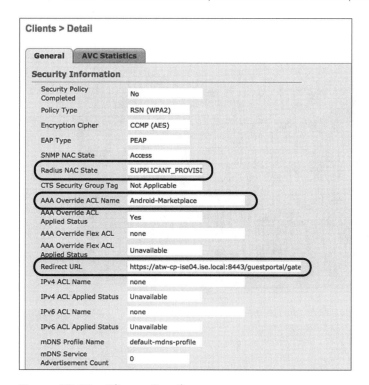

Figure 29-22   *Client > Details*

Figure 29-22 points out the most important fields for this exercise. If the Radius NAC State field shows RUN, then the RADIUS NAC setting was never enabled on the WLAN. This is a pretty common oversight. The fix is to enable RADIUS NAC in the controller, as described in Chapter 11.

The AAA Override ACL Name field must list the *exact* name that was noted in Step 1 and Figure 29-21.

The Redirect URL field should contain the URL pointing to ISE. Make note of the hostname.

3. Verify that DNS resolution is working from the client.

The URL redirect is automatically sent to the name stored in the ISE certificate, such as https://atw-cp-ise04.ise.local—which is visible in Figure 29-21 and Figure 29-22, as well as in the output in Step 2a. The client must be able to resolve this name with DNS. This is another common error, and easily correctable.

Sometimes, the issue may be that the entry was never made on the DNS server that the client is using, or that the ACL is not permitting DNS traffic. The ACLs are examined in Step 4.

To verify DNS from the client, you would normally use **ping** or **nslookup**, as shown in Figure 29-23. The **ping** may fail, depending on the ACL. However, you are looking for DNS resolution, not successful ICMP. Figure 29-23 demonstrates a successful DNS lookup, using both **ping** and **nslookup**.

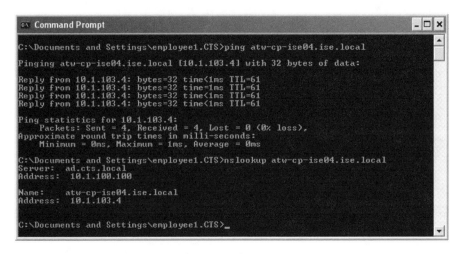

Figure 29-23 *Verifying DNS from the Client*

4. Examine the ACLs.

a. For wired devices, execute the **show ip access-list interface** *interface-name* command:

```
3560-X# sho ip access-list int g0/1

        permit udp host 10.1.41.102 any eq bootps
        permit udp host 10.1.41.102 any eq domain (4 matches)
        permit icmp host 10.1.41.102 any
        permit tcp host 10.1.41.102 host 10.1.100.232 eq 8443
        permit tcp host 10.1.41.102 host 10.1.100.232 eq 8905
        permit tcp host 10.1.41.102 host 10.1.100.232 eq 8909
        permit udp host 10.1.41.102 host 10.1.100.232 range 8905 8906
        permit udp host 10.1.41.102 host 10.1.100.232 eq 8909
```

As you see, the output of this **show** command displays the effective ACL that is applied to the interface, after applying the downloadable ACL.

b. Also for wired devices, you have to ensure that the redirection ACL is correct with the **show ip access-list** *access-list-name* command, as shown in the output that follows. This ACL will redirect only traffic that is permitted. Any traffic that is denied will bypass redirection.

```
3560-X# sho ip access-list ACL-WEBAUTH-REDIRECT

Extended IP access list ACL-WEBAUTH-REDIRECT
    10 deny udp any any eq domain (58523 matches)
    20 permit tcp any any eq www (7978448 matches)
    30 permit tcp any any eq 443 (416 matches)
```

Ensure that traffic is being redirected by looking for the matches for TCP ports 80 and 443.

c. With wireless access, only a single ACL is in effect. To examine the contents of the ACL and ensure it is named correctly, choose **Security > Access-Control-Lists**.

Ensure the name matches exactly what is sent in the authorization result noted in Step 1. If it does, edit the ACL to examine the individual rules, as shown in Figure 29-24.

Access Control Lists > Edit

General

Access List Name	ACL-WEBAUTH-REDIRECT
Deny Counters	134

Seq	Action	Source IP/Mask		Destination IP/Mask		Protocol	Source Port	Dest Port	DSCP	Direction	Number of Hits	
1	Permit	0.0.0.0 / 0.0.0.0		0.0.0.0 / 0.0.0.0		Any	Any	Any	Any	Outbound	27462	▾
2	Permit	0.0.0.0 / 0.0.0.0		10.130.1.0 / 255.255.255.0		Any	Any	Any	Any	Inbound	3095	▾
3	Permit	0.0.0.0 / 0.0.0.0		74.125.0.0 / 255.255.0.0		Any	Any	Any	Any	Inbound	323	▾
4	Permit	0.0.0.0 / 0.0.0.0		173.194.0.0 / 255.255.0.0		Any	Any	Any	Any	Inbound	21316	▾
5	Permit	0.0.0.0 / 0.0.0.0		173.227.0.0 / 255.255.0.0		Any	Any	Any	Any	Inbound	0	▾
6	Permit	0.0.0.0 / 0.0.0.0		206.111.0.0 / 255.255.0.0		Any	Any	Any	Any	Inbound	0	▾
7	Permit	0.0.0.0 / 0.0.0.0		12.150.127.0 / 255.255.255.0		Any	Any	Any	Any	Inbound	0	▾
8	Deny	0.0.0.0 / 0.0.0.0		0.0.0.0 / 0.0.0.0		TCP	Any	Any	Any	Inbound	3990	▾

Figure 29-24   *Verifying Airespace ACL*

Active Directory Is Disconnected

If you see that Active Directory is disconnected, such as shown in Figure 29-25, there is a built-in test tool you can use to identify why. The Test Connection tool has two options: basic test and detailed test. Most of the time, the basic test is enough to identify the problem. Nine times out of ten, the issue is a result of a time synchronization problem, as shown in Figure 29-26.

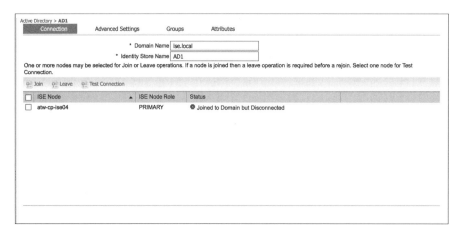

Figure 29-25   *Active Directory Disconnected*

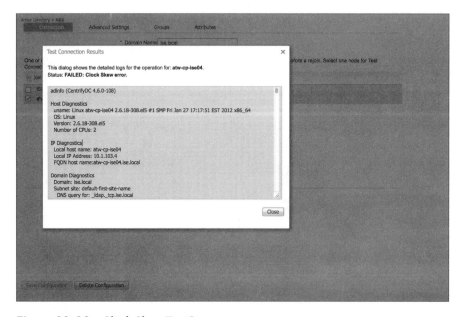

Figure 29-26   *Clock Skew Too Great*

Debug Situations: ISE Logs

If you are unable to isolate a root cause via the ISE GUI, it may be necessary to look into the log files. ISE maintains very detailed logging, and enables you to set the logging levels. If it becomes necessary to start debugging, perform the following steps:

1. Navigate to **Administration > Logging > Debug Log Configuration**.

2. Choose the appropriate ISE Policy Services Node (PSN).

3. Set the appropriate logs to debug level.

   For example, if you are troubleshooting authentication and authorizations, you would set the following logs to debug or trace as required:

   a. Basic AuthC Troubleshooting Logs: runtime-AAA and prrt-JNI

   b. AuthC Session ID Troubleshooting Logs: nsf, ns-session, runtime-AAA, and prrt-JNI

   c. Active Directory Troubleshooting Logs: identity-store-AD and Active Directory

4. Reproduce the problem and gather relevant seed information to aid in searching the logs, such as MAC Address, IP Address, sessionID, and so forth.

5. Navigate to **Operations > Download Logs** and choose the appropriate ISE node.

6. On the Debug Logs tab, download the logs.

7. Use an intelligent editor such as Notepad ++ (Windows) or TextWrangler (Mac) to parse the log files.

8. Once the issue has been isolated, return the log levels to their default levels.

The Support Bundle

Cisco TAC may ask for the support bundle, which contains the full ISE configuration and all logs. You can think of it as an equivalent of the **show tech-support** command on a Cisco IOS device. It allows the support engineer to re-create the environment in a lab, if necessary.

The bundle will save as a simple tar.gpg (GPG encrypted) file. The support bundle is automatically named with the date and time stamps in the following format: ise-support-bundle_ise-support-bundle-mm-dd-yyyy-hh-mm.tar.gpg.

You have the option to choose which logs you want to be part of your support bundle. For example, you can configure logs from a particular service to be part of your bundle.

The logs that you can download are categorized as follows:

- **Full configuration database:** If you choose this category, the ISE configuration database is saved into the support bundle and allows TAC to import this database configuration in another ISE node to re-create the scenario.

- **Debug logs:** This category captures bootstrap, application configuration, run-time, deployment, monitoring and reporting, and Public Key Infrastructure (PKI) information.

- **Local logs:** This category contains log messages from the various processes that run but are not collected by the MnT node.

- **Core files:** This category contains critical information that would help identify the cause of a crash. These logs are created if the application crashed and includes core dumps.

- **Monitoring and reporting logs:** This category contains information about the alarms and reports from the MnT node.

- **System logs:** This category contains the underlying OS (Application Deployment Engine [ADE-OS]) logs. These logs are not directly part of the ISE application itself.

There are two ways to create and download the support bundle: from the ISE GUI and from the command-line interface (CLI).

From the ISE GUI, perform the following steps:

1. Navigate to **Operations > Troubleshoot > Download Logs.**

2. Select the ISE node in the left pane.

3. Choose which categories of logs you want to include, which were described in the previous list.

4. Enter a password to use for encrypting the bundle.

5. Click **Create Support Bundle**, such as what is displayed in Figure 29-27.

From the CLI, use the **backup-logs** command, such as shown in Example 29-6.

Example 29-6   *Output of the* backup-logs *Command*

```
ATW-CP-ISE02/admin# backup-logs ATW-BACKUP repository NAS encryption-key plain
    ISE12345

% Creating log backup with timestamped filename: ATW-BACKUP-130128-1641.tar.gpg
% supportbundle in progress: Copying database config files...10% completed
% supportbundle in progress: Copying debug logs...20% completed
% supportbundle in progress: Copying local logs...30% completed
% supportbundle in progress: Copying monitor logs...50% completed
% supportbundle in progress: Copying ADEOS config files...50% completed
% supportbundle in progress: Moving support bundle to the repository...75% completed
% supportbundle in progress: Completing support bundle generation.....100% completed
```

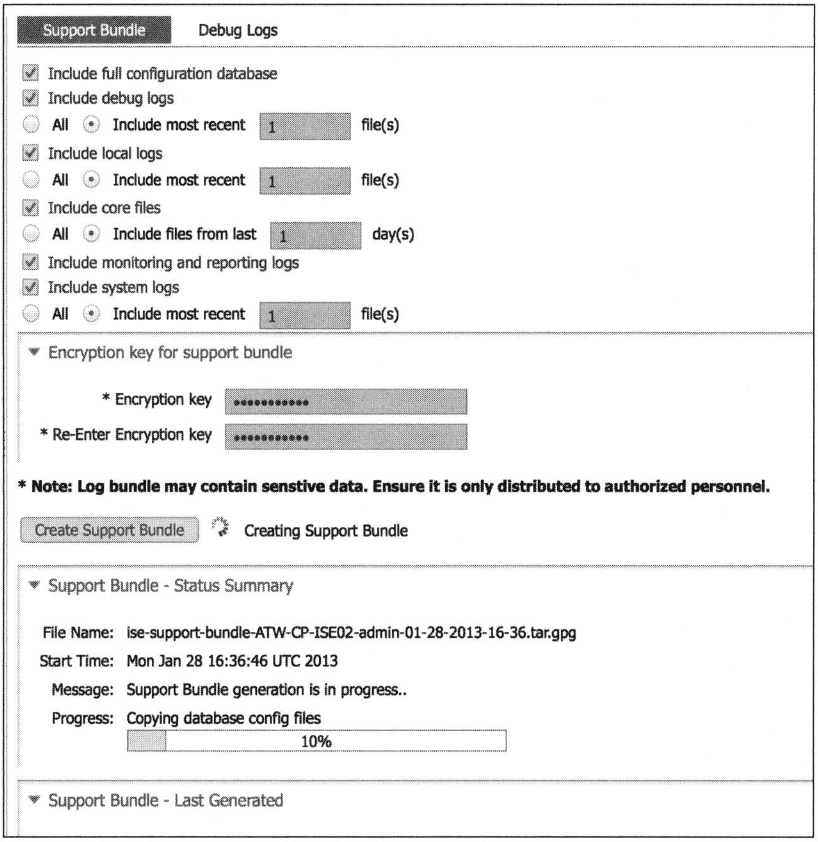

Figure 29-27   *Creating a Support Bundle from the GUI*

Common Error Messages and Alarms

In this section, we will examine some of the common error messages and alarms and look into possible causes and solutions.

EAP Connection Timeout

A common alarm is EAP Connection Timeout, as shown in Figure 29-28. This often means the client has rejected ISE's certificate. Some supplicants will prompt the user to accept an untrusted certificate only when the WLAN profile is being created. So, if the client happens to be authenticated by a different RADIUS server, and the client does not trust that new certificate, it will not sew up the TLS session between itself and the server.

This can happen in fail-over scenarios, or by updating/renewing the certificate on ISE, or even other ways. The EAP error will be that the client has not responded in 120 seconds, as shown in Figure 29-28.

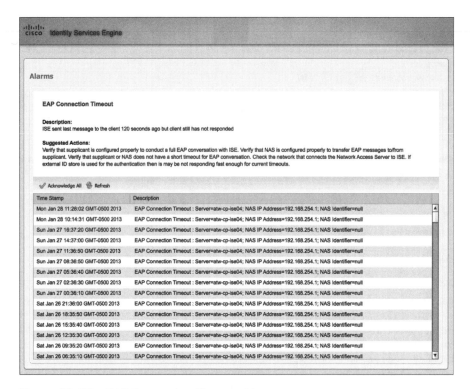

Figure 29-28   *EAP Connection Timeout Alarm*

This is seen very often in university settings, where students are able to bring in any device. Very specifically, Android devices seem to allow the end user to accept ISE's certificate only after the Wi-Fi profile is first built. If the certificate changes, the Android devices start rejecting the EAP session, and they do not send any notification to the NAD.

If you encounter this issue, try to identify the client that is rejecting the certificate and then fix this issue locally in the device's supplicant. For Android, forget the Wi-Fi network and then add it again.

Some supplicants, such as Cisco AnyConnect NAM, will send a message reporting that the certificate was rejected, and the error is more specific in ISE. You will see the specific failure reason shown in Figure 29-29: "12321: PEAP failed SSL/TLS handshake because the client rejected the ISE local-certificate."

Authentication Details

Source Timestamp	2013-01-28 17:09:18.834
Received Timestamp	2013-01-28 17:09:18.835
Policy Server	atw-cp-ise04
Event	5400 Authentication failed
Username	anonymous
User Type	
Endpoint Id	00:50:56:87:00:39
IP Address	
Identity Store	
Identity Group	
Audit Session Id	0A01283C0000005F0963992C
Authentication Method	dot1x
Authentication Protocol	PEAP
Service Type	Framed
Network Device	3560-X
Device Type	Switches#Access-Layer
Location	NorthAmerica#SJC
NAS IP Address	192.168.254.60
NAS Port Id	GigabitEthernet0/1
Authorization Profile	
Posture Status	
Security Group	
Failure Reason	12321 PEAP failed SSL/TLS handshake because the client rejected the ISE local-certificate

Figure 29-29   *When Supplicant Communicates the Failure*

Dynamic Authorization Failed

Dynamic Authorization is the official name for Change of Authorization (CoA). Cisco TAC personnel have said that it is very common for them to receive customer calls stating that they are receiving many Dynamic Authorization Failed errors in the Live Log, as shown in Figure 29-30. TAC has also told me that 99 percent of the time, the issue is a misconfiguration of the NAD.

To correct this on a switch, view the running configuration and ensure that ISE is correctly listed in the "aaa server radius dynamic-author" section of the configuration and that the server-key is exactly the same as the Shared Secret configured in ISE, as shown in Example 29-7.

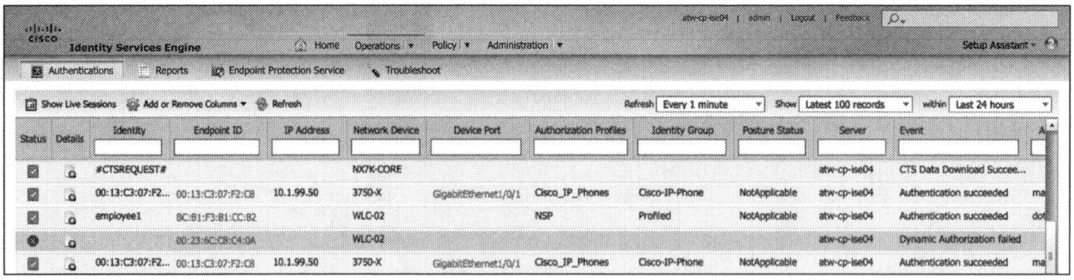

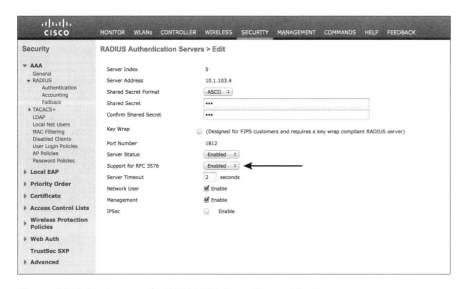

Figure 29-30 *Dynamic Authorization Failed Error*

Example 29-7 *Output of the* **show run | begin aaa server radius dynamic** *Command*

```
3560-X# show run | begin aaa server radius dynamic

aaa server radius dynamic-author
 client 10.1.103.231 server-key Cisco123
 client 10.1.103.4 server-key Cisco123
!
```

To correct the misconfiguration on the Wireless LAN Controller, navigate to **Security > AAA > RADIUS > Authentication**. Choose the ISE server from the list, and ensure that the Support for RFC 3576 drop-down list box is set to **Enabled**, as shown in Figure 29-31.

Figure 29-31 *Support for RFC 3576 Drop-Down List Box*

WebAuth Loop

If a user is enters their credentials correctly into the WebAuth Portal, but is repeatedly redirected back to the portal after logging in, the user is caught in what is known as a WebAuth loop. It means that a more specific Authorization Rule was not available, or that the order was incorrect. To correct this issue, you need to examine your Authorization Policy and ensure the correct policy does exist and is in the correct order.

Account Lockout

Quite often, an ISE proof of concept or pilot sits idle in a lab for a few weeks or months. When an administrator eventually returns to the GUI and tries to log in, they discover that the account password has expired and login is forbidden. In such cases, the administrator needs to reset the password from the CLI, as shown in Example 29-8.

Example 29-8   *Resetting the Administrative Password from SSH*

```
d$ ssh admin@atw-cp-ise04
admin@atw-cp-ise04's password:
Last login: Fri Apr  6 03:58:25 2013 from 10.154.13.123
atw-cp-ise04/admin# application reset-passwd ise ?

  <WORD>  Username for which password is to be reset (Max Size - 64)
atw-cp-ise04/admin# application reset-passwd ise admin
```

ISE Node Communication

Two of our colleagues, Craig Hyps and Ziad Serradine, created a very detailed diagram that documents all the communication between the nodes in a Secure Unified Access deployment. The diagram is so useful that someone from Cisco TAC printed it out on a plotter and hung it up in each AAA TAC engineer's cubical. Because the diagram is so useful, we have included it in Figure 29-32 for your reference.

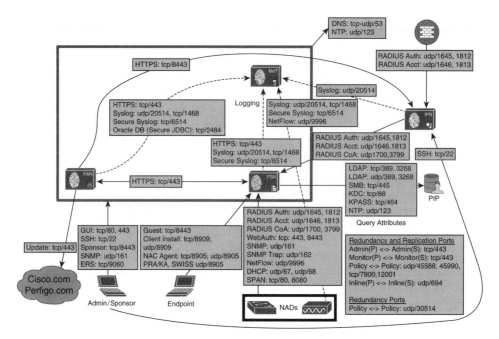

Figure 29-32   *ISE 1.2 Node Communications*

Summary

If you have gained nothing else from this chapter, you should at least take away the following lesson: when troubleshooting, always stay calm, take your time, and follow the flows.

If you can do that, you will be an expert troubleshooter in no time, and your understanding of the solution will grow exponentially. Cisco has also provided you with a number of tools to help solve common problems, so don't hesitate to use those tools.

Chapter 30

Backup, Patching, and Upgrading

This chapter examines a few items of importance for the ongoing maintenance of ISE. It looks at repositories, the different backup types, and patching the ISE deployment.

Repositories

Simply put, a repository is a location to store files. The repository may be local to ISE or positioned on a remote server. You may have more than one configured, but you certainly need at least one before you can perform backup or upgrade procedures. Repositories store all application upgrade bundles, support bundles, and system backups. It is recommended to have a repository of at least 10GB for small deployments (less than 100 endpoints), 100GB for medium deployments, and 200GB for large deployments.

Configuring a Repository

Repositories are added at the Maintenance tab of the System Properties of ISE. From the ISE GUI, perform the following steps:

1. Navigate to **Administration > System > Maintenance**.

2. Choose **Repository** on the left-hand side.

3. Click **Add** to add a new repository.

4. Give the repository a name and choose the type.

Multiple types of repositories are available. When adding a repository in the GUI, the GUI automatically displays the necessary fields. For example, a username and password is needed for an FTP repository, but not for a CD-ROM. Repository types include

- Disk
- FTP

- SFTP

- TFTP

- NFS

- CDROM

- HTTP

- HTTPS

The disk is used to provide a repository on the local hard disk. This is not used often, but sometimes, it can be helpful when Cisco TAC needs to export a support bundle quickly or other reactive needs. This type of repository needs a name and a path (such as /tac/ helpme/), as shown in Figure 30-1.

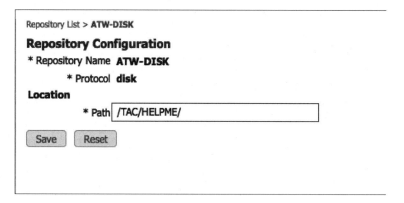

Figure 30-1   *DISK Repository*

FTP is the most common repository type. It uses File Transfer Protocol (FTP). It requires a server address or DNS name, along with the path, username, and password, as shown in Figure 30-2.

SFTP uses Secure File Transfer Protocol (SFTP). It requires a server address or DNS name along with the path, username, and password, as shown in Figure 30-3.

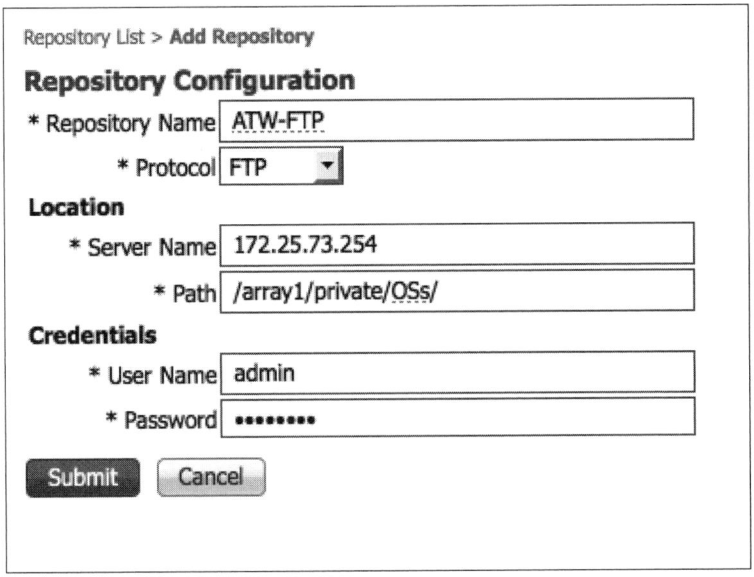

Repository List > **Add Repository**

Repository Configuration

* Repository Name ATW-FTP

* Protocol FTP ▼

Location

* Server Name 172.25.73.254

* Path /array1/private/OSs/

Credentials

* User Name admin

* Password ••••••••

Submit   Cancel

Figure 30-2 *FTP Repository*

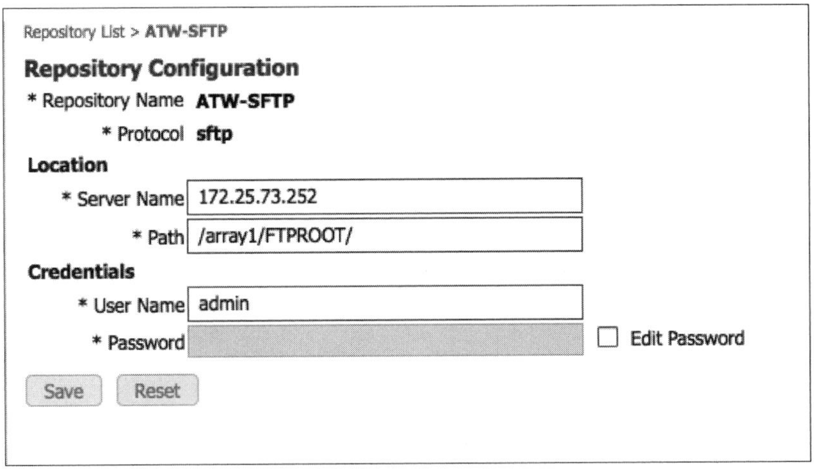

Repository List > **ATW-SFTP**

Repository Configuration

* Repository Name **ATW-SFTP**

* Protocol **sftp**

Location

* Server Name 172.25.73.252

* Path /array1/FTPROOT/

Credentials

* User Name admin

* Password [   ] ☐ Edit Password

Save   Reset

Figure 30-3 *SFTP Repository*

Note Before this type of repository works, you must trust the certificate of the SFTP server with the **host-key** command, as shown in Figure 30-4.

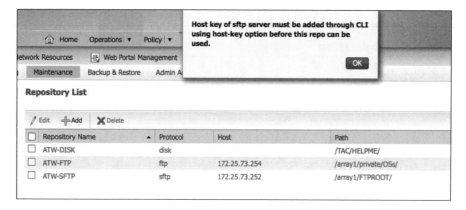

Figure 30-4   *Host-Key Required Pop-Up*

Example 30-1 shows truncated output of a **show running-config** command. As shown in the example, the repository was created and contains the URL as well as credentials.

Example 30-1   *Repository Output from* **show running-config**

```
atw-cp-ise02/admin#show run
! - Displaying only necessary information
repository ATW-SFTP
  url sftp://172.25.73.252/array1/FTPROOT/
  user admin password hash b5558b4ef1742747cc50723474f842818642df47
```

Next, you need to enter repository configuration mode to add the host key to the repository, in order to support SFTP, as shown in Example 30-2.

Example 30-2   *Adding the Host Key to the Repository*

```
atw-cp-ise02/admin# conf t
atw-cp-ise02/admin(config)# repository ATW-SFTP
% Warning: Host key of the server must be added using host-key command before sftp
repository can be used.
atw-cp-ise02/admin(config-Repository)# host-key host 172.25.73.254
host key fingerprint added
# Host 172.25.73.254 found: line 1 type RSA
1024 17:60:bb:44:2f:36:d8:df:6b:98:fb:63:7f:52:a7:a1 172.25.73.254 (RSA)
```

TFTP is not a common repository type for ISE. TFTP servers can often have drawbacks related to file sizes, and ISE packages usually exceed those file-size limitations. There are no credentials necessary, because TFTP is connectionless and does not use authentication credentials, as shown in Figure 30-5.

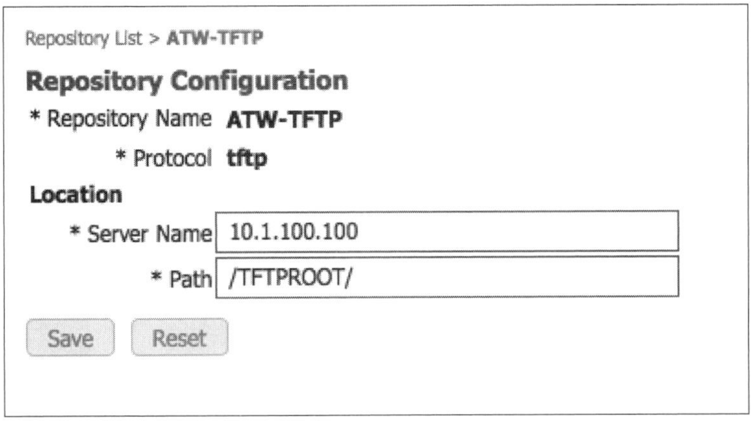

Repository List > **ATW-TFTP**

Repository Configuration

* Repository Name **ATW-TFTP**

        * Protocol **tftp**

Location

    * Server Name | 10.1.100.100

           * Path | /TFTPROOT/

Save   Reset

Figure 30-5 *TFTP Repository*

The Network File System (NFS) repository is fairly common, especially in environments with a storage-area network (SAN). NFS is usually a responsive and reliable transport mechanism for storage. This repository requires the NFS server, IP address or FQDN, and path and credentials, as shown in Figure 30-6.

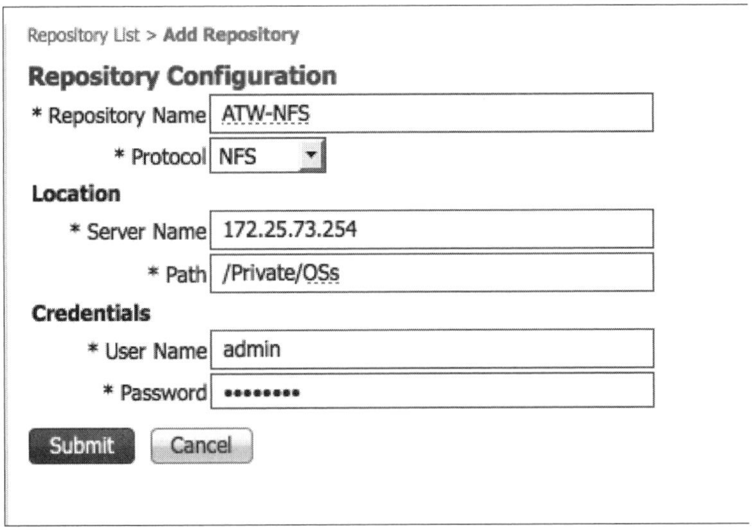

Repository List > **Add Repository**

Repository Configuration

* Repository Name | ATW-NFS

        * Protocol | NFS

Location

    * Server Name | 172.25.73.254

           * Path | /Private/OSs

Credentials

    * User Name | admin

      * Password | ••••••••

Submit   Cancel

Figure 30-6 *NFS Repository*

CD-ROM is a repository that is used with the physical CD-ROM/DVD-ROM drive of the 33x5 appliances (34x5 appliances have no drive) or the virtual CD drive with VMware, as shown in Figure 30-7.

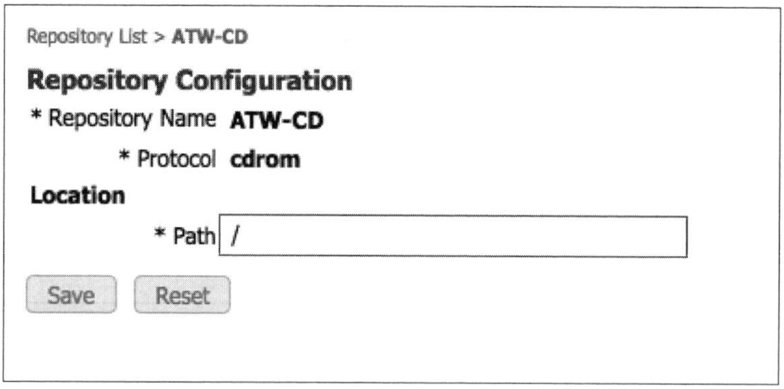

Repository List > **ATW-CD**

Repository Configuration
* Repository Name **ATW-CD**
      * Protocol **cdrom**
Location
    * Path `/`

  Save   Reset

Figure 30-7 *CD-ROM Repository*

HTTP is used for HTTP file storage. This repository does not support authentication credentials, just the path, as shown in Figure 30-8. Yes, an HTTP repository without the ability to authenticate is fairly useless, so don't expect this one to get much usage today unless it is only to download files.

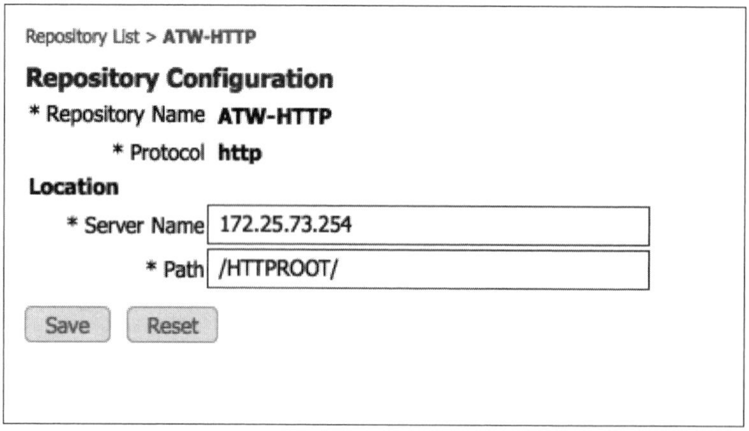

Repository List > **ATW-HTTP**

Repository Configuration
* Repository Name **ATW-HTTP**
    * Protocol **http**
Location
  * Server Name 172.25.73.254
     * Path /HTTPROOT/

  Save   Reset

Figure 30-8 *HTTP Repository*

HTTPS is used for HTTPS file storage. This repository does not provide authentication credentials, just the path, as shown in Figure 30-9. Yes, an HTTPS-encrypted repository type that does not provide enough security to authenticate the user is again pretty useless. So, don't expect this one to get too much usage today, either.

You may validate the repository at any time from the command line by using the **show repository** *repository-name* command, as shown in Example 30-3.

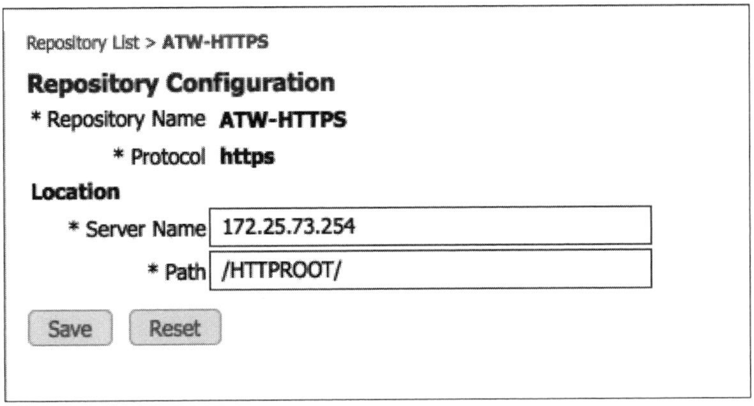

Repository List > **ATW-HTTPS**

Repository Configuration
* Repository Name **ATW-HTTPS**
      * Protocol **https**
Location
    * Server Name   172.25.73.254
      * Path   /HTTPROOT/

[Save]   [Reset]

Figure 30-9 *HTTP Repository*

Example 30-3 *Output of* show repository *Command*

```
atw-cp-ise02/admin# show repository ATW-CD
FILE NAME                            SIZE  MODIFIED TIME
==============================================================================
.discinfo                       102 Bytes  Tue Nov 13 18:38:10 2012
Server                             72 KB   Mon Nov 19 02:26:26 2012
TRANS.TBL                           1 KB   Mon Nov 19 02:26:26 2012
images                              2 KB   Mon Nov 19 02:25:36 2012
isolinux                            2 KB   Mon Nov 19 02:25:36 2012
ks.cfg                             24 KB   Mon Nov 19 02:25:36 2012
```

Backup

A repository is required before a backup procedure may be used. Backups can run from the Primary Administrative Node, Monitoring Node, or a Standalone Node. There are two types of backup: a configuration backup and an operational backup. The configuration backup supports the ISE database, all policies, objects, endpoints, rules, and ADE-OS configuration; the operational backup supports the monitoring (M&T) logs.

The backup operation creates a GNU Privacy Guard (GPG)-encrypted TAR file, containing the configuration database or the MNT log files, depending on the type of backup that was executed. TAR originally stood for Tape ARchive, and has been commonly used for file archival with UNIX operating systems for many years. For those of you without any UNIX/Linux background, think of it as being a lot like an encrypted ZIP file.

It is important to note that the backup TAR file is created on the local file system before it is moved to the repository. This is critically important for the disk size that an ISE vir-

tual machine was created with. There have been a number of TAC cases where the installation did not follow the recommended disk space size, and the deployment ran perfectly
fine, right up until the time a backup was required. There was not enough local disk space
for the backup to occur.

Backups may be run from the GUI or from the CLI. Figure 30-10 shows the main backup
screen. Figure 30-11 and Figure 30-12 show a backup being run, while Example 30-4
shows a backup being run from the CLI.

Figure 30-10   *Backup and Restore Screen*

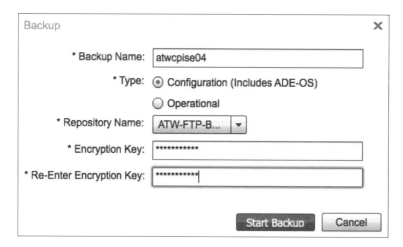

Figure 30-11   *On Demand Backup*

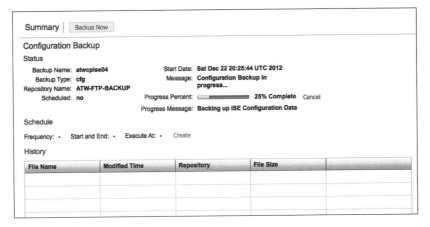

Figure 30-12 *Backup Progress*

Example 30-4   *CLI backup Command*

```
atw-cp-ise02/admin# backup Dec21Backup repository ATW-FTP ise-config encryption-key
plain ISE12345
% Creating backup with timestamped filename: Dec21Backup-CFG-121221-2119.tar.gpg
% backup in progress: Starting Backup...10% completed
% backup in progress: Validating ISE Node Role...20% completed
% backup in progress: Backing up ISE Configuration Data...25% completed
```

The list of available backups display on the Backup and Restore page, as shown in
Figure 30-13. Any of the listed backups may be restored by clicking the Restore link.
Restoration is covered in the next section.

Figure 30-13 *List of Backups*

Backups may also be scheduled. The schedule choices are one-time, daily, weekly, or monthly, as shown in Figure 30-14.

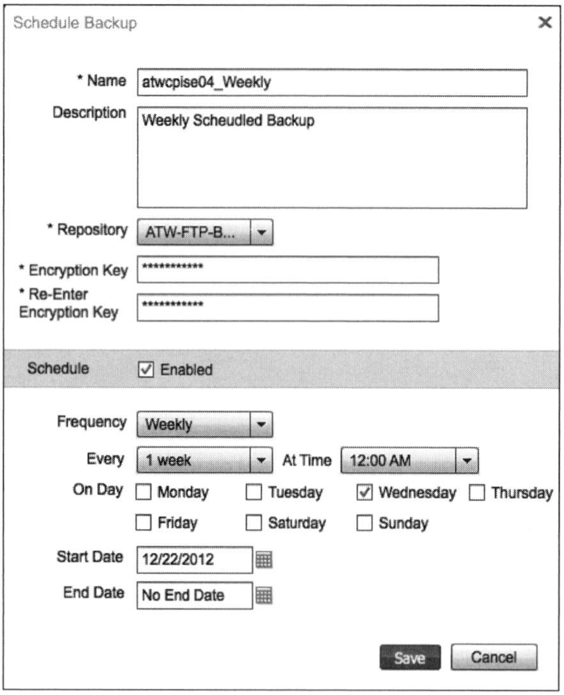

Figure 30-14   *Backup Schedule*

Restore

Each configuration backup contains the ADE-OS configuration and the ISE configuration. When performing a restore, you are presented with an option to restore the ADE-OS configuration or not.

Begin the restoration process by clicking the Restore link next to any of the existing backup's in the repository. You are then prompted to input the password to decrypt the backup, and whether you choose to restore ADE-OS configuration with the ISE configuration, as shown in Figure 30-15.

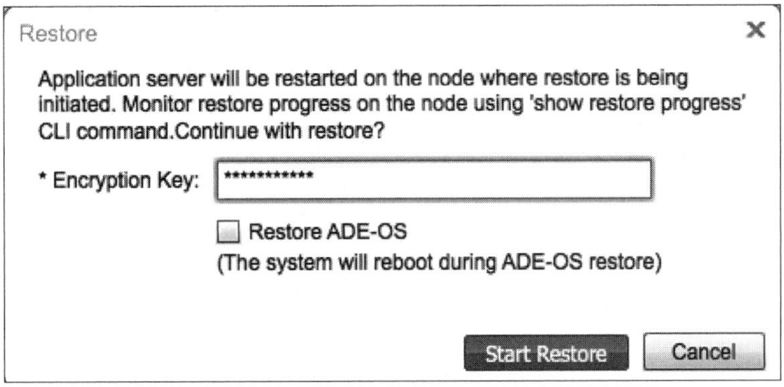

Restore   ✕

Application server will be restarted on the node where restore is being
initiated. Monitor restore progress on the node using 'show restore progress'
CLI command.Continue with restore?

* Encryption Key: [***********]

                        ☐ Restore ADE-OS
                        (The system will reboot during ADE-OS restore)

                                           [Start Restore]   [Cancel]

Figure 30-15 *Restoring a Configuration Backup*

Example 30-5 illustrates the CLI for performing a restore without the use of the GUI.

Example 30-5 *Restore CLI Showing the Optional* include-adeos *Command*

```
atw-cp-ise02/admin# restore atwcpise04-CFG-121222-2030.tar.gpg repository ATW-FTP ?
  encryption-key  Encryption-key used at time of backup
  include-adeos   Also restore ADE-OS configuration if included in backup
  <cr>            Carriage return.
System Upgrades and Patch Management
```

The patching of an ISE system, and upgrading the ISE system are two distinctly different activities.

Patching

Patches are released by Cisco on an as-needed basis. These are created to fix specific bugs, and they are cumulative. That means if Patch 3 is released, it will contain all bug fixes from Patch numbers 1 and 2.

Patches are downloaded from Cisco.com and are found along with the system software itself, under Support > Download Software > Products > Security > Access Control and Policy > Cisco Identity Services Engine, as shown in Figure 30-16.

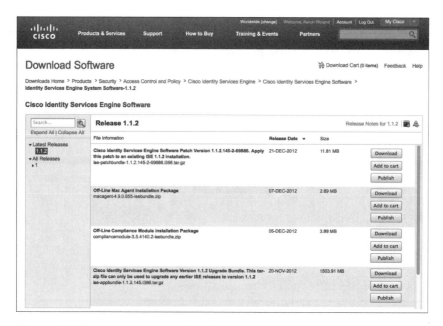

Figure 30-16   *Cisco.com Download Center*

The installation of the patch is completed on the primary admin node within the ISE GUI. The primary admin, in-turn, distributes the patch to all the other nodes within the ISE cube. There may be some downtime required for a patch, and if there, is documented in the Release notes.

To install a patch, perform the following steps:

1. Download the patch from Cisco.com.

2. Navigate to **Maintenance > Patch Management**.

3. Browse for the Downloaded Patch, as shown in Figure 30-17.

Figure 30-17   *Install the Patch*

4. Click **Install**.

5. A pop-up message displays, showing the MD5 hash to ensure that the file is unmodified from the original download. It provides a warning that you will be logged out while the patch is installed and that a restart of the application may occur, as shown in Figure 30-18.

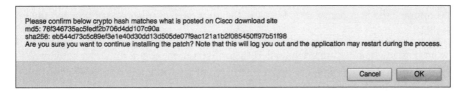

> Please confirm below crypto hash matches what is posted on Cisco download site
> md5: 78f346735ac5fedf2b706d4dd107c90a
> sha256: eb544d73c5c89ef3e1e40d30dd13d505de07f9ac121a1b2f085450ff97b51f98
> Are you sure you want to continue installing the patch? Note that this will log you out and the application may restart during the process.
>
> Cancel   OK

Figure 30-18   *Patch Install Pop-Up*

6. You can check to see the status of all the nodes at any time after the patch has been installed by clicking the **Node-Status** button, as shown in Figure 30-19.

Maintenance
- Patch Management
- Repository
- Data Purging

Installed Patches

Install   Rollback   Show Node Status

Patch Version

Node Status for Patch: 1

Nodes	Patch Status
10.65.172.68	Installed
10.42.8.43	Installed
10.42.8.44	Installed
10.42.8.41	Installed
10.42.8.42	Installed
10.42.7.63	Installed
10.42.7.64	Installed

Figure 30-19   *Node Status*

Patching has a quick Rollback option, just in case something goes awry. Simply highlight the patch and click **Rollback**.

Upgrading

Prior to ISE 1.2, you had to follow a split-domain upgrading model. The new model in 1.2 was designed to be more efficient and significantly reduce the upgrade time.

This new model is known as the Secondary PAN First (SPF) flow. This means that you should upgrade the Secondary PAN first and then upgrade all other nodes sequentially or in parallel.

Software upgrade bundles are downloaded from Cisco.com and are found along with the system software itself, under Support > Download Software > Products > Security > Access Control and Policy > Cisco Identity Services Engine.

Available images for download are .iso images for full installs and .tar.gz files available as upgrade bundles. For the upgrade procedure, download the latest .tar.gz upgrade bundle.

Ensure that you have a successful configuration and operational backup before beginning the upgrade procedure.

To follow the SPF flow for upgrade, perform the following steps:

1. Download the application upgrade .tar.gz bundle from Cisco.com, and place it in one of the repositories configured on ISE (such as the FTP repository).

2. On the Secondary PAN, execute the following CLI:

   ```
   ise/admin# application upgrade ise-appbundle-filename.tar.gz repository-name
   ```

   When the upgrade begins on the Secondary PAN, it automatically becomes the Primary PAN for the upgraded deployment. The PANs no longer speak to each other, because their versioning is different, as shown in Figure 30-20.

   Once the Secondary PAN has been successfully upgraded, the PSNs and MNT nodes may be upgraded one at a time or a few simultaneously. Always leave enough PSNs active to handle the authentication load of the entire deployment.

3. Upgrade one of the M&T nodes, so that a logging target will exist in the new deployment. To upgrade the M&T, simply repeat Step 2 on the M&T node itself.

4. Take each Policy Service Node "out of service" before beginning the upgrade process on that node.

   If using a Load-Balancer, all you need to do is mark the server as down to remove it from the VIP. If pointing directly to the Policy Service Nodes from the NADs, you must go into the NAD configuration and remove the server from the configuration.

   When the other PSNs are upgraded, they will just get the full database dump from Secondary PAN without requiring a full data-model upgrade. This saves a tremendous amount of time per PSN, because it does not need to upgrade the entire database, like the process for the PAN.

   Each of the PSNs upgraded automatically join the new PAN, and all logging continues to be sent to both MNT nodes, as shown in Figure 30-21.

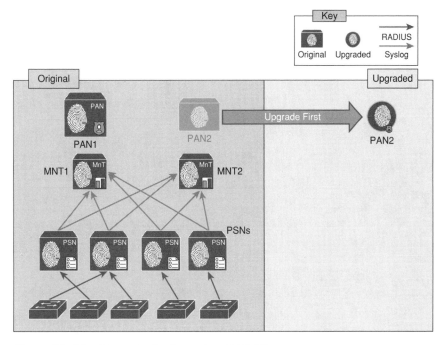

Figure 30-20   *Upgrade the Secondary PAN First*

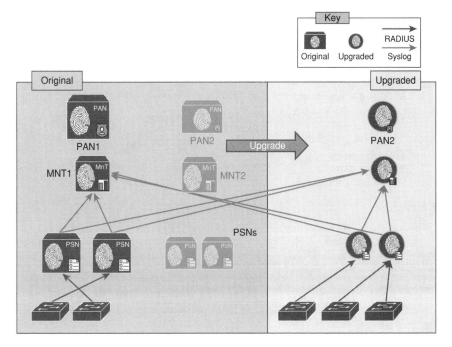

Figure 30-21   *Staged Upgrade*

5. Remember to take the PSNs out of service before upgrading them to ensure that you have limited the risk of end-user downtime, as shown in Figure 30-22.

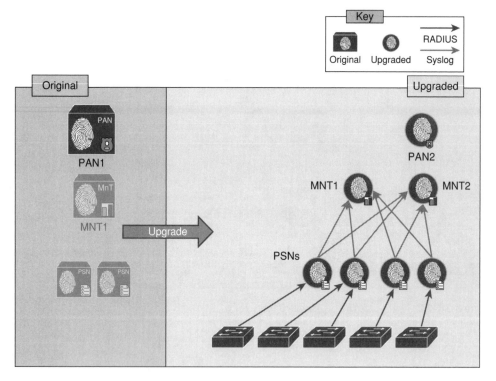

Figure 30-22   *Staged Upgrade: Primary PAN Is Last*

6. The last node to be upgraded should be the original Primary PAN. It will also receive a complete database dump from the Secondary PAN.

If you want the original primary PAN to be primary in the upgraded model, you need to manually promote it back to the primary role.

Summary

This chapter discussed the importance of repositories and the types of repositories available. It examined operational backups and configuration backups and how they are saved as encrypted "tarballs" on the repository. It also covered the importance of hard-drive space when performing backups. It demonstrated how patching is accomplished from a single location in the GUI and then distributed to all nodes in a deployment. Lastly, it examined the staged approach to upgrading and worked through the recommended upgrading procedures.

Sample User Community Deployment Messaging Material

This appendix provides sample messaging for you to use to inform your user population about what Identity Services Engine is, how to use it, and where to get help. This messaging is primarily tailored for the education environment but can be easily tailored for use in other environments. This appendix contains the following information and materials:

- Sample Identity Services Engine requirement change notification email

- Sample Identity Services Engine notice for a bulletin board or poster

- Sample Identity Services Engine letter to students

Feel free to modify and adapt these samples to your needs.

Sample Identity Services Engine Requirement Change Notification Email

The following email sample is meant to be sent out to the user community prior to the enforcement of a new posture assessment requirement or check in Identity Services Engine. It is recommended that you first roll out all new requirements as optional or monitor only, so that you can review the possible impact on your organization without actually causing any outage in the production environment. Then, after a set amount of time, make the new requirement mandatory. The sending of this email should coincide with the implementation of the optional requirement, to provide ample warning to the user community prior to the mandatory enforcement date. It should then be sent again immediately prior to the requirement being made mandatory.

To: Students and Faculty

From: ITD

Subject: NEW PC security updates required

Faculty and Students,

Starting tomorrow, September 23rd, there will be two new security require-
ments for all Windows PCs connected to the residential network. You may see
the NAC Agent prompt you to install these new security updates on your PC.
Please follow the instructions given to install these updates. You have a two-week
discretionary period within which to install the new updates before enforcement
begins.

In order to ensure uninterrupted network access, it is strongly recommended *that*
you install the new updates during this discretionary period. Please keep in
mind that these updates can take from 5 to 30 minutes to install depending on the
performance of your PC.

Starting October 8th, *the NAC system will initiate the enforcement of the new*
security updates. Once enforcement begins, any PC not running the required
security updates will be forced to install them before being allowed full network
access.

If you have any questions or need technical assistance, please go to the ITD ISE
support page at www.univ.com/nac/support *or call the help desk at x4000.*

Sample Identity Services Engine Notice for a Bulletin Board or Poster

The following announcement can be posted on internal websites, posted on bulletin
boards, or handed out as a flyer. Your implementation may differ, so please use this only
as a guideline. The objectives of this announcement are as follows:

- To inform the user community that the Identity Services Engine solution is in place, and to explain why

- To inform users how to employ the system

- To set expectations on its use

- To give references for obtaining more information

Connecting to the Campus Network

In an effort to reduce the threat posed by viruses and worms to the campus net-
work, the University has implemented the Cisco ISE network admission control
solution.

Here's what students need to know:

- All students living in the residence halls will be required to go through the new net- work policy controls to gain access to any campus network.

- Students with Windows PCs and Mac computers are required to install the Cisco NAC Agent and Cisco AnyConnect security software. This will be delivered to you automatically through the student web portal page.

- Students are required to authenticate to the network using their campus username and password.

- The PC being used will be checked to make sure it has the necessary security software and system patches installed before being allowed on to the network.

- Any PC that does not meet the security requirements will dynamically be placed into network quarantine and provided the necessary instructions and security software. Once the PC is certified, full network access will be restored.

- The Cisco Identity Services Engine solution does NOT access your personal files, block any applications, or monitor your network traffic.

Why is Cisco Identity Services Engine necessary?

Nearly all network outages or brown-outs experienced on the campus network are the result of virus-infected or severely compromised student PCs accessing the network. As a result, it has become necessary for the University to implement a network security system in order to minimize the risk posed by students who connect infected PCs to the campus network. This security solution will keep your computers much more secure, allowing them to resist the infection of viruses that may destroy your documents or render your PC unusable.

How to obtain the Cisco NAC Agent:

1. Plug into the campus network.

2. Open your web browser of choice. You will be redirected to the University login page.

3. Log in using your campus username and password.

4. You will be directed to install the Cisco NAC Agent and Cisco AnyConnect software.

5. Click the **Download** button and follow the installation wizard's instructions to install the software. Installation may require a reboot.

How to log in to the network:

1. Login is done using the Cisco AnyConnect Agent.

2. The agent login will happen automatically whenever your computer attempts to access the campus network.

3. If required, enter your username and password and click **Login**.

4. Follow the instructions given to remediate any failed security checks on your PC.

5. Once your PC is compliant, you will gain full network access.

Who to contact for help:

- Help Desk at x4000

- www.university.com/nac/support

- Email: Support@university.com

Additional information can be found at www.university.com/nac/support.

Sample Identity Services Engine Letter to Students

The following sample letter is intended to be added to the university's student handbook, which is typically sent to students before the beginning of the new school year. The letter serves two purposes: to inform students about the Identity Services Engine solution, and to instruct students on how to obtain the NAC Agent prior to arriving on campus.

Dear Student,

This letter is to inform you that the university's campus network is protected using a system called Cisco Identity Services Engine. This security solution was put into place in an effort to decrease the threat posed by viruses and worms on the university's network. The vast majority of previous network outages or slowness could be attributed directly to the outbreak of a computer virus or worm. These outbreaks also resulted in the widespread damage or loss of data on student PCs. An effective method of combating these outbreaks is to ensure that every PC connecting to the network is running an up-to-date antivirus software package and also has all of the latest Windows security patches installed. The Cisco Identity Services Engine security solution provides this capability to the University.

In order to be ready for the school year, you will need to download and install the NAC Agent on your Windows or Mac-based computer. Please make every effort to install the agent prior to arriving on campus. This will help make your arrival go that much smoother. The agent download can be found at www.university.com/agent. Just follow the instructions provided to complete the simple install. Should you have any questions or need technical assistance, please call the University help desk at 800-333-3333.

Thank you,

The ITD Staff

Sample ISE Deployment Questionnaire

This appendix provides a series of questions meant to help you determine the scope of your proposed ISE deployment. Most of this content comes from the *Cisco ISE High-level Design Guide* that is used by the Cisco ISE Certified Partners. Once you have answered the questions in each given table, you can then proceed to determine your Bill of Materials for Cisco ISE and your approximate project scope to plan for.

State Your Business Goals for ISE

Services	Wire (Yes or No)	Wireless (Yes or No)
Guest Services		
Device Profiling		
Host Posture Assessment		

Estimated Timelines

Phase	Number of Endpoints	Begin	End	Comments
Lab testing and qualification				
Final Design Review call with Cisco SME	—			
Production phase 1 (pilot)				
Production phase 2				
Production phase 3				

Customer Environment Summary

Deployment Summary	Response
Use cases in scope for design	
Wired?	
Wireless?	
VPN?	
Endpoint count	
Total endpoint count for entire deployment (endpoint count equals the sum of user and non-user devices)	
Total user endpoints (laptops, PCs, mobile devices, etc.)	
Total non-user endpoints that support 802.1x (i.e., IP-Phones, printers, BioMed, etc.)	
Total non-user endpoints that do not support 802.1x (i.e., IP cameras, badge readers, etc.)	
Concurrent endpoint count	
Max. number of endpoints online with ISE at any given time	
*ISE is licensed based on max. concurrent online users and devices.	
Total physical locations	
How many physical buildings/locations will you protect with ISE?	
Is your deployment geographically disperse?	
How many ISE Policy Service Node locations do you anticipate?	
Total number of network infrastructure devices	
Switches	
Wireless controllers	
VPN gateways	
Wireless Access Points	
IP-Phones (do they support dot1x?)	
Routers	
Other	

Topology Specifics

Required Information	Response
Network Access Devices	
Provide the general switch/controller model numbers/platforms deployed and Cisco IOS Software versions to be deployed to support ISE design.	
Client OS and Supplicant Types	
List all non-mobile client OS types and versions that will be used by non-guest users.	
Which 802.1x supplicant is used (native OS, AnyConnect NAM, other)?	
Number (general count for each type)?	
Please provide service pack details for Windows and OS types for Mac OS X.	
Mobile Devices (smartphones, tablets)	
List all vendor types and mobile OS versions deployed by non-guest users.	
Are mobile devices corporate- or employee-owned assets?	
Will you use a mobile device management system? If so, list the details.	
802.1X Authentication	
Will you be deploying 802.1x for wired, wireless, or both?	
Will you be using machine authentication, user authentication, or both?	
What percentage of your devices will not support 802.1x?	
Extensible Authentication Protocol (EAP) Types	
EAP types for users	
EAP types for machines	
Examples:	
PEAP (Username/password-based auth.)	
EAP-TLS (Certificate-based auth.)	
EAP-FAST	

Required Information	Response
ID Stores	
[EAP and ID Store Compatibility Reference]	
List the ID store to be used by each Auth. Type:	
802.1X machine auth.	
802.1X user auth.	
802.1X cert-based auth.	
MAB	
Web Authentication/Guests	
For Active Directory:	
Are there multiple domains?	
Are there multiple forests?	
Authorization	
Which enforcement types will be used? List wired/wireless.	
VLANs	
Downloadable ACLs	
Security Group Tags (SGTs/SGACLs)	
SmartPort macros	
Posture	
Will you be using host posture assessment?	
If so, which operating systems are in scope?	
Profiling	
List the primary device types to be profiled.	
Which probes will be deployed to collect the required data?	
If RSPAN or NetFlow is to be used, is there sufficient bandwidth between source SPAN/ NetFlow exporter and ISE Policy Service node used for profiling?	
Is profiling for visibility only or for use in Authorization Policy?	

Required Information	Response
ISE Nodes/Personas.	
Will high availability be deployed for ISE?	
Number and type of each ISE appliance (node).	
Define the personas assigned to each node (e.g., Administration, Monitoring, Policy Service, Inline Posture).	

Configuring the Microsoft CA for BYOD

As discussed in Chapter 17, "BYOD: Self-Service Onboarding and Registration," the vast majority of customers have been using the Microsoft Certificate Authority as their CA for BYOD. Therefore, we would be remiss not to include some information on how to configure the Microsoft CA for use in the BYOD solution.

CA Requirements

For the Microsoft CA to provide all the functions necessary, it must meet the following requirements:

- Windows 2008 R2 Enterprise Server.

- Certificate Enrollment Web Service and Certificate Enrollment Policy Web Service must be installed.

- The Windows 2008 R2 Enterprise Server must be joined to a domain.

- An enterprise CA is required. The Certificate Enrollment Web Service cannot be configured to work with a standalone CA.

Other Useful Information

- The Certificate Enrollment Web Service can be configured to work with an enterprise CA on the same server or a different server.

- The services can be installed on the same computer as the CA, Web Enrollment, Online Responder, and Network Device Enrollment Services (NDES) role services.

  - However, if you intend on using the NDES service for certificates issued to Cisco IOS device (for example, Cisco CVO deployment), you need to run Certificate Enrollment Web Services on a separate server than NDES.

- This is because of an IIS incompatibility with SCEP to IOS routers when NDES and CWES are running on the same server. If you do run on separate servers, review MS hotfixes listed in the next section.

Microsoft Hotfixes

- **http://support.microsoft.com/kb/2483564:** Renewal request for an SCEP certificate fails in Windows Server 2008 R2 if the certificate is managed by using NDES. This issue occurs because NDES does not support the GetCACaps operation.

- **http://support.microsoft.com/kb/2633200:** NDES does not submit certificate requests after the enterprise CA is restarted in Windows Server 2008 R2. You will see "The Network Device Enrollment Service cannot submit the certificate request (0x800706ba). The RPC server is unavailable" in the Event Viewer.

AD Account Roles

Use two different Active Directory (AD) accounts for the ongoing operation of the certificate authority and NDES. Those two accounts serve for the following roles:

- **SCEP administrator:** Used to install the NDES role service and must meet the following requirements:

    - Member of Domain Admins or Enterprise Admins group

    - Enroll permissions on the CA template (completed later)

- **SCEP service account:** Used by the NDES application pool for the application to "Run As". The account must meet the following requirements:

    - Member of the local IIS_IUSRS group

    - Request permission on the configured CA

    - *Read* and *enroll* permissions on configured device certificate templates

Configuration Steps

Create the Service Account

1. Add a new Active Directory user, such as SCEP_User.

2. Ensure that the user is added to the IIS_IUSRS local group.

Install AD Certificate Services

1. From Server Manager, select **Add Role.**

2. Select **Active Directory Certificate Services,** as shown in Figure C-1.

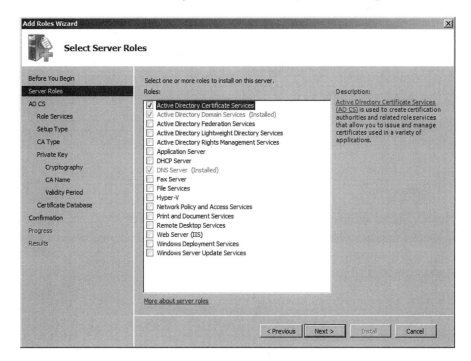

Figure C-1   *Add Active Directory Certificate Services*

3. Click **Next.**

4. Select **Certification Authority, Certification Authority Web Enrollment, Online Responder, and Certificate Enrollment Policy Web Service,** as shown in Figure C-2.

5. Click **Next.**

6. Choose **Enterprise to use Directory Services with the CA,** as shown in Figure C-3.

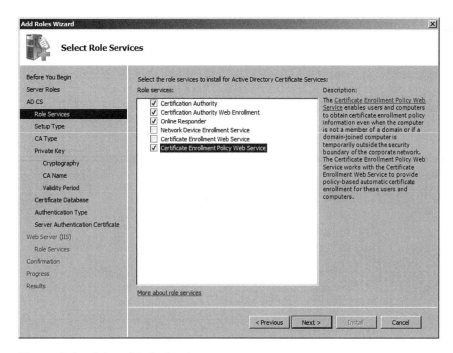

Figure C-2   *Selected Role Services*

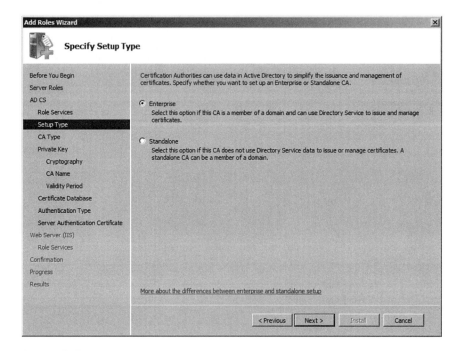

Figure C-3   *Enterprise CA Type*

7. Click **Next**.

8. Specify the CA type. If this is a new CA, it should be **root**, as shown in Figure C-4.

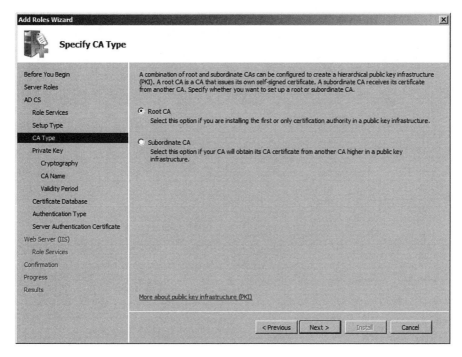

Figure C-4 *Root CA Type*

9. Click **Next**.

10. Create a new private key, as shown in Figure C-5.

11. Click **Next**.

12. Configure the Cryptography for the CA.

Most of the installations we have been involved with use the settings shown in Figure C-6.

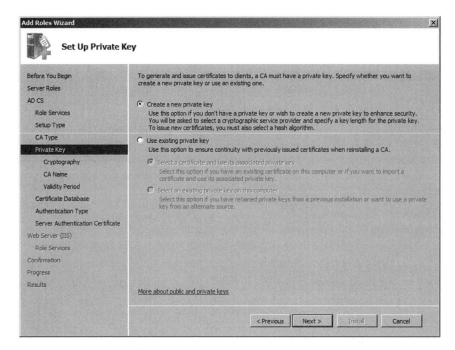

Figure C-5 *Set Up Private Key*

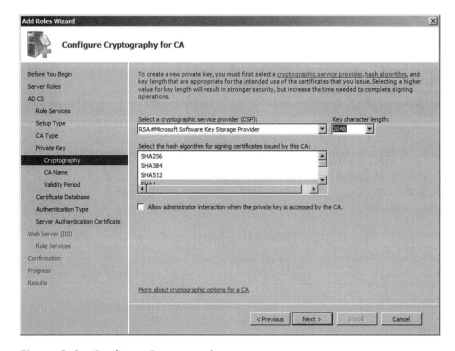

Figure C-6 *Configure Cryptography*

13. Click **Next.**

14. Configure the CA Name, as shown in Figure C-7.

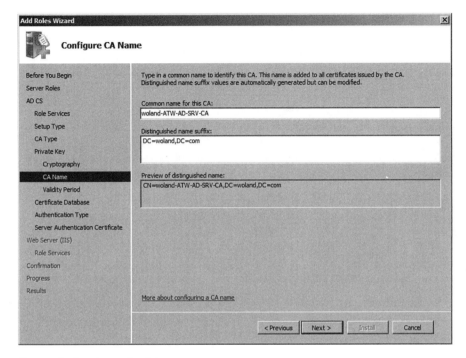

Figure C-7 *Name the CA*

15. Click **Next.**

16. Set the **Validity Period**, as shown in Figure C-8.

17. Click **Next.**

18. Set the location of the CA database, as shown in Figure C-9. The default is usually fine.

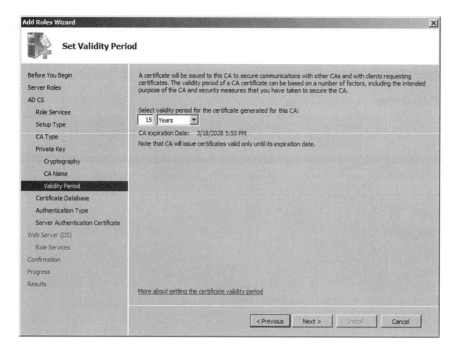

Figure C-8   *Validity Period*

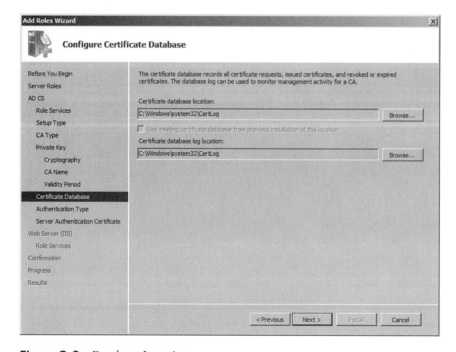

Figure C-9   *Database Location*

19. Click **Next.**

20. Set the authentication to use **Username and Password,** as shown in Figure C-10.

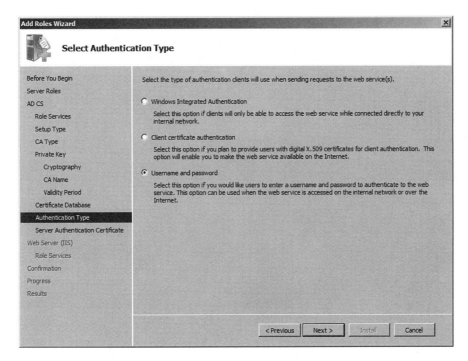

Figure C-10 *Authentication Type*

21. Click **Next.**

22. Choose the **Server Certificate**, as shown in Figure C-11.

23. Click **Next.**

24. Review your choices.

25. Click **Install.**

Now that the CA is installed, we can go back and add the remaining roles.

26. From Server Manager, select **Add Role Services** for the CA, as shown in Figure C-12.

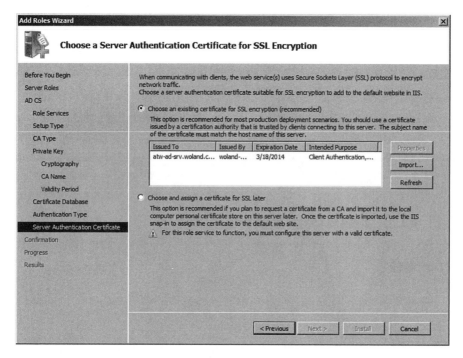

Figure C-11   *Choose the Server Certificate*

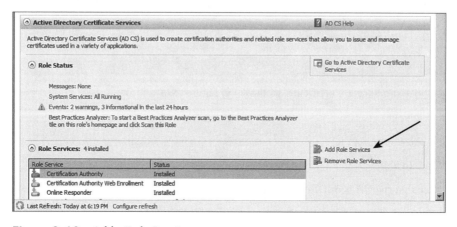

Figure C-12   *Add a Role Service*

27. Click **Next**.

28. Select **Network Device Enrollment Service** and **Certificate Enrollment Web Service**, as shown in Figure C-13.

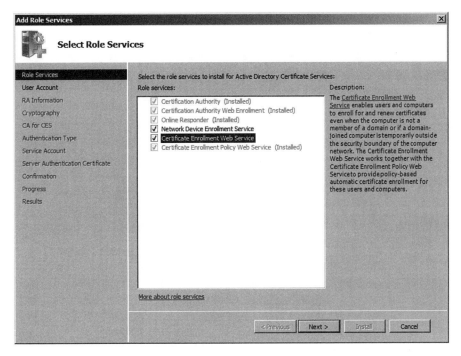

Figure C-13 *Select the Role Services*

29. Click **Next**.

30. Specify the Service Account User created previously, as shown in Figure C-14.

31. Click **Next**.

32. Fill in the registration authority data, as shown in Figure C-15.

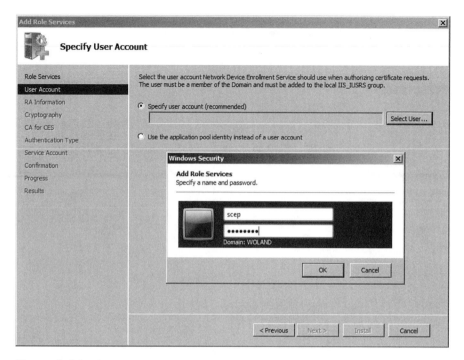

Figure C-14   *Service Account*

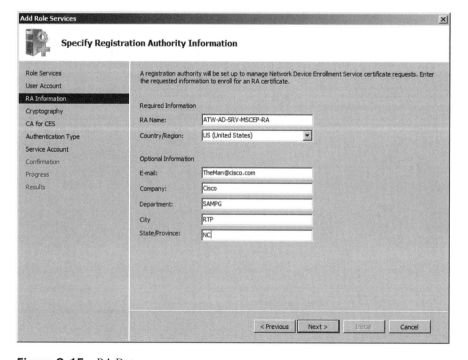

Figure C-15   *RA Data*

33. Click **Next**.

34. Set the RA cryptographic settings, as shown in Figure C-16.

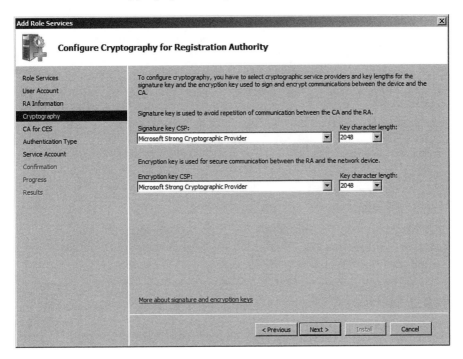

Figure C-16   *RA Cryptography*

35. Click **Next**.

36. Specify the CA for the Web services, as shown in Figure C-17.

37. Click **Next**.

38. Set Username and Password as **Authentication Type**, as shown in Figure C-18.

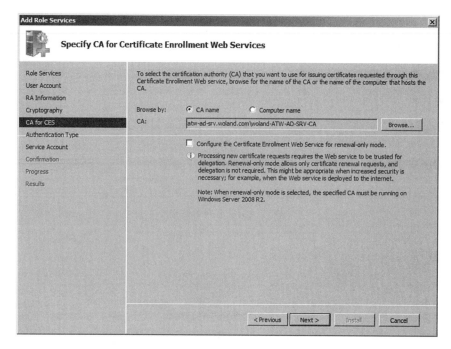

Figure C-17 *Web Services CA*

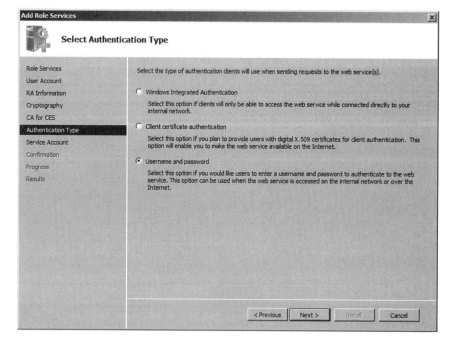

Figure C-18 *Authentication Type*

39. Click **Next.**

40. Specify the service account user again, as shown in Figure C-19.

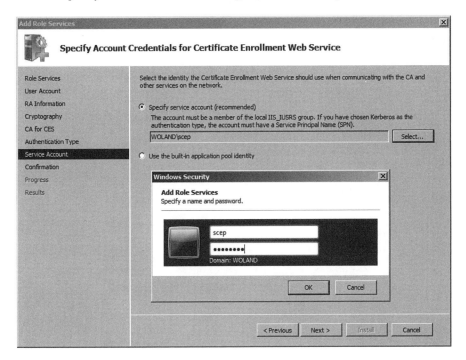

Figure C-19 *Service Account*

41. Click **Install.**

Configure the Certificate Template

1. Navigate to **Server Manager > Roles > AD Certificate Authority > Certificate Templates.**

2. Highlight the certificate template named **User** and choose **Duplicate**, as shown in Figure C-20.

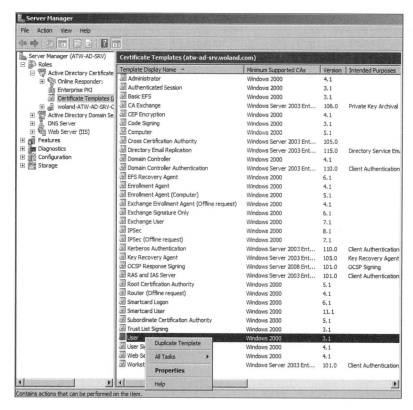

Figure C-20   *Duplicate the User Template*

3. Click **Next**.

4. Choose the **Template Version**. Either will work; the example screenshots are from a 2008 template version, as shown in Figure C-21.

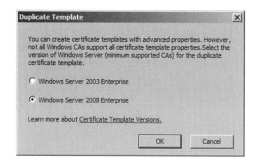

Figure C-21   *Template Version*

5. Click OK.

6. Name the certificate template and uncheck the **Publish in Active Directory** check box, as shown in Figure C-22.

Note This is an important check box, so ensure that it is not checked to avoid storage issues.

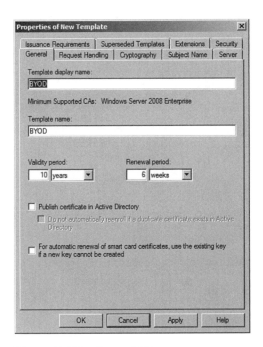

Figure C-22 *General Tab*

7. Click the **Request Handling** tab, as shown in Figure C-23:

- **Purpose:** States that the certificate will be used for signing and encrypting.

- Uncheck **allow private key to be exported** if you want to mark it as **nonexportable.**

- SCEP is an automated process; ensure **enroll subject without requiring any user input** is checked.

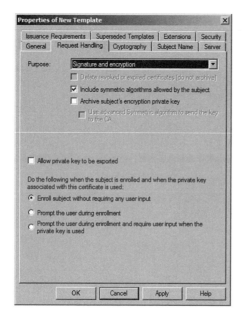

Figure C-23   *Request Handling Tab*

8. Click the **Subject Name** tab, as shown in Figure C-24.

9. The BYOD process is prebuilding the Certificate Signing Request; ensure that the **Supply in the Request** option is selected.

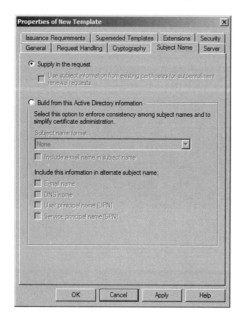

Figure C-24   *Subject Name Tab*

10. Click the **Extensions** tab, as shown in Figure C-25.

11. Click **Application Policies** and ensure that **client authentication** is listed.

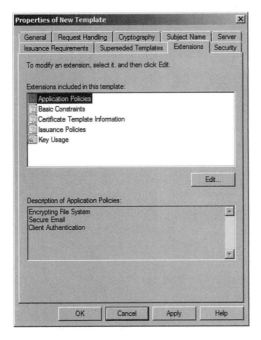

Figure C-25   *Application Policies*

12. Click **Issuance Policies,** as shown in Figure C-26.

13. Click **Edit,** then **Add.**

14. Select **All issuance policies.** This critical step ensures that the certificate is issued to the endpoint.

15. Click the **Security** tab, as shown in Figure C-27.

16. Add the service account user to have **full-control.**

17. Click **OK** to save the template.

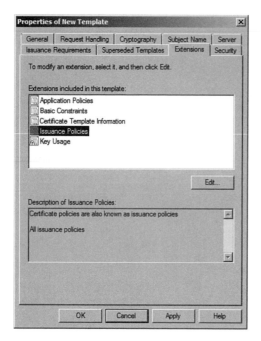

Figure C-26   *Issuance Policies*

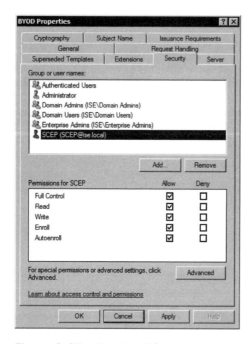

Figure C-27   *Security Tab*

Publish the Certificate Template

The template is created, but we have to choose it as one to be issued:

1. Go to **Server Manager > Roles > AD Certificate Authority > <your CA> > Certificate Templates**.

2. Right-click **New > Certificate Template to Issue**, as shown in Figure C-28.

3. Choose your new certificate template.

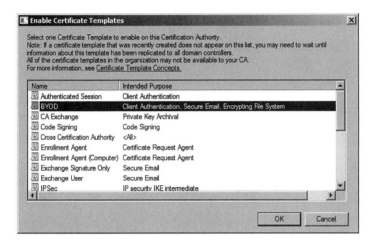

Figure C-28   *Certificate Template to Issue*

Edit the Registry

The service account user must have full control of the MSCEP registry key:

1. Open the Regedit application.

2. Select the **MSCEP** registry key from HKEY_LOCAL_MACHINE\Software\Microsoft\Cryptography\MSCEP, as shown in Figure C-29.

3. Right-click **MSCEP > Permissions**.

4. Add the **Service Account** and provide it **Full Control**, as shown in Figure C-30.

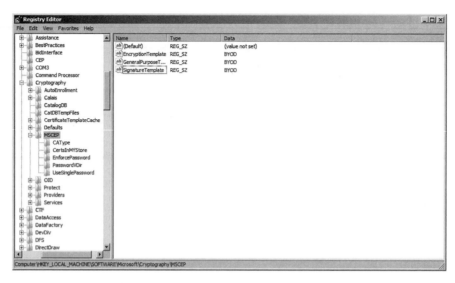

Figure C-29   *Regedit*

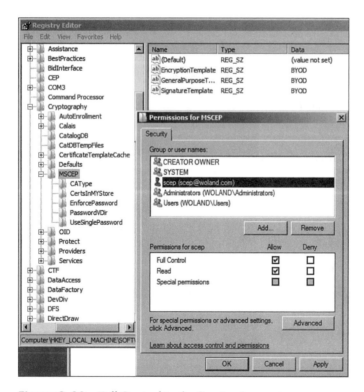

Figure C-30   *Full Control to the Service Account*

The Default Certificate Template for SCEP to issue is an IPsec template. You must change this to use the new User-Template.

5. From **HKLM > Software > Microsoft > Cryptography > MSCEP**, change the Three Registry Values to be the name of your newly created template (refer to Figure C-29).

While in Regedit, we must disable the UseSinglePassword setting.

6. From **HKLM > Software > Microsoft > Cryptography > MSCEP**, select the **UseSinglePassword Key**.

7. Change the value to **0**, as shown in Figure C-31.

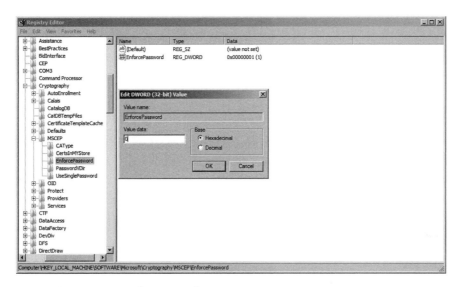

Figure C-31 *UseSinglePassword Setting*

You are finished! Reboot the server.

Useful Links

Microsoft Technet Article: Certificate Enrollment Web Services in Active Directory Certificate Services: http://tinyurl.com/aa6wro6

Microsoft Technet Article, AD CS: Deploying Network Device Enrollment Services: http://tinyurl.com/b47b6lb

Appendix D

Using a Cisco IOS Certificate Authority for BYOD Onboarding

This appendix shows an alternative for environments that do not have a production Certificate Authority (CA), such as the MS Certificate Authority for a proof of concept, or very small pilot. Cisco IOS on the Integrated Services Router (ISR) is capable of acting as a CA and supports SCEP with the ability to automatically issue the certificate. This works for many devices and should be sufficient for many proof of concept setups. See the section, "Important Notes," at the end of this appendix for information on some devices that may fail the certificate provisioning process.

For this appendix, a dedicated ISR has been set up to act as a CA. Figure D-1 displays the example topology.

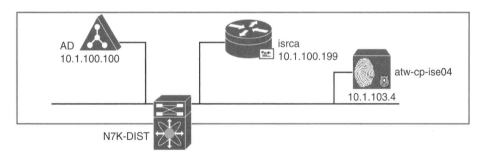

Figure D-1 *Topology Overview*

Set Hostname, Domain Name, and HTTP Server

Before generating any keys, ensure that a hostname and domain name have been configured within IOS (see Example D-1).

Example D-1   *Configure Hostname and Domain Name*

```
Router#conf t
Enter configuration commands, one per line.  End with CNTL/Z.
Router(config)#hostname atw-isr-ca
atw-isr-ca(config)#ip domain-name ise.local
```

The Cisco IOS CA server only supports enrollments done via Simple Certificate Enrollment Protocol (SCEP). To make this possible, the router must run the built-in Cisco IOS HTTP server. Use the **ip http server** command in order to enable it (see Example D-2).

Example D-2   *Generate the RSA Key Pair for the CA*

```
atw-isr-ca(config)#ip http server
atw-isr-ca(config)#
```

Generate and Export the RSA Key Pair for the Certificate Server

The first step is to generate the RSA key pair that the Cisco IOS CA server uses. Generate the RSA keys, as shown in Example D-3.

Example D-3   *Generate the RSA Key Pair for the CA*

```
atw-isr-ca(config)#crypto key generate rsa general-keys label isrca exportable
The name for the keys will be: isrca
Choose the size of the key modulus in the range of 360 to 4096 for your
  General Purpose Keys. Choosing a key modulus greater than 512 may take
  a few minutes.

How many bits in the modulus [512]: 2048
% Generating 2048 bit RSA keys, keys will be exportable...
[OK] (elapsed time was 12 seconds)

atw-isr-ca(config)#
Jan 10 16:51:06.471: %SSH-5-ENABLED: SSH 1.99 has been enabled
```

Note   You must use the same name for the key pair (key–label) that you plan to use for the certificate server (via the **crypto pki server cs–label** command, which is covered later).

Next, export the keys to NVRAM or TFTP. In Example D-4, NVRAM is used.

Example D-4 *Export the Keys*

```
atw-isr-ca(config)# crypto key export rsa isrca pem url nvram: 3des TrustSec123
% Key name: isrca
   Usage: General Purpose Key
Exporting public key...
Destination filename [isrca.pub]?
Writing file to nvram:isrca.pub
Exporting private key...
Destination filename [isrca.prv]?
Writing file to nvram:isrca.prv
atw-isr-ca(config)#
```

If you do not want the key to be exportable from your certificate server, import them back to the certificate server. However, import them as a non-exportable key pair. This way, the key cannot be removed again.

Configure the CA Server on the Router

Now that the router has been prepared with the foundational configuration, this section walks through the complete configuration process of the CA within IOS.

Enable the CA and Set the Database Level

Enable the CA server with the **crypto pki server** command. It is important to remember that the certificate server must use the same name as the key pair you just manually generated. Next, create a trustpoint that matches the CA name, as demonstrated in Example D-5.

Example D-5 *Enable the CA Server*

```
atw-isr-ca(config)#crypto pki server isrca
atw-isr-ca(cs-server)#exit
atw-isr-ca(config)#crypto pki trustpoint isrca
atw-isr-ca(ca-trustpoint)#rsakeypair isrca
atw-isr-ca(ca-trustpoint)#exit
```

If you want to specify the location where all database entries for the CA server are stored, use the **database url** command. If this command is not specified, all database entries are written to flash. Next, specify how much information is stored in the enrollment database with the **database level** command, as demonstrated in Example D-6:

- **Minimum** (default): Enough information is stored only to continue issuing new certificates without conflict.

- **Names:** Stores the data from the minimal level, plus the serial number and subject name of each certificate.

- **Complete:** In addition to the information given in the minimum and names levels, each issued certificate is written to the database.

> **Note**   The **complete** keyword produces a large amount of information. If it is issued, you should specify an external TFTP server in which to store the data via the **database url** command.

Example D-6   *Specify the Database URL and Information Level*

```
atw-isr-ca(config)#crypto pki server isrca
atw-isr-ca(cs-server)#database level names
```

Configure the CA Issuer Name

All CAs must have a name to present within the certificates they sign. The name should be in the Distinguished Name format of CN=, as shown here:

```
atw-isr-ca(cs-server)#issuer-name CN=isrca.ise.local
```

Set the Lifetimes of Certificates and the CRL

Specify the lifetime, in days, of a CA certificate or a certificate. Valid values range from 1 day to 1825 days. The default CA certificate lifetime is three years, and the default certificate lifetime is one year. The maximum certificate lifetime is one month less than the lifetime of the CA certificate.

Next, define the lifetime, in hours, of the CRL that is used by the certificate server. The maximum lifetime value is 336 hours (two weeks). The default value is 168 hours (one week).

It may also benefit you, for a proof of concept, to issue the **grant auto** command, as demonstrated in Example D-7. This automatically issues SCEP requests.

Example D-7   *Set the Lifetimes*

```
atw-isr-ca(cs-server)#lifetime ca-certificate 3650
atw-isr-ca(cs-server)#lifetime certificate 360
atw-isr-ca(cs-server)#lifetime crl 24
atw-isr-ca(cs-server)#grant auto
```

Define a CDP and Enable the CA Server

You may optionally specify a Certificate Revocation List (CRL) Distribution Point (CDP) that specifies a URL to store, update, and check the CRL. This is the last step, and the server may be enabled with the **no shutdown** command after all the steps have been completed, as demonstrated in Example D-8.

Example D-8 *Set the CDP and Enable the CA*

```
atw-isr-ca(cs-server)#cdp-url http://10.1.100.100/isrca.crl
atw-isr-ca(cs-server)#no shut
%Some server settings cannot be changed after CA certificate generation.
% Exporting Certificate Server signing certificate and keys...
%Some server settings cannot be changed after CA certificate generation.
% Please enter a passphrase to protect the private key
% or type Return to exit
Password:

Re-enter password:

% Certificate Server enabled.
atw-isr-ca(cs-server)#
Jan 10 18:59:43.803: %PKI-6-CS_ENABLED: Certificate server now enabled.
atw-isr-ca(cs-server)#
```

Important Notes

When configuring ISE to use the IOS CA for native supplicant provisioning, the URL for ISE to enroll is http://10.1.100.199/cgi-bin/pkiclient.exe, as shown in Figure D-2.

Figure D-2 *IOS CA SCEP RA Configuration*

At the time this book was written, there was a bug filed with Apple regarding the manufacturing installed certificate on newer iOS devices, as well as re-imaged iOS devices. The certificate that is installed on these devices has the subject name encoded in a way that does not follow the RFC. The RSA library used by Cisco IOS will not accept the broken encoding, and the certificate provisioning may fail.

Cisco is tracking this issue with bug id CSCud16869 and will resolve the bug when Apple releases a fix for the device certificates.

Sample Switch Configurations

This appendix includes some full sample configurations of various device types with multiple Cisco IOS versions, all designed to follow the guidelines and practices laid out in Chapter 11, "Bootstrapping Network Access Devices."

Catalyst 3000 Series, 12.2(55)SE

```
3560-X# sho run

Building configuration...

Current configuration : 22928 bytes
!
version 12.2
hostname 3560-X
logging monitor informational
username radius-test password 0 Cisco123
!
aaa new-model
!
!
aaa authentication dot1x default group radius
aaa authorization network default group radius
aaa accounting dot1x default start-stop group radius
!
!
aaa server radius dynamic-author
 client 10.1.103.231 server-key Cisco123
 client 10.1.103.4 server-key Cisco123
!
```

```
aaa session-id common
authentication mac-move permit
ip routing
!
ip domain-name cts.local
ip name-server 10.1.100.100
ip device tracking
!
!
crypto pki trustpoint TP-self-signed-4076357888
 enrollment selfsigned
 subject-name cn=IOS-Self-Signed-Certificate-4076357888
 revocation-check none
 rsakeypair TP-self-signed-4076357888
!
!
crypto pki certificate chain TP-self-signed-4076357888
 certificate self-signed 01
quit
!
dot1x system-auth-control
!
interface Loopback0
 ip address 192.168.254.60 255.255.255.255
!
interface <ALL EDGE PORTS>
 switchport access vlan 41
 switchport mode access
 switchport voice vlan 99
 ip access-group ACL-ALLOW in
 authentication event fail action next-method
 authentication event server dead action authorize vlan 41
 authentication event server dead action authorize voice
 authentication event server alive action reinitialize
 authentication host-mode multi-auth
 authentication open
 authentication order dot1x mab
 authentication priority dot1x mab
 authentication port-control auto
 authentication violation restrict
 mab
 dot1x pae authenticator
 dot1x timeout tx-period 10
 spanning-tree portfast
!
```

```
interface Vlan1
 no ip address
!
interface Vlan40
 ip address 10.1.40.60 255.255.255.0
!
!
ip http server
ip http secure-server
!
ip access-list extended ACL-AGENT-REDIRECT
 remark explicitly prevent DNS from being redirected to address a bug
 deny   udp any any eq domain
 remark redirect HTTP traffic only
 permit tcp any any eq www
 remark all other traffic will be implicitly denied from the redirection
ip access-list extended ACL-ALLOW
 permit ip any any
ip access-list extended ACL-DEFAULT
 remark DHCP
 permit udp any eq bootpc any eq bootps
 remark DNS
 permit udp any any eq domain
 remark Ping
 permit icmp any any
 remark PXE / TFTP
 permit udp any any eq tftp
 remark Drop all the rest
 deny   ip any any log
ip access-list extended ACL-WEBAUTH-REDIRECT
 remark explicitly prevent DNS from being redirected to accommodate certain switches
 deny   udp any any eq domain
 remark redirect all applicable traffic to the ISE Server
 permit tcp any any eq www
 permit tcp any any eq 443
 remark all other traffic will be implicitly denied from the redirection
!
ip radius source-interface Loopback0
logging origin-id ip
logging source-interface Loopback0
logging host 10.1.103.4 transport udp port 20514
!
snmp-server community CiscoPressRO RO
snmp-server trap-source Loopback0
snmp-server source-interface informs Loopback0
```

```
snmp-server host 10.1.103.231 version 2c CiscoPressRO
radius-server attribute 6 on-for-login-auth
radius-server attribute 8 include-in-access-req
radius-server attribute 25 access-request include
radius-server dead-criteria time 5 tries 3
radius-server host 10.1.103.231 auth-port 1812 acct-port 1813 key Cisco123
radius-server host 10.1.103.4 auth-port 1812 acct-port 1813 key Cisco123
radius-server vsa send accounting
radius-server vsa send authentication
!
end
```

Catalyst 3000 Series, 15.0(2)SE

```
C3750X# sho run brief

Building configuration...

Current configuration : 18936 bytes
!
version 15.0
no service pad
service timestamps debug datetime msec
service timestamps log datetime msec
no service password-encryption
!
hostname C3750X
!
boot-start-marker
boot-end-marker
!
logging monitor informational
!
username radius-test password 0 Cisco123
aaa new-model
!
!
aaa authentication dot1x default group radius
aaa authorization network default group radius
aaa accounting dot1x default start-stop group radius
!
!
aaa server radius dynamic-author
 client 10.1.103.231 server-key Cisco123
```

```
 client 10.1.103.4 server-key Cisco123
!
aaa session-id common
clock timezone EDT -1 0
authentication mac-move permit
ip routing
!
!
ip dhcp snooping vlan 10-13
ip dhcp snooping
ip domain-name cts.local
ip device tracking
!
!
device-sensor filter-list cdp list my_cdp_list
 tlv name device-name
 tlv name platform-type
!
device-sensor filter-list lldp list my_lldp_list
 tlv name port-id
 tlv name system-name
 tlv name system-description
!
device-sensor filter-list dhcp list my_dhcp_list
 option name host-name
 option name class-identifier
 option name client-identifier
device-sensor filter-spec dhcp include list my_dhcp_list
device-sensor filter-spec lldp include list my_lldp_list
device-sensor filter-spec cdp include list my_cdp_list
device-sensor accounting
device-sensor notify all-changes
!
epm logging
!
crypto pki trustpoint TP-self-signed-254914560
 enrollment selfsigned
 subject-name cn=IOS-Self-Signed-Certificate-254914560
 revocation-check none
 rsakeypair TP-self-signed-254914560
!
!
crypto pki certificate chain TP-self-signed-254914560
 certificate self-signed 01
cts role-based enforcement
```

```
!
dot1x system-auth-control
!
interface Loopback0
 ip address 192.168.254.1 255.255.255.255
!
interface <ALL EDGE PORTS>
 switchport access vlan 10
 switchport mode access
 switchport voice vlan 99
 ip access-group ACL-ALLOW in
 authentication event fail action next-method
 authentication event server dead action authorize vlan 10
 authentication event server dead action authorize voice
 authentication event server alive action reinitialize
 authentication host-mode multi-auth
 authentication open
 authentication order dot1x mab
 authentication priority dot1x mab
 authentication port-control auto
 authentication violation restrict
 mab
 dot1x pae authenticator
 dot1x timeout tx-period 10
 spanning-tree portfast
 ip dhcp snooping information option allow-untrusted
!
!
interface Vlan1
 no ip address
 shutdown
!
interface Vlan10
 ip address 10.1.10.1 255.255.255.0
!
interface Vlan20
 ip address 10.1.20.1 255.255.255.0
!
interface Vlan30
 ip address 10.1.30.1 255.255.255.0
!
interface Vlan99
 ip address 10.1.99.1 255.255.255.0
!
!
```

```
ip http server
ip http secure-server
!
!
ip access-list extended ACL-AGENT-REDIRECT
 remark explicitly prevent DNS from being redirected
 deny   udp any any eq domain
 remark redirect HTTP traffic only
 permit tcp any any eq www
 remark all other traffic will be implicitly denied from the redirection
ip access-list extended ACL-ALLOW
 permit ip any any
ip access-list extended ACL-DEFAULT
 remark DHCP
 permit udp any eq bootpc any eq bootps
 remark DNS
 permit udp any any eq domain
 remark Ping
 permit icmp any any
 remark PXE / TFTP
 permit udp any any eq tftp
 remark Drop all the rest
 deny   ip any any log
ip access-list extended ACL-WEBAUTH-REDIRECT
 remark explicitly prevent DNS from being redirected to address
 deny   udp any any eq domain
 remark redirect all applicable traffic to the ISE Server
 permit tcp any any eq www
 permit tcp any any eq 443
 remark all other traffic will be implicitly denied from the redirection
ip access-list extended AGENT-REDIRECT
 remark explicitly prevent DNS from being redirected to address
 deny   udp any any eq domain
 remark redirect HTTP traffic only
 permit tcp any any eq www
 remark all other traffic will be implicitly denied from the redirection
!
ip radius source-interface Loopback0
ip sla enable reaction-alerts
logging origin-id ip
logging source-interface Loopback0
logging host 10.1.103.4 transport udp port 20514
!
snmp-server community Cisco123 RO
snmp-server community TrustSecRO RO
```

```
snmp-server trap-source Loopback0
snmp-server source-interface informs Loopback0
snmp-server host 10.1.103.4 version 2c Cisco123  mac-notification
!
radius-server attribute 6 on-for-login-auth
radius-server attribute 8 include-in-access-req
radius-server attribute 25 access-request include
radius-server dead-criteria time 5 tries 3
radius-server vsa send accounting
radius-server vsa send authentication
!
radius server CP-VIP
 address ipv4 10.1.103.231 auth-port 1812 acct-port 1813
 automate-tester username radius-test
 key Cisco123
!
radius server CP-04
 address ipv4 10.1.103.4 auth-port 1812 acct-port 1813
 automate-tester username radius-test
 key Cisco123
!
end
```

Catalyst 4500 Series, IOS-XE 3.3.0 / 15.1(1)SG

```
4503# show run brief

Building configuration...
Current configuration : 35699 bytes
!
!
version 15.1
!
hostname 4503
!
!
username radius-test password 0 Cisco123
aaa new-model
!
!
aaa authentication dot1x default group radius
aaa authorization network default group radius
aaa accounting dot1x default start-stop group radius
!
```

```
!
aaa server radius dynamic-author
 client 10.1.103.231 server-key Cisco123
 client 10.1.103.4 server-key Cisco123
!
aaa session-id common
clock timezone EDT -1 0
!
ip domain-name cts.local
!
ip device tracking
!
device-sensor filter-list cdp list my_cdp_list
 tlv name device-name
 tlv name platform-type
!
device-sensor filter-list lldp list my_lldp_list
 tlv name port-id
 tlv name system-name
 tlv name system-description
!
device-sensor filter-list dhcp list my_dhcp_list
 option name host-name
 option name class-identifier
 option name client-identifier
device-sensor filter-spec dhcp include list my_dhcp_list
device-sensor filter-spec lldp include list my_lldp_list
device-sensor filter-spec cdp include list my_cdp_list
device-sensor accounting
device-sensor notify all-changes
epm logging
!
!
crypto pki trustpoint CISCO_IDEVID_SUDI
 revocation-check none
 rsakeypair CISCO_IDEVID_SUDI
!
crypto pki trustpoint CISCO_IDEVID_SUDI0
 revocation-check none
!
!
crypto pki certificate chain CISCO_IDEVID_SUDI
 certificate 238FC0E90000002BFCA1
 certificate ca 6A6967B3000000000003
crypto pki certificate chain CISCO_IDEVID_SUDI0
```

```
    certificate ca 5FF87B282B54DC8D42A315B568C9ADFF
    !
    dot1x system-auth-control
    !
    !
    vlan 40
     name jump
    !
    vlan 41
     name data
    !
    vlan 99
     name voice
    !
    interface <ALL EDGE PORTS>
     switchport access vlan 41
     switchport mode access
     switchport voice vlan 99
     ip access-group ACL-ALLOW in
     authentication event fail action next-method
     authentication event server dead action authorize vlan 41
     authentication event server dead action authorize voice
     authentication event server alive action reinitialize
     authentication host-mode multi-auth
     authentication open
     authentication order dot1x mab
     authentication priority dot1x mab
     authentication port-control auto
     authentication violation restrict
     mab
     dot1x pae authenticator
     dot1x timeout tx-period 10
     spanning-tree portfast
     ip dhcp snooping information option allow-untrusted
    !
    interface Vlan1
     no ip address
    !
    interface Vlan40
     ip address 10.1.40.2 255.255.255.0
    !
    ip http server
    ip http secure-server
    ip route 0.0.0.0 0.0.0.0 10.1.40.1
    !
```

```
ip access-list extended ACL-AGENT-REDIRECT
 remark explicitly prevent DNS from being redirected to address
 deny   udp any any eq domain
 remark redirect HTTP traffic only
 permit tcp any any eq www
 remark all other traffic will be implicitly denied from the redirection
ip access-list extended ACL-ALLOW
 permit ip any any
ip access-list extended ACL-DEFAULT
 remark DHCP
 permit udp any eq bootpc any eq bootps
 remark DNS
 permit udp any any eq domain
 remark Ping
 permit icmp any any
 remark PXE / TFTP
 permit udp any any eq tftp
 remark Drop all the rest
 deny   ip any any log
ip access-list extended ACL-WEBAUTH-REDIRECT
 remark explicitly prevent DNS from being redirected to address
 deny   udp any any eq domain
 remark redirect all applicable traffic to the ISE Server
 permit tcp any any eq www
 permit tcp any any eq 443
 remark all other traffic will be implicitly denied from the redirection
!
logging 10.1.103.4
!
snmp-server community Cisco123 RO
radius-server attribute 6 on-for-login-auth
radius-server attribute 8 include-in-access-req
radius-server attribute 25 access-request include
radius-server dead-criteria time 5 tries 3
radius-server host 10.1.103.231 auth-port 1812 acct-port 1813 test username radius-
test key Cisco123
radius-server host 10.1.103.4 auth-port 1812 acct-port 1813 test username radius-
test key Cisco123
radius-server vsa send accounting
radius-server vsa send authentication
!
end
```

Catalyst 6500 Series, 12.2(33)SXJ

```
hostname 6503
logging monitor informational
username radius-test password 0 Cisco123
!
aaa new-model
!
!
aaa authentication dot1x default group radius
aaa authorization network default group radius
aaa accounting dot1x default start-stop group radius
!
!
aaa server radius dynamic-author
 client 10.1.103.231 server-key Cisco123
 client 10.1.103.4 server-key Cisco123
!
aaa session-id common
authentication mac-move permit
ip routing
!
ip domain-name cts.local
ip name-server 10.1.100.100
ip device tracking
!
!
crypto pki trustpoint TP-self-signed-4076357888
 enrollment selfsigned
 subject-name cn=IOS-Self-Signed-Certificate-4076357888
 revocation-check none
 rsakeypair TP-self-signed-4076357888
!
!
crypto pki certificate chain TP-self-signed-4076357888
 certificate self-signed 01
quit
!
dot1x system-auth-control
!
interface Loopback0
 ip address 192.168.254.1 255.255.255.255
!
interface <ALL EDGE PORTS>
 switchport access vlan 10
```

```
 switchport mode access
 switchport voice vlan 99
 ip access-group ACL-ALLOW in
 authentication event fail action next-method
 authentication event server dead action authorize vlan 10
 authentication event server alive action reinitialize
 authentication host-mode multi-auth
 authentication open
 authentication order dot1x mab
 authentication priority dot1x mab
 authentication port-control auto
 authentication violation restrict
 mab
 dot1x pae authenticator
 dot1x timeout tx-period 10
 spanning-tree portfast
!
interface Vlan1
 no ip address
!
interface Vlan40
 ip address 10.1.40.1 255.255.255.0
!
!
ip http server
ip http secure-server
!
ip access-list extended ACL-AGENT-REDIRECT
 remark explicitly prevent DNS from being redirected to address a bug
 deny   udp any any eq domain
 remark redirect HTTP traffic only
 permit tcp any any eq www
 remark all other traffic will be implicitly denied from the redirection
 deny ip any any
ip access-list extended ACL-ALLOW
 permit ip any any
ip access-list extended ACL-DEFAULT
 remark DHCP
 permit udp any eq bootpc any eq bootps
 remark DNS
 permit udp any any eq domain
 remark Ping
 permit icmp any any
 remark PXE / TFTP
```

```
 permit udp any any eq tftp
 remark Drop all the rest
 deny   ip any any log
ip access-list extended ACL-WEBAUTH-REDIRECT
 remark explicitly prevent DNS from being redirected
 deny   udp any any eq domain
 remark redirect all applicable traffic to the ISE Server
 permit tcp any any eq www
 permit tcp any any eq 443
 deny ip any any
!
ip radius source-interface Loopback0
logging origin-id ip
logging source-interface Loopback0
logging host 10.1.103.4 transport udp port 20514
!
snmp-server community CiscoPressRO RO
snmp-server trap-source Loopback0
snmp-server source-interface informs Loopback0
radius-server attribute 6 on-for-login-auth
radius-server attribute 8 include-in-access-req
radius-server attribute 25 access-request include
radius-server dead-criteria time 5 tries 3
radius-server host 10.1.103.231 auth-port 1812 acct-port 1813 key Cisco123
radius-server host 10.1.103.4 auth-port 1812 acct-port 1813 key Cisco123
radius-server vsa send accounting
radius-server vsa send authentication
!
end
```

Index

Symbols

A

B

C

H

I

J-K

L

S

V

W-X-Y-Z